The Journals and Miscellaneous Notebooks

of

RALPH WALDO EMERSON

RALPH H. ORTH   *Chief Editor*

LINDA ALLARDT   HARRISON HAYFORD

J. E. PARSONS   SUSAN SUTTON SMITH

Editors

The Journals and Miscellaneous Notebooks

of

RALPH WALDO EMERSON

VOLUME XIV

1854–1861

EDITED BY

SUSAN SUTTON SMITH HARRISON HAYFORD

THE BELKNAP PRESS
OF HARVARD UNIVERSITY PRESS

Cambridge, Massachusetts
and London, England

1978

CENTER FOR EDITIONS OF
AMERICAN AUTHORS
AN APPROVED TEXT
MODERN LANGUAGE
ASSOCIATION OF AMERICA

®

Library of Congress Catalog Card Number: 60–11554
ISBN 0–674–48477–0

Typography by Burton J Jones
Printed in the U.S.A.

Preface

Miss Smith, the primary editor, has been responsible for the page-by-page study of the manuscripts and for the research, the notes, the introductory material, and the preparation of the text for the press. Mr. Hayford verified the text by independent readings of the journals.

The editors wish to thank a number of institutions and persons for help of various kinds. The Ralph Waldo Emerson Memorial Association has continued to provide regular grants-in-aid which have been indispensable to the progress of the edition. Miss Smith was aided by two Summer Faculty Research Grants from the Research Foundation of the State University of New York and a grant from the American Council of Learned Societies. The Center for Editions of American Authors of the Modern Language Association of America provided generous financial support for the work of both editors from grants made by the National Endowment for the Humanities of the National Foundation on the Arts and Humanities.

Among individuals who have given invaluable help in the preparation of this volume are Mary Sutton Smith, Sarah H. Bulgatz, Thomas Dixon Smith, Joan Wildman, Kendra Gaines, and Deborah Hayford Parker. Mary Leonard and Mary Sutton Smith transcribed the manuscript journals and notebooks. Professor William H. Gilman provided guidance and inspiration as Chief Editor and friend. The editors wish also to thank Professors Wallace E. Williams and James H. Justus, editors of Emerson's later lectures, for their generous help.

For other assistance and courtesies, thanks are also due to Miss Carolyn Jakeman, Professor William H. Bond, Miss Marte Shaw, and others of the staff of the Houghton Library; the staff of the Manuscript Division of the Library of Congress; the staffs of the James M. Milne Library of the State University of New York

College at Oneonta and the Widener Library; Professor Frederick Locke of the University of Rochester; and Mrs. John Dempsey of the Emerson House in Concord.

Unless otherwise noted, translations of classical quotations are from the Loeb Classical Library and are reprinted by permission of Harvard University Press and the Loeb Classical Library.

The edition title page reflects changes in the editorial group, all of whom have responsibilities of various kinds for the edition as a whole. The Chief Editor has the primary responsibility for the edition and for certification of individual volumes.

R. H. O.

Contents

Illustrations

Foreword to Volume XIV

The journals from 1854 to 1861 show the ripeness of Emerson's thought overshadowed by the gravest problem of his time, slavery. During these years he published two books, but as he entered his own middle fifties such accomplishments seemed harder and their price in time and energy higher. As he affirmed the necessity of examining the individual life, he wondered what advice would avail in an evil time when a national struggle grew surer and surer. *English Traits*, his richly ironic assessment of England as "the best of actual nations," the fruit of his English travel and years of reading, took shape in frigid midwestern hotel rooms in the winter of 1855–1856. *The Conduct of Life*, published in December 1860, addressed the fundamental problem of how a man ought to live without referring directly to the moral reef on which the lives of so many Americans were soon to be shattered.

Emerson found *English Traits* difficult to finish: he sent the first chapter to his publisher in October, 1855, but he was still working on the book at the Tremont House in Chicago in January, 1856, and on June 2 of that year he wrote to his brother William, "I have taken up again those weary refractory concluding chapters of the little English book." Evidence of his exasperation appeared in his journals: he headed one group of pages *"England, for the last time."*

He had been preparing, delivering, and refining the lectures in his "Conduct of Life" series since the early 1850's, but Emerson also found it difficult to complete this book. On June 6, 1860, he wrote to Moncure Conway, "It has cost me more time lately to do nothing, in many attempts to arrange & finish old MSS. for printing, than ever I think before to do what I could best. . . . They say, the

ix

ostrich hatches her egg by standing off & looking at it, and that is my present secret of authorship." On December 10, 1860, two days after *The Conduct of Life* was published, he wrote to his brother William, "I am ashamed to think what a relief is the delivery from this so little book."

While deprecating his own achievement, Emerson accomplished much in these years. In addition to completing *English Traits* and *The Conduct of Life*, Emerson wrote many of the lectures and articles that made up his next book, *Society and Solitude*: "Success," "Courage," and "Old Age," for example, first took shape as some of the lectures that made Emerson one of the best-known and best-paid performers on the lyceum circuit. Emerson also contributed often to *The Atlantic Monthly* after helping to found the magazine in 1857, completed several of his finest poems, and became one of the most notable speakers against slavery.

Publishing books didn't support the Emerson family; lecturing did. An arduous five- or six-month tour took Emerson back and forth across the frozen Mississippi several times every winter in the mid-fifties. In the winter of 1854–1855 Emerson had tried the experiment of touring with one or two lectures, "American Slavery" and his 1851 address on the Fugitive Slave Law; in the winter of 1855–1856 he returned to his usual pattern of a variety of lectures. He followed a demanding schedule: on December 25 and 26, 1855, he spoke at Salem, Massachusetts; on December 30, he wrote to Lidian from the Tremont House in Chicago, "I rode incessantly from Salem Mass, where I took the cars on Thursday morning, two days & two nights & was here at nine yesterday A.M. Tonight at eleven or else tomorrow at seven A.M. I go again to the Missisippi & across it to Davenport & then to Rock Island. But it is a little doubtful still as there is no arrival from that quarter whether snow and wind will allow me to reach the river. As for the crossing, once there, there is now no difficulty, for it is frozen." On this trip, the usual discomforts of western travel increased because none of the new shirts he had packed would button around his neck. As he noted in his journal when the mercury hit 27 or 28 degrees below zero in a two-week prairie cold snap, "This climate & people are a new test for the wares of a man of letters. All his thin watery matter freezes; 'tis only the smallest portion of alcohol that remains good. At the lyceum, the stout Illinoian, after a short trial, walks out of the hall." The committees told him that people wanted to hear humorists, and Emerson concluded that "Shakspeare or Franklin or Aesop coming to Illinois, would say, I must give my wisdom a comic form, instead of tragics or elegiacs, & well I know how to do it, and he is no master who cannot vary his forms, & carry his own end triumphantly through the most difficult."

Emerson found agreeable alternatives to the rigors of western journeying in his highly successful Boston lecture series at the Freeman Place Chapel in 1856, 1858, and 1859. Although these lectures were clearly announced as old, he drew good houses for many of the lectures eventually to become chapters in *The Conduct of Life* and *Society and Solitude*. After 1858, Emerson also spoke frequently in Boston before the "Parker Fraternity" or Twenty-eighth Congregational Fraternity, Theodore Parker's old congregation.

If Emerson succeeded as a lecturer in both West and East, the financial rewards were welcome: some of his investments, notably in Mad River & Lake Erie and Vermont & Canada railroad bonds and in the Atlantic Bank, had not turned out well. In his journal for 1857 he wrote ruefully: "I took such pains not to keep my money in the house, but to put it out of the reach of burglars by buying stock, & had no guess that I was putting it into the hands of these very burglars now grown wiser & standing dressed as Railway Directors." And he breaks into an 1859 entry on the flowing of the universe to ask, "What say you to the value of an estate invested in railroad stocks?"

In the years from 1855 to 1861 Emerson sought society as well as the solitude of his journal-keeping. He helped to organize the Saturday Club in September, 1856, becoming more of a social creature than ever before and writing warmly of the scholar's need for such diversions in "Clubs." From the society of Oliver Wendell Holmes, Henry Wadsworth Longfellow, and James Russell Lowell at the Parker House dinners, he could turn to his old companions of Concord walks and talks: Alcott, Channing, and Thoreau.

Thoreau's abrupt style of communication may have become more noticeable after sessions with the Boston literati, for Emerson remarked upon it in his journal: "It is curious that Thoreau goes to a house to say with little preface what he has just read or observed, delivers it in lump, is quite inattentive to any comment or thought which any of the company offer on the matter, nay, is merely interrupted by it, &, when he has finished his report, departs with precipitation." While he admired the patience with which Thoreau charmed woodchucks as he would never deign to charm his fellow men, Emerson sometimes felt that sitting in the woods could be carried too far. "My dear Henry," he wrote, "A frog was made to live in a swamp, but a man was not made to live in a swamp. Yours ever, R." At the same time, Emerson admired Thoreau's superiority to social pretense; as he noted in 1857, "Henry avoids commonplace, & talks birch bark to all comers, & reduces them all to the same insignificance." He was moved to awe by Thoreau's solitary quest, while paradoxically feeling that some failure or lack in himself prevented the experience from being more fully shared: in January 1858, after meeting Thoreau in his woods and admiring Thoreau's knowledge of nature — "How divine these studies! Here there is no taint of mortality. . . . How aristocratic, & of how defiant a beauty!" — Emerson remarked sadly, "I want animal spirits" and "I have not enough oil for my wheels."

Ellery Channing's easier enthusiasms apparently made him a less perplexing companion. Emerson noted his mastery of the "art of taking a walk" — "Can you bring home the summits of Wachusett & Monadnoc, & the Ucanoonuc, the savin fields of Lincoln, & the sedge & reeds of Flint Pond, the savage woods beyond Nut brook towards White Pond? He can" — but lamented Channing's inability to record his impressions in salable form.

Throughout this period Emerson continued his efforts to establish a fund for the benefit of another Concord friend whose talents proved unsalable, Amos Bronson Alcott. In 1856 he praised Alcott's "extraordinary insight" and sincerity: "For every opinion or sentence of Alcott, a reason may be sought & found, not in his will or fancy, but in the necessity of nature itself, which has daguerred that fatal impression on his susceptible soul. He is as good as a lens or a mirror, a beautiful susceptibility, every impression on which, is not to be reasoned against, or derided, but to be accounted for, &, until accounted for, registered as an (indisputable) addition to our catalogue of natural facts. There are defects in the lens, & errors of refraction & position, &c. to be allowed for, and it needs one acquainted with the lens by frequent use, to make these allowances; but 'tis the best instrument I have ever met with." Even Alcott had his limits, however, and in 1856 Emerson also wrote: "My son is coming to get his latin lesson without me. My son is coming to do without me. And I am coming to do without Plato, or Goethe, or Alcott."

As the ebb and flow of his friendships with Alcott, Channing, and Thoreau indicates, Emerson varied between cherishing his solitude and searching for a companion. His need to share his thoughts seems to have been most acute before the arrival of the unidentified friend or acquaintance of the remarkable 1859 journal entry: "I have now for more than a year, I believe, ceased to write in my Journal, in which I formerly wrote almost daily. I see few intellectual persons, & even those to no purpose, & sometimes believe that I have no new thoughts, and that my life is quite at an end. But the magnet that lies in my drawer for years, may believe it has no magnetism, and, on touching it with steel, it shows the old virtue; and, this morning, came by a man with knowledge & interests like mine, in his head, and suddenly I had thoughts again."

Emerson's intermittent conviction that he had "no new thoughts" and that his life was "quite at an end" seems to have been a continuation of his lifelong ambivalence about his role as a thinker, exacerbated by his own aging and the country's plight. In 1857 he had still his old fondness for thoughts: "Will he coax & stroke these deities? I do. I can no more manage these thoughts that come into my head than thunderbolts. But once get them written down, I come & look at them every day, & get wonted to their faces, & by & by, am so far used to them, that I see their family likeness, & can pair them & range them better, & if I once see where they belong, & join them in that order they will stay so." In 1858, as often before, he defended his way of life against charges of impracticality: "Greenough wittily called my speculations *masturbation*; but the artist life seems to me intolerably thin & superficial. I feel the reasonableness of what the lawyer or merchant or laborer has to allege against readers & thinkers, until I look at each of their wretched industries, and find them without end or aim." Sometimes, even as he exulted in his deliberately chosen path, he was struck by its loneliness: "I have been writing & speaking what were once called novelties, for twenty five or thirty years, & have not now one disciple. Why? Not that what I said was not true; not that it has not found intelligent receivers; but because it did not go from any wish in me to bring men to me, but to themselves." In 1859 he wrote gloomily, "I am a natural reader, and only a writer in the absence of natural writers. In a true time, I should never have written." In another mood, in 1859, he gloried in what he called the "Beatitudes of Intellect": "The joy which will not let me sit in my chair, which brings me bolt upright to my feet, & sends me striding around my room, like a tiger in his cage, and I cannot have composure & concentration enough even to set down in English words the thought which thrills me — is not that joy a certificate of the elevation? What if I never wrote a book or a line? For a moment, the eyes of my eyes were opened, the affirmative experience remains, & consoles through all suffering."

But the worth of solitary intellectual affirmation, even of all intellectual activity, was called into question by the events unfolding outside his study. News of New England men murdered in bloody Kansas and of the assault on Charles Sumner in the U.S. Senate in 1856 made it seem imperative for the scholar to leave his "honied thought" and take an active public stand on the side of the right. Influenced by events, by a growing friendship with Theodore Parker, and by the visits of John Brown to Concord in 1857 and 1859, Emerson spoke more loudly and more often for emancipation and even for war. He probably began his notebook WO Liberty, included in this volume, at about the same time he gave his address on the Fugitive Slave Law in New York in March, 1854. WO Liberty contains drafts or records of seven antislavery speeches, including some drafts for the March, 1854, speech, drafts for his "Speech on Affairs in Kansas" in September, 1856, and drafts for undelivered speeches on Senator Hale, a Free-Soil spokesman from New Hampshire, and against the return of fugitive slave Anthony Burns from Massachusetts to South Carolina. Almost one quarter of the pages in WO Liberty are devoted to drafts of Emerson's major address, "American Slavery," first given in Boston on January 25, 1855.

This separate notebook for ideas on slavery and human liberty afforded a special store of ammunition for Emerson's antislavery addresses; into it he copied many passages from his journals and notebooks of the early 1850's — BO, CO, IO, NO, VS — and added to them entries from later journals, new quotations from additional books, his own comments on unfolding events, and pertinent newspaper clippings. Emerson the scholar armed himself for his emergence from the study by marshaling his thoughts on liberty as he would have ranged his thoughts on any other topic. He also attempted topical poetry: WO Liberty and Journal VO contain drafts of an "Ode: Sung in the Town Hall, Concord, July 4, 1857," which called for the emancipation of the slaves.

If Emerson sometimes appealed to his carefully gathered authorities, as when Chief Justice Taney's words "servile races" in the 1857 Dred Scott decision recalled a French historian's vivid account of the Norman subjugation of the Saxons, he felt that the cause of liberty should need no justification by historical precedent. The appeal to the past he recognized as one of the most pernicious ploys of the enemy; in an 1857 entry headed "Against Whigs," he wrote, "Zoologists may dispute whether horse hairs in the water change to worms, but I find that whatever is old corrupts, & the past turns to snakes. The reverence for the deeds of our ancestors is a treacherous sentiment. Their merit was, not to reverence the old, but to honor the present moment, & we falsely cite them as examples of the very habit which they hated & defied." Instead of revering the founding fathers, Emerson felt that their compromise of 1789 had raised the devil for future generations, and he felt it might even have been better had America lost the Revolutionary War and won emancipation in the 1830's with other British colonies.

Moved to anger by the slavery of his own day, Emerson denounced the South and Southern sympathizers and temporizers in the North. In his journal for 1857 he wrote: "The shooting complexion, like the cobra capello & scorpion, grows in the South. It has no wisdom, no capacity of improvement: it looks, in every landscape, only for partridges, in every society, for duels. And, as it threatens life, all wise men brave or peaceable run away from the spider-man, as they run away from a black spider: for life to them is real & rich,

& not to be risked on any curiosity as to whether spider or spider-man can bite mortally, or only make a poisonous wound. With such a nation or a nation with a predominance of this complexion, war is the safest terms. That marks them, &, if they cross the lines, they can be dealt with as all fanged animals must be." In 1859 he wrote of "the insanity of the South" and said, "I see for such madness no hellebore, for such calamity no solution, but servile war & the Africanization of that country." Emerson's conviction that war was the only answer led to conflict with those bent on preserving the Union: when he attempted to speak at a meeting of the Massachusetts Anti-Slavery Society in Boston on January 24, 1861, before an audience whose sympathies were divided, he was drowned out with hisses, groans, and catcalls.

If Emerson regarded the South as mad, he reviled what he called the "cowardly" politics of Massachusetts; he privately excoriated the "class of privileged thieves that infest our politics" and wrote, "I knew some of these robbers born within sound of church bells, & rejoicing in good Christian New England names such as Douglas, Pierce, Cushing, Governor Gardner. There is a serious objection to hounding them out,—that they are nasty prey, which the noble hunter disdains. A good dog even must not be risked on such. They 'spoil his nose.'" Of the same politicians he wrote: "For these Cushings, & Hillards, & Co. one wants to say, as the minister to the Cape Cod farm, when requested to make a prayer,—'No, this land does not want a prayer, this land wants manure.'"

Comparing the two camps in 1856, Emerson felt that the side of right lacked cunning if not conviction and might prove unequal to a contest with the "earnest," "courteous" Carolinians and the forces of self-interest he contemned: "I go for those who have received a retaining fee to this party of freedom, before they came into this world. I would trust Garrison, I would trust Henry Thoreau, that they would make no compromises. I would trust Horace Greeley, I would trust my venerable friend Mr. Hoar, that they would be staunch for freedom to the death; but both of these would have a benevolent credulity in the honesty of the other party, that I think unsafe." Emerson now agreed with John Brown that mere unaided virtue appealing for strength to the "greatness of its wrongs" had provided protection neither for the Negro nor for the peace party in Kansas, and that force would be needed for the struggle ahead.

Even as he recognized that virtue alone won no battles, Emerson continued to believe that the *sine qua non* of real freedom, whether gained through laws or battle, was the knowledge of how a man should live, "the conduct of life." He remained the same seeker for truth he had always been as he judged himself and his allies: "We read the orientals, but remain occidental. The fewest men receive anything from their studies. The abolitionists are not better men for their zeal. They have neither abolished slavery in Carolina, nor in me. If they cannot break one fetter of mine, I cannot hope they will of any negro. They are bitter sterile people, whom I flee from, to the unpretentious whom they disparage." In 1858 he wrote, "The roarers for liberty turn out to be slaves themselves; the thunderers of the senate are poor creatures in the street, & when canvassing for votes. And when, in their own village, the question is how many honest men are there in town? men who will not take a petty advantage, & are severer watchers of themselves than of their debtor? Why, they are as rare among the reputable as among the unreputed; the great gentlemen, scornful & lofty, will do very shabby things: and a career of triumphantly logical reform has consumed all the domestic virtue & private charm of the athlete. His wife hates him, children do not love him, scholars dislike him, & he is miserable alone." The "infinitude of the private man" remained the one rock in a land of heaving earth through which he felt the tremors of the coming eruption.

Emerson's reading in the years from 1855 to 1861 reflected the diversity of his public and private interests. To bolster his antislavery arguments he read Francis Lieber's *Manual of Political Ethics* and copied Lieber's quotations from Blackstone, Coke, Cobbett, and Campbell; on the same subject he also read Ainsworth Rand Spofford's anonymous 1851 pamphlet *The Higher Law Tried by Reason and Authority*. Preparing for his first major address as an advocate of women's rights, to the Woman's Rights Convention in Boston in September, 1855, he consulted again his notes on the *Vishńu Puráña* and Lady Hutchinson's *Memoirs* of her husband. As he completed *English Traits* he continued reading Sir David Brewster's *Memoirs of the Life, Writings, and Discoveries of Sir Isaac Newton,* and Robert Southey's life of Nelson, and read *The Life and Letters of Barthold Georg Niebuhr, The Confidential Correspondence of Napoleon Bonaparte with his Brother Joseph,* Etienne Dumont's *Recollections of Mirabeau, and of the Two First Legislative Assemblies of France,* François Arago's *Biographies of Distinguished Scientific Men,* Pierre Lanfrey's *L'Eglise et les philosophes au dix-huitième siècle,* and Sainte-Beuve's *Causeries du Lundi.* In the summer of 1856 he read "an inestimable little book," Volume XV of the *Bibliotheca Indica,* Dr. E. Röer's translation of nine of the Upanishads. As he copied some passages from it into his journal he suddenly stopped and wrote what he then called the "Song of the Soul," published that November in the first issue of *The Atlantic Monthly* as "Brahma." In writing the poem he seemed to recall twenty years of readings in the *Vishńu Puráńa* and other Hindu writings and distill their spirit into four stanzas. Preparing for an article published in *The Atlantic Monthly* for April, 1858, on "Persian Poetry," he returned to Hammer-Purgstall's translations of Hafiz, Enweri, and Saadi and made more of his own translations from the German versions.

Throughout the period, for both public and private ends, Emerson reread and quoted his old favorites: Thomas Taylor's translations of Plato, Iamblichus, Plotinus, and Proclus; James John Garth Wilkinson's translations of Swedenborg; Mrs. Piozzi's *Anecdotes,* and Boswell's *Life of Johnson.* He found new favorites too, and felt that Benjamin Robert Haydon's autobiography shared some of the best qualities of Boswell.

He read Coventry Patmore's *The Angel in the House* in 1855 and found reason to revise upward his opinion of Tennyson. Though he wrote that "Many of Tennyson's poems, like 'Clara Vere de Vere,' are only the sublime of magazine poems, — admirable contributions for the 'Atlantic Monthly' of the current month, but not classic & eternal," he greeted the first four *Idyls of the King* enthusiastically in 1859: "What a heart-whole race is that which in the same year can turn out two such sovereign productions as the 'History of Friedrich,' and 'The Four Idyls.'" Among American poets Emerson read everything from Walt Whitman's *Leaves of Grass* to James

Russell Lowell's *Biglow Papers* to Ellery Channing's *Near Home*. Emerson's taste in novels also ranged widely: he read George Sand's *Consuelo* and perhaps *The Countess of Rudolstadt*, Elizabeth Gaskell's *Cranford*, and *Charles Auchester* and *Counterparts; or The Cross of Love*, both by Elizabeth Sara Sheppard. The last novel he recommended highly as a "talismanic book." Along with *The Atlantic Monthly*, Emerson read the *Revue des Deux Mondes* and *Atlantis*, a German-language magazine published first in Buffalo and then in Detroit and edited by a German exile of 1848, Christian Esselin. Emerson continued his eclectic, indeed, omnivorous reading along all the paths opened by his development as a public and private man.

Volume XIV includes five regular journals, RO, SO, VO, AC, and CL, covering a span of five and a half years; one miscellaneous notebook, WO Liberty (in the Moorfield Storey papers in the Library of Congress); and five pocket diaries, those for 1856, 1857, 1858, 1859, and 1860. A second pocket diary for 1859, listed in the editorial title list in *JMN*, I as Pocket Diary 10, has no entries by Emerson; two pages bear a description by Edward W. Emerson of a postoperative tonsillectomy patient at City Hospital. The major period covered in Volume XIV is July 1855 to January 1861, although Emerson probably began WO Liberty in 1854. Some of the journals in Volume XIV overlap one another in time: Journal AC overlaps with Journals VO and CL; Journal RO overlaps with Journal NO (*JMN*, XIII, 379–469); and Journals RO, SO, and VO overlap with Journal DO (*JMN*, XIII, 3–57).

Editorial technique. The editorial process follows that described in volume I and the slight modifications introduced in subsequent volumes of the edition. In volume XIV there is relatively little erased pencil writing, but in each case every effort has been made to recover the text. Use marks in the journals and notebooks comprising volume XIV have been carefully described, transcriptions and expansions of passages have been recorded, and uses in *English Traits, The Conduct of Life, Society and Solitude,* and other published works have been noted where possible, often with help from the locations supplied by Edward W. Emerson in the manuscripts.

In the manuscripts, Emerson's topical headings are sometimes underlined, sometimes set off by a rule or by enclosing straight or wavy lines; unless he seems to have intended something more than marking to identify the matter as a heading, the various forms are interpreted by setting the heading in italics. Whenever one of Emerson's hyphens coincides with the compositor's end-of-line hyphenation, two hyphens have been set, one at the end of the line and one at the beginning of the following line. When the text is quoted in the notes, no silent emendations are made; hence there are occasional variations between notes and text.

As in volumes XI, XII, and XIII, Emerson's own cross references to his other journals can be located through the use of the Appendix, which indicates where all of the journals published up to the volume in hand appear in the Harvard edition. Because the edition carries Emerson's manuscript pagination as well as its own, the reader can easily locate any cross reference to a journal already printed.

Numbering of "Fragments on Nature and Life" and "Fragments on the Poet and the Poetic Life" follows that assigned by Edward Emerson or by George S. Hubbell, *A Concordance to the Poems of Ralph Waldo Emerson.*

In accordance with the policies of the Center for Editions of American Authors, a list of silent emendations has been prepared; copies are to be deposited in the Rush Rhees Library of the University of Rochester, the Library of Congress, Houghton Library, Huntington Library, and Newberry Library. The following statement describes the silent or mostly silent emendations. These range from numerous — as with punctuation of items in a series, supplying periods at the ends of sentences if the next sentence begins with a capital, or expansion of contractions — to occasional, as with supplying quotation marks, dashes, or parentheses missing from intended pairs.

Emendation of prose. A period is silently added to any declarative sentence lacking terminal punctuation but followed in the same paragraph by a sentence beginning with a capital letter. If a declarative sentence lacking a period is followed by a sentence beginning with a small letter, either a bracketed semicolon is supplied, or a bracketed period is supplied and the small letter is silently capitalized.

In the second instance the reader will automatically know that the capital was originally a small letter. If a direct question lacking terminal punctuation is followed by a sentence in the same paragraph beginning with a capital the question mark is silently added. Punctuation of items in a series, since Emerson habitually set them off, is silently inserted. Small letters at the beginning of unquestionable paragraphs or of sentences which follow a sentence ending with a period are silently capitalized. Where indispensable for clarity a silent period is added to an abbreviation. Quotation marks, dashes, and parentheses missing from intended pairs have been silently supplied; so have quotation marks at the beginning of each of a series of quotations. Apostrophes have been silently inserted or normalized in possessives and contractions. Superscripts have been lowered and double or triple underscorings have been interpreted by small or large capitals. Common Emersonian contractions like y^t for *that*, y^e for *the*, *wh* for *which*, *wd* and *shd* for *would* and *should*, and *bo't* for *bought* are silently expanded. His dates have been regularly normalized by the silent insertion of commas and periods.

Emendation of poetry. On the whole, Emerson's poetry has been left as it stands in the manuscripts; apostrophes and some commas, periods, and question marks have been supplied, in accordance with the rules for emending prose, but only where Emerson's intention was unmistakable.

Certain materials are omitted, either silently or with descriptive annotation; these will not be reported in the list of emendations. Omitted silently are slips of the pen, false starts at words, careless repetitions of a single word, and Emerson's occasional carets under insertions (assimilated into the editor's insertion marks). Underscoring to indicate intended revisions is not reproduced. Omitted, but usually with descriptive annotation, are practice penmanship, isolated words or letters, and miscellaneous markings.

CHRONOLOGY 1855–1861

1855: July 21, Emerson writes to Walt Whitman praising *Leaves of Grass*; September 20, he speaks at the Woman's Rights Convention, Boston; September 29, he speaks at the dedication of Sleepy Hollow Cemetery in Concord; October 9, he sends Chapter I of *English Traits* to Phillips, Sampson and Company; November, Emerson lectures at eight Massachusetts towns and in Milford, N.H.; December, he lectures in eight cities and towns in New England, in Brooklyn, N.Y., and in Davenport, Iowa.

1856: January, Emerson lectures at Rock Island, La Salle, Dixon, Freeport, Galena, and Belvidere, Ill.; in Beloit, Janesville, and Waukesha, Wis.; Chicago, Galesburg, and Peoria, Ill.; Ann Arbor and Adrian, Mich.; Sandusky, Cleveland, Columbus, Akron, Hudson, and Ravenna, Ohio; and in Salem and Worcester, Mass.; January 13 and 14, he works to complete *English Traits* at the Tremont House in Chicago, Ill.; February, he lectures at five towns in Maine and eleven in Massachusetts; March, he lectures at seven towns in Massachusetts and at Dartmouth College; March 27–May 1, he gives six lectures at Freeman Place Chapel in Boston, receiving $770 as his share of the profits for the series; May 22, Charles Sumner is attacked by Preston Brooks on the floor of the U.S. Senate; May 24, John Brown kills five slavery adherents at Pottawatomie in revenge for a proslavery massacre at Lawrence, Kansas; May 26, Emerson addresses an indignation meeting at Concord on "The Assault on Mr. Sumner"; June 12–13, $1360 is raised as the result of a Kansas Relief Meeting in Concord; July, Emerson spends a week at Pigeon Cove, Mass.; August, John Brown makes a stand at Osawatomie against proslavery raiders from Missouri; August 6, *English Traits* is published in Boston; September 10, Emerson speaks at a Kansas Relief Meeting in Cambridge; September 13, at a Kansas Relief Meeting in Concord more than $510 is raised; September, Emerson helps to organize the Saturday Club; November, he lectures at six cities and towns in Massachusetts and Connecticut; November 4, James Buchanan is elected President of the United States; December, Emerson lectures at sixteen Massachusetts cities and towns.

1857: January, Emerson lectures at Concord and Woburn, Mass.; Concord, N.H.; Paterson, N.J.; Philadelphia, Pa.; Buffalo, Cortland, Rochester, and Syracuse, N.Y.; Columbus, Ohio; Chicago and Waukegan, Ill.; Lafayette, Ind.; Cincinnati, Sandusky, and Cleveland, Ohio; and Covington, Ky.; January 31–February 6, he gives four lectures in Cincinnati, Ohio; in February, he lectures in Jersey City, N.J.; Manchester, Wrentham, Salem, and Concord,

Mass.; and Newport, R.I.; March 6, the Dred Scott decision is handed down; also in March, Emerson lectures at seven Massachusetts towns and John Brown speaks in Concord; April, Emerson lectures at three Massachusetts towns; May, he helps to organize *The Atlantic Monthly*; October, he lectures at Watertown and Nantucket, Mass.; November, "The Chartist's Complaint," "Days," "Brahma," "The Romany Girl," and "Illusions" appear in the first issue of *The Atlantic Monthly*; also in November, Emerson lectures at Concord and Winchendon, Mass.; December, he lectures at ten towns in Massachusetts and Connecticut.

1858: January, Emerson lectures at four Massachusetts towns; February, he lectures at Philadelphia, Pa., and in Chicopee Falls and Springfield, Mass.; March 3–April 7, he gives six lectures at Freeman Place Chapel, Boston, receiving $884.08; April, he lectures at Worcester and Lynn, Mass.; June 11, the final action in Charles Bartlett's woodlot suit goes against Emerson, and Emerson is directed to pay damages of $25 and fees amounting to several times as much; July 8, Emerson moves the bodies of his mother and Waldo to his lot in Sleepy Hollow; August, Emerson spends two weeks with other members of the Saturday Club at the Adirondack camp of William J. Stillman; also in August, he visits the Forbeses at Naushon Island, Mass.; August 9, the first transatlantic cable is laid and September 9 the cable is broken; September 29, Emerson speaks at the Cattle Show of the Middlesex Agricultural Society at Concord; October, he lectures at Bangor, Maine; November, he gives five lectures at Salem, Mass.; November, he lectures at Peterboro, N.H., and Billerica, Mass.; December, he lectures at Boston, Mass., Burlington, Vt., Hartford, Conn., Brooklyn, N.Y., Philadelphia, Pa., Toronto and Hamilton, Ontario, and Salem and East Boston, Mass.; also in December, Emerson calculates his income from lectures in 1858 as $1988.

1859: January, Emerson lectures at Baltimore, Md.; Brooklyn, Albany, Auburn, Cortland, and Batavia, N.Y.; Cleveland, Ohio; Providence, R.I.; and Taunton, South Danvers, Boston, and Brighton, Mass.; January 25, he speaks at the Burns Festival centenary dinner in Boston; February, he gives four lectures at Lynn, Mass., and also lectures in Grafton, Auburndale, Concord, Cambridgeport, and Boston, Mass., and in Bangor, Maine; March 23–April 26, he gives six lectures at Freeman Place Chapel and the Music Hall in Boston, receiving $687.85; May, he lectures at Boston, Blackstone, and Natick, Mass.; May 27, Emerson's feeble-minded brother Robert Bulkeley Emerson dies at the age of fifty-two; June and July, Emerson lectures at Boston; also in July, he continues his efforts to establish the Alcott Life Annuity Fund; about July 15, he sprains his ankle severely in coming down Wachusett Mountain; August 29, he speaks at the Saturday Club dinner on Oliver Wendell Holmes's fiftieth birthday; September 9, Emerson's publishers, Phillips, Sampson & Company, suspend payment; October, Emerson lectures in Boston; October 16–18, John Brown seizes Harpers Ferry, Va., and is captured two days later; October 23, Emerson chooses Ticknor & Fields as his new publishers; October 31, John Brown is convicted of treason and murder; November, Emerson lectures at six towns and cities in Massachusetts; November 18, Emerson speaks at a Boston meeting for the relief of John Brown's family; December 2, John Brown is hanged, and Emerson speaks at Concord; also in December, Emerson lectures at nine New England cities and towns.

1860: January 6, Emerson speaks at a Salem meeting for the relief of the families of Brown and his men; Emerson lectures at Waltham, Worcester, and Salem, Mass.; Poughkeepsie, Saratoga, Hamilton, Rochester, Lima, Buffalo, Batavia, and Rochester, N.Y.; Toronto, Ontario; and Toledo, Ohio; February, he lectures at Yellow Springs and Cincinnati, Ohio; Lafayette, Ind.; Chicago and Rockford, Ill.; Madison, Milwaukee, Racine, and Kenosha, Wis.; Niles, Kalamazoo, Grand Rapids, Marshall, Ann Arbor, and Detroit, Mich.; Zanesville, Ohio; and Boston and New Bedford, Mass.; March, he lectures at Montreal, Quebec; Concord and Boston, Mass.; and New York; also in March, his reputation as a sympathizer with John Brown makes it necessary for him to cancel a projected lecture engagement in Philadelphia because of the possibility of disorder; also in March, Walt Whitman visits Emerson, who attempts unsuccessfully to dissuade him from including "Enfans d'Adam" in the new edition of *Leaves of Grass*; November 6, Abraham Lincoln is elected President of the U.S.; November, Emerson lectures at Boston and Concord, Mass.; November 26 or 27, he addresses the

Massachusetts State Teachers' Association convention in Concord; December 8, *The Conduct of Life* is published in Boston; also in December, Emerson lectures at nine cities and towns in Massachusetts, and in Concord and Nashua, N.H.

1861: January, Emerson lectures at Boston, Mass., and Elmira, Owego, Hornellsville, Cortland, Alfred, and Buffalo, N.Y.; January 24, he attempts to speak at the Massachusetts Anti-Slavery Society meeting in Boston but is shouted down.

SYMBOLS AND ABBREVIATIONS

⟨ ⟩	Cancellation
↑ ↓	Insertion or addition
/ /	Variant
‖ ... ‖	Unrecovered matter, normally unannotated. Three dots, one to five words; four dots, six to fifteen words; five dots, sixteen to thirty words. Matter lost by accidental mutilation but recovered conjecturally is inserted between the parallels.
⟨‖ ... ‖⟩	Unrecovered canceled matter
‖msm‖	Manuscript mutilated
[ ]	Editorial insertion
[...]	Editorial omission
[ ]	Emerson's square brackets
⌐ ⌐	Marginal matter inserted in text
[ ]	Page numbers of original manuscript
n	See Textual Notes
--	Two hyphens are set when the compositor's end-of-line hyphen coincides with Emerson's.
∧	Emerson's symbol for intended insertion
[R.W.E.]	Editorial substitution for Emerson's symbol of original authorship. See volume I, plate vii.
*	Emerson's note
epw	Erased pencil writing
☞ ☜ ✍	Hands pointing

ABBREVIATIONS AND SHORT TITLES IN FOOTNOTES

CEC   *The Correspondence of Emerson and Carlyle.* Edited by Joseph
        Slater. New York: Columbia University Press, 1964.

J   *Journals of Ralph Waldo Emerson.* Edited by Edward Waldo
        Emerson and Waldo Emerson Forbes. Boston and New York:
        Houghton Mifflin Co., 1909–1914. 10 vols.

JMN   *The Journals and Miscellaneous Notebooks of Ralph Waldo
        Emerson.* Ralph H. Orth, Chief Editor; Linda Allardt, Harrison
        Hayford, J. E. Parsons, Susan Sutton Smith, Editors (volume I
        edited by William H. Gilman, Alfred R. Ferguson, George P.
        Clark, and Merrell R. Davis; volumes II–VI, William H. Gil-
        man, Alfred R. Ferguson, Merrell R. Davis, Merton M. Sealts,
        Jr., Harrison Hayford; volumes VII–XI, William H. Gilman,
        Alfred R. Ferguson, Harrison Hayford, Ralph H. Orth, J. E.
        Parsons, A. W. Plumstead; volumes XII–XIII, William H. Gilman,
        Alfred R. Ferguson, Linda Allardt, Harrison Hayford, Ralph H.
        Orth, J. E. Parsons, A. W. Plumstead; volume XIV, Ralph H. Orth,
        Linda Allardt, Harrison Hayford, J. E. Parsons, Susan Sutton
        Smith). Cambridge: Harvard University Press, 1960–

Lectures *The Early Lectures of Ralph Waldo Emerson.* Volume I, 1833–
        1836, edited by Stephen E. Whicher and Robert E. Spiller; vol-
        ume II, 1836–1838, edited by Stephen E. Whicher, Robert E.
        Spiller, and Wallace E. Williams; volume III, 1838–1842, edited
        by Robert E. Spiller and Wallace E. Williams. Cambridge: Harvard
        University Press, 1959–1972.

Life   Ralph L. Rusk. *The Life of Ralph Waldo Emerson.* New York:
        Charles Scribner's Sons, 1949.

W   *The Complete Works of Ralph Waldo Emerson.* With a Bio-
        graphical Introduction and Notes, by Edward Waldo Emerson.
        Centenary Edition. Boston and New York: Houghton Mifflin Co.,
        1903–1904. 12 vols. I — *Nature Addresses and Lectures;* II —
        Essays, First Series; III — *Essays, Second Series;* IV — *Repre-
        sentative Men;* V — *English Traits;* VI — *Conduct of Life;*
        VII — *Society and Solitude;* VIII — *Letters and Social Aims;*
        IX — *Poems;* X — *Lectures and Biographical Sketches;* XI —
        Miscellanies; XII — *Natural History of Intellect.*

PART ONE

The Journals

$\mathcal{RO}$

1855–1856

Emerson began Journal RO in July, 1855, and used it through March, 1856. The earliest dated entry is July, 1855 (p. [11]), and the latest is January 9, 1856 (pp. [94]–[98]). It thus overlaps Journal NO, which he ended in August, 1855, by one month. Journal RO was written in from both ends to make two sequences. The earlier sequence, which dates from 1835, has been designated RO Mind by the editors and was published in *JMN*, V, 269–276. Two 1835 entries, however, one sentence and an early version of the "Concord Hymn," occur on pp. [127] and [129] in the later sequence.

The covers of the copybook, marbled brown and green over boards, measure 12.2 x 18.8 cm. The spine and spine strip are of brown paper. "RO" is centered in the upper half of the front cover, with "1855–6" centered beneath.

Including flyleaves (i, ii, 141, 142), there were 90 unlined leaves measuring 11.7 x 18.3 cm, but eighteen leaves, bearing what would have been pages 8–43 in sequential pagination, were cut out before pagination, as there is no gap at this point in Emerson's numbering. The leaf bearing pages 31–32 is cut out and is now Houghton MS. Am 1280.202(12) f49. The leaf bearing pages 33–34 is slit for 4.5 cm down from the top. Page 8 is mistakenly numbered 7. The pages are numbered in ink except for page 88 in pencil. Thirty-four pages are unnumbered: i, ii, 2, 4, 6, 10, 12, 14, 18, 20, 37, 52, 61, 69, 84, 89, 91, 109, 112, 113, 116, 124, 128, 129, 131, 132, 133, 134, 135, 136, 137, 140, 141, and 142. Eight pages are blank: 20, 22, 43, 48, 50, 52, 61, and 133. Pages 106, 108, 112, 114, 116, 118, 120, 122, 124, 126, 128, 130, 132, 134, 136, and 140 in the 1855 sequence bear writing from the separately paged RO Mind sequence of 1835, which, with reference to the 1855–1856 sequence, is upside down and runs from back to front.

[front cover]   RO

1855–6

[front cover verso] [blank]

3

[i]   R W Emerson
                            ———

                              RO
                            ——
                            1855–6

[ii]–[1] [Index material omitted]

[2] They do not forget a debt[.]

———

Superficial spleen, but at last tenderhearted.
Herein differing from ⟨the L⟩Rome ⁿ & the Latin nations.[1]

[3]   When I was born
             From all his ⟨tons⟩ ↑seas↓ of ⟨strength⟩ ↑wine↓ Fate filled
                a ⟨wine⟩ glass
             Saying, This be thy portion child, ⟨to have offered⟩ ↑this
                cup↓
             ⟨This cup⟩ Less ⁿ than a lily's thou shalt daily draw
             From my great ⟨store⟩ ↑flood↓; this cup nor less nor more
             If a new thought catch me with splendid ray
             ↑And I↓ throw ⁿ myself headlong into its heaven
             The needs of the first moment ⟨draw⟩ ↑suck↓ the wine
             And all the hours of the day
             Have a deformed old age
             So now when friends surround me
             And every day its book
             Or starbright scroll of some new genius
             The little cup will hold not ↑a↓ drop more
             And all is wasted
             Not to be husbanded for poorer days [2]

———

[1] "They do . . . debt" and "Superficial . . . nations.", struck through in ink
with single vertical use marks, are used in "Character," *W*, V, 137–138; cf. "Result," *W*, V, 299.
[2] "When I . . . poorer days", in pencil, underlies the ink inscription "*Errata
. . . dele* comma" on p. [3]. These lines are used in "The Day's Ration," ll. 1–5,
15–23, 25, *W*, IX, 138–139.

4

Errata of [n] *Eng. Traits*
Insert "Plutarch"

———

Correct conclusion of Wordsworth

———

   Loch Fyne

———

   amply sufficient for expenses

———

Coleridge

———

p 18   l. 4 & 5 dele quotation marks.

———

↑x↓ p. 231   "Stride" in heraldry
p 218   "Stability" of Eng. nation

———

"eaten" in Landor notice
p.

———

insert "coins"

———

insert ne [faire souffrir personne.]
p. 89   ventilated *for* ventilate
p 96   *dele* [n] comma

[4]   All substances the strong Chemist Time
           Melts down into that liquor of my life
           Friends foes facts fortunes beauty & disgust
           And whether I am angry or content
           /Crowned/Honored/ or insulted loved or impoverished
           All he distils into sidereal water
           And fills my little cup
           ↑And↓ heedless [n] how ⟨muc⟩ little it will hold
           How [n] much runs over ⟨in⟩on the desart
           Why need I volumes ⟨w⟩if one word suffice
           Why need I Italy where a humble copy
           Of one of Raphael's forms fills & o'erfills

My apprehension. Why need I travel
Who cannot circumnavigate the sea
Of ⁿ thoughts & things at home, but still ↑adjourn↓
↑Skip↓ the nearest matters for a thousand days [3]

Population of England ↑& Wales↓   16,921,888.
                        Scotland   2,888 742
                        Ireland   6,515 794

Population of Great Britain ⁿ ↑& Ireland↓ (and British
Isles)   27,475,271

Area of Great Britain, Ireland, Islands, & Malta. 120,500

[5]   Why honor the new men
         Who never understood the old

         Almost I am tempted to begin
         The inventory of my personal wealth
         And draw in lines length marble
         To sympathetic eyes the portraiture
         Of the fine angels that environ me
         One is a Greek in mind & face
         And doth establish to the latter times
         The truth of those old artists ⟨who⟩ ⁿ
         Who drew in marble or in bronze on vase & frieze
         Those perfect forms
                 Forms of a perfect simpleness
                 And beauty never in excess
         So bright so much
         So bright so positive so much in itself
         Yet so adapted to the thing it did [4]

---

[3] "All substances . . . days", in pencil, underlies the ink inscription "Population of England . . . 120,500" on p. [4]. These lines are used in "The Day's Ration," ll. 6–14, 26–32, *W*, IX, 138–139.

[4] "Why honor . . . thing it did", in pencil, underlies the ink inscription "Population . . . miles." on p. [5].

Population of the United States in 1850   23,191,876
Area of the States & Territories   2,983 153, square miles.

[6]   For either I will marry with a star
            Or I will labor in a factory.

            So perfect in her action that it seemed
            She condescended if she spoke and though

            She spoke better than all the rest she did not speak
            Worthy of her, and well she loved the Greek, as if it
                were
            Her mother tongue.[5]

[7]   So perfect in her action that it seemed
            She condescended if she spoke and
            although
            She spoke ⟨as well as others⟩ ↑better than all↓, did not
                speak
            Worthy of her
            And well she loved the Greek as if it were
            Her mother tongue [6]

            And yet the best of angels live alone.[7]

            She seemed to commune with herself & say
            For either I will marry with a star,
            Or I will labor in a factory.

[5] "For either . . . factory." is in pencil; "For either . . . tongue." is struck
through in pencil with a vertical use mark. See *JMN*, VIII, 452, 475.

[6] "So perfect . . . Her mother tongue", in pencil, is struck through in pencil
with a vertical use mark. "Her mother tongue" underlies the first line of the ink
inscription following.

[7] For "And yet . . . alone.", see Emerson's paraphrases of Swedenborg in *JMN*,
XIII, 8 and 44: " 'There are also Angels who do not live consociated, but separate,
house & house; these dwell in the midst of heaven because they are the best of
angels.' " See *A Treatise Concerning Heaven and its Wonders, and also Concerning
Hell . . . , From the Latin of Emanuel Swedenborg* (London, 1823), p. 116. This
book is in Emerson's library. See p. [35] below.

> So perfect in her action, one would say,
> She condescended if she added speech,
> And though she spoke
> Better than all the rest, she did not speak
> Worthy of her.
> She read in many books
> And loved the Greek as t'were her mother tongue

[8] [8] A Scholar is a man with this inconvenience, that, when you ask him his opinion of any matter, he must go home & look up his manuscripts to know.ⁿ ⟨what his⟩
How strange,ⁿ said Choate, All the English to this day love or hate Charles Fox so much, that they cannot understand the history of Greece.

[eighteen leaves torn out] [9]
[9] il reno⟨v⟩uvela cette /politesse/complaisance/ c'est à dire pour ⟨du⟩ ↑le↓ poisson, qu'il ⟨eut⟩ ↑avait↓ deja montré↑e↓ pour ⟨des⟩ ↑les↓ oeufs.

                     Go without fire one day in year [10]

"No man can get a high price, till he asks it."

          Edw. H Ladd   5 Dec
          Julia E. Marvin   29 Lynde St

[10] Collingwood was five years at sea without landing.
        ———

          Purpurea intexti tollant aulaea Britanni.
          ———————

                    Virgil [11]
                    C[harles] K[ing] N[ewcomb]

---

[8] Emerson numbered two pages 7; the editors have regularized the second to 8.

[9] The leaves were torn out before pagination. Letters and words or portions of words in French are visible on the stubs.

[10] "Go . . . year", in pencil, is used in "Land," *W*, V, 39–40; see *JMN*, X, 182, and p. [18] below.

[11] *Georgics*, III, 25: "the inwoven Britons raise the purple curtains." There is a short rule before and above "Britanni.", and a wavy line begins to the right of

"And chiefly that tall fern
So stately of the Queen Osmunda named
Plant lovelier in its own retired abode
⟨By⟩ On Grasmere's beach than Naiad by the side
Of Grecian brook or lady of the mere
Sole sitting ⟨on⟩by the Shores of old Romance"
Wordsw[or]th ["Poems on the Naming of Places," IV, ll. 33–38,]
III 160 [12]

[11]   1855   July
Loyalty is a subreligion, & men walk by their loyalty as if among the forms of gods. Politeness is the ritual of the social church, as prayers are of the heavenly worshippers. Thus the aristocracy are a gentle blessing to a well-willing people. Every one who values time, & has tasted the delight of select companionship, will respect every social guard which [12] our manners can establish tending to secure from the intrusion of frivolous & distasteful people. The jealousy of every class to guard itself is a testimony to the reality they have found in life.

When a man once knows that he is rightly made, let him dismiss [13] all notions about Aristocracy & exclusive marque as superstitions, so far as he is concerned. Every body who is good for anything, & real, is open & ready for him as real.[13] Power loves power & seeks for it as one athirst[.]

[14] It must be believed that St George ↑when he↓ conquered the dragon ⟨took his heart into his own he⟩ absorbed his nature[.]

[15] Life is safe in England[.]

"*Virgil*" and extends for approximately 5 cm in the right margin. Near the beginning of July, 1855, mystic and former close friend Charles King Newcomb (1820–1894) had written Emerson a "Swedenborgian, rhapsodical letter"; see *L*, IV, 516--517.
   [12] *The Poetical Works of William Wordsworth*, 4 vols. (Boston, 1824), in Emerson's library.
   [13] "Loyalty is . . . real.", struck through in ink with vertical use marks on pp. [11], [12], and [13], is used in "Aristocracy," *W*, V, 186–188. For "Every one who . . . people.", see *JMN*, XIII, 406.

Advantages once confined to men of family are now open to the whole middle class.

'Tis a fiction that they are men of the conquest. 'Tis wide open to vigor, & 'tis all newly come in.[14]

Ridicule the natural antagonist of Terror. See *Causeries de S. B.* Vol III p. 10.[15]

[16] For Gymnastics of Intellect or favorable conditions see a passage from Rousseau's Confessions, ap[ud]. *Causeries de S[ainte]. B[euve].* [1851–1862,] ⟨p⟩Vol. III. p. 75

La marche a quelque chose qui anime et avive mes idées[.] [16] [*Ibid.*]

[17] One more point:[n] they are propagandist, with their steam, galvanism, & liberty[.]

Adoptive

Sebastian Cabot, Alcuin, Asser, Van Dyke, Erasmus, Handel, Kneller, Herschel, Romilly, Ricardo, Fuseli, Schomburgk, Rothschild

[18] "Climate of England," said Luttrel, "on a fair day, looking up a chimney; on a foul day, looking down one."

Mr Paulet of Liverpool told me that, in his experience, he found he could do without a fire ↑in his house,↓ about one day in the year.[17]

---

[14] "Tis a fiction . . . come in." is in pencil. "Life is . . . England" and "Advantages . . . class.", struck through in ink with single vertical use marks, are used in "Ability," *W*, V, 82, and "Aristocracy," *W*, V, 196. With "Tis a fiction . . . come in.", cf. "Aristocracy," *W*, V, 196–197.

[15] Charles Augustin Sainte-Beuve, *Causeries du Lundi*, 15 vols. (Paris, 1851–1862). Emerson withdrew volumes 3 and 4 of this work from the Boston Athenaeum December 31, 1853–March 23, 1854; volume 5 March 24–April 20, 1854; and volume 8 November 23–December 7, 1854.

[16] This quotation, translated, is used in "Country Life," *W*, XII, 141–142.

[17] The entries on p. [18], struck through in ink with a vertical use mark, are used in "Land," *W*, V, 39–40. See p. [9] above.

[19] *London*
S⟨i⟩ydney Smith said, "A few yards in London cement or dissolve friendship."[18]

[20] [blank]
[21] *Race.* The interest of the subject of race that everybody is delighted to find advantages which cannot be attributed to climate; ⟨sea,⟩ soil; sea; or local resources, like mines & quarries; but to superior brain.[19]

[22] [blank]
[23] Spleen, an[n] organ found in an Englishman, not found in the American, & differencing the two nations.[20]

[24] Dr Johnson said, "Every man is a rascal as soon as he is sick."

"A man who is afraid of anything is a scoundrel." [21]

[25]   *Nobil volgar eloquenza*[22]
"Let me take off this great-coat[,] I sweat like a wolf."

[26] Morals
'Tis wonderful where the moral influences come from, since no man

---

[18] Smith's remark, struck through in ink with a vertical use mark, is used in "Considerations by the Way," *W*, VI, 247.

[19] This entry, struck through in ink with a vertical use mark, is used in "Race," *W*, V, 46. See p. [137] below.

[20] This entry, struck through in ink with a vertical use mark, is used in "Character," *W*, V, 138.

[21] "Dr Johnson . . . sick.' ", struck through in ink with a vertical use mark, is used in "Considerations by the Way," *W*, VI, 263. Cf. Hester Lynch Piozzi, *Anecdotes of the Late Samuel Johnson, LL.D.*, as reprinted in *Johnsonian Miscellanies*, arranged and edited by George Birkbeck Hill, 2 vols. (London, 1897), I, 267: "It is so *very* difficult (said he always) for a sick man not to be a scoundrel." Johnson's second remark is quoted in William Johnston, *England As It Is, Political, Social, and Industrial, in the Middle of the Nineteenth Century*, 2 vols. (London, 1851), II, 88; Emerson withdrew this work from the Boston Athenaeum August 13–23, 1852.

[22] The Italian, translated as "noble vulgar speech," is used in "Literature," *W*, V, 234.

is a moralist. 'Tis like the generation of the atmosphere, which is a secret.

[27] Coleridge is one of those who save England from the reproach of no longer possessing in the land the appreciation of ⟨the⟩ what highest wit the land has yielded, as, Shakspeare, Spenser, Herbert, &c. But for Coleridge, and a lurking taciturn or rarely-speaking minority, one would say that, in Germany, & in America, is the best mind of England rightly respected. And that is the sure sign of national decay, [28] when the Bramins can no longer read & understand the Braminical science & philosophy.[23]

Health   that's beauty   long days because   eyes are good   & circulations keep 'em warm in cold rooms & read Plato as I did with a wool smell [24]

System of reliefs
Wo↑r↓dsworth

[29] ↑L[ouis].↓ Napoleon the ⟨Em⟩present emperor is a plucky fellow who writes spirited terms for his general Pelissier to offer the Russians, & bolder far than the English would have dictated.[25] He means to teach them how robbers rob.

See below, p 76

[30]   Trifles
Lone women readers, &c ↑wish to live with good housekeepers, &↓ ⟨don't⟩ ↑never↓ learn that good housekeepers cordially hate anybody who does not dine at the family hour.

[23] "Coleridge is . . . philosophy.", struck through in ink with a discontinuous vertical use mark on pp. [27] and [28], is used in "Literature," W, V, 248–249.
[24] "Health . . . smell", struck through in ink with one vertical and one diagonal use mark, is used in "Success," W, VII, 297.
[25] Aimable Jean Jacques Pélissier, duc de Malakoff (1794–1864), commanded the 1st army corps in the Crimean War (1854–55) and represented France at the Congress of Paris in February and March, 1856, to negotiate the peace.

[31]²⁶ Why need you vote? If new power is here, if a character which solves old tough questions, which puts me & all the rest in the wrong, tries and condemns our religion, customs, laws, & opens new careers to young receptive men & women, you can well leave voting to the old dead people. Those whom you teach, & those whom you half teach, will fast enough make themselves considered & strong with their new insight, & votes⟨.⟩ will follow from all the dull.

[32] Marriage is bad enough, but is far the best solution that has yet been offered of the woman's problem. Fourierism, or ⟨Mahometism⟩ ↑Mormonism↓, or the New York Socialis⟨ts⟩m, are not solutions that any high woman will accept as even approximate to her ideas of well-being.²⁷

⟨"Ceremony" out of Marlowe⟩

[33]   *Woman*
Mrs Hutchinson's sinking of her substance into attributes of her husband. *NO* 148 ²⁸

And the new movement is only a tide shared by the spirits of man & woman, & you may proceed in a faith that whatever the woman's heart is prompted to desire, the man's mind is simultaneously prompted to execute[.] ²⁹

[34] *Woman*
I think it impossible to separate their education & interests.

---

²⁶ The leaf bearing pp. [31] and [32] has been cut out and is now f49 of "Address at the Woman's Rights Convention, Sept. 20, 1855" [Houghton MS. Am 1280.202(12)]. The original page number, "31", and the period after "votes" are canceled in pencil. "(We may ask, to be sure) lec Report" and beneath this "95" are written at the top of p. [31] in a hand not Emerson's. This paragraph is used in "Woman," *W*, XII, 420–421.

²⁷ "Marriage . . . wellbeing." is struck through in ink and in pencil with single vertical use marks.

²⁸ This entry is struck through in ink with a diagonal use mark; the quotation from Lucy Hutchinson in Journal NO, p. [148], is used in "Woman," *W*, XI, 407.

²⁹ "And the . . . execute", struck through in pencil with a vertical use mark, is used in "Woman," *W*, XI, 426.

The policy of defending their property is good; and if the women demand ⟨political equality⟩ votes, offices, & political equality as an Elder & Eldress are of equal power in the Shaker Families, refuse it not. 'Tis very cheap wit that finds it so funny. Certainly all my points would be sooner carried in the state if women voted.[30]

[35] Woman.

"Take the first advice of a woman, & not the second."

Women more than all are the element & kingdom of illusion. They see only through Claude Lorraine & how dare anyone — I dare not — pluck away the coulisses, stage effects, & ceremonies, by which they live. ↑TU 277↓ [31]

The cruel human race suffer no exempts, no sisters of charity

TU 157

Yet "the best of angels live alone." [32]

[36] man wants a wife to every mood of his mind   AB 97

Vishnu Purana says "Women with ease attain the same sphere as their husbands with toil." [33]   S 211

They can't keep the conversation impersonal.   HO 138

[30] "I think . . . voted." is struck through in ink and in pencil with single vertical use marks; "I think . . . interests.", struck through in pencil with one vertical use mark, and "The policy . . . voted.", struck through with another, are used in "Woman," W, XI, 425, 419, and 420.
[31] "Take . . . they live." is struck through in ink with a vertical use mark; "'Take . . . the second.'", struck through in pencil with two vertical use marks, is used in "Woman," W, XI, 405; "Women . . . live.", struck through in pencil with a vertical use mark that is a continuation of one of those through the first sentence, is used in "Illusions," W, VI, 315–316. The leaf bearing p. [277] is missing from Journal TU.
[32] The quotation from Swedenborg's A Treatise Concerning Heaven . . . and Hell . . . , 1823, p. 116, to which this entry refers is used in "Society and Solitude," W, VII, 6. See p. [7] above.
[33] The Vishńu Puráńa, A System of Hindu Mythology and Tradition, trans. H. H. Wilson (London, 1840), p. 628; this work is in Emerson's library. This entry, struck through in ink and pencil with single vertical use marks, is used in "Woman," W, XI, 406–407.

They wish to interest,ⁿ not to affright.   [HO] 139
    The convention should be holden in the Sculpture Gallery
                                                    CO 264

Woman moulds the lawgiver, & ↑so↓ writes the law.   ⟨B⟩*CO* 264

Will is the rudder, & sentiment the sail. When woman affects to
steer, the rudder is only a masked sail.   ⟨C⟩*BO* 180 [34]

[37] There is unbelief in a cigar, in wine, in all luxury. The poet
doubts his access to the grand sources of inspiration, doubts the con-
tinuance of the supplies, & steals to these shabby pots.

———

Women as most impressionable are the best index of the coming hour.
                                                    AZ 113
When they take up art or trade it is only as a resource or substitute
not a legitimate primary object[.] [35]   *AZ* 165

[38] When Red Jacket heard somebody complaining of want of time
he said gruffly, "Well, I suppose, you have all there is." [36]

[39] "De Greeks be Godes, de Greeks be Godes," said Fuseli, striding
up & down among the Elgin marbles.

What adoptive arms their genius has, hospitable to ability from every
land. Fuseli, Kneller, Romilly, Ricardo, Schomburgk, Asser. ↑Handel,
Herschel,↓

---

[34] "Vishnu . . . Gallery" is struck through in pencil with a diagonal use mark;
"The convention . . . law." and "Will . . . sail." are struck through in pencil
with single vertical use marks; "The convention . . . sail." is struck through in ink
with a diagonal use mark. "They can't . . . impersonal.", "Woman moulds . . .
law.", and "Will . . . sail." are used in "Woman," *W*, XI, 418, 425, and 407.

[35] "Women . . . object" is struck through in ink and in pencil with single
vertical use marks; "Women . . . hour." is used in "Fate," *W*, VI, 44; "When
. . . object", struck through in pencil with a vertical use mark, is used in "Woman,"
W, XI, 407.

[36] This entry, struck through in ink with a vertical use mark, is used in "Works
and Days," *W*, VII, 178.

"We ask no favors, & we will do what we like with our own," is their surly tone —
"A peerage or Westminster" said Nelson. "I have no illusion left, but the Abp. Canterbury," said the joking Smith.[37]

[40] All the barriers to rank only whet the thirst & enhance the prize.[38]
They will not play chess with you, unless you let them give you a rook or a knight.

[41] Nature has impressed periodical or secular impulses to emigrate on savage men, as upon lemings, rats, & birds.

The church is an institution of God. Yes, but is not wit, & wise men, & good judgment whether a thing be so or no, also institutions of God, & older than the other? [39]

[42] Never to assume an obscure cause, when an obvious one exists, is a rule of the mind. It is therefore a little violent↑ — ↓is it not?↑ — ↓ to contradict the universal traditions of mankind, in regard to the eastern origin of nations, by assuming independent creation of ⟨many⟩ ↑a several↓ race⟨s⟩ for each country.

[43] [blank]
[44]   ↑*Premium on Individualism*↓
In each change of industry, whole classes & populations are sacrificed ↑like caterpillars;↓ as when cotton takes the place of linen, or railroads of turnpikes. Or ⟨in⟩by the inclosing of a common ⟨ground⟩ by land lords. Then society is admonished of the mischief of the division of labor, which [45] makes one man a pin- or a buckle-maker, or any other specialty; & all are ruined except such as are proper individuals,

---

[37] " 'We ask . . . tone—' " and " 'I have . . . Smith." are struck through in ink with single vertical use marks; " 'A peerage . . . Smith." is used in "Aristocracy," *W*, V, 197. For Nelson's remark, see *JMN*, XIII, 319.
    [38] "All . . . prize.", struck through in ink with two vertical use marks, is used in "Aristocracy," *W*, V, 197.
    [39] This paragraph is in pencil.

capable of thought, and of new choice & application of their talent to new labor.[40]

[46] Sleepy Hollow
The blazing evidence of immortality is our dissatisfaction with any other solution.
　　　All great natures love stability[.] [41]

　　　Our fear of death is like our fear that summer will be short, but when we have had our swing of pleasure, our fill of fruit, & our swelter of heat, we say, we have had our day; & rest of brain & affection please.
If life was ⟨bad⟩ ↑a disease,↓ then death will be only a varioloid.

　　　[47] Shelley's tombs of Pompeii   [AZ 66]

　　　Death no longer perfumed

"When we pronounce the name of man, we pronounce the belief of immortality." *Lieber* [42]

"Death takes us away from ill things, not from good." [43]

[48] [blank]
　　　[49] ↑Bible is an old Cremona.   *NO* 190↓ [44]
　　　He causes the wrath of man to praise him, & the remainder of wrath he shall restrain.

---

[40] This paragraph, struck through in ink with a vertical use mark on p. [44] and in ink with one vertical and two diagonal use marks on p. [45], is used in "Wealth," *W*, V, 167.
　　[41] "The blazing . . . stability", struck through in ink with a vertical use mark, is used in "Sleepy Hollow Cemetery," *W*, XI, 436; Emerson spoke at the consecration of the Concord cemetery on September 29, 1855.
　　[42] Emerson was familiar with Francis Lieber's *Manual of Political Ethics*, 2 vols. (Boston, 1838–1839), which he withdrew from the Boston Athenaeum July 8–25, 1854; see Notebook WO Liberty, pp. [3] and [27] below.
　　[43] The entries on p. [47] are struck through in ink with a vertical use mark; the quotation from Shelley is used in "Immortality," *W*, VIII, 325–326; " 'When . . . good.' " is used in "Sleepy Hollow Cemetery," *W*, XI, 436.
　　[44] "Bible . . . Cremona.", struck through in ink with three vertical use marks, is used in "Quotation and Originality," *W*, VIII, 182.

↑There is↓ no[n] man who is not indebted to his vices, as no plant that is ↑not↓ fed from manures. All that is asked is that the man steadily meliorates, & that the plant grows upward, & converts the base into the better nature.[45]

[50] [blank]

    [51] Superlative. 'Twas[n] a great discovery to me, that, when a lady says, "she shall die," she means, take a nap.

    Dr P[arkman]. was sent to procure an angel to do cooking.[46]

I want a horse that will run all day like a wolf.

Mr ⟨‖ … ‖⟩ said the mare was good, but she was as old as the north star.[47]

It did not suffice S. Buttrick to say the pines were killed, but "they were as dead as Julius Caesar."

[52] [blank]

[53] It would not be good for architecture, the law of Turkey, which puts every house, ⟨‖ … ‖⟩on the death of its master, at the Grand Seignior's disposal.[48]

    [54] The ⟨poet⟩ English poet must be as large as London, by no means in the commercial or economic way, — large producer, shipper, jobber, or banker, — but in a real way, drawing as much water, consuming as much ⟨vitality,⟩ oxygen, physical, & metaphysical, [55] as any the ablest-bodied, strongest-willed commander in the market, exchange, law courts, or shipyards of the Metropolis.[49]

---

    [45] "He causes . . . nature." and "He causes . . . manures." are struck through in ink with single vertical use marks; these three sentences are used in "Considerations by the Way," *W*, VI, 258–259. For "He causes . . . manures.", see *JMN*, XIII, 459. With "He causes . . . restrain.", cf. Ps. 76:10: "Surely the wrath of man shall praise thee: the remainder of wrath shalt thou restrain."

    [46] This sentence, quoting the Reverend Francis Parkman (1788–1852), pastor of the New North Church, Boston, is struck through in ink with two vertical use marks and used in "Considerations by the Way," *W*, VI, 275. See *JMN*, XIII, 24.

    [47] For "Mr ⟨‖ … ‖⟩ . . . star.", see *JMN*, XIII, 282.

    [48] In Sir Paul Ricaut's *The Present State of the Ottoman Empire. Containing the Maxims of the Turkish Politie*, . . . (London, 1668), which Emerson owned, Turkish laws and customs concerning the inheritance of property are described on pp. 5 and 70–71.

    [49] This entry is struck through in ink on p. [54] with a vertical use mark.

When I see the waves of Lake Michigan toss in the bleak snow storm, I see how small ⟨th⟩& inadequate the common poet is. But Tennyson with his eagle over the sea, has shown his sufficiency.

[56] *Naturel*
But who dare draw out the linch pin from the wagon wheel? [50]

The defence of Whiggery, is, that they like a man with 1800 years in him.[51]

[57] Madame de Rambouillet made a new era in the Hotels of the nobility, by getting the horses out, & the Sch⟨a⟩olars in.[52]

Aristocracy. First come first served.

[58] There is no rich man like the selfreliant: this is royalty. He walks in a long street. Once for all he has abdicated second-thoughts, and asks no leave of others' eyes, & makes lanes & alleys palatial.

[59] What talent had this second Charles, that he could hold his place among the Wrens, Hookes, Newtons, Flamsteeds, Halleys, Bentleys, Pettys, Coventrys, that clustered in ⟨t⟩his "Royal Society" & atone for the harpies & dragons and all unclean⟨s⟩ beasts which masqueraded in titles around him? Manners, the manners of power, sense enough to see his advantage, & Manners up to it; that is his cheap secret, and a boundless subserviency corresponding in the people. [60] Just what happens in every two persons who meet on any affair; one instantly perceives that he has the key of the situation, that his will comprehends the other's will, as the cat does the mouse,

---

"The ⟨poet⟩ English . . . way," is used in "Literature," *W*, V, 257. A page-wide rule in pencil separates the two entries on p. [55]; beneath it, in pencil, in a hand not Emerson's, is the notation "This should be *1856* Jan. 11, 12, Chicago, Waukesha &c *RO* p 100" referring to the entry about Lake Michigan.

[50] This sentence, struck through in ink with one vertical and one diagonal use mark, is used in "Considerations by the Way," *W*, VI, 258. See *JMN*, XIII, 459.

[51] This sentence, in pencil, is struck through in pencil with a vertical use mark.

[52] This sentence, struck through in ink with a vertical use mark, is used in "Clubs," *W*, VII, 243; cf. "Woman," *W*, XI, 415.

& he has only to use courtesy, & furnish goodnatured reasons to his victim, to cover up the chain, lest he be shamed into resistance.[53]

[61] [blank]

[62] Sidney Smith says, you will never break down in a speech, if you have walked twelve miles the same day.[54]

Alcott had much to say of there being more in a man than was contained in his skin;   as I say, a man is as his relatedness. But I was struck with the late superiority he showed. The inter-locutors were all better than he; he seemed childish & helpless, not apprehending or answering their remarks aright, ⟨But⟩ⁿ they masters of their weapons. But by &[55] [64₁] by, when he got upon a thought like an Indian seizing by the mane & mounting a wild horse of the desart, he overrode them all & showed such mastery & took up time & nature like a boy's marble in his hand as to vindicate himself[.]

   [63] Oct. 4
      Last night a dream within a dream. I fancied I woke up, & found myself out walking in ⟨the⟩ ↑my↓ cornfield. James was dis-turbed, & came out & called, who's there?[56] I, though a little confused how I came there, answered, "it was I." Presently, I walked off, & found I had lost my way. I inquired what town it was, & was told *Lisbon*. I ↑was↓ got by & by into a railroad car; but was a long way from home; &c &c — & was furthermore astonished again to wake really.
      [64₂] Imperfection or want that we suffer from in dreams, as, to go on a journey without a hat, or be in a ⟨j⟩large assembly without your coat, what is the theory of that? o professor of Metaphysics!

      [53] "Manners, the manners . . . resistance.", struck through in ink and in pencil with single vertical use marks on pp. [59] and [60], is used in "Behavior," *W*, VI, 183–184.
      [54] This sentence is used in "Inspiration," *W*, VIII, 280, and "Country Life," *W*, XII, 141. A question mark between two vertical lines appears in the right margin immediately after "twelve".
      [55] "Alcott . . . But by &", in pencil, is continued in pencil at the bottom of p. [64] under a page-wide rule in pencil.
      [56] James Burke was Emerson's Irish handyman. See Journal AC, pp. [252] and [276] below.

[65] Wide the gulf between genius & talent. The men we know deal with their thoughts as jewellers with jewels which they sell but must not wear; like ⟨architects⟩ ↑carpenters↓ with houses too fine for such as they to live in. The mystic is as good as his gold & jewels, good as his house that he builds, goes always in purple apparel, a glistering angel.

[66] In the solitary man of whom I wrote elsewhere, who must walk miles & miles to get the twitchings out of his face, the starts ↑&↓ shoves↓ out of his arms & shoulders, is to be noted the remorse running to despair of his social gaucheries, and he exclaimed, "God may forgive sins, but awkwardness has no forgiveness in heaven or on earth." [57]

[67] Treadwell, like Macaulay ↑& Brewster↓ sees the high place of Bacon, without being able to account for it, & thinks it a mistake. But he is there by specific gravity or levity of spirit, not by any feat he did, or ⟨in⟩ ↑by↓ tutoring more or less of Newton & his followers, but by birthright, like the aristocracy of heaven. [58]

[68] In England, the refined gardening & building

_____

In England, sure of gentlemen.

_____

[69] Wordsworth ⟨was true⟩ honored himself by his adherence to truth & was ⟨co⟩ willing not to shine. But he surprized by the ⟨speedy⟩ ↑hard↓ limits of his thought[.] [59]

[70] At the Albion, we found that Mr W[oodman].'s mushrooms tasted like the roof of a house. [60]

[57] This paragraph, struck through in ink with a diagonal use mark, is used in "Society and Solitude," *W*, VII, 5.
[58] This paragraph, struck through in ink with two diagonal use marks, is used in "Literature," *W*, V, 248.
[59] These two sentences, struck through in ink with a vertical use mark, are used in "First Visit to England," *W*, V, 24.
[60] The Albion Hotel was at the corner of Tremont and Beacon Streets in Boston. At one of the Albion dinners that preceded the formation of the Saturday Club,

The Indians told Columbus that tobacco took away fatigue.[61]

Trebellius one of the 5 writers of the Augustan history in the 4th Century, says, "Galli, quibus insitum est esse leves," [62]

And see the identity of traits between the French & the ancient Gauls, in Article ⁿ *Julius Cesar*. [*Nouvelle*] *Biog[raphie]*. *Generale* [Paris, 1855, IX, 470]

[71] ——
loss of confidence in judges

——

The ermine is a fierce animal[.]

——

Colleges should have a real examination or test, before granting diplomas, as by competition for valuable prizes, so having ⟨your⟩ rivals or enemies to adjudicate the crown, and this will come to be suggested & enforced by the neighborhood of the race-course at Cambridge, by the pugilistic prize fights, by regattas, & cattle-shows. A fair mode is to propose ⟨really hard⟩ problems[,] chemical, mathematical, botanical, never yet solved, and rewards for the solution. The old custom of defending a thesis against all comers, was a fair test, *when there were comers.*

[72] Time was when we built castles in the air, — of the American College. Allston, Greenough, Nuttall, Audubon, Fremont, Irving, were to fill the chairs.[63]

---

lawyer Horatio Woodman (1821–1879) cooked mushrooms at the table. Music critic John Sullivan Dwight (1813–1893), deputed to try this novelty, bravely tasted and gave this report. For this anecdote and for other information on the Saturday Club, the Adirondack Club, and the founding of *The Atlantic Monthly* throughout this volume, the editors are indebted to Edward Waldo Emerson, *The Early Years of the Saturday Club 1855–1870* (Boston, 1918).

[61] This sentence is struck through in ink with a vertical use mark.

[62] "The Gauls, whose nature it is to be frivolous" (Ed.). Trebellius Pollio was one of six real or supposed writers on late Roman history.

[63] Washington Allston (1779–1843), American artist and author; Horatio Greenough (1805–1852) and his brother Richard Saltonstall Greenough (1819–1904), American sculptors; Thomas Nuttall (1786–1859), onetime curator of the Botanical Garden at Harvard, the author of *A Manual of the Ornithology of the United States and Canada*, 1832; John James Audubon (1785–1851); John Charles Frémont (1813–1890); and Washington Irving (1783–1859).

[73] Cardinal Wolsey was magnificent.
Magnificence is the *genius* of wealth.

[74] God forbid I should complain of being excluded by this
or that man or circle from this or that privilege. On the contrary,
the most absolute submission on my part attends it. For do I not
know that these parties are all eager to invite high merit to this
privilege; and, that, on the instant ⟨of⟩ [75] when that merit is
demonstrated by me, or by any, they will fly to greet it, & will open
every door to it, & bear it on their arms with joy unfeigned.

[76] In this mixed world, men are so heterogeneous in composition, & in the exigences they must daily meet, that the most amiable
proprietor is glad of a bull-dog to represent him in his orchard, & of
a cossack in his watch-man. It is skepticism this, — yes, but a saint is a
skeptic once in twenty four hours.[64]

[77] The House of Commons[n] sits frequently 14, 15, & even 16
hours; whilst ⟨the House of Lords⟩ "it has been observed by an irreverent
wit, that⟨"⟩ the Lords sit scarcely long enough to boil an egg."
                    Ed. Rev Jan 1854 [pp. 124, 127][65]
till at length the time arrives, when, in the words of Sir F[rancis]. Baring,
"any man who occupies the time of the ⟨h⟩House is a public enemy"
                                      Ib[*id*]. [p. 129]
The Charitable Trusts bill proposed by Lord Brougham in 1816 has at
length become a law in 1853, [78][66] and Lord J. Russell said that this
was about the ordinary period for bringing any considerable measure to
maturity.   Ed[*inburgh*] R[*eview*,] Jan 1854 [*Ibid.*]

⟨Don't be a bore.⟩ Every body is a bore to somebody. Better sit
at home alone.

———

People who offend all others, never suspect themselves, but
think others only to blame.

———

[64] "In this . . . orchard," is struck through in ink with a vertical use mark.
    [65] "The Machinery of Parliamentary Legislation," *Edinburgh Review*, XCIX
(Jan. 1854), pp. 121–141.
    [66] A page-wide rule and "from p. 77", enclosed in a line at bottom and right,
separate the conclusion of this quotation at the bottom of p. [78] from "⟨Dont be
. . . blame." at the top of the page.

[79] English have more constitution than other people,—that which yields the supplies of the day,—the enough & to spare,—giving magnificence to wealth, courage to war, genius in poetry, enterprise in trade, invention in mechanics, petulance & projects to youth.[n][67]

Marshall was a good specimen; so much blood he did not know what [80] to do with it[;] drank vast quantities of brandy like water, spent quantities of strength on swimming, hunting, riding, walking, & ready for the most absurd frolics, with the gravity of the Eumenides.[68]

They do not hesitate.

[81] Marcelle says, she took cold in coming into the world, & has had a cold ever since.[69]
Mr Blanchard ↑the carpenter↓ in Concord,[n] ⟨th⟩reading in the newspaper the sale of building lots on Lake Street, in Chicago, "can't hardly believe that any lands can ⟨bring⟩ ↑be worth↓ so much money, so far off."

[82] The radiation of manners the boundless America gives opportunity as wide as the morning, & the effect is to change the peak of the mountain into a vast table land, where millions can share the privilege of this handful of patricians.

[83] What said Consuelo of the lessons she had given the nobles on manners from the stage? Genius invents fine manners also, which the baron & the baroness copy very fast, & better the instruction. They stereotype the lesson they have learned into a mode.[70]

[67] This sentence, struck through in ink with a vertical use mark, is used in "Character," W, V, 132.
[68] "Marshall . . . Eumenides.", struck through in ink with a vertical use mark on p. [80], is used in "Character," W, V, 132.
[69] This sentence, struck through in ink with a vertical use mark, is used in "Behavior," W, VI, 185. See Journal VO, p. [269] below.
[70] This paragraph, struck through in ink with a vertical use mark, is used in "Behavior," W, VI, 170. George Sand's Consuelo, trans. Fayette Robinson (New York, 1851), is in Emerson's library.

[84] ↑Caloric↓
"I have no enthusiasm for nature," said George Sand, "which the slightest chill will not instantly destroy." [71]   ↑printed↓

The only safe rule in politics is always to believe that the worst will be done.

[85] Davenport, Iowa, Dec., 31, 1855
Le Claire House
"No gentleman permitted to sit at the table without his coat" [72]
"No gambling permitted in the House."

                            Rules of the house

I have crossed the Missisippi on foot three times.
Soft coal which comes to Rock Island from about /12/8/ miles, sells for 16 cents a bushel: wood at [n] 6.00 per cord.[73] They talk "quarter sections." I will take a [86] quarter section of that pie. Leclaire being a halfbreed of the Sacs & Foxes (& of French Canadian) had a right to a location of a square mile of land & with a more than Indian sagacity of choosing his warpath, he chose his lot ⟨abo⟩ one, above the rapids, & the other below the rapids, at Rock Island. ⟨His house⟩ He chose his lot 30 years ago, & now the *railroad* ⟨runs⟩ *to the Pacific runs directly through his* ⟨house⟩ *log-house*, which is occupied by the company for wood & other purposes. His property has risen to the value of 5 or 600 000 dollars. He is 57 years old, & weighs 308 pounds.[74]

    [87] I have seen a country gentleman cut himself all up into pieces by the critical introvertive habit. When disconcerted by an odd person, he addressed himself, "O my wit! Why do you not help me at this pinch?" When he found himself silent in a noisy set, he cried, "O my animal spirits! to the rescue! holla!"

---

    [71] This sentence, struck through in ink with one vertical and one diagonal use mark, is used in "Inspiration," *W*, VIII, 289–290, and "Country Life," *W*, XII, 140.
    [72] This sentence, struck through in ink with a diagonal use mark, is used in "Behavior," *W*, VI, 173.
    [73] The number "8" is inserted in pencil.
    [74] "Leclaire being . . . 308 pounds." is in pencil.

[88] In Rock Island I am advertised as "the celebrated Metaphysician"[;] in Davenport as "the Essayist & Poet." [75]

Dixon	3500 souls	
Davenport	8000	?
Rock Island	7500	?
La Salle	1500	?
Galena	1200	
Elgin	4000	
Beloit	5↑000↓ [76]	
Peoria	13000	
Chicago	⟨7⟩90 000	
Cleveland	45 000	
Columbus	24 000	

[89] In Dixon I talked with Mr Dixon the pioneer founder of the city.[77] His full length portrait was hanging in the town-hall where we were. He is 80 years old & a great favorite with the people, his family have all died, but some grand-children remain. He who has made so many rich is a poor man, which, it seems, is a common fortune here; Sutter the Californian discoverer of gold, is poor. It looks as if one must have a talent for misfortune to miss so many opportunities as these men who have owned the whole [90] township & not saved a competence. He is a correct quiet man[,] was first a tailor, then a stage owner, & mail agent, &c. I went down the Galena river, once Bean river, Fève, then Fever, now Galena River, four or five miles in a sleigh, with Mr McMasters to the Marsden Lead, so called, a valuable lead mine, & went into it. Marsden, it seems, was a ↑poor↓ farmer here; ⟨poor⟩ & sold out his place, & went to California; found no gold, & came back ⟨here⟩,[n] & bought his [91] land again, &, in digging to clear out a spring of water, stumbled on this most

[75] This entry is in pencil. Emerson lectured at Davenport, Iowa, on December 31, 1855, and on "England and the English" at Rock Island, Illinois, on January 1, 1856. See Pocket Diary 7, p. [15] below.

[76] The "ooo" added to "Beloit   5" is in pencil.

[77] Emerson lectured on "Beauty" in Dixon, Illinois, on January 3, 1856. See Pocket Diary 7, p. [15] below.

valuable lead (leed), as they call it, of lead-ore. They can get up 7000 lb. of the ore in a day (by a couple of laborers), and the smelters will come to the spot, & buy the ore at 3 cents a pound; so that he found California here. He at once called in his brothers, & divided the mine with them. One of them sold out his share↑, one sixth,↓ ("foolishly") for 12 000 dollars; the others retain theirs.

[92] Mr Shetland said, 75 or 100 000 dollars ⟨w⟩had already been derived from this mine, & perhaps as much more remains. ⟨M⟩Hon. Mr Turner of Freeport said to me, that it is not usually the first settlers, who become rich, but the second comers: the first, he said, are often visionary men, the second are practical. The first two settlers of Rockford died insolvent, & he named similar cases in other towns[,] I think Beloit. I read at the bottom of a map of Wisconsin, that the motto of the State-seal of Wisconsin, is, "*Civilitas successit Barbarum.*"[78]

[93] An idealist, if he have the sensibilities & habits of those whom I know, is very ungrateful. He craves & enjoys every chemical property, and every elemental force, loves pure air, water, light, caloric, wheat, flesh, salt, & sugar, the blood ⟨bounding⟩ ↑coursing↓ in his own veins, and the grasp of friendly hands; & uses the meat he eats to preach against matter as malignant, & to praise mind, which he very hollowly & treacherously serves. Beware of hypocrisy.

[94]   ↑1856, Jan 9, Beloit.↓
I fancied in this fierce cold weather, mercury varying from 20 to 30 degrees below zero, for the last week, that Illinois lands would be at a discount,ⁿ and the agent who at Dixon was selling great tracts, would be better advised to keep them for milder days, since a hundred miles of prairie in such days as these are not worth the poorest shed or cellar in the towns. But my easy landlord assured me "we had no cold weather in Illinois, only now & then Indian Summers & cool nights." He looked [95] merrily at his windowpanes, opaque with a stratum of frost, & said, that his was a fashionable first class hotel, with window-lights of ground glass.

This climate & people are a new test for the wares of a man of

[78] "Civilization follows barbarism" (Ed.), territorial motto of Minnesota.

letters. All his thin watery matter freezes; 'tis only the smallest portion of alcohol that remains good. At the lyceum, the stout Illinoian, after a short trial, walks out of the hall. The Committee tell you that the people want a hearty laugh, & Stark, & Saxe, & Park Benjamin, [96] who give them that, are heard with joy. Well I think with Gov. Reynolds, the people are always right, (in a sense,) & that the man of letters is to say, these are the new conditions to which I must conform.[79] The architect who is asked to build a house to go upon the sea, must not build a parthenon or a square house, but a ship. And Shakspeare or Franklin or Aesop coming to Illinois, would say, I must give my [97] wisdom a comic form, instead of tragics or elegiacs, & well I know to do it, and ⟨N⟩he is no master who cannot vary his forms, & carry his own end triumphantly through the most difficult.

[98] Mr Sweet, a telegraph agent on the Chicago & Rock River line, said, he can tell the name of the operator, by the accent of his dispatch, by the ⟨a⟩ear, just as readily as he knows the handwriting of his friends. Every operator has his own manner or accent. An operator usually reads more correctly & quickly by the ear, than by the eye. Some good operators never learn to read by the ear. Boys make the best operators, and, in six months, a boy of 16 was worth 45 dollars a month in an office at Chicago. The rule of their experience is never to establish a telegraph line until after a railroad is built. It cannot sooner pay.

[99] At Beloit, on Tuesday night, ↑8 Jan[uar]y↓ the mercury was at 27 & 28 below Zero. It has been bitterly cold for a fortnight. ↑A cold night they call a singer.↓

The hard times of Illinois were from 1837 to 1845 & onward, when pork was worth 12 shillings a hundred, & men journeyed with loads of wheat & pork a hundred miles or more to Chicago, & sold their

---

[79] John Godfrey Saxe (1816–1887), American poet and editor of the Burlington, Vermont, *Sentinel*, was best known for his humorous verse. Park Benjamin (1809–1864) was an American editor and minor poet. Emerson met John Reynolds (1788–1865), onetime governor of Illinois, in Springfield in 1853; see *JMN*, XI, 531. For his statement that "the people are always right", see *JMN*, XIII, 397.

wheat for 26 cents a bushel, & were obliged to sell their team to get home again. Mr Jenks[,] a stage agent & livery stable keeper[,] told us of his experiences & when he left Chicago to go eastward he would not have given $3.00 for a warranty deed of the State of Illinois.

[100] Hoosier meant Southerner. Hoosiers & Yankees would fight for the land. Yankees when fighting men would fight by the day: the Hoosiers are good to begin, but they *cave*.

Judge[n] Emmons ↑Esq↓ of Michigan said to me that he had said he wished it might be a criminal offence to bring an English lawbook into a court in this country, so foolish & mischievous is our slavery to Eng. precedent. The word commerce has had only an Eng meaning & has been made to follow only the petty exigences of Eng. experience but the commerce of rivers & the commerce of roads & the commerce of air balloons must add an American extension to the pondhole of "admiralty." [80]

[101] There are times when the intellect is so active, that every thing seems to run to meet it. Its supplies are found without much thought as to studies. Knowledge runs to the man, & the man runs to knowledge. In spring, when the snow melts, the maple trees run with sugar, & you cannot get tubs fast enough. But it is only for a few days. The hunter on the prairie at the right season, has no need of choosing his ground. East, west, by the river, by the timber, near the farm, from the farm, he is everywhere by his game.

[102] Here is a road, *Mich[iga]n Southern*, which runs through four sovereign states, a judicial being, which has no judicial sovereign. ↑Ohio,[n] Ind., Mich., Ill.↓
Franchise has to yield to eminent domain, & the remedy is appraisal & payment of damages. But unfortunately, when, as now, the Mich. Central is to be ⟨re⟩bereaved of its monopoly, which it had bought & paid for, the jury to appraise the damage done is taken from the

---

[80] "he wished . . . 'admiralty.' ", struck through in ink with a vertical use mark, is used in "Power," *W*, VI, 62.

population aggrieved by the Mich. Central. I asked, why not take a jury from other states?

[103] People here are alive to a benefaction derived from railroads which is inexpressibly great, & vastly exceeding any intentional philanthropy on record. What is the benefit by a Howard or a Bell & Lancaster or an Alfred or an Elizabeth Fry or any lover less or larger compared with the involuntary blessing wrought on nations by the selfish capitalists who built the Illinois Central & the Mich. Central[?] [81]
↑Meantime, my banker here at Adrian, Mr Lyon, is of opinion, that, to run on a bank for gold, is a criminal offence, & ought to be punished by ⟨s⟩the state's prison! He delights[,] he frankly told me[,] to make such people pay 3 & 4 percent a month for money.↓

[104] Seek things in their purity. Well, we try, on each subject we accost, to ascend to principles; to dip our pen in the blackest of the pot; and, to be sure, find the cause of the trait in some organ, as spleen, or bone, or blood. We are not nearer. We are still outside. Nature itself is nothing but a skin, and all these but coarser cuticles. [105] A god or genius sits regent over every plant & animal, and causes this, & knits this to that, after an order or plan which is intellectual. The botanist, the physicist is not then the man deepest immersed in nature, as if he were ready to bear apples or to shoot out four legs, but one filled with the light↑est↓ ⟨air⟩ & purest air who sympathizes with the ⟨light⟩ ↑creative↓ spirit, ⟨of⟩ [106] ⟨of the world, &⟩ anticipates the tendency, & where the bird will next alight, — being ⟨it⟩↑him↓self full of the same tendency.
[...] [82]

[107] Hospitality consists in a little fire, a little food, ↑but enough,↓ & an immense quiet. In England, it is a great deal of fine food, & of fire & immense decorum.

[81] This paragraph, struck through in ink with a vertical use mark, is used in "Considerations by the Way," *W*, VI, 256.
[82] From this point on, material from Journal RO Mind, printed in *JMN*, V, is indicated by [...].

[108] [...]
[109]   Mem.
1855, 9 Oct. Sent Chapter I. of "English Traits," to P. S. & Co [83]

1856 6 Aug[us]t *English Traits* published

[110] [...]
       [111] A man in Illinois told me he had been able to distinguish
a horse from a cow on the prairie, with the naked eye at the distance
of five miles.
       The lumber sold at the Chicago market in the last year was
336 000 000 feet, said Mr Campbell of LaSalle. Mr. A. C. Harding,
of Monmouth said he would sell his farm of 1300 acres at M. 50
miles I think west of Peoria, containing ten buildings, 2 good orchards,
at $50 per acre & a part of it at $40[.]
The wild grass on the bottom lands when not fed, grows 14 ft. high.[84]

[112] [...]
       [113] It is observed ⟨h⟩that the emigrant usually keeps his own
line of latitude.

       "In the American backwoods is there nothing of those social & ar-
tistic enjoyments which ennoble man, whilst they dissatisfy him. What man
would live without the poesy of sounds, colors, & rhymes? Unhappy people that is condemned to this privation!" *German Paper*

[114] [...]
       [115] My friend had great abilities, & a genial temper, & no
vices, but he had one defect which ruined all. He could not speak in
the tone of the people. ⟨In the⟩ There seemed to be some paralysis
on his will, that, when he met men on common terms, he spoke
weakly, & from the point, like a silly girl. His consciousness of the
fault only made it worse. He envied every woodsawyer & drover in
the bar room their manly speech.

       [83] "P. S." is Phillips, Sampson & Co., Emerson's publisher. Emerson wrote to
Moses Dresser Phillips on October 9, 1855, "Here is the first of say, sixteen or seventeen chapters" (*L*, IV, 533).
       [84] "A man . . . five miles." and "The wild . . . high.", struck through in
pencil with single vertical use marks, are used in "Country Life," *W*, XII, 143–144.

But Mirabeau had *le don terrible de la familiarité*. He whose sympathy goes lowest, dread him, o kings! [85]

[116] [...]
    [117] Most people prefer nuts in their shells, as they then have the pleasure of overcoming a small difficulty[.]

Wm Little came to church & heard my sermon against minding trifles. He told me, ⟨he should⟩ had he preached ↑the↓ sho⟨l⟩uld have taken the other side. Probably not one hearer besides thought so far on the subject.

Mr ——, gardener of Phila.[,] had a friend in Eng[lan]d who was butler to a duke. When he went to Eng[lan]d he was very kindly entertained by the butler & at last with wine of which he said [118] "I don't let the duke himself have any of this."

The railroads have ⟨tried⟩ pretended low fares, and, instead of 75 cents, I pay for a passage to Boston from Concord, 60 cents; & the trip costs one hour instead of 2½ hours. Well, I have really paid, in the depreciation of my railroad stock, six or seven hundred dollars a year, for the last [...] [119] few years, or, say, a hundred a year, since the roads were built. And I shall be glad to know that I am at the end of my losses on this head.

————

A writer in the B[oston]. Transcript says, that "just in proportion to the morality of a people, will be the expansion of the credit system." Which sounds to me like better polit[ical]. economy than I often hear.

[120] [...]
    [121] ⟨The result of⟩ "Spiritualism" or the rappings is a new

[85] "My friend . . . o kings!", struck through in ink with three vertical use marks, is used in "Society and Solitude," *W*, VII, 3–4. For Mirabeau's familiarity, see Pierre Etienne Louis Dumont, *Recollections of Mirabeau, and the Two First Legislative Assemblies of France* (Philadelphia, 1833), pp. 49–50. Emerson withdrew this book from the Boston Athenaeum July 26–August 12, 1854. See *JMN*, XIII, 275.

test, like blue litmus, or other chemical test, to try catechisms with. It detects organic skepticism in the very heads of the church.[86]

[122] [...]
[123] *Lectures*

    1 France
    ——
    2 Eng[lish]. Civ[ilization].
    ——
    6 Poetry
    7 Beauty
    8 The Scholar
    3 Anglo-American
    5 The Age
    4 Stonehenge

⟨France⟩
England
↑France↓
America
Stonehenge
The Age
⟨Poetry⟩ ↑Beauty↓
⟨Beauty⟩ ↑Poetry↓
    ↑Scholar↓

For "*Beauty*." Use of gems, in "Pericles & Aspasia"; in C[harles] K[ing] N[ewcomb]'s "Cleone"; in "Angel in the House." [87]

Man off his centre.[88]

---

[86] This paragraph, struck through in pencil with two vertical use marks, is used in "Demonology," *W*, X, 26. See also Journal SO, p. [261] below.

[87] For the use of gems, see Walter Savage Landor, *Pericles and Aspasia*, 2 vols. (London, 1836), I, 24–25: "The Goddesses are in the right . . . their ears are marble, but I do not believe any one of them would tell us that women were made to be the settings of pearls and emeralds." This work is in Emerson's library. The manuscript of Charles King Newcomb's unpublished poem "Cleone" is in the Brown University library. Emerson owned Coventry Kersey Dighton Patmore's *The Angel in the House* . . . (London, 1854) and quotes from a passage on gems on p. [131] below. For Emerson's use of gems in "Beauty," see *W*, VI, 304–305.

[88] This entry is used in "Behavior," *W*, VI, 180. See p. [131] below.

and "author offering truth which is taken without him."

[124] [...]
[125] They called ⟨F⟩old France a despotism tempered with epigrams. Wherever the epigrams grow, they are pretty sure to make room for themselves ↑& temper ↑any↓ despotisms.↓ⁿ What can you do with a Talleyrand? "Sire, no government has prospered that has resisted me." So in politics with De Retz, or with Webster. "Where shall I go?" said Webster. There is [126] [...] [127] the Whig party & the Democratic party & Mr Webster. It soon appears that the Epigram, or Webster, is a party too. Much more in the Courts, where he was really sovereign.
↑What to do with a man who successively converted five censors into 5 advocates — Beaumarchais↓ [89]

Choate said, that a man once a candidate for the Presidency, it was impossible to get that *virus* quite out of ⟨t⟩his constitution: as Everett, Webster, Cass, down to Pratt & Mellen.[90]

In looking at a sunset we seem to lose our identity [91]

[128] [...]
[129]   On this green bank by this soft flood
    Their flag to April's breeze unfurled
    Here once the embattled farmers stood
    And fired the shot heard round the world.

    The foe long since in silence slept
    A↑l↓ike the conqueror silent sleeps
    And Time the ruined bridge hath swept
    Down the dark stream which seaward creeps

---

[89] This sentence is used in "Clubs," *W*, VII, 240. See *JMN*, XIII, 408, and Journal VO, p. [154] below.

[90] Daniel Webster (1782–1852) failed to win the Whig nomination for the presidency in 1852; Lewis Cass (1782–1866) was the unsuccessful Democratic candidate for the presidency in 1848. Daniel Pratt (1809–1887) was a vagrant whose chief delusion was that he had been elected to the presidency and was being kept out of office by a coalition of unscrupulous rivals. Mellen has not been identified.

[91] This sentence from RO Mind, in pencil and upside down, appears at the bottom of p. [127].

On this green bank by this lone stream
We set today the votive stone
That memory may their deed redeem
When like our sires our sons are gone.

Spirit that made those heroes dare
To die or leave their children free
Bid Time & Nature gently spare
The shaft we raise to them & thee [92]

[130] [...]
[131] N. Wood, Esq. says, the clients say, 'Tis not the money, I
should like that you should have it, but I want to fight this man
(in law), and let him know that he is not to ride over me.

———

The Eyes tell in an instant if the man is off his centre, or no.[93]

———

Diamonds, plumes, colors, &c. says Patmore, "suit her better than
themselves." [94]

[132] [...]
[133] [blank]
[134] [...]
[135]   English Traits
                 Chap. 1.   First Visit
                     2   Voyage
                     3   Land
                     4   Race
                     5   Ability
                     6   Manners   .
                     7   Truth

[92] The stanzas on p. [129], in pencil, are a version of "Concord Hymn," W, IX,
158–159. They are from the 1835 sequence.
[93] This sentence, struck through in ink with a vertical use mark, is used in "Behavior," W, VI, 180. See p. [123] above.
[94] The Angel in the House . . . , 1854, p. 60. This entry is used in "Woman,"
W, XI, 411–412.

[136] [...]

[137] I celebrate the Eng Nation but I do not know that it is a race. Race piques, because we wish to know that what we do well is personal to us, that ↑fortune,↓ ⟨climate⟩ ↑air↓, laws, religion, numbers, had no part in it, that a Chinaman or a ⟨French⟩ Portugueze or a Russian or a Malay educated in England will not do the same thing in the next generation[.]

[138] Question of race is to quality of mind. How came such a man as Herbert?

Another measure is spawning power
Another —   chosen men
      Where do new discoveries appear [95]

[139] Eng. Race have Character
         ↑balance↓
      Genius
      discoveries
      physique
      assimilating power

[95] "Question . . . appear" is struck through in ink with three diagonal use marks. No ink came out of the pen for the whole of one use mark and half of another. "How came . . . Herbert?" is used in "Race," *W*, V, 47.

[140] [96] *English Traits sent to*
    Mrs [Lydia Maria] Child
Mrs [Anna Jackson] Lowell
C[yrus]. A[ugustus]. Bartol
⟨Mrs Agassiz⟩
Mrs [Paulina Tucker] Nash
Miss [Elizabeth Palmer] Peabody
G[eorge]. P[artridge]. Bradford
Elizabeth Hoar
E[benezer]. R[ockwood]. Hoar
S[amuel] G[ray] Ward
S Clark
Edw[ard]. Bangs
J[ames]. E[lliot]. Cabot
Mr [Barzillai] Frost
W.⟨H⟩O. White ↑W.⟨H⟩O. W?↓
T[heodore]. Parker
H[enry] D[avid] Thoreau
W[illiam]. E[llery]. Channing
C[harles] K[ing] Newcomb
W[illiam]. Emerson
A[mos] B[ronson] Alcott

Mrs [Susan Bridge] Jackson
Mrs Jackson

---

[96] The list on p. [140] is in two columns, indicated by a break. "F C Lowell", "J M Cheney", and "⟨Judge Hoar⟩", all on p. [140], are in pencil. Of those who have not been previously identified or are not easily recognizable, Lydia Maria Child (1802–1880) was an American abolitionist and author; Cyrus Augustus Bartol was a Boston pastor; Paulina Tucker Nash was Emerson's sister-in-law; Elizabeth Palmer Peabody operated a bookshop in Boston; Dr. George Partridge Bradford had been a friend of Emerson since they were students at Harvard Divinity School; Elizabeth Hoar had been engaged to Emerson's brother Charles at the time of his death in May, 1836; Ebenezer Rockwood Hoar (1816–1895) was a lawyer, congressman (1873–1875), and later attorney general; Samuel Gray Ward (1817–1907), Harvard graduate and a Boston banker, was a close friend of Emerson; "S Clark" may be Sarah Freeman Clarke, sister of James Freeman Clarke, Unitarian clergyman. in Boston; Edward Bangs was a young Harvard graduate of Boston, studying law; Barzillai Frost was minister of the First Parish Church in Concord; "W. O. White" may be William Abijah White, an editor of

N[athaniel] L[angdon] Frothingham
H[enry]. W[adsworth]. Longfellow
W[illiam]. Emerson, Jr.
Mrs J[ulia Ward]. Howe
Mrs [Caroline Sturgis] Tappan
Miss [Ida] Agassiz
F A Sanborn
⟨Judge Hoar⟩W[illiam] H[enry] Furness
Sam[ue]l Bradford
Miss M[ary]. H[owland]. Russell
J[ames] W[arner] Ward   Cincinnati

---

temperance journals and lecturer on antislavery; Susan Bridge Jackson was the wife of Emerson's brother-in-law Charles Thomas Jackson; Nathaniel Langdon Frothingham was pastor of Boston's First Church; Caroline Sturgis, who had been a close friend of Emerson since 1838, had married William Tappan of New York; Ida Agassiz was the daughter of Louis Agassiz; "F A Sanborn" is probably a mistake for Franklin Benjamin Sanborn (1831–1917), who opened a school in Concord in May, 1855; William Henry Furness, Emerson's friend since boyhood, was minister of the First Unitarian Church in Philadelphia; Samuel Bradford, a lifelong friend from Boston, was treasurer of two Philadelphia coal companies; Mary Howland Russell, daughter of Nathaniel Russell, was a Plymouth friend; James Warner Ward (b. 1817), poet and botanist, who later taught at the Female College of Ohio and edited the *Botanical Magazine*, had visited the Mammoth Cave with Emerson in 1850; Francis Cabot Lowell was Emerson's classmate at Harvard and friend; John Milton Cheney, Emerson's classmate at Harvard, was cashier of the Middlesex Institution for Savings in Concord; Mary Preston Stearns was the wife of George Luther Stearns of Medford, antislavery advocate; "J M Bundy" may be the "Bundy" of Journal SO, p. [20], described in "Society and Solitude" as "a backwoodsman, who had been sent to the University" (*W*, VII, 11–12); "G. C. Vaughan" may be John C. Vaughan, a South Carolina abolitionist and editor of the free-soil daily, *Free Democrat*; a William W. Welch wrote to Emerson in February and May, 1856 (*L*, VI, 620); "Mrs Jackson" has not been identified. In the list on p. [141], historian Arthur Helps entertained Emerson in England on July 8 and 9, 1848; James John Garth Wilkinson (1812–1899) was a translator of Swedenborg; Edwin Wilkins Field (1804–1871) was a law reformer and artist; William Edward Forster (1818–1886), Quaker, reformer, and statesman, was also a friend of the Carlyles; Alexander Ireland, editor and friend, encouraged and organized Emerson's 1847–1848 trip to England; William Stirling wrote to Emerson in June and July of 1848 (*L*, VI, 595); Emerson had lodged with his British publisher, John Chapman, in 1848; Emerson met the painter William Bell Scott (1811–1890) in England; Dr. Samuel Brown (1817–1856), a physicist and chemist who had entertained Margaret Fuller, was Emerson's host during his stay in Edinburgh.

38

F[rancis] C[abot] Lowell
J[ohn] M[ilton] Cheney
Mrs [Mary Preston] Stearns
J M Bundy
G. ⟨R⟩C. Vaughan
W[illiam]. W. Welch
[...]

[141] A[rthur] Helps
T[homas] Carlyle
A[rthur] H[ugh] Clough
C[hristopher]. P[earse]. Cranch
[James John Garth] Wilkinson
Edw↑in↓. Field
⟨E⟩W[illiam]. E[dward]. Forster
Alex[ander]. Ireland
W[illiam]. Stirling, Esq.
J[ohn] Chapman
J[ane Welsh]. Carlyle
H[arriet]. Martineau
W[illiam]. B[ell]. Scott
Sam[ue]l Brown
W[illiam]. Allingham

[142] [blank]
[inside back cover] [blank]

$\mathcal{SO}$

1856–1857

Emerson began Journal SO in March, 1856, as he notes on p. [i], and used it through February, 1857. The first dated entry is April 5, [1856]; the last is February 7, 1857. A brief later entry, dated 1869, appears on p. [156].

The covers of the copybook, gray paper marbled with red, yellow, and blue over boards, measure 17.8 x 21.3 cm. The spine strip and the protective corners on the front and back covers are of tan leather. "SO" is written on the spine, in the upper right corner of the front cover, and in both outer corners of the back cover. "1856" is centered in the upper half of the front cover.

Including flyleaves (i, 1, 296, 297), there were 152 unlined leaves, measuring 17.2 x 20.7 cm, but the leaf bearing what would have been pages 195–196 in sequential pagination was cut out before pagination; page 197 is unnumbered, and Emerson numbered the verso of 197 as 200. The leaves bearing pages 212–213 and 268–279 are torn out; Emerson numbered what would have been page 281 in sequential pagination 280. He numbered the three pages following page 292 as follows: 291½, 292½, 293. He numbered the front flyleaf verso as "1"; odd numbers regularly appear on the verso and even numbers on the recto of pages to page 280. Emerson numbered three pages 111, and two pages each 186, 201, and 230. The editors have added subscript numbers to distinguish the trio and pairs. One page was misnumbered and corrected: ⟨3⟩4. The pages are numbered in ink except for the following twenty in pencil: 3, 34, 81, 85–90, 93, 143, 145, 147, 161, 163, 194, 243, 245, 247, 258. Thirty-five pages are unnumbered: i, 2, 7, 9, 11, 39, 50, 57, 58, 62, 94, 100, 122, 124, 127, 128, 130, 144, 181, 195, 214–216, 233, 234, 238, 240, 244, 246, 248, 256, 283, 284, 288, 297. Pages 91, 141, 151, 153, 159, and 249 were numbered first in pencil and then in ink. Twenty-eight pages are blank: 1, 7, 17, 22, 57, 62, 71, 97, 99, 103, 115, 124, 127, 128, 144, 145, 154, 162, 163, 181, 200, 245, 246, 248, 264, and 283–285.

A single sheet of unwatermarked white paper measuring 20 x 24.1 cm, which has been folded in half, is laid in inside the back cover; the editors have designated this pages 297a–297b. Also laid in inside the back cover is a blue sheet, faintly ruled, measuring 20 x 12.3 cm. This sheet is headed "Pantheism", and a note by Edward W. Emerson reads, "Very probably this is Thoreau's writing."

[front cover]   SO

1856

[front cover verso] [1]   ↑*Examined in Jan. 1878*↓

[Index material omitted]

[i] [Index material omitted]   March, 1856

SO
———

Nunc pellite curas cras ingens iterabimus aequor [2]
[Horace, *Odes*, I, vii, 31–32]

[1] [blank]
[2] To the illustration of Monomania.
    Muldar the chemist requires ↑as the first condition↓ of a chemist, that he shall know nothing of Philosophy.

Balzac describes Seraphelus as looking down with that deep blue eye over the mountain cleft abime sur abime and Esselin contrasts the desart deeps of astronomy with the peopled deeps of the heart of man.[3]
The ⟨people in the⟩ parishioner when ⟨M⟩Rev Mr M took off his rubbers thought him ⟨the⟩ like the antique statue of the Boy taking the thorn from his foot.[4]

[1] The entries on the front cover verso and p. [i] are in pencil.
[2] "Now banish care . . . To-morrow we will take again our course over the mighty main."
[3] Gerardus Johannes Mulder (1802–1880), a Dutch chemist, isolated fibrin from blood; Christian Esselen edited and published *Atlantis: Eine Monatsschrift für Wissenschaft, Politik und Poesie* in Detroit and later in Buffalo. Emerson's library contains most of the issues for 1855, 1856, and 1857. This is Emerson's translation of a passage from the issue of June, 1855.
[4] "Balzac . . . foot." is in pencil.

[3]⁵ The Two Ways. California not discovered by Geologists. It was chance but not Chaos.

Olmstead's Bad Economy of Slavery.⁶
What said Newton of the temporary or hypothetical character of gravity?

Two ways. The love of gold led to the planting of California. & Australia   went for asses and found a kingdom for men. So the greatest piece of benefit is not a Howard or Alfred, but an Illinois Central Railroad[.] ⁷

[⟨3⟩4] Two ways again. The most important effect of Copernicus was not on astronomy but on Calvinism, — tapping the Conceit of Man ↑and geology introduces new measures of antiquity.↓

Now & then leaps a word or a fact to light which is no man's invention, but the common instinct. Thus, "all men are born free and equal" — though denied by all politics, is the key-word of our modern civilization.
Many things we have that are not set down in the bill.

[5] 1856, Dec. 3. I have been reading some of Trench's translations of Calderon, and I miss the expected power. He has not genius. His fancy is sprightly, but his construction is ⟨s⟩merely mechanical. The mark of genius, is, that it has not only thoughts, but ⟨⟨the⟩also⟩ the copula that joins them is also a thought.⁸ It does not take some well--known fable, & use it, ↑if↓ a little more prettily, ⟨bu⟩yet to the same predictable ends, as others; but its fable & its use & end are un-predictable & its own. 'Tis the difference between the carpenter who

⁵ The entries on pp. [3] and [4] are written in ink over substantially the same matter in pencil.

⁶ Frederick Law Olmsted (1822–1903) published *A Journey in the Seaboard Slaves States* in 1856.

⁷ See Journal RO, p. [103] above. Cf. "Considerations by the Way," *W*, VI, 256; for "went . . . men.", see I Sam. 9–11.

⁸ "The mark . . . thought." is marked with a vertical pencil line in the left margin. Emerson withdrew Richard Chenevix Trench, *Calderon, his life and genius, with specimens of his plays* (New York, 1856), from the Boston Athenaeum December 3, 1856–March 12, 1857.

makes a box, & the mother who bears a child. The box was all in the
carpenter; but the [6] child was not ⟨of the mother or the father⟩
↑all in the parents.↓ They knew no more of the child's formation than
they did of their own. They were merely channels through which
the chi↑l↓d's nature flowed from quite another & eternal power. And
the child is as much a wonder to them, as to any: &, like the child
Jesus, shall, as he matures, convert & guide them as if he were the
Parent.

[7] [blank]
[8] C. N. Emerson, Esq. of Great Barrington told me a good college
story. His father, Rev. Sam. E. of Manchester, was at Williamstown
College, I think; at all events, the thing occurred there.[9] ⟨Baldwin⟩It
was the custom for the senior class to choose by ballot the Valedic-
torian orator, as he was called, that is, the one of their number who
should have the first honors at Commencement. The class wished to
choose Baldwin, who, though otherwise deserving, had received some
college censure, [9] and, I believe, had been suspended. The government brought all their influence to bear to secure the election of
Justin Edwards. The result of the ballot was 15 for Baldwin, 15 for
Edwards; Baldwin voting for Edwards, & Edwards not voting at all.
Several ballotings were had with the same result. The President sent
for Edwards, & told him that the government thought it altogether
proper [10] that he should be elected. But how to secure it? Edwards
said, that he could not vote for himself↑.↓ ⟨without Baldwin's finding
it out⟩ The President thought it proper that Edwards should vote
for himself. Edwards said, Baldwin would find it out, & then would
not vote for him, & then there would still be a tie. The President told
him to say nothing about it. And, at the next ballot, Edwards voted
for himself, [11] and the ballot stood 1⟨7⟩6 against 15, & he was
elected. Edwards had the oration, but his class absented themselves
at the delivery. Mr Emerson ⟨tol⟩said, that his father told him that
↑in his lifetime↓ he never would go to hear Dr Edwards, (who became
the head of the Andover Institution) preach, and used to say to him,

---

[9] Charles Noble Emerson (1821–1869), a cousin, was the son of Samuel Moody
Emerson (1785–1841), who was graduated from Williams College in 1810 and
preached at Manchester, Mass. (1821–1839).

"My son, whatever you do, never do anything mean." Baldwin, on the following year, was coming to Commencement [12] at Williamstown, & stepping to the door of the tavern at ↑Pittsfield↓,[10] to see ⟨the⟩a thundershower, was struck by lightning, & killed.

Mr Robinson's account of the Constitutional Convention, & the members, as Wilson, & Sumner, ↑& Banks,↓ on any difficulty or squall, running to Boutwell — [11]

Sir Stephen Lakeman

[13][12] Rockwell said, Toucey would not try titles with you, but sheltered himself in a general remark, "I don't want to hear your old Federal doctrines[.]"[13]

Stand up & stand long enough to be a party & give us somewhat to appeal to & we in the Southern states will rise.

[14] 'Tis strange, that Sir John Franklin & his picked men, with all the resources of English art, perished of famine where Esquimaux lived, & found them, & continue to live.[14]

Herschel said, ⟨Science⟩ ↑chemistry↓ had made such progress, that it would no longer be, that men would perish of famine, for sawdust could be made into food. And yet men in Sligo & Cape Verd & N. York have been dying of famine ever since. 'Tis answered, Yes, [15] you can convert woolen & cotton rags into sugar, but 'tis very ex-

---

[10] "Pittsfield" is inserted in pencil.

[11] The Massachusetts Constitutional Convention of 1853. George Sewell Boutwell (1818–1905) was Free-Soil governor in 1851–1852. "Mr Robinson's . . . Lakeman" is in pencil; for Sir Stephen Lakeman, see *JMN*, VI, 324.

[12] The entries on p. [13] are in pencil.

[13] Isaac Toucey (1792–1869) was Democratic governor of Connecticut, congressman, senator, and cabinet member; Julius Rockwell was a Republican senator from Lenox, Massachusetts. The punctuation in this sentence is added in pencil.

[14] Sir John Franklin (1786–1847) led an expedition in 1845 to discover a northwest passage and died in the Arctic. See *JMN*, V, 25.

pensive; & 'tis like Duke of ⟨Norfolk's⟩ Sussex's recommendation, that the poor should eat curry.

[16] 'Tis a geographic problem whether the Missisippi running from the depressed polar zone to the elevated equatorial region, 2500 miles, — does it not run up hill?

———

Alcott thinks Conventions, the Newspaper, the Lecture, & Conversation, to be our American achievments; which he ascribes to Garrison, Greeley, RWE, & himself!

———

[17] [blank]
[18] ↑Manners↓
If you talk with J[ames]. K. M↑ills↓ or J[ohn]. M[urray]. F[orbes]. or any other State Street man, ⟨⟨they⟩ ↑he↓ at once impress↑es↓⟩ you ↑find↓ that you are talking with ⟨S⟩all State Street, and if you are impressionable to that force, why they ⟨are⟩ have great advantage, are very strong men.[15] But if you talk with H[enry] ↑D[avid]↓ T[horeau] or C[harles] K[ing] N[ewcomb], or A[mos] B[ronson] A[lcott], you talk with only one man; he brings only his own ⟨deep⟩ force. But for that very reason that ⟨this⟩ ↑the conventional↓[16] requires softness or impressionability to [19] the dear little urbanities in you, if you abound in your own sense, ⟨if you are ⟨stron⟩ sound & rich in yourself,⟩ they are weak, & soon at your mercy. ⟨Then it presently appears, that⟩ ↑But↓ the others, (those wise hermits) who speak from their thought, speak from the deep heart of man, from a far wider public, the public of all sane & good men, from[17] [20] a broad humanity; and Greek & Syrian, Parthian & Chinese, Cherokee & Canaka, hear ⟨you⟩ ↑them↓[18] speaking in their own tongue. Bundy told me, that, when he heard the young men at the law-school talk

———

[15] James K. Mills helped establish the manufacturing towns of Chicopee and Holyoke. John Murray Forbes (1814–1898), later father-in-law of Emerson's daughter Edith, began as a China merchant and became president of the Michigan Central and the Chicago, Burlington, & Quincy railroads.

[16] The cancellation and insertion are in pencil.

[17] "the deep . . . men, from" is struck through with four diagonal use marks, one in ink and three in pencil.

[18] The cancellation and insertion are in ink over pencil.

together, he seemed to himself a boor; but when he ⟨got⟩ ↑caught↓ one of them alone, then *they* were the boors, & he was ↑the↓ better man.[19]

[21] Mr Eaton of Malden told me, that when Father Taylor was about going to Europe, he heard him preach, & he said, "To be sure, I am sorry to leave my own babes, — but he who takes care of every whale, & can give him a ton of herrings for a breakfast, will ⟨see that⟩ find food for my babes." [20]

[22] [blank]
[23]   Surface
Nineteen twentieths of their nourishment,[n] the trees owe to the air.[21]

———

The Rock of Ages is diffused into the mineral air.[22]

———

Blessed wonderful nature, without depth, but with immeasureable lateral spaces, — has only the thickness of a shingle or a slate.   See U 119

———

Skim it with a dipper[.]

———

[24] ↑Surface↓
        All life is surface-affair.
        Most diseases are cutane⟨us⟩ous.
        The matter proceeds from the manner.
W 138,   *RS* 36   *O* 185   *RO* 104   *SO* 11⟨7⟩8
        All men's life superficial   D 289 [23]

———

[19] "Bundy . . . man.", struck through in ink with two vertical use marks, is used in "Society and Solitude," *W*, VII, 11–12. Cf. *JMN*, XIII, 40.
[20] Edward Taylor (1793–1871) was the pastor of the Seamen's Bethel in Boston.
[21] This sentence, struck through in pencil with a vertical use mark, is used in "Instinct and Inspiration," *W*, XII, 80–81, and "Concord Walks," *W*, XII, 178.
[22] "The Rock . . . air." is struck through in pencil with a vertical use mark; cf. "Fragments on Nature and Life," XXIV, *W*, IX, 355, and Journal VO, pp. [83], [232], and [236] below.
[23] "Surface" and "W 138 . . . D 289" are in pencil.

Nature itself is nothing but a skin, & all these but coarser cuticles.   *RO* 104

———

Χρως δήλοει, the skin showeth, said the rotting Pherecydes.[24]

———

Old rogues soon show themselves.

———

———

Hahnemann said, that ⅞ of the chronic maladies affecting the human frame are forms of *psora*, & that all such are referable to 3 types of skin disease. *W* 138

[25] Life a surface affair, & our difference a difference of impressionability. *SO* 118

[26] Wise man was Napoleon. "The ⟨strength⟩kindness of Kings consists in strength & strict justice." He sees the same law running through all things. "Whatever they may tell you, believe that one fights with cannon as with fists;"—"When once the fire is begun, the least want of ammunition renders what you have done already, useless."
I find it easy to translate all his technics into all of mine, & his official advices are ↑to me↓ more literary & philosophical ⟨to me⟩ than the Memoires of the Academy.[25] ↑See in *Atlantis* for Feb., 1856, p. 118 ↑120↓ how Carnot translated mechanics into politics.↓

[27] "For your Sicilian Expedition, you should start too formidable to be attacked, you should abandon every position in your rear, except the defence of your Capital, & should act entirely on the aggressive against the

[24] Pherecydes was "eaten up with Lice"; he showed his friends "the condition of his whole Body: Saying 'χερι δήλα, the skin sheweth'" (Thomas Stanley, *The History of Philosophy* . . . [London, 1701], p. 59, in Emerson's library). See *JMN*, XI, 13, n. 38.
[25] "'The ⟨strength⟩kindness . . . advices" is struck through with two vertical use marks, one in pencil and one in ink; the entry is overwritten by "Printed" downward from "He sees" to "believe", and "printed" is written in ink in the left margin from "is begun," to "have done". The quotations are from *The Confidential Correspondence of Napoleon Bonaparte with his Brother Joseph, sometime King of Spain*, 2 vols. (New York, 1856), I, 181, 121. "'Whatever . . . useless.'" is used in "Greatness," *W*, VIII, 314.

enemy, who can attempt nothing when once you have accomplished your landing." Such is the art of war: you will see many men who ⟨will⟩ can fight well, but none who understand how to apply this principle." [Napoleon, *The Confidential Correspondence* . . . , 1856,] Vol I p 170 [26]

[28] "You are losing confidence in Salicetti. I can imagine no greater misfortune for you than to alienate so valuable a man." "Roederer belongs to the men who always destroy those to whom they are attached, — whether from want of tact, or of good fortune, it does not signify." [*Ibid.*, I, 308–309]

Culture

I see you are no wiser than ¾ of mankind, who do not appreciate the difference which exists between troops. You cannot replace with foreigners such troops as I have given you. [*Ibid.*, I, 273]

[29] "One can't make a man of imagination, like Roederer, understand that the great art is to be governed by time; that what ought not to be done till 1810, can't be done in 1807. The Gallic temperament can't submit to wait upon time; & yet it is by doing so, that I have gained all my success." [*Ibid.*, I, 237–238]

France. M. de [n] Sartine found in Vienna, the rogue, whom the Vienna police had prayed him to find in Paris.[27]

[30] "No general is satisfied unless he has an army. Answer him (St Cyr,), that a general always has enough troops, if he knows how to employ them, & if, instead of sleeping in town, he bivouacs with his men." [28] [*Ibid.*, I, 151]

"Your ministers are always cracking their whips." [*Ibid.*, I, 253]

England. "Her conduct is decided not by general politics, but by internal intrigues." [29] [*Ibid.*, I, 215]

[26] Two pencil lines are drawn in the left margin downward from "should start" to "attacked' ".
[27] In *JMN*, VIII, 156, Emerson cites the story of M. de Sartines from the *Memoirs of the Duchess d'Abrantès* [trans. from the French], 8 vols. (London, 1831–1835), III, 332–333. See also *JMN*, VI, 359.
[28] "a general . . . men.' ", marked with a vertical ink line in the left margin, is used in "Works and Days," *W*, VIII, 176.
[29] This quotation, struck through in ink with a vertical use mark, is used in "Result," *W*, V, 299.

[31] "In war, all is⟨; opin⟩opinion; opinion as to the enemy, opinion as to oneself. After the loss of a battle, the physical difference in the loss of the conqueror & of the conquered, is little; the moral difference is enormous,ⁿ as we see from the effect which two or three squadrons may produce on a beaten army." [*Ibid.*,] ↑vol↓ I. p. 363 —

[32]   ↑To Joseph Bonaparte↓
"I am not accustomed to let my policy be governed by the gossip of Paris, & I am sorry that you attach so much importance to it. My people under all circumstances has found it good to trust everything to me, & the present question is too complicated to be understood by a Parisian citizen." [*Ibid.*,] Vol. I. p. 74

"My people will always be of one opinion when it knows that I am pleased, because it proves that its interests have been protected." [*Ibid.*, I,] — 75

"I trust nothing to chance, but what I say, I do, or I die." [*Ibid.*, I,] ↑p.↓ 75

[33] "I should see Naples in revolt, as a father sees his children in the small pox; the crisis is salutary, provided it does not ↑too much↓ weaken the constitution." [*Ibid.*, I, 190]

"March 1, 1807. Neither the staff, nor the colonels, nor the other regimental officers have taken off their clothes for the last two months, some not for four months, (I myself have been a fortnight without taking off my boots,) in the middle of snow & mud, without bread, wine, or brandy, living on potatoes & meat, making [34] long marches & countermarches without any sort of comfort, fighting with our bayonets frequently under grape-shot. x x x In such fatigues, every one has been more or less ill, except myself; for I never was stronger, I have grown fat." [*Ibid.*,] Vol I. p 236

"I ask from you only one thing, — be master." [30] [*Ibid.*, I, 87]

[35] 1856. December. One would say that such a dinner party as L. desires, could only be arranged on the Resurrection Day; — ⁿ Zeus of Crete, Pericles of Athens, Rabelais of Paris, Shakspeare of Stratford, Lord Bacon, Dr Franklin, Montaigne, Columbus, Mr Alcott, & Tom Appleton, &c. &c.

[30] This quotation is used in "Greatness," *W*, VIII, 315.

[36] 1857. January, Chicago, Tremont House.

"In 1838," said Dr Boynton, "I came here to Waukegan & there were not so many houses as there are towns now." He got in to the train at Evansville, a town a year & a half old, where are now 600 inhabitants, a Biblical Institute, or Divinity School of the Methodists, to which a Mrs Garrett lately gave some land in Chicago appraised at $125,000, but which, when they came to sell it, the worser half brought $160 000, & the value of the whole donation, 'tis thought, will be half a million. They had in the same [37] town a College, — a thriving institution, which unfortunately blew down one night, — but I believe they raised it again the next day, or built another, & no doubt in a few weeks it will eclipse Cambridge & ⟨Oxford⟩ ↑Yale↓! 'Tis very droll to hear the comic stories of the rising values here, which, ludicrous though they seem, are justified by facts presently. Mr Corwin's story of land offered for 50 000, and an hour given to consider of it. The buyer [38] made up his mind to take it, but he could not have it; it was five minutes past the hour, & it was now worth $60,000. After dinner, he resolved to give the price, but he had overstayed the time ↑again,↓ & it was already 70,000; & it became 80,000, before night, — when he bought it. I believe it was Mr Corwin's joke, but the solemn citizen who stood by, heard it approvingly, & said, "Yes, that is about the fair growth of Chicago *per* hour." However a quite [39] parallel case to this, I am told, actually occurred in the sale of the "American House" lot, which rose in a day from perhaps $40 000 to 50, 60, 70, 80, or 90,000, at which price it was sold. Mr Foster of Evansville, when I asked about the once rival towns which competed with Chicago, sa↑i↓d, "Yes, at New City they once thought there was to be the great centre, & built 60 houses." [31] "Was there not a ⟨har⟩ river [40] & harbor there?" "O yes, there was a guzzle out of a sandbank, but now there are still the 60 houses, &, when he ⟨was th⟩ passed by the last time, there was one owl, which was the only inhabitant."

Mr ↑W. B.↓ Ogden told me that he came here ↑from New York↓ 21 years ago. In N. Y. he had in association with some others

---

[31] "I asked . . . houses.' " is struck through in pencil with a very faint curved vertical use mark. "Evansville" is Evanston, Ill.; the college (p. [37]) is Northwestern University.

⟨bought⟩made a large purchase here to the amount of $100,000. He had never been here, but wished to have a reason for coming, ⟨out here⟩ beyond merely seeing the country; had never then been beyond Buffalo westward. [41] He ⁿ arrived here one morning 11 June, 1836. He learned that one of the parties ↑of whom↓ he had purchased,ⁿ ⟨of,⟩ was in the house, on his arrival at the tavern or fort, & this person sent for him to come up & see him. ↑This↓ Mr Bronson had heard some rumor that his brother had sold the land to a company in N. Y. but hoped it was not so. Mr O. showed him his deed. Bronson said it was all right, but it was injudicious in his brother. O. said he was glad to hear that, for he had feared he had made a foolish bargain. While he was in B.'s room, somebody tapped at the door, & wished to know if the man who represented *block no. 1*, was here? Mr O. knew nothing of it; but B. told ⟨him,⟩ ↑the man,↓ yes, Ogden represented that purchase. "Well, will you sell Block no. 1?" O. ⟨said⟩ ↑replied↓, "he knew nothing of it, but after breakfast he would (see p. 46)

↑Kings↓
"A king is but the first of subjects."
Frederic of Prussia [32]

[42] In & out.
Ship steered by compass instead of by the stars [33]

————

Dogma of immanence

————

    ↑the actual is the ideal↓
"Was wirklich ist, das ist vernunfti⟨ch⟩g"
alles begreifen heisst alles verziechen

————

"The ground of everything is immanent in that thing."

[32] "Kings . . . Prussia", at the top of p. [41], is separated from the other entry on the page by a page-wide rule. "In & out." is separated from the other entries on p. [42] by a wavy, curved pencil line. For the "Dogma of immanence" and Hegel's "Whatever is true is reasonable", see also pp. [109]–[110] below.
[33] "Ship . . . compass" is used in "Civilization," *W*, VII, 24.

Self supporting institutions, like farms,   states prisons,
a man who maintains himself.
a chimney which consumes its own smoke.
a steamship which makes fresh water out of salt.[34]

[43] Sin is, when a man trifles with himself, & is untrue to his own constitution.
Every thing is the cause of itself[.]

We have seen art coming back to veracity.

Napoleon, from pedantry of old tactics to the making the art of war a piece of common sense.

Carlyle, armed with the same realism in his speculation on society & [44] government, red tape, &c.

Wagner, in Music. The old musicians said, "the worse text the better score." Wagner said, "the ⟨sco⟩ text must be fixed to the score, & from the first invention."

Nor let the musician think he can be a frivolous person & a parasite; he must be musician throughout, in his vote, in his economy, in his prayer.

[45] Allston said, "His art should make the artist happy."[35]

"A strong nature feels itself brought into the world for its own development, & not for the approbation of the public."   Goethe[36]

[46] ↑(see p. 41)↓
go & see the land." After breakfast, they crossed in a little boat, &

---

[34] "Self supporting . . . salt." is used in "Civilization," *W*, VII, 25.
[35] This sentence is rewritten in ink over the same matter in pencil. Allston expressed this sentiment in "Sonnet: To my venerable Friend, the President of the Royal Academy" in *The Sylphs of the Seasons, with other Poems* (Cambridge, Mass., 1813), p. 154.
[36] "Goethe as a Man of Science," *Westminster Review*, LVIII (Oct. 1852), 259. See *JMN*, XIII, 105.

looked about in the swamp & woods, & came to a stake. "Here" said Bronson, "is Block no. 1." Well, they were followed by several persons, &, among others, the one he had seen. These came up, & the man said, "What will you take for this property?" O. said, "he knew nothing of its value, but if they would make him an offer, he would inform himself, & answer." The man said, "We will give you $35,000. for eight blocks from ↑No.↓ 1 to ↑No.↓ 8." O. ⟨looked in his face to see if he was joking, "but⟩ ↑said↓ "I ^{n} never altered a muscle of my face, but I looked him in the face, to see if he were joking, & expected they would all laugh; but they all looked solemn, & the speaker no more crazy than the rest. So I took Bronson's arm, & walked apart, & said, is this a joke, or are they crazy? or is this the value of the land?" "Yes ^{n} this is the supposed value." "Is ^{n} it worth more?" "Perhaps, ^{n} but you must wait." "So ^{n} I went back, & said as gravely as I could, that I would take it; ^{n} but I expected them to laugh, but that would (turn to p. 51)

[47] Here we stand, silent, unknown, dumb as mountains, inspiring curiosity in each other, and what we wish to know is whether there be ↑in you↓ an interior organization as finished & excellent as the body. For if there be, then is there a rider to the horse; then has nature a lord. Blow the horn at the gate of Egremont Castle, which none but the heir of Egremont can blow.[37]   Encore!

[48]   ↑*Say it again.*↓
     The outward organization is admirable, the geology, the astronomy, the anatomy, ↑all↓ excellent; but 'tis all a half; &, enlarge it by astronomy never so far, remains a half; it requires a will as perfectly organized⟨,⟩: — a perfect freedom is the only counterpart to ⟨the perfect⟩ nature. When that is born, & ripened, & tried, — & says, "Here stand I, I cannot otherwise," — Nature surrenders as meekly as the ass on which Jesus rode.[38]

[37] This entry is struck through in pencil with a vertical use mark; "For if . . . lord.", struck through in pencil with two vertical use marks, is used in "Country Life," W, XII, 167.
     [38] This paragraph is struck through in pencil with one vertical use mark; "The outward . . . nature." is struck through in pencil with another; "The outward

[49]   *Positive Degree*

———

Jonathan Phillips said of Dr Channing, "I have known him long, I have studied his character, & I believe him to be capable of virtue." [39]

———

"Chee said, I see little use for eloquence." [40]

———

[50] The God of statesmen is only an Emperor. "Whereupon, I pray God to keep you in his holy & honorable protection," writes Napoleon always in conclusion. [41]

———

[51] ↑(continued from page 46)↓
not harm me." But the man said, "Well we will pay 10 per cent down, & we will pay it now." But I said we will go back to the tavern.ⁿ But the ↑man↓ was uneasy, & wished to pay now. "I said, 'I shall not vary from what I have said.' But the man inclined to pay now. So he took out of his pocket ten $1000. notes of the U.S. Bank, & I put them in my waistcoat pocket." And from that time ⟨he⟩ ↑Mr Ogden↓ proceeded to sell piece after piece of the land (about 150 acres) till in one year he had nearly sold the whole for $1,000,000.

———

[52] matter of words, you say,
They call it freedom. I call it lockjaw.
⟨'Tis⟩You say, "'tis lavender;" ⟨S⟩I say, 'tis bilgewater. [42]

———

. . . organized⟨,⟩" is used in "Country Life," *W*, XII, 165–166. The quotation is from Luther's speech at the Diet of Worms, April 18, 1521.

[39] This remark by Jonathan M. Phillips (1778–1861), close friend of the Emerson family, philanthropist, and early member of the Transcendental Club, is used in "The Superlative," *W*, X, 167.

[40] "The Morals of Confucius," in *The Phenix; A Collection of Old and Rare Fragments* (New York, 1835), p. 101. See *JMN*, VI, 387.

[41] *The Confidential Correspondence* . . . , 1856, I, 233, 259, 282, 285, et passim.

[42] "tis lavender . . . bilgewater.", struck through in pencil with a horizontal use mark or perhaps canceled, is used in "Speech on Affairs in Kansas," *W*, XI, 259. See *JMN*, XIII, 339.

There are four sweets in my confectionary, — sugar, ⟨life⟩ ↑beauty↓, freedom, & revenge, said egyptiacus[.]

——

Husbands & wives recite goose melodies. E 222

[53] Civilization has taken away hearths, altars, urns, ashes, grey hair, teeth, so that, L. says, we can no longer speak poetically of ourselves.

[54] With the deluge of Natural Science, "the moral & political freedom of men came to be treated as an illusion, following the eternal necessit⟨ies⟩y of Nature. ⟨Thinking⟩ Thought was degraded to a bodily action ⟨or inflammation⟩. Physiologists ⟨mainly English⟩ made minute observations on ⟨the movement of⟩ the nerves of the brain. Phrenology unfolded the character out of the form of the skull. Kant's Categorical imperative was quite forgotten. But, what is noticeable, with this reform from the Natural Science, [55][43] quite no change happened in *praxis*. In public opinion, in public morals, in civic life, in criminal law ⟨which⟩quite no change of the old praxis, ⟨occurred⟩which was founded on the theory of responsibility & freedom of the will, — occurred."

See Atlantis, July   43

[56] Black star, builders of dungeons in the air [44]

"Thro' nature's ample range in thought to ⟨stroll⟩ ↑rove↓, And start at man the single mourner there." Young [*Night Thoughts*, "Night VII," ll. 700–701]

[57] [blank]
[58]   *Conduct of Life*
Good is a good doctor. Bad is a better   NO 259
                                        192

Boyden & his boys [45] [NO 260]

[43] "Whether a man is a ninepin?" is inserted at the top of p. [55] and set off by a horizontal rule.
[44] This entry, in pencil, is used in "Considerations by the Way," *W*, VI, 265. Cf. *JMN*, XIII, 457.
[45] "Good . . . boys" is struck through in ink with a vertical use mark; the passages cited are used in "Considerations by the Way," *W*, VI, 253 and 258–259.

He who has a thousand friends   NO 145 [46]
Sympathy of eye & hand. *NO* 256 [47]
Who dare draw out the linch pin? [NO 260] [48]

> 'Tis said, best men are moulded of their faults.
> [Shakespeare, *Measure for Measure*, V, i, 434; NO 54]

―――

Settlement of California; tub to whale; overruling of evil to good. [49]
IO 79, 80, 81.
RO 49

―――

See NO 54 [50]

―――

Househunting, &c   *NO* 112   important for Culture [51]

―――

You must begin at the beginning, & you must take all the steps.
NO 118[–119] [52]

―――

[59]   This ↑passing↓ hour is an edifice
              Which the Omnipotent cannot rebuild. [53]

―――

Entering into the game, & outshooting God with his own bow. *GH* 79

―――

Conduct of Life, see *LM* 3

―――

[46] "He . . . friends" is struck through in ink with a vertical use mark. The reference is to "He who has a thousand friends, has not enough; and he who has one foe, has too many," attributed to 'Ali ibn-abi-Tālib (600?–661), son-in-law of Mohammed. Emerson's source is not known.
   [47] The journal passage referred to is used in "Works and Days," *W*, VII, 157.
   [48] This sentence is struck through in ink with a vertical use mark; see Journal RO, p. [56] above.
   [49] "'Tis said . . . good." is struck through in ink with a vertical use mark; the quotation and the four journal passages cited are used in "Considerations by the Way," *W*, VI, 258 and 255–256.
   [50] This notation and the rule above it are in pencil.
   [51] This entry is struck through in ink with a curved vertical use mark.
   [52] This entry is struck through in ink with a diagonal use mark.
   [53] These lines are used as an epigraph for "Works and Days," *W*, VII, 156, and in "Fragments on Nature and Life," V, *W*, IX, 350.

Culture has no enemies; instanced in William of Wykeham. *RS* 165

———

3 classes. Conservers, Reformers, & Geniuses. *J* 115

———

Temperance, the plantain. *J* 141

———

Will ↑is↓ a particular; habit a massive force. Speech a particular, manners a mass.

———

Bores are good too: they may help you to a good indignation, if not to a sympathy. *J* 77

———

[60] ———
Some play at chess, some at cards, some at the stock exchange; I prefer to play at Cause & Effect.

———

   Few valuable lives, most are cases for a gun. AB 115 [54]

———

The friction of the social machine absorbs almost all the power applied. see *W* 17

———

[61] "Study for eternity smiled on me," says Van Helmont.[55]
It were a good rule ⟨for⟩to read some lines at least, every day, that shall not be of the day's occasion or task, but of "study for eternity."

"While we are musing on these subjects, according to the remark of Varro, we are adding to the length of our lives; for life properly consists in being awake"   *Bohn's Pliny.*   p 6 [56]

↑See NO 126↓

———

   [54] This entry, struck through in pencil with a vertical use mark, is used in "Considerations by the Way," *W*, VI, 248.
   [55] Jean Baptiste van Helmont, *Oriatrike or, Physick refined. The Common Errors therein Refuted, and the Whole Art Reformed & Rectified* . . . Now faithfully rendered into English by J[ohn]. C[handler]. . . . (London, 1662), p. 12. The quotation is used in "The Celebration of Intellect," *W*, XII, 131. See *JMN*, XI, 202.
   [56] *The Natural History of Pliny*, trans. John Bostock and H. T. Riley, 6 vols. (London, 1855–1857), vol. 1. "'While . . . our lives;" is used in "Works and Days," *W*, VII, 179.

I value myself, not as I do the duty of the day, but of the remote day, &c. *DO* 192 [57]

[62] [blank]

[63] The ⟨J⟩Missouri & the Missisippi after their Junction run 40 miles side by side in the same bed ⟨without⟩ before they fully mix. The rate of Interest in Illinois runs from 10 to 40 per cent; [n] in Boston, from 5 to 10 & 12 per cent; yet does not the capital of Boston realize this difference of level & flow down into Illinois. Well, in England & in America there is the widest ⟨steepest a great⟩ difference of altitude between the [64] culture of the↑ir↓ scholars & that of the Germans, and here are in America a nation of Germans living with the ⟨or⟩ organon of Hegel in their hands, which makes the discoveries & thinking of the Eng↑lish↓ & Americans look of a Chinese narrowness, and yet good easy dunces that we are, we never suspect our inferiority.[58]

[65] Woman should find in man her guardian. Silently she looks for that, & when she finds, as she instantly does, that he is not, she betakes her to her own defences, & does the best she can. But when he is her guardian, all goes well for both.[59]

[66] Your subject is quite indifferent, if you really speak out. If I met Shakspeare, or Montaigne, or Goethe, I should only aim to understand correctly what they said: they might talk of what they would. When ⟨they⟩ ↑people↓ object to me my topics of England, or France, or Nat. History, 'tis only that they fear I shall not think on these subjects, but shall consult my ease, & repeat ⟨some⟩ [60] commonplaces. The way to the centre is everywhere equally short[.]

[67] "A general has always troops enough, if he only knows how

---

[57] For "I value . . . day, &c.", see also Journal VO, p. [15] below.
[58] This entry is struck through in pencil with single vertical use marks on pp. [63] and [64].
[59] This paragraph is used in "Woman," *W*, XI, 426.
[60] "some" is canceled in pencil.

to employ those he has, & bivouacs with them," said Bonaparte.[61]
⟨Every atom embodies the soul of the world, &⟩ Every[n] breath of air
is the carrier of the universal mind. Thus, for subjects, I do not know
what is more tedious than Dedications, or pieces of flattery to
Grandees. Yet ⟨it would not do to skip them lest⟩ in Hafiz, it would
not do to skip them, since his ↑dare-devil↓ [68] muse ⟨⟨& the poetry
of the world⟩⟩ is never better shown.

A practical man is the hobby of the age. Well, when I read German
philosophy, or wrote verses, I was willing to concede there might
be too much of th⟨is⟩ese, & that the western pioneer with axe on his
shoulder, & still moving west ⟨when⟩ as the settlements approached
him, had his merits. But when I went to Illinois, they told me that
the founders of the towns [69] as ↑of↓ Dixon, of Rockford, of San
Francisco, St Louis, were visionary men, & ⟨became⟩ always remained
poor; that, after them, came practical men, who made fortunes.[62]
On further consideration of this ⟨qu⟩ practical quality, by which our
people are proud to be marked, I concede its excellence; but practice
or practicalness consists in the consequent or logical following out of
a good theory.*

[70] Here are[n] they practical i.e. they confound the means
with the ends, & lose the ends thereby out of sight —   freedom,
worth, & beauty of life.[63]

[71] [blank]
[72] No matter how many centuries of culture have preceded,
the new man always finds himself standing on the brink of Chaos.
'Tis because the man is by much the larger half; and, though we
exaggerate his tools & sciences, ⟨the⟩yet the moment we face a hero
or a sage, the arts & civilizations are *peu de cas*.[64]

* See *Atlantis* Feb. 1855 p 109

---

[61] See p. [30] above.
[62] See Journal RO, pp. [89]–[92] above.
[63] "Here . . . life." is in pencil.
[64] "the new . . . *peu de cas*." is struck through in pencil with a vertical use

[73] We no longer measure by miles but by orbits of Neptune[.]
The old six thousand years of chronology is a kitchen clock[,] no
more a measure of time than ⟨an egg-glass⟩ an hour-glass or an egg-
-glass since the durations of geologic periods have come in use[.] [65]
      ↑printed↓

A[mos]. B[ronson]. A[lcott]. saw the *Midsummers Night's dream*,
↑played,↓ & said, it was a phallus to which fathers could carry their
daughters, & each had their own thoughts, without suspecting that
the other had the same.

[74] *Qu'est ce qu'un classique?* [66]
The classic art was the art of necessity: modern romantic art bears
the stamp of caprice & chance. This is the most general distinction we
can give between classic & romantic art.
The difference between classic & romantic exists herein, that the one
is the product of inclination, of caprice, of ⟨accident,⟩ hap-hazard,
whilst, ⟨on the contrary,⟩ the classic carries its law & necessity within
itself.[67]
[75] In this view, the politics of monarchy, wherein all hangs on
the accidents of the life & temper of a single person, may be called
romantic politics: the democratic, on the other hand, where the
power proceeds organically from the people, & ⟨the⟩ is responsible
to them, are classic politics, — the politics of necessity & self-government, against the politics of whim.[68]
    Republics run into romance when they lose sight of the inner
necessity & organism that must be in their laws, & act from whim.
Wagner made music again classic.

---

mark; "No matter . . . Chaos.", struck through in pencil with a vertical use mark
and a curved vertical use mark, is used in "Works and Days," *W*, VII, 163–164.

    [65] "We no . . . use" is struck through with two vertical use marks, one in
pencil and one in ink; "The old . . . use" is used in "Progress of Culture," *W*,
VIII, 212.

    [66] The title of one of Sainte-Beuve's most famous essays; see *Causeries du Lundi,*
1852, III, 31–44.

    [67] "This is . . . romantic art." is struck through in ink with five vertical use
marks. Sainte-Beuve's question, translated; "the classic . . . chance."; and "The
difference . . . itself." are used in "Art and Criticism," *W*, XII, 303–304.

    [68] "the politics of monarchy . . . classic politics," is used in "Art and Criticism,"
W, XII, 304. "Atlantis" is inserted at the top of p. [75].

[76] Goethe says, "I call classic the sound, & romantic the sick." [69]

These are German definitions.
Saint Beuve defines classic
"un auteur qui a fait faire un pas de plus, à découvert quelque verité, qui a rendu sa pensée sous une forme large et grande, saine et belle en soi, &c." I abridge much. See [Sainte-Beuve,] *Causeries* [*du Lundi*, 1851–1862,] T[ome] 3, p. 34

Eugene Sue, Dumas, &c., when they begin a story, do not know ⟨whe⟩ how it will end; but Walter Scott when he began the Bride of Lammermoor had no choice, nor Shakspeare in Macbeth. [77] But ↑Mme↓ George Sand, though she writes fast & miscellaneously, is yet fundamentally classic & necessitated: and I, who tack things strangely enough together, & consult my ease rather than my strength, & often write *on the other side*, am yet an adorer of the *One*.

To be classic, then, *de rigueur*, is the ⟨mark⟩ ↑prerogative↓ of a vigorous mind who is able to execute what he conceives.

The classic ⟨evolves⟩ ↑unfolds↓; the romantic adds.[70]
The discovery of America is an antique or classic work. See *E* 196 *VO* 254

[78] [71] Of great cities you cannot compute the influences. In the farthest colonies, in New Orleans, in New York, in Montreal, in Guiana, in Gaudaloupe, a middle aged gentleman is just embarking with all his property to fulfil the dream of his life, & spend his old age in Paris; so that a fortune falls to that city every day. Astronomers come because there only can they find companions. The chemist,

[69] This quotation, struck through in pencil with a vertical use mark, is used in "Art and Criticism," *W*, XII, 304.
[70] This sentence is used in "Art and Criticism," *W*, XII, 304.
[71] The entry on this page is rewritten in ink over substantially the same matter in erased pencil. "Paris", written at the top of the page as a heading, is partially erased above "Of great". "Of great . . . grande⟨s⟩es." is used in "Boston," *W*, XII, 187.

geologist, Musician, Artist, because there only are grande⟨s⟩es. A handsome leg, a graceful girl, comes to the ballet. Sevres[n] porcelain, Gobelin⟨,⟩ tapestry, ⟨Sevres Porcelain Gob⟩Rebellious youth comes to satisfy his passions. Babinet — an inventor of a ragout, a modiste who has invented a bonnet

[79] Sick & frivolous people spend all their day in going to bed, & in getting up again, & have no time left: hypochondriacs, whose employment & avocation is to be sick.

[80] Property goes before persons, as the Railroad company advertises a freight-train with a passenger-car attached.

↑Apr. 5,↓ Walden fired a cannonade yesterday of a hundred guns, but not in honor of the birth of Napoleon[.] [72]

M[ary]. M[oody]. E[merson]. said of Tallyrand, that he was not organized for ⟨a⟩ ↑the↓ ⟨f⟩Future ⟨s⟩State.

M. M. E. is jealous of all the newer friends of her friends & cannot bear either C[aroline]. S[turgis]. [Tappan] or A[mos]. B[ronson]. A[lcott]. or the fame of A[nna]. H[azard]. B[arker]. W[ard].[n] [73] She reminds one in these days of ⟨o⟩an old aristocrat, say Queen Elizabeth shaking the Duchess of   on her deathbed. — or of Sarah of Marlborough, as she walks with her stick to the oyster shop.

[81] "If 'tis n't one thing, 'tis another."

[82] I think I can show that France cleaves to the form, & loses the substance, as; in the famous unities of her drama; and in her poetry itself; in the whole "C↑l↓assicality" of her turn of mind, which is only apery; (definition of *classic*)

---

[72] Cf. "May-Day," ll. 104–106, *W*, IX, 166.

[73] Anna Hazard Barker was the wife of Samuel Gray Ward; Emerson had attended their wedding October 5, 1840. See *JMN*, VII, 404, and p. [175] below.

↑For↓ France doth ape the lion's shape.

———

Classic & Romantic

Menander's speech, "that he had finished the comedy, all but the verses." And Burke who studied the statistics of his speech, but left the illustration & ornament to the impulse of speaking.

[83]   Greatness

———

The men who are not measured men of 5 & 6 feet. Z[A] 165

———

Greatness   Z[A] 166

———

"For Laughter never looked upon his brow."
            Giles Fletcher. ["Christ's Victory and Triumph
                                    on Earth," stanza 12]

"The last luxury Fin Chin gave up in his economizing, was his giving." [74]

———

People like a rattling town, where a great deal of business is done, &c.[75] Student shuns all this. They like to be in a state of exaggeration. Manly greatness consists in being so much that the wash of the sea, the observed passage of the stars, or the *almost heard* current of time is event enough. Let not the noise of what you call events disturb me. AZ 33[–34]

[84] [76] *Greatness*
                    Niebuhr   *NO* 42

———

"They sing enough who life blood have."
            [Channing, "To the Muse," l. 30]   NO 19

———

"Eternal beings only have a real existence" Proclus [77]

———

[74] For these two quotations, see *JMN*, IX, 36.
[75] "People . . . &c." is used in "The Superlative," *W*, X, 174.
[76] The entries on this page, except for "*Greatness* . . . have.' ", are in pencil.
[77] *The Six Books of Proclus . . . on the Theology of Plato*, trans. Thomas Taylor, 2 vols. (London, 1816), II, 464; this edition is in Emerson's library. See *JMN*, XIII, 408.

The vote of a prophet is equal to a hundred hands[.]

___

Suppose the ⟨Marathon⟩Thermopylae ⟨400⟩300 had paired off[.] [78]

___

Osric Great in the present   K 19 [79]

___

Price of the picture shows how false our state. *D* 56, 238,[80]

___

Ozman   F[2] 37

___

Blessed is the man who has no powers.

[85] [81] It is base to remember

___

Books the destruction of literature   NO 201

___

The Cid's Swords &c   *NO* 214 [82]

___

Alfred   *NO* 224
And Niewenheis   *NO* 229

___

All the transcendent ⟨men⟩ writers, 'tis doubtful who they were.
W 1 [83]

___

[78] "The vote . . . paired off" is struck through in pencil with three diagonal use marks, and the individual entries are struck through in pencil with single diagonal use marks. See *JMN*, XIII, 297 and 49, respectively. The first entry is from *Select Works of Plotinus*, trans. Thomas Taylor (London, 1817), p. 522, in Emerson's library. Both entries are used in "Considerations by the Way," *W*, VI, 249–250.
[79] The passage from Journal K is used in "Worship," *W*, VI, 234. Emerson changed the name to Benedict in the essay.
[80] The paragraph referred to in Journal D, p. [238], is used in the lecture "The School."
[81] All entries on p. [85] are in pencil except "Swedenborg . . . *TO* 131)".
[82] For "The Cid's Swords", see also Journal VO, p. [6] below.
[83] This sentence, struck through in ink with a vertical use mark, is used in "Plato; or, the Philosopher," *W*, IV, 41.

He that made the world lets that speak for him, & does not employ a town crier. *W* 44

———

Indians don't think white man with his brow of care has succeeded[.] [84] SO 177

Swedenborg & Behmen great, because, —   (see *TO* 131)

[86]   Hurry is for slaves

———

The celestial mind incapable of care, peeping, or discourtesy. TU 230 [85]

↑Homage paid to a great man the expression of our hope. [86] *NO* 52↓

———

Those only can sleep who do not care to sleep, & those only write or act well, who do not respect the writing or the act. [87]

———

"A man is already of consequence in the world, when it is known that we can implicitly rely upon him." Bulwer [88]

———

Immense force of men whose part is taken   *Z* 163;
illustrated also to me by seeing Robert Owen in society. [89]

[87]   Thy voice is sweet, Musketaquid,[n]
            ⟨&⟩ repeats the music of the rain
            but sweeter ⟨is the⟩ ↑⟨flows⟩ rivers↓ silent ⟨stream⟩ ↑flit↓
            ⟨which flows ever⟩ through thee

[84] This sentence, struck through in pencil with a diagonal use mark, is used in "Illusions," *W*, VI, 323.

[85] "Hurry . . . TU 230" and the short rule below "Hurry" are in pencil with punctuation in ink. The entry in Journal TU is cross-indexed under Alcottiana in Notebook Amos Bronson Alcott, p. [1].

[86] This sentence is used in "Progress of Culture," *W*, VIII, 226–227.

[87] This sentence, struck through in pencil and in ink with single vertical use marks, is used in "Works and Days," *W*, VII, 182.

[88] This quotation is used in "Character," *W*, X, 102. See Journal VO, p. [13] below.

[89] Emerson continues his entries on "Greatness" on p. [93] below.

as thou through ⟨the land⟩ ↑Concord plain↓.
Thou art shut in thy banks;
but the stream I love, flows
in thy water, & flows through ⟨me⟩ rocks & through the
air & through rays of light as well, & through darkness, & through
men & women. I hear & see the inundation & eternal spending of the
stream in winter & in summer in men & animals, in passion & thought.
Happy are they who can hear it[.] [90]

[88] The property proves too much for the man, and now all
the men of science, art, intellect, are pretty sure to degenerate into
selfish housekeepers dependent on wine, coffee, furnace, gas-light, &
furniture. ⟨Well, t⟩Then⟨,⟩ things swing the other way, & we suddenly
find that civilization crowed too soon, that what we bragged as
triumphs were treacheries; that we ↑have↓ ⟨taken the⟩ ↑opened the
wrong door, and let the↓ enemy into the castle; ⟨by mistake,⟩ that
civilization was a mistake; that ⟨a pent-house⟩ nothing is [89] so
vulgar as a great warehouse of rooms full of furniture & ⟨‖ … ‖⟩
trumpery; that, ⟨the best wisdom were⟩ in the circumstances, the best
wisdom were an auction or a fire; since the ↑foxes &↓ birds have the
right of it, with a warm hole to fend the weather, and no more; that
a pent-house to fend the sun & wind & rain, is the ⟨right⟩ house which
makes no tax on the owner's time & thought, and which he can leave
when the sun ⟨is warm⟩ reaches noon.

[90] ↑From p 87 continued↓
I see thy brimming eddying stream,
And thy enchantment
For thou changest every rock in thy bed
Into a gem
All is ⟨real⟩ opal & agate
And at will thou pavest with diamonds
Take them away from thy stream

[90] The entry on p. [87] is struck through in ink with a vertical use mark; see
pp. [90] and [194] below, Journal VO, pp. [78]–[79] below, and "Two Rivers,"
ll. 1–8, W, IX, 248. The cancellations and insertions are in pencil.

66

And they are poor shards & flints
So is it with me today [91]

What need ↑have↓ I of book or priest
⟨When all my stars are⟩ ↑And every star is↓ Bethlehem
    star⟨s⟩
And I have as many as there are
Yellow flowers in the grass.
So many saints & saviours,
↑So many high behaviours,↓
Are there to him
Who is himself, as thou,[n] ⟨art⟩ alive
And only sees what he doth give.[92]

[91] *Monochord*

M[ary] M[oody] E[merson] cannot sympathize with children. I know several persons whose world is only large enough for one person, and ⟨though⟩ each of them↑, though he↓ were to be the last man, would, like the executioner in Hood's poem, guillotine the last but one.[93] 'Tis A's misfortune, & T's,

---

↑E[lizabeth] H[oar] said ↑of M. M. E.,↓ she[n] thinks much more of her bonnet & of other peoples' bonnets than they do, & sends E[lizabeth]. from Dan to Beersheba to find a bonnet that does not conform; while Mrs. H[oar]., whom she severely taxes with conforming, is satisfied with anything she finds in the shops. She[n] [92] tramples on the common humanities all day, & they rise as ghosts & torment her at night.↓ [94]

---

[91] With "I see . . . today", cf. "Two Rivers," ll. 9–16, *W*, IX, 248. The cancellation and the page-wide rule beneath these lines are in pencil.

[92] "What need . . . give." is used in "Fragments on the Poet and the Poetic Gift," XXVIII, *W*, IX, 333.

[93] "several persons . . . one." is struck through in ink with a vertical use mark; "each of . . . one." is used in "Society and Solitude," *W*, VII, 3. Hood's poem is "The Last Man"; see *Selected Poems of Thomas Hood*, ed. John Clubbe (Cambridge, Mass.: Harvard University Press, 1970), pp. 134–141.

[94] "tramples . . . night." at the bottom of p. [92], continued from p. [91], is separated from the other entries on the page by a page-wide rule; lines in ink connect the top and bottom of "E H said . . . shops. She" with the continuation.

↑*Kings & Nobles*↓

"Tycho Brahe refused (1574) for a long time to publish his observations upon the remarkable star in Cassiopeia, lest he should thus cast a stain upon his nobility." *Brewster. Life of* Newton. I. p. 259.[95]

———

↑Fame↓

Copernicus's discoveries "insinuated themselves into ecclesiastical minds by the very reluctance of their author to bring them into notice." Brewster — [*ibid.,*] vol I p 256
⟨C⟩He died, 1543.

[93] *Greatness*   Continued from p. 86
How a noble person dwarfs a nation of underlings. HO 112
Great leaders may wake up one morning to their great mistake. *HO* 257.
Philosophy of Wa↑i↓ting. *RS* 42

To the grand interest a superficial success is of no account. It prospers as well in mistake as in luck; in obstruction & nonsense, as well as among the angels. It reckons fortunes mere paint. Difficulty is its delight. Perplexity its noonday.[96]

———

"For Zeus hates those who are busybodies, & do too much." *Euripides.*
                              See Aristotle's Ethics. (Bohn). p. 164.[97]

[94] English idea of good is of that which perishes in the using, and the world is becoming English. The spirit of art & science are strangers to Eng. mind. She occasionally produces an artist, like Turner, or a philosopher like Coleridge, ⟨b⟩or a naturalist like Brown, or Owen, but they breathe not the English atmosphere, but are strangers there, & import their thoughts from Germany: nor do they exert any adequate influence on the national spirit [95] &, with

[95] Sir David Brewster, *Memoirs of the Life, Writings and Discoveries of Sir Isaac Newton,* 2 vols. (Edinburgh, 1855).
[96] "Philosophy . . . noonday." is struck through in pencil with two vertical use marks; "To the grand . . . noonday." is used in "Aristocracy," *W,* X, 59.
[97] *The Nichomachean Ethics of Aristotle,* trans. R[obert] W[illiam] Browne (London, 1850), p. 164. The quotation, struck through in ink with one diagonal and two vertical use marks, is used in "Success," *W,* VII, 312.

the exception of the good sense, or application of means to ends, in which they surpass all, everything in England is factitious, special, & limited. — This is the amount of the Pilot's report of my lecture, & not bad. —

[96] At the sale of the ↑two↓ Catholic Colleges of St. Peter & St. Paul, Prior Park, North Bath, "the Bollandist Lives of the Saints brought $575.00[.]"

[97] [blank]
[98] ↑States.↓
A man to get the advantage of the ideal man, turns himself into several men, by using his eyes today, when he is loving; & tomorrow, when he is ⟨ra⟩spiteful; & the third day, when he is merry; & so on; as the astronomer uses the earth as a cart to carry him to the two ends of its orbit, to find the parallax of a star.

[99] [blank]
[100] I thought at New Bedford, ↑(see *DO* 185)↓ that, the mind is always true; though the premises are false, the conclusions are right: and this self-reliance which belongs to every healthy human being, is proof of it; proof that not he, but the soul of the world, is in him; &, in proportion as it penetrates his miserable crust of partiality, saith, Here am I, here is the whole. Therefore we require absoluteness in every body, absoluteness in the orator, in the poet, in the hero, in all manners.
                    ↑Copied in *ML* 69↓ [98]

[101] And if they have it not, they simulate it.
"The greatest pride of a man consists herein, that the recognition of him by others is nowise necessary to him." *Atl*[*antis*]. [99]

"Radicalism consists in an unconditioned subordination of the personality under the thing, under the principle." *Atl*[*antis*].

---

[98] This insertion is in pencil; the entry on p. [100] is struck through with two diagonal use marks in pencil.
[99] "And if . . . *Atl*." is struck through in pencil with a diagonal use mark.

———

See also *JK* 107

———

[102] "True freedom consists in the limitation of the same. None must have the freedom to be un-free, neither an individual, nor a state." *Atl*[*antis*].

> I never knew but one
> ↑Could↓ do ⁿ what thou hast done
> Give me back the song of birds
> Into plainest English words
> Or articulate
> The sough of the wind as I sate [100]

[103] [blank]
[104]   *German Language.*
Gemuth
Anschauung   poetic vision
Wirksamkeit   activity
Geist   esprit
Gehalt — ⟨and⟩ ↑substance↓   inhalt. ↑contents — ↓
begriff — the unsplit   godhead;   ↑general idea.↓
Anschauen — insee   ↑insight↓
Verausserung — externisation
das fassliche — comprehensibility, illusion,
Philister, — snob —
motive, — means (in art) calculated to produce an effect.
Thatsach   fact   matter of fact
aufgabe   problem
lockern   to loosen
vertrag   treaty [101]

[105] ↑Science↓
                    Critical value

---

[100] These six lines are in pencil.
[101] "insight" is added in pencil; some of the German words and most of the English equivalents are probably added.

enlarged our measures
it's upset Calvinism
it mitigates the ferocity of law
'tis a blue litmus, or test, — this new
⟨Rappings⟩ neurology to show the skepticism
    of the Church. RO 121
Value of new astronomy   DO 191 [102]

[106] Science on tiptoe, on stilts.
Science in scraps.
Science in stampede
Science of number One
Was it moral
did it make head clear & heart better
Science desart

Its merit
Tendency to unity
belief that as my farm, so is the Solar system.
Its critical value
It upset Calvinism
It enlarged our measures

[107] What a barren witted pate am I, says the scholar; I will go see whether I have lost my reason. He ⟨finds⟩ seeks companions, he ⟨g⟩seeks intelligent persons, whether more wise or less wise than he, who give him provocation, and, at once, & very easily, the old motion begins in his brain, thoughts, fancies, humors, flow, the horizon broadens, the cloud lifts, & the infinite opulence of things is again shown him. But the right conditions must be observed. ⟨H⟩Principally he must have leave to be himself. We go to dine with M. & N. & O. & P. And, to be sure, they begin to be something else than [108] they were, they play tricks, they dance jigs, they pun, they tell stories, they try many fantastic tricks, under some supersti-

---

[102] The heading is inserted in pencil near the top of the page, and the other entries begin more than halfway down the page.

tion that there must be excitement & elevation, and ↑they↓ kill conversation at once. It is only on natural ground that they can be rich.
Keep the ground, feel the roots, domesticate yourself[.]
↑I think of ↑Andrew[s]↓ Norton who did not like toasts & sentiments
because they interfered with the hilarity of the occasion.↓

But one of these ruffians who is conceited, who thinks only of himself,
& values nature only as it feeds & exhibits him, is equally a pest with
the roisterers. There must be infinite reception as well as giving.
↑What kind of↓ a ⁿ pump ↑is↓ that ↑which↓ cannot ⟨suck⟩ ↑draw↓, but
only deliver⟨,⟩ ↑?↓ ⟨is good for nothing.⟩ [103]

[109] I think the Germans have ⟨a probity and⟩ an integrity of
mind which sets their science above all other. They have not this
Science in scraps, this Science on stilts. They have posed certain
philosophical facts on which all is built, the doctrine of *immanence*,
as it is called, by which every thing is the cause of itself, or stands
there for its own, and repeats in its own all other, [110] "the ground
of every thing is immanent in that thing." [104]

Every thing is organic — freedom also, not to add, but to ↑grow &↓
unfold.

They purify, they sweeten, they warm & ennoble, by seeing the heart
to be indispensable[.]

Not in scraps, not on stilts.

In music, it was once the doctrine, the text is nothing, the score is
all, ⟨but Wag⟩ and even, the worse the ⟨score⟩ text, the better the
score; but Wagner said the text must be fixed to the score, [111₁]
& from the first   must be inspired with the score.[105]

---

[103] This entry is struck through on p. [107] with two vertical use marks in
pencil and one in ink, on p. [108] with one vertical use mark in ink and another
in pencil; "But one . . . giving." is struck through in pencil with a vertical use
mark. "What a . . . giving." is used in "Clubs," *W*, VII, 229, 231–232, and 233.
[104] See p. [42] above.
[105] See p. [44] above.

So in Chemistry, Muldar said ⟨No⟩ ↑For a↓ good chemist, the first condition is, he shall know nothing of philosophy; but Oersted & Humboldt saw & said, that Chemistry must be the handmaid of moral Science.[106] Do you not see how nature avenges herself of the pedantry? The wits excluded from the academ⟨es⟩ies met in clubs & threw the academy into the shade.

[111₂] A carpenter built a house 5 stories high, perfect & beautiful on every floor, but forgot to put in the stairs.

Do you

[111₃] If he bought a book, we all went & bought the same book.

[112] 1857, Feb. 7
Johnny Gourgas wrote for his verses
       "The Hunter's life
       Is full of strife
       But the hunter's gun
       Is better than the poet's fun."

'Tis of small importance what becomes of the practice of life, said B. R., if only the theory is satisfactory.

"I can well wait," said E[lizabeth]. H[oar]., "all winter, if sure to blossom an apple tree in spring; but not, if, perhaps, I am dead wood, & ought to burn now."

[113] I know a song which blasts, ⟨those who hear it⟩ like the lightning, those who hear it, changes their color & shape, & utterly dissipates them. It is more hurtful than the taste of strychnine, or the kiss of the asp. It is called Time.[107]

---

[106] For Muldar, see p. [2] above. Hans Christian Oersted, *The Soul in Nature* . . . , trans. Leonora and Joanna B. Horner (London, 1852), is in Emerson's library.
   [107] This entry is struck through in ink with three diagonal use marks; cf. the "Song of a Runic Bard" from William Godwin's *Life of Geoffrey Chaucer* (*with*

I know a song which though it be sung never so loud, few can hear, — ↑only↓ six or seven or eight persons: yet they who hear it become young again. [114] When it is sung, the stars twinkle gladly, & the moon bends nearer the earth.

↑(See below, p. 172)↓

I know a song which is more hurtful ⟨to those who hear it⟩ⁿ than strychnine or the kiss of the asp. It blasts those who hear it, changes their color & shape, & dissipates their substance. It is called Time.

> Yet they who hear it shed their age
> And take their youth again [108]

[115] [blank]
[116] Whipple said of the author of "Leaves of Grass," that he had every leaf but the fig leaf.[109]

The audience that assembled to hear my lectures in these six weeks was called, "the *effete* of Boston." Apr. 26

[117] As Linnaeus delighted in finding that seven stamened flower which alone gave him a seventh class, or filled a gap in his system, so I know a man who served as intermediate between two notable acquaintances of mine, not else to be approximated: & ⟨E⟩W[illiam]. E[llery]. C[hanning]. served as a companion of H[enry]. D[avid]. T[horeau]; & T[horeau]. of C[hanning].

[118] In conversation, we come out of our egg-shell existence into the great Dome, & see the Zeni↑t↓h over us & the Nadir under us.

All life is a surface-affair, &, 'tis curious, our difference of wit

---

Memoirs of John of Gaunt), 2 vols. (London, 1803), II, 452, *JMN*, I, 371, and "Poetry and Imagination," *W*, VIII, 59.

[108] These two lines in pencil, struck through in pencil with a vertical use mark, are used in "Merlin's Song," ll. 12–13, *W*, IX, 218.

[109] Edwin Percy Whipple (1819–1886), essayist and critic.

only a difference in impressionability, or power to appreciate faint & fainter & infinitely faint voices & visions, or thinner & impal[p]abler laminae.[110]

↑See above p. 24↓ [111]

[119] Charles Auchester
The Counterparts
My First Season

Kate Coventry

Cranford
John Halifax [112]

[120] "The natural & the cultivated man differ herein, that Nature rules the one, & the other rules nature. To be sure, no man is purely the one or the other. Every man is a mixture of free activity & received impressions." *Atlantis*. March 1856 p 165

[121] Subject for lecture, is, the art of taking a walk. I would not ask W[illiam]. E[llery]. C[hanning]., like the little girl, "Mamma wishes, Sir, you would begin to be funny." Indeed quite the reverse; for his written fun is very bad — and as to his serious letter, the very best, that to Ward in Europe, is un⟨p⟩reproducible. Would you bottle

---

[110] "In conversation . . . impressionability," is struck through in ink with a discontinuous diagonal use mark; "All life . . . laminae." is struck through in pencil with a vertical use mark; "In conversation . . . under us.", struck through in pencil with a vertical use mark, is used in "Considerations by the Way," *W*, VI, 271; "All life . . . visions," is used in "Success," *W*, VII, 297.

[111] The insertion is in pencil.

[112] The purpose of this list of recent English novels is not known. Two of the novels by Elizabeth Sara Sheppard, *Charles Auchester; a memorial* (New York, 1853), and *Counterparts; or, The cross of love*, 3 vols. (London, 1854), are in Emerson's library. The other novels are Sheppard, *My First Season* (London, 1855); G. J. Whyte Melville, *Kate Coventry; An autobiography* (London, 1856); Elizabeth Cleghorn Gaskell, *Cranford* (London, 1853); and D. M. Mulock, afterwards Craik, *John Halifax, Gentleman*, 3 vols. (London, 1856). For *Charles Auchester*, see Journal CL, pp. [18] and [117] below; for *Counterparts*, see Journal AC, pp. [30]–[31], [236], and [248], and Journal CL, p. [117] below.

the efflux of a June noon, & sell it in your shop? but if he could be engaged again into kindly letters, he has that which none else could give. But 'tis rare & rich compound of gods & dwarfs, & best of humanity, that goes to walk. Can you bring home the summits of Wachusett[n] [122] & Monadnoc, & the Uncanoonuc, the savin fields of Lincoln, & the sedge & reeds of Flint Pond, the savage woods beyond ⟨n⟩Nut brook towards White Pond? He can.

[123] Do you think I am in such great terror of being shot, I, who am only waiting to shuffle off my corporeal jacket to scud away into the *back*[n] stars, & put diameters of the solar system & millions of sidereal orbits between me & all souls, there to wear out ages in solitude, & forget memory itself, if it be possible? [113]

_____

[124] [blank]
        [125] In the conversation, what helpless callow birds we are, each waiting for other, — total inadequacy of power to reach the walls of the vast sky that compasses us in, until at last a thought, a principle appears, from some more active mind; then, each catches by the mane one or other of these strong goers, like horses of the prairie, & rides up & down among worlds & natures.[114]

↑(See below, p. 155.)↓

        [126] It is curious that Thoreau goes to a house to say with little preface what he has just read or observed, delivers it in lump, is quite inattentive to ⟨what⟩ any comment or thought which any of the company offer on the matter, nay, i⟨n⟩s merely interrupted by it, &, when he has finished⟨,⟩ his report, departs with precipitation.

[127]–[128] [blank]
[129]   *England, for the last time.*

_____

        Many-headed-ness.

[113] This entry, struck through in ink with two vertical use marks and in pencil with another, is used in "Society and Solitude," *W*, VII, 5. It is marked with rules at beginning and end, possibly for emphasis.
        [114] "at last . . . natures.", struck through in pencil with two vertical use marks, is used in "Inspiration," *W*, VIII, 293.

They do "em*body*"[n] as Wordsworth said, more than others. Their culture, compared with the Americans they walk with, made the last seem like bags of bones. See *DO* 134

They are still living on the men of the 16 century.

Do they occupy themselves about matters of general & lasting import(?), like the Germans or the Hindoos; or upon trifles ↑& a corporeal civilization?↓[115]

[130] What said Napoleon, that "her conduct was decided not by general politics, but by /petty/internal/ intrigues."
    [Napoleon, *The Confidential Correspondence* ..., 1856, I, 215]

⟨English⟩ History[n] of Greece or Rome ⟨is⟩ written by Englishmen is English party pamphlets.[116]

" 'Tis the peculiar & inimitable excellence of the ⟨Eng⟩British legislation that no law can anticipate the progress of public opinion."
                                        Niebuhr III. p. 111.[117]

They laugh you down: they treat the rule of right as a puerile enthusiasm: they sacrifice the right to the pleasant & convenient & wonted. See *NO* 2 [118]

---

[115] "They do . . . bones." is struck through in ink with a diagonal use mark. "Many-headed-ness.", struck through in ink with a diagonal use mark, is used in "Result," *W*, V, 303. "They do . . . others." is used in "Result," *W*, V, 305; "Their . . . bones." is used in "Personal," *W*, V, 295. "Do they . . . civilization?", struck through in ink with a vertical use mark, is used in "Result," *W*, V, 304.

[116] For "What said . . . intrigues.' ", see p. [30] above; for "⟨English⟩ . . . pamphlets.", see *JMN*, XIII, 388.

[117] Barthold Georg Niebuhr, *The Life and Letters of Barthold Georg Niebuhr; with essays on his character and influence by* [Baron] Bunsen, [Johannes] Brandis, and [Johann Wilhelm] Loebell, 3 vols. (London, 1852); Emerson withdrew volume 3 from the Harvard College Library on May 18, 1855. See *JMN*, XIII, 439.

[118] "What said . . . intrigues.' ", struck through in ink with a diagonal use mark, "⟨English⟩ history . . . pamphlets.", struck through in ink with a diagonal use mark; and "Tis the . . . opinion.' ", struck through in ink with a vertical use

[131] Fifteen years will restore the relative positions of Eng[lan]d & France, thought [Reinhold] S[olger]., because France makes conquests, & Eng[lan]d /retains/holds/ them.[119]

Atlantic is the sieve through which only or chiefly the liberal, bold, *America-loving* part of each city, clan, or family, pass hither.

Great plenteousness of Eng[lish]. nature.[120]

England can only fall by suicide.

[132] Economical geology, Economical astronomy, with a view (to[n] annexation, if it could be,)[n] to navigation. And chemistry & natural history, for utility. Yes, rightly enough: but is there no right wishing to know what is, without reaping a rent or commission?[n] Now their natural history is profane. They do not know the bird, the fish, the tree, they describe. The ambition that "hurries them after ⟨the⟩ truth, takes away the power to attain it[.]"

This charge that I make against English science, ⟨which⟩ ↑that it↓ bereaves nature of its charm; lies equally against all European[n] science.[121]

[133] Voltaire's definition of Eng[lish]. science ↑of↓ gov[ernmen]t ↑is↓, "that in which the prince[,] omnipotent for good, has his hands tied from doing harm."[122]

---

mark, are used in "Result," *W*, V, 299 and 305. "They laugh you down:" is used in "Literature," *W*, V, 255.

[119] See *JMN*, XIII, 410. Reinhold Solger, a minor writer of fiction and verse who had emigrated to the United States from Germany in 1853, was a teacher at F. B. Sanborn's school in Concord. See *L*, IV, 498, p. [282] below, and Journal VO, pp. [160]–[161] below.

[120] "Great . . . nature.", struck through in ink with a vertical use mark, is used in "Result," *W*, V, 302.

[121] "This charge . . . science." is struck through in ink with two vertical use marks.

[122] Voltaire's definition, from Lettre VIII of the *Lettres sur l'Angleterre*, is quoted in Pierre Lanfrey, *L'Eglise et les philosophes au dix-huitième siècle* (Paris, 1855), p. 115.

[134] Eng[lish]. Result
     Best of actual nations. You see the poor best you have got.
Epitome of modern times, & Rome of today.[123] Broad-fronted broad-
-bottomed Teutons

———

England tender-hearted. Rome was not.

———

magnificent theory of colony. *IO* 39

———

falls only by suicide

———

they constitute the mod↑ern↓ world; stand foursquare to the compass.

———

Great richness of nature.

———

Every thing is the instrument of their contumacious *naturel*.[124]

———

↑They have↓ given importance to individualism.

———

[135] Every Englishman expects to kick ⟨th⟩all those below him, &
to be kicked by all those above him.

                                        ↑"Quid vult, valde vult."↓
English have Character. They are not demonstrative, but reticent;
and are like a dull good horse who lets every nag ⟨run by⟩ pass him,
but with whip & spur will pass every racer on the field: of slow blood,
"but being moved," (shall I finish?) *"perplexed in the extreme."* [125]

---

[123] See *JMN*, XIII, 248.
[124] "Best . . . not." is struck through in ink with a vertical use mark; "they
constitute . . . compass." and "Every thing . . . naturel." are struck through in
ink with single diagonal use marks; "Great . . . nature." is struck through in ink
with two vertical use marks; these entries are expanded in "Result," *W*, V, 299,
302, and 306.
[125] "Every . . . above him.", struck through in ink with two diagonal use
marks, and " 'Quid . . . field?", struck through in ink with three diagonal use
marks, are used in "Result," *W*, V, 305–306, where the Latin is translated "What
they do they do with a will." With " '*but being . . . extreme.*' ", cf. Shakespeare,
Othello, V, ii, 345–346.

[136] with difficulty ideal; he is the most conditioned man, as if having the best conditions, he could not bring himself to forfeit them.[126]

English are worldly.

↑The fagging of the schools is repeated in the classes of Society.↓ ⟨As⟩ He[n] shows no mercy to those below him, as he looks for none from those above him: indeed any forbearance from his superiors surprises him, & they suffer in his good opinion.[127]

[137] Few pure English geniuses; — Shakspeare; & Milton ⟨is⟩ in his poems; But what shall one do with Dryden? Chaucer is far from symmetrical, and only pleases by pieces. But Homer by wholes, & Æschylus; & Plato by an equal whole, & Raphael by every work, & not by a merit here & there, & merits counterbalanced. Dante is great from first to last.

[138] All our talk about a nation is a superficial symptomatic trifling. We ⟨don't⟩ can't go deep enough into the tremendous biography of the Spirit who ↑never↓ manifests himself ↑entire↓ in one, ⟨& another, as the⟩ ↑but delegates his energy in parts or spasms to vicious & defective men.↓ ⟨habit of the man shows itself in the skin, or in a finger, or in a disease of the eye or the ear.⟩
↑But the wealth of the magazine is seen in the plenteousness of Eng[lish]. nature. Many headedness↓ [128]

[139] The English genius is much indebted to the sea; ↑& air. NO 173↓ ⟨indebted⟩ also to the advantageous position of the middle class who are always the source of letters. Hence ↑their many headedness &↓ the vast plenty of their aesthetic production. In America, it

---

[126] See *JMN*, XIII, 300.
[127] "with difficulty . . . them.", struck through in ink with a diagonal use mark, and "The fagging . . . opinion.", struck through in ink with a vertical use mark, are used in "Literature," *W*, V, 252, and "Result," *W*, V, 306, respectively.
[128] The entries on p. [138] are struck through in ink with a diagonal use mark. "All . . . defective men.", "But . . . nature.", and "Many headedness" are used in "Result," *W*, V, 302–303.

will be one day still better, from the careful elementary education
⟨of such a vast population⟩ of robust middle & lower class boys.

———————

Probability of the Eng[lish]. tongue becoming the universal
language [129]

[140] This winterly man's virtues come out in private life. Truth
in private life & ⟨treachery⟩ ↑untruth↓ in public [130]

————

Eng[lan]d always in a state of arrested development

————

Every one of them is 2000 years old. A⟨n⟩s many new ideas as you
like, provided you will cast them in the old forms: [131] but thoughts
that will & must make their own, we will not have. But can you run
a locomotive on a turnpike, or ⟨turn⟩ ↑curry & groom↓ a horse into a
locomotive?

Nor even am I quite sure that Shakspeare ⟨himself⟩ will answer the
questions of 1856, or ⟨Newton⟩ whether we have not exhausted the
benefit of Newton.

[141] In the delegation of the parts of Jove to the races of men, one
would say, that, the Greeks sprung from his eyes, the Germans from
his brain, the Romans from his virility, the English from his hands.

↑Their mind in a state of arrested development[,] a divine cripple
like Vulcan[,] a blind savant like Huber or Sanderson. They do not
occupy themselves on matters of general & lasting import but on a
corporeal civilization. Their political conduct not decided by general

———————

[129] "& air.   NO 173" is inserted in pencil. "⟨indebted⟩ also . . . production.",
struck through in ink with one vertical and two diagonal use marks, and "Probability . . . language", struck through in ink with a vertical use mark, are used in
"Result," *W*, V, 303.
     [130] "This winterly . . . public" is struck through in ink with a vertical use
mark; the cancellation and insertion are in pencil.
     [131] "Engd . . . forms:" is struck through in ink with a diagonal use mark.
"Engd . . . development" is used in "Result," *W*, V, 304; "Every . . . old." is
used in "Literature," *W*, V, 252.

views but by internal intrigues & personal & family interest. The history of Greece & Rome is written by them as Eng[lish]. party pamphlets.↓ [132]

[142] ⟨But⟩ England is rich & wise beyond all, but lives on her capital; & new forms are looming up, new & gigantic thoughts, which cannot dress themselves ⟨in⟩out of any ↑old↓ wardrobe[.]

English Science when I see its faults & its achievements seems an ⟨illustrious⟩ ↑divine↓ cripple, ↑like Vulcan,↓ or a blind scholar like Huber or Sanderson.[133]

---

[143] I am to say what is strange, but it so happened, that the higher were the persons in the social scale ↑I conversed with↓ the less ⟨pecul was⟩ marked was their ⟨pe⟩ national accent, the more I found them like the most cultivated persons in America[.]

[144]–[145] [blank]
[146] "Mathematics," said Copernicus to the Pope, "are written for mathematicians." [Brewster, *Life of Newton*, 1855, I, 257–258]

[147] See what a cometary train man carries with him of animals to serve him, & of plants, stones, ⟨&⟩ gases, & imponderable elements.[134]

[148] The ⟨whole⟩ comfort of Alcott's mind is, the connexion in which he sees whatever he sees. He is never dazzled by a spot of

---

[132] The entries on p. [141] are struck through in ink with a vertical use mark. "Their mind . . . pamphlets.", inserted after the second entry on p. [142], "English Science . . . Sanderson.", was written, is used in "Result," *W*, V, 299 and 304. François Huber (1750–1831) was a blind Swiss naturalist, Nicholas Sanderson (1682–1739) a blind English mathematician. For "The history of . . . pamphlets.", see p. [130] above.

[133] "⟨But⟩ England . . . wardrobe" is struck through in ink with a vertical use mark. "English Science . . . Sanderson." is struck through in ink with a diagonal use mark.

[134] This sentence, struck through in ink with two diagonal use marks, is used in "Considerations by the Way," *W*, VI, 247.

colour, or a gleam of light, to value that thing by itself; but forever
& ever is prepossessed by the undivided One behind it & all. I do not
know where to find in men or books a mind so valuable to faith.
H⟨e⟩is ↑own invariable faith↓ inspires faith, in others.ⁿ ⟨by his ↑own↓
invariable faith.⟩ I valued Miss Bacon's studies of Shakspeare, simply
for the belief it showed in cause & effect; [135] that a first-rate genius
was not a prodigy⟨,⟩ & stupefying anomaly, but built up step by step
[149] as a tree or a house is, with a sufficient cause, ⟨for⟩ (and one
that, with diligence, might be found or assigned,) for every difference
& every superiority to the dunce or average man. For every opinion
or sentence of Alcott, ⟨in⟩ a reason may be sought & found, not in
his will or fancy, but in the necessity of nature itself, which has
daguerred that fatal impression on his susceptible soul. He is as good
as a [150] lens or a mirror, a beautiful susceptibility, every impression
on which, is not to be reasoned against, or derided, but to be accounted
for, &, until accounted for, ⟨religiously⟩ re⟨c⟩gistered as an (indisputable) addition to our catalogue of natural facts. There are defects in
the lens, & errors of refraction & position, &c. to be allowed for, and
it needs one acquainted with the lens by frequent use, to make these
allowances; but 'tis the best instrument I have ever met with.

[151] Every man looks a piece of luck, but he is a piece of the
mosaic accurately measured & ground to fit into the gap he fills, such
as Parker or Garrison, or Carlyle, or Hegel is, and with good optics,
I suppose, we should find as nice fitting, down to the bores & loafers.[136]

[152] I admire that poetry which no man wrote, no poet⟨ry⟩
less than the genius of humanity itself, & which is to be read in a
mythology, in the effect of pictures, or sculptures, or drama, or cities,
↑or sciences,↓ on me.

My son is coming to get his latin lesson without me. My son is coming

[135] Delia Salter Bacon (1811–1859), author of *Philosophy of the Plays of
Shakspere Unfolded* (Boston, 1857), worked in England (1853–1857) to prove her
theory that Shakespearean plays were written by a group headed by Lord Bacon. See
Journal VO, pp. [55] and [58] below, and *JMN*, XIII, 25–26.
[136] This paragraph is struck through in ink with a diagonal use mark; "Every
man . . . fills," is used in "Fate," *W*, VI, 42.

to do without me. And I am coming to do without Plato, or Goethe, or Alcott.

[153] To carry temperance very high & very thoroughly into life & into intellect, & that with insight of its necessity & efficacy! Wise men read very sharply all your private history in your look, gait, speech, writing, & whole performance.

"Manner is power." [137]

[154] [blank]
[155]   ↑Conversation↓
I ought to have said above, ↑(p. 125)↓ in respect to Conversation, that our habit is squalid & beggarly. ⟨We think⟩ An assembly of men & women think they are each poor, defective, pointed at. They think that the success which will satisfy them & others, is, a good trade; or well reputed & lucrative employment; a good marriage; a legacy, or patrimony; & the like. This is forlorn, & they feel sore & sensitive. Now if one comes who can illuminate this dark cold house of theirs, & show them their sleeping [156] & unsuspected riches, what gifts they have, ↑how indispensable each is,↓ what magicians' powers over nature & men, what access to poetry, & those powers which constitute character, he is Plutus, he is a god, he a pure benefactor.   ↑*See next page.*↓

They have all been to California, & all have come back millionaires.[138]
          ↑printed↓

          ↑P 155 is crossed as if printed; but I do not think it is. 1869↓

---

[137] "Wise men . . . power.'" is struck through in ink with a vertical use mark; "Wise men . . . performance." is used in "Behavior," *W*, VI, 177.

[138] This entry is struck through in ink on p. [155] with a discontinuous diagonal use mark and in pencil with a vertical use mark; "& unsuspected . . . character," is struck through in pencil with a vertical use mark; "& unsuspected . . . millionaires." is struck through in ink with a diagonal use mark; "They have . . . millionaires." is struck through in ink with five vertical use marks. The entry is used in "Considerations by the Way," *W*, VI, 271–272.

[157]   ↑Conversation↓

In a parlor, the unexpectedness of the effects. When we go to
Faneuil Hall, we ⟨expect⟩ ↑look for↓ important events; facts, thoughts,
& persuasions, that bear on them. But in your parlor, to find your
companion who sits by your side start up into a more potent than
Demosthenes, &, in an instant, work a revolution that makes Athens
& England & Washington Politics — old carrion & dust-barrels, —
because his suggestions require new ways [158] of living, new books,
new men, new arts & sciences, — yes the lecture & the book seem
vapid. Eloquence is forever a power that shoves usurpers from their
thrones, & sits down on them by allowance & acclaim of all.[139]

Conversation or eloquence, it is to be remembered, is an art in which
a man has all mankind for his competitors; for it is that which all are
practising every day,[n] while they live.[140]

[159] Conversation.

These black coats never can speak ⟨but when⟩ ↑until↓ they meet
a black coat; then their tongues are loosed, & chatter like blackbirds.
The "practical" folks in the rail-car meet daily, & to their discourse
there is no end.

How can a man be concealed? ☞ [141]

[160] ↑Conversation↓

A man cannot utter many ⟨words, or, at least a few⟩ sentences,
⟨in conversation,⟩ without announcing to intelligent ears exactly
where he stands in life & thought, namely whether in the kingdom of
the senses & the understanding; in that of truths & the reasoning;
or in that of ideas & imagination; in the realm of the intuitions &
duty.[142]

---

[139] A pencil line in the left margin marks "Eloquence . . . all."
[140] This sentence, struck through in ink with a diagonal use mark and in pencil
with a vertical one, is used in "Considerations by the Way," *W*, VI, 270–271.
[141] The hand points upwards and to the right at the entry on p. [160]; with
"How can . . . concealed?", cf. *JMN*, VI, 391.
[142] This paragraph, struck through in ink with one vertical use mark and in

[161] Once more for Alcott it is to be said, that he is sincerely & necessarily engaged to his task & not wilfully or ostentatiously or pecuniarily.

———

Mr Johnson at Manchester said, of him, "he is universally competent. Whatever question is asked, he is prepared for."

[162]–[163] [blank]
      [164] Collins shall not insert Newton's name (with his solution of the Problems) in The Phil[osophical]. Transactions. ↑He writes↓ "It would perhaps increase my acquaintance, the thing which I chiefly study to decline." [143]   [Brewster,] Life. [of Newton, 1855,] I. 69

E[dwin]. Whipple said, He could not walk along Washington St with a man, but he perceived he should have to dissolve the union with him presently. There must always be compromise.

      [165] *Maupertuis' Theorem*

La quantité d'action nécessaire pour produire un changement dans le mouvement des corps est toujours un minimum.

———

Il entendait par quantité d'action le produit d'une masse par sa vitesse et par l'espace qu'elle parcourt.

      See "Principes de l'equilibre, et du mouvement" de Carnot. 2d Edit. p. 163

———

                              Biog. Universelle ad verb. Maupertuis
↑See *Carnot*, below, p. 169 SO↓

      [166] I shall go far, & see many, before I find such an extraordinary insight ⟨i⟩as Alcott's. In his fine talk, last evening, he ran up & down the scale of ⟨existence⟩ powers, with as much ease &

———

pencil with another, is used in "Worship," *W*, VI, 224. The cancellation of "words, or, at least a few" is marked with parentheses.
      [143] "Collins . . . decline.' ", struck through in ink with a vertical use mark and in pencil with another, is used in "Society and Solitude," *W*, VII, 5.

pre↑c↓ision as a squirrel the wires of his cage, & is never dazzled by his means, or by any particular, & a fine heroic action or a poetic passage would make no impression on him, because he expects heroism & poetry in All. Ideal purity, the poet, the [167] artist, the man, must have. I have never seen any person who so fortifies the believer, so confutes the skeptic. And the almost uniform rejection of this man by men of parts, ↑Carlyle & Browning inclusive,↓ & by women of piety, might make one despair of ⟨the race.⟩ ↑society.↓ If he came with a cannonade of acclati↓m⟨ation⟩ from all nations, as the first wit on the planet, ⟨they⟩ ↑these masters↓ would ⟨sus⟩ receive him, & he would sustain the reputation: or if they could find him in a book a thousand [168] years old, with a legend of miracles appended, there would be churches of disciples: but now they wish to know if his coat is out at the elbow, or whether some body did not hear from somebody, that he had got a new hat, &c. &c. He has faults, no doubt, but I may safely know no more about them than he does; and some that are most severely imputed to him are only the omissions of a preoccupied mind.

[169] Paris vaut bien un messe.[144]

———

Her great names are Carnot & Francis Arago. The last did not duck to the second Napoleon, nor did ⟨the first⟩ ↑Carnot↓ nor Lafayette to the first↑.↓ ⟨Napoleon.⟩
Carnot's Theorem was, "Avoid sudden alterations of speed; since the loss of living power is equal to the living power which all the parts of the machine or system would possess, if you should give to every one ⟨them⟩of them the speed which it lost in the moment when the sudden alteration occurred." [n]
↑(See above, p. 165.)↓   See Atlantis Feb. 1856 p. 118

[170]   *Education*
Don't let them eat their seed-corn; don't let them anticipate, or ante-date, & be young men, before they have finished their boyhood.

[144] The supposed remark of Henri IV in 1593 when he became a convert to Roman Catholicism as a step toward winning Paris and the crown of France. See *JMN*, VI, 208.

Let them have the fields & woods, & learn their secret & the base & foot-ball, & wrestling, & brickbats, & suck all the strength & courage that lies for them in these games; let them ride bareback, & catch their horse in his pasture, let them hook & spear their fish, & shin a post and a tall tree, ⟨⟨before they⟩go a-hunting⟩ & shoot their partridge & trap the woodchuck, before they begin to dress like collegians, & sing in serenades, & make polite calls.

[171] 'Tis curious that there is not only ⟨a mythology⟩ an apothe⟨a⟩osis of every power or faculty of mind & body, but also of every element, material, & tool, we use; as, of ↑fire, water, air, earth,↓ the hammer of Thor, the shoe of Mercury, the belt of Venus, the bracelet, balance, waterpot,

[172]   *Wafthrudnir* [145]
The horse taught me something, the titmouse whispered a secret in my ear, & the lespedeza looked at me, as I passed. Will the Academicians, in their "Annual Report," please tell me what they said?

[173] One man is born to explain bones & animal architectures; and one, the expression of crooked & casual lines, spots on a turtle, or on the leaf of a plant; & one, machines, & the application of coil springs & steam & waterwheels to the weaving of cloth or paper; & one, morals; & one, a pot of brandy, & poisons; and the laws of disease are as beautiful as the laws of health. Let each mind his own, & declare his own.

[174] When the interlocutor at last asks a question which only Odin could ask, the startled giant replies, "Not one knows what in the old time *Thou* saidest in the ear of thy son. With death on my mouth have I uttered the fate-words of the genealogy of the Æsir. With Odin contended I in wise words. Thou must ever the wisest be." [146]   ↑printed in ⟨Soci⟩ "Clubs."↓

---

[145] Wafthrudnir was a giant in Norse mythology who asked questions the hearer must answer or forfeit his life.

[146] This paragraph, struck through in ink with a vertical use mark, is used in "Clubs," *W*, VII, 238.

Well, every true soul sees that this is true of itself. It has that to disclose which none knows beside; that which it whispered in the ear of Balder, when he climbed the funeral pile.

[175] *The affirmative.* ⟨t⟩To awake in man & to raise the feeling of his worth; to educate his feeling & his judgment, that he must scorn himself for a bad action.

My friend A[nna]. H[azard]. B[arker]. W[ard].ⁿ refuses to tell her children whether the act was right or wrong, but sends them away to find out what *the little voice* says, and at night they shall tell her.

[176] ↑*Negative*↓   *Spots in the Sun*
Newton writes to young Aston, ⟨no⟩going abroad, not to notice any affront that may be offered him, for nobody in England will know that he received any! [147] And Goethe believed that spectacles made the wearer conceited!

[177] Out upon your Cathedral! I had rather have a basket.

Hume's doctrine was, that the circumstances vary, but that the amount of happiness did not. The beggar cracking his fleas under a hedge, & the duke ↑trolling by↓ in his chariot, ⟨rolling by,⟩ had different means, but the same quantity of pleasant excitement; & I observe that my German friend believes the same thing. Yoganidra, the goddess of illusion, is stronger than the Titans, & stronger than Apollo? The Indians say that they do not think the white man with his brow of care, always toiling, & afraid of wet & cold, keeping within doors, has any advantage of them.[148]

[178] cockchafer, may-fly, sucker, trout

[147] Brewster, *Memoirs of the Life, Writings and Discoveries of Sir Isaac Newton,* 1855, I, 387.
[148] "Hume's doctrine . . . Yoganidra," is struck through in ink with a vertical use mark, and "Yoganidra . . . them." is struck through in ink with another; "Hume's doctrine . . . excitement;" is used in "Works and Days," *W,* VII, 173; "Yoganidra . . . them." is used in "Illusions," *W,* VI, 313 and 323.

It must be admitted, that civilization is onerous & expensive; hideous
expense to keep it up; let it go, & be Indians again; but why Indians,
that is costly too; the m⟨i⟩ud-turtle & trout life is easier & cheaper;
& oyster, cheaper still. *Pater ipse colendi haud facilem* ↑*esse*↓ *viam
voluit, curis acuens mortalia corda.*[149] Play out the game, act well
your part[,] and if the gods have blundered, we will not.

[179] I have but one military recollection in all my life. In 1813
or 1814, all Boston, young & old, turned out to build the fortifications
on Noddle's Island; and, ⟨with the rest,⟩ the Schoolmaster at the
Latin School announced to the boys, that, if we wished, we might all
go on a certain day to work on the Island. I went with the rest in the
ferry boat, & spent ⟨the⟩ ↑a summer↓ day; but I cannot remember
that I did any kind of work. I remember only the pains we took to
get water in our tin pails, to relieve our intolerable thirst. I am afraid
⟨there is⟩ no valuable [180] effect of my labor ⟨remaining⟩ ↑remains↓
in the existing defences.[150]

———

Culture. Set a dog on him; set a highwayman on him; set a woman
on him; try him with money.[151]

King Alfred, King Richard, Cromwell, George Borrow, even,
might stand these tests.

[181] [blank]
[182] ↑21 May↓
Yesterday to the ⟨S⟩Sawmill Brook with Henry.[152] He was in search
of yellow violet (pubescens) and menyanthes which he ⟨found⟩ waded

[149] Virgil, *Georgics*, I, 121–123: "pater ipse colendi haud facilem esse viam
voluit, primusque per artem movit agros, curis acuens mortalia corda": "The great
Father himself has willed that the path of husbandry should not be smooth, and he
first made art awake the fields, sharpening men's wits by care."
[150] See *Life*, pp. 39–40, where the year is given as 1814. Noddle's Island is now
part of Logan Airport, in Boston.
[151] "Set a dog . . . highwayman on him;", struck through in ink with a vertical use mark, is used in "Considerations by the Way," *W*, VI, 261.
[152] One Saw Mill Brook runs into the Concord River a mile downstream from
Concord village; a second Saw Mill Brook, more frequently visited by Thoreau, runs
under the Cambridge Turnpike about a mile and a quarter southeast of Emerson's
house.

into the water for. & which he concluded, on examination, had been
out five days. Having found his flowers, he drew out of his breast
pocket his diary & read the names of all the plants that should bloom
on this day, 20 May; whereof he keeps account as a banker ↑when↓
his notes fall due. rubus triflora, guerens⟨,⟩   , vaccinium   ,
&c. The cyprop⟨æ⟩edium not due 'till tomorrow. Then we diverged
to the brook,ⁿ where was viburnum dentatum,ⁿ arrowhead. But his
attention was drawn to the redstart which flew [183] about with its
cheah cheah chevet, & presently to two fine grosbeaks[,] rosebreasted,
whose brilliant scarlet "made the rash gazer wipe his eye," & which
he brought nearer with his spy glass, ⟨his pockets are full of twine &c
also,⟩ ⟨then to the note of a bird⟩ & whose fine clear note he compares
to that of a "tanager who has got rid of his hoarseness," then he heard
a note which he calls that of the nightwarbler, ⟨w⟩ a bird he has
never ⟨seen⟩ ↑identified↓, has been in search of for twelve years;
which, always, when he sees, is in [184] the act of diving down into
a tree or bush, & which 'tis vain to seek; ⟨a bird⟩ the only bird that
sings indifferently by night & by day. I told him, he must beware
of finding & booking him, lest life should have nothing more to show
him. He said, "What you seek in vain for half your life, one day you
come full upon all the family at dinner. — You seek him like a dream,
and as soon as you find him, you become his prey." He thinks he
could tell by the flowers what day of the month it is, within two
days. [185] We found saxifraga Pennsylvanica and ⟨saxifraga⟩
↑chrysosplenium↓ oppositifolium, by Everett's spring, and stellaria &
cerastium ↑and arabis rhemboidea↓ & veronica anagallis, which he
thinks handsomer than the cultivated *veronica*,ⁿ *forget me not.*
Solidago odora, he says, is common in Concord, & penny royal ⟨is one
of the *herbs*⟩ he gathers in quantity as *herbs* every season. *Shad
blossom* is no longer a *pyrus*, which is now confined to choke berry.
Shad blossom is Amelan⟨tia⟩↑chier↓ botryapi⟨s⟩um & A.   , Shad
blossom because it comes when ↑the↓ shad come.¹⁵³

---

¹⁵³ "examination [p. [182]] . . . hoarseness,'" is struck through in pencil
with single vertical use marks on pp. [182] and [183]; "then he . . . sees, is in"
is struck through in ink with a diagonal use mark on p. [183]; p. [184] is struck
through in ink with a vertical use mark. This long entry is used in "Thoreau," *W*,
X, 470–471. For " 'made . . . eye,' " cf. George Herbert, "Virtue," l. 6.

[1861] ⟨The w⟩Water ⟨seems to be⟩ ↑is↓ the first gardener[;] ⟨when you find him⟩ he always plants ⟨a⟩grasses & flowers about his dwelling. There came Henry with music-book under his arm, to press flowers in; with telescope in his pocket, to see the birds, & microscope to count stamens; with a diary, jacknife, & twine, in stout shoes, & strong grey ⟨pantal⟩ trowsers, ready to brave the shrub oaks & smilax, & to climb the tree for a hawk's nest. His strong legs when he wades were no insignificant part of his armour.[154] Two Alders we have, and one of them is here on the northern border of its habitat.

[1862] I am impressed at the Indignation Meeting last night, as ever, on like occasions, with the sweet nitrous oxide gas which the speakers seem to breathe. Once they taste it, they cling like mad to the bladder, & will not let it go. And it is so plain to me that eloquence, like swimming, is an art which all men might learn, though so few do. It only needs, that they should once be pushed off into the water, overhead, without corks, and after a mad struggle or two, they find their [187] poise, & the use of their arms, & henceforward they possess this new & wonderful element. The most hard-fisted disagreeably virile & ⟨paraly⟩ thought-paralyzing companion turns out in a public assembly to be the most fluent, various, & effective orator. Now you find what all that excess of power which so chafed & fretted you tête a tête, is for.[155]

[188] Affectation also has its place in a fine character, namely, of cordiality to your blood relations.[156]

Sumner's attack is of no importance. It is only a leaf of the tree, it is not Sumner who must be avenged, but the tree must be cut

[154] "There came . . . armour.", struck through in ink with a vertical use mark, is used in "Thoreau," *W*, X, 469–470.

[155] "the sweet . . . is for." is struck through in ink with single vertical use marks on pp. [1862] and [187]; "And it . . . is for.", struck through in pencil with single vertical use marks on pp. [1862] and [187], is used in "Eloquence," *W*, VIII, 119. After the May 22, 1856, assault upon Charles Sumner in the U.S. Senate, "Indignation Meetings" were held in most northern towns and cities. Emerson spoke at the "meeting in Concord on the 26th, to Consider the outrage upon Mr. Sumner"; see Notebook WO Liberty, p. [143] below.

[156] See Journal CL, p. [242] below.

down. But this stroke rouses the feeling of the people, & shows every body where they are. All feel it. Those who affect not to feel it must perforce share the shame, nor will [189] hiding their heads & pretending other tasks & a preoccupied mind, deceive themselves or us. We are all in this boat of the State, & cannot dodge the duties.
This history teaches the fatal blunder of going into false position. Let us not compromise again, or accept the aid of evil agents.
Our position, of the free states, very like that of covenanters against the cavaliers.
Massachusetts uniformly retreats from her resolutions.
Suppose we raise soldiers in Mass[achuse]tts[.]
Suppose we ⟨c⟩propose a Northern Union.

[190] ⟨T⟩How can I describe the English defect, except as the immorality of Eng[lish]. science? ⁿ As if the fung⟨o⟩us of their Church had ⟨super⟩ eaten out their native morals, & superseded them.

———

⟨England as⟩ ↑English mind↓ turns ⟨all⟩ ↑every abstraction↓ that it feeds upon ⟨at instantly⟩ into a daily fact, a portable ⟨useful⟩ utensil, a working institution.[157]

———

[191] ——
———

F. P said, "I think I don't care so much for what they say, as I do for what makes them say it."

———

2 June. The finest day the high noon of the year, went with Thoreau in a wagon to Perez Blood's auction;[158] found the myrica flowering; it had already ↑begun to↓ shed its pollen one day, the lowest flowers being effete; found the English hawthorn on Mrs Ripley's hill, ready to bloom; went up the Asabet, & found the *Azalea Nudicaulis* in full bloom, a beautiful show, the *viola muhlenbergi*, the *ranunculus recurvatus*; saw *swamp white oak*, (chestnut-like leaves) *white maple,*

---

[157] This sentence is struck through in ink with a diagonal use mark.
[158] The Concord farmer Perez Blood had died; he had "spent much of his inheritance on a telescope, globes, and books on astronomy" (*J*, IX, 47, n. 1). See *JMN*, X, 315.

red maple,   —no *chestnut oak* on the river—[192] Henry
told his story of the *Ephemera,* the manna of the fi⟨s⟩shes, which falls
like a snow storm one day in the year, only on this river, not on the
Concord, high up in the air as he can see, & blundering down to the
river,—(the shad-fly,) the true angler's fly; the fish die of repletion
when it comes, the kingfisher⟨'⟩s wait for their prey.[159] Around us
the pepeepee of the king bird kind was noisy. He showed the history
of the river from the banks, the male & female bank, the ponte⟨r⟩deria
keeps the female bank, on whichever side.

[193] "Avec un⟨e⟩ grand génie, il faut une grande volonté." [160]

"Les faiblesses de Voltaire! Que nous importe à nous ses heritiers sous
benefice d'inventaire? *Nous ne sommes solidaires que de ses vertus.*" Lanfrey. p.92 [161]

[194]   Thy ⟨⟨d⟩murmuring⟩ ↑summer↓ voice Musketaquit
              Repeats the music of the rain
              But sweeter rivers silent flit
              Thro' thee as thou thro' Concord plain
                   Thou in thy banks must dwell
                   But
                   The stream I follow freely flows
                        The str
                   Thro' thee, thro' rocks, thro' air, as well,
                   Thro' light, thro' men, it gaily goes [162]

                                                    ―――――――――

[195]–[196₁] [leaf cut out] [163]
      [197₁] The hour is coming when the strongest will not be strong
enough.[164]

---

[159] With the story of the *Ephemera,* cf. "Thoreau," *W,* X, 466.

[160] Lanfrey, *L'Eglise et les philosophes* . . . , 1855, p. 93.

[161] *Ibid.*; Emerson supplies the italics.

[162] These lines, in pencil, are struck through in pencil with a vertical use mark;
cf. pp. [87] and [90] above, Journal VO, pp. [78]–[79] below, and "Two Rivers," ll. 1–8, *W,* IX, 248.

[163] The leaf bearing what would have been pp. [195]–[196] in sequential
pagination was cut out before pagination; p. [197₂] is unnumbered, and the verso
of [197₂] is numbered [200]. Emerson numbered two pages [201].

[164] This sentence, struck through in ink with a diagonal use mark, is used in
"Speech on Affairs in Kansas," *W,* XI, 262.

I go for those who have received a retaining fee to this party of freedom, before they came into this world. I would trust Garrison, I would trust Henry Thoreau, that they would make no compromises. I would trust Horace Greeley, I would trust my venerable friend Mr Hoar, that they would be staunch for freedom to the death; but both of ⟨them⟩ ↑these↓ would have a benevolent credulity in the honesty of the other party, that I think unsafe.[165]

[196₂] The vote of a prophet is worth a hundred hands.[166]

⟨The⟩ If he knows it to be ⟨decisive⟩ the true vote, it will be decisive of the question for his country.

[197₂] The want of profound sincerity is the cause of failures. South Carolina is in earnest.

——

I see the courtesy of the Carolinians, but I know meanwhile that the only reason why they do not plant a cannon before Faneuil Hall, & blow Bunker Hill monument to fragments, as a nuisance, is because they have not the power. They are fast acquiring the power, & if they get it, they will do it.

[200] [blank]
    [201₁] There are men who as soon as they are born take a bee--line to the axe of the inquisitor, like Jordano Bruno[.] [167]

in France, the fagots for Vanini
in ⟨E⟩Italy, the fagots for Bruno
in England, the pillory for DeFoe
in New England, the whipping post for the Quakers.

Algernon Sydney a tragic character; and Sumner is; no humor.

---

[165] The cancellation and insertion are in pencil.
[166] See p. [84] above. This sentence is marked by a curved line above and at the left.
[167] This sentence, struck through in ink with two diagonal use marks, is used in "Courage," W, VII, 274.

Wonderful the way in which we are saved by this unfailing supply of the moral element[.]

[201₂]   June 14.
12 June, at our Kansas relief meeting, in Concord, $962. were subscribed on the spot. Yesterday, the subscription had amounted to ↑$1130.00↓ and it will probably reach 1200. or one per cent on the valuation of the town.

↑$13⟨5⟩60. I believe was the final amount.↓ ¹⁶⁸

$1360. was the sum of the subscription in June. In September ↑13↓, was held another Kansas ⟨r⟩Relief meeting to hear the Report of Mr Sanborn, and the new subscription has reached ↑$510.↓ whilst an additional subscription among the ladies, for clothing, amounts to upwards of ↑$130.↓ more.¹⁶⁹
Sept. 13,

[202] *Cant*
"A character more common in the modern world is that of ⟨the⟩ ambition without belief, [with the mask of religion, deceiving men to enslave them,] seeing in a dogma nothing but a two edged glaive" to strike them down.
          —see Lanfrey [*L'Eglise et les philosophes*..., 1855,] p. 144

↑*Voltaire.*↓
Voltaire enrolled fashion on his side, — the mode, — good society, — ;
il est de bon ton d'etre libre penseur.
          [Lanfrey, *L'Eglise et les philosophes*..., 1855, pp. 144–145]
To get the hurra on our side, is well; but if you are a gentleman ⟨it

---

¹⁶⁸ This sentence is inserted in pencil, and "13" is inserted in pencil in the second sentence below.
¹⁶⁹ F. B. Sanborn reported on emigrant roads to Kansas through Nebraska and Iowa for the Kansas State Committee of Massachusetts and the Committee for Middlesex County. A clipping from the Boston *Evening Telegraph* for Monday, September 1, 1856, bearing this report is laid in inside the back cover of Notebook WO Liberty below.

is essential that⟩ you ↑must↓ have the hurra of gentlemen ⟨also⟩ on your side.

[203] ⟨For years the government has been an obstruction⟩
The government has been an obstruction, & nothing but an obstruction. The people by themselves would have settled Iowa, & Utah, & Kansas, in a sufficient way. The gov[ernmen]t has made all the mischief.[170] This for the people; then for the upper classes, who acquiesce in ⟨the⟩ what they call law & order of a gov[ernmen]t which [204] exists for fraud & ⟨s⟩violence, — they are properly paid by its excessive vulgarity. The refined Boston upholds a gang of Rhynderses, & Toombses, & Brookses, before whom it is obliged to be very quiet & dapper like a dear little rabbit as it is, among the wolves. The Choates & Winthrops, and, at long interval, the Hillards, we see through them very clearly, — ↑&↓ their abject attitude.[171]

[205] ⟨The⟩ Experience[n] has shown that the aggregate of the spendings of the poor is more than equivalent to the large spending of the rich, to enrich a London or Paris. It is shoes & cotton cloth, it is an appleparing machine ↑at a dime, newspaper at 2 cents,↓ or a lamp, or a knife scourer, that draws the shillings from millions, which none is too poor to buy, whilst the fine ho⟨r⟩↑u↓se, or the good horse, or the brave equipage, has only a few hundreds or a few scores of customers.

[206] I was to say at the end of my narrative of Wordsworth, that I find nothing in the disparaging speeches of the Londoners about

[170] "For years . . . obstruction" is finger-wiped and struck through in ink with six diagonal marks to cancel; "The government . . . mischief.", struck through in ink with a vertical use mark, is used in "Speech on Affairs in Kansas," *W*, XI, 258–259.
[171] Isaiah Rynders was a U.S. marshal and Tammany leader in New York City; Robert Augustus Toombs (1810–1885), Georgia member of the U.S. House of Representatives, was said to have helped South Carolina representative Preston Brooks (1819–1857) to plan his May 22, 1856, attack on Senator Charles Sumner; Emerson refers to Rufus Choate (1799–1859), a Boston lawyer and U.S. senator from Massachusetts; Robert Charles Winthrop (1809–1894), U.S. representative and senator from Massachusetts; and George Stillman Hillard (1808–1879), a Boston lawyer and supporter of the Fugitive Slave Law.

him, that would not easily be said of a faithful scholar who rated
things after his own scale, & not by the conventional. He almost alone
in his generation has treated the mind well.[172]

[207] *Jesuits*

——— "et chaque fois que le dogme embarrassa la marche triomphante des
conquerants, ils laissèrent le dogme en chemin."
                    Lanfrey [*L'Eglise et les philosophes* ..., 1855,] p 180

"Malesherbes avait compris de bonne heure que toutes les libertés sont solidaires." [*Ibid.*,] p. 194 [195]

[208] Montesquieu said
"Dans les pays ou l'on a le malheur d'avoir une religion que Dieu n'a pas
donnée, il est toujours necessaire qu'elle s'accorde avec la morale." Ap[ud]
                              Lanfrey [*ibid.*,] p. 156

↑*Literature*↓
"Le temps fera distinguer ce que nous avons pensé de ce que nous
avons écrit," ↑said Diderot & Voltaire↓[.] [*Ibid.*, p. 161]

[209]
———

     Les femmes du dix huitième siècle, à peu d'exceptions près, sont plus
grandes par le coeur que par le caractère. *Lanfrey* [*ibid.*,] p. 201

lorsqu'on cherche à preciser le role et l'influence des femmes a une epoque
donnée, une chose frappe tout d'abord⟨,⟩ l'esprit, c'est leur radicale inapti-
tude à generaliser, à embrasser de vastes horizons, a dégager les causes de
⟨c⟩leurs effets.
Est ce à dire qu'elles soient condamnées a perpétuité aux servitudes intel-
lectuelles ou seulement à ce rôle, noble assurement, mais un peu sacrifié,
— des Sabines, — ? [*Ibid.*,] p 202 [173]

---

[172] This entry is struck through in pencil with a vertical use mark; cf. "Personal," *W*, V, 297–298.
[173] "p 202" is written in the lower left corner of p. [210] and set off from the
entries on that page by a curved line.

[210] "It is the quality of words that they imply a speaker."
↑Miss Bacon↓ [174]

↑Professor↓ Poikilus had one advantage over the rest of the University, that when the ⟨audience⟩ ↑class↓ gaped or began to diminish, he would with great celerity throw his heels into the air, & stand upon his head, & continue his lecture in that posture, a ⟨feat⟩ ↑turn↓ which seemed to invigorate his audience, who would ⟨cheerfully⟩ listen with ⟨great⟩ ↑marked↓ cheerfulness as long as he would speak to them in that ⟨position.⟩ ↑attitude.↓

[211] "Cette grace plus belle ↑encore↓ que la beauté." [Lanfrey, *ibid.*, p. 214]

Three or four odes of Wordsworth[:] the Dion, the Ode, the ⟨Alcestis⟩ ↑Laodamia↓

Then I think the *Ode on the Immortality* the high-water mark which the intellect has reached in this age. A new step has been taken ⟨a⟩ new means have been employed. No cou⟨r⟩rage has surpassed that, & a way made through the void by this finer Columbus. [175]

[212]–[213] [leaf torn out]
[214] & make him whole at last by ⟨its own⟩ compensations of its own.

For what avail the plough & sail,
Or /life or song/land or life/, if Freedom fail?

↑espial denial dial trial↓ [176]

One other thing remains to be said about th⟨e⟩at English reserved force, this namely, if I can say it,—that in the island they

---

[174] For Delia Salter Bacon, see p. [148] above and Journal VO, pp. [55] and [58] below; the insertion is in pencil.
[175] "Three . . . Laodamia" is struck through in pencil with a vertical use mark; "Then . . . Columbus.", struck through in pencil with a vertical use mark, is used in "Personal," *W*, V, 298.
[176] These words are in pencil.

never let out all the length of all the reins, there is ↑Berserkir fight,↓ no burning of the ships, no abandonment & ecstasy of will & intellect like that which marked France in 1789, and the Arabians ⟨in⟩of Mahomet. But who would see the [215] uncoiling of ⟨the⟩ ↑that tremendous↓ spring, the ⟨vast & measureless indulgence⟩ ↑explosion↓ of this centennial & millennial husbanding of force must look at the colonization which sails & marches in all climates, ⟨especially⟩ ↑mainly↓ in the /temperate Zones,/ ⟨imperial⟩ belt of empire,/ to the peaceful conquest of the globe.[177]

[216] ⟨I was also to say that as⟩ ↑On my ⟨return⟩ ↑way↓ from Edinburgh↓ I had recorded my[n] earlier visit to Wordsworth many years before. I must not omit my later interview. I believe he did not well know my name until ↑after↓ I left him.
And as I have recorded on a visit to W. many years before I must not forget this second interview.[178]

[217] W⟨a⟩hen I said of Ellery's ↑new↓ verses that "they were as good as the old ones"; "Yes," said Ward, "but ⟨they⟩ ↑those↓ were excellent promise, & now he does no more."
He has a ⟨fine⟩ more poetic temperament than any other in America, but the artistic executive power of completing a design, he has not. His poetry is like the artless ⟨whistling⟩ ↑warbling↓ of a vireo, which ⟨whistles⟩ ⟨↑warbles↓⟩ ↑whistles↓ prettily ⟨enough⟩ all day & all summer in the elm, but never ⟨a⟩ rounds a tune, nor ⟨has any power to⟩ ↑can↓ increase the value of melody by the power of composition & cuneiform determination. He must have construction also.

[218] 23 July. Returned from Pigeon Cove, where we have made acquaintance with the sea, for seven days. 'Tis a noble friendly power, and seemed to say to me, "Why so late & slow to come to me? Am I

[177] This paragraph, struck through in ink with a diagonal use mark and in pencil with two diagonal use marks on p. [214] and in ink with a vertical use mark on p. [215], is used in "Result," *W*, V, 303–304.
[178] "On my . . . him." is struck through in pencil with a wavy vertical use mark; "And as . . . interview.", struck through in pencil with a vertical use mark, is used in "Personal," *W*, V, 294.

not here always, thy proper summer home? Is not my voice thy
needful music; my breath, thy heal[t]hful climate in the heats; my
touch, thy cure? Was ever building like my terraces? Was ever couch
so magnificent as mine? L⟨ay⟩ie down on my warm ledges and learn
that a very [219] little hut is all you need. I have made thy architecture superfluous, and it is paltry beside mine. Here are twenty Romes
& Ninevehs & Karnacs in ruins together, obelisk & pyramid and
Giants' Causeway here they all are prostrate or half piled[.]"
And behold the sea, the opaline, plentiful & strong, yet beautiful as
the rose or the rainbow, full of food, nourisher of men, purger of the
world, creating a sweet climate, and, in its unchangeable ebb & flow,
[220] and in its beauty at a few furlongs, giving a hint of that which
changes not, & is perfect.[179]

For the sea, see also *CD* 7

Good nature is stronger than tomahawks.[180]

---

[221] Things go in pairs; and that, I suppose, is the reason why
a gentleman when he has told a good thing, immediately tells it
again.[181]

> Michel Angelo & Raphael
> Beaumont & Fletcher
> Newton & Flamsteed

And the Bigelows

[222] "Until man is able to compress the ether like leather, there will be
no end of misery, except through the knowledge of God." [S'wétás'wa-
tara] *Upanishad.*[182]

---

[179] With this entry, struck through in pencil with single vertical use marks on
pp. [218], [219], and [220], cf. "Seashore," ll. 1–17, *W*, IX, 242.
[180] This sentence is used in "Clubs," *W*, VII, 233; see Journal AC, p. [155]
below.
[181] "Things . . . again.", struck through in pencil with a vertical use mark,
is used in "Clubs," *W*, VII, 230.
[182] *The Taittaríya, Aitaréya, . . . Upanishads*, trans. E. Röer (Calcutta, 1853),
vol. XV of *Bibliotheca Indica . . .* , p. 68. On May 1, 1857, Emerson asked the
Boston Athenaeum to procure this for his use, and it is in Emerson's library.

"From whom the sun rises, & in whom it sets again, him all the gods entered; from him none is separated; this is that." [Katha Upanishad, p. 111]

"What is here, the same is there, & what is there, the same is here. He proceeds from death to death, who beholds here difference." [*Ibid.*]

[223] "The body is the consumer of food.

Food is founded upon food." [Taittiríya Upanishad, p. 22]

"Hunger & thirst spoke to him, 'Do thou prepare for us.'" [Aitaréya Upanishad, p. 29]

[224] "He (Brahma, or the Soul) does not move; is swifter than the mind: not the gods (the senses) did obtain him, he was gone before. Standing, he outstrips all the other gods, how fast soever they run." [Vájasanéya Sanhitá Upanishad, p. 72]

"He moves, he does not move, he is far, & also near." [*Ibid.*]

Brahma was once victorious for the sake of the gods. By the victory of Brahma, the gods obtained [225] majesty. They reflected, ⟨t⟩To us belongs this victory, this majesty. He knew their delusion, he manifested himself to them. They did not know him & asked each other, "⟨i⟩Is this being worthy of adoration?" They spoke to Agni; "Iataveda, ascertain whether this being is worthy of adoration." He replied, "Be it so." He ran up to Brahma. Brahma said, "Who art thou?" He answered, "I am Agni." Brahma asked him, "What power [226] hast thou?" Agni replied, "I can burn whatsoever there is on earth." Brahma placed a blade of grass before him saying, "Burn this." Approaching it with all his might, he could not burn it. He returned, saying, "I could not ascertain whether this being is worthy of adoration." Then they spoke to Vaju. "Vaju ascertain whether this being is worthy of adoration." He replied, "Be it so." He ran up to him. Brahma said, "Who art thou?" [227] He answered, "I am Vaju." Brahma asked him, "What power hast thou?" Vaju replied, "I can sweep away whatsoever there is on earth." He placed a blade of grass before him, saying, "Sweep away this." Approaching it with all his might, he could not sweep it away. Returning he said, "I could not ascertain whether this being is worthy adoration." Then they [228] spoke to Indra, "Maghavan, ascertain whether this being is worthy of adoration." He replied, "Be it so." Indra ran up to him. Brahma disappeared before him. As Indra is the most powerful of the gods, Brahma disappeared to show of how little avail his power was to obtain a knowledge of Brahma.   [Talavakára Upanishad, pp. 83–84]

[229]   ↑*Song of the Soul*↓
        If the ↑red↓ slayer think, ⟨I⟩ ↑he↓ slay↑s↓,
        Or if the slain think, ⟨I am⟩ ↑he is↓ slain,

⟨He⟩ ↑They↓ know⟨s⟩ not well the subtle way↑s↓
I keep & pass & turn again.

⟨What is⟩ ↑Far or↓ forgot to me is near,
⟨And night & splendor⟩ ↑Shadow & sunlight↓ are the same,
⟨Things disappeared⟩ ↑The vanished gods↓ ⟨to me⟩ ↑not
    less↓ appear,
⟨Alike to⟩ [n] ↑And one to↓ me are shame & fame.

They reckon ill who leave me out,
⟨And⟩ When [n] ↑me↓ they fly ⟨me⟩, I⟨'m⟩ ↑am↓ the wings
⟨Of⟩ ↑I am↓ the doubter ⟨I am⟩ ↑&↓ the doubt
And I the hymn the bramin sings.

The ↑strong↓ gods ⟨desire⟩ ↑pine↓ /to know thy rede/for
    my abode/
⟨The gods desire⟩ ↑But pine↓ in vain the sacred Seven,
But thou,[n] firm holder of the good,
Hast turned thy back on heaven

The strong gods pine⟨d⟩ for my abode
And pine in vain the sacred Seven
But thou ⟨joy-scorning, loving⟩ ↑meek lover of the↓ good,
Find me,[n] & turn thy back on heaven.[183]

[230₁] [184] "Know that which does not see by the eye, and by which they
see the eyes, as Brahma, & not what is worshipped as this." [Talavakára
Upanishad, p. 79]
"Know that which does not think by the mind, & by which they say the
mind is thought, as Brahma, & not what is worshipped as this." [*Ibid.*]

[183] These lines, struck through in ink with single vertical use marks on pp.
[229] and [230₁], are the first version of "Brahma," *W*, IX, 195. The first version
of the fourth stanza is written beneath other entries on p. [230₁]; "Secret", above
and to the left of the first line of this stanza, may be a variant for "strong". The
second version of stanza four is written at the bottom of p. [229].
[184] Emerson numbered two pages [230] in ink. Page [232] in sequential
pagination is numbered [231], and pp. [233] and [234], unnumbered, become
[232] and [233]. There is no page numbered [234].

[230₂] "The soul declared by an inferior man is not easy to be known but when it is declared by a teacher who beholds no difference, there is no doubt concerning it. The soul being more subtle than what is subtle, is not to be obtained by arguing. I know, worldly happiness is transient, for that firm one is not obtained by what is not firm." [Katha Upanishad, p. 104]

[231] A grander legend than western literature contains, is the story of Nachiketas. Gautama wished to obtain heaven by the sacrifice of all his property. His son Nachiketas was present when ⟨all⟩ his flocks & herds & all he had were brought ⟨as⟩ for the sacrifice. The son reflected; these cows can not bring happiness. Then he said, "My father, to whom wilt thou give me?" The father was silent. Twice, & a third time, the son repeated his question. The father enraged, said, "I give thee to Death." To the house of Yama, or D↑e↓ath, [232] the son Nachiketas went. (To save his veracity the father sent him to the abode of Yama, where in Yama's absence, he abode three nights.) The wives of Yama, on ⟨his⟩ ↑Yama's↓ return, reproach him that a Brahmana has dwelled three nights in his house without taking food, and they say,

"Hope, expectation, meeting with the good, friendly words, pious gifts, sons, & cattle,—all this loses the man of little sense in whose house a Brahmana dwells without taking food."

Then Yama said, "O Brahmana, [233] because thou, a venerable guest, hast tarried in my house 3 nights without taking food, let there be salutation to thee, & welfare to me. Moreover choose three boons instead."

Nachiketas ↑said↓, "O Death! Let Gautama be appeased in mind, & forget his anger against me. This I choose for the first boon."

Yama said, "Through my favor, Gautama will remember Thee with love as before⟨,⟩."

[235] Nachiketas said, "Thou hast, O Death! a recollection of the fire by which heaven is gained; make it known to me who have faith. This I choose as the second boon." Yama then explained to him the nature of the fire which is placed in the cavity of the heart & the manner of performing the rite; & declared that henceforth it should be known by his name, as the Nachiketas fire. [236] "Choose the third boon, O Nachiketas." Nachiketas said, "There is this inquiry;

some say, the soul exists after ↑the↓ death of man: others say, it does not exist. This I should like to know, instructed by thee. Such is the third of the boons."

Yama said, "For this question, it was inquired of old, even by the gods; for it is not easy to understand it: subtle is its nature: choose another boon, O Nachiketas, do not compel me to this: release me from this boon." [237] Nachiketas said, "Even by the gods was it inquired, and as to what thou sayest, O death! 'that it is not easy to understand it' there is no other speaker to be found like thee; ↑If thou dost not declare it, who can?↓ [185] there is no other boon like this."

Yama said, "Choose sons & grandsons who may live a hundred years; choose herds of cattle, choose elephants, & gold, & horses; choose the wide-expanded earth, and live thyself as many years as thou listeth. [238] Or, if thou knowest a boon like this, choose it together with wealth & far-extending life. Be a king, O Nachiketas! on the wide earth. I will make thee the enjoyer of all desires. All those desires that are difficult to gain in the world of mortals, all those, ask thou at thy pleasure, those fair ⟨ones⟩ ↑nymphs↓ of heaven with their chariots, with their musical instruments; for the like of them are not to be gained by men. I will give them to thee, but do not ask [239] the question of the state of the Soul after death."

Nachiketas said, "All those enjoyments are of yesterday: they wear out the glory of all the senses; and more, the life of ⟨them⟩ ↑all↓ is short. With thee remain thy horses & ⟨thy⟩ elephants, with thee the dance & song. ⟨Man is not satisfied with wealth⟩ If we should obtain wealth & behold thee, we live only as long as thou pleasest.[186] The boon which I choose I have said."

[240] Yama said, "One thing is good, another ⟨what⟩ is pleasant. Blessed is he who takes the good, but he who chooses the pleasant loses the object of man. But thou considering the objects of desire, whether pleasant, as a son, & prosperity, or of beautiful shape, as the heavenly nymphs, hast abandoned them, O Nachiketas! Thou hast not chosen the ⟨way⟩ road of wealth on which so many men perish.

These two, ignorance (whose object is what is pleasant) & knowledge

---

[185] The insertion is in pencil.
[186] "they wear . . . senses;" and "& behold thee," are set off by penciled square brackets.

(whose object is what is good) are known to be far asunder, & to lead to different goals. Believing this world exists, & not the other, the careless youth is subject to my sway.

[241] Of the soul is wonderful the speaker, ingenious the receiver, wonderful the knower. That soul declared by an inferior man is not easily to be known, as it ⟨a⟩is to be thought of in various ways; but when it is declared by a teacher who beholds no difference, there is no doubt concerning it. The soul being more subtle than what is subtle, is not to be obtained by arguing.

[242] That knowledge, O dearest, for which thou hast asked is not to be obtained by argument, but it is easy to understand it when declared by a teacher who knows no difference. Thou art persevering as to the truth. May there be for us another enquirer like thee, O Nachi⟨c⟩ketas. I know, worldly happiness is transient, for that firm one is not to be obtained by what is not firm. Thou, O Nachiketas! although thou hast beheld the parad⟨a⟩ise where all desires are fulfilled, where every fear ceases [243] yet wise by firmness thou hast abandoned it.

The wise, by means of union of the intellect with the Soul, thinking him whom it is hard to behold, whose abode is impervious, who exists from times of old, — leaves both grief & joy.

Thee, ⟨I⟩O Nachiketas, I believe a house whose door is open to Brahma."

Nachiketas said, "Then make known to me the being which thou beholdest, [244] different from virtue, different from vice, different from this whole of effects & causes, from past, future, & present time."

Yama said; "The word is *Om*. This sound means Brahma, means the supreme; whoever knows /this sound/him/, obtains whatever he wishes.[187] Who knows this is adored. The soul is not born, nor does it die, it was not produced from any one, nor was any produced from it.[188] Unborn[,][n] eternal[,] it is not slain though the body is slain[,]

↑Continued on p 247↓

[245]–[246] [blank]

---

[187] "The word . . . sound means", "means", and "this sound" are set off by penciled square brackets.

[188] The punctuation in this sentence is added in pencil.

[247] subtler than what is subtle, greater than what is great. Sitting it goes far; sleeping, it goes everywhere. Who else save myself is able to comprehend the god who rejoices & not rejoices? Thinking, the soul as unbodily among bodies, firm among the fleeting things, and wise casts off all grief. The soul cannot be gained by knowledge, not by understanding, not by manifold science. It can be obtained by the soul, by which it is desired. His soul reveals its own truth[.]" [189]

[248] [blank]
[249] Walks.
For walking, you must have a broken country. ⟨There is no walking⟩ In[n] Illinois, they all ride, there is no walk in that country. The reason is, an ⟨inch⟩ ↑furlong↓ of it is as good as a hundred miles.[190]   See RO 111

Dr Johnson.

Collingwood 5 years at sea without landing. [RO 10]

Sidney Smith and his 12 miles.

Rousseau, la marche. See *RO* 16

De Quincey & Wordsworth

The woes also:[n] housekeepers cordially hate anybody who does not dine at the family hour.[191]

---

[189] The final quotation marks and the horizontal rules following have been inserted in pencil. Pp. [231]–[233], [235]–[244], and [247], Emerson's abridgement of the Katha Upanishad, *The . . . Upanishads*, 1853, pp. 99–106, struck through in ink with single diagonal use marks on pp. [233], [235], [236], [243], and [247], and with single vertical use marks on pp. [237]–[242] and [244], are used in "Immortality," *W*, VIII, 349–352. "That soul declared . . . arguing." (p. [241]) and "I know, worldly . . . firm." (p. [242]) also occur on p. [230₂] above.
[190] "For walking . . . miles." is used in "Country Life," *W*, XII, 143. "See RO 111" is separated from this entry by a short rule.
[191] For Sidney Smith, see Journal RO, p. [62] above; for "The woes . . . hour.", see Journal RO, p. [30] above.

[250]   *Walks*

Nature impressed periodic or secular impulses to emigrate on savage men, as upon lemings, rats, & birds.

And the seashore is the natural home of us in July.[192] See *above* p 218, 251.

[251] The swimmer standing on the land dreads the plunge, yet, having plunged, enjoys the water. The living fear death, yet dying enjoy the new life.

How the landscape mocks the weakness of man! It is vast, beautiful, complete, & alive; and we can only dibble & step about, & dot it a little. The gulf between our seeing & doing is a symbol of that between faith & experience.

At Niagara, I noticed that as quick as I got out of the wetting of the Fall, ⟨it⟩all the grandeur changed into beauty. You cannot keep it grand[,] [252] it is so quickly beautiful. And ⟨at⟩ the sea at Pigeon Cove gave me daily the same experience. It is great & formidable when you lie down in it among the rocks; but on the shore, at one rod's distance, it is changed instantly into a beauty as of gems & clouds.[193]   ↑see *SO* 220↓

                    ↑printed I believe in ⟨"Conduct of Life."⟩↓ [194]

[253] Pseudo Spiritualism

————————

This mesmerism is high life below stairs, or Momus playing Jove in the kitchens of Olympus. [Y 219]

————

The love of mesmerism is a low curiosity or lust of structure & is

———

[192] "Nature . . . July." is struck through in pencil with a vertical use mark; "Nature . . . birds." is used in "Country Life," *W*, XII, 135; see Journal VO, p. [109] below.

[193] "At Niagara . . . clouds.", struck through in pencil on pp. [251] and [252] with single vertical use marks, is used in "Country Life," *W*, XII, 153.

[194] The insertion and cancellation are in pencil.

separated by celestial diameters from the love of spiritual truth.
[O 346] [195]

The new man. Neither Herodotus nor Homer nor Moses nor
G↑i↓bbon nor Voltaire have told the story as he knows it. His prudence
is a new prudence[,] his charity a new charity &c   O 144[-145] [196]

[254]   ↑Demonology↓
   There are many things of which a wise man would wish to be
ignorant, and this is one of them. Shun them, as you would shun the
secrets of the undertaker, of the butcher, the secrets of the jakes &
the dead-cart. The ⟨experts⟩ ↑adepts↓ ⟨have⟩ are they who have
mistaken flatulence, for inspiration. If ⟨these⟩ this drivel ⟨of ideots⟩
which they report as the voice ⟨w⟩of spirits were really such, ⟨suicide,
& of a⟩ ↑we must find out a more↓ decisive ⟨kind, would come into
vogue.⟩ ↑suicide.↓ [197]

In Swedenborg, the spirits have the dumps. See also *TU* 123

Miss Brindle. *GO* 15 [198]

[255] Aug. 8. A walk about Conantum with Henry Thoreau &
saw some of his botanical rarities.[199] The *Vitis sinuata* of Pursh and a
vitis only rarely yielding a sinuated leaf and a small ivy-leafed
grape, with small inedible fruit: saw the only slippery elm in Concord
& under it the only *parietaria* which he knows in town; three or four
galiums, three or four polygonums, three [256] Lespedezas & des-
modums (?) or hedysa⟨rus,⟩rums, eleceampane, pennyroyal, mugil-

---

   [195] "This mesmerism . . . truth.", struck through in pencil with one continuous and one discontinuous vertical use mark, is used in "Demonology," *W*, X, 25–26.
   [196] This entry is struck through in ink with two diagonal use marks.
   [197] "There are . . . suicide." is struck through in ink with a vertical use mark;
"There are . . . dead-cart.", struck through in pencil with a vertical use mark, is
used in "Demonology," *W*, X, 21; "The ⟨experts⟩ . . . suicide." is used in "Demonology," *W*, X, 26.
   [198] The entry in Journal GO describes "Miss Bridge" as a "mantuamaker in
Concord" who "became a *Medium*".
   [199] The cliffs of Conantum overlook Fair Haven Bay on the Sudbury River
about two miles south of Concord center.

leta (?) lechea, looking like hypericum, saw on the lanceolate thistle the ants & their milch cows the aphides, both larger than we are wont to see.

Saw spleen wort, a fern, — and the beaked hazel; ⟨T⟩the low & early blue berry is the *vaccinium pennsylvanicum*[,] the large & conspicuous huckleberry is *resinosum*, another is *vacillans*, [257] the huckleberry bird, which I used to call pinewarbler, is a sparrow, *fringilla pusilla*, the *Asclepias* has a stronger tension in its fibre than hemp, or than any other plant. All the asclepias kind have this strong fibre. Henry expatiated on the omniscience of the Indians. Found calamint or basil and gerardia quercifolia[.]

14 Aug[us]t A walk again with Henry, & found *Solidago Odora*, pellucid points on the leaves: found two polygalas with checkerberry scent. [258] Found pinesap, Hypopythis. And Aarons--rod *in bloom* which is rare; and a tall shrub unknown to Henry near & like the arrow-wood solidago altissima, & gigantea, three lecheas, major, incana, &   ; laurus benzoin. But I was taken with the aspects of the forest, & thought to Nero advertising for a luxury a walk in the woods should have been offered. 'Tis one of the secrets for dodging old age.[200]

[259] Among the good subjects for lectures is the Club.
If one were sure, when he goes to the city, to find at No. 49 Tremont Row, what scholars were abroad after the morning studies were ended.[201]

[Demonology] *Pseudo-Spiritualism.*
History of man is a series of conspiracies to win from nature some advantage without paying for it. 'Tis very curious to see what grand powers we have a hint of, and are mad to grasp, yet how slow Heaven is to trust us with edge-tools.[202]   See *Intell*[ect]. Lect. II p. 43

---

[200] "But I . . . age.", struck through in pencil with a vertical use mark, is used in "Country Life," *W*, XII, 147. A pencil line in the right margin marks "Tis one . . . age."
[201] "Among . . . ended." is struck through in pencil with a diagonal use mark; "If one . . . ended." is used in "Clubs," *W*, VII, 244.
[202] "History . . . edge-tools.", struck through with two vertical use marks, one in ink and one in pencil, is used in "Demonology," *W*, X, 20.

[260]   *Pseudo Spiritualism*
I say to the rapping tables
            "I well believe
            Thou wilt not utter what thou dost not know,
            And so far will I trust you, gentle *wood*." [203]

———

It agrees with Swedenborg in tenets. See *IO* 124

———

They are ignorant of all that is healthy & useful & beautiful to know, &, by law of kind, dunces seeking dunces in the dark of what they call the spiritual world,[n] ↑preferring snores & gastric noises to the voice of any muse[.]↓ [204]   See IO 242   ↑Demonology↓

[261] [Demonology]   ↑Pseudo spirit↓
    The rapping⟨s⟩ a new test like blue litmus, or other chemical absorbent, to try catechisms with. It detects organic skepticism in the very heads of the Church.[205]

Dreams may explain the magnetic *directed* dream. Dreams are the sequel of waking knowledge   &c   C [134–]135 [206]

———

Mesmerised is part & parcel of the mesmeriser[.]

———

Could you mesmerise yourself!

———

The amount of information I obtain from these mesmerised, is, that ↑pain is very unpleasing,↓ my shoes are made of leather, &c ↑that the cock crows in the morning, that there is a great deal of water in the high seas.↓ O 295

———

[203] Emerson's version of *I Henry IV*, II, iii, 113–115, struck through in ink with a vertical use mark, is used in "Demonology," *W*, X, 26. See *JMN*, XIII, 298.
    [204] "They are . . . muse", struck through in ink with a discontinuous vertical use mark, is used in "Demonology," *W*, X, 26. The entries on p. [260] are struck through in pencil with a vertical use mark.
    [205] "The rapping⟨s⟩ . . . Church.", struck through in ink with a vertical use mark, is used in "Demonology," *W*, X, 26. See Journal RO, p. [121] above.
    [206] The expanded form of this entry is used in "Demonology," *W*, X, 8–9.

[262]   ↑Pseudo Spiritism↓
Mrs Brindle   GO 15 [207]

———

We used to ask triumphantly, where was a ghost that could bear the smell of printer's ink? &c. but 'tis the peculiarity of this sorcery that it has stood in the teeth of the press, nay, uses the press largely for its own propagandism.

"The oracles assert, that the impressions of characters & other divine visions appear in aether." See *U* 120

———

All New Hampshire learning to walk on its thumbs. J 119 [208]

———

The Black Art

———

Bettine says the reason spirits so seldom appear is that they do not like phantoms, ugly phantoms[n] [263] such as the men are. See the passage, *Correspondence* with Goethe, Vol. I, 191 [209]

The only objection to spiritism is, that it is in the wrong hands. New powers are to be looked for. Who has found the limits of human intelligence?[n] But not in the vile.

[264] [blank]

[265] "Si Dieu a fait l'homme a son image, l'homme le lui a bien rendu." ap[ud]. *Chateaubriand.*

If God made man in his image, man has repaid him.
↑printed↓ [210]

———

[207] See p. [254] above.
[208] The entry in Journal J is used in the lecture "Manners and Customs of New England."
[209] Bettina Brentano von Arnim, *Goethe's Correspondence with a Child* . . . , 3 vols. (London, 1839), in Emerson's library.
[210] The quotation used by Chateaubriand is from Voltaire's *Le Sottisier*, XXXII, *Faits détachés*. Struck through in ink with a vertical use mark and in pencil with a diagonal use mark, it is used in translation in "Character," *W*, X, 104. "printed" is inserted in pencil. See Journal VO, p. [274] below.

Nov. 15. Walk with Ellery, who finds in nature, or man, that whatever is done for beauty or in sport, is excellent; but the moment there's any use in it or any kind of talent, 'tis very bad & stupid. The fox sparrows & the blue snowbirds pleased him & the watercresses which we saw in the brook, but which, he said, were not in any botany.

[266] There are people who give you their society in large saturating doses.[211]

Men who wish to inspire terror seem thereby to confess themselves cowards. ⟨They use the⟩ Why do they rely on it, but because they know how potent it is on themselves? [212]   ↑printed↓

[267] Agassiz said, "the best meteorologist was his corns."

[268]–[279] [213] [six leaves torn out]
[280]   ↑Samuel Hoar↓
[b]y which on each occasion it was tried & found wanting. ↑I am sorry to say↓ he [n] could not be elected a second time to Congress from Middlesex. And so in his own town when some important end was to be gained, as, for instance, when the County Commissioners refused to rebuild the ↑burned↓ Court House on the belief that the courts would be transferred from Concord to Lowell[,] all parties combined to send Mr Hoar to the Legislature, where his presence & speech secured the rebuilding, &, of course, also having answered our end [281] we passed by him, & elected somebody else at the next term.[214]

[282] 'Tis a trait of France, that it rapidly acquires & rapidly loses. This is confirmed by Montalembert's statement that the Collegiate institutions of France, in the Middle Age, were identical with those

---

[211] This sentence, struck through in ink with a vertical use mark, is used in "Behavior," *W*, VI, 173.

[212] "Men who . . . themselves?", struck through in ink with a vertical use mark, is used in "Courage," *W*, VII, 271.

[213] Traces of writing, in which no letters are discernible, are visible on the stubs of pp. [278] and [279].

[214] "[b]y which . . . term.", struck through in ink on p. [280] with a vertical use mark, is used in "Samuel Hoar," *W*, X, 443.

of England; & the Oxford history, lately, has been helped by examination of the history of French Universitiés, which explains the Oxford foundations & usages ⁿ at the present day; which are lost in France, except in the Record. ↑l'histoire de l'université de Paris, par Du Boulay.↓ ²¹⁵

Mem. Dr Solger's remark about French Conquests.²¹⁶

[283]–[285] [blank]

[286] I speak badly whilst I speak for feats. Feats are no measure of the heaven of intellect. It is profoundly solitary, it is unprofitable, it is to be despised & forgotten of men. If I recall the happiest hours of existence, those which really make man an inmate of ↑a↓ better world, it is a lonely & undescribed joy; but it is the ⟨angel⟩ ↑door↓ ⟨that ⟨invites us⟩ ↑leads↓⟩ to joys that ear hath not heard nor eye seen[.] ²¹⁷

[287] To answer a question so as to admit of no reply, is the test of a man,ⁿ to touch bottom every time.

                                        ↑printed in "Clubs"↓

————

↑*Fate*↓

'Tis a very composite force that which we know. I figure to myself men struggling in the waves of the ocean, & driven about here & there; they glance intelligently at each other now & then. Well, they have a right to their eyebeams, & all the rest is Fate.²¹⁸

[288] Knowing is the measure[,] for I suppose it will be conceded, that the nobility of a company or of a period is always to be estimated by the depth ⁿ of the ideas from which they live, & to which, of course, they appeal.

²¹⁵ César Egasse Du Boulay, *Historia Universitatis Parisiensis*, 6 vols. (Paris, 1665–1673).

²¹⁶ See p. [131] above and Journal VO, pp. [160]–[161] below.

²¹⁷ With "ear hath . . . seen", cf. Shakespeare, *A Midsummer Night's Dream*, IV, i, 213–215.

²¹⁸ "To answer . . . Fate." is struck through with two vertical use marks, one in ink and one in pencil; "To answer . . . time." is used in "Clubs," *W*, VII, 239; "I figure . . . Fate." is used in "Fate," *W*, VI, 19.

Quantum scimus sumus,[219] a proper enjoyment, a thrill of pleasure connected with a new perception
⟨thought⟩ knowledge the only elegance.

[289] [220] 'Tis in knowing, that man differs from a dog, ⟨not in doing,⟩ for ↑otherwise↓ he cannot compare ⟨with⟩⟨in doing,⟩ with a steam engine [n] ↑or the self acting spinning mule which is never tired & makes no fault.↓ [221] And he that can define, he that can answer a question so as to admit of no further answer, is the best man. And rightly do the old Norse fables in a bold barbarous manner show this; for heroes & gods set themselves at once on a game of question & answer, and the heads of speakers are at stake[.]

[290] Nature is not enjoyed or enjoyable, until man finds his completion[.]

Svend Vonved, Gylfis Mocking, Waft⟨h⟩hrudnir, are such.[222]

And, in the Indian ⟨tra⟩ legends, King, courtier, God, make the most romantic sacrifices for knowledge. Buddhists say, "he who has well made Bana shall never be born into any hell." And Plato's Adrastia, "he [n] who had known a truth shall be safe from harm until another period." [n] [223]

[291] Waste for "The Scholar."
Apology for the subject, that it is the health of all. Every man is a Scholar potentially, & does not need any one good so much as this of right thought. "Calm pleasures here abide, majestic pains."

[219] "We are what we know" (Ed.). Emerson's source was probably James Marsh's edition of Coleridge's *Aids to Reflection* (Burlington, Vt., 1829), p. 257, n. 10, where, however, it occurs as "quantum *sumus, scimus.*" See *JMN*, IX, 369.

[220] The entry on p. [289] is struck through in pencil with a vertical use mark.

[221] This sentence is struck through in ink with a vertical use mark.

[222] The page-wide rule above this entry is in pencil. For Svend Vonved, see Journal AC, p. [177] below.

[223] The quotation from Plato is from *The Six Books of Proclus . . .* , 1816, I, 260. The quotation is used in "Experience," *W*, III, 84, "Quotation and Originality," *W*, VIII, 177, and "Immortality," *W*, VIII, 340. See *JMN*, XIII, 302.

Coleridge's silent revolutions,

1. When the clerisy fell from the church. A scholar was once a priest, but the church clung to ⟨form⟩ ritual, & the scholar clung to joy, low as well as high, & so the separation was a mutual fault. But I think ⟨that⟩ ↑it↓ a schism which must be healed. The true scholar is the church: only, the duties [292] of intellect must be owned.

Down with these dapper trimmers & sycophants, & let us have masculine & divine men, ⟨drawing⟩ formidable lawgivers, Pythagoras, Plato, Aristotle, who warp the Churches of the world from their traditions, & penetrate them through & through with original perception[.]

Rabelais is somebody, & Luther ↑is↓ & Erasmus. Intellectual man lives in perpetual victory[.] [224]   E 352

> Sacre rushaski
> Zac

[291½] Henry B. Harrison, Esq. New Haven

Halfheaded men, who, by vicious organization, see only the object directly before them, & that in vast proportions, so as to engage their whole heat & faculty in the encounter with it. It awakens in them eloquence, industry, & passion; whilst people around them, in their accosting of the same object, are liable to returns of frigidity & indifference, from being forced to see both sides, — many sides, — & therefore cannot get up any [292½] furious zeal, as if this were the only point to be carried. Of course, such ⟨men⟩ monomaniacs, (like Quincy Adams or Calhoun, in politics) seem to be deities to those near them, interested in the same things, because these have great endowments all bent on one focus[.]

[293] The other point which interested A[lbert]. T[racy]. was the ⟨in⟩ ridiculous fame of the rhetoricians.[225] In a senate or other

---

[224] A small slash or rule follows "victory"; with this sentence, cf. "Worship," W, VI, 237.

[225] Emerson apparently met Albert H. Tracy (1793–1859), a Buffalo attorney, in December, 1856, or January, 1857 (L, V, 53). See JMN, XIII, 30, and Journal VO, p. [25] below.

business committee, all depends on a few men with working talent. They do every thing, & value men only as they can forward the work. But some ⟨fellow⟩ ↑new man↓ comes there who has ⟨a talent for speaking⟩ no ⟨n⟩ capacity for helping them at all, can't do the first thing, is insignificant, & nobody, but has a talent for speaking; this fellow gets up & makes a speech which is printed & read all over the Union, & at once becomes famous & takes the lead in public mind over [294] all these ⟨really powerful⟩ ↑executive↓ men who, of course, are full of indignation to find one who has no tact or skill, & knows he has none, put over them, by means of this ⟨loud⟩ talking ↑-power↓ which they despise.[226]

John Randolph said, there was one quality which was very rare, commonsense. He had been boy & man 24 years in this body (H[ouse]. [of] R[epresentatives].) & he had known one man who had it; he wouldn't say, he had known but one; he wouldn't say he had known more than one; but he had seen one man who had it in a remarkable degree; — his name was Roger Sherman. That man had made this remark; "when you are in the majority, vote, [295] when you are in the minority, talk." Well, Mr President, I am in the minority in this body, & I talk.

↑Tracy↓
A[lbert]. H T[racy]. said, "Mass[achuse]tts was full of rhetoricians." I forgot to tell him, that every twelfth man in Mass[achusetts]. was a shoemaker, & that Erastus Bigelow, Uriah Boyden, Nathaniel Bowditch and Mason of Taunton were not[n] ↑rhetoricians, & the rail--road projectors all over U.S.↓ & the merchants who planned so many voyages ⟨whi⟩ of vessels which distribute their cargoes at New York, & make so much of the importance of that city, did not so much create speeches, as business. — [227]

---

[226] "The other point . . . despise.", struck through in ink with single vertical use marks on pp. [293] and [294], is used in "Eloquence," *W*, VII, 75–76.

[227] Erastus Bigelow (1814–1879) invented power looms for use in carpet weaving; Uriah Boyden (1804–1879) devised an improved turbine water wheel; Nathaniel Bowditch (1773–1838), mathematician and astronomer, published the best-known work on practical navigation; William Mason (1808–1883) invented a

[296] Hayden of Springfield[,] a young naturalist[,] went to Nebraska.

↑H[enry]. S[tephens].↓ Randall of Cortland writes the life of Jefferson[.] [228]

The English limitariness in literature is the inevitable result of their social condition; as the people that are the best off, they wish to stay where they are.

"And then, Mr ↑John↓ Wistar, pray tell me ↑for↓ what purpose Jesus Christ came into the world?"—
"My dear sir, 'tis very hard to say for what purpose any man came into the world," replied the Quaker.[229]

---

[297] [Index material omitted] [230]
[297a] [231] *Books*

> Love of reading,— what is that? It is to exchange ⟨those⟩ stupid hours ⟨which come in each life,⟩ for delightful hours.
> ⟨The || ... ||⟩Many times the reading of a book ↑has↓ made the fortune of the reader,— has decided his way of life. The reading of Voyages & travels has ⟨filled the boys⟩ waked the boy's ambition & curiosity, & made him a sailor, & an explorer of new countries all his life, a powerful merchant, ⟨a military hero,⟩ a good soldier, [297b] a pure patriot, or a successful student of science[.]

[inside back cover] [Index material omitted]

---

device for spinning cotton and a self-acting mule and began building locomotives in 1852.

[228] *The Life of Thomas Jefferson*, 3 vols. (New York, 1858). See *L*, V, 105.

[229] John Wistar was a member of a prominent Philadelphia family. Emerson attended one of the celebrated "Wistar parties," which had grown out of gatherings held at the home of the noted physician Caspar Wistar (1761–1818), in January, 1854 (*L*, IV, 415).

[230] The page bears a preliminary index, in pencil and not alphabetical, and six index entries in ink at right, alphabetized additions to the index on the facing page (inside back cover).

[231] For a physical description of pp. [297a]–[297b], see the bibliographical headnote to Journal SO.

$\mathcal{VO}$

1857–1858

Emerson began Journal VO in early 1857; on p. [19] he refers to
John Brown's March, 1857, speech in Town Hall, Concord. The earliest
dated entry is May 2, [1857] (pp. [65]–[66]) and the latest is June 7,
1858 (pp. [292]–[293]). Brief later entries, dated 1865 and 1874,
appear on pp. [67] and [84] respectively.

The covers of the copybook, gray paper marbled with red, yellow, and blue
over boards, measure 17.8 x 21.3 cm. The spine strip and the protective corners on
the front and back covers are of tan leather. "VO" is written in the upper and lower
right corners of the front cover, in the upper left corner of the back cover, and in
crayon on the lower left corner of the back cover. The date "1857" is written to
the right of center in the upper half of the front cover. Thirteen lines, from 1 to
1.5 cm long, appear at the lower right corner of the back cover.

Including flyleaves (i, ii, 299, 300), there were 152 unlined leaves measuring
17.2 x 20.8 cm, but the leaf bearing pages 171–172 is torn out. Upper portions of
the leaves bearing pages 141–142 and 169–170 are torn out. In his pagination, Emerson repeated pages 274 and 275; he then added a superscript "a" in pencil to the
second of each pair. Seven pages were misnumbered and corrected in ink: 3⟨2⟩8,
1⟨4⟩98, 1⟨4⟩99, ⟨⟨15⟩200⟩ 200, ⟨15⟩204 204, ⟨155⟩ 205, and ⟨15⟩206. Three pages
are misnumbered in pencil and corrected in ink: ⟨276⟩278, ⟨278⟩280, and 2⟨79⟩81.
Pages 222 and 223 are numbered 22 and 23. The pages are numbered in ink except
for the following twenty-three in pencil: 50, 54–56, 58, 64, 70, 76, 78, 99, 105,
110, 112, 114, 115, 117, 120, 176, 178, 180–182, and 282. Twenty pages are unnumbered: i, ii, 1, 2, 12, 13, 57, 95, 113, 116, 121, 177, 179, 183, 197, 231, 233,
239, 241, and 300. Six pages were numbered first in pencil and then in ink: 48, 60,
62, 66, 68, and 72. Twenty-two pages are blank: ii, 1, 2, 12, 14, 18, 46, 54, 57,
64, 94, 95, 120, 122, 149, 195, 204, 206, 218, 222, 223, and 267.

[front cover]   VO

1857

VO

[front cover verso] [1]   ↑Examined Sept '77↓

_____

[Etienne] Vacherot. Histoire Critique de l'Ecole d'Alexandrie. Paris, Librairie Philosophique de Ladrange. 1846. 3 vols. 8 Vo

_____

a note from Charles Attwood
_____

Illa cantat nec tacemus
Ni tacero desinam
Perderem musas tacendo
        Cat[ullus]. *Pervig[ilium] Ven[eris]* [n 2]

[Index material omitted]   ↑1877 Feb↓

[i] R. W. Emerson.   1857

VO

[Index material omitted]

O Hafiz, give me thought
In fiery figures cast,
For all beside is naught,
All else is din & blast.[3]

_____

[1] "Examined Sept 77" and the rule beneath it are in pencil; the index material on the front cover verso is in pencil except for one entry. A curving line in the left margin marks "Vacherot. Histoire . . . Attwood". "1877 Feb" is enclosed at left and top by a line.

[2] Emerson paraphrases and alters three lines from *Pervigilium Veneris*, XXII: "illa cantat, nos tacemus: quando ver venit meum? quando fiam uti chelidon ut tacere desinam? perdidi musam tacendo, nec me Apollo respicit," "She sings, we are mute: when is my spring coming? when shall I be as the swallow, that I may cease to be voiceless? I have lost the Muse in silence, nor does Apollo regard me."

[3] Emerson's English version of four lines from *Der Diwan von Mohammed Schemsed-din Hafis*, trans. Joseph von Hammer-Purgstall, 2 vols. (Stuttgart and Tübingen, 1812–1813), II, 135; this book is in Emerson's library. See p. [77] below.

↑This Book searched through February '77.↓ [4]

[ii] [blank]
[1]–[2] [blank]
[3]   *Inspiration.*

"The gods," says Homer, "ever give to mortals their apportioned share of reason only ⟨for⟩on one day." [5]

Dii Majores.

Jupiter, Juno, Minerva, Neptune,
Vesta, Apollo, Diana, Ceres,
Mercury, Venus, Mars, Vulcan.

Pindar p 233 [6]

[4] Pindar in one of his poems represented Agamedes & Trophonius as rewarded by sudden death for building the temple of Apollo. He was afterwards referred by the priestess on his inquiring what was best for mankind, to his own verses. He understood this reply as an intimation of his death, which soon after took place.

Bohn's [Odes of] Pindar. [1852,] p. xi

[5] "Do you suppose, prince, that Raffaelle would not have been the greatest genius among painters, even though, unfortunately, he should have been born without hands?"

Lessing— Emilia Galeotti [I, iv]

[6] ↑Royal roads.↓
↑1.↓ "The Cid said," he never obtained his swords by barter or trade, but won them in fight." [7] ↑2.↓ The life is sacred in each house

---

[4] This notation, enclosed by a short rule above and a line to the left, is in pencil; the index entry is in pencil.

[5] This sentence is used in "Works and Days," *W*, VII, 178. Cf. *Odyssey*, XVIII, 136–137, "τοῖος γὰρ νόος ἐστὶν ἐπιχθονίων ἀχθρώπων οἷον ἐπ' ἦμαρ ἄγῃσι πατὴρ ἀνδρῶν τε θεῶν τε.": "for the spirit of men upon the earth is even such as the day which the father of gods and men brings upon them."

[6] *The Odes of Pindar, Literally Translated into English Prose, by Dawson W. Turner* (London: Henry G. Bohn, 1852), p. 233, in Emerson's library. The "twelve Sovereign Gods" are listed in a note to Antistrophe III of Pindar's Olympic Ode X. "*Dii Majores . . . Vulcan.*" is rewritten in ink over substantially the same matter in pencil; "Pindar p 233" is in pencil. See *JMN*, XIII, 380.

[7] Robert Southey, *Chronicle of the Cid* (Lowell, 1846), p. 313. This book is in Emerson's library.

that did not enter the house by any door, but was born into it.

↑3.↓ There are royal roads, as when one finds the way to the sea by following the river; or, when one derives insight from good will.

↑4.↓   ☞ 8

[7] ↑4.↓ "He is gifted with genius who knoweth much by natural talent, but those who have learnt, boisterous in gabbling like daws, clamor in fruitless fashion against the divine bird of Zeus." [*Odes of*] *Pindar* [1852,]

p 15

↑*Pindar*↓

"Neither by sea nor by land canst thou find the way to the Hyperboreans." [9] *Pindar.* [*Ibid.*, p. xxii]

"There are many swift darts under my elbow, within my quiver, which have a voice for those with understanding, but to the crowd they need interpreters." [10] [*Ibid.*]

[8]   Retsch's men & animals all run to hair & nails.[11]

[9]   Agassiz

Errata

p 27   weigh the standing of the four great branches of the animal Kingdom

St Antony   *TU* 106

Newton & Cuvier calvinistic   *TU* 123

Vol. 2. p 534   ⟨f⟩Concept↑i↓on & fecundation intellectual acts.

p. 578. *matter* does not exist as such, but only as specific things.

Vol I. p. 306, Table showing geologic place of mammalia.[12]

[10] The ⟨turtes⟩turtles in Cambridge, on the publication of this book ↑of Agassiz,↓ should hold an indignation meeting, & migrate

---

[8] The hand sign points to "4. He is . . . fashion" inserted beneath a short rule at the bottom of p. [7]; "against the . . . *Pindar* p 15" is at the top of p [8].

[9] This quotation is used in "Inspiration," *W*, VIII, 294.

[10] This quotation is used in "Quotation and Originality," *W*, VIII, 202–203.

[11] This sentence is in pencil. For Retsch, see *JMN*, XIII, 441.

[12] The entries on p. [9] refer to Jean Louis Rodolphe Agassiz, *Contributions to the Natural History of the United States of America*, 4 vols. (Boston, 1857–1863). "Agassiz . . . *TU* 123" is in pencil.

from the Charles River, with Chelydra serpentina marching ⟨a⟩at the head, and "Death to Agassiz!" inscribed on their shields.[13]

↑*Naturalists.*↓

No matter what /they/savants ⁿ/ say, tortoise, or shark, or sheep, or ostrich, it is always man they have in their thought, both professor & public are surreptitiously studying man ⟨which⟩ ↑whom↓ they would gladly read directly, if they could. 'Tis a vast Aesop's Fable, which ↑prates about lions & foxes & storks, but↓ [11] means you⟨, you, you,⟩ ↑& me↓ from beginning to end.

⟨⟨VO⟩ NO 273   235, 106⟩NO 273, 235, 106,
The important fact in his book, is, that, when the turtle is born, ⟨the⟩ ↑its↓ ovary is already full of eggs.[14]

―――

If nat↑tural↓ philosophy is faithfully written, moral philosophy need not be, for /it/that/ will find itself expressed in these *theses* to a perceptive soul. *See below* p. 140

―――

Agassiz discovered "the coincidence between the embryonic develop-ment of beings, & the gradation which is wrought from age to age in organic forms."
      (*Revue des D[eux]. M[ondes]*.   1 Sept. 1857)   *A. Laugel*.[15]

[12] [blank]
[13] "A Man is already of consequence in the world, when it is known that we can implicitly rely on him." *Bulwer*.[16]

[14] [blank]

―――――

[13] "of Agassiz" is inserted in pencil and then traced in ink with a comma added; this entry is followed by a short rule and a curved rule above the inserted "*Natural-ists.*"
      [14] "VO" is erased pencil; "NO 273   235, 106" was written first in pencil and partially erased, then written in ink with commas added after "273" and "106"; "the" is canceled and "its" is inserted in pencil.
      [15] Auguste Laugel, "Un Naturaliste, M. Agassiz et ses travaux," *Revue des Deux Mondes*, Sept. 1, 1857, pp. 77–108; Emerson translates this sentence from pp. 94–95. See Journal AC, p. [39] below. Emerson withdrew this volume from the Boston Athenaeum January 21–March 3 and July 7–August 12, 1858.
      [16] This quotation is used in "Character," *W*, X, 102. See Journal SO, p. [86] above.

[15]   *Works & days.*

———

"A general has always troops enough, if he only knows how to employ those he has, & bivouacs with them," said Bonaparte[.] [17] [*The Confidential Correspondence . . . , 1856, I, 151*]

I value myself not as I do the duty of the day, but of the remote day, &c[.]   *DO* 192

———

〈This〉 ↑The passing↓ 〈hour〉 ↑moment↓ is an edifice
Which the Omnipotent cannot rebuild.[18]

———

The man is by much the larger half, &, though we exaggerate his tools & sciences, as soon as we face a hero or a sage, arts & civilizations *peu de cas*[.] [19]

[16] Hear what the morning says & believe that. *BO* 148

———

Days   *TU* 41

———

Somewhat finer in the sky than we have senses to appreciate.[20]
                                        TU 160

———

age of ages.

———

I owe to genius always the same debt, of lifting the curtain from the

———

[17] This sentence is struck through in ink with a wavy diagonal use mark. See Journal SO, pp. [30] and [67] above.

[18] With these lines, struck through in ink with a wavy diagonal use mark, cf. "Fragments on Nature and Life," V, *W*, IX, 350, and the motto of "Works and Days," *W*, VII, 156. See Journal SO, p.[59] above, and Journal AC, p. [5] below.

[19] "I value . . . day, &c" and "The man . . . *peu de cas*" are struck through in ink with wavy diagonal use marks. For "I value . . . day, &c", see Journal SO, p. [61] above.

[20] "Hear . . . that." and "Somewhat . . . appreciate.", struck through in ink with single wavy diagonal use marks, are used in "Country Life," *W*, XII, 156–157. For "Somewhat . . . appreciate.", see p. [103] below.

common, & showing me that gods are sitting disguised in this seeming gang of gypsies & pedlers.   E 118 [21]

"When we wake in the morning there is a thought already up & waiting for us." See *TO* 51 [22]

———

Use of history to give value to the present hour. That is good which commends [17] to me my country, my climate, my means & materials, my associates. Jones Very thought it an honor to wash his own face: hc sccms to me more sane than men who hold themselves cheap.[23]   ↑printed in↓

[18] [blank]
[19] Captain John Brown of Kansas gave a good account of himself in the Town Hall, last night, to a meeting of Citizens. One of his good points was, the folly of the peace party in Kansas, who believed, that their strength lay in the greatness of their wrongs, & so discountenanced resistance. He wished to know if their wrong was greater than the negro's, & what kind of strength that gave to the negro?
[20] He believes on his own experience that one good, believing, strong-minded man is worth a hundred, nay twenty thousand men without character, for a settler in a new country; & that the right men will give a permanent direction to the fortunes of a state. For one of these bullying[,] drinking rowdies, — he seemed to think cholera, smallpox & consumption were as valuable recruits.[24]
[21] The first man who went in to Kansas from Missouri to interfere in the elections, he thought, had a perfect right to be shot.
He gave a circumstantial account of the battle at Black-Jack, where 23 Missourians surrendered to 9 abolitionists.

[21] This sentence (actually found in Journal E, p. [318]), struck through in ink with a diagonal use mark, is used in "Works and Days," *W*, VII, 176.
[22] In Notebook TO, Emerson quotes Thoreau: "H.D.T. says, that when he wakes in the morning, he finds a thought already in his mind, waiting for him. The ground is preoccupied."
[23] "Jones Very . . . face:" is struck through in ink with six vertical use marks, and "he seems . . . cheap." is struck through in ink with two; "Use of . . . cheap." is used in "Works and Days," *W*, VII, 177.
[24] Thoreau introduced Emerson to John Brown in March, 1857. "One of . . . negro?" and "He believes . . . recruits." are used in "Courage," *W*, VII, 260 and 270.

[22] He had 3000 sheep in Ohio, & would instantly detect a strange sheep in his flock. A cow can tell its calf by ⟨the eye⟩ secret signal, he thinks, by the eye, to run away or to lie down & hide itself.[25] He always makes friends with his horse or mule, ⟦or with the deer ⟨on⟩that visit his Ohio farm⟧ & when he sleeps on his horse, as he does as readily as in his bed, his horse does not start or endanger him.

[23] Brown described the expensiveness of war in a country where every thing that is to be eaten or worn or used by man or beast ⟨is to⟩ ↑must↓ be ⟨conveyed⟩ ↑dragged↓ a long distance on wheels.

"God protects us in winter," he said; "No Missourian can be⟨e⟩ seen in the country until the grass comes up again."

[24] Most men are insolvent, or, promise ⟨much more⟩ by their countenance, & conversation, & by their early endeavor, much more ↑than↓ they ever perform. Charles N[ewcomb]. did, & Burrill C[urtis]. & Coleridge did, & Carlyle.[26]

Men's conscience, I once wrote, is local in spots & veins, here & there, & not in healthy circulation through their system, so that they are unexpectedly good in some passage, & when [25] you infer that they may be depended on in some other case, they heavily disappoint you. Well, so is their thought. Albert Tracy dazzles with his intellectual light, but is a wretched hunker in politics, & hunks in social & practical life. And I learn from the ⟨phre⟩photograph & daguerre men, that almost all faces & forms ⟨that⟩ ↑which↓ come to their shops to be copied, are irregular & unsymmetrical[,] [26] have one eye blue & one grey, ⟨one⟩ the nose is not straight, & one shoulder is higher than the other. The man is physically as well as metaphysically a thing of shreds & patches, ⟨&⟩borrowed unequally from his good & bad ancestors, — a misfit from the start.[27]

[25] Cf. "John Brown: Speech at Salem," *W*, XI, 279.

[26] "Most . . . perform." is used in "Immortality," *W*, VIII, 338–339. Burrill Curtis, native of Rhode Island and onetime member of Brook Farm, later moved to Concord.

[27] "And I . . . start.", struck through in ink with a vertical use mark on p. [25] and two vertical use marks, one wiped, on p. [26], is used in "Beauty," *W*,

[27] The democratic party is the ⟨th⟩party of the Poor marshalled against the Rich. They are sure they are excluded from rich houses & society, & they vote with the poor against you. That is the sting that exasperates them, & makes a strong party. But they are always officered by ⟨the⟩ a few ↑self-seeking↓ deserters from the Rich or Whig Party. They know the incapacity of ⟨the⟩ ↑their own↓ rank & file, and would reject one of their own nobodies as a leader. A few rich men or Whigs are therefore always ready to accept the place of Captain & Major & Colonel & President, & wear their [28] colors for the rewards which are only to be given to the officers, & never to rank & file. But these leaders are Whigs, & associate with Whigs, that is, they are the dining, drinking, & dancing ↑& investing↓ class, & by no means the digging & hoeing class.

_____   See also *SO* 204

[29] But 'tis of no use to tell me, as Brown & others do, that the Southerner is not a better fighter than the Northerner, — when I see, that uniformly a Southern minority prevails, & gives the law. Why, but because the Southerner ⟨shows fight,⟩ ↑is a fighting man,↓ & the Northerner ⟨fears?⟩ ↑is not.↓
1857.

[30] [28]   ⟨For gods do not⟩ ↑Nor think that gods↓ receive the prayer
              In ear & heart, but find ⟨them⟩ ↑it↓ there [29]

              Think not the gods receive thy prayer
              In ear & heart, but find it there.

[31]   ⟨Of limber knees & twisted spine⟩
              ⟨And⟩ ↑Whose↓ meager bodies peak & pine
              With limber knees & twisted spine

              And paints with white & red the moors
              To draw the nations out of doors

_____
VI, 299. For Albert H. Tracy, Buffalo lawyer, see Journal SO, pp. [293]–[295] above.
      [28] The entries on pp. [30] and [31] are in pencil.
      [29] These two lines are struck through in pencil with a diagonal use mark.

Or earth with red volcano charmed

[32]   ⟨Y⟩*Rhetoric.*
You shall never say, "I beg not to be mis-understood," or, only in the case, when you are afraid that what is called a better meaning will be taken, when you wish to insist on a worse.

Another rule is; omit all the negative propositions. I fear, Agassiz takes quite too much time & space in denying popular science. He should ⟨shock⟩ ↑electrify↓ us by perpetual affirmations [n] [33] unexplained.[30]

[34]   ↑*Superlative.*↓
When a man says to me, "I have the intensest love of nature," at once I know that he has none.

"The freedom of man consists herein, that he is his own aim."

"Every man who stamps his personality on his life is the true natural & free man."
                    Atlantis, Feb. 1857. p. 142
                                        See below, *VO* 254

[35] I ⟨w⟩once knew of a man who drew a poor gir⟨h⟩l into his chamber. The girl quickly came to her penitence, & said she was bitterly ashamed. "Ashamed" said the man, "What is there ↑to↓ be ashamed of?" The speeches of our statesmen at Washington are much in the same clear key of correct sentiment, or like Talleyrand's reply to Bonaparte when he asked, "what is all this about non-intervention?" — "Sire, it means about the same as intervention." [n]

[36] Lord Normanby says of the French aristocracy in 1848, "Country retirement in their own land has done more for them than exile in foreign parts formerly did." [31]

---

[30] "shock" is canceled and "electrify" inserted in pencil on p. [32].

[31] Constantine Henry Phipps (1797–1863), first Marquis of Normanby, MP, lord lieutenant of Ireland, and minister to the court of Tuscany, was the author of romantic novels and sketches. See Journal AC, p. [246] below.

A deputy said of Guizot, "il ne pratique pas toutes ses maximes, mais il maxime toutes les pratiques."

Guizot said, "the government would not engage itself for the future from the Tribune; — to promise was sometimes worse than to act, since [37] to promise destroyed what existed without attempting to replace it."

Lord Normanby when in Florence had the foible of desiring to appear young. He quarreled with Landor who published a letter against the ex-minister which ended with these words, "If we were not both, my lord, two miserable old dotards trembling on the brink of the grave, this letter would be more pointed than it is."

One source of sublime prophecy
Coleridge's
Mine

The two ways

Providence deigns a supply of oxygen & of moral element[.]
There are men who are born to go to Kansas, men born to take a bee line to an axe[.] [32]

[3⟨2⟩8] Nature who made the lock, knows where to find the key.

――――

↑Skeptic↓
I find no more flagrant proof of skepticism than th⟨is⟩e toleration of slavery. Another is, this running of the girls into popery. They know nothing of religions, & the grounds of the sects; they know that they do like music, & Mozart's masses; & Bach's, & run into the Catholic Church, where these are.
[39] Another is, this mummery of rapping & pseudo spiritualism[.]

The absence of moral feeling in the white man is not felt as such.

                                         CO 59

―――――

[32] "One source . . . axe" is in pencil. For "men born . . . axe", see Journal SO, p. [201₁] above.

From high to higher forces
The scale of power uprears,
The heroes on their horses,
The gods upon the spheres [33]

Thebadel et Messpot Messku Marathonz Salamoley
Eurymedopz Pelofib Lenetratpi Mantisi Phocilp
Granitif Istit Arbtib Alextis Aritet Aegtas.[34]

1	2	3	4	5	6	7	8	9	0
BO	DF	GH	JKZ	L	MN	PQ	RS	TV	WX

[40]   Anaesthetic
Power of mind to withdraw from pain. "Some have been burned
& not apprehended it; some transfixed with spits, do not perceive it;
others that are struck on their shoulders with axes, or their ar⟨e⟩ms
struck with knives, & are not conscious of what is done to them."
Iamblĩ̃chus [35]

[41]
———

The man of the world bows with a vertical movement of the head,

[33] These four lines are used in "Fragments on Nature and Life," IV, *W*, IX, 349.

[34] Richard Grey, in his *Memoria Technica or, Method of Artificial Memory . . .* (London, 1806), p. 5, describes a cipher for remembering dates which Emerson used in *JMN*, III, 265, and *JMN*, IV, 234:

a	e	i	o	u	au	oi	ei	ou	y	th
1	2	3	4	5	6	7	8	9	0	00
b	d	t	f	l	s	p	k	n	z	

Included in the events signified by the mnemonic words in this entry are the battle of Marathon, 490 B.C., "Marathonz"; the battle of Eurymedon, c. 467 B.C., "Eurymedopz"; the battle of Granicus, c. 334 B.C., "Granitif"; and the battle of Issus, 333 B.C., "Istit".

[35] *Iamblichus on the Mysteries of the Egyptians, Chaldeans, and Assyrians, translated from the Greek by Thomas Taylor* (Chiswick, 1821), p. 122. This book is in Emerson's library. In this paragraph, the period after "pain" is in pencil, as are the crosses of the "t's" in the "with" of "with spits," "with axes," and "with knives," the crosses of the "t's" in "struck" and "what", and the dot of the "i" in "with axes,".

up & down. My Stoic used a horizontal Salutation, as if always saying No.

———

↑Palsy↓

————

> I batter the wheel of heaven,
> When it rolls not rightly by;
> I am not one of the snivellers
> Who fall thereon, & die.
> *Hafiz.*[36]

C[harles]. K[ing]. N[ewcomb]. says, "Daniel Webster contents me as a nature, but is nothing as a person."

[42] I suppose the same impulse of the air entering into the trachea of an ass will bray, & into the trachea of a nightingale will sing. Inspiration is as the receiver.[37]

[43] "We cannot speak rightly about the ⟨g⟩Gods, without the Gods." *Iamblichus* [*on the Mysteries of the Egyptians, Chaldeans, and Assyrians . . . , 1821, p. 164*]

> ⟨And⟩ ↑Then↓ what must be the splendor of that soul
> ⟨Buried⟩ ↑Prisoned↓ in Anna's beauty for its ⟨tomb⟩ ↑tent↓.

See Iamblichus [*ibid.,*] p. 171 [38]

↑I remember that↓ I expect↑ed↓ a revival in the churches to be caused by the reading of Iamblichus.

paradigm   phasmata, pleromas, mundane   archons [39]

---

[36] These four lines, struck through in ink with one vertical and one diagonal use mark, are Emerson's version of four lines from *Der Diwan von . . . Hafis,* 1812–1813, II, 125; they are used in "Persian Poetry," *W,* VIII, 244–245.

[37] See Journal AC, p. [176] below.

[38] A footnote to p. 171 quotes Philolaus, who says "that the soul is conjoined to the body on account of certain punishments, and that it is buried in it as in a sepulchre."

[39] These five words are in pencil.

[44] I see the ⟨same⟩ selfsame energy & action in a boy at football, that I admire in the intellectual play of Burke or Pindar.

———

Who has ever found the boundaries of the human intelligence?

———

↑*Art.*↓

All your facts, my dear doctor, leave us outside, but a good word lets us into the world: such is the eternal precedence of literature.

[45] ——
the thumb of Michel Angelo.

———

↑What a damning verdict when we say of a man, Bad-looking!↓ How dare I meet him, lest I should find he wears ear-rings, or has long hair braided into a disgusting queue!

'Tis the law that each ⟨life⟩ ↑kind↓ when it becomes aware of a higher life, gladly abandons its own, & exchanges it for that.
What would become of a fox who found out that it was a fox?

[46] [blank]
[47] Calvert said, that, when Frye had sung at his chambers in Paris to a French company, they were much struck with his person & performance, & one of the guests made his compliments to Calvert, & told him how much he admired Frye; "*C'est un bel homme*; quel visage! c'est précisement la figure de Jesus," and, turning to Bryan, who stood by with his white hair & beard, he suddenly added, "*et vous êtes le Pere* ⟨e⟩*Eternel.*" [40]

[48] *Conduct of Life.*
A man can spare nothing; wants whitest ⟨night⟩day & blackest night &c &c. see *CO* 261   *HO* 207
Leasts. *BO* 56

———

[40] George Henry Calvert (1803–1889), poet and essayist, Harvard 1823, spent a number of years abroad in the 1820s, 1840s, and 1850s; the identity of Frye and of Bryan has not been established. See *JMN*, VI, 359–360.

Better one cultivated than a nation of others   *VS* 40

———

"Wisdom is not found in the hand of those that live at their ease." *Job.*[41]

Despotism necessary to the generatization of a state.
Theory of Hum↑an↓ Progression. p. 449 [42]
French Revolution useful. *IO.* 527

———

Of common & uncommon people. W 128

———

What are common people made for? W 128

———

Saxons loving shipwrecks. T 124

———

[49] ↑*Power of opinion*↓
'Tis a small part of the guarding that police & armies do; the main guard is, the fear & superstition of men themselves. The reverence for the Bible has saved a million crimes, which the people were bad enough to commit. "Thou shalt not kill," guards London.[43]

[50]   ↑*Art.*↓
You cannot make a cheap palace.

[51] Because our education is defective, because we are superficial & ill-read, we were forced to make the most of that position, of ignorance; to idealize ignorance. Hence America is a vast Know-Nothing Party, & we disparage books, & cry up intuition. With a few clever men we have made a reputable thing of that, & denouncing libraries & severe culture, & magnifying the motherwit [52] swagger of bright boys from the country colleges, we have even come ↑so far as↓ to

[41] Kenelm Digby, *Two Treatises: In the one of which, the Nature of Bodies; In the other, The Nature of Mans Soule, is looked into:* . . . (London, 1645), *Nature of Mans Soule,* p. 119; the two treatises are separately paginated. See *JMN,* XIII, 165, and p. [205] below.
    [42] Patrick Edward Dove, *The Theory of Human Progression and Natural Probability of a Reign of Justice* (Boston, 1851), in Emerson's library. See *JMN,* XIII, 178 and 291.
    [43] See *JMN,* XIII, 237.

deceive every body, except ourselves, into an admiration of un-learning and inspiration forsooth.

[53] I have an arrow that can find its mark. ↑A mastiff that will bite without a bark.↓ [44]

[54] [blank]
[55] [45]   ↑Miss Delia Bacon↓

___

Si non errasset fecer⟨i⟩at illa minus[.] [46]

___

The author I bade rush to her proofs without digression or episode[.]

___

"No man or woman has ever thought or written more sincerely than the author of this book" Hawthorne p xii [47]

↑Raleigh "a western man."↓
parallelism of ⟨S⟩aⁿ passage of B[acon]. & of S[hakespeare]. [*Philosophy of the Plays of Shakspere Unfolded*, 1857,] p. 153

" 'Tis the school of a criticism much more severe than the criticism which calls its freedom in question." [*Ibid.*,] p. lxxx

"Historical key to that Art of Delivery & Tradition by means of which the secrets of the Elizabethan Age are conveyed." [*Ibid.*,] p. l

[56] [48] All the great masters, — doubtful who they were   *W* 1
Club founded on Shakspeare   *TU* 264

___

[44] This sentence is in pencil.

[45] The entries on p. [55] are in pencil, except for "Miss Delia Bacon" and "Si . . . minus".

[46] "Had she not erred, she had achieved less." Emerson seems to have revised a favorite quotation — "Si non errasset, fecerat ille minus,": "Had it not erred, it had achieved less," Martial, *Epigrams*, I, xxi — to suit Delia Salter Bacon. See *JMN*, VI, 73, and *JMN*, IX, 360.

[47] Preface to Delia Salter Bacon, *The Philosophy of the Plays of Shakspere Unfolded*, 1857, in Emerson's library.

[48] The entries on p. [56] are in pencil, except for "If the ⟨picture⟩ . . . *NO* 257" with the rules above and below it and "see also . . . *IT* 44" with the rules above and below it.

See SO 148

———

If the ⟨picture⟩ ↑book↓ is good who cares who made it? *NO* 257 [49]

———

↑If the book is good, who does not care who made it?↓

———

She has the virtue to believe ⁿ in cause & effect[.]

———

see also the quotation from Muller. *IT* 44 [50]

———

[57] [blank]
[58] [51] Miss B[acon]. has read much in these plays that the critics of the Athenaeum, &c, never read there & will never read.

Some men come into the park for sport & gymnastics. Plenty of people come thither to hunt as an end. But these first have another end[:] they are hunters of men[.]

[59] Shakspeare's Plays published in 1623, three years after Plymouth Colony. If they had been published first, the good forefathers had never been able to come away.

[60] We are called a very patient people. Our assemblies are much more passive in the hands of their orators than the English. We do not cough down or roar down the heaviest proser, nor smother by dissent the most unpalatable & injurious. ⟨I think it very discreditable that we should be⟩ ↑'Tis a pity that our decorum should make us↓ such lambs & rabbits ⟨⟨through our decorum⟩⟩ in the claws of these [61] wolves & foxes of the caucus. We encourage them to tear us by ⟨their⟩ ↑our↓ tameness. They drop their hypocrisy quite too early, & are not at the pains to hide their claw under velvet,↑ — from↓ the dear innocents that we are.

———

[49] The entry from Journal NO, p. [257], "If the ⟨picture⟩ . . . it?", is used in "Greatness," *W*, VIII, 312.
[50] On p. [44] of Notebook IT, Emerson gives the quotation: " 'Poesy drawing within its circle all that is glorious & inspiring, gave itself but little concern as to where its flowers originally grew.' J.O. Muller".
[51] The entries on p. [58] are in pencil.

Who would see fun must be on hand at seven.

[62] The hater of property & of government takes care to have his warranty-deed recorded, and the book written against Fame & learning has the author's name on the title-page.

talkers against talking, writers against writing

> If wishes would carry me over the land
> I would /greet/ride/ ⟨a⟩with loose bridle today
> I would greet every tree wi[t]h a grasp of my hand
> ⟨Take a draught⟩ ↑Make my cup↓ of each fountain ⟨&c⟩
> ↑my↓ bath in the bay [52]

[63] [53]
> For joy & beauty planted it
> With faerie gardens cheered,
> And boding Fancy haunted it
> With men & women weird.[54]

> What ailed them in these fields impearled
> My children all aghast
> Or dreaming on the future world
> Or suffering from the ⟨old⟩ past

[64] [blank]
[65] ↑2 May.↓
Walk yesterday first day of May with Henry T[horeau]. to Goose Pond, & to the "Red chokeberry Lane." [55] Found sedge flowering, & salix humilis later than s. discolor; found Lycopodium dendroides & lucidulum; found Chimaphila maculata the only patch of it in town. Found Senecio & even solidago in the water already forward, & the Sawmill-brook much adorned with hellebore veratrum viride.

[52] "talkers against . . . bay" is in pencil.
[53] The entries on p. [63] are in pencil.
[54] These four lines are used in "Fragments on Nature and Life," X, W, IX, 340. See p. [226] below.
[55] Goose Pond is a small pond northeast of Walden Pond about one and one-half miles south of Concord center.

Saw the white-throated sparrow with a strong white stripe on the top of his head[.]

[66] Saw a stump of a ↑canoe-↓birch-tree newly cut down, which had bled a barrel.ⁿ From a white birch, H. cut a strip of bark to show how a naturalist would make the best box to carry a plant or other specimen requiring care. & thought the woodman would make a better hat of birch-bark than of felt, ↑yes,↓ & pantaloons too, — hat, with cockade of lichens, thrown in. — I told him the Birkebeiners of the Heimskringla had been before him.[56]

[67] We will make a book on walking, 'tis certain, & have easy lessons for beginners. "Walking in ten Lessons." Pulsifer, &, it seems, Collier, have already taken ground. Thoreau, Channing, Rice, Pulsifer, Collier, & I. H. had found, he said, lately a fungus which was a perfect Phallus; & in the books one is noted *Obscoenum*[.]

1865. I have since seen this very undesirable neighbor under my study window.

[68] "It is because he is not mercenary, that his soldiers will enrich him." D Buen

The legs of the throne↑s↓ are the plough, & the oar, ↑the anvil↓ & the sewing-machine.[57]

[69] A deep sympathy with intellect is what we require for any conversation, & it is hard to find among scholars.

⟨It is not⟩ Inⁿ writing, it is not propositions that are of the first need, but to watch & tenderly cherish the intellectual & moral sensibilities[,] ↑those↓ fountains of right thoughts, & woo them to stay & make their home with us. Whilst they abide with us, we shall not think or write amiss.[58]

[70] In the house

---

[56] For the Birkebeiners, see *JMN*, XIII, 133.

[57] This sentence is struck through in pencil with a diagonal use mark; the "s" of "thrones" has been inserted or improved in pencil.

[58] This paragraph is struck through in pencil with a vertical use mark.

[71] Woods, Lord Abercorn, & the Roman watering of sycamores with wine, & the botanic wonder & price of a tree.[59] And the aerial nourishment 19/20 of the timber: the top of the tree being a taproot thrust into the public pocket of the world. This a *highwayman*. And in proportion to the foliation is the ⟨lig⟩ wood. They ⟨reserve⟩ give us all our wreaths, but they reserve finer. For a wreath has worth & beauty according to the head on which it falls. A wreath dies on ↑touching↓ the head of a ⟨politician⟩ president[.]

2 leaves to a fascicle of a Norway pine; 3 to a ⟨white⟩yellow; 5 to a white.

[72]   ↑1857↓

October 14th, the New York & Boston Banks suspended specie payment. And, as usual in hard times, there are all sorts of petty & local reasons given for the pressure, but none that explain it to me. I suppose the reasons are not of yesterday or today; that the same danger has often approached & been avoided or postponed. 'Tis like that destruction of St Petersburgh, which ⟨has⟩ was threatened by Kohl, which may come whenever a great freshet in the Neva shall coincide with a long prevalence [n] [73] of Northwest (?) wind.[60] 'Tis like the jam which the ice ⟨mak⟩ or the logs make in our rivers: There is ample room for all the ice & all the logs to go ⟨on⟩down stream, — was, & is, & shall be; — but, by unfavorable circumstances, they are heaped together in a dead lock, so as to dam up the back water, till it accumulates to a deluge, & bursts at last, carrying bridges, houses, & half towns, to destruction.

But I take it as an inevitable [74] incident to this money of civilization. Paper-money is a wonderful convenience, which builds up cities & nations, but it has this danger in it, like a camphene lamp, or a steam-boiler, it will sometimes explode. So excellent a tool we cannot spare, but must take it with its risks. We know the dangers of the railroad but we prefer it with its dangers to the old coach. & we

[59] For Lord Abercorn's comment on trees, see *JMN*, XIII, 444; this paragraph is used in "Concord Walks," *W*, XII, 178.

[60] Emerson owned Johann George Kohl's *Russia. St. Petersburg, Moscow, Kharkoff, Riga, Odessa, the German Provinces on the Baltic, the Steppes, the Crimea, and the Interior of the Empire* (London, 1844).

must not forego the high civility of paper & credit, though once in twenty years it breaks the banks, & puts all exchange & traffic ⟨in⟩at a stand. ↑See p 79↓

[75] The imagination gives all the value to the day. If we walk, if we work, if we talk, it is how many strokes vibrate on the mystic string. That is, how many diameters we draw or are drawn quite through from matter to spirit, how many laws ⟨ann⟩ enunciated that are true to the common sense & to soul.[61] ↑To be Printed in Poetry & Criticism↓

[76] But 'tis the Northwind that thinks, & whatever it blows through,—is it pinewood or biped,—thinks rightly & beautifully.

———————

↑Receptivity.↓
'Tis the receptivity that is rare, 'tis this I value, the occasions I cannot scientifically tabulate; the motive or disposing circumstances I could never catalogue; but now one form, or color, or word, or companion, or book, or work, & now another strikes the mystic invisible string, ⟨&⟩ I ⟨hear delighted⟩ ↑listen with joy↓.[62] [77] And the day is good that has the most perceptions.

II. 137.   "O Hafiz, give me thoughts,
           ⟨If thoughts⟩ ↑For ⟨&⟩ pearls of thought↓ thou hast;
           All ⟨else is⟩ beside is n⟨o⟩aught
           ⟨Empty chatter & ⟨noise⟩ ↑blast↓⟩
           All ↑else↓ is din & blast"

           O Hafiz, give me thought
           ⟨Thought⟩ In^{n} /golden image/fiery fancy/ cast;
           For all beside is n⟨o⟩aught
           All else is din & blast.

———————

[61] This paragraph, struck through in ink with two diagonal use marks forming an "x" and in pencil with one vertical and three diagonal use marks, is used in "Poetry and Imagination," *W*, VIII, 15–16. One penciled diagonal ends in a curved line partially encircling "To be . . . Criticism" inserted in pencil.
[62] "hear delighted" is canceled and "listen with joy" is inserted in pencil.

O Hafiz, give me thought(s)ⁿ
In fiery ⟨fancies⟩ ↑figures↓ cast;
For all beside is naught, —
All else is din & blast.⁶³

[78]   Thy summer voice, Musketaquit,
Repeats the music of the rain;
But sweeter rivers ⟨silent⟩ ↑pulsing↓ flit
Thro' thee, as thou thro' Concord plain.
Thou in thy narrow banks art pent; —
The stream I love unbounded ⟨flows⟩ ↑goes↓
Thro' ⟨stream⟩flood & sea & firmament
Thro' light, thro' life, it forward flows.ⁿ

I see the inundation sweet
↑I hear↓ the ⁿ ⟨eternal⟩ spending of the stream,
Thro' years, thro' men, thro' nature fleet
Thro' passion, thought, thro' power & dream

Musketaquit ⟨is⟩ a goblin strong
Of shard & flint makes jewels gay
They lose their grief who hear his song
And where he winds is the day of day

[79]   Musketaquit is a goblin strong
Of shards & flints makes jewels gay
⟨And whither he winds makes a new day⟩
⟨Forget your⟩ ↑They lose their↓ grief ⟨to⟩ ↑who↓ hear his
    song
And where he winds is the day of day

So ↑& better↓ fares my /stream/flood/
Who drink it shall not thirst again
No darkness stains its equal gleam
Its flowers are stars its boys are gods

⁶³ These three stanzas are Emerson's versions of four lines from *Der Diwan von
. . . Hafis*, 1812–1813, II, 135. See p. [i] above.

So forth & better fares my stream
Who drink it shall not thirst again
No darkness stains its equal gleam
And ages drop in it like rain.[64]

The financial panic has the value of a test. Nobody knows how far each of these bank⟨s⟩ers & traders blows up his little airball on what infinitely small supply of soap & water. They all float in the air alike as balloons or planets, if you will, ⟨but when⟩ ↑untill↓ they strike ⟨any⟩ one another, or any house. — But this panic is a severer examiner than any committee of Bank Commissioners to find out how much specie all this paper represents, & how much real value[.]

[80] These enjoyers have abdicated all high claims; they saw early in the course that they stood no chance for coming in for the plate, & they decline the strife, & say, well, we will keep ourselves for the "scrub-race." "The man," said Proclus, "who has not subdued his passions, the universe uses him as a brute." And these fellows squalidly accept their tavern joys.

———

[81]———   ↑"Christ's College," Cambridge, England.↓
Sir C[hristopher]. Wren said, ⟨If⟩Show me where to lay the first stone, & I will build you another Christ's College. Well, it is even so in Nature. All the parts are so cunningly co-adapted, & overlap, that, one is led forever on, in an endless Circle, & cannot find a beginning.[65]

———

↑Memory   472↑, 172,↓↓ [66]

———

⁶⁴ The entries on pp. [78] and [79] are early versions of "Two Rivers," *W*, IX, 248; see Journal SO, pp. [87], [90], and [194] above. The stanzas on p. [78] are struck through in ink with a vertical use mark; in the final stanza "is" is canceled in pencil. The stanzas on p. [79] are in pencil under "The financial . . . real value" in ink; "Musketaquit . . . gods" is struck through in pencil with two vertical use marks.

⁶⁵ "Sir C. Wren . . . beginning.", struck through in ink with a vertical use mark and in pencil with a wavy diagonal use mark, is used in "Fate," *W*, VI, 36; for Wren's remark, see *JMN*, XIII, 301. " 'Christ's College . . . England." is inserted in pencil.

⁶⁶ ", 172," is added in pencil.

Drive the nail overnight, & clinch it next morning. ↑Yes, and drive it this week, & clinch it next; & this year, & clinch it the next.↓ [67]

[82] A man signing himself Geo. Ross (of Madison, Wis.) & who seems to be drunk, writes me, that "the secret of drunkenness, is, that it insulates us in thought, whilst it unites us in feeling."

———

Victor Hugo said, "An idea steeped in verse, becomes suddenly more incisive & more brilliant; the iron becomes steel." [68] ↑printed↓

———

[83] The Rock of Ages dissolves himself into the mineral air, & thus becomes the foundation of mortal frames. [69]

1⟨8⟩9 May, ↑1857.↓ I saw Peter Kaufmann in N. Y., a man of much intellectual power, and of expansive moral sympathy & purposes; another Benjamin Franklin in his practical skill & tastes. Unhappily, he is without imagination, the more to be regretted, that his life has kept him [84] invariably *bourgeois*. His bonhommie & philanthropy occasionally changed his face to a wonderful degree, as if a young man looked out of an old mask.

———

↑1874, February,

> On looking — I fear too late — into the singular Diary which Kaufmann sent me many years ago, I grieve that I neglected it until now. It is very imaginative & doubtless sincere, & indicates a far more intellectual person than I suspected in our short & singular meeting in New York. Alas I have never heard from him, or of him, since, & ⟨never⟩ I fear that this total silence on my part must have pained & alienated him.↓ [70]

[67] "Drive the . . . next.", struck through in pencil with one vertical and one diagonal use mark, is used in "Memory," *W*, XII, 107, where it is credited to Thomas Fuller. See Journal AC, p. [33] below.

[68] "Victor Hugo . . . steel.' ", struck through in ink with three diagonal use marks, is used in "Poetry and Imagination," *W*, VIII, 53. The quotation is a translation from Hugo's Preface to *Cromwell*.

[69] With this sentence, cf. "Fragments on Nature and Life," XXIV, *W*, IX, 335, and Journal SO, p. [23] above, and pp. [232] and [236] below.

[70] Peter Kaufmann sent Emerson an eighty-page history of his life and exposi-

[85] 25 May.

Yesterday, at the Cliff, with a family party, & H[enry]. D[avid]. T[horeau]. & Ricketson,[71] found the trailing Arbutus, & the Corydalis. H. D. T. has found new willows, & has a natural *Salictum*, where the seeds gather and plant themselves, near the railroad. Saw the *Salix rostrata; discolor; humilis*; I think, he finds ⟨12 or⟩ 1⟨3⟩4. — At this time of the year, the old leaves of the forest are gone, & the new not yet opened, & for a few days the view of the landscape is more open.

[86] At home, D[aniel]. R↑icketson↓. expressed some sad views of life & religion. A thunderstorm is a terror to him, and his theism was judaical. Henry thought a new pear-tree was more to purpose, &c. but said better, that an ecstasy was never interrupted. A theology of this kind is as good a meter or yardstick as any other. If I can be scared by a highwayman or a thunderclap, I should say, my performances were not very high, & should at once be mended.

[87]   ↑1857↓

Thursday, 28 May. ⟨I⟩We kept Agassiz's ↑fiftieth↓ birthday at the Club. Three or four strangers were present, to wit, Dresel, Felton, Holmes, & Hillard. For the rest, we had Agassiz, Pierce, Ward, Motley, Longfellow, Lowell, Whipple, Dwight, Woodman, & J. Cabot was due, but did not come.[72] Agassiz brought what had just been sent him, the last coloured plates to conclude the First Volume

---

tion of his philosophical views on April 27, 1857; Emerson traveled to New York to meet him on May 19; see *L*, V, 73–74, 77.

[71] Emerson's Cliff or "the Cliff" overlooks Walden Pond from the south about two miles south of Concord center. Daniel Ricketson of New Bedford, Massachusetts, was a friend and correspondent of Thoreau.

[72] In late 1855 and early 1856 the Saturday Club, which met for dinner at the Parker House hotel once a month, "generally sitting from three o'clock until nine" was formed. The original members, in 1856, were Louis Agassiz, Richard Henry Dana, Jr., John Sullivan Dwight, Ralph Waldo Emerson, Ebenezer Rockwood Hoar, James Russell Lowell, John Lothrop Motley, Benjamin Peirce, Samuel Gray Ward, Edwin Percy Whipple, and Horatio Woodman. Henry Wadsworth Longfellow, Oliver Wendell Holmes, and Cornelius Conway Felton became members in 1857. James Elliot Cabot did not become a member until 1861. Dresel has not been identified.

of his "Contributions, &c", which will now be published incontinently.[73] The flower of the feast was the reading of three poems, written by our three poets, for the occasion. [88] The first by Longfellow, who presided; [74] the second, by Holmes; the third, by Lowell; all excellent in their way.

↑May↓ 30. Walk this P M with Henry T[horeau]. Found the *perfoliate uvularia* for the first time in Lincoln by Flint's Pond,[75] found the *chestnut sided warbler*, which, I doubt not, I have seen already, & mistaken for the *particolored*. Heard the note of the latter, which resembles a locust-sound. Saw the cuckoo. Examined the young oak leaves by way of comparing the black, scarlet, & red, [89] & think the penetrating the bark of the first to find the yellow quercitrum must be for me the final test. Found the chestnut-oak, in Lincoln, on Thompson's land, not far from his boat-house, near large old chestnuts. Saw the two poplars, grandidentata, & tremuliforma, which are both good for the powder-mills. Henry thinks, that planting acres of barren land by running a furrow every four feet across the ⟨ac⟩field, with a plough, & following it with a planter, supplied with pine seed, would be lucrative. He proposes to plant my Wyman lot so. Go in September, ⟨to⟩& gather white-pine ↑cones↓ n

---

See p. 91

[90] Physiologie du Gout
L↑ongfellow↓. avoids greedy smokers.[76] A cigar lasts one hour: but is not allowed to lose fire.

I make little blue skies of my own, my dear.

---

[73] For Agassiz's *Contributions to the Natural History of the United States of America*, see p. [9] above.

[74] Longfellow's poem is printed in Edward W. Emerson, *The Early Years of the Saturday Club 1855–1870*, 1918, pp. 131–132.

[75] Flint's or Sandy Pond is in the town of Lincoln two and one-half miles southeast of Concord center.

[76] The insertion is in ink over the same in pencil. Emerson had been introduced to Brillat-Savarin's *Physiologie du Goût* (Paris, 1825) by his friend and fellow Saturday Club member Samuel Gray Ward.

"Give me the luxuries, the necessaries may take their chance." [77]

And the appendix to this, is S[amuel]. G[ray]. W[ard].'s rule; that the last thing an invalid is to give up, is, the going out to places of amusement, — the theatre, balls, concerts, &c.
And Sir George Cornewall Lewis's saying, that "Life would be tolerable, if it were not for the pleasures." [78]

[91] Continued from p 89

---

with a hook at the end of a long pole, & ⟨you⟩let them dry & open in a chamber at home. Add acorns, & birch-seed, & pitch-pines. He thinks, it would be ⟨good⟩ profitable to buy cheap land & plant it so. ⟨Hen⟩Edward Gardner at Nantucket sells the land at an advanced price as soon as he has planted it. It is a woodlot. Henry says, that the Flora of Massachusetts embraces almost all the important plants of America. We have all the willows but one or two, all the oaks but one or two[.]
   Furrows 8 feet apart & stick a pine along each at every 4 feet.

[92] Παντα ρει, said Heraclitus.[79]

[93] I do not count the ⟨days⟩hours I spend in ⟨h⟩the woods, though I forget my affairs there & my books. ⟨For⟩ And, when there, I wander h⟨ere⟩ither & th⟨ere⟩ither; any bird, any plant, any spring, detains me. I do not hurry ⟨back⟩ ↑homewards↓ for I think all affairs may be postponed to this walking. And it is for this idleness that all my businesses exist[.]

   [77] In *The Autocrat of the Breakfast Table* (Boston, 1858), p. 143, Oliver Wendell Holmes attributes this "glorious epicurean paradox" to John Lothrop Motley. See p. [87] above.
   [78] Sir George Cornewall Lewis (1806–1863), statesman and man of letters, was editor of the *Edinburgh Review* from 1852 to 1855. The "t's" in "their chance.'" and "the pleasures.'" are crossed in pencil, and the periods in "S. G. W." are in pencil.
   [79] "πάντα ῥεῖ,": "All things flow," is attributed to Heraclitus.

> I do not count the hours I spend
> In wandering by the sea [80]

[94]–[95] [blank]

[96] Our young men have nothing to do. Let them plant the land with good trees; let them cut the sea with good boats. Their friends like them best, if they do nothing new or important, but win a living in the quietest old ways of shop & office.

[97] The New Journal [81]
Note the good things said of the Dial praising, dispraising, & advising in *R* 47.

Your magazine should be the Bible of the Americans.
Dial has not piety.
It should be waited for by all the newspapers & journals. Abolitionists should get their leading from it, & not be able to shun it as they do.

——

'Tis always a favorable time to establish a new Journal, & now it is.
Essential to new book a new spirit
authors have a new idea, higher life — [82]

AB 108

——

Halle Literary Gazette. *BO* 187

——

See *CO* 277

---

[80] The entries on p. [93] are in pencil; the second is used in "Waldeinsamkeit," ll. 1–2, *W*, IX 249. See pp. [227]–[229] below.

[81] The entries on pp. [97] and [98] refer to the founding of *The Atlantic Monthly*. On May 16, 1857, Emerson attended a dinner given by publisher Moses Dresser Phillips; the other guests were Henry Wadsworth Longfellow, James Russell Lowell, John Lothrop Motley, Oliver Wendell Holmes, James Elliott Cabot, and Francis H. Underwood. During the five-hour meeting, Lowell accepted the editorship, and Holmes gave the new magazine its name. The first issue appeared in November, 1857. See *L*, V, 76–78.

[82] "Essential . . . life—" is in ink over substantially the same matter in erased pencil.

[98] "Atlantic"
See of Criticism & Tennyson   *IO* 18   *BO* 126
                                           RO 55
Dickens said, I will outamerica America   *N* 72

[99] T[homas]. Taylor   *R* 65   ↑*V* 2 3 4 5↓
Proclus   *AB* 103 [83]
            VO 43

[100] Wealth. See *BO* 140

[101] My naturalist has perfect magnanimity, he has no secrets, he will show you where his rare plants are, where the rare birds breed, carry you to the heron's haunt, or even to his most prized botanical swamp, confiding, I doubt not, that you can never find it again, yet willing to take his risks.[84]

[102]   May 20, 1858
Yesterday walked with H. D. T. to the spring in Everett's pasture and found *Ranunculus Abortivus* and *bulbosus*, and the *Equisetum hiemale*, scouring rush, and Saxifraga /Pennsylvanica/Virginiana/ and golden saxifrage or chryso[s]plenium oppositifolium[;] heard a note of Henry's night warbler and saw at Gourgas's pond two ⟨y⟩Yellow-legs ⟨looking⟩ ↑flying↓ like ducks, only with a curlew cry (tell tales) and a pair of tatl⟨r⟩ers who continued their researches in the water without regard to our spyglasses. Saw *rana sylvatica*

[103] Massachusetts has a good climate, but it needs a little anthracite coal.

   In Boston we pity ↑N Y. &↓ the whole uncochituated creation[.] [85]
Somewhat finer in our sky & climate than we appreciate. *TU* 160

---

[83] "V 2 3 4 5" and "Proclus   *AB* 103" are in pencil.
[84] This paragraph is used in "Thoreau," *W*, X, 472.
[85] Lake Cochituate is a Boston reservoir. See *JMN*, XI, 130.

Perhaps the landscape is peopled with a race of daemons who move at a faster rate than men, so fast as just to escape our organ of sight.

———

Bottle the efflux of a June noon, & bring home the tops of Uncanoonuc.[86] *SO* 121

———

Natural & cultivated man. *SO* 120

———

Of walking see *SO* 249
of landscape   *SO* 251

[104] To the pomologist the young June moon had a sad reminder of the print of a curculio on his blue plum. And shall the canary bird only remind him of yellow fever? & the fireflies of incendiaries? [87]

[105] robin: gull: duck: fish

[106] June 9. Yesterday a walk with H[enry] D[avid] T[horeau] in search of *Actaea alba,* which we found, but only one plant, & the petals were shed. The (pl)shrub also we saw which had puzzled him last year, & which was only *Viburnum nudum* grown more erect in the damp woods than usual. We found at Cyrus Smith's the (*Juglans nigra*) Black Walnut in flower.[88] It blooms with the pignut, /C⟨h⟩ar⟨i⟩ya/ Juglans/ *glabra,* & not with the Butternut, *Juglans cinerea.* I do not find Black Walnut in Bigelow. Henry praises Bigelow's descriptions of plants; [107] but knows sixty plants not recorded in his Edition of Bigelow (1840).[89] We saw the hairy wood-

———

[86] "Massachusetts . . . coal.", "Somewhat finer . . . appreciate.", and "Bottle . . . Uncanoonuc.", struck through in ink with diagonal use marks, are used in "Country Life," *W,* XII, 139 and 156–157. There are pencil checkmarks before "Massachusetts" and after "TU 160", before "Perhaps" and after "sight.", before "Bottle" and after "Uncanoonuc.", and after "SO 251". Mt. Uncanoonuc, in New Hampshire, is 1,321 ft. high. For "Somewhat finer . . . appreciate.", see p. [16] above.

[87] This paragraph is struck through in pencil with a diagonal use mark. For "robin . . . fish", directly below, see *JMN,* XI, 58.

[88] Cyrus Smith lived on the Cambridge Turnpike about two miles southeast of Emerson's home.

[89] Jacob Bigelow, *Florula Bostoniensis,* 3rd ed. (Boston, 1840), was the standard manual of New England botany.

pecker watching his chirping brood in an apple tree in Wyman's orchard. ↑Spider will show whether the hole is inhabited or not.↓ The red maples are conspicuous in these days with red keys. Saw *white swamp oak*, under the handsome pleached elm on the road from the manse to Peter Hutchinson's.[90] The day was joyfully bright & warm, but, at night, coldish again.

Saw the leather-colored or dead-oak-leaf-colored *rana sylvatica*.

In the morning we saw Krigia.

[108] On Sunday (6 June) on our walk along the river bank, the air was full of the ephemerides, which Henry celebrates as the manna of the fishes.

[109]   *Concord Walks* for a subject.
See the praises of the woods. *CD* 44
White days. Yellow days. ↑dog days↓

———

Country gentleman raises monuments to Van Mons. CD 99

———

gardens, trees in clumps, bath in the brook, arboretum, fireworks over water.

———

Fast Day   *W* 52 [91]

———

Garden. J 130

———

dew & fire. J 96

———

Malpighi's effects of atmosphere   TU 40

———

Marvell's verses, "Mower in the Garden"

———

In last days of August, & first of September, the woods are full of agarics.

———

[90] Peter Hutchinson lived south of the Great Meadows along the Concord River about one mile east of the old manse along "Peter's Path."

[91] "dog days" and "Fast Day   *W* 52" and the rule above it are in pencil.

the barberry trade.

———

Travel & walking have this apology, that nature has impressed periodical or secular impulses to emigrate on savage men, as upon lemings, rats, & birds.[92]

[110] Sydney Smith's rule, 12 ⟨br⟩Miles [93]

For success, to be sure we esteem it a test in other people, since we do first in ourselves. We respect ourselves more if we have succeeded.[94]

Scholar & Times

Could I make you feel your indispensableness, — & yet it behoves first to show you the joy of your high place. You have the keys. You deal with design & the methods. Here lies this wide aboriginal Nature, old beyond figures, ↑yet↓ new & entire, the silver flame which flashes up the sky, — no aeons can date it, yet there it burns as delicately[n] [111] as the ⟨flash⟩passing cinder of the firefly ↑with the lightness of a new petal↓. Here you rest & work in this element of Space, whose bewildering ⟨immensity⟩[n] circuits make all the Universe a dot on its margin, dwarfing the gods.

To teach us the first lesson of humility, God set down man in these two vastitudes of Space and Time, yet is he such an incorrigible peacock that he thinks them only a perch to show his dirty feathers on.

[112] Relation is between fate & us
Secret of the world is the tie between person & event
Person makes event; & event, person;

Every planet gets its living
Every ⟨bird⟩ ↑wren or↓ dragon ⟨man devil makes⟩ its lair

---

[92] This sentence, in pencil, is used in "Country Life," *W*, XII, 135; see Journal SO, p. [250] above.

[93] For Sydney Smith's rule, see Journal RO, p. [62], and Journal SO, p. [249] above.

[94] "For success . . . succeeded.", struck through in pencil with a diagonal use mark, is used in "Success," *W*, VII, 286. See Journal AC, p. [177] below.

Every Zone its own
⟨Angels ray out light⟩
Devils ray out darkness, & angels light

And, as the vegetable eye makes leaf, pericarp, root or bark ⟨or apple⟩ or[n] thorn, as the need is, ⟨so⟩ and as the primal animal cell makes a stomach or a mouth or an eye or a nail according to the want; so, the world throws its life into a hero or a shepherd; so it puts it where it is [113] wanted[;] Dante & Columbus are Italians then; they would be Americans & ⟨Prussians⟩Germans today[.]

Turtle in swamp
wader on beaches
camel in sand
goat on mountain
fish in s⟨a⟩ea
eyes in light
Every Zone its ⟨fauna⟩ flora & fauna
animals hybernate, or wake when dinner is ready
↑food, parasite, enemy, census,↓
Same fitness between a man & his time & event
⟨Pericles & St John⟩
Man comes when world is ready for him.
And ⟨as event⟩ things ripen, new men ⟨Pericles,
St John, Bonaparte⟩
Hercules comes first, & St John afterwards.
& Shakspeare ↑at last.↓

[114] What we accept in generals, we deny in particulars.
But the ⟨same⟩ applicability is not capricious, ⟨but the same adjustment⟩ ↑this applicability↓ by which planets subside & crystallize & clothe themselves with forests & animate themselves with /animals/ beasts/ & men will not stop; but will continue ⟨to work⟩ into finer particulars, & from finer to finest evermore.

[115] For every creature has a sphere & a predisposing power.
He is not possible unless the invisible things are right for him as well as the visible[.]

There ⟨is a great deal⟩ ↑are↓ more belongings to every creature than his lair & his food. He is full of instincts that must be met, & he has predisposing power that bends & fits all that is near to his use. He is not possible until the invisible things are right for him as well as the visible. What changes then in sky & earth, & in finer skies & earths ↑than ours,↓ does not the appearance of some Dante or Columbus apprize us of! [95]

[116]   They strew in the path of kings ↑& czars↓
            Jewels & gems of price
            ⟨O⟩But for thy head I will pluck down stars
            And pave thy way with eyes.

            I have sought for thee a ⟨worthy home⟩ ↑costlier dome↓
            ⟨Kings have⟩ ↑Than Mahmoud's↓ palace high
            ⟨But⟩ ↑And↓ thou return↑ed shall↓ find thy ⟨Rome⟩ ↑home↓
            In the apple of love's eye.

            They strew in the path of Kings & Czars
                Jewels & pearls of price,
            But for thy head I will pluck down stars,
                And pave thy way with eyes.

            I have sought for thee a costlier dome
                Than Mahmoud's palace high,
            And thou returned shall find thy home
                In the apple of love's eye.

[117]   They strew in the path of Kings
            Jewels & gems of price
            ⟨But I will crown⟩ ↑I will pluck down for↓ thy head with
                stars
            And pave thy way with eyes.

[95] The entries on pp. [112]–[115], in pencil, are struck through in pencil with single vertical use marks, and "For every . . . visible" on p. [115] is struck through in pencil with a vertical use mark; "Secret of . . . person;" (p. [112]), "And, as . . . today" (pp. [112]–[113]), and "For every . . . apprize us of!" (p. [115]) are used in "Fate," *W*, VI, 39 and 37.

I cannot find thee a worthy home
W⟨‖ ... ‖⟩
Kings have a palace ⟨proud⟩ ↑high↓
But thou returning find thy Rome
Than ⟨‖ ... ‖⟩
In the apple ⟨‖ ... ‖⟩ eye

↑My eye↓ upon ⁿ thy beauty fell ⟨mine eye⟩
Upon thy lutes my ear
And so ⟨upon them both abode⟩ ↑with eye & ear t'was
    well↓
⟨This time⟩ ↑For both↓ a ⟨happy⟩ ↑joyful↓ cheer

My eye upon thy beauty fell
Upon thy lute my ear
And so with eye & ear 'twas well
For both a happy cheer.[96]

[118]   O sun! take off thy hood of clouds,
            O land! take off thy chain,
            And fill the world with happy mood
            And love from main to main

            Ye shall not on thy charter day
            Disloyally withhold
            Their household rights from captive men
            By pirates bought & sold

            Ah little knew the innocent
            In ⟨pangs of b⟩ throes of birth forlorn
            That wolves & foxes waited for
            Their victim to be born.[97]

[96] The entries on pp. [116] and [117] are Emerson's English versions of eight
lines from *Der Diwan von . . . Hafis*, 1812–1813, II, 192. The first two stanzas
on p. [116] are in pencil and erased pencil; the first two stanzas on p. [117],
struck through in pencil with two vertical use marks, are in erased pencil, and the
second two, struck through in pencil with a vertical use mark, are in pencil. The first
version on p. [116] is used in "Persian Poetry," *W*, VIII, 260.
[97] These three stanzas, struck through in pencil with a vertical use mark, are in

[119] Against Whigs. ⟨'Tis very doubtful⟩ ↑Zoologists may dispute↓ whether horse hairs in the water ⟨turn⟩ ↑change↓ to ⟨s⟩worms, but I find that ⟨corr that⟩ whatever is old corrupts, & the past turns to snakes. The reverence for the deeds of our ancestors is a treacherous sentiment. ⟨What ⟨they did⟩ was precisely⟩ Their[n] merit, was, not to reverence the old, but to honor the present moment. & we falsely cite them as examples of the very habit which they hated & defied.[98] ↑Memory is bitter.↓

———
———

Works & Days. See *IO* 9

———

↑printed↓

[120] [blank]

[121] Wednesday, 8 July, 1857. This morning I had the remains of my mother & of my son Waldo removed from the tomb of ⟨the⟩Mrs Ripley to my lot in "Sleepy Hollow." The sun shone brightly on the coffins, of which Waldo's was well preserved — now fifteen years. I ventured to look into the coffin. I gave a few white-oak leaves to ⟨bo⟩each coffin, after they were put in the new vault, & the vault was then covered with two slabs of granite.

[122] [blank]

[123] There is certainly a convenience in the money scale in the absence of finer metres. In the South a slave is bluntly but accurately valued at 500 to 1000 dollars, if a good working field hand; if a mechanic, as carpenter or smith, at 12, 15, or 2⟨2⟩0 hundred.[99] A Mulatto girl, if beautiful, rises at once very naturally to high estimation. If beautiful & sprightly-witted, one who is a joy when present, a perpetual entertainment to the eye, &, when absent, a happy remembrance, $2500 & upwards of our money[.]

---

pencil. Cf. "Ode: Sung in the Town Hall, Concord, July 4, 1857," *W*, IX, 199–200. See also Notebook WO Liberty, pp. [228₂]–[239] below.

[98] "⟨Tis very . . . defied.", struck through in ink with two vertical use marks, is used in "Works and Days," *W*, VII, 177. For "the past turns to snakes.", see *JMN*, XI, 30.

[99] This sentence is used in "Aristocracy," *W*, X, 48.

[124] [*Clubs*]

In the East, they buy their wives at stipulated prices. Well, shall I not estimate, when the finer ⟨scale⟩ anthropometer is wanting, my social properties so? In our club, no man shall be admitted who is not worth in his skin 500,000. One of them, I hold worth a million; for he bows to facts, has no impertinent will, & nobody has come to the bottom of his wit, to the end of his resources. So, in my house, I shall not deign to count myself by my poor taxable estate 20 or 30 thousand, but each of my [125] children is worth, on leaving school, ⟨100,000⟩a hundred thousand, as being able to think, speak, feel & act correctly, — able to fill the vacant hours, & ⟨carry⟩ keep life up to a high point. Bonaparte was right⟨,⟩ ↑in saying,↓ ⁿ "I have three hundred millions in my treasury, & I would give them all for Ney." [100]

[126] Sunday, 19 July, 1857. A visit to Josiah Quincy, Jr., on his old place at Quincy, which has been in the family for seven generations since 1635, and the deed by which the place is holden is an *order* on the first page of the Records of the Town of Boston, "*Ordered*, that Edmund Quincy &   (one other named party) lay out 800 acres at Mount Wollaston." There lives the old President, now 85 years old, in the house built by his father in 1770; & Josiah Jr. in a new house built by Billings, 7 years ago. ⟨The land⟩ [127] They ⁿ hold 500 acres, & the land runs down to the sea. From the piazza in the rear of the house of J.↑Q.↓ Jr. you may see every ship that comes in or goes out of Boston, and most of the islands in the harbor. 'Tis the best placed house I know. The old man I visited on Saturday evening, & on Sunday he came & spent the evening with us at his son's house. He is the most fortunate of men. Old John Adams said that of him; & his good fortune has followed [128] to this hour. His son said to me, "My father has thrown ten times, & every time got doublets." Yet he was engaged to a lady whose existence he did not know of, 7 days before, & she proved the best ⟨wife⟩ ⁿ ↑of wives↓. I made a very pleasant acquaintance with young Josiah 3d, the poet of "Lyteria." And ↑I↓ like him better than his

[100] This quotation is used, with "two hundred millions", in "Napoleon," *W*, IV, 244.

poem. Charles Francis Adams also was there in the Sunday Evening. Old Quincy [129] still reads & writes with vigor & steadiness 2 or 3 hours every ⟨eve⟩night after tea till ten. He has just finished his "Life of J. Q. Adams." [101]

[130] Montaigne's story of the man who learned courage from the hare weighs with me. 'Tis the best use of Fate to teach us courage like the Turk. Go face the burglar, or the fire at sea, or ⟨the⟩ whatever danger lies in the way of duty, knowing you are guarded by the omnipotence of Destiny. If you believe in Fate to your harm, believe it, at least, for your good. And, one more lesson learn, — to balance the ugly fact of temperament [n] [131] & race, which pulls you down, — this, namely, that, by that cunning co-presence of the two elements, which we find throughout nature, what ever lames you, or paralyzes you, drags in with it the divinity in some form to repay. [102]

[132] [103] Peirce at Cambridge Observatory told me, that what we call a fine night is often no ⟨fine⟩ good night for the telescope; that the sky is not clear for astronomical observation, perhaps more than one night in a month. Of course, they hate to be annoyed by visiters at such times & I can well believe it. My days & hours for observation & record are as few: not every undisturbed day is good for the Muse. The day [133] comes once in a month, & 'tis likely on that day the idle visiter drops in, thinking his coming no intrusion.

"Herschel found that, in England, there are not above a hundred hours in a year, during which the heavens can be advantageously observed with a telescope of forty feet, furnished with a magnifying power of a thousand." *Arago.* p. 179 [104]

[101] Josiah Quincy, *Memoir of the Life of John Quincy Adams* (Boston, 1858).

[102] This paragraph is struck through in ink with single vertical use marks on pp. [130] and [131]. "Tis the best . . . good.", struck through in pencil with a vertical use mark, is used in "Fate," *W*, VI, 24; "And, one . . . repay.", struck through in pencil with single vertical use marks on pp. [130] and [131], is used in "Fate," *W*, VI, 47–48.

[103] The entries on pp. [132] and [133] are struck through in pencil with single diagonal use marks.

[104] François Arago, *Biographies of Distinguished Scientific Men*, trans. W. H. Smyth, Baden Powell, and Robert Grant (London, 1857). Emerson withdrew this book from the Boston Athenaeum October 31, 1857–January 14, 1858.

So, few stars & few thoughts; see below, p. 256

[134] Milton wrote to his own ear. *H* 21

No cymbal clashed[,] no clarion rang at the advent of ideas.[105]
All poems are unfinished   H 112
Life of a poet a catalogue   D 366
Every man tries his hand at poetry somewhere, but most men don't
know which their poems are.

[135]   26 July
Ellery Channing thinks that these frogs at Walden are very curious
but final facts; that they will never be disappointed by finding themselves raised to "a higher state of intelligence." * [106] He persists in his
bad opinion of orchards & farming; declares, that the only success
he ever had with the former, was, that he once paid a cent ⟨&⟩for a
russetin apple; and farming, he thinks, is an attempt to outwit God
with a hoe: that they plant a great many potatoes, with much ado;
but it is doubtful if they ever get the seed again.

[136] 28 July. Yesterday the best day of the year we spent in the
afternoon on the river. ↑A sky of Calcutta,↓ light,ⁿ air, clouds, water,
banks, birds, grass, pads, lilies, were in perfection, and it was delicious to live. Ellery & I went up the South Branch, & took a bath
from the bank behind Cyrus Hubbard, ⟨opp⟩ where the river makes
a bend.[107] Blackbirds ↑in hundreds;↓ swallows in tens sitting on the

* The "Sacontala" ends with a prayer of the King, —
        "And may the purple selfexistent God,
        Whose vital energy pervades all space,
        From future transmigrations save my Soul!"

[105] "Milton . . . ideas." is struck through in pencil with a diagonal use mark
[106] Emerson's footnote is written at the bottom of p. [134]. Kálidása, *Sákoon-
talá; or, The lost ring; an Indian drama*, trans. Monier Williams (Hertford, 1855)
p. 227. The volume is in Emerson's library.
[107] The Sudbury River changes its course from northwest to northeast abou
three-quarters of a mile from Cyrus Hubbard's house and about one and one-hal
miles southwest of Concord center. Thoreau refers to a spot just downstream fron
the bend on the east bank as "Hubbard's Bath."

telegraph lines; & one heron (ardea minor) assisted. In these perfect pictures, one thinks what weary nonsense is all this painful collection of rubbish, — [137] pictures of rubbish masters, — in the total neglect of this & every ⟨other⟩ lovely river valley, where the multitudinous life & beauty makes these pictures ridiculous cold chalk & ochre. Ellery complains of ↑the new↓ pedantry in T[horeau?]., as a dry rot, which consumes, as the ↑famed↓ Yacht "America" perishes now in ⟨E⟩Liverpool, for all its fine model. —

[138] Faraday's Lecture at the Royal Institution. Feb. 27, 1857, on the Conservation of Force.

The received idea of gravitating force, is, "a simple attractive force exerted between any two particles or masses, at every sensible distance, but with a strength varying inversely as the square of the distance."

Extracts.

"a grain of water is known to have electric relations equivalent to a very powerful flash of lightning. — ⁿ It may therefore be supposed that a very large [139] apparent amount of the force causing the phenomena of gravitation may be the equivalent of a very small change in the unknown condition of the bodies whose attraction is varying by change of distance. ↑[See below *VO* 220]↓ Many considerations urge my mind toward the idea of a cause of gravity which is not resident in the particles of matter merely, but constantly in them ⟨& in all⟩& all space."

"indestructibility of ↑individual↓ matter"
"a particle of oxygen is ever a particle of oxygen, — nothing can in the least wear it"

[140] Faraday is an excellent writer, and a wise man. And whilst I read him, I think, that, if natural philosophy is faithfully written, moral philosophy ⟨w⟩ need not be, for it will find itself expressed in these theses to a perceptive soul.[107a] ↑That is, we shall read off the ⟨Com⟩Commandments & Gospels in Chemistry — without need of translation; as we read a latin or a french book to Scholars without translation.↓

[107a] See p. [11] above.

[141] [108] ||msm|| [abo]ve thirty y[ears] & can count on my fingers all the sane men ⟨I ever saw⟩ that ever came to me. Were I to insist on silence ⟨& solitude⟩ until I was fully met, & all my faculty called out & tasked by my companion, I should have a solitary time of it. ⟨So we⟩ Those who visit me are young men, imperfect persons, people with some partial thought, or local culture, [142] ||msm|| Each man too has six or seven leading thoughts or observations, and his talk with a stranger, ⟨i⟩as it rises or falls, is usually a pure or a diluted statement of these, until they are all told. Then, if the stranger has not evinced the power to excite & draw him out, they live thenceforward in heavy relation, as people [143] who know each other to disadvantage, & who have nothing to expect from each other.

[144]   *Thoughts.*

Will he coax & stroke these deities? I do. I can no more manage these thoughts that come into my head than thunderbolts. But ⟨w⟩once get them written down, I come & look at them every day, & get w⟨n⟩onted to their faces, & by & by, am so far used to them, that I see their family likeness, & can pair them & range them better, & if I once see where they belong, & ⟨put⟩ ↑join↓ them ⟨so⟩ ↑in that order↓ they will [145] stay so.

[146] In the house of Mahmoud, the guests discussed gardens, architecture, diamonds, horses, chess, the natural history of certain trees, as, the palm, sandal-tree,   wines, amber, steel, flowers,

[147] In *"Tarare,"* Beaumarchais directed to be sung "majestically," ⟨the verses⟩ by ⟨n⟩*Nature* & the *Genius of* ⟨f⟩*Fire*, the verses,

> *"Mortel, qui que tu sois, prince, brahme, ou soldat,*
> *Homme, ta^n grandeur sur la terre*
> *N'appartient point à ton état,*
> *Elle est toute à ton caractère."* [109]

---

[108] A strip from 5 to 3.5 cm wide is torn away from the top of the leaf bearing pp. [141] and [142]. Emerson indexed p. [141] under Conversation and Society.
[109] See Pierre Augustin Caron de Beaumarchais, *Tarare, Opéra en cinq actes* . . . (Paris, 1787), p. 79.

At the top or at the end of all illusions, I set the cheat which still leads us to work & live for appearances, in spite of our conviction in all sane hours that it is only what we [148] really are that avails with friends, with strangers or with fate or fortune.[110]

All

"It must not be imagined that any force or fraction of a force can be ever annihilated. All that which is not found in the useful effect produced by the motive power, nor in the amount of force which it retains after having acted, must have gone towards the shaking & destroying of the machine." Arago. [*Biographies of Distinguished Scientific Men*, 1857,] Life
of Carnot p[p. 303–]304

[149] [blank]

[150] August 2. Yesterday with Ellery at Flint's Pond. The pond was in its summer glory, the chestnuts in flower, ⟨one⟩two fishermen in a boat, thundertops in the sky, and the whole picture a study of all the secrets of landscape. "A place for every thing, & everything in place;" "No waste & no want;" "Each minds his own part, & none overdo & none interfere," — these & the like rules of good householding are kept here in nature. ⟨And t⟩The great afternoon spends like [151] fireworks, or festival of the gods, with a tranquil exultation, as of a boy that has launched his first boat, or his little balloon, & the experiment succeeds.

E said, You must come here to see it! It can never be imagined. You must come here to see it, or you have lost your day.

'Tis an objection, I said, to astronomy, that you light your candle at both ends. After you have got through the day [152] & 'tis necessary you should give attention to the business of sleeping, all hands are called; here come Canopus, Aldebaran, & all stars, & you are to begin again.

The woods were in the⟨ir↓⟩ best, high grown again, & flecked with spots of pure sunshine everywhere, — paths for Una & her lamb; say better, fit for the stoutest farmers & the greatest scholars.

---

[110] "At the top . . . fortune.", struck through in ink with a vertical use mark on p. [147] and with three vertical use marks on p. [148], is used in "Illusions," *W*, VI, 326.

[153] Reading is a languid pleasure and we must forget our books ⟨before we can⟩ ↑to↓ see the landscape's royal looks.[111]

> Inspired we must [n] forget our books,
> To see the landscape's royal looks.

[154] "What can be done with a man," says the biographer of Beaumarchais, "who converts successively five censors into five advocates?"[112]

The Indian can call a muskrat swimming in the river to the side where he stands, & make him land. "See muskrat, me go talk with em." He can go into the lakes, & be paddled round & round ten or twenty times & then can go off in straight line "to camp," or to Oldtown.⟨"⟩ White man cannot; & Indian can't tell how he does it. He can give you a [155] new tea every night, & a soup every day; lily soup; hemlock tea;   tea from the snowberry↑, chiogenes hixpidula,↓ is best. He can cut a string from spruce root, as you cannot. Joseph Polis is the hunter who went with Henry T[horeau]. & Edward Hoar.[113]
An Indian has his knowledge for use, & it only appears in use. Most white men that we know have theirs for talking purposes. ↑*Cornus Sericeus* is the *kinnik kinnik*↓ [.]

[156] The evil⟨l⟩s we suffer are the just measure of those we have done.[114]

↑*Truth.*↓ "Truth," says Buchner, "hides an inner attraction in itself, beside which all other respects easily vanish." *ap. Frauenstadt.*

---

[111] This sentence is struck through in ink with a vertical use mark and in pencil with a diagonal use mark; cf. "Waldeinsamkeit," ll. 41–44, *W*, IX, 250.

[112] This sentence, struck through in ink with three vertical use marks, is used in "Clubs," *W*, VII, 240. See Journal RO, p. [127] above.

[113] The trip with Joseph Polis, from July 20 to August 3, 1857, is described in "The Allegash and East Branch," *The Maine Woods* (Boston, 1864).

[114] This sentence is struck through in ink with a vertical use mark.

"De par le Roi, défense à Dieu
D'opérer miracle en ce lieu!"

"By royal decree, we prohibit the ⟨g⟩Gods
To work any miracle near these Sods."

I have quite forgotten in what garden this compliment to religion
was paid.[115]

[157] Sept. 4. Yesterday with Henry T[horeau]. at the Estabrook
Farm & Ebba Hubbard's swamp, to see the yellow birches, which
grow larger than I have seen them elsewhere.[116] The biggest measured, at 5 ft. from the ground, /10/ten/ feet, 5 inches in circum-
ference. We found bass, black ash, a large old white thorn (Crataegus)
tree, fever-bush abounding, a huge ivy running up from the base
round a   tree, to the height of 20 or 30 feet, like a hairy snake,
Osmunda regalis, white mint, penny royal, calamint, aster corymbosa,
the ⟨[pass to page 160]⟩ [158] bay-berry, Amphicarpaea,[n] botrychium
↑onoclea, brake tripartite,↓
A valuable walk through the savage fertile houseless land, where
we saw pigeons & marsh-hawks, &, ere we left it, the mists, which
denote the haunt of the elder Gods, were rising.[117]
Henry said of the railroad whistle, that nature had made up her
mind not to hear it, she knew better than to wake up. And, "the fact
you tell, is of no value, 'tis only the impression." [118]

[159] Curious that the best thing I saw in ⟨M C⟩ ↑Mammoth Cave,↓
was an illusion[.]
But I have had many experiences like that & many men have[.]
Our conversation with nature is not quite what it seems. The sunset
glories are not quite so real as ⟨we⟩ childhood thought them, & the

---

[115] This couplet "was posted on the church of Médard, one of the Jansenist
congregations in the seventeenth century. The Jansenists had alleged miracles in support of their heresy" (J, IX, 112).
    [116] The Estabrook Farm or Easterbrook Country is about two miles north of
Concord center along the old Carlisle Road.
    [117] With this sentence, cf. "Waldeinsamkeit," ll. 33–36, W, IX, 250.
    [118] These two sentences are used in "Thoreau," W, X, 463 and 471.

part that our organization plays in them is ⟨quite⟩ too large. The same subjectiveness interferes everywhere.[119]

[160] ↑*Doctor Solger*↓ [120]
Clovis Chlovich Ludovicus Louis
When the event is past & remote, how insignificant the greatest, compared with the piquancy of the present! The Professor interrogates Annie in the class about Odoacer & Alaric. Annie can't[n] remember, but suggests that Odoacer was defeated; and the Professor says "No, he defeated the Romans." But 'tis plain to the hearer, that 'tis of no importance at all about Odoacer, & ⟨a⟩'tis a great deal of importance about Annie; & if she says he was defeated, why he had better a great deal ↑have↓ been defeated, than give [161] her a moment's mortification & annoy. ↑⟨Odoacer if there was a particle of a gentleman in him would have said, let me be defeated a thousand times.⟩↓ [121] The other lesson we[*] got from the lecture was the pathetic one, that the poor Goths or Germans must needs come into the Empire when Valens was an Arian, & therefore all Goths & Germans must be[n] Arians, & not of the Orthodox Catholic prevailing Athanasian Creed. In this first germ, one sees us nailed to the north wall of opposition, & foreordained to be pale protestants, ⟨fre⟩ Unitarians, freesoilers, Abolitionists.

[162] What baulks all language, is, the broad, radiating, immensely distributive action of Nature or Spirit. If it were linear, if it were

* How we failed to be Catholics.

[119] The entries on p. [159], struck through in ink with a vertical use mark, are used in "Illusions," *W*, VI, 310–311. "Mammoth Cave," is encircled in ink. See Emerson's description of his visit to Mammoth Cave in June, 1850, in "Illusions," *W*, VI, 309–310. See *JMN*, XIII, 60.
[120] "*Doctor Solger*" is inserted as a heading between the first two lines on the page and is set off at top, right, and bottom by a curved line. See Journal SO, p. [282] above.
[121] The paragraph to this point, struck through in ink on p. [160] with one discontinuous vertical use mark and two vertical use marks and on p. [161] with two vertical use marks through "her . . . annoy." and one vertical use mark through "her . . . times.)", is used in "Success," *W*, VII, 304–305.

successive, step by step, jet ⟨by⟩after jet, like our small human agency, we could follow it ⟨in our description⟩ with language; but it mocks us.

———

↑*Greatness.*↓

Every human being whom history selects is some child of fate, full of fate, who did what he did by this strong arm; as the wood-chopper, by using the force of gravity,[122] [163] lets the planet chop his stick, so these men perceived each that he had inherited some trick of nature, a voice, or a face, or a sympathy, or a brutish courage, or skill, some fascination, which prevailed with his fellow↑s↓, & he gladly threw himself on this, seeing how much it served him, though this all belonged to the kingdom of fate, & not to the sphere of souls.

[164] The doses of heaven are homoeopathic. How little it is that differences the man from the woman; the animal from the plant; the most like, from the most unlike things!

———

↑Maximum & minimum.↓

———

The sun is as much a creature of fate as any worm which his heat engenders in the mud of earth. Large & small are nothing. Given a vesicle you have the Cosmos.[123]

[165] The physician goes on stimulating the diseased patient. But 'tis the fever that is fed on the rich diet, & not the patient.

When the poet goes to Europe for his subject, he avows his want of primary vision[.]

All English are precisians, & require ⟨an⟩ ↑a↓ rigid outline drawing. But the result is a dead bird. The manners of the bird, which is the

———

[122] "What baulks . . . mocks us." and "Every human . . . gravity," are struck through in pencil with wavy diagonal use marks.
[123] This paragraph is rewritten in ink over substantially the same matter in pencil.

heart of the thing, they cannot have, for Nature is alive & ⟨flowing into⟩ ascending.[124]

[166] "For the living out of doors, & simple fare, & gymnastic exercises, & the morals of companions, produce the greatest effect in the way of virtue & ↑of↓ vice."

Timaeus, Locrian. [Locrus] *Plato*   Vol. VI. p[p. 165–]166 [125]

Here again is the *Circumstance* in Fate, so potent or, shall I say, here the unity of things intimating that the moral is the highest chemistry. Put the atoms all right in their best order, & you get the unsophisticated countryman, body & mind in [167] equal health; the crystallization is not interfered with, nor hastened, & the perfect diamond results.

[168] Surfaces. Good writing sips the foam of the cup. There are infinite degrees of delicacy in the use of the hands; and good workmen are so distinguished from laborers; & good horsemen, from rude riders; & people of elegant manners, from the vulgar. In writing, it is not less. Montaigne dwells always at the surface, & can chip of↑f↓ a scale, where a coarser hand & eye finds only ⟨a⟩sol↑i↓d wall.

[169] [126] ||msm||

Determination of blood is all one with intrinsic value. If a man is set on collecting diamonds, or Arabian horses, or an arboretum, or a particular piece of land, or a telescope, his heat makes the value.

[170] ||msm||

---

[124] This paragraph is struck through in ink with two vertical use marks, and "But the . . . bird." is struck through in ink with three vertical use marks.

[125] *Works, A New and literal version, chiefly from the text of Stallbaum . . . ,* 6 vols. (London, 1848–1854); this work is in Emerson's library. This quotation, struck through in pencil with a diagonal use mark, is used in "Country Life," *W*, XII, 142.

[126] Approximately 2 cm. of the top of the leaf bearing pp. [169] and [170] are torn away. Emerson indexed p. [169] under Bias, Bias or Determination, Determination, Heat makes Value, Subjectiveness, and Wealth, and p. [170] under Abolitionist.

⟨They⟩ ↑We↓ read the orientals, but remain occidental. The fewest men receive anything from their studies. The abolitionists are not better men for their zeal. They have neither abolished slavery ⟨nor⟩ in Carolina, nor in me. If they cannot break one fetter of mine, I cannot hope they will of ⟨the⟩ any negro. They are bitter sterile people, whom I flee from, to the unpretentious whom they disparage. I see them to be logically right, but to the [171]–[172] [leaf torn out] [127]

[173] The eye is final; what it tells is the last stroke of nature. Beyond color we cannot go.

Gauss, I believe it is[,] who writes books that nobody can understand but himself, & himself only in his best hours. And Pierce & Gould & others in Cambridge are piqued with the like ambition.[128] But I fancy more the wit of Defoe, & Cervantes, & Montaigne, who make deep & abstruse things popular. & I like the spirit of Kean who said,[n] [174] "the boxes, say you? a fig for the boxes; — the Pit rose to me," and of Mrs Stowe who had three audiences for "Uncle Tom," the parlor, & the kitchen, & the nursery.[129]

[175] Henry avoids commonplace, & talks birch bark to all comers, & reduces them all to the same insignificance.

[176] [130] Alcott returns to the lunar theory & thinks we must justify the ancients.
talked well of the Atlantic.

---

[127] Emerson indexed p. [172] under France.

[128] Karl Friedrich Gauss (1777–1855), German mathematician and astronomer, was director and professor of astronomy at the Göttingen observatory from 1807; Benjamin Peirce (1809–1880), American mathematician and astronomer, was professor at Harvard, 1833–1880; Benjamin Apthorp Gould (1824–1896), American astronomer, founded and edited the *Astronomical Journal*.

[129] The Kean anecdote appears in a review of Brian Waller Proctor's *Life of Edmund Kean* (London, 1835) in the *Quarterly Review*, LIV (July 1835), 115; see *JMN*, XI, 185. For the comment about *Uncle Tom's Cabin*, see *JMN*, XIII, 121, and "Success", *W*, VII, 286.

[130] The entries on pp. [176]–[181] are in pencil.

Good novels, ⟨o⟩O yes, but never a marriage, no new quality, no change of character, no marriage, have not baked a loaf. Ideas have not yet got possession, though they say they have. Does J. P. hold his money for the public benefit?ⁿ does he establish a press for the dissemination of truth? or sustain men apt for that? Who holds wealth for the public good? No, but all for themselves or some worthless son. ⟨Nonthinkers⟩ Theⁿ publishers dictate, & do not yet know their places.

[177] A journal is an assuming to guide the age — very propre & necessary to be done, & good news that it shall be so. — But this Journal, is this it? His solar eye looked over the list, without much comfort. This the Dodona? this the Sais? Has Apollo spoken? In this, the sentiment of freedom is the sting which all feel in common. A northern sentiment, the only tie; & the manifest conveniency of having a good vent for such wares as scholars have.
There is this discrepancy in the nature of the thing. Each of the contributors is content that the thing be to the [178] largest aims; but when he is asked for his contribution, he considers where his strength lies: he has certain experiences which have impressed him lately, & which he can combine, but no choice, or a very narrow choice among such. And the best the Editor can do, is, to see that nothing goes into the Book but important pieces. Every ⟨piece⟩ ↑chapter↓ ⟨s⟩must be something sterling; ⟨n⟩some record of real experiences. It suffices that it be weighty. ⟨'Tis of no⟩ It matters not [179] whether 'tis upon Religion, or Balloons, or kneebuckles, so only that there was nothing fantastic or factitious in the subject & writing. Great scope & illumination ought to be in the Editor, to draw from the best in the land, & to defy the public, if he is only sure himself that the piece has worth, & is right. Publics are very placable, & will soon find out when they have a Master. The value of ↑money↓Capital is to be able to hold out for a few months, & go on printing, until the discerning minority of the [180] public have found out that the Book is right, & must be humbly & thankfully accepted, & abandon themselves to this direction, too happy that they have got something good & wise to admire & to obey.

Alcott makes his large demand on the ⟨l⟩*Lecture*, that it is the University of the people, & 'tis time they should know at the end of the season what their professors have taught this winter: & it should be gathered by a good reporter in a book what Beecher, Whipple, Parker, [181] Bellows, King, ↑Solger,↓ & Emerson, have taught. But the Lecturer was not ⟨qu⟩ allowed to be quite simple, as if he were on his conscience to unfold himself to a college class. But he knew his audience, & used the "adulatory" & "confectionary" arts, (according to Plato,) to keep them in their seats. He treats them as children; and Mercantile Libraries & Lyceums will all vote, if the question be virtually put to them, — we prefer to be entertained, nay, we must be entertained.

[182]   ↑*Alcott.*↓

My friend has magnificent views, & looks habitually to the government of the County; of the state; of Nature. Nothing less. His natural attitude explains Plato. When has Plato found a genial critic? No, always a silly village wondering what he could be at? What he said about women? Did he mean Athens, or Hippias, or the Thirty? None of it at all, but just what you mean, when you come to the morning mountains, & say, the soul made the world, & should govern it, and the right radiancy of the soul from the centre outward, making nature, & [183] distributing it to the care of wise souls, would be thus & thus. Here is my sketch; speaking really or scientifically, & not in your conventional gabble.

Alcott thinks Socrates would not have known his own remark when Plato repeated it! [131]

———

People do not see that their opinion of the world is a confession also of character. We can only see what we are, and if we misbehave, ⟨o⟩we suspect others.[132]

---

[131] This sentence and the paragraph above it are in pencil; the heading "*Alcott.*" on p. [182] is inserted in ink.

[132] This entry, struck through in ink with a vertical use mark, is used in "Worship," *W*, VI, 224.

[184] ⟨The⟩ 'Tis a proverb that "the air of Madrid will not put out a candle," that is to say, it will kill a man.

[185] What an obstinate illusion is that which in youth gives respect to the old! And, presently, whilst we are yet young, & all our mates are ⟨b⟩mere youths & boyish, one Dick or Harry among them prematurely sports a bald head, or a grey one, which does not deceive us, who know how frivolous he is, but does not less deceive ⟨all⟩ his juniors & the public, who presently treat him with a most inadequate respect: & this lets us into the secret, that the venerable forms we knew in our childhood were just such impostors.[133]

[186]   Dreams.
I owe real knowledge & even alarming hints[n] to dreams, & wonder to see people extracting emptiness from mahogany tables, when there is vaticination in their dreams. For the soul in dreams has a subtle synthetic power which it will not exert under the sharp eyes of day. It does not like to be watched or looked upon, & flies to real twilights, as the rappers do in their wretched mummeries. If in dreams you see loose & luxurious pictures, an inevitable tie drags in the sequel of cruelty & malignity[.]

[187] If you swallow the devil's bait, you will have a horizon full of dragons shortly.
——
When I higgled for my dime & half dime in the dream, & lost, — the parrots on the chimney tops & church pinnacles scoffed at me, Ho! ho!

[188] The shooting complexion, like the cobra capello & scorpion, grows in the South. It has no wisdom, no capacity of improvement: it looks, in every landscape, only for partridges, in every society, for duels. And, as it threatens life, all wise men brave or ⟨otherwise⟩ peaceable run away from ⟨it⟩ the spider-man, as they run away from

---

[133] This paragraph, struck through in pencil with two vertical use marks, is used in "Old Age," *W*, VII, 316.

a black spider: for life to them is real & rich, & not to be risked on any curiosity as to whether spider or spider-man can bite mortally, or only make a poisonous wound. With such a nation or a [189] nation with a predominance of this complexion, war is the safest terms. That marks them, &, if they cross the lines, they can be dealt with as all fanged animals ⟨are⟩ must be.

———

The contrary temperament. The wrong thing always mounts to their lips, & they raise their voices at the moment when the person they are disparaging chances upon them.

[190] Is there no ⟨term⟩ check to this class of privileged thieves that infest our politics? ⁿ We mark & lock up the petty thief or we raise the hue & cry in the street, and do not hesitate to draw our revolvers out of the box, when ⟨h⟩one is in the house. But here are certain well dressed well-bred fellows, infinitely more mischievous, who get into the government & rob without stint, & without disgrace. They do it with a high hand, & by the device of having a party to whitewash them, to abet [191] the act, & lie, & vote for them. And ⟨us⟩ often each of the larger rogues has his newspaper, called "his organ," to say that it was not stealing, this which he did; that if there was stealing, it was you who stole, & not he. ↑See Talleyrand, *Supra VO* 35↓ There is no abominable act which these men ↑will not↓ do, & ↑they↓ are not abominated. No meanness below their stooping; yet is there no loathsomeness which their party & the "organ" will not strain its elastic larynx to swallow, & then to crow for it. ⟨Douglas, Cushing⟩ [192] ⟨Pierce, Gard⟨e⟩ner,⟩ I knew some of these robbers born within sound of church bells, & rejoicing in good Christian New England names such as Douglas, Pierce, Cushing, ↑Gov[erno]r↓ Gardner.¹³⁴ There is a serious objection to hounding them out,— that ⟨it⟩ they are nasty prey, which the noble hunter disdains. A good dog even must not be risked on such. They "spoil his nose."

---

¹³⁴ Emerson probably refers to Democrats Stephen Arnold Douglas (1813–1861), U.S. senator and author of the Kansas-Nebraska Bill (1854), Franklin Pierce (1804–1869), president of the United States (1853–1857), Caleb Cushing (1800–1879), U.S. attorney general (1853–1857), and to Henry Joseph Gardner (1818–1892), three-time Know-Nothing governor of Massachusetts.

I took such pains ⟨to put⟩ⁿ ↑not to keep↓ my money ⟨out⟩ in the house, but to put it out of the reach of burglars by buying stock, & had no guess that I was putting it into the hands of these very burglars now grown wiser & standing dressed ⟨in⟩ as Railway Directors.[134a]

[193] Wisdom has its root in goodness, & not goodness its root in wisdom. A thought is embosomed in a sentiment, which broadens indefinitely around it, and the attempt to detach & blazon the thought by itself, is like a show of cut flowers.

For these Cushings, & Hillards, & Co. one wants to say, as the minister to the Cape Cod farm, when requested to make a prayer, — "No, this land does not want a prayer, this land wants manure."[135]

> " 'Tis Virtue which they want, & wanting it,
> Honor no garment to their backs can fit."
>   *Ben Jonson*   Cynthia's Revels. [V, xi, 117–118][136]

[194] ⟨It occurred that⟩ Weⁿ live among the people of many eras, the blacks, the reds, the browns, & the blondes; these are the last. ↑See *infra* p 211↓[137]

Fate.

At Lisbon, an earthquake killed men like flies, & the cholera & the small pox have proved as mortal to some tribes, as a frost to the crickets, ↑nations↓ who filled the summer with noise & are ⟨silent in one⟩ suddenly silent in one night.[138]

Wonders of Arnica. I must surely see the plant growing. Where's Henry? If Louis XVI had only in his pocket a ⟨|| ... ||⟩phial of

[134a] See Journal RO, pp. [118]–[119] above.

[135] "For these . . . manure.' " is used in "The Fortune of the Republic," *W*, XI, 520.

[136] *The Works of Ben Jonson*, 6 vols. (London, 1716); this edition, except for vol. 2, is in Emerson's library. The title actually reads "*The Works of Ben. Johnson.*" This quotation is used in "The Fortune of the Republic," *W*, XI, 520. See *JMN*, XI, 250.

[137] This insertion is in pencil.

[138] This sentence, struck through in ink and pencil with single vertical use marks, is used in "Fate," *W*, VI, 7–8.

arnica, Father Edgeworth could have attached his falling head to his body, & with a little arnica made all whole again, & altered the fate of Europe.[139]

[195] [blank]

[196] It was a sublime sounding fact which we used to hear of Egyptian temples, that the foundation stones showed carving on their under sides, showing that old as they were, they were ruins of an older civilization. And I found in Sicily, that the church in Syracuse, was an antique temple of Diana; but that was a mushroom to the Egyptian. ⟨Well, b)But ⟨the⟩ Geology will show that first primaeval ⟨carving⟩ carved stone to have been a stratum ⟨crystallized &⟩ precipitated & ⟨then⟩ crystallized in what far aeons [197] of ⟨time⟩ uncounted time! ⟨Well,⟩ Neither[n] then were the particles & atoms new & raw, but mellowed & charred & decomposed from older mixtures, when, when, & where to reach their youth? A particle of azote or carbon is & remains azote & carbon, "nothing can in the least wear it." Well, the like aerugo, sacred rust & smell of an immeasurable antiquity, is on all with which we deal or of which we are.[140]

> "And the ruby bricks
> Of the human blood
> Have of old been wicks
> In God's halls that stood."

as Wilkinson huskily sings.[141]

[1⟨4⟩98] Do we suppose it is newer with our thoughts? Do they come to us as for the first time? ⟨or are they⟩ ↑these↓ wandering stars & sparks of truth that shone for eternity, & casually beamed this instant on us? The memory is made up of older memories, the blaze of genius owes its depth to our delighted recognition of the truth,

---

[139] Henry Essex Edgeworth de Firmont (1745–1807), Irish confessor to Louis XVI, attended him on the scaffold.

[140] "It was . . . antiquity," is struck through in pencil on pp. [196] and [197] with single wavy diagonal use marks.

[141] James John Garth Wilkinson, *Improvisations from the Spirit* (London, 1857), p. 45; this book is in Emerson's library.

as something older than the oldest, & which we knew ↑⟨bef⟩aforetime,↓ whether in the body or out of the body we cannot tell, God knoweth.[142]

[1⟨4⟩99] I recalled today — for the first time for many years — old lines of Moore that once delighted me —

_____

the song of the Peri

_____

Lar's lonely chamber

_____

Lines about Campbell, I think

_____

"True bard & simple as the race
Of true born poets always are
When stooping from their starry place
The⟨r⟩y're ↑children↓ near, tho' gods afar" [143]

[⟨⟨15⟩200⟩ 200] This ⟨detachment⟩ banishment to the rocks & ⟨the⟩ echoes ⟨this is not to be borne⟩ no metaphysics can make right or tolerable.[144]

Feb. 27

Felton told of Agassiz that when some one applied to him to read lectures, or some other paying employment, he answered, "I can't waste my time in earning money."
Dr Holmes told a story of John Hunter, that, being interrupted by a professional call, when he was dissecting a tiger, he said, "Do you think I can leave my work for your damned guinea?"

[201]   English Whim.
In 1844 Mr R H Gurney, a banker of Norwich, said, on his cross examination before a Railway Committee, "I have never travelled

[142] "Do we suppose . . . knoweth." is struck through in pencil with a wavy diagonal use mark.
[143] Emerson owned Thomas Moore's *Melodies, National Airs, Miscellaneous Poems and the Odes of Anacreon* (Boston, 1853). He printed the "Song of the Peri" and "To Campbell" in *Parnassus*. "children" is written in pencil and overwritten in ink.
[144] This sentence, struck through in pencil with a vertical use mark, is used in "Society and Solitude," *W*, VII, 10.

by rails. I am an enemy to them. I have opposed the Norwich Railway. I have left a sum of money in my will to oppose railroads."
"I was put in witness box," said Stephenson before the Parliamentary Comm↑i↓ttee, some said, *"He's a foreigner."* "No," others replied, "he's mad."

↑'Twas believed in this country that↓ an[n] Englishman offered a youth £10,000[n] for a hundred thousand used ⟨post⟩ ↑letter-↓stamps ↑of different nations,↓ to paper his chamber with.

---

[202]   This problem of solitude & society ⟨is⟩ here[n] again, as so often, nature delights to put us b⟨‖ ... ‖⟩etween extreme antagonisms, & our safety is in the skill with which we ⟨draw b⟩keep the diagonal line. Life is transition, & we must draw elements from both sides. Solitude is fatal, & Society fatal: we must keep our head in one, & our hands in the other, & mix the cup of life from both.[145] There's no teaching on this head, any more than elsewhere. We can celebrate the facts we observe, 'tis a hymn of praise to the Deity, *but each will read* [203] *only what he already knows.* On all the rest his eyes will shut.

Generalization. The studies of Cuvier showed that the classification of animals must be based on organs. But Bichat showed that the organs depended on the tissues, & so undermined Cuvier's system. But /newer inquirers/Schwann/ showed that tissues depended on cellular structure, & so undermined Bichat. And, when the microscope is improved, we shall have the cells analysed, & all will be electricity, or somewhat else.

[⟨15⟩204 204] [blank]
[⟨155⟩ 205] We should no more complain of the ⟨difficulties⟩ obstructions which make success in poetry, oratory, or in character difficult, than we should ⟨r⟩complain of the iron walls of the ⟨rifle⟩ ↑gun↓ which hinder the shot from scattering here & there. It was walled

---

[145] This paragraph is struck through in ink with three vertical use marks and in pencil with one; one of the ink use marks is wiped. "Here again . . . line." and "Solitude . . . other," are used in "Society and Solitude," *W*, VII, 15.

round with iron tube with that purpose to give it irresistible force in one direction. I hate these cheap successes of every idle whimsical boy & girl. I like the successes of George Stephenson, & Columbus, well-won, hard-earned, by ↑50↓ years of work, ↑a sleepless eye↓ & an invincible will. ↑Do you not know that "wisdom is not found in the hands of those who live at their ease?" (*Job*)↓ [146]

[⟨15⟩206] [blank]
[207]   *Instinct.*
The girl deserts the parlor to hear the delightful naiveté of the Milesians ⟨of⟩in the kitchen. The boy runs as gladly from the tutors & parents to the ⟨life &⟩ uproarious ⟨spirits⟩ ↑life↓ he finds in the market & the wharf. The college is not so wise as the shop, nor the quarterdeck as the forecastle. ↑Note↓ the [n] inexhaustible interest of the white man about the Indian, & the trapper, & hunter, & sailor. — Then how ⟨much⟩ awful are the hints of wit we detect in the horse & dog, & still more in the animals we have not demoralized, like the tiger & the eagle. By what compass the geese steer, & the herrings migrate, ⟨in the sea,⟩ we would [208] so gladly know. What ⟨that dog⟩ the house dog knows, & how he knows it, piques us more than all we heard ↑today↓ from the chair of metaphysics. If Bowen or Sir William Hamilton were to lecture & at the same hour, ⟨with⟩ ↑in which↓ George Melvin ↑or Joe Polis, the Bangor Indian,↓ would tell us what the↑y↓ knew of owls or of muskrats, Sir William would be deserted. [147]

[209] 'Twas a Pythagorean rule
επι γης ριη πλειν   ↑Don't sail on the ground.↓

[146] "we should ⟨r⟩complain . . . one direction." is struck through in ink with two vertical use marks. "We should no more . . . girl." is used in "Progress of Culture," W, VIII, 231. "a sleepless eye" is inserted in pencil and overwritten in ink. For Emerson's source of the Biblical quotation, see p. [48] above.
[147] "The girl . . . wharf." is used in "Clubs," W, VII, 246. "The college . . . metaphysics.", struck through in pencil with a vertical use mark and a wavy diagonal use mark on p. [207] and two vertical use marks on p. [208], is used in "Country Life," W, XII, 161. Francis Bowen (1811–1890) was an American philosopher and professor at Harvard from 1853; Sir William Hamilton (1788–1856) was a Scottish philosopher and professor at Edinburgh. George Melvin was a Concord pot-hunter and fisher; for Joe Polis, see p. [155] above.

What is civilization?
What is the individual?

Studies.
Haüy
Arnica [148]

[210] When a man defines his position, it must be his organic position, — that which[n] he *must* occupy: then it is interesting, as every piece of natural history is: but not his expedient or selected position. For fraud & cunning are essentially *un*interesting.

Works & Days.
The world is enigmatical, everything said, & everything known or done, & must not be taken literally, but genially. We must be at the top of our condition to understand anything rightly.[149]
↑printed??↓

[211] *Corpora non agunt nisi soluta.*[150] Hence, 'tis not the disgusting politics of "Know Nothing" parties that can serve or hinder, when the nations are in exodus & flux. *Nature aime les croisements*, and Germany, China, Turk, Russ, & Kanaka, are crossing the sea, & intermarrying, race with race, and ships are built capacious enough to carry the people of a county. ↑See above, p. 194↓ [151]

↑printed in *"Works & Days"*↓

[148] René Just Haüy (1743–1822), French mineralogist, was one of the founders of crystallography; see *JMN*, XI, 398. For arnica, see p. [194] above.
[149] "The world . . . rightly.", struck through in pencil with one diagonal and three vertical use marks, is used in "Works and Days," *W*, VII, 180; see *JMN*, IX, 351. "printed??" is inserted in pencil.
[150] "*Corpora . . . soluta.*" is used in "The Fortune of the Republic," *W*, XI, 533. See *JMN*, X, 112, where it is translated "They do not exert themselves unless unfettered" (Ed.), or "Bodies act only when freed" (*J*, VII, 307, n. 1). See *JMN*, XI, 184.
[151] "Hence, tis . . . county.", struck through in ink and pencil with single ver-

M Tissenet   DO 46

[212] If a true metaphysician should come, he would accompany each man through his own (the student's) mind, & would point at this ⟨cryp⟩ treasure-crypt, & at that, indicating immense wealth lying here & there, which the student would joyfully perceive, & pass on from hall to hall, from recess to recess, ever to more interior & causal forces, being minded to come over again on the same tracks by himself, [213] at future leisure & explore more nearly the treasures now only verified. But such ⟨n⟩as we now call metaphysicians, the Lockes, & Reids, & Stewarts, &c., are no more than the *valets de place* & *custodi* wh⟨ich⟩o lead travellers through the curiosities of Rome or Verona, & say over by rote the legends that have been repeated from father to son, "Molto antic⟨ho⟩o, signore;" "un tempio," "c'era battaglia," &c. &c.[152]

[214] Why does the name of a chapter "on Memory," shoot a little chill to the mind of each auditor?
There are few facts known on the subject of Memory. In the minds of most men it is nothing but a calender. ↑On↓ such ⁿ a day, I paid my note: on the next, my cow calved: on the next, I cut my finger: on the next, the Banks suspended payment. But another man's memory is the history of science & art & civility & thought. ↑& there are men whose memory is the history of their country during their active life.↓ And still another's [215] memory deals with laws & perceptions that are the platonic reminiscence of the Cosmos.[153] "You may perish out of your senses, but not out of your memory & imagination," said Alcott. But he says nothing satisfactory about either of these two immense powers. All that is good is his ranking them so high. I tell him, that no people have imagination. 'Tis the rarest gift. Imagina-

---

tical use marks, is used in "Works and Days," *W*, VII, 162. "See above, p. 194" is inserted in pencil. For *"Nature aime les croisements,"* see *JMN*, IX, 50.

[152] This paragraph is struck through in pencil with single wavy diagonal use marks on pp. [212] and [213].

[153] "In the minds . . . Cosmos.", struck through in pencil with one vertical and two wavy diagonal use marks on p. [214] and two vertical use marks on p. [215], is used in "Memory," *W*, XII, 96.

tion is the ⟨interpreter⟩ ↑nomination↓ of the causal facts, — the
⟨‖ . . . ‖⟩laws of the soul, — by the physical facts. [216] All physical
facts are words for spiritual facts, & ⟨th⟩Imagination, by naming them,
is the Interpreter, ⟨as⟩ showing us the Unity of the world.

[217] Most men are cowed by society, & say good things to you
in private, but will not stand to them in public. And we require such
a solitude as shall hold us to our order when we are in the street
↑or in ⟨the⟩ palace⟨.⟩.s.↓
These wonderful horses need to be driven by fine hands. The conditions are met, if we keep our independence, yet are not excluded.[154]
We must come to the club, yet ⟨with⟩ ↑in↓ ⟨our⟩ boots ⟨on, & our hats
under the chair⟩ ↑& spurs↓ ready to depart on the instant our private
alarm-clock strikes.
I listen to every prompting of honor, believing that it can deliver
itself through all the maze of relations to the end of nature.

[218] [blank]
[219] Nature does not like criticism. There is much that a wise
man would not know. See how she never shows the skeleton, but
covers it up, weaves her tissues & folds & integuments, the sun shall
not shine on it, the eye shall not see it. Who & what are you that
would lay it bare? & what a ghastly[n] grinning fragment have you
got at last, which you call a man! [155] That is criticism.
And jokes are of the same bastard kind. As soon as the company betray
the delight in jokes, we shall have no Olympus. Nothing comes of
it but vacancy & self reproach. True wit never made us laugh.[156]

---

[154] "Most men . . . excluded.", struck through in ink with a vertical use mark,
is used in "Society and Solitude," *W*, VII, 15.

[155] "There is . . . man!" is struck through in pencil with a wavy diagonal use
mark. "See how . . . bare?", struck through in ink with one diagonal and three
vertical use marks, is used in "Success," *W*, VII, 308–309. For "See how . . . see
it.", see *JMN*, XIII, 4.

[156] "As soon as . . . Olympus." is struck through in ink and pencil with single
vertical use marks; "As soon as . . . laugh." is used in "Social Aims," *W*, VIII,
98. See *JMN*, XIII, 389.

[220] The day is great & final: the night is for the day, but the day is not for the night.[157]

The ripe fruit is dropped at last without violence, yet the lightning fell, & the storm raged, & the strata were deposited & then uptorn & bent back, & chaos moved from beneath, to create & flavor that fruit. ↑See above p 13⟨8⟩9↓

[221] ↑Naiveté.↓

Uses of nature, to be sure! —

Why, this is foremost. What we value, all we value, is the *naturel*, or peculiar quality of each man; &, in a large healthy ⟨man⟩ individual, this is the antagonist of gravitation, vegetation, chemistry, nay, of matter itself, & as good ↑at least↓ as they. This is the saliency, the principle of levity, ⟨of volatilization,⟩ the *sal volatile*, which is the ⟨counter, or⟩ balance, or offset, to the mountains & masses. This is forever a surprise, and engaging, and a man is therefore & thus wonderful & lovely. Now Homer, Shakspeare, Burns, Scott, Voltaire, Rabelais, Montaigne, Hafiz, have those spirits or intuitions &

———————————

pass to p. 224 [158]

[[2]22]–[[2]23] [blank]

[224] are ⟨the⟩[n] magnetic, or interesting to all men. We are curious about them, can't be satiated with watching the primal springs, & their movements, wish to know their law, if we could.[159] Well, every man has the like potency in him, more or less. ⟨The use of nature the⟩ This wit is related to the secret of the world, to the primitive power,

———————————

[157] This sentence, struck through in ink with a vertical use mark and in pencil with one wavy diagonal and two vertical use marks, is used in "Success," *W*, VII, 307.

[158] "all we . . . levity," and "the *sal volatile* . . . lovely." are struck through in pencil with single vertical use marks. "What we . . . masses." is used in "Country Life," *W*, XII, 163. "This is the . . . masses." is enclosed in penciled square brackets, and "of volatilization," is canceled in pencil. "This is forever . . . lovely." is used in "Concord Walks," *W*, XII, 179. "pass to p. 224" is enclosed at left and above by a line.

[159] "We are . . . movements," is struck through in pencil with one vertical and one diagonal use mark, and "are curious . . . movements," is set off by pencil parentheses; these markings are probably intended to cancel.

the incessant creation. It is ⟨therefore⟩ in harmony with gravity, & the orbit of stars, & the growth of grass, & the angles of crystals.[160] There is no luck or choice about it, [225] but law in it, from first to last. It is the next finer ascent or metamorphosis of gravity, chemistry, vegetation, anima⟨te⟩l life, the same thing, on the next higher plane; as the *morale* is a still higher ascent or metamorphosis, & kindred to it. But the essence of it is, that it be native ↑&↓ⁿ intuitive. All ⟨animals⟩ facts in nature interest ⟨me⟩ ↑us↓, because they are deep, & not accidental, ⟨or⟩ especially ⟨⟨interfered with or⟩⟩ ↑not↓ tampered with, adulterated, doctored, or betraying any lower will, any quacking or falsehood. ⟨All⟩ ↑Animals,ⁿ Indians, ⟨fools⟩ & farmers,↓ children, interest us so, & ⟨fools & farmers &⟩

[226₁] ⟨Now the⟩ But this native force has most unequal ⟨vivacity or⟩ temperament. In the vast mass, it sleeps, and is hard to awaken. In Rabelais, Homer, & Shakspeare, & Cervantes, it is fortunately free, & escapes in fine jets, illuminating the time & place where they are. It ⟨is in the not less⟩ ↑subsists↓ in the whole population, but is ↑⟨in them⟩ more or less↓ torpid. Then the problem was, to free it. It was found, that ↑new aspects of nature, mountains, forests,↓ sea-air, ⟨that⟩ change of place, ⟨that⟩ cities, & travel had a good effect of disengaging this volatile principle. And the Mediterranean sea, & the Atlantic ↑ocean↓ have this ↑medical↓ value in the history of man.

[227₁] But ⟨whilst⟩ it was early discovered, that the low will or selfishness of the individual could be disengaged at the same time & blend with this spirit or genius, & instantly rots it. Better have none. Cities are sure to corrupt it.

[226₂]   See p. 93
⟨The race⟩ ↑Cities↓ of mortals wobegone
Fantastic care derides
But in the ⟨cheerful landscape lone⟩
⟨Stern benefit⟨s re⟩⟩ abides

⟨The shine⟩ ↑Sheen↓ⁿ will tarnish, honey ↑will↓ cloy
⟨The⟩ ↑And↓ merry is only a ⟨face⟩ ↑mask↓ of sad

[160] "it is ⟨therefore⟩ . . . crystals." is struck through in pencil with two vertical use marks; "This wit . . . crystals." is used in "Country Life," *W*, XII, 163.

But sober with a fund of joy
The woods ⟨their hermit had⟩ ↑at heart are glad↓

For joy & beauty planted it
With faerie gardens
And boding time[?] haunted it
With men ‖ . . . ‖ weird [161]

[227₂]   I do not count the hours I spend
In wandering by the sea
The forest is my ↑loyal↓ friend
Like God he uses me
Dodona [*words*]
[*3–5 w*]
↑⟨And⟩↓ If ⟨then I left⟩ ↑[*1 w*]↓ [*1 w*] delight
My thoughts to home rebound
I should reckon it a flight
To the higher cheer I found

In learned academic hall
The ⟨lecturer speaks⟩ ↑⟨Don't   praelect⟩↓ ↑praelects↓ for
     hours
But ⟨mid his pauses⟩ ↑in each pause↓ I hear the call
Of robins out of doors [162]

[228] [163]   And oft at home mid tasks I heed
I heed how wears the day
We must not halt while fiercely speed
The spans of life away

---

[161] "See p. 93 . . . weird", in pencil, is struck through in pencil with a curved use mark; it underlies the ink inscription on p. [226]. "⟨The race⟩ . . . glad" is used in "Waldeinsamkeit," ll. 13–20, *W*, IX, 249. "For joy . . . weird" is used in "Fragments on Nature and Life," X, *W*, IX, 340. See p. [63] above.

[162] "I do not . . . doors" is in erased pencil and underlies the ink inscription on p. [227]. "I do not . . . found" is struck through in pencil with a vertical use mark; "I do not . . . uses me" is used in "Waldeinsamkeit," ll. 1–4, *W*, IX, 249. "In learned . . . doors" is used in "Walden," ll. 33–36, *W*, IX, 372.

[163] The entries on pp. [228]–[233] are in pencil.

But here amid the hills ⟨m⟩sublime,
Or there along the /moors/oaken glade/
O what have I to do with time
For this the day was made

In learned College hall⟨s⟩
The Doctor ⟨fills⟩ ↑load[s]↓ the hours
But in each pause I hear the call⟨s⟩
Of robins out of doors [164]

[229]   An idleness like this
Crowns all thy dull affairs
Nor fetch to match /in wood & stone/one hour/
You shall not bring
The fancies found in books
Leave authors' eyes & fetch your own
To ⟨‖ . . . ‖⟩face the landscape's looks

And paints with white & red the moors
To draw the nations out of doors

Or earth with red volcano charred [165]

[230]   Time & Thought the high surveyors

The Doctor in the College hall⟨s⟩
Praelects thro' dreary hours
But in each pause I hear the call⟨s⟩
Of Robin out of doors [166]

[164] "And oft . . . life away" and "In learned . . . doors" are used in "Walden," ll. 41–44 and 33–36, W, IX, 372. "But here . . . made" is used in "Waldeinsamkeit," ll. 9–12, W, IX, 249.

[165] "Nor fetch . . . looks" and "An idleness . . . looks", struck through in
pencil with vertical use marks, are used in "Waldeinsamkeit," ll. 41–48, W, IX,
250–251. "And paints . . . doors" is used in "Fragments on Nature and Life," XIII,
W, IX, 341.

[166] "Time & . . . surveyors" is used in "Song of Nature," l. 33, W, IX, 245.
"The Doctor . . . doors" is used in "Walden," ll. 33–36, W, IX, 372.

[231]   She had wealth of mornings in her year
And planets in her sky,
⟨But⟩ She ⁿ chose the best thy heart to cheer
Thy beauty to supply. —
⟨& many come to the stream⟩
⟨And⟩⟨n⟩Now younger lovers find the stream
The willow & the vine
But aye to me the happiest seem
To draw the dregs of wine

[232]   ⟨For 'tis my faith the northwind thinks⟩
↑↑The air is↓ ⟨well &⟩ wise the wind thinks well↓
And all thro' which it blows
If plant or ⟨man⟩ ↑brain↓ if ⟨sedge or pinks⟩ ↑egg or cell↓
Or bird or biped, knows

The Rock of Ages melts alway
Into the mineral air
To yield the base quarry whence /we/to/ build
⟨Wise man & woman fair⟩
Fair world & tenant fair
The spirit's mansion fair
Thought & its mansion fair [167]

[233]   Room for the shadows on the plain
Of ⟨mighty⟩ ↑skirting↓ hills to lie

Room for the hills upon the plain
To spread their shadows long

Here the great planter plants
Of worlds the fruitful grain
And with a million spells enchants

[167] "To yield . . . its mansion fair" is struck through in pencil with a diagonal use mark; "The air . . . knows" is used in "Walden," ll. 37-40, W, IX, 372; "The Rock . . . its mansion fair" is used in "Fragments on Nature and Life," XXIV, W, IX, 355. See Journal SO, pp. [23] and [83] above.

⟨The eyes of men in pain⟩
Proud wit that pores in vain [168]

Vain wit but to pure virgin bold
Or humble daring boy
Told what could not ⟨b⟩again be told
But moulded into joy

[234]   Here is the mill that wove the robe
Of sky & broidered /stars/cloth/
⟨That cast the coc⟩
That carved the cockle & cast the globe
Spawned the kinds & set the bars [169]

Literature is a softened image of facts: & has all the beauty which the Claude mirror gives to familiar objects by mere reflection.

Our thesis is, ↑1.↓ that ⟨nature⟩ alone ⟨interests man, as⟩ man seems the object of nature. What vast schemes & performance for his good in layers of coal,[n] in tempering of air, in adapting of food, & animals, & materials; Owen's molar tooth, and Buffon's famous remark.[170] (?) [n] Agassiz has expanded this & confirmed it. Nature is for man not man for nature.

2. That whatever we study in nature 'tis always found to be [235] the study of man. That gives the edge to the inquiry. If you could once show an independency & foreignness in nature, we should never care for it more. Man is the husband of the world, and it makes no difference how far you extend nature astronomically, or microscopically, man follows, & is still the half, & the larger half[.]

[168] "Room for the shadows . . . vain" is used in "Waldeinsamkeit," ll. 4–8 and 21–24, W, IX, 249–250.

[169] "Here is . . . bars", in pencil, is struck through in pencil with a vertical use mark; it underlies the ink inscription "Literature . . . reflection." at the top of p. [234].

[170] Georges-Louis Leclerc, Comte de Buffon, "les choses sont hors de l'homme, le style est l'homme même," Discours sur le style, prononcé à l'Académie française, le jour de sa réception, le 25 août 1753. See JMN, XIII, 352.

But this study has its stern purifying corrective effect. Man's egotism will not be found there; Man's crime or folly will be filtered out. 'Tis only moral & rational ⟨nature⟩ man, that nature subserves.

> Broad plains that give the shadows room
> Of skirting hills to lie
> washed by the stream that gives & takes
> The colors of the sky
>
> Broad plain that room for shadows makes
> Of skirting hills to lie,
> Washed by the stream that gives & takes
> The colors of the sky.[171]

[236] [172] Patterns of all that yet was made
> And grace that gladly wins
> Words for all thoughts that can be said
> And youth which aye begins
>
> The Rock of ages melts alway
> Into the mineral air
> To yield the quarry whence to build
> Thought & its mansion fair

[237] Here the great Planter plants
> Of fruitful worlds the grain
> And with a million spells enchants
> The souls that walk in pain.[173]
>
> Here are the types of all he made;
> ⟨An⟩The grace that gladly wins,

---

[171] These two stanzas, in partially erased pencil and struck through in pencil with a vertical use mark, underlie the ink inscription on p. [235]; the second version is used in "Waldeinsamkeit," ll. 5–8, *W*, IX, 249.

[172] The entries on p. [236] are in pencil. "The Rock . . . fair" is used in "Fragments on Nature and Life," XXIV, *W*, IX, 355. See p. [232] above.

[173] "Here . . . pain.", struck through in ink with a vertical use mark, is used in "Waldeinsamkeit," ll. 21–24, *W*, IX, 250. See p. [233] above.

Words for all tho'ts that can be said,
And youth which aye begins.

Here works the craft that wove the robe
Of sky & broidered stars
That carved the cockle, cast the globe,
Scooped ⟨the⟩ sea↑ts↓, & set ⟨its⟩ ↑their↓ bars.

He to the gentle virgin bold
Or humble careless boy
Tells what cannot ⟨again⟩ ↑with words↓ be told
But moulded into joy

[238][174] Here in secret veins of air
Blows the ↑sweet↓ breath of song
Who ⟨find⟩ scale those ↑echoing↓ cliffs are few & rare
Though they to all belong

As
What need is here of Thebes or Rome
Or lands of Eastern day
Here I am most at home
And hence I cannot stray

[239][175] ↑Down↓ in [n] yon low ↑water↓ nook
↑Where↓ the [n] bearded mists divide
The gray old gods that Chaos knew
The sires of nature hide

Down in yon watery nook
Where bearded mists divide

[174] The entries on p. [238] are in pencil. "Here in . . . belong", struck through in pencil with a vertical use mark, is used in "Waldeinsamkeit," ll. 37–40, W, IX, 250. "What need . . . stray" is used in "Walden," ll. 45–48, W, IX, 372.
[175] The entries on p. [239], in pencil and struck through in pencil with a diagonal use mark, are used in "Waldeinsamkeit," ll. 33–40, W, IX, 250. The first four lines are partially erased. See p. [238] above. For a prose version of the two stanzas "Down in . . . hide", see p. [158] above.

The gray old gods that Chaos knew
The sires of nature hide

⟨Up here⟩ ↑Aloft↓ in secret veins of air
Blows the sweet breath of song
⟨And⟩ ↑Ah↓ few to scale those mountains dare
Though they to all belong

[240] [176]   In learned College hall⟨s⟩
The doctors /stretch/drone through/ the hours,
But in each pause I hear the call
Of robins out of doors

And oft at home mid tasks I heed,
I heed how wears the day,
We must not halt, while fiercely speed
The spans of life away.

What boots it here of ⟨G⟩Thebes, or Rome,
Or lands of Eastern day?
In forests I am still at home.
And there I cannot stray.

[241] [177]   Down in yon watery nook
Where bearded mists divide,
The gray old gods that chaos knew,
The sires of nature hide.

⟨Ab⟩Aloft in secret veins of air,
Blows the sweet breath of song;
Ah! few to scale those mountains dare,
Though they to all belong.

[176] The entries on p. [240] are used in "Walden," ll. 33–36 and 41–48, W, IX, 372. See p. [238] above.
[177] The entries on p. [241], in pencil, are used in "Waldeinsamkeit," ll. 33–40, W, IX, 250. See pp. [238] and [239] above.

[242]

'Tis curious that sickness & other hurtful accidents should some-times exalt certain mental powers, as, memory, fancy, &c.

Test of the poet his science of love
Does he not know the mystery well?
Never was poet of late or of yore
Who was not tremulous with love-lore

⟨The art that⟩
The craft that is older than Saturn & Jove
Test of the poet ⟨is⟩his science of love,
The science is older than Saturn or Jove,
Never was poet of late or of yore
Who was not tremulous with love lore.

The test of a bard is his knowledge of love,
That knowledge is older than Saturn or Jove,
Never was poet of late or of yore
Who was not tremulous with love-lore.[178]

[243]

Layard found in Nineveh, beneath the relics of the 8th Century be-fore Christ, another previously buried Nineveh, whose works of art are of a more exquisite character
     ap. E[lizabeth]. P[almer]. P[eabody].'s Essay Ms.[179]

We remember an image.

"The Theogony of Hesiod, which is really ill-remembered history," E. P. P.

---

[178] "Test of the poet his . . . Jove" and "Test of the poet ⟨is⟩his . . . love-lore.", struck through in ink with vertical use marks, are used in "Casella," *W*, IX, 296.
[179] For Elizabeth Palmer Peabody's essay on "Primeval History," see *L*, V, 135.

"Malus, ↑Captain of Engineers,↓ went to the Egyptian Campaign & was attached to the advanced guard of the invading army: he encamped on the road ⟨to⟩from Ramanièh. The corps of engineers had neither materiel nor troops. An officer was deprived of the commonest necessaries. 'Wanting a picquet to which to attach my horse, I tied him to my leg: I slept & [244] dreamed peaceably of the pleasures of Europe.'"
    Arago, Biog.[*raphies of Distinguished Scientific Men*, 1857,] p 364

    ↑See, of desperate circumstances, V 123↓

Fontenelle (?) said, "When a learned man speaks to instruct other men, & exactly in that line of instruction they wish to ⟨in⟩acquire, he does them a favor: but if he speaks only to show off his ↑own↓ learning, they do him a favor in listening." Arago. [*Ibid.*,] p 360 [180]

    Fascination of individuals for *LO*   see V 73 [181]

[245] Degrees of power   *V* 129

    Le Play, Les ouvriers Européens.
    Histoire de la renaissance, Michelet.
    It is towards the 10 Century that the *Chansons de Roland* began. They were old in 1166. Their modern form is, say, 1100
        Quatre Fils Aymon. See Michelet. p. XVIII.[182]
"The 12 century is an aurora; the 14th, a sunset," said Fauriel.[183]
"There is a certain village where the whole population reproduces still at the present day the features of the ancient seigneurs↑.↓ ⟨of⟩ I speak of the Mirabeaus" Michelet [*Histoire de France* . . .] Renaissance [1855, p. 29]

─────

"God the Father during 15 Centuries has no altar." [*Ibid.*, p. 46] [184]

───────

[180] Arago ascribes the quotation to "the oldest and most ingenious of your interpreters" in the French Academy.
    [181] "See, of . . . V 123" and "Fascination . . . see V 73" are in pencil, as is "Degrees . . . V 129" on p. [245].
    [182] Jules Michelet, *Histoire de France au seizième siècle: Renaissance* (Paris, 1855).
    [183] Claude Charles Fauriel, *Histoire de la Poésie Provençale*, 3 vols. (Paris, 1847). See Journal CL, p. [167] below.
    [184] Two vertical lines in the left margin mark this sentence.

[246]   *Pace.*

The miracle in Safford & in Corinne or Corella is only the accelera-
tion of the processes which take place slower in the writer. And we
say, in relating any body's bon mot, that he replied *instantly* so &
so, whilst *l'esprit d'escalier*, though it were better, is not valued.

———

We remember an image.

[247] Nothing befals us which we do not invite.

In nature we find ourselves expressed.

'Tis curious ⟨our⟩ what the show of nature does for us. We find
ourselves expressed in it, but we cannot translate it into ⟨English⟩
↑words↓. 'Tis easier to read Greek, to read Sanscrit, to cipher out the
arrowheaded character, than to interpret these familiar symbols of
snow & grass, animals, rocks, seas, & skies.[185] [248] ⟨We⟩ 'Tis even
much to name these very things. Thus Thomson's "Seasons" and the
best parts of many old & many new poets, are nothing but simple
enumerations, by a person who felt the⟨ir⟩ beauty of the common
sights & sounds, without the least attempt to draw a moral, or affix
any meaning to them.[186] The charm of the Hindoo writings is a
lively painting of these elements of fire, water, winds, clouds, [249]
without a hint of what they signify.

[250] ↑Rev. Mr↓ Stone ↑of Bolton↓ thought Bacon monotonous, &
'tis certain that Shakspeare is *murionous.*[187]

---

[185] "Nothing . . . invite." is marked with two vertical pencil lines in the left
margin. With "In nature . . . expressed." and "We find . . . expressed in it," cf.
"Concord Walks," *W*, XII, 179. "'Tis easier . . . skies.", struck through in pencil
with two vertical use marks, is used in "Poetry and Imagination," *W*, VIII, 22.

[186] "'Tis even . . . to them.", struck through in pencil with a vertical use mark,
is used in "Poetry and Imagination," *W*, VIII, 22–23; cf. "Country Life," *W*, XII,
164.

[187] Thomas Treadwell Stone (1801–1895), a popular liberal preacher and antislavery lecturer, had been a contributor to *The Dial*. "of Bolton" is in pencil overwritten in ink. On December 23, 1857, according to the records of the Concord Lyceum, the "Reverend Thomas T. Stone delivered the first of a course of Six Lectures
upon *English Language and Literature*."

Stone said that he did not find Wordsworth's ode true for him. Every spring ⟨was⟩is more beautiful than the last.[188]

↑printed "Success"↓

Bacon is worldly. Shakspeare defies the world even, through Falstaff & the clown, with his spirituel fun.

[251] Miscellany is as bad as drunkenness[.]
They ri⟨g⟩ng their bells backward when there is a fire[.]
    to steer by a planet & not by a star
    love eats his way through Alps of opposition

" 'Tis a man's perdition to be safe when he ought to perish for God" [189]

———

    Ring your bells backward, loyal towers!
    And warn the land of harm.

[252] Sulphur in every egg all over the world. Whence comes the sulphur? Limestone in seawater. Where do the corallines get it? Ask Dr Jackson.[190]
↑Ans.↓ Sulphur is present in most soils, & lime in seawater.

———

The saddest fact I know under the ⟨law⟩ ↑category↓ of *Compensation*, is, that, when we look at an object, we turn away from every other object in the universe.

———

Answer. The redress is that we find every other object in that.

[253] My philosophy holds to a few laws, ↑1.↓ *Identity*, whence comes the fact that *metaphysical* ↑*faculties* &↓ *facts are the transcendency of physical.* ⟨&⟩2. Flowing, or transition, or shooting the

———

[188] "Stone said . . . last.", struck through in ink with a vertical use mark, is used in "Success," *W*, VII, 299. See Journal AC, p. [47] below.

[189] A versified form of this sentence is used in the quatrain "Sacrifice," *W*, IX, 296, and in "Character," *W*, X, 96.

[190] Dr. Charles Thomas Jackson (1805–1880), Emerson's brother-in-law, was a chemist and mineralogist.

gulf, the perpetual striving to ascend to a higher platform, the same thing in new & higher forms[.]

[254]   ↑*High Criticism.*↓

You must draw your rule from the genius of that which you do, & not from by-ends. Don't make a novel to establish a principle of polit[ical]. economy. You will spoil both. Do not set out to make your school of design lucrative to the pupils: you will fail in the art & in the profit. Don't set out to please, — you will displease. Don't set out to teach theism from your Nat[ural]. History, like Paley & Agassiz. You spoil both. * The Augsburg *Allgemeine Zeitung* deprecates an Observatory founded for the benefit of Navigation! *

"Seekest thou great things? Seek them not." [191]

[255]   *Country Life*
In the water party, the skipper was the best company: the scholars made puns.

"The stars cast or inject their imagination or influence into the air." *Bacon*

"Air is the soul & essence of things," said An⟨ax⟩aximenes.[192]

Excellent paper on *Zweck* in *Atlantis* of Feb., 1857. p. 144 [193]

* *March, 1874.* That Observatory has been established to the great benefit of Navigators.

[191] "*The Augsburg . . . not.' " is struck through in pencil with a vertical use mark. "You must . . . Navigation!*", struck through in pencil with two vertical use marks, is used in "Art and Criticism," *W*, XII, 304. " 'Seekest . . . not.' ", Jer. 45:5, is used in "Considerations by the Way," *W*, VI, 278, and "Greatness," *W*, VIII, 313.

[192] " 'Air . . . An⟨ax⟩aximenes." is written in pencil and overwritten in ink with punctuation added. "In the . . . puns." and " 'The stars . . . *Bacon*", struck through in pencil with single vertical use marks, and " 'Air . . . An⟨ax⟩aximenes." are used in "Country Life," *W*, XII, 141 and 161. For "In the . . . puns.", see *JMN*, IX, 282.

[193] See p. [34] above: "The freedom of man consists herein, that he is his own aim."

[256]   ↑*Few stars, few thoughts.*↓

⟨When I was a boy t⟩They ⟨said,⟩ ↑say,↓ that, though the stars appear so numberless, you cannot count more than a thousand. Well, there are few thoughts. Count the books & you would think there was immense wealth; but any expert knows that there are few thoughts which have emerged in his time. Shut him up in a closet, & he could soon tell them all. They are quoted, contradicted, modified, but the amount remains computably small.[194]

[257] "masterly inactivity" "wise passiveness" see how much has been made of that feather stolen from the plume of Carlyle by Calhoun & others.

———

(see above, p. 132)

The ballads got their excellence, as perhaps Homer & the Cid did, by being conventional stories conventionally treated, with conventional rhymes & tunes & images, done over & over, until, at last, all the strokes were right, & t1e faults were ⟨omitted⟩ thrown away. Thus Logan got his "sought[n] him east, & sought him west," &c. Somebody even borrowed *"Parcite dum propero, mergite dum redeo."* See Child's Edition   Vol II p 176[195]

[258] Society is very swift in its instincts, &, if you do not belong to it, resists & sneers at you, or, ⟨what is more efficient,⟩ quietly drops you. The first weapon enrages the party attacked; ⟨but⟩ the second is still more effective, but is not to be resisted, as ⟨it⟩ ↑the date of the transaction↓ is not easily found ⟨out⟩. I have seen people grow up & grow old under this infliction, & never suspect the truth, ascribing the solitude, which acted on them very injuriously, to any cause but the right one.[196]

---

[194] This paragraph is struck through in pencil with a wavy diagonal use mark.
[195] Francis James Child, *English and Scottish Ballads*, 8 vols. (Boston, 1857–1858); this work is in Emerson's library. The poem "The Drowned Lovers," by John Logan, to which Emerson refers, is on pp. 175–180. " '*Parcite . . . redeo.*' ": "Spare me while I hasten, o'erwhelm me when I return." Martial, *Epigrams*, XXV. The Latin is used in "Quotation and Originality," *W*, VIII, 186. See p. [269] below.
[196] This paragraph, struck through in ink with a vertical use mark, is used in "Behavior," *W*, VI, 186.

[259] The reason why the Greek mythology obtains to this day, is that it is more catholic than any other.

———

If men should take off their clothes, I think the aristocracy would not be less, but more pronounced than now.

———

If men were as thick as snowflakes,——— millions of flakes, but there is still but one snowflake: but every man ↑is↓ a door to a single deep secret.

———

The ancients to make a god added to the human figure ⁿ [260] some brutal exaggeration, as the leonine head of Jove, the bull-neck of Hercules; and Michel Angelo add⟨d⟩ed horns to give mysterious strength to the head of Moses. So Webster impressed by his superb animality, & was strong as a nature, though weak in character. His understanding & his demonstrative talents were invigorated from these low sources, but ⟨of⟩ ↑he had↓ the ⟨most⟩ vulgar ambition, & his power was only that of a ⟨handy⟩ lawyer,* ¹⁹⁷ & [261] ↑it↓ perished utterly, even before his death. What is called his fame — only marks the imbecility of those who invoke it.

————

Sentiment is always color, as thought is form. When I talked with Goodson, on a Sunday morning, ⟨of Catholic Churches⟩ in Cincinnati, of Catholic Churches, how warm & rich & sufficient was the hour & conversation: as the colors of the sunset, whilst we gaze, make life so great; but now ⟨nothing⟩ ↑no memory↓ remains of conversation or sunset.¹⁹⁸

[262] ↑Young↓ people ⁿ talk of moments when their brain seemed bursting with the multitude of thoughts. It was a false alarm. It was

↑* No, he was a skilful statesman & a great orator.↓

---

¹⁹⁷ Emerson's footnote is at the bottom of p. [260] beneath a page-wide rule. "handy" is canceled in pencil.

¹⁹⁸ "Sentiment . . . form." and "the colors . . . great;" are used in "Success," *W*, VII, 300. Emerson met John E. Goodson of Cincinnati in 1850; see *JMN*, XI, 260 and 514.

an illusion of sentiment, which acts like a multiplying-glass, & a Claude mirror, at the same time. *See above*, p. 256[199]
But remember the high value of sentiment to deepen or fix the thought, as when Wordsworth told me that a thought born & united to a sentiment was κτημα ες αει or, ⟨wh⟩ as I wrote elsewhere, we never attain a perfect sincerity in our speech, unless we feel a degree of tenderness.[200] See *TO* ⟨2⟩245

[263] Jan. 1858. The question is, — have you got the interesting facts? That yours have cost you time & labor, & that you are a person of wonderful parts, & of wonderful fame, ↑in the society or town in which you live↓ is nothing to the purpose. Society is a respecter of persons, but nature is not, & I am not. 'Tis fatal that I do not care a rush for all you have recorded, — cannot read it, if I should try. Henry T[horeau]. says, the Indians know better natural history than you, they with their type fish, & fingers the sons of hands.

I should go to the Naturalist with a new feeling, if he had promised to teach me what birds say to each other at midsummer, & what when they convene in autumn.[201]

[264] I found Henry T. yesterday in my woods. He thought nothing to be hoped from you, if this bit of mould under your feet was not sweeter to you to eat, than any other in this world, or in any world.[202] We talked of the willows. He says, 'tis impossible to tell when they push the bud (which so marks the arrival of spring) out of its dark scales. It is done & doing all winter. It is begun in the previous autumn. It seems one steady push from autumn to spring. I say, How divine these studies! Here there is no taint of mortality. ↑See

---

[199] "Young . . . p. 256" is struck through in pencil with a wavy diagonal use mark.
[200] "κτημα ἐς ἀεί": "a possession for all time." Thucydides, *The History of the Peloponnesian War*, I, 22, 4. Emerson renders the Greek phrase "what was good today was good forever" in *JMN*, X, 557, and in "First Visit to England," *W*, V, 23.
[201] "in the society . . . live" is in pencil. With "I should . . . autumn.", cf. Journal AC, p. [111] below.
[202] This sentence, struck through in pencil with two vertical use marks and one diagonal use mark, is used in "Thoreau," *W*, X, 469. "printed" is written vertically in the left margin in pencil.

WA 303↓ How aristocratic, & of how defiant a beauty! This is the garden [265] of Edelweisen. He says, Wachusett is 27 miles from Fairhaven, and Monadnoc about 50.[203]

↑I want animal spirits[.]↓[204]

I have not oil enough for my wheels.

Bonaparte asked Talleyrand what they meant by this term nonintervention? Talleyrand replied, "It means about the same as intervention"[205] See p 35

---

[266] Perhaps it would be a safe episode to the Intellect chapters, to give an account of the gentleman in search of the Practical, as illustrated by the history of the turbine, which is valued here at $100 000, & there is discarded as useless, and on which there seems no settled verdict to be had. J[ohn]. Bright of Rochdale said, the use of machinery in America & in England went by fancy: & my search for the pioneers in Illinois & Wisconsin, — "they were visionary men, not practical, & all bankrupted." And my western banker, at Adrian, & Mr Hooper's at Lexington, may serve to show what practical people are.

[267][blank]
    [268] Jan. 28. The panegyrics of Hafiz addressed to his Shahs & Agas show poetry, but they show deficient civilization. The finest genius in England or France would feel the absurdity of fabling such things to his queen or Emperor about their saddle, as Hafiz & Enweri do not stick at.

When a dog barks on the stage of a theatre, the audience are interested. What acting can take their attention from the dog? But

---

[203] Two vertical pencil lines in the left margin mark "He says, . . . 50."
[204] This sentence and the rule above it are in pencil.
[205] "Bonaparte . . . intervention' " is struck through in ink with three diagonal use marks.

if in the real action which their scene represents, a dog had barked, it would not have been ⟨minded⟩ ↑heard↓.

[269]   "Thou art roaring ower loud, Clyde water!
        Thy streams are ower strang;
        Make me thy wreck, when I come back,
        But spare me when I gang."

Parcite dum propero, mergite dum redeo.[206] [Martial, *Epigrams*, XXV]

People who caught cold in coming into the world, & have increased their cold ever since.[207]

[270] The politics of Massachusetts are cowardly. O for a Roman breath, & the courage that advances & dictates! When we get an advantage, as in Congress, the other day, it is because our adversary has made a fault, & not that we have made a thrust.[208]
↑printed↓

Why do we not say, We are abolitionists of the most absolute abolition, as every man that is a man must be? Only the Hottentots, only the barbarous or semibarbarous societies are not. We do [271] not try to alter your laws in Alabama, nor yours in Japan, or the Fee Jee Islands; but we do not admit them or permit a trace of them here. Nor shall we suffer you to carry your Thuggism north, south, east, or west ↑into↓ a single rod of territory which we control. We intend to set & keep a *cordon sanitaire* all around the infected district, & by no means suffer the pestilence to spread.

[272] At Springfield, I told Lamoureux that I thought metaphysics owed very little to the French mind. What we owe is not to the

[206] "Spare me while I hasten, o'erwhelm me when I return"; see p. [257] above. "'Thou art . . . gang.'" is from Child, *English and Scottish Ballads*, 1857–1858, II, 177. "'Thou art . . . redeo." is used in "Quotation and Originality," *W*, VIII, 186.
[207] This sentence, struck through in ink with a vertical use mark, is used in "Behavior," *W*, VI, 185. See Journal RO, p. [81] above.
[208] This entry, struck through in ink with two vertical and two discontinuous vertical use marks, is used in "Courage," *W*, VII, 259.

professors, but to the incidental remarks of a few deep men, namely, to Montaigne, ↑Ma⟨e⟩lebranche,↓ Pascal, & Montesquieu.* n 209 The analytic mind ⟨I⟩ will not carry us far. Taking to pieces is the trade of those who cannot ⟨make⟩ ↑construct↓. In a healthy mind, the love of wholes, the power of generalizing, is usually joined with a keen appreciation of differences. But they are so bent on the aim & genius of the [273] thing, that they don't mind the surface faults. But minds of low & surface power pounce on some fault of expression, of rhetoric, or petty mis-statement of fact, and quite lose sight of the main purpose. I knew a lady who ⟨knew w⟩ thought she knew she had heard my discourse before, because the word "*Arena*" was in both of the two discourses.

↑The↓ English think, if you add a hundred facts, you will have made a right step towards a theory; if you add a thousand, so much the nearer. But these lines never meet. A good mind infers from two or three [274] facts, or from one, as readily as from a legion. Witness Kepler, Newton, Dalton, &c., who are born with ⟨an aptitude⟩ a taste for the manners of nature, & catch the whole tune from a few bars.

———   ———

↑From p 271↓

It is impossible to be a gentleman, & not be an abolitionist. For a gentleman is one ⟨who imparts of his nobleness⟩ who is fulfilled with all nobleness, & imparts it; is the natural defender & raiser of the weak & oppressed; ⟨But⟩ like the Cid. But these are snobs. In the southern country, their idea of a gentleman is a striker. ⟨H⟩There are abundance of their gentlemen garrotting &c in N. Y. streets.

[275] "Meanwhile the Cardinal Ippolite, in whom all my best hopes were placed, being dead, I began to understand that the promises of this world

* [Yet we must remember DesCartes & Malebranche; ⟨&⟩if Cousin is only a pupil of Hegel.]

209 Emerson's footnote is inserted after the end of this paragraph on p. [273].

are for the most part vain phantoms; & that to confide in one's self, & become something of worth & value, is the best & safest course."

Vasari, Vol 5 p 509 [210]

↑Printed in "Success"↓

——

1858

1776

82   years count the age of the Union, and yet they say the nation is as old & infirm as a man is with those years. Now a building is not in its prime till after 500 years. Nor should a nation be; and we aged at 80!

[274a][n] The populace ⟨instantly⟩ drag down the gods to their own level, and give them their egotism. Whilst in nature is none at all, God keeping ⟨absolutely⟩ out of sight. And ⟨is⟩ known only as pure law, though resistless. "Si Dieu a fait l'homme à son image, l'homme lui l'a bien rendu." [211] (?) ↑*Chateaubriand*↓

Thorwaldsen said, "⟨P⟩Clay was the life, plaster the death, & marble the resurrection," — of the statue.[212]

[275a][n] Here is Mr Rare⟨e⟩y in London showing in 1858 how to tame a horse by appealing to his heart & his mind. 'Tis as it should be, only we have been rather slow about it. It ought to be as old as Homer & Theseus, at least. So the taming or the conquering of a dog is not yet a science. And the language of birds is a fable still. I think the fame of Theseus has come down a peg or two, since the appearance of Mr Rarey. His maxim is, "he who would tame a horse must not know fear or anger."

[210] Giorgio Vasari, *Lives of the most eminent Painters, Sculptors, and Architects* . . . , trans. Mrs. Jonathan Foster, 5 vols. (London, 1850–1852); this work is in Emerson's library. This quotation, struck through in ink with three vertical use marks, is used in "Success," *W*, VII, 290–291. One use mark is extended to enclose "Printed" at top and left.

[211] "The populace . . . rendu.' ", struck through in ink with a vertical use mark, is used in "Character," *W*, X, 104. The quotation is actually from Voltaire, *Le Sottisier*, XXXII, *Faits détachés*; see Journal SO, p. [265] above.

[212] Bertel Thorvaldsen or Thorwaldsen (1768–1844) was a Danish sculptor.

[276] It seems as if there should be new Olympian games in which the unsolved questions should be proposed for prizes. *What is imagination? Will?*
↑*Which is first, truth or goodness?*↓
Nor can we dispose of these gods by saying, *these are simple acts of one power.*
I admit the perpetual Pertinence of the ⟨question⟩reference to amount of manhood or humanity. What have all your inquiries or skills or reforms ⟨‖ ... ‖⟩by you inaugurated, profited you? The r⟨al⟩oarers for liberty turn out to be slaves themselves; the thunderers of the Senate are poor creatures in the street, & when canvassing for votes. And when, in their own village, the question is how many honest men are there in town? men who will not take a petty advantage, & are severer [277] watchers of themselves than of their debtor? Why, they are as rare among ⟨them⟩ the reputable as among the unreputed; the great gentlemen, scornful & lofty, will do very shabby things: and a career of triumphantly logical reform has consumed all the domestic virtue & private charm of the athlete. His wife hates him, children do not love him, scholars dislike him, & he is miserable alone.

———

Glout morceaux ↑apple↓ perfect in the centre of a barrel of Baldwins this 20 February 1858[.] ↑As good today, 15 Feb. 1864↓

—————

↑*Races.*↓

———

All the children born in the last three years or 8 years should be charged with love of liberty, for their parents have been filled with Kansas & antislavery.
1858

[⟨276⟩278] [213]   *German*
    Thatsach   fact, matter of fact,
aufgabe   problem
lochern   to loosen
vertrag   treaty

[213] The entries on pp. [278] and [279] are in pencil.

uebereinkommen,   convention, understanding
Entscheidung   Decision
welt-anschauung

[279] complete head
⟨stars⟩ sky sun a million ⟨times⟩ repetitions

———

Moral sense makes genius in spite even of disowning by genius.[214]

———

Why moral sentiment is laming?

———

My theory ⟨of three days ago⟩ of the present basis of society being brutish, each feeding on other; but the ⟨true⟩ basis of intell[ect]. & morals is aid, & the more angels more room[.]

———

Write the way you look. Write what you do; not write one thing, think one thing, & handle another; row & back water. 'Tis the constitution not the institution[.] [215]

———

Snowflake is a small glacier, glacier a large snowflake[.]

———

[⟨278⟩280] Mystery of the animal led M. Angelo to give horns to Moses.[216]

———

You are too historical by half. I show you a grievance, & you proceed to inquire, not if it is ⟨wrong⟩ mischievous, but if it is old. I point the redress, & you ⟨only⟩ inquire about a constitutional precedent for the redress. That which only requires perception, — mischiefs that are rank & intolerable, which only need ⟨the glance of the eye⟩ to be seen, to be hated & attacked, with you are ground for argument, & you are already preparing to defend them. [2⟨79⟩81] The reliance

———

[214] "Moral sense . . . by genius." is struck through in pencil with a diagonal use mark.
[215] "Write the . . . institution" is struck through in pencil with a vertical use mark.
[216] This sentence and the rule following it are in pencil. See p. [260] above.

on simple perception constitutes genius & heroism; and that is the religion before us.

———

Wordsworth's "Prelude" is not quite solid enough in its texture: it is rather a poetical pamphlet; though proceeding from a new & genuine experience. It is like Milton's "*Areopagitica*," an immortal pamp[h]let.

↑Many of↓ Tennyson's poems, ⟨many of them,⟩ like "Clara Vere de Vere," are only the sublime of magazine poems, — admirable contributions for the "Atlantic [282] Monthly" of the current month, but not classic & eternal.

In this solitude of [2 w]
P [3–5 w]

Milton would have raised his eyebrow a little at such pieces. But the "Ulysses" he would have approved.

The quaking earth did quake in rhyme
Seas ebbed & flowed with clanging chime

The sun athwart the cloud thought it no sin
To use my land to put his rainbows in [217]

[↑*Eloquence*↓]
What unreckoned elements the orator carries with him, for example, ⟨th⟩ silence. He performs as much or more with judicious pauses, as by his best stroke.

[283] We can't afford to take the horse out of Montaigne's Essays.

———

[217] "In this solitude of . . . P" is in erased pencil. "The quaking . . . rainbows in" is in pencil. "The quaking . . . chime" is struck through in pencil with a vertical use mark. "The sun . . . rainbows in" is used in "Fragments on Nature and Life," IX, *W*, IX, 340.

[284]   I⟨2⟩I May

Yesterday with Henry T. at the pond saw the creeper *vesey vesey vesey*. *Yorick is the*[n] *veery, or Wilson's Thrush.* The ⟨ee⟩lamprey-eel was seen by Wetherell building the pebble nest in the river. The dead sucker so often seen in the river needs a great deal of air & hence perhaps dies when detained below. The trout was seen to kill the pickerel by darting at him & tearing off a fin every time. I hear the account of the man who lives in the wilderness of Maine with respect, but with despair. ⟨'Tis the⟩ It needs the doing hand to make the seeing eye, & my imbecile hands leave me always helpless & ignorant, ⟨&⟩after so many years in the country. The beauty of [285] the spectacle I fully feel, but 'tis strange that more than the miracle of the plant & any animal is the ⟨mere⟩ impression of mere mass of broken land & water, say a mountain, precipices, & water-falls, or the ocean side, and stars. These affect us more than anything except men & women. But neither is Henry's hermit, 45 miles from the nearest house, important, until we know what he is now, what he thinks of it on his return, & after a year. Perhaps he has found it foolish & wasteful to spend a [286] tenth or a twentieth of his active life with a muskrat & fried fishes. ↑I tell him that a man was not made to live in a swamp, but a frog.*↓ [218] The charm which Henry T. uses for bird & frog & mink, is patience. They will not come to him, or show him aught, until he becomes a log among the logs, sitting still for hours in the same place; then they come around him & to him, & show themselves at home.[219] ↑Peabody-bird[;]↓ *Pee-pee*, pee pee pee[,] five bars, — that is the note of the *myrtle bird*. ⟨n⟩Penetrating and like the note of the meadow lark.

[287] Rowse said that a portrait should be made by a few continuous strokes giving the great lines, ⟨and that⟩ ↑but↓ if made by labor & by

* If God meant him to live in a swamp, he would have made him a frog.

---

[218] Emerson's footnote, "If God . . . frog.", is inserted beneath a page-wide rule at the bottom of p. [287].

[219] "The charm . . . & to him," is struck through in pencil with a vertical use mark. Cf. "Thoreau," *W*, X, 469.

many corrections, ↑though it↓ became at last ⟨perfect,⟩ ↑accurate,↓ it would give an artist no pleasure, — would look muddy. Any body could make a likeness by main strength⟨, but an artist⟩. ⁿ 220

———

See the contrast of these two pages, 286   287.

[288] We are all better in attack than in defence. It is very easy to make acute objections to any style of life, but the objector is quite as vulnerable. Greenough wittily called my ⟨|| ... ||⟩speculations *masturbation*; 221 but the artist life seems to me intolerably thin & superficial. I feel the reasonableness of what the lawyer or merchant or laborer has to allege against readers & thinkers, until I look at each of their wretched industries, and find them without [289] end or aim.

———

↑*monotone*↓
Chicadee dee, says the titmouse; *peē peē* pee pee pee, says the myrtle bird, ↑"Peabody bird"↓ each as long as he lives; & the man who hears, goes all his life saying his one proverb too.

———

↑My dear Henry,↓
    A frog was made to live in a swamp, but a man was not made to live in a swamp. ↑Yours ever,
                        R.↓ 222

———

[290] Nature overloads the bias, overshoots the mark, to hit the mark. Her end of reproduction & care of young is so dear to her, that she demoralizes the universe of men with this immense superfluity of attraction in all directions to woman: & see what carnage in relations results! Nothing is so hypocritical as the abuse in all journals, — & at the South, especially, — of Mormonism & Free-Love Socialism. These men who write the paragraphs in the "Herald" & "Observer," have just come from their brothel, or, in [291] Carolina, from their

———

220 Samuel Worcester Rowse (1822–1901), painter, illustrator, and lithographer, made a crayon sketch of Emerson in June, 1858. See *L*, V, 114.
    221 See *JMN*, XIII, 84.
    222 See p. [286] above.

Mulattoes. How then can you say, that, in nature is always a minimum of force to effect a change? It is a maximum.

———

Nature has two ways of hiding her things, by light, & by darkness. We never see mosses, lichens, grasses, birds, or insects, which are near us every day, on account of our preoccupied mind. When our attention is at last called to them, they seem the only things worth minding.

[292] 185⟨7⟩8
⟨7⟩8 June. I spent the evening of 7↑th↓ June at the American House, with J. S. Babcock, the carpenter, Mr Rowse's friend — a man of much reading, & a very active & independent mind, with an exclusive respect for intellectual power, ⟨lef⟩ not much sensibility to morals, though meaning to be fair, & of little hope for the race. The bully, he thinks, the great god of the people, &, if Sumner had killed Brooks, ⟨the⟩he thought the people would have worsh⟨p⟩ipped Sumner. Now, all the west despised him. I tried to show him how much the genius of Burke was indebted to his affection; what insight good will ⟨m⟩gives, & what [293] eyewaters all the virtues are, as humility, love, courage, &c & what a blindman's buff ⟨conceit⟩ self-conceit makes. And he was candid enough. I told him, that, whatever was dreary & repels, is not power, but the lack of power, — which he allowed. He struggled hard for Webster, who is his idol. He thought the masses admire Cushing, Burlingame, Wise,[223] or any man who has done the feat, — who has succeeded.
His opinions on books, — which he has read a good deal, — were his own, & just.

[294] A man of ↑eminently↓ fortunate aspects who is cordially hailed as bringing the glitter of the Muse & good omen into certain houses, ⟨is not the less of a dreary & withering aspect, & that⟩ ↑has↓, in spite of himself, & to his deep regret, in other quarters, a dreary & withering aspect.

[223] Anson Burlingame (1820–1870) was a member of the House of Representatives from 1855 to 1861; Henry Alexander Wise (1806–1876) was a member of the House of Representatives from 1833 to 1844.

[295] ⟨It is well thought that⟩ ↑What is↓ the benefit of the doctrine of Fate⟨, is, that,⟩↑? because↓ under that form we learn the lesson of the immutability & universality of law.[224]

Why preach to us the doctrine of Fate? Because under that form we learn the immutability & universality of Law.

[296] English politics are ever agreeable reading on this side the water, whilst our own are the reverse. 'Tis partly that the virulent element is taken out by our ⟨position⟩ disinterested position as spectat⟨u⟩ors like tobacco smoke⟨d⟩ strained through water, or the gas cleansed through water on its way to the jet, and partly the distinction of the persons who act in them, who, for the most part, are highly-bred men.

[297] Wealth consists in having at every moment a commanding position as ⟨respects⟩ ↑regards↓ your ends. A man in debt has it not. Every hour is bringing certain opportunities to do somewhat desire-able. But we are not free to use today, or ↑to↓ promise tomorrow, because we are already mortgaged to yesterday, having eaten our cake before we had earned it. Leisure, tranquillity, grace, & strength, belong to economy.

Calvert mows his grass. Kant wears the same hat for 20 years. Minot never rides. Francis stays at home, and [298] H. goes to work every day; and each of these are free & able to the new day, free & great as it, whilst the debtor is ⟨worried &⟩ perplexed in the extreme, &, because he is low in his own esteem, ⟨falls in rank⟩ loses rank in the world.[225]

———

A great aim infuses itself alike into hours and ages. Quality makes all moments indifferent, and character pervades all acts. Time is the quality of the moment.
Not feats but forces.

---

[224] "What is . . . law." is struck through in ink with a diagonal use mark.
[225] For "perplexed in the extreme," see Shakespeare, *Othello*, V, ii, 346.

[299] ↑FATE↓

He ⟨said &⟩ saw ↑& spoke↓ truly who said, When you have come to your highest thought, you say what is already known to ⟨every man⟩ the common man.

———

Your fate is what you ⟨are⟩ do, because first it is what you are.

———

[300] [Index material omitted]
[inside back cover] [Index material omitted]

$\mathcal{AC}$

1858–1859

There are almost no dates in Journal AC: the earliest dated entry is February 4, 1859 (p. [30]), and the latest is May 25, [1859] (p. [278]). It was used as a notebook and probably overlaps regular journal VO by five to six months. When Journal VO was full Emerson began to use AC, but only after much time had elapsed: see his statement that he has not written in his journal "for more than a year" (p. [136]).

The covers of the copybook, gray paper marbled with red, yellow, and blue over boards, measure 17.8 x 21.4 cm. The spine strip and the protective corners on the front and back covers are of tan leather. "AC" and beneath this "1859" are written in the upper right corner of the front cover, and "AC" is written in crayon in the upper left corner of the back cover.

Including the flyleaves (1, 2, 301, 302) there were 152 unlined leaves measuring 17.2 x 20.8 cm., but the leaves bearing pages 165–166, 167–168, and 169–170 are torn out. In his pagination, Emerson repeated pages 260 and 261; the editors have added subscript numbers to distinguish the two pairs. Twenty-one pages were misnumbered and corrected: 6⟨7⟩9, 18⟨7⟩8, 18⟨8⟩9, 23⟨7⟩8, 2⟨38⟩40, 2⟨39⟩41, 24⟨1⟩4, 24⟨2⟩5, 24⟨3⟩6, 24⟨4⟩7, 24⟨5⟩8, 2⟨47⟩50, 2⟨48⟩51, 2⟨49⟩52, 25⟨0⟩3, 25⟨3⟩6, 25⟨4⟩7, 2⟨58⟩60, ⟨3⟩286, ⟨3⟩287, and ⟨3⟩288. The pages are numbered in ink except for the following thirty-nine in pencil: 1, 39, 42–44, 54, 78, 104, 106, 110, 190, 192, 193, 196, 198, 202–209, 212, 214, 216, 218, 219, 222, 223, 230, 232, 234, 239, 248, 249, 298, 300, and 302. Forty-one pages are unnumbered: 22, 23, 38, 55, 93–95, 98, 101, 105, 112, 114, 115, 127–129, 135, 137, 158, 159, 171, 175, 179, 191, 194, 195, 197, 199, 201, 211, 213, 215, 217, 221, 233, 235, 269, 277, 281, 299, and 301. Four pages were numbered first in pencil and then in ink: 46, 47, 102, and 108. Twenty-nine pages are blank: 38, 40, 42, 46, 56, 58, 60, 94, 104, 112, 114–116, 126–129, 158, 159, 175, 179, 190, 191, 222, 229, 235, 283, 300, and 301.

[front cover]   AC
                                                     1859

[front cover verso] ¹ Country Life   [Index material omitted]
Works & Days
Powers of mind
⟨Memory⟩ Powers
Natural Meth↑od↓ Nat[ural] System
Memory Perception Imagination
        Memory is the copula[.]
        Imagination follows the metamorphosis[.]

"Earth smiled with flowers, — forth rushed the god to light."

[Index material omitted]

[1] ² ↑Examined October, '77↓

                        AC—
                        1859

¹ The entries on the front cover verso are in pencil except for " 'Earth smiled . . . light.' "
² The entries on p. [1] are in pencil except for "AC — 1859" in ink.
³ This list may be related to the group of six lectures Emerson gave at the Freeman Place Chapel on the "Natural Method of Mental Philosophy" from March 3 to April 7, 1858.

Transition $\pi\alpha\nu\tau\alpha\ \rho\epsilon\iota$ [4]
Rhetoric

[2]   Country-Life.
        joy of naturalists   AZ 270

———

The savant led *from* the road by the whole distance of his apparent
progress on it. *WA* 286 [5]
The secret of nature untold

———

Therien [6]

———

Peroration   *WA* 272

———

Nature not enjoyed or enjoyable till man finds his completion

[3]   *Works & Days*
Leasts   surfaces
M. Tissenet   *DO* 46
Exodus
The progress of arts is not justified by progress of melioration,[n] but
↑is attended↓ by increased crime. Newgate Calendar out of use;
superseded by London Times & N. Y. Tribune

———

That is good which commends the present hour & place, my climate,
my country, my plight to me. Jones Very washed his face, &c. *VO* 17 [7]

[4] ———
        I value morals, because it enhances today. AB 46

———

    [4] See Journal VO, p. [92] above.
    [5] "The savant . . . on it.", struck through in ink with four vertical use marks,
is used in "Beauty," *W*, VI, 282.
    [6] Alek Therien was the French-Canadian woodchopper described by Thoreau
in chapter 6 of *Walden*.
    [7] "Exodus . . . *VO* 17" and "That is . . . *VO* 17" are struck through in ink
with single diagonal use marks. "Newgate . . . Tribune" and "That is . . . face,
&c." are used in "Works and Days," *W*, VII, 165 and 177.

Mystic goes drest in jewels.

———

The Everlasting New which reigns in Nature & hangs the same roses on our bushes which charmed the Roman & Chaldaan. *WA* 274

———

⟨Therien⟩ Osric great in present time   [K 19]

———

A ⟨conclusi peroration. WA 272⟩

———

I value myself as I do the duty of the remote day. *DO* 192

———

Men are a ⟨near⟩ ↑far↓sighted people. We can see well into the Dark Ages; guess into the Future; but what is rolled & muffled in impenetrable ⟨clouds⟩ ↑folds↓, is Today.
Life a carnival. Nobody drops his domino. *S* 115
Hurry is for slaves.[8]

[5] Eternal beings only have a real existence.[9]

> This ↑shining↓ hour is an edifice
> Which the Omnipotent cannot rebuild [10]

———

> They sing enow who life blood have
> [Channing, "To the Muse," l. 30]

I owe to Genius always the same debt of lifting the curtain from the Common, & showing me that gods are sitting disguised in this seeming gang of gypsies & pedlers.[11]

———

[8] "Mystic . . . jewels." and "The Everlasting . . . Chaldaan." are struck through in ink with single diagonal use marks; "The Everlasting . . . Chaldaan.", struck through in pencil with a vertical use mark and in ink with four vertical use marks, is used in "Works and Days," *W*, VII, 174. "Life . . . domino." is used in "Illusions," *W*, VI, 312–313. For "Hurry is for slaves.", see p. [197] below.

[9] See Journal SO, p. [84] above.

[10] These two lines are used in "Fragments on Nature and Life," V, *W*, IX, 350. See Journal VO, p. [15] above.

[11] This sentence, struck through in ink with a diagonal use mark, is used in "Powers and Laws of Thought," *W*, XII, 43.

Use of history to give value to the present hour [12]

———

Age of Ages

———

The doses of heaven are homoeopathic. VO 164
Thought like the weather; take it as it comes. *GH* 47 or 97 [actually 47]

———

Alfred, *NO* 224   Niewenheis, *NO* 229

———

Pis aller S 283 [13]
We in them not they in us.[14] O 247

Infra Pass to p 41

[6]   *Loci*
Quotation. *Index* p. 293
Surfaces & Leasts   *SO* 24, *S* 181,
Rhetoric
Hafiz
Faraday, Carnot, Arago   *VO* 148,
Practical   *SO* 293   *VO* 266
Questions, Wafthrudnir   *SO* 174

———

Melioration

———

Dreams   & Demonology, Infra 223,

———

Greatness

———

Sensibility   impressionability. *AC* 47

———

[12] This entry, struck through in ink with a diagonal use mark, is used in "Works and Days," *W*, VII, 177.

[13] The entry in Notebook S (Salvage), p. [283], reads "Do not imagine that I should work for the future, if my services were accepted or acceptable in the present. Immortality, as you call it, is my *pis aller*."

[14] This sentence is used in "Inspiration," *W*, VIII, 279.

Classic & Romantic. *SO* 74   *VO* 254, *AC* 59 [15]

——

[7]   *Powers of the Mind.*
    A stern enumeration will find few thoughts. All that is known
of love or memory is soon told; and hardly Goethe, Coleridge, or
Alcott will have added more than one observation apiece.

——

the false alarm   *VO* 261
Æsculapian   NO 249   *TO* 210
    &
Anaesthetic   IT 61 ↑or 68 or 60↓ VO 40 ⟨T⟩

——

The new audience   TO 220 [16]

——

Few astronomical hours, & few metaphysical:
Also few stars, and few thoughts.   *VO* 132 256

——

A thought would destroy most persons[.] [17]

[8]   ↑Powers of the Mind.↓
    Excellence of this subject that 'tis always fit, & that every fact
is pure value. Even if our theory be wrong, thoughts are things that
require no system to make them pertinent, but they make everything
else impertinent. See of ↑key to↓ Montaigne, *TO* 134

——

Power of opinion. *SO* 31

——

Feats

——

Sympathy

——

[15] ", *AC* 59" is in pencil.
[16] "or 68 or 60" and "The new . . . TO 220" and the rules above and below
it are in pencil. "A stern . . . or 60" is struck through in ink with a diagonal use
mark.
[17] "Few astronomical . . . persons" is struck through in ink with a diagonal
use mark.

Moral foundation

———

Who has found the boundary of human intelligence? [18]

———

[9] When the vesper-bell rings the warrior drops his sword, the smith his hammer, the child his toys, & ↑all↓ compose themselves to prayer.

⟨H⟩The ↑philosopher↓ would gladly devote himself to such a god. NO 246

———

New Olympian games   VO 276

———

Metaphysics owes little to the French mind, or to the ⟨Metaphysician⟩ professional metaphysician.

———

A man is taxed for his poll.

———

You cannot think too highly of a man.
Every step of science, of material art, has its echo, reason, & cause in the mind itself.

———

"My greatest discovery was ↑Michael↓ Faraday." ↑Sir H. Davy.↓ [19]

———

[10] The reliance on simple perception constitutes genius & heroism. And that is the religion before us.

———

A belief in its thoughts, 'tis this which the age lacks.

———

Originality. AC 64 [20]

———

[18] "Excellence . . . SO 31", "Sympathy", and "Who has . . . intelligence?" are struck through in ink with single diagonal use marks.

[19] "Metaphysics . . . metaphysician.", "A man . . . man.", and " 'My greatest . . . Davy." are struck through in ink with single diagonal use marks. " 'My greatest . . . Davy." is used in "Greatness," W, VIII, 306; see JMN, IX, 179. See p. [57] below.

[20] "& heroism . . . AC 64" is struck through in ink with two diagonal use marks.

One is made of porcelain, & the other of putty.

[11] *Cid.*
God how joyful was my Cid with the fleecy beard! [21]
        [Robert Southey, *Chronicle of the Cid*, 1846, p. 155]
"Glad was the Cid; never had he such joy; for tidings were come to him of what he loved best." [*Ibid.*, p. 254]
"Hear what he sat↓d who was born in happy hour—" [*ibid.*, p. 255]
He replies to the herald, "Tell him ↑that↓ I am not a man to be besieged." [*Ibid.*, p. 280]
He gave a feast, & "so well did he prepare for them, that all were joyful, & agreed in one thing, that they had not eaten better ⟨in⟩for three years." [22] [*Ibid.*, p. 269]
               Cid. see p. 242

[12] Use of life is to learn metonomy[.]
All thought is analogizing[.]

Wholes & details
NO 262, 269.
Truth = gravitation. *TO* 102 [23]

"If, however, as we maintain, all the intellectual faculties are likewise senses, & if their objects are real outward ↑like those of the visible world↓" —
IT 5   ↑Wilkinson Preface to Swedenborg p. 6 —↓

[13]   *Natural Method*
                TO 293

    Battery   *DO*

1. Identity,
      ———
      ↑Science of wholes & of particulars↓
      ———

2. Bipolarity, Centrality or Gravitation
          Centrifugence

[21] This quotation is used in "Old Age," *W*, VII, 322.
[22] This quotation is used in "Clubs," *W*, VII, 248.
[23] "Wholes . . . *TO* 102" is in pencil.

3. Circulation, or conversation
    Metamorphosis, or realization or incarnation
        All truth rushes to act   TO 105

    Sex, in creation & apprehension
        in croisement
    Hunger, or curiosity
    Eating, or perceiving
    Digesting, or assimilating or using
    Gestation in detachment.   parturition   *IT* 76
    Hybernation
    Gravitation   RS 234
    Contagion. Superinduction [24] *IT* ⟨2⟩ 74

    [14] The fermentations go on. *TO* 30

Balance of knowing & expression. Air is kept vital by circulation; water is, & blood. Kvasir choked with his own wisdom. *TO* 22

    Will & idea are man & woman. *TO* 57

    Metaphysics the transcendency of physics.
    All thought analogizes.

———

"Analogy is identity of ratio, the most beautiful of all bonds."
                                            in Timaeus

Iterations or rhymes in Nature are an idea of science & a guide. IT 62

———

Symbolism of nature is thus explained, because the mental series exactly tallies with the material series.
                        &c &c   *IT 62* [25]

[24] "Contagion." and "Superinduction" are struck through in pencil with single diagonal use marks.

[25] On p. [14] "The fermentations . . . *TO* 30", "Metaphysics . . . analogizes.", " 'Analogy . . . bonds.' ", and "Symbolism . . . &c &c" are struck through in pencil with single diagonal use marks. " 'Analogy . . . bonds.' " is probably a paraphrase of a passage in *The Works of Plato* . . . , trans. Floyer Sydenham and Thomas Taylor, 5 vols. (London, 1804), II, 479–480; this work is in Emerson's library. See *JMN*, XIII, 5.

[15] Every new perception attended with a thrill of pleasure.

TO 202

M. was a vigorous cock let into the coop of a farmhouse.

TU 127

Every atom displaces every other atom; every ⟨sphere⟩soul unspheres every other soul. *CO* 208.

———

These spiritual crises are periods of as certain recurrence, in some form, to every mind, as are dentition & puberty. C 134

All natural functions attended by their own pleasure[:] so are metaphysical; classification, imagination, memory[.] [26] TO 238

[16] [27] Life in the animal is one, but has many functions[.] & the intel[lectual]. power now reasons, now follows the proteus, now remembers.

[17] Van Mons and his pear in state of melioration; to be liquid & plastic; that our reading or doing or knowing should react on us,— that is all in all. See *VO* 70

Wisdom consists in keeping the soul liquid; in resisting the tendency to too rapid petrifaction.[28]

———

NO 86

———

As caloric to matter so is love to mind[.]

Identity. Napoleon sees the same law running through all things. "⟨w⟩Whatever they tell you, believe that one fights with cannon as with fists." *SO* 26 I find it easy to translate all his technics into all of

[26] "Every new . . . pleasure.", "These spiritual . . . puberty.", and "All natural . . . memory" are struck through in pencil with single diagonal use marks. "Every new . . . pleasure." is used in "Clubs," *W*, VII, 227.

[27] The entries on p. [16] are in pencil.

[28] See *JMN*, IX, 322.

mine, & Carnot's & Maupertuis' & laws of architecture. So it is that every *nat*[ural]. law is a moral law[.] [29]

[18] all diff↑erence↓. is quantitative

Highest val↑ue↓ of nat[ural]. Hist[ory]   *TO* 6

The fermentations go on. *TO* 30   37   38
οι ρεουτες [30]
porosity
Kvasir choked. TO 22
Nature a kind of adulterated reason.

↑Newton↓
To know is to re-know. Newton used less, & not more will: 'tis to lie parallel to the currents of nature. ⟨TO⟩ *IT* 49
vegetation   IT 49
How advance of nat[ural]. science is to help. *TO* 235
How gravity reaches up into the sacred soul   *TU* 138 [31]

[19]   ⟨Imagination⟩
⟨Hafiz⟩
The doctrine of metamorphosis a fruitful aperçu.

Mask of nature is variety: our education is through surfaces & partit↑c↓ulars; & multitudes remain in the babe or animal state, & never see or know more: but in the measure in which there is wit, we learn that we are alike; that a fundamental unity or agreement

[29] "*Identity*. . . . moral law" is struck through in pencil with one vertical and two diagonal use marks. " ⟨w⟩Whatever . . . fists.' " is quoted from *The Confidential Correspondence* . . . , 1856, I, 121. " ⟨w⟩Whatever . . . mine," is used in "Greatness," *W*, VIII, 314.

[30] Cf. Plato, *Theaetetus*, 181A (τοὺς ῥέοντας), an allusion to Heraclitus and his followers. The phrase is rendered as "the flowing philosophers" by Thomas Taylor in *The Works of Plato* . . . , 1804, IV, 56. See *JMN*, XIII, 98, 387, and 408.

[31] On p. [18], "Highest value . . . TO 6" and "How advance . . . TU 138" are struck through in pencil with single diagonal use marks; "To know . . . ⟨TO⟩ *IT* 49" is struck through in pencil with two diagonal use marks. The "erence" in "difference" and "ue" in "value" are added in pencil, perhaps by Emerson.

exists, without which there could be neither marriage, nor politics, nor literature, nor science.[32]

[20] We are born with an indestructible conviction that the reason why our fellow does not think as we do, is, because of some fraud he practises on himself. He holds up his milk. He checks the flow of his opinion. Yes, & we look in his eye, & see that he ⟨thinks so⟩ ↑knows it↓ too, & hides his eye: there is mud at the bottom of his eye.

Well, when we have recognized this unity of men we find the correspondence of man to nature.[33]

[21] p. 111   Michel Angelo ⟨sonnette⟩ ↑madrigal 51↓
        Alas, Alas, that I am betrayed
        By my flying days, ⟨it⟩ ↑it is↓ then the looking glass,
        Not the mind, if self love do not tarnish it
        Alas that he who foolish frets in desire
        Not heeding the flying time
        Finds himself, like me, at one ⟨point⟩ ↑instant↓, old.
        Nor know I how to repent, nor do I make myself ready,
        Nor advise myself with death at the door.
            Enemy of myself
        Vainly I pour out plaints & sighs
        Since there is no harm equal to lost time

---

p 112 follows a better form of the same
        Wo is me woe's me when I think
        Of my spent years I find not one
        Among so many days; not one was mine.
        Hopes which betrayed me, vain longing,
[22]   Tears, love, fiery glow, & sigh,

[32] This paragraph is struck through in ink with a diagonal use mark.
[33] "conviction that . . . nature.", struck through in pencil with a diagonal use mark, is used in "Clubs," W, VII, 234.

> For not one mortal affection is longer new to me *
> Held me fast, & now, I know it, & learn it,[34]
> And from goodness & truth ever severed,
> Go I forth, from day to day, further;
> Ever the shadows grow longer; ever deeper
> Sinks for me the sun;
> And I am ready to fall infirm & ⟨worn⟩ out↑worn."↓

Michel Angelo's Poems
   p. 112 [35]

[23] *Michel Angelo.*

> "The best artist has not any conception
> Which one ⟨single⟩ ↑block of↓ marble does not contain
> Within its surface, ⟨and⟩ ↑yet↓ alone arrives at this
> The hand which obeys the ⟨intellect⟩ ↑mind↓.
>
> ↑So lurks↓ ⟨The ⟨evil⟩ ↑ill↓ I shun, & the good I ⟨propose
>   to myself⟩ ↑seek↓⟩
> In thee, O lovely, proud, & divine dame!
> ⟨So conceals itself,⟩ ↑The ill I shun, the good I follow,↓
>   &, because I no longer live,
> I find my art fail of the desired /effect/attainment/.
>
> Not love, ⟨therefore⟩ ↑then↓, nor thy beauty,
> Nor fortune, nor cruelty, must bear the blame
> Of my harm, nor my destiny, nor lot,

* Grimm's translation runs

> "New to me is not↑hing↓ ⟨one⟩ which /blinds/dazzles/
>   beguiles/ men,"

---

[34] Emerson enclosed the footnoted line and the line following it in parentheses. His footnote translates Herman Friedrich Grimm, *Essays* (Hannover, 1859), p. 250; this book is in Emerson's library.

[35] The entries on pp. [21] and [22] are Emerson's translations of Michelangelo's Madrigale LI and LII from *Rime di Michelangelo Buonarroti il vecchio . . .* (Paris, 1821); this book is in Emerson's library. "p. 111 . . . the same" on p. [21] is in pencil, and "51" is partially encircled in pencil.

If within thy heart, thou bearest ⟨at once⟩ ↑both↓
Death & pity, & ⟨that⟩ my low genius
Knows not (burning there) to draw thence aught but
    death."

[24]   The best artist has never a conception
Which a block of marble does not contain
Within its surface, yet ⟨arrives at this⟩ ↑can find it there↓
⟨Alone⟩Only the ↑unerring↓ hand which strictly serves the
    mind

So lurks in thee, ⟨dame,⟩ /lovely,/fair//proud,/divine,/
    heavenly dame/
The ill I shun, the good I ⟨seek⟩ claim
And because I no longer am ⟨rightly⟩ ↑well↓ alive
I find my art ⟨failing of the desired attainment⟩ ↑miss that
    for which I strive↓

Not love then nor thy beauty
Nor fortune nor cruelty nor great disdain
Nor destiny nor fate must bear the blame of my pain

If ↑whilst↓ within thy heart thou bear⟨est⟩
Both death & pity, my low genius
Has no skill (with all its fire) to draw thence aught but
    death,
Cannot carve out the life but death alone [36]

[25]   Affirmative.
Negro & Negro holder are of one class, and, like animal & vegetable,
feed on each other. What one eats robs the rest; they are mutually
destructive: but thought & virtue help, and science & genius would
serve all[.] *DO* 116

---

[36] The entries on pp. [23] and [24] and [28] and [29] are versions of Emerson's translation of Sonetto I, *Rime di Michelangelo Buonarroti* . . . , 1821, p. 3. The version on p. [29] is struck through in ink with a discontinuous vertical use mark; cf. "Sonnet of Michel Angelo Buonarotti," *W*, IX, 298.

affirmative in pictures. *DO* 1
Don't discourage young people   *DO* 179
"Think on living"   *DO* 1,

———

Vulgar people show great acuteness in stating objections.

———

Spin some yards of helpful twine, — no ragbag gay —

———

[26] Nature does not like Criticism. Covers up the skeleton. *VO* 219

———

Always the weeping Church

———

To answer a question so as to admit of no reply, is the test of a ⟨master,⟩ man; — to touch bottom every time.[37]

———

[27] "Avec un grand génie, il faut une grande volonté." [38]
                    [Lanfrey, *L'Eglise et les philosophes* . . . , 1855, p. 53]

———

And Mirabeau said to Lafayette "You must marry me;" "My impulsion is necessary to your virtue." [39]

———

[28]   ↑*Michel Angelo, Sonnet I.*↓

       The ⟨artist⟩ ↑sculptor↓ never dreamed a form
       Which the marble does not hold
       In its white block, yet that shall find
       Only the unerring hand ⟨which strictly serves the mind⟩
         ↑& bold↓
       Which strictly serves the mind.

       So lurk⟨s⟩ in thee, fair, proud, & heavenly dame!
       The ill I shun, the good I claim,

[37] Cf. "He that can define, he that can answer a question so as to admit of no further answer, is the best man." "Clubs," *W*, VII, 235.
[38] See Journal SO, p. [193] above.
[39] Quoted in Sainte-Beuve, *Causeries du Lundi,* 1851–1862, IV, 86. See *JMN,* XIII, 275.

I, alas! no more alive
Miss the aim whereto I strive.

Not love, ⟨then⟩ nor beauty's ⁿ pride,
Nor fortune, nor thy coldness, can I chide,
If, whilst within thy heart abide
Both death & pity, my unequal skill
Cannot carve out the life, but death & ill.

[29]   The ⟨best⟩ artist ⟨has never a design⟩ ↑never dreamed a
            form↓
Which ↑the↓ marble ⟨block⟩ d⟨id⟩oes not ⟨contain⟩ ↑hold↓
In its white block, yet can it find
Therein
Only the unerring hand which strictly serves the mind

So lurks in thee, fair, proud, & heavenly dame,
The ill I shun, the good I claim,
⟨And for that I⟩ ↑I alas↓ no more ⟨am well⟩ alive
⟨I see my art⟩ Miss ⁿ ⟨that for which⟩ ↑the aim whereto↓
            I strive.

Not love, then, nor thy ⟨grace⟩ pride
Nor fortune nor thy coldness or disdain
Nor fate ⟨must bear the blame of this my pain⟩ ↑can I
            chide↓
If, whilst within thy heart abide
Both death & pity, this low skill of mine
Cannot carve out the life, but death ⟨alone⟩ ↑& ill & bane↓

[30] To M[argaret]. P. F↑orbes↓.
        I send you back "Counterparts," a talismanic book, full
of secrets guarded so well that no profaner eye can read. For the
gem will, I doubt not, be taken by most for a dull pebble, whilst you
are sure you have seen it shoot rays of green, blue, & rosy fire. I
don't know when a novel has contained so many searching glances
into the house of life, & given the reader this [31] joy of sincere

conversation rightly made the culmination of interest. Genius always treats us well, & we are not turned rudely out of doors at the end of the story, by a prosperity exclusively the hero's, but are delighted to find he means *us*. What a discovery to know there is an Author of "Counterparts" hidden among these slow British people! Send to Caroline T[appan]. to meet you at an Evening with the Author of "C↑ounterparts,"↓ⁿ in London. — Feb. 14, 1859.[40]

[32] Memory should be tenacious   bite
                              accessible   choice
                                                                  pace
                                                               logic [41]

Michel's answer to G. Strozzi pocms p 136
            Sweet to me is sleep; sweeter, to be stone,
            Whilst wrong & shame ⟨endure⟩ ↑⟨spread⟩ live & grow,↓
            Not to see, not to feel is ⟨great gain⟩ ↑boon↓
            ⟨Therefore,⟩ ↑Hence,↓ not to wake me, pray speak low! [42]

            Sweet is sleep — Ah sweeter, to be stone,
            Whilst wrong & shame exist & grow;
            Not to see, not to feel, is boon,
            Then not to wake me, pray speak low!

[33]   Memory
Foundations of Nineveh.[43] VO 196

Why is memory cold   *VO* 214
             bitter   *VO* 119

———

[40] Margaret P. Forbes was the sister of John Murray Forbes. For *Counterparts; or, The cross of love*, 1854, by Elizabeth Sara Sheppard, see Journal SO, p. [119] above.

[41] "bite   choice   pace   logic" is struck through in pencil with a wavy diagonal use mark.

[42] These four lines, struck through in ink with a diagonal use mark, are Emerson's translation of the "Riposta, In Persona della Notte," *Rime di Michelangelo Buonarroti* . . . , 1821.

[43] This entry is struck through in pencil with three wavy diagonal use marks.

Yes, & drive the nail this week, & clinch it the next, ⟨&⟩ ↑drive it↓ this year, & clinch it the next.[44]

———

Our Ninevite thoughts which are made up of older. *VO* 196, 243.

————

———

↑*Good of evil*↓
'Tis curious that sickness & hurtful accidents should sometimes exalt certain mental powers, as memory, fancy, &c.

[34] Bite or tenacity of certain minds.   *O* 3⟨2⟩5, 52.
Power & necessity of repeating itself which belongs to every mind. A man can write but one book: the courage which comes from having done the thing before. —

———

Lysimachus

———

            Memory is alive, & has a will of its own[.]

[35] The past will not sleep: it works still. With every new fact &c. IT 13 [45]

It seems as if all had the ⟨same⟩ power, but great difference in ⟨pace⟩ degree. One ↑who↓ remembers a little more than I, with equal opportunity, is a prodigy to me. Then difference in pace makes a miracle not less. But the high difference is, in ⟨q⟩the quality of association by which ⟨he⟩ ↑each↓ remembers, whether by puns, or by principles.[46] The moment I discover that this man observes & recalls [36] ⟨by cause & effect, &⟩ not by yellow string or a knot in his handkerchief or Gray's Mnemonics, but ↑by cause & effect,↓ by the axis of the globe, or the axis of nature, every word of his represents the harmony of the Kosmos, and I am as in the presence of Jove.

[44] This sentence, enclosed in penciled square brackets, is used in "Memory," *W*, XII, 107. See Journal VO, p. [81] above.
    [45] This entry is struck through in ink with three diagonal use marks.
    [46] This sentence is used in "Memory," *W*, XII, 96.

[37]   Individualism
The populace give the gods their egotism   *VO* 274

——

Subjectiveness

——

Miscellany is as bad as drunkenness.

——

"Every man who stamps his personality on his life is the true, free, & brave man." [47]

[38] [blank]
[39] Pace
            We call ourselves fast men[.]
            Nature too is faster than she was[.]

        Auguste Laugel   Rev[ue]. des deux
                            Mondes, 1 Sept., 1857.
Agassiz discovered "the coincidence between the embryonic development of beings, & the gradation which is wrought from age to age in organic forms." [48]

[40] [blank]
[41]   Works & Days (continued from p. 5)

——

Strychnine cannot compare with time [49]   DO 169

——

Osman   F 37

——

---

[47] This quotation is struck through in pencil with a wavy diagonal use mark; see p. [59] below. For "Miscellany . . . drunkenness.", see Journal VO, p. [251] above.

[48] A vertical line separates "Auguste Laugel" from "Rev. des . . . 1857." "Agassiz . . . forms." is written in ink over the same matter in erased pencil. Emerson translates this sentence from Auguste Laugel, "Un Naturaliste, M. Agassiz et ses Travaux," *Revue des Deux Mondes*, Sept. 1, 1857, pp. 94–95. See Journal VO, p. [11] above. "Pace . . . 1857." is in pencil: "s'est operée" in erased pencil appears above "is wrought".

[49] This sentence, struck through in ink with a vertical use mark, is used in "Old Age," *W*, VII, 319.

"The day is immeasureably long to him who knows how to value & use it,"
Goethe [50]

[42] [blank]
[43]   ⟨Generalization⟩ [51]
Generalization   *HO* 189

[44]   Latter Day Pamphlet
                                                Jesuitism

To T[homas]. C[arlyle]. 1854
                        It required courage & conditions that
feuilletonists are not the persons to name or qualify this writing
Rabelais in 1850. And to do this alone! You must even choose your
tune to suit yourself. We must let Arctic navigators & deep sea divers
wear what astonishing coats, & eat what meats, wheat or whale, they
like, without criticism —
[45] "You would come to America, when Frederic was disposed of."
Speed to Frederic, then. America is growing furiously, towns on
towns, states on states, & the cities, & wealth which is always interesting, — for from wealth power cannot be divorced, — is piled in
architectural mountains. California↑n↓ quartz mountains dumped
down in New York, to be repiled architecturally along shore from
Canada to Cuba, & thence westward to California again. Come & see.
John Bull interests you at home, & is all your subject. Come & see the
Jonathanization of John[.] [52]

[46] [blank]
[47]   Miscellany
        Impressionability

                "the sky seemed not a sky ↑of earth↓
        and with what motion moved the clouds"
                    [Wordsworth, *The Prelude*, I, 338–339]

[50] Quoted in Sarah Austin, *Characteristics of Goethe: from the German of Falk,
von Müller, etc.*, 3 vols. (London, 1833), II, 297. See *JMN*, VI, 386.

[51] The heading "Generalization", in pencil, is canceled in pencil.

[52] The entry on pp. [44] and [45] is an excerpt from a letter to Carlyle, March
11, 1854, where "Jesuitism," one of Carlyle's *Latter Day Pamphlets*, is mentioned
(*CEC*, pp. 497–499). "furiously, towns . . . California again.", on p. [45], is
struck through in ink with two vertical use marks. The dashes after "interesting," and
"divorced," are in pencil.

"a light that never was on sea or land"

_____

"the houses were in the air, any grey night — " [n]

_____

made the "surface of the earth work like a sea" — See "Prelude" [I, 473–475] p. 22 [53]

When the mountains begin to dislimn, we are in a high state.

_____

↑T[homas].↓ T[readwell]. Stone did not find Wordsworth's Ode true to him: he was more impressionable as he grew older.[54] *VO* 250

_____

immense porosity

_____

See [Notebook] M[ary] M[oody] E[merson] II p.

[48]   Miscellany

          _____

↑*Object & Subject*↓

_____

↑*What object?*↓

My sheriff ought not to be forgotten down in Maine, who had ↑once↓ tasted a cordial, ↑but did not know the name of it,↓ at some hotel in New York, many years before, & had been tasting liquors at all places in all the United States ↑ever since↓ in the faint hope that he might yet cry *Eureka*, it is the same.

_____

immense porosity

_____

[49]   *Miscellany.*
          _____

Introduction to "Works & Days."
The Union already old. *VO* 275

_____

[53] William Wordsworth, *The Prelude; or, Growth of a Poet's Mind* (New York, 1850); in Emerson's library. Emerson quotes " 'a light . . . land' ", l. 15 of Wordsworth's "Elegiac Stanzas Suggested by a Picture of Peele Castle in a Storm," in "Beauty," *W*, VI, 303. "Miscellany" and "of earth" are in pencil, and quotation marks and comma are added to " 'the houses . . . night — ' " in pencil.
[54] This sentence is used in "Success," *W*, VII, 299.

When the Right gets an advantage, 'tis by the fault of the Malignants.
VO 270 [55]

I read that
We are marked by abundance of crimes, & of great inventions. We are ashamed ↑on account of the↑se↓ ⟨one⟩↓ to be men; ⟨by the one⟩ and proud to be born at this time, ⟨by the other⟩ ↑on account of those↓[.]
Every great invention finds the means ready to carry it out. Thus when ⟨galvanic battery⟩ ↑electric telegraph↓ is ready, guttapercha is found.
When commerce is vastly enlarged, California & Australia yield gold. Telegraph & railroad suit America[.] [56]
                              ↑Printed in "Works & Days"↓

[50] When Europe is overcrowded, America[,] California open, & a corn chamber is found in the west.[57]

But every stride of science or of use⟨s⟩ful arts has its echo, its reason, or its cause, in the mind itself. Every victory won from nature should impart to man new feeling of worth.

But now the man does not look greater for its arts, but little; & one wonders where the arts come from, in which this little huckster fusses about so complacently. No equal poetry celebrates them.[58] And, as I said, the greatness of centuries [51]* is born of the paltriness of the

---

[55] "The Union . . . VO 275" and "When the . . . VO 270" are enclosed in penciled square brackets.
    [56] "We are marked . . . to be men;" is struck through in pencil with a diagonal use mark; "Every great . . . America" is struck through in pencil with a wavy, discontinuous diagonal use mark; "Thus when . . . America" is struck through in ink with three diagonal use marks. "Every great . . . gold." is used in "Works and Days," W, VII, 161.
    [57] This sentence, struck through in ink with two diagonal use marks, is used in "Works and Days," W, VII, 161.
    [58] Two discontinuous parallel vertical pencil lines in the left margin mark "& one . . . celebrates them."

hours, so the greatness of arts stands now in contrast with the pettiness of the men.↑* The greatest meliorator is Trade.↓ [59]

We have not a religious reference to thought. We are absurdly historical. ⟨See our squabbles in Congress.⟩ When an outrage is charged on human rights, instead of instant redress, the government answers, "the form in which ⟨you⟩ the wrong alleged was done, was strictly routinary; and the manner in which you propose to redress it is ⟨unusual;⟩ ↑not;↓ and it would be so dreadful to have an [52] unaccustomed statute." [n]

Better endure tyranny according to law a thousand years, than irregular & unconstitutional happiness for a day. ⟨I⟩One thinks of the patient who charmed the physician by the frightful detail of symptoms. "My dear sir," exclaimed the Doctor, at last, "↑let me embrace you;↓ do you know you have a malady which has long been supposed to have become extinct."

Want of reference to thought[:] I ⟨stand in a street in which⟩ ↑dreamed I stood in [a] city of↓ beheaded men, ⟨walk about⟩ where the decapitated trunks continued to walk about.[60]

> [53] *A belief in its thoughts, 'tis this which the age lacks.*
> ↑*Whig*↓

                                        ↑Of course he had rather↓
⟨Better⟩ ↑⟨forgetful of the first principles of politeness, forgetful that it is better to⟩↓ ⟨be slain by a regular⟩ ↑die in the hands of a↓ physician, than to be cured by a quack.

↑*Printed in "Works & Days." see p. 149↓

[59] Both asterisks on p. [51] refer to the same footnote at the bottom of p. [51]. "is born . . . paltriness of the" is struck through in ink with four diagonal use marks; "The greatest . . . Trade." is struck through in pencil with a diagonal use mark and in ink with five diagonal use marks and marked with two parallel vertical lines in the left margin. "the greatness [p. [50]] . . . Trade." is used in "Works and Days," *W*, VII, 166.

[60] Two vertical pencil lines in the left margin mark "Better endure . . . . a day." "in which" and "walk about" are canceled in pencil as well as in ink, and the comma after "men" is added in pencil. For the source of " 'My dear sir,' . . . extinct.' ", see *JMN*, XIII, 457.

Franklin said, "Go home, & tell the Americans to get children as fast as possible." [61]

[54] Thos[e] poor benighted fellows in Kansas, how entirely they mistake the question! they ⟨a⟩complaining of the wrong, when the gov[ernmen]t shows them plainly that the forms ⟨were⟩ of law were observed. "But it was the Missourians that voted, & not we." — "What of that? here is the certificate signed by the Assessor." — "But they will kill me if I vote." — "What of that? here is the seal." — "But they ⟨invented the names &⟩ forged the [55] votes, & invented the names of voters." "What of that? here is signature & countersign as the law directs."

Those ⟨wr⟩ benighted Kansas men who wish to be unconstitutionally happy & free.
deaf to the assurances of the gov[ernmen]t that all their rights have been taken away by the strictest forms of law.

[56] [blank]
[57]   Miscellany.

"My greatest discovery was the discovery of Michael Faraday."
                                        Davy. [62]

"Sirs & Mesdames," said the Englishman to the spirits, "you are welcome to your specialty, but I must insist on mine. It is not the habit of my countrymen nor of myself, to talk with any person to whom I have not been properly introduced."

——   Pseudospirit

See the story of Mr Osborn. *HO* 49

[58] [blank]

[61] "*A belief* . . . *lacks.*" is struck through in ink with a diagonal use mark. "⟨Better⟩ ⟨forgetful . . . possible.'⟩" is enclosed in penciled square brackets.
[62] " 'My greatest . . . Davy.'" is struck through in ink with a diagonal use mark. See p. [9] above.

[59]   Miscellany
Classic & Romantic
     Dumas, when he begins his story, does not know ⟨where⟩ ↑how↓ it is to end. Our politics are of the same hand-to-mouth kind, not of great necessity, but of small expedients.

Of *Zweck*, see the *Atlantis*, Feb. 1857. p. 144
See *VO* p. 254

"The freedom of man consists herein, that he is his own aim."

"Every man who stamps his personality on his life is the true, natural, & free man." [63]

[60] [blank]
[61]   *Miscellany.*
The sublime fact, that the State is older than any particular states.
                    Atlantis, May 1856 [64]
"Human rights," says Atlantis, "are as the human type itself. Ever the same, as we see in ⟨Gree⟩ Egyptian mummies & in Greek statues, it alters ever, but the alterations are ⟨for⟩ ever for its advantage."
He is free who owns himself.
"Smartness" is the only political ⟨property capacity⟩ ↑eigenschaft↓ of an American politician[.]
"The political incapacity of the German plainly showed itself in the last revolution⟨s⟩-years, ⟨in Europe⟩ and in Europe is become pro-[v]erbial[.]"
[62] In the world of thoughts there is no crime & no sorrow more
Goethe had *urkraftige Behagen*
"the circumstances of our social & civic life can be so fitted as to pro-

------

[63] The reference to Zweck concerns the article "Hat die Welt einen Zweck?", *Atlantis*, VI, ii, 136–144. See Journal VO, p. [34] above. The two quotations on p. [59] are Emerson's translations of sentences on p. 142 of this article. With " 'Every man . . . man.' ", cf. p. [37] above. For "Dumas, when . . . end", see Journal SO, p. [76] above.
     [64] The entries on pp. [61] and [62] are Emerson's translations of passages from "Mai-Betrachtungen," *Atlantis*, IV, v, 321–323. "In the world . . . more", p. [62], is struck through in ink with a diagonal use mark.

duce such a normal harmonious man as Goethe; and 'tis a proof
that man & society are not so bad as we sometimes think."
"Every poet is a credit to his environment & age therefore."

[63] ↑K[ing].↓ Frederick said of Voltaire, "He is good for
nothing but to ↑be↓ read." 'Tis the definition of the literary scamp.

"Without illusion is no poesy possible." says Atlantis.   p 389   May
                                                                    1856

[64]   Miscellany.
For the chapter on Quotation, much is to be said on the matter of
originality. We ⟨say⟩ have said all our life, whoever is original, I am
not. What have I that I have not received? Let every ⟨giver⟩ creditor
take his own, & what would be left? ⁿ 'Tis the sea again, which, ↑if
you stop all the rivers,↓ Amasis can drink up.
Yet this is true, & not true. Every man brings a certain difference of
angle to the identical picture which [65] makes all new.
But this makes originality, that the beholder of this particular knot
of things or thoughts has the habit of recurrence to Universal views.
The boy in the school or in the sitting room at home sits there
adorned with all the color, health, & power which the ⟨out door life⟩
day spent out of doors has lent him. The man interests in the same
way, not for what he does in our presence, at the table, or in his chair,
but for the authentic [66] tokens he gives us of powers in the landscape, over ships, railroads, cities, or other outdoor organizations.
The girl charms us with the distant contributions which she reconciles.
She has ⟨the air⟩ inherited the feature which manly joy & energy
↑of her ancestors↓ formed long ago, softened & masked under this
present beauty, & she brings the hint of the romance of fields &
forests & forest brooks, of the sunsets, [67] & music, & all-various
figures that deck it. A ⟨pale⟩ white invalid that sits in a chamber is
⟨bereft of attraction⟩ ↑good for nothing↓. To be isolated, is to be sick,
& so far dead. That is, ⟨our⟩ the life of the *All* must stream through
us, to make the man & the moment great. And the same ⟨thing⟩ ↑law↓
takes place in thought that the mind has gone out of its little parlor
⟨there⟩ into the great sky of Universal ⟨propositions⟩ truths, & has not

come back the same it went, but ennobled, [68] & with the necessity
of going back habitually to the same firmament ⟨& generosities⟩ &
importing its generosities into all its particular thought. He who
compares all his traditions with this eternal standard — He who
cannot be astonished by any tinsel or clap-trap or smartness or pop-
gun; for the immensities & eternities, from which he newly came, to
which he familiarly returns, have once for all put it out of [6⟨7⟩9]
his power to be surprised ⟨with⟩ ↑by↓ trifles: That man conveys the
same ecstasy in which he lives, in some degree, into every thing he
says; it is in his manners & ↑feeds↓ the root of his life. It is the magic
of nature, that the whole life of the universe concentrates itself on
⟨to⟩ its every point.[65]

[70]   Miscellany
Miscellany
"Ah, maam," said my dear old cook, the Genius of Abundance, whom my
baby↑-niece↓ appropriately christened Meat, — "And are there Protestants
who fast?" "Perfectly true, indeed." "Oh, ⟨&⟩and[n] did the martyrs go
through all they suffered, to leave us that?"
                                        Miss Cobb's "Ride" &c [65a]

[71]   Miscellany —
Men are mad with revivals in the churches. Whose fault is it? If you
talk with the gravest & best citizen, the moment the topic of religion
is broached, he loses his wits: he runs into a childish superstition. His
face looks infatuated. Men's faculties are torpid, & do not act on that
side. If you could make them feel that th⟨at⟩is also was most properly
the domain [72] of reflection; that every one was ⟨so⟩ to act as for
the benefit of the public or Universal Man; that his welfare was
sacred; ⟨his⟩ injury to him was injury to the malefactor, — then [66]

[65] The entries on pp. [64]–[69] are struck through in ink with single diagonal
use marks on pp. [66], [67], [68], and [69]; "We ⟨say⟩ . . . which", p.
[64], is struck through in ink with a diagonal use mark, and p. [65] is struck
through in ink with two diagonal use marks in the form of an "x." "of her ancestors", p. [66], is in pencil overwritten in ink. "To be isolated . . . great.",
p. [67], is struck through in pencil with two vertical use marks.
[65a] Frances Power Cobbe (1822–1904), English writer and philanthropist, published numerous accounts of her travels. In Journal WA, p. [211], Emerson refers
to this quotation as "Story of Cook in Miss Cobb's 'Ride to Baalbec' ".
[66] This entry is marked by two parallel vertical pencil lines in the right margin

[73] The other thought was the revolution of society, that is promised in every meeting of men of thought. That state of mind in which they find themselves, those truths which are at once patent to them, condemn our customs & laws & people as irrational, & require new: show that we are living after customs whose root of thought has died out: point at a health so potent that all elements, all planets serve it, & [74] it has no need to ask succor for its flaggings from narcotics & alcohol; a health & perception to which the earth speaks & the heaven glows.

[75] The ⟨first⟩ ↑fundamental↓ fact is the correspondence of the human being to the world, ↑correspondence & impressionability[,]↓ so that every change in that writes a record on the mind.[67]

⟨Auburn⟩
Edward says, that Cicero was a postmaster who kept in with the strongest side.

[76] 'Tis very important in writing that you ⟨shou⟩ do not lose your presence of mind. Despair is no muse, & he who finds himself hurried, & gives up carrying his point this time, writes in vain. Goethe had the *"urkraftige behagen,"* [68] the stout comfortableness, the stomach for the fight, and you must.

[77] Correspondence ↑of the mind↓ to the world. ⟨of the mind⟩ Obedience of the mind to the laws. Vital obedience or sympathy. Then, in the Perfection of this correspondence or expressiveness, the health & force of man consists[.]
    Hence intellect is Aesculapian[.] [69]

---

on p. [71] and a single vertical pencil line in the left margin on p. [72]. "If you talk . . . infatuated." is struck through in pencil with two vertical use marks.
    [67] This sentence, struck through in ink with a discontinuous diagonal use mark, is used in "Success," *W*, VII, 300.
    [68] See p. [62] above. "Despair is no muse," is used in "Considerations by the Way," *W*, VI, 265.
    [69] "Correspondence . . . Aesculapian" is struck through in ink with a diagonal use mark; "Correspondence . . . consists", struck through in pencil with a vertical use mark, is used in "Success," *W*, VII, 300–301.

Greatness.

κινητικον aboriginal mover.[70] Great men are they that see that spiritual is greater than any material force; that thoughts rule the world.[71] But a thought which does not go to embody or externize itself, is no thought.

[78]   Reason or universality
He is original who is admitted to that.[72]
Conversation shows it   *TO* 277
And it derives from Morals. Or is conditioned or characterized thereby.

[79] Certain facts are very significant[:]
that the religions are obsolete, as shown in the fact that the reforms do not proceed from the churches, but the churches are church yards great interests are confided to fools: voluntary servitude in reading nations.
Society is revolutionized & a vast future promised ⟨in⟩ whenever two contemplative men meet. Do you suppose there is any doubt? ⁿ Every thought rushes to light, — rushes to body. That which cannot be externized is no thought.[73]

[80] An immense future is before us. We are so bad & know it. These forms & customs rattle so. A reform such as never was, — a revolution that shall ⟨h⟩leave no hypocrisy a crown[.]

[81]   *Miscellany*
The powers are four, ⟨Perception⟩ ↑Imagination↓ Reason — Perception,   ↑Memory.↓
First, there is an identity running through things, so that ↑the↓ one we look at, is only a variation of the last, & of the next. Each is equal ⟨to the other,⟩ &, ⟨if⟩ whatever organ or process you note in this, you

[70] See *JMN*, XI, 297.

[71] This sentence, enclosed in penciled square brackets, is used in "Progress of Culture," *W*, VIII, 229.

[72] "Reason . . . that." is struck through in pencil with a vertical use mark.

[73] "that the religions . . . but the churches" and "Society is . . . Every tho't" are each marked by two parallel vertical pencil lines in the left margin.

shall find its counterpart in that. If you take man, he has breathing, sight, organs for taking food, for digesting, expelling, locomotion, reproduction,   and if you take a muskrat, ⟨it⟩ you find their equivalents [82] breathing, locomotion, eating, expelling, protection from cold, house building, reproduction, & care of the young.
In short, 'tis only ⟨a⟩ man modified to live in a mud-hole,ⁿ a fish in like manner to swim in sea
and a mollusk[.]

Well, in this invisible ⟨ocean⟩ fine ocean where the mind of man inhabits, all these functions reappear,—every one of them subject to the same great laws of centrality or gravity and to centrifugence. Repose, self rest, possession, brooding on the one; & bipolarity; rest & flowing. [pulse or alternation, come & go, ebb & flow of power, easy transmiss[ion]. & reflect[ion].] *TO 238*]

[83] ↑7 vols. of latent heat to 1 patent; 7 silences to 1 word.↓
There is the same hunger for food. We call it ⟨now⟩ curiosity; there is the same need of seizing it: we call it perception, the same assimilation of the food to the eater: ↑↑We call it culture:↓ simple recipiency ↑is↓ the virtue of space, not of man.↓
The phenomena of sex reappear, as creation, in one mind, apprehension in the other. A powerful mind impresses itself on a whole nation of minds, as the male in some ⟨inferior⟩ species impregnates multitudes, & is the parent of innumerable posterity.
[84] What do you suppose is the census of the Aristotelian minds, or of the Platonists, ⟨or of the Cartesians,⟩ or of the followers of St Paul, ↑or of Des Cartes↓ or of Luther or of Voltaire? ⟨of Goethe?⟩ or Swedenborg, or Goethe? Nature loves to cross her stocks; [74] & does the ⟨e⟩ variety & blending of talents less appear in new minds that have been bred under Napoleon & under Goethe? IT 74

Composite minds. Like Burke? *B 31*

[85] Well, if the analogy of two great sexes animate the world, the gestation ↑or ⟨births⟩ bringing forth↓ of the mind is seen in the act of detachment.

[74] For "Nature loves . . . stocks;", see Journal VO, p. [211] above.

↑Life is incessant parturition[.]↓
Viviparous & oviparous minds.
Some minds choke from too much store, too little vent.
Some discharge ↑their activity↓ in volleys, & some need a siphon.
CO 278
⟨roots are⟩ Health is in the balance of the take & give; roots are made by trees best, when leaves & wood are made best.
⟨Life is incessant parturition⟩ [75]

[86] The *va et vient*, the ebb & flow, the pendulum, the alternation, the fits of easy transmission & reception, the pulsation, the undulation which seems to be a fundamental secret of nature[,] exists in intellect. Nature masks under ostentatious ⟨multitude of⟩ subdivision & manifold particulars the poverty of her ⟨principles⟩ elements, the rigid economy of her rules. [76]

[87] Now we say that as the differences are superficial between James & John, & the agreements like two leaves of a tree, so is it between a man & a planet that they also are leaves of a tree[:] all the parts & properties of one are in the other.
Then we add that as man & his planet are analogous, so the same laws which are found in these run up into the ⟨invisible world⟩ mind, chemistry, polarity, undulation, gravity, centrifugence,
and that hereby we acquire the key to these ⟨exceeding⟩ dark, skulking hide & seek, blindman's play of Thoughts, namely, by the

---

[75] The entries on pp. [81]–[85] are struck through in pencil with single diagonal use marks on pp. [84] and [85] and in pencil with two diagonal use marks on p. [83]. The entries on p. [81] are struck through in pencil with a wavy diagonal use mark; "you note . . . equivalents", p. [81], is struck through in pencil with a second wavy diagonal use mark. The entries on p. [82] are struck through in pencil with two wavy diagonal use marks. On p. [82], the first "t" in "in short, 'tis" is crossed in pencil and the apostrophe is added in pencil; the "t's" in "to the same great laws" are crossed in pencil; the comma in "come & go, ebb" is added in pencil; and "ion" is added in pencil to "transmiss." and "reflect" in a hand not Emerson's. "If you take [p. [81]] . . . a mollusk" and "Life is . . . oviparous minds.", p. [85], are used in "Powers and Laws of Thought," *W*, XII, 22, 18.

[76] "The *va* . . . intellect." is enclosed in pencil square brackets. The "*v*" in "*va*" is mended in pencil. "Nature masks . . . rules." is struck through in ink with a vertical use mark.

solar microscope of Analogy. 'Tis the key of the Universe[;] Nature shows ⟨all⟩ everything once, everything in great bodies somewhere. This distributes worlds[.] [77]

[88] I described to you the world of thought. The mystery is great. Who shall penetrate those caverns with thorolights? Who shall come in & plant instruments, & take the height of those stars? Who shall fix its solstice or its mid-summer? [78]

[89]   Imagination
⟨The⟩ ↑Often the best↓ gift to men is a new symbol. IT 63 [79]
The use of life is to learn metonomy[.]

[90]   Individual
Each man excellent in his own way by reason of not apprehending gift of another. You can't make any paint stick but your own[.] [80]

Self symmetry of L. da Vinci   *LO* 105

[91]   *Self-possession*
         Strength enters as the moral element enters. *NO* 53
As caloric to matter, so ↑is↓ love to the mind   *E* 175
Every principle a war note
Good will makes insight, as one finds his way to the sea, by embarking on a river (*J* 129) or uses the Cid's way of procuring swords[.] [81]
↑Let me show how the cards beat the players[.]↓

---

[77] The entry on p. [87] is struck through in ink with one vertical and one diagonal use mark.
[78] This paragraph is struck through in pencil with a wavy diagonal use mark; "I described . . . stars?" is struck through in pencil with one diagonal and three vertical use marks.
[79] "⟨The⟩ Often" is preceded by a penciled square bracket.
[80] "Each man . . . your own", struck through in pencil with five vertical and four wavy diagonal use marks, is used in "Powers and Laws of Thought," *W*, XII, 53.
[81] "or uses the Cid's way" is enclosed in pencil brackets; "As caloric . . . mind" and "Good will . . . river", struck through in pencil with single vertical use marks, are used in "Success," *W*, VII, 309. For the Cid's swords, see Journal VO, p. [6] above.

Art lies not in making object prominent but choosing the
prominent. ↑trachea↓
impossible to conceal your opinion
Should[n] ↑is↓ the genius of the /antique/classic/ drama; not *would*
↑of the Renaisance[.]↓

Fouché
    Should is the genius of the antique or classic drama; & *would*
    of the Rena⟨sis⟩isance.[82]

[92] No man passes for that with another as with self. TU 65

⟨Not⟩ This[n] would furnish, if he would obey its light, to each
the best telescope that could be offered for the study of the world.
The excess of this is monotones[.][n]
    The defect is dispersers[.]
        Miscellany is bad as drunkenness.[83]

Then soldiers who argue,
    Then ⟨Goddard⟩ Ball the swaggerer,
    Then Chigi the trifler,[84]

[93]   Conduct of intellect
Every toper knows the way to tavern   *TO* 57
What ebb & flow of power   60

Could you show me! *TO* 93,
    Love the day. Nature covers up her skeletons. *DO* 1
'Tis easy to discour↑a↓ge, but to help is hard   *DO* 179

[82] "*Should* . . . Renaisance" is paraphrased from Goethe, "Shakspeare und kein
Ende," *Werke*, 55 vols. (Stuttgart and Tübingen, 1822–1833), XLV, 45, 47. See
JMN, VI, 228. A vertical ink line in the left margin marks "Let me . . . not
would of the Renaisance"; "not *would* of the Renaisance" has an ink "x" above "not"
and pencil lines above, at right, and beneath it. For "Let me . . . players", see
JMN, VI, 94. For Fouché see p. [102] below.
  [83] "the defect . . . drunkenness." is struck through in ink with a vertical use
mark.
  [84] For Chigi, see *JMN*, XIII, 372.

What does he add? and, what state of mind does he leave me in?

TO 133 [85]

See how the good soul educates the youth of the universe. *TO* 150,
Live the Day & the Azure.
study for eternity   *TO* 92

[94] [blank]
[95]   I hold of the Maker not of the Made,
           I sit with the Cause ↑or↓ grim⟨ly⟩ or glad [86]

[96]   Diseases
Autobiography usurps the largest part & sometimes the whole of the
discourse of very worthy persons.[87]

[97]   Great is the mind
       Ah! if we knew how to use it! Ah ⟨if we⟩ could you show me in
every torpid hour how I could wake to full belief, & earnest labor.
⟨But see how we⟩ A man should know his way to his nectar. But see
how we use it, how the memory, how the mind,

I propose then to[n] ⟨give some hints for the⟩ draw from the mind
itself some lights for the ⟨mans⟩ rule of it even at the risk of repeating
old sayings[.]

[98] ↑1.↓ It must be by & through your individualism. Opinions
are organic. Every man who stamps his personality on his life is great
& free. 'Tis a wonderful instrument, a sympathy with the whole frame
of things. Write what you are.

Yet we do not believe our own thought. We import the religion of
other nations: we are tickled by names that have a glorious sound.

---

[85] "Love the . . . skeletons." is struck through in ink with a diagonal use
mark; "Tis easy . . . hard" and "What does . . . in?" are struck through in pencil
with single diagonal use marks.
      [86] These lines are used in "Fragments on the Poet and the Poetic Gift," XVII,
W, IX, 331.
      [87] This sentence is struck through in ink with a vertical use mark.

We quote our opinions. We dote on the distant & the old. ⟨We are bored⟩ We shun to be asked our opinion on a new man, — a new question. What, no [99] precedent? ⁿ — & the gravest courts in the country shrink to ⟨answer⟩ ↑decide↓ a new question. — What a calamity! & will wait for months & years for some ⟨precedent⟩ ↑case↓ to turn up that can be strained into a precedent, & throw on ⟨others the⟩ ↑a↓ bolder party the onus of an initiative. They do not carry a counsel in their breasts.

[100] It does not need to pump your brains, & force thought to think well. O no: right thought comes spontaneously; ⟨but⟩ it comes like the breath of the morning wind, comes daily, like our daily bread, to those who ⟨pray & those who wait on⟩ ↑love it & obey↓ it, itⁿ comes duly. When we wake, our thought is there waiting for us. Yes, but it comes to health & temperance & willingness to believe, [101] to those who use ⟨that⟩ ↑what↓ they have, and embody their thoughts in action.   ↑To shake off from our shoes the dust of Europe & Asia.↓

Whether I listen to the "lordly music flowing from the illimitable years" or whether I interrogate the future with the immense cravings of hope.[88]

[102]   *Self possession*

Pingo in aeternitatem.[89] *TO* 92

⟨Fouché & his poniards.[90] Sanctorius. Lord Coke⟩

---

[88] The entries on pp. [97]–[101] are struck through in pencil with single wavy diagonal use marks on pp. [98], [99], and [100]; "Ah! if . . . sayings", p. [97], is struck through in pencil with a wavy diagonal use mark. P. [99] is struck through in ink with a vertical use mark, as is "precedent? . . . decide". "to those . . . Asia.", p. [101], is used in "Theodore Parker," *W*, XI, 287. "Yet we . . . breasts.", pp. [98]–[99], and "To shake . . . Asia.", p. [101], are used in "Success," *W*, VII, 292. The page-wide rule on p. [101] is in pencil.
[89] "I paint for eternity": this quotation is used in "The Celebration of Intellect," *W*, XII, 131.
[90] See *JMN*, XI, 312, and "Culture," *W*, VI, 132.

⟨Love the day[.]   Washington & Kane⟩
———
Scholar teaches the dominion of substances & not of shows; we pass for what we are.

[103]   Immortality.
                 Space to fulfil our idea.
                 A love of life so disproportioned to particulars, points at immense reserves.

                 "eternal existence proved from my idea of activity" [91]

The mind must be ruled
1. By & through your individualism
Opinions are organic—

[104] [blank]
[105] [92] Love. All the renovation of Spring connects itself with love; the marriage of the plants, the wedding of the birds, the pairing of all animals. Even the frog & his mate have a new & gayer coat for this benign occasion[.]

[106]   Leasts
The air of plague hospitals cannot be discriminated by the chemist from the air of the Alps. The potent virus fatal to human life eludes his scales & tests. It has no size, or weight, or visible extension.
———
Doses of heaven are homoeopathic[.]
_____

"Send me tribute," said Tyrconnel, "or else—."
O'Neal's [n] answer was, "I owe you none, and if—"

[107] George Minott said, "he set out to ⟨go⟩ ↑walk↓ to the woods with ⟨Mr⟩Edmund Hosmer, but he found that one ↑of his↓ legs did not want to go."

———
[91] This quotation is used in "Immortality," *W*, VIII, 342. With "a love . . . reserves.", cf. "Immortality," *W*, VIII, 337.
[92] The entries on pp. [105] and [106] are in pencil.

Ann O'Brien says, that Ann Kelly has been teaching the parrot to say "gingerbread," & he mad⟨a⟩e ⟨b⟩a beautiful offer to say it. ↑See p. 184↓

———

"Thou talk of a free exercise of religion!" said Essex to Tirone: "Thou carest as much for religion as my horse." [93]

[108] 'Tis certain, that whenever Miss Cavendish came into town, the grate broke in the furnace & let down the fire; the water pipes burst overnight with frost; the lamp chimneys broke; the cook fell ill; — was neither cake nor bread ⟨to⟩in the house; and the Express man was gone two minutes before our order was sent⟨.⟩ ↑to him.↓

———

↑Brag↓   Went a-fishing & caught a mermaid.

———

"He was riding on his Jersey wagon."

———

I don't care if he ascended to heaven in his Jersey wagon.

———

Snow with the taste of wine, — and, I suppose, all the rain in [109] that country was whiskey.
"Bursting of lakes"
Cow with two bodies milked ⟨three⟩ ↑four times↓ a day.

[110]   *Spring verses.*

[111]   ⟨s⟩*Spring* —
What a joy to believe that nature loved me. I received hints in my dreams —
I found the friends I went to seek on the way to my door. *S* 93   *V* 43

[93] George Minott and Edmund Hosmer were Emerson's Concord neighbors. "Ann O'Brien . . . say it." is struck through in ink with two diagonal use marks in the form of an "x"; " 'Thou talk . . . horse.' " is written in ink over substantially the same matter in pencil; the preceding rule and the opening quotation mark are in pencil.

We shall know what the social birds say in their autumn councils[.] [94]

Mallows: [n] first sign ⟨of sympathy of the⟩ celestial ⟨powers⟩ ↑natures↓ show of sympathy with ours below. [95]

Pythagoras. See T. [173]

> Spring cold with dropping rain
> ⟨Brings⟩ Willows & lilacs brings again
> The whistling of unnumbered birds
> And ⟨lowi⟩ trumpet lowing of the herds [96]

[112] [blank]

[113]   *Flux.*

παντα ρει. [97]

Nature is in continual flux. Every body is an hourly mercury of the state of its Soul.

[114]–[116] [blank]

[117] "Thought, in conformity with its nature, must ↑act↓ according to Nature's Eternal laws, so that ⟨its⟩ irrational flights are in opposition to its fundamental essence."   Oersted [*The Soul in Nature* . . . , 1852,]

p 123 [98]

[118] The fool in ↑Goethe's↓ "Helena" when paper currency was invented, said, "what do you say—this is money? I will go & buy me a farm"; and Mephistopheles points to the fact that the fool is the only one of the set who does a wise thing. [99] I saw the same thing occur the other day, when the two girls passed me. The accom-

---

[94] This sentence is struck through in ink with a vertical use mark; see Journal VO, p. [263] above.

[95] This entry, drawn from *Iamblichus' Life of Pythagoras*, trans. Thomas Taylor (London, 1818), pp. 79–80, is used in "Country Life," *W*, XII, 150–151.

[96] These four lines, struck through in ink with three diagonal use marks, are used in "May-Day," ll. 182–185, *W*, IX, 169.

[97] See p. [1] above.

[98] This quotation is struck through in pencil with a diagonal use mark. See Journal SO, p. [111] above.

[99] This episode from Part Two of *Faust* occurs not in the "Helena," Act III, but in the Lustgarten scene of Act I, ll. 6155–6173.

plished & promising young man chose, with the approbation of all surrounding society, the pretty girl, who went through all her steps unexceptionably. But the real person, the fine hearted [119] witty sister, fit for all the range of real life, was left, & to her a foolish youth passionately attached himself, & said, "I shall be wretched & undone, b⟨y⟩ut you I must have." And he was right, & the other not.

[120]   *Ripple Pond*

The rippling of the pond under a gusty south wind ⟨delights the eye⟩ gives the like delight to the eye, as the fitful play of the same wind on the Aeolian harp to the ear. Or the darting & scud of ripples is like the auroral shootings in the night heaven.[100]

[121] W[illiam]. E[llery]. C[hanning].'s poetry is wanting in clear statement. Rembrandt makes effects without details, gives you the effect of a sharp nose or a gazing eye, when, if you look close, there is no point to the nose, & no eye is drawn. ↑W[illiam].↓ Hunt admires this, & ↑in his own painting,↓ puts his eye in deep shadow; but I miss the eye, & the face seems to nod for want of it.[101] & Ellery makes a hazy indefinite impression, as of miscellaneous music, without any theme or tune. Still, it is an autumnal [122] air & like the smell of the ↑herb↓ "Life Everlasting" & syngenesious flowers.

"Near Home" is a poem which would delight the heart of Wordsworth, though genuinely original, & with a simplicity of plan which allows the writer to leave out all the prose. 'Tis a series of sketches of natural objects, such as abound in N. England, enwreathed by the thoughts they suggest to a contemplative [123] pilgrim,

"Unsleeping truths by which wheels on Heaven's prime." [102]

---

[100] This paragraph is versified in "Fragments on the Poet and the Poetic Gift," I, ll. 35–42, *W*, IX, 321–322. Ripple Pond or Little Goose Pond is a mile and three-quarters southeast of Concord center.

[101] "in his own painting," is in pencil. Newport painter William Morris Hunt had painted Chief Justice Lemuel Shaw, and Edward W. Emerson says that Emerson had this portrait in mind (*J*, IX, 180).

[102] William Ellery Channing, *Near Home. A Poem* (Boston, 1858), p. 6; this book is in Emerson's library. The quotation is the final line of the dedicatory poem "To Henry [Thoreau]."

There is a neglect of superficial correctness, which looks a little studied, as if perhaps the poet challenged notice to his subtler melody. & strokes of skill which recall the great Masters. There is nothing conventional in the thought, or the illustration, but "thoughts that voluntary move harmonious numbers," [103] [124] & pictures seen by an instructed eye.

[125] Jefferson says in a letter to Judge Roane "The great object of my fear is the federal judiciary. That body, like gravity, ever acting with noiseless foot & unalarming ⟨step⟩advance, gaining ground step by step, & holding what it gains, is ingulphing insidiously the special governments into the jaws of that which /feeds↑?↓/↑eats?↓/ them." Jefferson's works Vol VII. p 212 [104]

[126]–[129] [blank]
[130] Illusions.
One is the belief that W — is large & cosmical, does not strut nor pinch his lips, but hospitably receives you with laughter & intimate graces, and ⟨we⟩you set him down so on your table of constants. The fact is he is *timed* to you; and to the next man he meets though as apprehensive as yourself, he is not *timed*, and is stilted, struts, & pinches his lips.

[131] I am a natural ⟨w⟩reader, & only a writer in the absence of natural writers. In a true time, I should never have written.

[132] The village of Amherst is eagerly discussing the authorship of a paper signed Bifid which appeared in the College Magazine. 'Tis said, if the Faculty knew his name, the author would be expelled from the college. Ten miles off,[n] nobody ever heard of the magazine, or ever will hear of it. In London 'tis of equal interest today whether Lord Palmerston wrote the leader in Wednesday's Times.

[133] In literary circles they still discuss the question who wrote Junius, — a matter of supreme unimportance, like the others. But in

---

[103] Milton, *Paradise Lost*, III, 37–38.
[104] *The Writings of Thomas Jefferson* . . . , 9 vols. (Washington, D.C., 1854).

the whole world none discuss the question who wrote Hamlet & Lear and the Sonnets, which concerns mankind.

[134] You can always tell an English book by the confusion of ideas; a German, by the ideal order. Thus an English speculator shows the wonders of electricity, & talks of its leaving poetry far behind, &c, or, perhaps, that it will yet show poetry new materials, &c.

———

↑*Illusion. See above, no poetry without illusion*—↓ Yet poetry is in nature just as much as carbon is: love ⟨exists⟩ & wonder & the delight in suddenly seen analogy exist as [135] necessarily as space, or heat, or Canada thistles; and have their legitimate functions: and where they have no play, the impatience of the mind betrays precisely the distance from the truth, —— the truth which satisfies the mind & affections, & leaves the real & the ideal in equilibrium which constitutes happiness.

[136] I have now for more than a year, I believe, ceased ⟨almost wholly⟩ to write in my Journal, in which I formerly wrote almost daily. I see few intellectual persons, & even those to no purpose, & sometimes believe that I have no new thoughts, and that my life is quite at an end. But the magnet that lies in my drawer for years, may believe it has no magnetism, and, ⟨at the⟩ ↑on↓ touching it with steel, it [137] shows the old virtue; and, this morning, came by a man with knowledge & interests like mine, in his head, and suddenly I had thoughts again.[105]

[138] Races. There are female races, which, mixing with male races, produce a better man.

[139] The ⟨dull⟩ ↑solid↓ men complain that the idealist leaves out the fundamental facts; the poetic men complain that ⟨they⟩ ↑the solid men↓ leave the sky out.[106]   ↑Printed?↓

———

[105] "But the magnet . . . again." is struck through in pencil with two wavy diagonal use marks on p. [136] and one wavy diagonal use mark on p. [137].

[106] This sentence, struck through in pencil with a diagonal use mark, is used in "Poetry and Imagination," W, VIII, 71. "Printed?" is in pencil.

Among the words to be gazetted pray insert the offensive American-
ism "*balance*" for *remainder*, and, what always accompanies it in this
Albany Hammond's book, "*lay*" for lie.[107]
"I am very particular"
Sneak [108]

[140]   ↑*Pace*↓   παντα ρει [109]
   The world is reckoned by dull men a dead subject, whilst i⟨s⟩t
↑is↓ quick & blazing. The house & farm are thought ⟨solid⟩ fixed &
lasting, whilst they are rushing to ruin every moment. The difference
between skilful & unskilful men is, — that the one class are timed to
this movement, & move with it, can shoot flying, can load as they go,
can read as they run, can write in a cab; whilst the heavy men [141]
wait for the eagle to alight, for the swallow to ⟨come⟩ roost like ⟨a
hen⟩ ↑a barn fowl↓, for the river to run by, for the pause in the conversation, which never comes till the guests take their hats.

[142] Rarey can tame a wild horse, but can he ↑make↓ wild a tame
horse, it were better[.] [110]
Channing[,] who writes a poem for our fields[,] begins to help us.
That is construction, & better than running to Charlemagne & Alfred
for subjects.
   Secondary men & primary men. These travellers to Europe, these
readers of books, these youths rushing into counting rooms of successful merchants, are all imitators, and we get only the same product
weaker. But the man who never so slowly & patiently works out
[143] his ⟨own⟩ native thought, is a primary person. The girl who
does not visit, but ⟨has⟩ ↑follows↓ her native tastes & objects, draws
Boston to her. If she do not follow fashion, fashion follows her.

   [144] Why do I hide in a library, read books, or write them,
& skulk in the woods, & not dictate to these fellows, who, you say,

---

[107] "this Albany Hammond's book" may be one of the works of Jabez Delano
Hammond (1778–1855): *The History of Political Parties in the State of New York*,
3 vols. (Auburn and Syracuse, 1842, 1848), or his *On the Evidence, Independent
of Written Revelation, of the Immortality of the Soul* (1851).
   [108] " 'I am very particular' " and "Sneak" are in pencil.
   [109] "*Pace*" is in pencil. For "πάντα ῥεῖ", see pp. [1] and [113] above.
   [110] For Rarey, see p. [147] below. "make" is in pencil.

dictate to me, as they should not? Why?[n] but because in my bones is none of the magnetism which flows in theirs⟨?⟩. They inundate ⟨me &⟩ all men with their streams. I have a reception & a perception, which they have not, but it is rare & casual, and yet drives me forth to ↑watch↓ these workers, ⟨&,⟩[n] if so be I may derive ⟨the occasion of⟩ ↑from their performance↓ a new insight ⟨from the performance.⟩ ↑for mine.↓ But [145] there are no equal terms for me & them. They all unwittingly perform for me the part of the gymnotus on the fish.[111]

[146] Every man has the whole capital in him, but does not know how to turn it. Every man knows all that Plato or Kant can teach him. When they have got out the proposition at last, 'tis something which he recognizes & feels himself entirely competent. He *was* already that which they ⟨so profoundly⟩ say, ↑& was that more profoundly than they can say it.↓ Yet, from the inertness & phlegm of his ⟨mixing⟩ ↑nature↓, the seldomness with which a spark passes from him, he ⟨lives⟩ ↑exists as↓ a flint, he that should be a sun.

"No author ever wrote ⟨or⟩ ↑no↓ speaker ever said anything to compare with what the most ordinary man can feel." J. C. Thompson.[112]

[147] *Rarey* taught the English to tame horses
Morphy to play chess
Steers to build yachts
Bigelow to make carpets
Hoe to build a printing press
↑Waltham to make watches↓
Colt to make a revolver
The Springfield man to make muskets

———

↑*Heenan* to box.↓
See a passage on the Theory of the Know Nothings   *VO* 51 [113]

[111] Two parallel vertical pencil lines in the left margin mark "there are . . . fish."

[112] Possibly the J.C. Thompson who wrote to Emerson on January 18, 1865. See pp. [150] and [153] below.

[113] Emerson's all-American list includes John Solomon Rarey (1827–1866), a horse tamer, who went to England late in 1857 and gave an exhibition before Queen Victoria; Paul Charles Morphy (1837–1884), who was world's chess master,

We impatient Americans! If we ⟨rode⟩ ↑came↓ on the wires of the telegraph, yet, on arriving, every one would be striving to get ahead of the rest.

[148] ⟨‖ ... ‖⟩Ellery said, looking at a golden rod, — "ah! here they are. These things consume a great deal of time. I don't know but they are of more importance than any other of our investments."

But what shall I say of culture? It occurred that we check our interest in ⟨histories⟩ ↑books↓ of civil history & of natural history by the thought, — well, how have my ⟨o⟩readings in that kind hitherto helped me? I have found my new fact, my new [149] ⟨t⟩ pretended law just propounded by Decandolle, by Blainville, by McLeay, gave me no advantage in my dry talk with Adams or Hosmer.[114] The mind is saturated with a few facts, with one fact, and can hold no more; is not reinforced by adding twenty atmospheres, when one fills it.

You must love the day, you must come from the azure, you must not leave the sky out.[115]

Another ⟨thing⟩ ↑word↓ on culture, my experience is ⟨very⟩ever [150] crying, that, I lose my days, & am barren of all thoughts for

---

1857–1859; George Steers (1820–1856), naval architect and yacht designer, builder of the *America*, who revolutionized yacht design on both sides of the Atlantic; Erastus Brigham Bigelow (1814–1879), who invented power looms for use in power weaving; Robert Hoe (1784–1833), who invented the rotary press and web press; Samuel Colt (1814–1862), who invented the revolver; and John Carmel Heenan (1835–1873), pugilist, who fought the English champion to a draw in April, 1860. Waltham, Massachusetts, was famous for its watches; the U.S. Armory at Springfield, Massachusetts, was famous for the development of the Springfield army rifle. "Waltham" and "See a . . . *VO* 51" are in pencil.

[114] Augustin Pyrame de Candolle (1778–1841), Swiss botanist, and his son Alphonse Louis Pierre Pyrame de Candolle (1806–1893) attempted to set forth a complete natural system of plant classification; Henri Marie Ducrotay de Blainville (1777–1850), French zoologist and physician, succeeded Cuvier as professor in the Museum of Natural History, Paris; William Sharp Macleay (1792–1865) zoologist, propounded a natural system of classification. Abel Adams, Boston banker, was Emerson's friend and financial adviser.

[115] This sentence, struck through in pencil with two vertical use marks, is used in "Behavior," *W*, VI, 196. See p. [139] above and p. [171] below.

want of any person to talk with. ↑"The Understanding can no⟨t⟩ ↑more↓ empty itself by its *own* action ⟨any more⟩ than ↑can↓ a deal box."↓ [116] Thompson

————

Expression, Sensibility, Poet.
It is not they who call out loudest who are most hurt.

[151] The doctrine of latent heat is a key to the history of intellect. There is as much heat used in the conversion of ice to water as in raising water __ degrees; and there is the total amount of mind that Newton shows later, really active in the infant ⟨n⟩Newton, in acquiring the knowledge of the first sensible objects. When we ⟨first⟩ remember our first mental action, it does not seem unworthy or unequal to the latest.

[152]   She walked in flowers around my field
             As June herself around the sphere [117]

[153] "A republican gov[ernmen]t, so far from proving that all men are ↑free &↓ equal, owes its merit to the very reverse, — that it does away with artificial distinctions by which natural inferiority is disguised, & superiority kept under."
                                    J. C. Thompson
                                    ↑Who is he?↓ [118]

You must distinguish between people, in your serving, and leave alone those frivolous drones who exist only to be carted about, who have no object in life. If any body has a thought or is in good earnest about anything [154] worthy, serve him. "He ought to be forraded," as the dollar-giving peasant said to Bellows,[119] "A man that has them 'ere sentiments ought to be forraded." Leave the others to fertilize the ground like guano.

———

[116] "Another ⟨thing⟩ . . . deal box.' ", struck through in pencil with single vertical use marks on pp. [149] and [150], is used in "Clubs," *W*, VII, 227.
[117] These lines, in pencil, are used in "Fragments on Nature and Life," XIII, *W*, IX, 351.
[118] "Who is he?" is in pencil. See pp. [146] and [150] above.
[119] "Bellows" is probably Henry Whitney Bellows (1814–1882), a Unitarian clergyman in New York City, active in civil-service reform.

Supreme Court United States declares "that negroes have no rights which white men are bound to respect."   ? ? ?

[155] Conversation

↑*old pale* of Hobbes↓ [120]

Intellectual construction. *SO* 5

Toucey would not try titles. *SO* 13

Talk with J[ohn]. M[urray]. F[orbes]. or G[eorge]. R. R↑ussell↓ [121] & you talk with State street; ⁿ not so with C[harles]. K[ing]. N[ew-comb]. *SO* 18

Nature no depth but immeasureable lateral spaces. *SO* 23

Life a surface affair; health & disease cutaneous;
Nature a skin.   *SO* 2⟨2⟩4, 25, 118,
⟨Science of⟩ power of color [122]

How delightful, after the conceited ruffians, is Whipple's ⁿ radiant playful wit. Good nature stronger than tomahawks[.] [123]

[156] Things go in pairs[.] [124] *SO* 221

Scholar in age goes out to see if he have lost his wits. *SO* 107

———

Needs provocation. AC 149.

———

Alcott sees things in connexion. *SO* 148

People made for efficient speakers are thereby poor companions.
                          SO 186

[120] "*old pale* of Hobbes" is in pencil.

[121] George R. Russell may be the same George Russell listed as a member of the Town and Country Club in *JMN*, XI, 237.

[122] "Nature no . . . color" is struck through in pencil with two diagonal use marks.

[123] "How delightful . . . tomahawks", struck through in pencil with a diagonal use mark, is used in "Clubs," *W*, VII, 233. For "Good . . . tomahawks", see Journal SO, p. [220] above.

[124] This entry, struck through in pencil with two vertical use marks, is used in "Clubs," *W*, VII, 230.

Mystic goes drest in jewels[.]

Things said for conversation are chalk eggs.[125] Don't *say* things; what you are stands over you the while, & thunders, so that I cannot hear what you say to the contrary.

↑printed perhaps in Society & Solitude↓ [126]

[157]   "For now a few have all, & all have nought."
Spenser. Mother Hubberds Tale.[127]

"I think I don't care so much for what they say, as I do for what makes them say it." [128]

———

W B G[reene].   see *XO* 11 [129]

———

—

    ↑*Gifts*↓

    Who was it ⟨who, in a liberal fit bought a ticket *through*,[n] & made⟩ ↑who wishing to make↓ a present ⟨of it⟩ to the engineer on the locomotive⟨?⟩ ↑bought him a season ticket?↓

[158]–[159] [blank]
    [160] Will you see me at 7 o'clock? I have nothing particular to say, thank God!

---

[125] See *JMN*, IX, 15. For "Mystic . . . jewels", see Journal RO, p. [65], and p. [4] above.

[126] "Mystic goes . . . jewels" and "printed perhaps . . . Solitude" are in pencil; a pencil use mark extends to curve around the left end of "printed". "Things said . . . contrary.", struck through in pencil with two diagonal use marks, is used in "Social Aims," *W*, VIII, 96.

[127] Edmund Spenser, *Prosopopoia: or Mother Hubberds Tale*, l. 141. " 'For now . . . Tale." and the rule beneath it are in pencil.

[128] This quotation, struck through in pencil with a diagonal use mark, is used in "Social Aims," *W*, VIII, 96. See Journal SO, p. [191] above.

[129] The entry from Emerson's Notebook XO reads: "W. B. Green said, 'when he fell into a barroom, he was glad to tell a few coon stories to be acquainted with the company, & afterwards they got along together the better.' "; it is used in "Clubs," *W*, VII, 246. William Batchelder Greene (1819–1878) was a Unitarian minister, member of the Town and Country Club, and author of a pamphlet, "Transcendentalism" (1849).

[161]   Classic & Romantic
See *SO* 74, 75, 76, 77, 82

[162]   He must have a style
          ___

He only is a well made man who has a good determination.
                                                   Culture [130]

          ___

⟨Antony⟩ ↑Telemachus↓ must have a style,
↑Yet he must be versatile↓

[163] For "Culture," it occurred last night, that certain state-
ments must be made, quite omitted, I fear, in my Essay.

                         ↑a style↓

A cultivated person must have a strong ⟨*naturel*⟩ ↑motherwit↓, invincible by his culture, which thankfully & skilfully uses all books;
arts; facilities & elegances of intercourse; but is never subdued & lost
in these.[131]

A cultivated person must be versatile, or have various susceptibility,
& not be sterile & cast iron. ↑Hence the tacit rules of society to sink
the shop, the profession, or specialty, of each *convive*. A specialty he
must have, & be master in it, & then leave it behind him as much
as his dictionary.↓
   [164] A Cultivated Person must look at every object for itself,
& without affection. Bonaparte, though an egoist *à l'outrance*, could
criticize a play, a ⟨a⟩building, a character, a picture, on universal
grounds, & give of every thing a new opinion. ↑printed↓ But an
indigent egotism appears in most men's judgments. Though they
talk of the object before them, you can see they are thinking of
themselves.   ↑printed?↓

   [130] "He only . . . *Culture*" is struck through in ink with four vertical use
marks. See *JMN*, XI, 198.
   [131] "A cultivated . . . these." is struck through in pencil with a vertical use
mark, and "his culture . . . these." is struck through in ink with two vertical use
marks. This paragraph is used in "Culture," *W*, VI, 134.

↑The number of conceited people is so great, that it must subserve great uses in nature, like sexual passion.↓ [132]

[165]–[170] [three leaves torn out] [133]
[171] melancholy swainish natures, on whom speech makes no impression; and others, who are not only swainish, but who are prompt to take oath that swainishness is the highest culture; and, though their wit is good for you alone, when your friends come, you must bolt these out.[134]

1. You shall be somebody[.]
2. You shall have catholicity[.]
3. You shall ⟨live⟩ know the power of the imagination[.]

————

You shall come from the Azure[.] [135]

————

You shall be intellectual.

————

[172] I delight in persons who clearly perceive the transcendant superiority of Shakspeare to all other writers. I delight in the votaries of the genius of Plato. Because this clear love does not consist with self-conceit.ⁿ

Not so, when I see youths coming to me with their books & poems. I soon discover that they are egotists & wish my homage.[136]

---

[132] "But an . . . passion." is struck through in pencil with a vertical use mark; "Though they . . . themselves." and "The number . . . passion." are both struck through in ink and pencil with single vertical use marks; and "Though they . . . passion." is struck through in ink with a vertical use mark. "A Cultivated . . . affection.", struck through in pencil with a diagonal use mark, and "Bonaparte . . . opinion.", struck through in ink with a vertical use mark, are used in "Culture," *W*, VI, 158. "But an . . . passion." is used in "Culture," *W*, VI, 134–135.
[133] Emerson indexed p. [168] under Conversation and p. [170] under Clubs.
[134] "that swainishness . . . out." is struck through in ink with a vertical use mark; "melancholy swainish . . . out.", struck through in pencil with two vertical use marks, is used in "Social Aims," *W*, VIII, 97.
[135] "You shall come from the Azure", struck through in pencil with two diagonal use marks, is used in "Behavior," *W*, VI, 196. See p. [149] above.
[136] The entry on p. [172] is struck through in pencil with a vertical use mark; "I delight in persons . . . writers." is struck through in ink with three vertical use marks. "I delight in persons . . . self-conceit." is used in "Culture," *W*, VI, 142.

[173] Culture is a pagan. It marks intellectual values, but ↑is↓ not lost in them, not the fool of them, but holding them under control, & socially. Yes, a reference to Society is part of the idea of Culture, — science of a gentleman, art of a gentleman, poetry in a gentleman,   intellectually held, that is, for their own sake, for what they are, for their universal beauty & worth, & not for economy, which degrades them.

But not over-intellectually, that is, not to an ecstasy, entrancing the man, but redounding to his beauty & glory[.]

[174] I am forced to add that the cultivated person must have a moral determination.

There will be a certain toleration, a letting be & letting do, a consideration & allowance for the faults of others, but a severity to his own. Sportive ⟨& playful⟩ in manner, inexorable in act. Then in one of my truest gentlemen is an impossibility of taking an advantage. He will not foreclose a mortgage. ↑Such is Frank C. Lowell.↓

[175] [blank]

[176] Events are not as the brute circumstance that falls, but as the life which they fall upon. ⟨Tha⟩Out of the same ⟨atoms of⟩ carbon & ammonia, ⟨in the soil,⟩ the rose will make a rose, and the nettle a nettle. ⟨The⟩ The same air in the trachea of an ass will bray, in the trachea of a nightingale will sing.[137]

[177] For success, to be sure, we esteem it a test in other people, since we do first in ourselves. We respect ourselves more if we have succeeded.   ↑Copied from *VO* 110↓
↑If the man is not well mixed, he needs do some great feat as fine or expiation. *AB* 19↓

> Success shall be in thy courser tall
> Success in thyself which is best of all [138]
>   See *NO* p. 1,

[137] See Journal VO, p. [42] above.
[138] These two lines are from a Danish ballad, "Svend Vonved," translated by George Borrow in *Romantic Ballads, translated from the Danish; and Miscellaneous*

⟨Self⟩ Determination[n] of the blood makes value. *VO* 169
Money-value an anthropometer. *VO* 123

See Bonaparte's[n] feats. T 97
    Sugar from turn↑i↓ps, &c.
Sentiment is color, & thought is form. VO 261
Color VO 173

---

[178] For Fate Lecture remember *VO* p. 130 [139]
Success
    EO 13. We are results
Those who conquer, — Victory was born with them. S 149
    determination of the blood makes value. *VO* 169

"Good fortune accompanied Alfred in all things like a gift of God."
⟨Asser⟩ *Asser*.[140]

---

immense porosity

---

[179] [blank]
[180] I have been writing & speaking what were once called novelties, for twenty five or thirty years, & have not now one disciple. Why? Not that what I said was not true; not that it has not found intelligent receivers but because it did not go from ⟨me to⟩ any wish in me to bring men to me, but to themselves. I delight in driving them from me. What could I do, if they came to me? they would interrupt & ⟨bother⟩ encumber me. [181] This is my boast that I have no school ⟨or following⟩ ↑& no↓ follower. I should account it a measure of the impurity of insight, if it did not create independence.

Pieces (London, 1826), p. 64, ll. 38–39; "For success . . . all" is struck through in pencil with a diagonal use mark; "For success . . . succeeded." and "Success shall . . . all" are used in "Success," *W*, VII, 286–287.

[139] "For Fate . . . p. 130", in pencil, is struck through in ink with a curved diagonal use mark.

[140] Reinhold Pauli, *The Life of Alfred the Great*, trans. from the German (London, 1853), p. 67; this book is in Emerson's library. This quotation is used in "Success," *W*, VII, 295. See *JMN*, XIII, 450.

[182] ↑Here came the subsoil plougher H[enry]. J[ames].↓
H. J.'s correspondent is Kimball in Franklin, N. H.

The ease with which people use the word spiritual to cover what is antagonistic to spiritual, ⟨seems to⟩ suggests the possibility of a searching tuition in that direction. I fancy, that, if you give me a class of intelligent youths & maidens, I could bring them to see the essential distinctions which I see; & could exercise them in [183] that ↑high↓ department, so that they should not let go what they had seen. Spiritual is that which is its own evidence; which is self-executing; which cannot be conceived not to be; that which sets aside you & me, & can very well let us drop, but not we it. The existence & history of Christ are doubted & denied by ⟨multitudes of⟩ ↑some↓ learned & critical persons in perfect good faith. Of course, the existence & history of Christ are not a spiritual reality, for they could not deny the existence of justice, of love, of the laws of time & space[.]

[184] H[enry]. J[ames]. said of woman, "that the flesh said, it is for me, & the spirit said, it is for me."

Ann ↑O'Brien↓ says, "that A. K↑elley↓. is trying to teach the parrot to say 'gingerbread,' and, the other day, the parrot made a beautiful offer to say it."

———

French have no word for "awe," & none for "earnest," says Mlle. Leclerc.
A parrot has few duties[.]

[185] A man finds out that there is somewhat in him that knows more than he does.
Then he comes presently to the curious question, who's who? which of these two is really me? the one that knows more, or the one that knows less? the little fellow, or the big fellow? [141]

[186] Personality
No man's egotism covers his personality.

[141] This entry is marked by two parallel vertical pencil lines in the left margin.

Personality is identical with the interest of the Universe. The mind is obedient to the heavenly vision; suffers no regard to self to interfere. Egotism looks after the little Timothy ⟨or⟩ that it is, & much overestimates the importance of Timothy. Egotism is a kind of buckram that [187] gives momentary strength ⟨to⟩ & concentration to human beings & seems to be much used in ⟨the⟩ Nature for fabrics in which local & spasmodic energy are required. Four or five men in this country[,] of indispensable impo[r]tance to the carrying on of American life, are rank egotists, whom we could ill spare. Either of them would be a national loss. But it spoils them for me; they are not [18⟨7⟩8] good for conversation. And it is plain that they have much education to undergo, to reach simplicity & poetry.[142]

Broad as God is the Personality we want, & which all great souls have or aspire to have. We stand for God.[143] Knights in Romance must be majestic & compel reverence, & accept no conditions or disparagments. Henry Clay says, "I thank my God that he has given me a soul incapable of fear [18⟨8⟩9] of the anger of any other being besides himself."

Send the divingbell of Memory down, — see the immense relations of every symbol —

A man has the Universe in his belly, as Henry VIII had a Pope.[144]

[190]–[191] [blank]
[192][145]   *Success* —
        Value of the Present

Nature & Life superficial
the great *now*

---

[142] "Egotism is [p. [186]] . . . poetry.", struck through in pencil with single vertical use marks on pp. [186], [187], and [188] and an additional discontinuous vertical use mark on p. [187], is used in "Success," *W*, VII, 289.
[143] "Broad . . . for God." is struck through in pencil with a diagonal use mark. For the remark by Henry Clay directly below, see *JMN*, VI, 205–206.
[144] See *JMN*, VI, 208.
[145] The entries on pp. [192]–[214] are in pencil.

the susceptible subject
　Nature no depth, but wide lateral spaces
　Nature is a skin[.]

　And health is in ⟨openness to⟩ impressionability.
　Man overflows & makes his bibles & Homers so great[.]

[193] A man whose heart is in that thing he does, loses no time, & ↑lets slip↓ no aids[.]

After you have pumped your brains for thoughts & verses, there is a better poetry hinted in whistling a tune on your walk —
　The greatness of basking in Nature & of disdaining progress.[146]
I state a fact which every thoughtful soul will recognize[.]

　[194] Nature utilizes all our foibles[.]

　utilizes misers, egotists, fanatics,
↑But education (right) rules nature↓
　Aim, whether at the Essence or at the Wages
　Courage
　Cheerfulness
　Affirming
　Plaindealing　　sight of the selfexecuting law

[195]　　Feats
　Every man can do one[.]
though some ripen too slow like Isabella⟨s⟩ grapes; yet the tendency
a pregnant argument

[196] [brag of the world]
　↑World shaken with our engineries.↓
Success. We may well make it a test[.]

　The present, the whistle of the boy, the piping of the bird, is better than your literary results[.]

[146] "A man . . . aids", "After you . . . walk —", and "The greatness . . . progress." are struck through in pencil with single vertical use marks.

How great hearted it is to do ⟨your⟩ ↑the↓ work you love, without care, & without counting the hours.[147] How happy the sympathetic & susceptible[:] The slipper
                            & Odoacer
                                            and sensibility to thoughts.
    Life is a surface affair and 'tis relatedness that magnifies[.]

Feel yourself & be not daunted by things. 'Tis the fulness of man
[197] that runs over into ↑so many↓ objects.

Poverty of our stereotype criticism; one Homer, one Shakspeare, —
but in the happy present we do not find Shakspeare or Homer over-
great, only to have been translators of the happy present, & every
man & woman are great possibilities.[148]

This now, this tranquil well founded ⟨far⟩ wide seeing is no busy-
body no fussey express rider —
Such a one said to me, "I will pardon you that you do so much, & you
me that I do nothing."

    Hurry is for slaves; & ⟨one of the⟩ Marcus Antoninus said, Zeus
hates busybodies.[149]

    [198] It does not make *tours de force* nor overstimulate you

---

[147] "The present . . . hours." is struck through in pencil with a vertical use
mark; "The present . . . results" is used in "Success," *W*, VII, 297.
    [148] "The slipper . . . man", p. [196], struck through in ink with a discon-
tinuous diagonal use mark, "Feel yourself . . . man", p. [196], struck through
in pencil with a vertical use mark, and "that runs . . . possibilities.", struck through
in pencil with a vertical use mark, are used in "Success," *W*, VII, 295–297 and 304–
305.
    [149] "This now . . . nothing.' " is struck through in pencil with a vertical use
mark. For " 'I will . . . nothing.' ", see *JMN*, XI, 428, where the remark is attributed to Caroline Sturgis Tappan; see also *JMN*, XIII, 396. For "Zeus hates
busybodies.", a quotation from *The Nichomachean Ethics of Aristotle*, 1850, p. 164,
see Journal SO, p. [93] above. "This now . . . busybodies.", struck through in
pencil with a discontinuous diagonal use mark, is used in "Success," *W*, VII, 311–
312.

to be at the head of your class, ⟨to lie with cold feet & hot head⟩ &
drive ᴺ you to consumption[.] ¹⁵⁰

[199] It loves, it cheers, it approves
it finds itself all-related
it is rich in the poorest place
it is optimist
it is brave[.]
↑Affirms;↓ ⟨I⟩it hates negations, criticism, sneer,
It loves the self-executing ᴺ laws
the immense porosity of nature.

This power works by love,
            by courage,
            by faith[.]
It cheers & affirms[.]

[200] The earth is shaken by our engineries. We are feeling
our youth & ↑nerve &↓ bone. We have the power of land & sea, &
know the use of these. We count our census, we read our growing
valuations, we survey our map, ⟨&⟩ which becomes speedily old, our
railway, telegraph. We interfere ↑in S. America,↓ in Canton, & Japan,
& discover Antarctic continents & polar sea. We are the brag of the
world, & value ourselves by these feats[.]

[201] 'Tis the way of the world; 'tis the law of youth & of
youthful organization. Men are made each with some triumphant
superiority, which, th[r]ough some adaptation of fingers or ear or
eye or ciphering or pugilistic or musical or literary craft which enriches
the ⟨w⟩ community with a new art[.]
    Giotto could draw a perfect circle —
    Erwin could build a minster
    Olaf could run round the oars of his galley

¹⁵⁰ This sentence, struck through in pencil with a diagonal use mark, is used
in "Success," *W*, VII, 302.

[202] ↑*Feats.*↓

Ojeda could run out swiftly on a ⟨board⟩ plank projected from the top of a tower & return[.]

Byron, Sheridan, Bernini —

Columbus,

Cook,

Simpson

Kane

C. B. Stowe

These are all feats[.]

Success

And these are arts to be thankful for[,] but chiefly as they show the general wealth[.]

[203] But there comes quickly the fury ⟨of⟩ⁿ for reward

pretention instead of performance

Nelson   Brougham

And we are deeply tainted with that as our bankruptcy may show[.]

But it is not talent but sensibility which is best.

And why⟨,⟩? because talent confines, & centrality puts us in rapport with all.[151]

[204] The greatness of humility.

Find your superiority in not wishing superiority. Find the riches of love which possesses that which it adores; the riches of poverty; the immensity of today; the height of lowliness; the age of ages.[152]

---

[151] The entries on pp. [200]–[203], struck through in pencil with single vertical use marks on pp. [200] and [201], with a curved vertical use mark on p. [202], and with a discontinuous vertical use mark on p. [203] are used in "Success," *W*, VII, 283–286, 295. For "Ojeda . . . return", cf. Arthur Helps, *The Spanish Conquest in America* . . . , 4 vols. (New York, 1856–1857), I, 282–283.

[152] The entry on p. [204] is struck through in pencil with a vertical use mark; "find your . . . ages." is used in "The Sovereignty of Ethics," *W*, X, 194.

[205] We adore success[.]
'Tis very undiscriminating —
We like results, but do not ask the vital question ⟨whether⟩ ↑what↓ the success cost. If it cost the health & life of the gladiator, he paid too much. If it was his to do, 'tis well. But if it was a tour de force —

We grasp & pull down, & would pull down God if we could. 'Tis malignant & if a man get 10,000 votes, admire him; but if another ↑get↓ 20,000 the Universe of fools turns round to the new man [206] ⟨& puff &⟩ⁿ and Excellence is lost sight of in this hunger for performance

———

'Tis ¹⁵³

[207] Let us rather prefer the private power of each person, — the door into nature that is opened to him; that which each can, let him do, satisfied with his task & its instructions & its happiness.

Then, over all, let him value the sensibility ⟨that loves⟩ that receives, that believes, ⟨that affirms that dares &⟩ that loves, that dares, that affirms[.] ¹⁵⁴

[208] I value M. Angelo's saying There is something I can do —

I value a man's trust in his fortune, when it is a hearing of voices that call him to his task; when he is conscious of a great work laid on him to do, & that nature cannot afford to lose him until it is done.¹⁵⁵

[209] *Courage.* Each has his own as his talent, but the courage of the ⟨horse⟩ cat is one, & of the horse, another. The dog that scorns

¹⁵³ "& puff . . . performance" is struck through in pencil with two vertical use marks. "& puff &" and "'Tis" are each partially enclosed in pencil. "and Excellence . . . performance" is used in "Success," *W*, VII, 290.
¹⁵⁴ This sentence, struck through in pencil with a vertical use mark, is used in "The Preacher," *W*, X, 230.
¹⁵⁵ "I value M. Angelo's . . . do —" is struck through in pencil with a curved diagonal use mark; "I value a man's . . . done." is struck through in pencil with a vertical use mark.

to fight, will fight for his master. The llama that will carry a load if you caress him, will ⟨die⟩ refuse food & die if he is beaten. The fury of onset is one, & calm endurance another[.] [156]

⟨There is a courage⟩

Every creature has a courage ⟨fit for his⟩ of his constitution, fit for his duties. Archimedes the courage of a geometer to stick to his diagram in the siege of the city, — & the soldier his, [210] to strike at Archimedes. Each is strong relying on his own, ⟨each weak⟩ ↑& betrayed↓ when he ⟨apes the courage of others⟩ seeks in himself the courage of others.[157]

Is there only one courage?

[211]   Success a natural standard

Value of feats
We must value them[.]
But we come to value reward & not excellence[.]
Then comes in Mischief & the hells.
Malignity

M Angelo
Self trust
Our talent is our door

But that must lead us to central intelligence
[212] And that leads us (⟨to⟩strange to say) to surface.

Sensibility
    shown in youth
    shown in love
    shown in hospitality of mind

---

[156] This paragraph, struck through in pencil with a vertical use mark, is used in "Courage," *W*, VII, 267.

[157] This paragraph, struck through on p. [209] with a vertical use mark in pencil, is used in "Courage," *W*, VII, 270. For "Each is . . . others.", see *JMN*, IX, 112.

Courage
Anti-Egotism
Affirming

[213] Popular idea of success again extends to the very gods
Success to me which is not success to all
Fortune a Genius
Fortunate men
Fortunate youth
not depending on ⟨the⟩ virtue or the weal of the world, but on the luck of one.
'Tis the ⟨very⟩ midsummer madness — 'tis conceit. —
As long as I am in my place I am safe. The best [214] lightning rod is your own spine. Is there not some better insurance against cholera than abstaining from salads.

[215] These feats that we extol ⟨are not⟩ do not signify so much as we say. These wonderful arts that we boast are ⟨all⟩ of very recent origin. ⟨but⟩ They are ⟨great⟩ local conveniences, but nowise necessary. ⟨to greatness⟩ All the great men of the world have got along very well without them. Newton ⟨had no⟩ ↑was a great man without↓ ⟨g⟩telegraph or gas or rubber shoes or lucifer match, or [216] steam engine, or ether.
⟨Nor had⟩ ↑So was↓ Shakspeare
⟨nor⟩ ↑&↓ Alfred ⟨⟨nor⟩& Julius Caesar ⟨nor⟩& Socrates ⟨nor⟩⟩& Scipio ⟨nor⟩& Socrates. ⟨Yet all these achieved greatness. In⟩ The⟨r⟩se are local conveniences, but how easy to go now to parts of the world where not only all these arts are wanting but where they are despised. [217] The Arabs[,] the most dignified people on the planet[,] do not want them, and are yet easily able to impress on the Frenchman or American who visits them the respect of a great man[.] [158]

[218] ↑Bacon or↓ Kant, or Hegel, propound some maxim which is

[158] The entries on pp. [215]–[217], struck through in pencil with a diagonal use mark on p. [215], with one wavy discontinuous use mark and one curved use mark on p. [216], and with one curved diagonal use mark on p. [217], are used in "Success," W, VII, 287–288.

the key note of philosophy thenceforward; but I am more interested to know, that, when at last they hurled out their deep word, it is only some familiar experience of every man in the street.[159]

↑Printed?↓

[219] The ⟨wo⟩ populace says, with Horne Tooke, "If you would be powerful, pretend to be powerful." I prefer to say, with the old prophet Jeremiah, "Seekest thou great things, seek them not"; or, what was said of a great Spanish prince, "the more you took from him, the greater he appeared." Plus on lui ôte, plus il est grand.[160] ↑Printed, I believe.↓

[220] [161] Believe the faintest of your presentiments against the testimony of all sacred & profane history. A great man is always a contradiction to his age & to foregoing history. If Plato had not been, you would say, no Plato could be. If Jesus had not been, would not ⟨all mankind⟩ ↑the Skeptic↓ deny the possibility of so just a life? And yet steadily in the heart of every man, the possib⟨u⟩ility of a greater than Plato, of a greater than Jesus, was always affirmed, and is affirmed; for every man [221] carries with him the vision of the Perfect. And the highest actual that fulfils any part of this promise ⟨instantly⟩ exalts the Ideal just so much higher, & it can no more be attained than he can set his foot on the horizon which flies before him.

---

[159] "Bacon . . . the street.", struck through in ink with one vertical use mark and in pencil with one curving diagonal use mark, is used in "Success," W, VII, 301. "Printed?", below, is in pencil.

[160] Horne Tooke's remark is quoted by Coleridge, *Specimens of the Table Talk of the Late Samuel Taylor Coleridge*, 2 vols. in 1 (New York, 1835), II, 27; this edition is in Emerson's library; see JMN, VII, 100. The paragraph, struck through in pencil with one vertical and one diagonal use mark, is used in "Considerations by the Way," W, VI, 278, and "Greatness," W, VIII, 313. For " 'Seekest thou . . . not;' ", see Jer. 45:5 and JMN, VIII, 387. For "Plus on . . . grand.", see JMN, XIII, 291. "Printed, I believe.", below, is in pencil.

[161] On p. [220], the commas after "would say", "every man", "than Plato", "than Jesus", and "always affirmed" are in pencil; "all mankind" is canceled and "the Skeptic" is inserted in pencil and then in ink; in "in the heart" the "i" is dotted in pencil and the second "t" is crossed in pencil; in "than Plato" the first "t" is crossed in pencil; and in "than Jesus" the "t" is crossed in pencil.

See too ("Tendencies" p. 10.) a good page about the impossibility
of wiping out the superiority of manners that annoys us[.] [162]

↑??↓

↑see "Tendencies"↓

[222] [blank]
[223] For ↑Pseudo↓Spiritism, it shows that no man almost is fit to
give evidence. Then I say to the best, these matters are quite too
important than that I can rest them on any legends. If I have no
facts such as you allege, I can very well wait for them. I am content
& occupied with such miracles as I know. If any others are important
to me, they will certainly be shown to me.[163]

[224] Once more. The same things which you tell, or much better,
I could well accept, if they were told me by poets,[n] or of great &
worthy persons. That the hero had intimations ⟨o⟩preternatural of
what it behoved him to know, — that a noble lover should be apprized
by omens, or by presentiments, of what had befallen his friend in
some distant place, [225] is agreeable ⟨enough to my belief⟩ ↑to
believe↓; but angels do not appear ⟨because⟩ ↑to ask why↓ Mr ⟨Harris
forgot to⟩ ↑Smith did not↓ send home his cabbages ↑or Dick, his
⟨shoes⟩new shoes.↓

[226] How well these orators help themselves each with his anecdote.
Swift with his boy that was whipped, & la⟨g⟩ughed at the master
still, and, on being asked, why? said, "I was laughing to think how
you are sold; I ain't the boy." ——
And * Howe ↑of ⟨Canada⟩ Nova Scotia,↓ with his shillaleh among

↑* At the Burns Centenial in Boston.↓ [164]

[162] See "Tendencies," *Lectures*, III, 304–305. "??" and "See 'Tendencies' ", below, are in pencil.
[163] "Pseudo" is inserted in pencil and overwritten in ink. "Demonology", in
blue-black ink, is written vertically in the upper left-hand margin of p. [223],
probably by Edward Emerson. The paragraph, struck through in ink with a vertical use mark, is used in "Demonology," *W*, X, 13.
[164] At the Burns Centennial dinner at the Parker House on January 25, 1859,
Holmes, Lowell, and Whittier read poems they had written for the occasion, and
Emerson spoke; see "Robert Burns," *W*, XI, 437–443.

the double barrelled guns & 6 barrel revolvers, — ⁿ "Here goes for the instrument that never missed fire," which he applied to his unprepared speech among the prepared speeches, and again his being expected to speak for old Scotland as well as for Nova Scotia; with his Irishman who being asked which he liked best, the bacon or [227] the beans? ⁿ said, "the bacon was excellent, but the beans /speak/spake/ for themselves." And Lord Radstock's apology was not bad, of the sot in the ditch who "belonged to the Temperance Reform," — "My brother is the great Temperance Orator, and I travel with him; I am the *Sad Example*."

[228] We had much talk at the Adirondac Club on Everett's extraordinary jump into the arms of Bonner. For the matter of the money he earns for Mount Vernon, he might earn more by exhibiting himself for an hour a day in a ridiculous posture. I had occasion to describe Poikilos (   ) who entertained the audience by standing on his head.[165]

Anth↑r↓opomorphists in this that we cannot let moral distinctions be, but must mould them into human shape. "Mere morality" means not put into ↑a↓ personal master of morals.

[229] [blank]

---

[165] The Adirondac Club consisted of those members of the Saturday Club of Boston who, in the first two weeks of August, 1858, made an excursion to a camp set up by the painter and journalist William J. Stillman on Follensby Pond in the wildest part of the Adirondacks. See *JMN*, XIII, 34–35 and 55–56. The party consisted of Stillman, Emerson, Louis Agassiz, James Russell Lowell, Ebenezer Rockwood Hoar, John Holmes (brother of Oliver Wendell), Prof. Jeffries Wyman, Dr. Estes Howe, Dr. Amos Binney, Horatio Woodman, and several guides. Stillman's painting of "Philosophers' Camp" is reproduced in *W*, IX, 184. Edward Everett, former governor of Massachusetts, had accepted the offer of Bonner, editor of the *New York Ledger*, of a large price for contributing articles during 1858 in order to help purchase and restore Washington's home. "Everett's timid holding aloof from the cause of Freedom in his own day, while he busied himself in a strange way in order to establish a Memorial to its champion in the last century, was very displeasing to these Northern patriots" (*J*, IX, 193). For "Professor Poikilos" or "Poikilus", see Journal SO, p. [210] above.

[230]¹⁶⁶   Hie to the woods the citizen
          To the ⟨|| ... ||⟩deep sea ⟨the⟩ye landsmen ⟨hie⟩down
          Off to the hills ye aldermen
          And empty leave the town
                Go purge your blood in ⟨wave⟩ ↑lake↓ & wood
                To honor born of hardihood

          Your town is full of gentle names
          By Patriots ⟨borne⟩ ↑once↓ were watchwords made
          The warcry names are muffled shames
          ↑The men are menials made↓
          But who would dare a name to wear
          The foe of freedom everywhere

[231]   The rocky nook ⟨had⟩ ↑with↓ hillocks three
          Looked Eastward from the farms
          And twice a day the flowing sea
          Took Boston in its arms
          The /days/times/ were poor the men it bore
          ⟨Were marked⟩ for
                    ⟨trusty seamen on the shore⟩
          ⟨In ships⟩
          ↑And↓ sailed ⁿ ⟨every sea⟩ ↑for bread↓ to every shore

          The ⟨waves that⟩ ↑billows↓ rocked him on the deep
          Made the sea boy free
          The winds that sung the boy to sleep
          Breathed daring liberty
          The honest waves refuse to slaves
          The empire of the ocean caves

[232]   The rocky nook with hilltops three
          Looked eastward from the farms
          And twice a day the flowing sea
          Took Boston in its arms

¹⁶⁶ The entries on pp. [230]–[234], in pencil, are early versions of "Boston,"
W, IX, 212–217.

The ⟨men⟩ ↑youth↓ of yore were stout & poor
And sailed for bread to every shore

The waves that rocked them on the deep
Made them as free & bold
The winds that sung the boy to sleep
Sang freedom uncontrolled
The honest waves refuse to slaves
The empire of the ocean caves

[233]   O once when they were poor & brave
They minded well their task
Was nought too high for them to crave
They gave what they did ask

[234]   The land that has no song
Shall have a song today
The granite rock is dumb too long
The ⟨stone is rolled away⟩ ↑earth has much to say↓
For you can teach the lightning speech
And round the earth your voices reach

[235] [blank]
[236] The greatest benefit of London seems today to be this, that, in such a vast number of persons & conditions, one can believe there is room for such people as we read of ⟨no⟩in novels to exist, such, for instance, as the heroes & heroines of "Counterparts." [167]

[237] Nobody can read in M[ary]. M[oody]. E[merson].'s MSS. or in the conversation of old-school people, without seeing that Milton and Young had a religious authority in their mind, & no wise the slight, merely entertaining quality of modern bards. And Plato, Aristotle, Plotinus, how venerable & organic as Nature, they are in ⟨her⟩ ↑M.M.E.'s↓ mind!

---

[167] This paragraph, struck through in ink with a vertical use mark and in pencil with a wavy diagonal use mark, is used in "Culture," W, VI, 150. For *Counterparts; or, The cross of love* by Elizabeth Sara Sheppard, see Journal SO, p. [119] above.

What a subject is her mind & life for the finest novel. And I wish I were younger, or that my daughters [23⟨7⟩8] would aspire to draw this portrait. And when I read Dante, the other day, & his periphrases to signify with more adequateness Christ or ⟨the⟩ Jehovah,— who, do you think, I was reminded of? who but M.M.E, & her ⟨jour⟩eloquent theology? [168]

[239] At every parting with people who interest us at all, how the sense of demerit is forced upon each!

[2⟨38⟩40] Here dies the amiable & worthy Prescott amid a chorus of eulogies, and, if you believe the American & almost the English newspapers for a year or two back, he is the very Muse of History. And meantime here has come into the country 3 months ago a book of *Carlyle*, History of Frederick, infinitely the wittiest book that ever was written, a book that one would think the English people would rise up ⟨a⟩in mass to thank him for, ↑⟨the donation⟩↓ by cordial acclamation & congratulate themselves [2⟨39⟩41] that such a head existed among them, and ↑much↓sympathising & on its own account reading-America would make a new treaty extraordinary of joyful grateful delight with England, in acknowledgment of such ⟨an obligation;⟩ ↑a donation,—↓a book with so many memorable & heroic facts, working directly, too, to practice,— with new heroes, things unvoiced before, with a range of thought & wisdom, the largest & the most colloquially elastic, that ever was, [242] not so much applying as inosculating to every need & sensibility of a man, so that I do not so much read a sterotype page, ⟨&⟩ ↑as↓ I see the eyes of the writer looking into my eyes; all the way, chuckling with undertones & hums & winks & shrugs, & ↑long↓ commanding glances, and stereoscoping every figure that passes & every hill, river, wood, hummock, & pebble in the long perspective,   and with↑al↓ a [n] book [243] that is a Judgment Day, too, for its moral verdict on the men & nations & manners of modern ⟨days.⟩ times. With its wonderful ⟨mn⟩ new ⟨mnemoni⟩ system of mnemonics,

---

[168] The entries on pp. [237] and [238], struck through in ink with single vertical use marks, are used in "Mary Moody Emerson," *W*, X, 402–403.

whereby great & insignificant ⟨dull⟩ men are ineffaceably ticketed & marked in the memory by what they were, had, & did.

And this book ⟨I hav⟩ makes no noise:ⁿ I have hardly seen a notice of it in any newspaper or journal,ⁿ [24⟨1⟩4] and you would think there was no such book; but the secret interior wits & heart↑s↓ of men take note of it, not the less surely. They have said nothing lately in praise of the air, or of fire, or of the blessing of love, and yet, I suppose, they are sensible of these, & not less of this Book, which is like these.[169]

[24⟨2⟩5] There is a good deal of water in the high seas[.]

———

A certain quantity of power belongs to a certain quantity of faculty, and whoever ⟨wants⟩ ↑claims↓ more power than is the legitimate attraction of his faculty is an adventurer[.]

Lect[ure]. on Nat[ural]. Aristocracy [170]

[24⟨3⟩6] "In the morning — solitude," said Pythagoras. By all means, give the youth solitude, that nature may speak to his imagination, as it does never in company; and, for the like reason, give him a chamber alone; and that was the best thing I found in College.[171]

Lord Normanby says of the French Aristocracy, "Country retirement in their own land has done more for them than foreign travel once did." ↑VO 36↓

[24⟨4⟩7] ↑There's always some deuce of a new thing coming up that tries you.↓

[169] "*Carlyle*, History . . . themselves", p. [240], and the entries on pp. [241]–[244], struck through in pencil with single vertical use marks, are used in "Art and Criticism," *W*, XII, 298–299. William Hickling Prescott (1776–1859) had died on January 28, 1859. Emerson began reading volume one of *Frederick the Great* in the American edition before he received his copy from Carlyle. See Emerson's letter to Carlyle, May 1, 1859 (*CEC*, pp. 527–528).

[170] The entries on p. [245] are in pencil. "A certain . . . faculty," is used in "The Celebration of Intellect," *W*, XII, 121. For "There is . . . seas", see Journal SO, p. [261] above.

[171] This paragraph, struck through in ink with a vertical use mark, is used in "Culture," *W*, VI, 156. Emerson's source for Pythagoras' remark is *Iamblichus' Life of Pythagoras*, 1818, pp. 70–71; see *JMN*, VI, 381.

What a Critic is the Age! Calvinism ↑how coherent! how sufficing! how poetic! It↓ stood well every test but the telescope. When that showed the Copernican system to be true, it was too ridiculous to pretend that our little ⟨asteroid⟩ⁿ spec of an earth was the central point of nature, &c.

⟨Well,⟩ Whenⁿ India was explored, & the wonderful riches of Indian theologic literature found, that dispelled once for all the dream about Christianity being the sole revelation,—for, here in India

                                        pass to p. 250 [172]

[24⟨5⟩8] [173] Subjects
Carlyle
Counterparts
Channing
Pseudospiritism
Rhetoric
Manners
Demonology
Love
Wait till there is more production
The weight of him who adds the weight of the Earth
↑Immense force of him whose part is taken. Z 163↓
    An opinion of a lawyer
    An opinion of a judge
    An opinion of mankind

[249] Nantucket
Quotation
                          Success
                          Morals
                          Clubs
                          Clubs
                          Classic & Romantic

[172] "pass to p. 250" is encircled by a line.
[173] The entries on pp. [248] and [249] are in pencil.

Novels
Rhetoric
Carlyle [174]

[2⟨47⟩50]—there in China, were the same principles, the same grandeurs, the ⟨same⟩ ↑like↓ depths moral & intellectual.

Well, we still maintained that we were the true men,—we were believers,—the rest were heathen. Now comes this doctrine of the ↑pseudo-↓spiritists to explain to us that we are not Christians, are not believers, but totally unbelieving.

[2⟨48⟩51] The game of question & answer[:] Sphinx, Asgard, Gungradir, Svend Vonved

Gov. Reynolds, See *NO* 46, 109

Hyde Earl of Rochester & Guilford

SO 289, 287, 174.

"Do you not think I could understand any business in Eng[lan]d in a month?" said Roch↑ester↓. "Yes, my lord," said L. K. Guilford, "but I think you would understand it better in two months."

Clubs

Esprit de corps, *Corporate spirit,* one of the most steady & inflexible prin[c]iples of human action [175]

Webster had the head of a bull dog, but the heart of a spaniel.

[2⟨49⟩52] When James Burke was ⟨coming⟩ ↑driving↓ home from ⟨driving⟩ ↑carrying↓ Ellen T[ucker]. E[merson]. in my wagon to the Concord station, the bolt of the wagon broke, & James was thrown out, & the horse ran home with the shafts. James was much hurt, but he thought only of the horse, & picked himself up the best

[174] A pencil line above and at the left sets off "Novels", "Rhetoric", and "Carlyle".

[175] "Hyde Earl . . . Guilford", "Do you . . . months.' ", and "Esprit . . . action" are struck through in pencil with single vertical use marks; "Hyde Earl . . . months.' " is used in "Clubs," *W*, VII, 239.

he could, & limped home ⟨and said How lucky it was that Ellen was not in the wagon⟩ comforting himself ↑how lucky it was↓ that "it did not happen when Miss Ellen was in the wagon." [176]

[25⟨0⟩3] Now & then, rarely comes a stout man like Luther, Montaigne, Pascal, Herbert, who utters a thought or feeling in a virile manner, and it is unforgettable. Then follow any number of spiritual eunuchs and women, who talk about that thought, imply it, in pages & volumes. Thus ⟨S⟩Novalis said, "Spinoza was a God--intoxicated man." [177] Samuel Hopkins said, "A man must be willing to be damned for the glory of God."
[254] George Fox said, "That which men trample on must be thy food." Swedenborg said, "the older the angels are, the more beautiful."
⟨The⟩ Rabbia said

Eastern poet said, "when the jubilant ⟨soul⟩ ↑Omar↓ prays, the ninth heaven vibrates to the tread of the Soul." [178]

↑S.↓ Augustine said,

Herbert said, "Let me not love thee, if I love thee not," [179]

↑J[ones].↓ Very said,

[255] Each of these male words being cast into the apprehension of pious souls delight & occupy them, and they say them over in every form of song, prayer, & discourse. ⟨And⟩ Such is Silesius Angelus, such is Upham, such Alger, such Pusey & his men.

Great bands of female souls who only receive the spermatic aura & brood on the same but add nothing.

[176] James Burke was Emerson's Irish laborer, "my saint of an Irishman" (*L*, V, 172). See p. [276] below.
[177] Attributed to Novalis by Carlyle in "Novalis," *Foreign Review*, IV (July 1829), 130. See *JMN*, VI, 209.
[178] This sentence is versified in "Character," *W*, X, 101.
[179] George Herbert, "Affliction," I, 66. See *JMN*, VI, 230.

[25⟨3⟩6] Do not spend one moment on the last; they are mere publishers & ⟨weakeners⟩ ↑diluters↓ & critics.

[25⟨4⟩7]   ↑See Gulistan↓
'Tis amusing to see Henry's ↑constant↓ assumption that the science is or should have been complete, & he has just found that they had neglected to describe the seeds, or count the sepals, or mark a variety. The ignorant scoundrels have not been in Concord. I mildly suggest that "what is every body's business is nobody's"; besides, who said they had? —besides, what were you sent for but ⟨for⟩ ↑to make↓ this observation? [180]

[258] Sentiment is materialized: that dear excellence of English intellect, *materialized intellect*, like *Kyanized wood*, has already come into fashion.

———

[259] "The deepest speculations are ↑but↓ difficult trifles, if they be not employed to guide men's actions in the path of virtue." Kenelm Digby
Memoirs p. 265 [181]

———

[2⟨58⟩60₁] ↑Poverty's praise.↓
And when he goes he carries
no more baggage than a bird.

If ↑bright↓ the sun, ⟨lie bright,⟩ he tarries;
All day his song is heard;
And when he goes, he carries
No more baggage than a bird [182]

[180] This paragraph, struck through in ink with a diagonal use mark and in pencil with one vertical and four diagonal use marks, is used in "Thoreau," *W*, X, 479–480. "See Gulistan" is in pencil with the "G" overwritten in ink; Emerson's Notebook OP Gulistan collects accounts of Concord friends. This paragraph occurs there on pp. [133]–[134].
[181] *Private Memoirs of Sir Kenelm Digby . . . Written by Himself . . .* (London, 1827); in Emerson's library. Emerson withdrew this book from the Boston Athenaeum June 22–August 14, 1855.
[182] These four lines are used in "Fragments on the Poet and the Poetic Gift," XXXIII, *W*, IX, 334.

[261₁] I think better of those ⟨that⟩ ↑who↓ neglect honors than of those who seek them[.] K[enelm] D[igby] [183]

Were it not fit subject for poem, to send a soul to doom ⟨by⟩ in the charge of an Angel, and trace the Angel's vain attempts to find a hell for it,—the assimilating energy of Osman converting every place into the one thing needful, & every hobgoblin into the best company. "I love low company," said Sprague, & says Osman, "What hell could be found for such an incorrigible Montaigne always Montaigne[.] The hero is always where he is[.]" [184]

[260₂] Reality rules destiny. They may well fear fate who have any infirmity of habit & aim. But he who rests on what is, & what he is, has a destiny above destiny, & can make mouths at fortune.[185]

[261₂] There are better pleasures than to be first. I keenly enjoyed Caroline's pointed remark, after we had both known Charles New-comb, that "no one could compare with him in ⟨geniu⟩ original genius," though I knew that she saw, as I saw, that his mind was far richer than mine, which ↑fact↓ nobody but she and I knew or suspected. Nay, I rejoiced in this very proof of her perception. And now, sixteen years later, we two alone possess this secret still.[186]

[262] The French wittily describe the English on a steamboat as each endeavoring to draw around himself an impassable space detaching him from his countrymen, in which he shall stand alone[,] clean & miserable. The French pay for their brilliant social cultivation herein, that they all write alike. I cannot tell whose book I am reading without looking on the cover; you would think all the novels & all the critic[i]sm were written by one & the same man.

[183] This sentence is in pencil. *Private Memoirs of Sir Kenelm Digby* . . . , 1827, p. 282: "For I judge more nobly of those that neglect honours, than of those who seek them."

[184] "The hero . . . is' " is written at the bottom of p. [260₁]. With "Were it . . . incorrigible", struck through in ink with a vertical use mark, cf. "Behavior," *W*, VI, 193–194. " 'I love . . . Sprague," is used in "Clubs," *W*, VII, 246.

[185] "Reality rules . . . at fortune." is marked by a vertical pencil line in the left margin.

[186] "Caroline" is Caroline Sturgis Tappan.

[263] Antony had heard too well the knell of thought & genius in the stertorous voice of the rector to have the smallest inclination to the church.

People live like these boys who watch for a sleigh-ride & mount on the f↑i↓rst that passes, & when they meet another that they know, swing themselves on to that, & ride in another direction, until a third passes, & they change again; 'tis no matter where they go, as long as there is snow & company[.]

[264] People masquerade before us in their fortunes & titles & connexion as Professors or Senators or great lawyers & impose on the frivolous, yes, & a good deal on each other, by these fames, at least it is a point of prudent good manners to treat these reputations tenderly as if they were real. But the sad realist knows these fellows at a glance, & they know him, as when ↑in Paris↓ the chief of the Police enters the ballroom, so many diamonded pretenders shrink & make themselves as inconspicuous as they can, or give him [265] a supplicating glance as they pass. "I had received," said Aunt Mary, "the fatal gift of penetration." And these Cassandras are ⟨never extinct⟩ always born. S[arah]. M[argaret]. F[uller] was one, & C[aroline]. S[turgis]. hardly less, & C[harles]. K[ing]. N[ewcomb]. a Delphic Oracle.[187]

[266] Modern Criticism has whitewashed Richard III; ↑Cromwell;↓ Froude has made out of Henry VIII. a good family man; Robespierre is a genuine patriot & tender philanthropist;
'Tis almost Caesar Borgia's turn to become a saint. Meantime, the other process now begins, and For↑ts?↓chammer has blackwashed Socrates[.] [188]

---

[187] "People masquerade [p. [264]] . . . always born.", struck through in ink with a vertical use mark on p. [264] and two vertical use marks on p. [265], is used in "Behavior," W, VI, 188. One vertical use mark on p. [265] is inadvertently extended through the final sentence of the paragraph, then finger-wiped.

[188] "Modern Criticism . . . Socrates" is struck through in pencil with a vertical use mark. Emerson probably refers to Peter Wilhelm Forchhammer, *Die Athener und Sokrates; die Gesetzlichen und der Revolutionär* (Berlin, 1837).

[267] Criticism See *TO* 24. The two handles.

_____

Herrick the most remarkable example of the low style. See *Herrick*
                                    Vol II p. 161   217

What does "farced" (p 162) mean?
         ↑"maunds" p 181↓
Herrick names himself in his verses, & his mother & brother[.] II
                              169, 190, 248

    "Jocund his muse was, but his life was chaste" II, p 198

    his rhymes are "else," "also," "ho," & "to"

_____

Because of his low style, he is a good example of the modernness of
an old Eng[lish]. writer.

_____

    His capital advantage over all is that he discovered his subject
where he stood, between his feet, in his house, [268] pantry, barn,
village, & neighbors, poultry yard, gossip & scandal of his set, their
feasts & holidays. Like Montaigne in this, that his subject cost him
nothing, & he knew what he spake of and he took his views level, so
that he had all his strength, the easiness of strength: he took what
he knew, & "took it easy," as we say.[189]

"Business" is comic when a hairdresser says "business is dull;" or
when a soldier says to his enemy, ⟨we⟩ ↑"I↓ have not come here now
on business."

[269] Guy, Merlin, Homer, Bard
Mars, Jove, ⟨Ossian⟩ Gray

[189] "Herrick the most . . . p. 161   217", p. [267], is struck through in pencil
with a vertical use mark. " 'Jocund his . . . house,", p. [267], is struck through in
pencil with one vertical use mark, and "Because of . . . house,", p. [267], with
two. "pantry, barn . . . say.", struck through in pencil with a vertical use mark,
is written on the lower half of p. [268], separated from the entry above it, " 'Business' is . . . business.' ", by a page-wide rule. "Herrick the most . . . style." and
"Because of . . . writer.", p. [267], and "he discovered [p. [267]] . . . say."
are used in "Art and Criticism," *W*, XII, 296. Emerson's references are to *The
Poetical Works of Robert Herrick*, 2 vols. (London, 1825), in his library.

Orpheus, Taliessin, Pindar, Gr[eek] Poet, Druid
Priest, Seer, Bard, Khan, Cid, Christ, Jove
Minstrel

[270] The people ⟨were⟩ ↑looked↓ melancholy & spiteful as if
bewitched, Hollan told Aubrey[.]

"The divine art of printing frightened away Robin Goodfellow & the
fairies"

"Fairies lingered till people became readers"

___

books versus fairies.

Ben Jonson's last masque "Time Vindicated."

> "One is ⟨m⟩his printer in disguise & keeps
> His press in a hollow tree, where to conceal him
> He works by glow-worm light, the moon's too open;
> The other zealous rag is his compositor"

↑B.↓ Jonson called the newspaper "a weekly cheat to draw money," &
thought it an ephemeral taste easily to be put down." *C. Knight.* "*Once
on a time*" [190]

[271] Prince Napoleon | sons of Louis & Hortense [191]
and Louis Napoleon
    ↑(now Emperor)↓

Prince Napoleon married his cousin Princess Charlotte, daughter
of Joseph Bonaparte; ↑and for his second wife Clotilde[,]
daughter of Victor Emanuel, King of Italy.↓

_____

↑*Eyes*↓

↑"those↓ furtive inclinations avowed by the eye, though dis⟨avowed⟩sembled
by the lips." Lamartine

[190] For "Time Vindicated", see *The Works of Ben Jonson*, 1716, VI, 6. Charles
Knight, *Once Upon a Time*, 2 vols. (London, 1854), I, 59.
[191] "Prince Napoleon" and "and Louis Napoleon" are joined at the right by a
pencil brace with an arrow at its center pointing to "sons of Louis & Hortense"; the
ampersand is in pencil.

"his head had the air of leaning downwards in order not to humble the crowd." — L[amartine] [192]

[272] Shall I blame my mother, whitest of women, because she was not a gipsy, & gave me no swarthy ferocity? or my father, because he came of a lettered race, & had no porter's shoulders?

[273] Emperor of Austria says, that "knowing too much only gives people the headache."
Strange that our government ⟨should never,⟩ so stupid as it is, should never blunder into a good measure. In Utah the leading issues are not those of our parties, yet the government invariably adopts the bad side. We have no character. In the European crisis, we should be of great weight, if we had character. But Austria & France & Russia can ⟨plausibly⟩ say, look at ⟨the⟩ America, 'Tis worse than we.

[274] I think that the religious revolution ought to have shaken by this time the security of the European tyrannies. Napoleon writes, "By the grace of God, & *by the will of the French people*[,]" but Austria & Russia still write, "By the grace of God," and the cohesion of /that/the/ system is in that dilapidated religion. Well, here we think meanly enough of Unitarianism. 'Tis here a mere spec of whitewash, because the mind of our culture has already left it behind. Nobody goes to church or longer ⟨has ears for⟩ ↑holds↓ [275] the Christian traditions. We rest on the moral nature, & the whole world shortly must. One would think, then, poor little Unitarianism would have sapped these thrones[.]

[276] There is no strong performance without a little fanaticism in the performer. That field yonder did not get such digging, ditching, ⟨&⟩ filling, & planting for any pay. A fanaticism lucky for the owner did it. ↑James B↑urke↓ opened my hay as fiercely on Sunday as on Monday.↓
Neither can any account be given of the fervid work in M[ary]. M[oody]. E[merson].'s manuscripts, but the vehement religion which would not let her sleep, nor sit, but write, write, night & day, year

[192] " 'those furtive . . . crowd.' — L" is struck through in ink with a diagonal use mark; " 'his head . . . crowd.' " is used in "Behavior," W, VI, 182–183.

after year. And C[harles]. K[ing]. N[ewcomb]. had this ⟨Daemων⟩ Δαιμων dazzling his eyes, & driving his pen. Unweariable fanaticism⟨s⟩ (which, ⟨to⟩ if it could give account of itself to itself, were [277] lost,) — is the Troll that

> "by night threshed the corn
> Which ten day laborers could not end." [193]
>   [Milton, "L'Allegro," ll. 108–109]

Cushing, & Banks, & Wilson, are ⟨all⟩ its victims, &, by means of it, vanquishers of men. But they whose eyes are prematurely opened with broad common-sense views, are hopeless dilettanti, & must obey these madmen.

Bonaparte rightly sighed for his soldiers of 1789.

[278]   May 25

The warblers at this season make much of the beauty & interest of the woods. The↑y↓ are so elegant in form & coat, and many of them here but for a short time; the Blackburnian warbler rarely seen by H[enry]. D[avid]. T[horeau] — [n]; the trees still allowing you to see far. Their small ⟨leaves⟩ ↑leaflets↓ do not vie with the spaces of the sky, — but let in the vision high — ↑and↓ (yesterday) Concord was all Sicily.

[279] Glad of Ellery's cordial praise of Carlyle's History, which, he thinks well entitled to be called a "Work," & far superior to his early books. Wonders at his imagination which can invest with such interest to himself these (one would think) hopeless details of German story. He is the only man who knows. — What a reader! how competent to give light now on the politics of Europe!
Today this History appears the best of all histories.[194]

[280] Alcott said, "Jove is in his reserves."

'Tis worth remembering in connexion with what I have so often to say of surface, that our whole skill is in that direction. Carlyle's

---

[193] This quotation is used in "Character," W, V, 135.
[194] Emerson received vol. 3 of Carlyle's *Frederick the Great* in late April, 1859 (CEC, p. 527). For " 'Jove . . . reserves.' ", directly below, see JMN, XIII, 329.

Friedrich is a great book; opens new extension to history. How much event, personality, nationality, is there disclosed, or hinted at, & will draw multitudes of scholars to its exploring & illustration! So with every new vein that is opened. [281] Wide, east & west, north & south, immense lateral spaces,—but the sum & upshot of all, the aim & theory,—is in few steps, or one; seen in an instant, or never seen. Vast surface, short diameter.

[282] For "Success," add the circumstance of the *Claqueurs* of the French theatre.

Also, CL 83

The climate of Sahara is ⟨described as⟩ day after day, sunstroke after sunstroke with a frosty shadow between.

[283] [blank]

    [284] *Historical pairs.*   ↑Agamemnon & Ulysses↓
                                          ↑Arthur & Merlin↓
Æschylus & Sophocles; ↑Socrates & Plato;↓
↑Paul & John   Caesar & Pompey,   Brutus & Caesar,↓
Michel Angelo & Raffaelle
Corneille & Racine
Shakspeare & Milton
⟨|| . . . ||⟩   ↑Demosthenes & Cicero↓
             ↑Burke & Fox↓
Voltaire & Rousseau
Goethe & Schiller
Cuvier & Geoffroi St Hilaire
Owen & Agassiz
Beethoven & Mozart
⟨Paul & John⟩
Webster & Everett
Eldon & Romilly
⟨Fox & Burke⟩
↑Kant & Hegel↓ [195]

[195] "Paul & John", in pencil parentheses, is canceled in ink; "Fox & Burke", in pencil parentheses, is canceled in pencil.

[285] Raffaelle's letter to Count Castiglione is as follows,
"On account of Galatea, I should reckon myself a great master, were ⟨only⟩ there in it only half of the great things which your excellency writes me. I recognize, nevertheless, in your words, the love which you bear me. Besides, I must say to you, that, in order to paint a beautiful female form, I must see many of them, & certainly under the condition that your Excellency stand near me in order to select the finest. But whilst still a [⟨3⟩286] right judgment is as rare as beautiful women are, therefore I use a certain idea which subsists in my mind. Whether this possesses genuine artistic excellence, I know not, but I strive to reach it; & so I commend myself to your Excellency."

See Grimm's Essays, p. 194 [196]

When people come to see us, we foolishly talk, lest we be inhospitable. But the wise way, is, to ⟨pr⟩ let nature bear the expense of the conversation.

[⟨3⟩287] Instinct & Inspiration
The two ways.
⟨Our shopping⟩ The Understanding is a sort of shop clerk: it is for petty ends. It has nothing catholic or noble in power or aim. It is the "Preceptor of a Prince."
direct, omniscient, ⟨almighty,⟩ self-contained, needing no ally. [197]

[⟨3⟩288]   *Egotism.*
'Tis pity to see egotism for its poverty. All must talk about themselves, for 'tis all they know, but genius never needs to allude to his personality, as every ⟨creature &⟩ person & creature he has seen serves him as an exponent of his private experience. So the↓ communicates ⟨his se⟩ all his secrets, and endless autobiography, & never

---

[196] This entry is Emerson's translation of Herman Friedrich Grimm, *Essays*, 1859, pp. 194–195. "See Grimm's . . . p. 194" is enclosed on three sides by a line.
[197] "almighty," is canceled in ink and pencil.

lets on that he means himself.   ↑See M[ary] M[oody] E[merson], I.
p. 50, 73, Remember Dr Chauncey's prayer.↓   ↑Dante ☞↓ 198

[289] ↑Dante.↓

Dante cannot utter a few lines but I am informed what transcendent eyes he had, as, for example,

"un foco
Ch' emisperio di tenebre vincia."
[Inferno, iv, 68–69]

How many millions would have looked at candles, lamps, & fires, &
planets, all their days, & never noticed this measure of their illuminating force, "of conquering a hemisphere of the darkness." Yet he says
nothing about his own eyes.

[290]   Inspiration.

What marks right mental action is always newness, ignoring of
the past; & the elasticity of the present object, — which makes all the
magnitudes & magnates quite unnecessary. This is what we mean
when we say your subject is absolutely indifferent. You need not write
the History of the World, nor the Fall of Man, nor ↑King↓ Arthur,
nor Iliad, nor Christianity; but write of hay, or of cattleshows, or
trade sales, or of a ship, or of Ellen, or Alcott, or [291] of a couple
of school-boys, if only you can be the fanatic of your subject, & find
a fibre reaching from it to the core of your heart, so that all your
affection & all your thought ↑can↓ freely play.

[292]   ↑Tennyson.↓
England is solvent, no matter what rubbish & hypocrisy of Palmer-
stons & Malmesburys & D'Israelis she may have, for here comes
Tennyson's poem, indicating a ⟨perfect⟩ ↑supreme↓ social culture, a
perfect insight, & the possession of all the weapons & all the functions
of a man, with the skill to wield them which Homer, Aristophanes,
or Dante had.[199] The long promise to pay that runs over ages from

---

[198] The hand sign points to the entry on p. [289]. Two of Dr. Charles Chauncy's prayers are given in "Eloquence," W, VIII, 127–128.
[199] Idyls of the King (Boston, 1859), in Emerson's Library.

Chaucer, Spenser, Milton, Ben Jonson,—the long promise to write
[293] the national poem of Arthur, Tennyson at last keeps, in these
low selfdespising times; Taliessin & Ossian are at last edited, revised,
expurgated, distilled. The national poem needed a national man.
And the blood is still so rich, & healthful, that, at last ↑in Tennyson↓
a national soul comes to the Olympic games ⟨in Tennyson,⟩—equal
to the task. He is the Pisistratus, ⟨that⟩ who collects & publishes the
Homer, ripened at last by the infusion of so many harvests, & henceforth unchangeable ⁿ [294] & immortal.

↑Bard.↓

A ⟨history⟩ collection there should be of those fables which are
agreeable to the human mind. One is the orator or singer who can
control all minds. The perfect ⟨min⟩ poet again is described in Taliessin's songs, in Mabinogion. Tennyson has drawn Merlin.

[295] England forever! What a secular genius is that which begins
its purpose of writing the Arthur Epic with Chaucer, & slowly ripens
it until now, in 1859, it is ⟨|| ... ||⟩done! And what a heart-whole race
is that which in the same year can turn out two such sovereign productions as the "History of Friedrich," and "The Four Idyls."
Channing's remark is that there is a prose tone running through the
book, and certainly he has flat lines e.g. the four lines "Forgetful"
&c p. [11] [296₁] which contrast badly with a similar iteration in
Shakspeare's Henry VI., the ↑dying↓ soliloquy of Warwick, which
is alive. And such a line occurs sometimes, as,
         "You hardly know me yet" ²⁰⁰
Again C. ⟨makes the⟩ objects, that he has taken this old legend,
instead of a theme of today.

---

²⁰⁰ In "The Marriage of Geraint," ll. 50–54, five successive lines begin with
"Forgetful":
         Forgetful of his promise to the king,
         Forgetful of the falcon and the hunt,
         Forgetful of the tilt and tournament,
         Forgetful of his glory and his name,
         Forgetful of his princedom and its cares.
For "the dying soliloquy of Warwick", see *Henry VI*, Part 3, V, ii, 5–28. "you
hardly know me yet" is from "Merlin and Vivien," l. 353.

But he has known how to universalize his fable [297₁] & fill it with his experience & wisdom. The eternal moral shines.

But what landscape, & what words⟨,⟩! "the stammering thunder" [201]

[296₂] Great arts   little men
greatness begot of paltriness
The greatest meliorator is Trade
A
Every victory over nature ought to recommend to man the height of his nature but one wonders who did it[.]
Each man has a knack ⟨|| ... ||⟩ is in veins & spots the great brain equal symmetrical   the great brain fed from a great heart does not appear

[297₂] Every one has more to hide than he has to show or is lamed by his excellence[.] [202]

[298] [203]   Works & Days, *Conclusion*
        Thus we climb from the activity of our hands to the inner faculties which rule them, from local skills & the ⟨poor⟩ ↑huckstering↓ economy of time which values the amount to the finer economy which respects the quality & the right we have to the work, or the fidelity with which it flows from ourselves to the depth of thought it betrays
        to its universality or that its roots are in eternity & not in time. Then it flows from character[,] that sublime [299] health which values one moment as another & makes us great in all conditions in

[201] Cf. "And deafened with the stammering cracks and claps," "Merlin and Vivien," l. 940.
[202] On p. [296], "Great arts . . . appear", in pencil, is overwritten by "which contrast . . . fable" in ink; on p. [297] "Every one . . . excellence", in pencil, is overwritten by "& fill . . . thunder'" in ink. For "Great Arts . . . Trade", see pp. [50] and [51] above. "Great Arts . . . excellence" is used in "Works and Days," *W*, VII, 166.
[203] The entries on pp. [298] and [299] are in pencil.

youth & age and is the only definition we have of Freedom & Power[.] [204] ↑printed in "Society & Solitude"↓

[300]–[301] [blank]
[302] [Index material omitted]
[inside back cover] [Index material omitted]

---

[204] This paragraph, struck through in pencil with one vertical and one diagonal use mark on p. [298] and with two vertical and two diagonal use marks on p. [299], is used in "Works and Days," *W*, VII, 185.

CL

1859–1861

Although the earliest dated entry in Journal CL is August 16, 1859 (p. [49]), Emerson seems to have begun using it in May or June, 1859; the reference to Choate's death (p. [29]) was probably written around July 15–20. The latest dated entry is January 19, 1861 (pp. [284]–[285]).

The covers of the copybook, brown paper marbled with red and blue over boards, measure 17.8 x 21.4 cm. The protective corners on the front and back covers are of tan leather; the original spine strip, probably of the same tan leather, has been replaced in rebacking. "1859–60" is centered in the upper half of the front cover. Both front and back covers show ink blots, wiped and unwiped, and several lines of blotted writing are visible on the upper half of the back cover.

Including flyleaves (i, ii, 291, 292), there were 148 unlined leaves measuring 17.4 x 20.6 cm, but the leaves bearing pages 73–80 have been cut out, and the leaves bearing pages 179–180 and 249–250 have been torn out. The leaves that would have been pages 165–166 and 167–168 in sequential pagination were torn out before pagination, as there is no gap at this point in Emerson's numbering. In his pagination, Emerson repeated pages 136 and 137; the editors have added subscript numbers to distinguish the two pairs. Five pages were misnumbered and corrected: 8⟨6⟩5, 10⟨6⟩4, 10⟨7⟩5, 1⟨4⟩84, and 28⟨4⟩6. The verso of page 281 was numbered 282 and then mistakenly changed: 28⟨2⟩4. The editors have regularized this to 282. Most of the pages are numbered in ink, but two are numbered in pencil: 213 and 247, and twenty-five are unnumbered: 14, 15, 46, 47, 57, 81, 97, 114, 161, 188, 223, 230, 232–235, 238, 239, 267, and 287–292. Twenty pages are blank: 2, 6, 10, 15, 46, 47, 63, 102, 130, 146, 163, 178, 208, 232–235, 238, 239, and 291. The leaves bearing pages i–ii, 1–2, and 3–4, once torn out, are now reattached to the front cover verso and page 5 with a strip of stiff white paper; the leaves bearing pages 287–288 and 291–292, once torn out, are now reattached to page 286 and the inside back cover with a strip of stiff white paper. The leaf bearing pages 289 and 290 is laid in between pages 288 and 291.

Laid in between pages 66 and 67 is a blue sheet 11.3 x 18.3 cm bearing a printed "Song, For the Festival of the Concord School, Nawshawtuck, July 15th, 1859" and an identifying note in Edward Emerson's hand.

[front cover]   1859–60

[front cover verso] [1] [Index material omitted]

[i]   1859–60.   R. W. Emerson
                                    Concord. Mass.

"Aliis laetus, sapiens sibi." [2]

CL

[ii] [3]   ↑*Reverse*↓
            Elmira
            Owego
               B   Waterbury
    ↑*Direct*↓
      Binghamton   Elmira
      Owego   Owego
      Elmira   Kalamazoo
    J M Johnson   ↑*Walker*↓ Binghamton
                                    Alfred   N.Y.

                                    Sandusky O
                                    Ashland O
                                    Oberlin O

                                    Pittsburg

[1]   1860 [4]
           Nov 15
             16

[1] The entries on the front cover verso are in pencil.
[2] "Outwardly joyous, inwardly wise" (Ed.). The Latin is used in "Considerations by the Way," W, VI, 265. This epigraph, "CL," and the line beneath are encircled in pencil.
[3] The entries on p. [ii] are in pencil.
[4] The entries on p. [1] are Emerson's tentative lecture schedule for December, 1860, and January–March, 1861. The list is in three columns, beginning with Nov 15, Dec 24, and Feb 17. Emerson also listed lecture engagements for the season in Pocket Diary 12 below. "And" (November 28) is in pencil and canceled in pencil;

```
       17
       18  S.
       19  M.
       20  [Parker] Fraternity Boston
       21  W
       22  Th
       23  F
       24  S
       25  Su
       26  M
       27  Tu Lynn
       28  W      ⟨And⟩
       29  Th Thanksgiving
       30  F.
  Dec   1  S.
        2  ⟨M⟩ S
        3  ⟨Tu⟩ M
        4  ⟨W⟩ Tu   And[over]
        5  ⟨Th⟩ ⟨Chelsea⟩W. Roxbury
        6  ⟨F⟩Th    Chelsea
        7  ⟨S⟩Fri      And[over]
        8  Sat
        9  ⟨M⟩Sun
       10  ⟨T⟩Mon
       11  ⟨W⟩Tu ⟨Lynn⟩ ↑Concord↓ ↑N.H↓
       12  ⟨Th⟩W. ⟨Concord⟩Bedford
       13  Th    Andover
       14  F    ⟨And⟩Beeson?
       15  S
```

"Thanksgiving" (November 29) is in pencil; "And" (December 4), "⟨Chelsea⟩" (December 5), "And" (December 7), "Concord" (December 11), "⟨Concord⟩" (December 12), "Andover" (December 13), "⟨And⟩" (December 14), "Music Hall" (January 6), "A" (January 8), "W ⟨E⟩" (January 9), "Th O" (January 10), "F" (January 11), "S" (January 12), "S Cortland" (January 13), "M Alfred? Corning" (January 14), "Sandusky?" (January 20), "Tu" (February 5), "N. Haven?" (February 7), "Tu So Danvers?" (February 12), "⟨Concord N H?⟩" (February 19), and "⟨Augusta?⟩" (February 20) are in pencil. "So Danvers/?/" (February 5) and "Concord N H?" (February 19) are canceled in pencil.

16 Su
17 M
18 Dowse Institute [Cambridgeport]
19 W   Salem
20 Th
21 F
22 S
23 Su
Dec 24 M.
25 Tu. Dowse Institute [Cambridgeport]
26 Wed Nashua
27 Th.
28 Fr Andover
29 Sat
30 S
31 M.
1861
Jan 1 Tu
2.
3.
4.
5.
6. Music Hall [Boston]
7 M
8 Tu A
9. W ⟨E⟩Elmira
10. Th   O[wego]
11. F   Hornellsville
12. S
13 S   Cortland
14 M   Alfred? Corning
15 Buffalo
16 W
17 Th
18 F
19 Sat
20 S   Sandusky?

      21 M

      22 Tu

      23 W

      24 Th

      25 F

      26 Sat

      27 S

      28 M

      29 Tu

      30 W

      31 Th

Feb 1 F

       2

       3

       4

       5 Tu ⟨So Danvers/?/⟩

       6

       7 N. Haven?

       8

       9

     10

     11

     12 Tu   So Danvers?

     13 Augusta

     14

     15

     16

     17

     18

     19 ⟨Concord N H?⟩

     20 ⟨Augusta?⟩Gloucester

     21

     22

     23

     24 Portland

     25

     26

27
28
⟨29⟩
March 1
2
3
4
5
6
7
8
9
10
11

[2] [blank]

[3] I learned that the rhyme is there in the theme, thought, & im⟨g⟩age, themselves. I learned that there is a beyond to every place, & the bird moving through the air by successive dartings taught me.

[4] Simonides made an epigram in commendation of his memory[.]
(See it in Bentley's Works Vol I p 110)

Μνημη δ' ου τινα φημι Σιμωνιδη ισοφαριζειν
Ογδωκονταετει παιδι Λεωπρεπεος.

Nobody has a memory like to Simonides who am 80 years of age, the son of Leoprepes.[5]

[5] The sky looks indignantly on all that is doubtful & obscure in man[.]

⟨And aye⟩ ↑I saw↓ the sky looked scornful down
On all was mean in man
⟨And⟩ ↑Heard↓ airy tongues ⟨that told⟩ ↑⟨taunted⟩↓ ↑that taunt↓ the town
Achieve it, if you can.

[5] *The Works of Richard Bentley, D.D. Collected and Edited by the Rev. Alexander Dyce*, 3 vols. (London, 1836–1838), I, 111.

Methought the sky looked scornful down
On all was base in man,
And airy tongues did taunt the town
Achieve it, if you can.[6]

[6] [blank]

[7] Certain persons utter oracles, as Bettine, as Aunt Mary, as Alcott, & Charles Newcomb. We hear awestruck that the ancients recognized an *omen* or *fatum*, now & then, in chance words spoken; and we cast about & wonder what these oracles were. And ⟨now & then⟩ we hear some remark which explains our own character, or foible, or circumstance, and ↑it↓ do↑es↓ not occur to us that this is the very ⟨thing⟩ ↑chance↓ ⟨they⟩ ↑those ancients↓ considered. This is the omen & *fatum*↑.↓ ⟨& oracle.⟩ But these oracles [8] are simply perceptions of the intellect; &, whenever the intellect acts, there is an oracle. An omen or fatum is that of Pindar; see *VO* 4

[9] Nature wishes that woman should attract man, but she has cunningly made them with a little sarcasm in expression, which seems to say, "Yes, I am willing to attract, but to attract a little better kind of man than any I yet see." [7]

[10] [blank]
[11] Bridle him.
Yes, but he takes the bridle in his teeth
Scourge him
He is refreshed by blows.
Imprison him
No prison will hold him
He invented locks & bolts & can unlock his own. This is he ⟨that⟩ who invented the electric horse. He can swim across the ocean, & arrive in Asia at an earlier date than he left New York.

---

[6] The two versions of the quatrain are in pencil. The first is struck through in pencil with a diagonal mark, perhaps to cancel it. Cf. "Walden," ll. 21–24, *W*, IX, 371. For "The sky . . . obscure in man", see *JMN*, XI, 109.
[7] This entry, struck through in ink with two vertical use marks, is used in "Beauty," *W*, VI, 296.

Throw him to the lions. But this is Androcles, Van Amburg; the lions lick his feet.

Fire will not burn him, but plays the part of Saint Irenaeus' ⟨Martyr⟩ⁿ flames, — namely of a wall, or a [12] vaulted shrine bending ⟨ornamentally⟩ around & over him, without harm⟨ing him⟩.[8]

[13] The south has too large concession to begin with.

"Was ever magnanimity so enormous as mine? I did not pitch him out of the window," said ⟨W⟩John Wilson.[9]
⟨Gosse's testimony⟩

Disunion excellent, if it is just disunion enough, but if it go too far, 'tis bad.
Is the Union a conveniency only like the ↑U. S.↓ Bank, which ⟨allowed⟩ ↑enabled↓ a man to put in his pocket bills which were current everywhere, — and so ⟨this⟩ made us citizens from Canada to the Gulf.
The insanity of the South. I acquit them of guilt on that plea. "But [14] never more be officer of mine." [10]
They come to our colleges. They ⟨were a⟩travel in Europe. They marry here. They hear at Columbia College Dr Lieber's lectures.[11]
Europeans go, like Gosse, into Alabama, & write as he, about the damnation, & such is the *Esprit du corps* that their reason is dethroned.[12]

[8] "Scourge him . . . blows." and "No prison . . . him", struck through in ink with single horizontal and diagonal use marks, "Throw him . . . feet.", struck through in ink with a diagonal use mark, and "Fire will . . . harm⟨ing him⟩." are used in "Worship," *W*, VI, 199, and *W*, IX, 279–280. Isaac H. Van Amburgh (1811–1865), American animal trainer, was the first man to put his head into a lion's mouth. Saint Irenaeus was a bishop of Lyons in the second century.
[9] This story is told in *JMN*, X, 223–224 and 564–565. According to *J*, VII, 396, n. 1, Emerson used the story in an unsuccessful attempt to quiet a mob that broke up a meeting of the Massachusetts Anti-Slavery Society in 1861.
[10] Cf. Shakespeare, *Othello*, II, iii, 250.
[11] Francis Lieber (1800–1872) was professor of history and political economy at Columbia from 1857 to 1865.
[12] Philip Henry Gosse (1810–1888), English naturalist, published *Letters from*

I see for such madness no hellebore[,] for such calamity no solution[,] but servile war & the Africanization of that country.[13]

[15] [blank]
    [16] All things have an accompaniment of magic. If the fact seems plain & thoroughly known to thee, 'tis plain thou knowest nothing about it.
    ↑The painter came at last to say with alarm, "I have at last painted a picture which contents me."   See infra p. 21↓[14]

    Magic needs finer organs, & its own time. You must not look at ⟨a⟩ firefl⟨y⟩ies by daylight.

    A man must be a mystic or worshipper, he must carry with him an unsounded secret, or he is worthless. See the poor Unitarian with his dreary superficiality. He is a bare coat & pantaloons.

    [17] Look at the tree, & it becometh fruitful. But also look not at the tree; ↑if you↓ guard ⟨not⟩ against ⟨cro⟩worms by ↑so much as↓ a spoonful of salt, ⟨or⟩ it will be ⟨bored to death.⟩ honeycombed by borers.

    See below, ↑CL 170↓ what is said, ⟨of⟩ "Power, as such, is not known to the angels." CL 170   It must be magically easy.

    [18] Bettine is a wise child with her wit, humor, will, & pure inspirations. She utters oracles & is the best critic of Goethe. Her talk about ⟨music, & about⟩ manners & character, is like Charles Auchester's.[15] But he has no wit like her fine things about the "flat

---

Alabama, (*U.S.*): *Chiefly Relating to Natural History* (London, 1859) after living seven or eight months in Alabama. Emerson withdrew this book from the Boston Athenaeum March 23–30, 1861.
    [13] This sentence, struck through in ink with two vertical use marks, is used in "American Civilization," *W*, XI, 298.
    [14] This entry is in pencil. "Allston" is inserted in pencil before "The painter" in a hand probably not Emerson's.
    [15] For Elizabeth Sara Sheppard's novel *Charles Auchester, a memorial*, see *JMN*, XIII, 338 and 382, and Journal SO, p. [119] above.

seventh." (Vol. I, 282) [16] ↑And Mme. de Stael, & Jacobi.↓ How
clearly she sees the defects of his mind & working! How superior
she is to him, & cunningly hints it, ↑(See Vol I. p 310)↓ & he never
dares own it. ↑He thanks her "for every bright glance into a spiritual
life, which, without you, I should perhaps never again have ex-
perienced." Never *again*! Mean fellow! As if he ha⟨s⟩d or could
anticipate a thought of hers! [Vol II 178]↓

[19] 'Tis easy to see that Carlyle has learned of Goethe his
literary manners, & how to be condescending & courteous, & yet to
keep himself always in rein.

But ⟨in the letter⟩ when Bettine writes from Vienna her admirable
reports of her conversation with Beethoven, Goethe in his reply
comes at last out of his shell, & pays a homage to Beethoven he has
not expressed for any other; calls himself a "layman" before this
"demon-possessed person," and offers to meet him at Carlsbad. &c.

(Vol II. p. 217)

↑But, in Varnhagen's [n] ⟨Bettine⟩ journals, Bettine makes a far
different appearance, & never to her advantage.↓

[20] Bettine says of the Frau Rath, "She let me do as I pleased, &
gave my manner of being no name." [*Ibid.*, II, 34]

"I am in low esteem with the Philistines who find a row of talents valuable
in a woman, — but not the woman herself without these." II. 10.

[21]   ↑*Bettine*↓
"I see also artists contented with their ability, whilst genius vanishes; they
measure with one another, & will find the measure of their own greatness
still the highest; but have no idea that the smallest scale of genius requires
unmeasurable inspiration." II. 342.

[16] This quotation and those on pp. [18]–[21] are from Bettina Brentano von
Arnim, *Goethe's Correspondence with a Child*, 1839.

[22] The good invention by which everybody is provided with somebody who is glad to see him.[17]

↑printed ↑in↓ "Society & Solitude," p. 205↓

[23] [18] ↑Illusion.↓
All is riddle, & the key to a riddle is another riddle.

See for the illusion that may deceive the elect, *BL* 239

[24]   Manners
Fuseli said of Northcote, that he looked like a rat which had seen a cat.[19]

[25] As soon [as] the intellect awakes, all things make a musical impression. It is comedy without laughter. Everything in the human world, fashionist, millionaire, presidents, academics, are toy people in a toy-house — [20]

Illusions
    Berkeley,   Viasa,
              ↑This passage transferred to "Love." *L* 136↓
The Capital illusion of love is to have the cosmical beauty or moral or material or even sexual excellency so suggested by one person, as to give him or her the benefit of all. Truly, in a deep sense, *puella minima pars sui.*
⟨illusion of time⟩
↑'Tis[n] as if we mistook the aurora & meteors for part of the fire-works.↓ [21]
of pleasure   ———

---

[17] "The good . . . him.", struck through in ink with a vertical use mark, is used in "Clubs," *W*, VII, 229.
[18] The entries on p. [23] are struck through in ink and pencil with single vertical use marks; "All . . . riddle." is used in "Illusions," *W*, VI, 313. *BL* is Emerson's notebook Book of Lectures.
[19] This sentence, struck through in ink with a vertical use mark, is used in "Behavior," *W*, VI, 185. James Northcote (1746–1831) was an English historical and portrait painter.
[20] This paragraph is struck through in ink with a diagonal use mark.
[21] "The Capital . . . fireworks." is struck through in pencil with one vertical

[26] Illusion of time, which is very deep. Who has disposed of it? or come to the conviction which the old Philosopher expressed[?] [22]

We live by our admiration, faith,

Illusion of property

self

[27] Very little reliance must be put on the common stories of Mr Webster's or of Mr Choate's learning, their Greek, or their varied literature. That ice won't bear. Reading! to what purpose did they read?[n] I allow them the merit of that reading which appears in their opinions, tastes, beliefs, ↑& practice.↓ They read that they might know, — did they not? Well, these men did not know: they blundered. They were utterly ignorant of that whi↑c↓h every boy & girl of fifteen knows perfectly, the rights of men [28] & women, and this old talking lubber among his dictionaries, & Leipsic editions of Lysias, had lost his knowledge.

But Mr A. of the Suffolk Bank, & Mr B. of the Merchant's Insurance, & Mr C. President of the City Exchange, say, he was a very learned man, &, that, at Sharon Springs, he devoured a trunk of books.[23]

[29] Poor Choate, — he ⟨was⟩is properly punished for his hypocritical church deaconing, &c. by having this poor dunce of a Dr Adams braying over his grave — that Jesus Christ is getting on,

and one diagonal use mark; cf. "Illusions," W, VI, 319. The Latin may be translated "The girl is the least part of herself"; see JMN, VIII, 367. A pencil line curves from above "The Capital . . . fireworks." down the left margin and around to "This passage . . . L 136".

[22] "Illusion . . . expressed", struck through in ink with a vertical use mark, is used in "Illusions," W, VI, 319.

[23] The entries on pp. [27] and [28], struck through in pencil on p. [27] with two vertical use marks and on p. [28] with one, are used in "The Man of Letters," W, X, 256.

↑for↓ Mr Choate has signified his good opinion. Even the old Jehovah himself, good times must be coming to Him; for Mr Choate, &c [24]

———

Fame is the impression that a fine soul makes of itself. Many a man has done no one thing up to his fame. Yet the fame was inevitable. See *CL* 55

[30]   *Persians.*

"In any piece of ground where springs of naphtha or petroleum obtain, by merely sticking an iron tube in the earth, & applying a light to the upper end, the mineral oil will burn till the tube is decomposed, or for a vast number of years."

Guthrie: "Tour through the Taurida" ap[ud]. Southey [25]

[31] In reading prose, I am sensible as soon as a sentence drags, but in reading poetry, as soon as one word drags.[26]

Of Adam ⁿ Smith, "but had I known that he loved rhyme as much as you say he does, I should have hugged him;" said Johnson.
Boswell p. 118 [27]

[32] What David says, "Each may be king over himself."

A will that inquires, "Dare I?," and a man whose will is his law.

"I promised no Constancy, all within me is mightier than I myself; I cannot rule, I cannot will, I must let all happen as it may." Bettine [*Goethe's Correspondence with a Child,* 1839,] II 92 [93]

[24] Rufus Choate, Boston lawyer and U.S. senator from Massachusetts, died on July 13, 1859; a memorial meeting was held on July 23 at Faneuil Hall with Edward Everett as the principal speaker. See Journal SO, p. [204] above.

[25] *Southey's Common-Place Book. Second Series. Special Collections,* ed. John Wood Warter (London, 1850), p. 420. The quotation, struck through in pencil with a wavy diagonal use mark, is used in "Resources," *W*, VIII, 141–142. Emerson withdrew this book from the Boston Athenaeum March 31–May 1, 1860.

[26] This sentence, struck through in pencil with a wavy diagonal use mark, is used in "Poetry and Imagination," *W*, VIII, 54.

[27] *The Life of Samuel Johnson* (London, 1827), in Emerson's library. The quotation from Boswell, struck through in pencil with a wavy diagonal use mark, is used in "Address at the Opening of the Concord Free Public Library," *W*, XI, 503–504.

[33] "that bearing, which as much surpasses beauty, as it bids defiance to ugliness." *Bettine* [28]

[34] When the railroad bridge breaks, or the road is washed away by the freshet, it is because the Company breaks, and its integrity is ⟨washed away⟩ corrupted.   Shall the "groundworks be all one cracking & ⟨disease?⟩ ↑pulverization?↓"

A park of artillery & not a spoonful of powder

33.[n] *Henry VIII.* it is ordered, "that no person above the age of twenty-four shall shoot with the lightflight arrow at a distance under 220 yards." 220 yds., then, was the effective range for fighting purposes of the heavy war arrow[.] [29]
↑Latimer says, ⟨his⟩ ↑my↓ father taught ⟨him⟩ ↑me↓ "how to lay my body in the bow, — not to draw with strength of arm, as other nations do, but with the strength of the body." Froude II. 96.↓ [30]

[35] [Alcott said, that Cowley considered the use of a University for the cherishing of gifted persons.] [31]

↑It is true there is but one institution.↓ It is true that the University & the Church, which should be counterbalancing institutions & independent, do now express the sentiment of the popular politics, & the popular optimism, whatever it be. Harvard College has no voice in Harvard College, but Statestreet votes it down on every ballot. Every thing [36] will be permitted there which goes to adorn Boston Whiggism; is it geology, ⟨a⟩Astronomy, Poetry, antiquities, art, rhetoric, but, that which it exists for, — to be a fountain of novelties out of heaven, — a Delphi uttering warning & ravishing oracles to ⟨control⟩ elevate & lead mankind, — *that* it shall not be permitted to do or to think of. On the contrary every generosity of thought is

[28] The quotation is struck through in ink with a vertical use mark.
[29] *The Statutes of the Realm*, 9 vols. in 10 (London, 1810–1827), III, 838. A curved line separates this entry from the next.
[30] James Anthony Froude, *History of England from the Fall of Wolsey to the Death of Elizabeth*, 2 vols. (London, 1856). Emerson withdrew this volume from the Boston Athenaeum August 16–18, 1859.
[31] See also p. [209] below.

suspect↑ed,↓ & gets a bad name. [37] And all the young men come out decrepit ⟨b⟩Bostonians; not a poet, not a prophet, not a daemon, but is gagged & stifled, or driven away. All that is sought in the ⟨tutors⟩ ↑instruction↓ is drilling tutors, & not inspirers.[32]

See what is said on this matter, *GO* 221

See ↑poor↓ Unitarianism now at its solemn feast piteously speaking to a Calvinistic Bunkum, about the "work", the "higher life", &c. ⟨with ⟨|| ... ||⟩ & ⟨MST⟩ⁿ & ⟨SSL⟩ for orators and S. O.!⟩——[33]

[38] The spring is an inundation of love. The marriage of the plants, the marriage of bird, beast, reptile, of the animal world, & of man, is the aim of all this new glory of color & form[.]

> And love's inundation poured
> Over space & race abroad [34]

[39] Our doctrine must begin with ⟨the Eternal,⟩ the Necessary & Eternal, & discriminate ↑Fate↓ from the Necessary ⟨Fate⟩.ⁿ There is no limitation about the Eternal↑.↓ ⟨the soul⟩ Thought, Will is co--eternal with the world; and, as soon as intellect is awaked in any man, it ⟨ascends so far,⟩ shares so far of the eternity,—is of the Maker not of the Made. But Fate is the name we give to the action of that one eternal all-various Necessity on the brute myriads whether [40] in things, animals, or in men in whom the intellect pure is not yet opened. To such it is only a burning wall which hurts those who run against it[.]

The great day in the man is the birth ⟨of mind in him⟩ of perception, which instantly throws him on the party of the Eternal. He sees what must be, and that it ⟨no⟩is not [41] more that which must be, than it is that which should be, ⟨or,⟩ ↑or↓ what is best. To be, then

---

[32] This paragraph is used in "The Celebration of Intellect," *W*, XII, 126.

[33] "⟨|| ... ||⟩", "MST", and "SSL" are very heavily canceled with many strokes of the pen.

[34] "And love's . . . abroad", in pencil, is struck through in pencil with a diagonal use mark.

becomes the infinite good, & breath is jubilation. A breath of Will blows through the Universe eternally in the direction of the right or necessary; it is the air which all intellects ⟨inspire⟩ inhale & exhale, and all things are blown or moved by it in ⟨orbit &⟩ order & orbit.[35]

The secret of the Will is that it ⟨does⟩ ↑doth↓ what it knows absolutely good to be done, & so is greater than itself, & is divine in doing. Whilst ↑o↓the↑r↓ choices ⟨of an animal quadruped[n] [42] or biped⟩ are ⟨the choices⟩ of an appetite or of a disease, as of an itching skin, or of a thief, or sot, or ⟨assa⟩ striker.

———

Nature is the memory of the mind, said A[lcott].

———

But come how it will, the only men of any account in nature are the three or five we have beheld who have a will. Then we say, here is a man, & men obey [43] him; his body is sweet, & not putrid like others; his words are loaded, and all around him is eventful.

Come, then, count your reasons,

↑1.↓ The belief in Fate is unwholesome, and ⟨we⟩ can only be good where it teaches the strength of nature to man.

↑2.↓ We only value a stroke of will; He alone is happy who has will; The rest are herds.

He uses, they are used.[36]

↑3.↓ This will derives from the [44] aboriginal Nature, is perception of the Eternal Necessity[.]

It rests on God himself, & that is its power to shock, that it

---

[35] "more that . . . jubilation." is struck through in ink with a vertical use mark; "A breath . . . orbit.", struck through in ink with a vertical use mark, is used in "Fate," *W*, VI, 27–28.
[36] "We only . . . used." is struck through in pencil with two vertical use marks; "He alone . . . used." is used in "Powers and Laws of Thought," *W*, XII, 46.

betrays his presence in this loafer; but it winds through dark channels, & one knows not how it arrived here.

It is a sharing of the true order of the world, & a push in that interest & direction.

It is born, freedom, in the intellect.   On that bright [45] moment when we are born into thought, we are instantaneously uplifted out of the rank we had. Now we are of the Maker, not of the Made. Now all things have such a look as the horse has which we drive.
↑Nature is no longer intrusive, but↓ all [n] things make a pictorial, musical impression.[37] Perception distances this mob which so rubbed against ⟨me⟩us.[n]
But is there not another element, or, people who are strong through love alone?

[46]–[47] [blank]
[48] The parrot has good uses for a detached family. Poll is a socialist & knits a neighborhood very soon. Every child stops before the gate to say, "Poll wants a cracker," & is promptly answered by Poll. When there is a lull,—to prevent all life going to ennui, Poll scolds & screeches; then, if you feed her & talk to her, rallies, & shows her refinement by the sudden gentleness & delicacy of her tones. If she cannot say all that she is reputed to say, she still, as Ann O'Brien affirmed, "makes a beautiful offer to say it." ⟨☞⟩ [49] Then what a terrible test of people's truth was Poll. To hear what they told of her!↓ [38]

T. Appleton says, that ⟨all⟩he thinks, that all Bostonians, when they die, if they are good, go to Paris.[39]

---

[37] This sentence is struck through in ink with five finger-wiped diagonal marks, perhaps intended to cancel.
[38] The hand sign at the bottom of p. [48] points to "Then . . . of her!" at the bottom of p. [49] under a page-wide rule. "A devoted attendant of Mr. Emerson's children made them a present of a parrot, who, perched on the scraper of the sunny southeast doorstep in summer, endeavored to keep things pleasant in the neighborhood," J, IX, 218–219. See Journal AC, pp. [107] and [184] above.
[39] Thomas Gold Appleton (1812–1884) was a Boston wit and friend of Emerson.

Aug. 16. I saw Dr. H[enry]. J. Bigelow's bird Mino, ⟨a black⟩ about the size of a cat-bird, black, with a yellow collar. His speech was articulate as a man's. "What's your name?" "How d'ye do?" "Go way," "Doctor Bigelow,"ⁿ "Mino," and a loud whistle, like ⟨as of⟩ a locomotive's, were his utterances.

[50] παντα ρει. You think a farm & broad acres a solid property but its ⟨whole⟩ value is flowing like water. It requires as much watching as if you were decanting wine from a hogshead.ⁿ Bent the farmer knows what ↑to↓ do with it, & decants wine; but a blunderhead Minns comes out of Cornhill & ⟨'tis⟩ it all leaks away. So is it with houses as with ships. What say you to the permanent value of an [51] estate invested in railroad stocks[?] [40]

[52] The secret of the charm which English castles & cathedrals have for us is in the ⟨arrival of the belief⟩ ↑conviction they impress↓ that the art & ⟨the artist &⟩ the race that made these is utterly gone. 'Tis fine to tell us, that chemically ⟨yonder magical⟩ diamond is identical with ⟨this⟩ coal-cinder, ⟨of⟩ if there is no science in the world that can re-form such a crystal; and I must respect the men who built Westminster Abbey, since they have left no posterity who can do the like.

[53]   ↑Beatitudes of Intellect.↓
Am I not, one of these days, to write consecutively of the beatitude of intellect? It is too great for feeble souls, and they are overexcited. The wineglass shakes, & ⟨all⟩ the wine is spilled. What then? ⟨Is not that⟩ ↑The↓ joy which will not let me sit in my chair, which brings me bolt upright to my feet, & sends me striding around my room, like a tiger in his cage, and I cannot have composure & concentration enough even to set down in English words the thought which thrills me — isⁿ not that joy a ⟨sufficient⟩ [54] certificate of the ⟨reality & height of the privilege?⟩ ↑elevation?↓ What if I never write a book or a line?ⁿ ⟨If I have had⟩ ↑For a moment,↓ the eyes

----

[40] "You think . . . stocks", struck through in ink with a diagonal use mark on p. [50] and a horizontal use mark on p. [51], is used in "Wealth," W, VI, 119. For "πάντα ρεῖ", see Journal VO, p. [92], and Journal AC, p. [4] above.

of my eyes ↑were↓ opened, ⟨for a moment,⟩ the affirmative experience remains, ⟨forever,⟩ⁿ & consoles through all suffering.

> For ⟨use, for⟩ art, for music, overthrilled
> The wineglass shakes, the wine is spilled
>
> Him art, him music overthrilled,
> The wine glass shakes, the wine is spilled [41]

[55] The remorse of an offender, & the self-banishment into which he runs, are the triumphs of the divine law.

↑I admire those undescribable hints that power gives of itself.↓ I find sublime that essence of the man which makes him pass for more than his performances, though he never told his secret; ⟨knows⟩ ↑is aware↓ that a few private persons alone know him, & not one of them thoroughly.[42] ⟨those undescribable hints that power gives of itself.⟩

[56] 'Tis a great misfortune of certain temperaments that they are by their own force or ⟨dete⟩too much determination thrown out of all sympathy, and are therefore inconvertible. They cannot be made to see when they are in the wrong, & when they are rushing to ruin, taking the bits in their teeth, they are then triumphantly assured of their innocency, & mere Phocions, scorning the universe of objectors. ⟨No⟩ Argument,ⁿ appeal to bystanders, [57] to a world of bystanders, masses of opposing fact, all is wasted, 'tis only oil to flame, only mountains of confirmation to their insanity. In these tragic cases ↑their own↓ talent, acuteness cannot help them, even Genius, as in ⟨the⟩M[ary]. M[oody]. E[merson]., only widens the hopeless chasm.

[58] [43]   *Clubs*

Latimer's lesson. *CL* 34

---

[41] The first version of this couplet is in pencil; cf. "Fragments on the Poet and the Poetic Gift," XVI, *W*, IX, 330.

[42] "is aware" and the cancellation of "knows" are in pencil.

[43] The entries on p. [58] are in pencil.

Goethe's remark, "a few reasonable words" [44]

———

All men are competitors in this art[.]

———

Touchstone

———

Books have their limits.[45] *CL* 187

———

Wendell Phillips & Cassius Clay   *CL* [220–221]

———

The answer to G. F. Train's saying, in a N. Y. speech, that slavery was a divine institution.[46]

———

Use of friendship. *CL* 248

———

Pairs. *CL* 244

———

Alcott & the Club. *CL* 250

———

A scholar who gets high place has some convivial talent. *GL* 329[–330]

———

[59] What is the ⟨interest⟩ poetic interest of the lost Pleiad for so many minds? Each nun or hermit in the country-towns has hea⟨d⟩rd, that there were once seven stars, & now the eye can count but six. (No matter about the fact; it is a numerous cluster, & more or fewer can be counted, as your eyes are better or worse.) But the legend is, as I have said, & each nun or hermit is struck with the circumstance [60] & writes solitary verses about it. What is the charm of the incident? I think because it is to each a symbol of [n] lost thoughts.

The pace of nature is so slow. Why not from strength to strength, from miracle to miracle, & not as now with this retardation, as if

———

[44] *Wilhelm Meisters Lehrjahre*, Bk. V, ch. 1: "One ought, every day at least, to hear a little song, read a good poem, see a fine picture, and, if it were possible, to speak a few reasonable words."

[45] This sentence is struck through in ink with two vertical use marks.

[46] George Francis Train (1829–1904) was an American merchant, promoter, and author.

Nature had sprained her foot, & ↑makes↓ plenteous stopping at little stations.⁴⁷

[61] The correct writer will have a wide effect, as if he had written a dictionary for his people.

The privilege of thought is that it dates from itself. Winckelmann dates from Pericles or Augustus or the Renaissance; Hallam from the Revival, or the Reformation; Coleridge from Shakspeare; but the intellect from itself.⁴⁸ ⟨And that makes the interest of⟩ ↑We like↓ a person of will & of thought [62] ⟨that⟩ ↑because↓ there is nobody behind his chair. It is the year one, and the Emperor is here.

———

The right answer to Archimedes's "Δος που οτω," &c, is Who couldn't? ⁴⁹

———

↑As we say, the real dictionary is the correct writer, (see *infra* p 94)↓

The publisher's advertisements are very well, but the author ⟨cro⟩blotting out a weak sentence, or adding a happy thought, is the best bookseller.

———

[63] [blank]
[64]   *one wrong step.*
On Wachusett, I sprained my foot.⁵⁰ It was slow to heal, & I went to the doctors. Dr H. Bigelow said, "a splint, & absolute rest;" Dr Russell said, "⟨a splint⟩rest yes; but a splint, no." Dr Bartlett said, "neither splint nor rest, but go & walk." Dr Russell said, "⟨b⟩Pour water on the foot, but it must be warm." Dr Jackson said, "stand in a trout brook all day."

---

⁴⁷ This paragraph, struck through in pencil with a single vertical use mark, is used in "Powers and Laws of Thought," *W*, XII, 49.

⁴⁸ The first sentence is struck through in ink with a diagonal use mark and in pencil with a vertical zigzag; "Winckelmann . . . itself." is set off by a vertical pencil mark in the left margin. Cf. "Fate," *W*, VI, 26.

⁴⁹ For "Δός μοι πού στῶ καὶ κινῶ τὴν γῆν," "Give me a place to stand on and I will move the earth," traditionally ascribed to Archimedes, see *JMN*, VI, 210.

⁵⁰ Emerson sprained his foot on an excursion to Mt. Wachusett at the end of July or early in August, 1859; recovery took two or three months. See *J*, IX, 219–220.

[65] The philanthropies are all duns, & hated as duns. ⟨are hated.⟩ⁿ But art is worse.

When I sprained my foot I soon found it was all one as if I had sprained my head, if I must sit in my chair. Then I thought nature had sprained her foot; and that King Lear had never sprained his, or he would have thought there were worse evils than unkind daughters. When I see a man unhappy, I ask, has ⟨he⟩ a sprained foot brought him to *this* pass? [51]

[66]   Aug. 20
Home is a good place in August. We have plenty of sopsavines, & Moscow Transparents, & the sweet apple we call Early Bough (?). Our Early pears — (Madeleine /?/)ⁿ are past, but ⟨b⟩Bloodgoods are ripe & ripening. And apricot plums, (ifⁿ we had more trees than the one survivor!)ⁿ are mature.

[67] All knowledge gives superiority, & it makes so little difference in what direction. 'Tis so wonderful to expound an Assyrian inscription! but 'tis not less to know ↑a↓ Greek or German ⟨more⟩ word that I do not know; or to see through a galvanic battery, or a chemical combining, or a binomial theorem, which I see⟨k⟩ not at all.

[68] Dread the collectors. Whether of books, of shells, of coins, of eggs, of newspapers, they become alike trustless. Their hunger overrides their honesty. A *forte* always makes a foible.

Remember Norton's story of the gentleman who passed the antique coin which he believed to be an unique around his dinner-table, & lost it. One guest alone refused to be searched, and, after it was found on the floor, excused his refusal by announcing that he had a duplicate of the coin at that moment in his pocket.

[69]   *Subjects*
    ⟨Works & Days⟩

[51] "When I . . . foot;" is used in "Address at the Opening of the Concord Free Public Library," *W*, XI, 502–503. Cf. Shakespeare, *King Lear*, III, iv, 65.

⟨Clubs⟩
⟨Country Life⟩
Classes of Men
Criticism
⟨Success⟩

[70]   ↑Civilization imperfect.↓
"In 1849 when the cholera was in Boston, one cellar was reported
by the police to be occupied nightly as a sleeping apartment by 39 persons.
In another, the tide had risen so high, that it was necessary to approach
the bedside of a patient by means of a plank which was laid from one stool
to another while the dead body of an infant was actually *sailing* about the
room in its coffin."
                    Dr H. G. Clark's (City Physician's report. p. 172) [52]

[71]   ↑Civilization imperfect.↓
British Board of Health conclude "that half the attainable period of
human life is lost to all who are born."

————

Compel them to be clean.* [53]

————

In Ward ⟨4⟩7, the number of deaths in a year is about twice the
number in Ward 6. See Census &c p. 57,

[72] H[olmes] not a heavy man nor a heavy companion nor a heavy
writer[.] [54]

[73]–[80] [four leaves cut out] [55]

* Manners are to make them endurable to each other[.]

---

[52] Henry Grafton Clark, *Report of the Committee of Internal Health on the
Asiatic Cholera, Together with a Report of the City Physician on the Cholera Hospital* (Boston, 1849), pp. 172–173.
    [53] "Compel . . . clean." is struck through in pencil with two diagonal use
marks; "Manners . . . other" is struck through in ink with two diagonal use
marks and in pencil with one.
    [54] See pp. [81] and [87]–[100] below. This entry is in pencil.
    [55] Words and portions of words and letters are visible on the stubs of pp. [75],
[76], and [79], including: p. [75]: "& ‖ . . . ‖ an‖ . . . ‖" (one-line space) "the
‖ . . . ‖ our ‖ . . . ‖ tha‖ . . . ‖ ers ‖ . . . ‖ aga‖ . . . ‖ both‖ . . . ‖"; p. [76]: "‖ . . . ‖al"

[81] The tired traveller who sees the Atlantic covers, says Well ⟨there is⟩ ↑there comes↓ the Autocrat to bring me one half hour's absolute relief from the vacant mind. And to Perception wherever it appears I hail ⟨with d⟩ the inextinguishable mystery with joy. Who is Wendell Holmes[?] if it shines through him[,] it is not his[,] it ⟨is⟩belongs to all of us[,] & we hail it as our own[.] [56]

[82] I find Haydon's Autobiography one of the best books.[57] He admired Boswell's Johnson, & his book is precious like that. His estimate of himself & his sanguine folly of hoping important results from every compliment or polite look with which any of his great men smoothed their leave-taking, reminds me of Alcott's Journals fifty times. How weak & how strong these English are!

[83] The way to make a man famous ↑is↓ to tell the result, & skip the means. Sir George Beaumont made the town rush to Wilkie, by describing him as "a young man who came to London, saw a picture of Teniers, went home, & at once painted the Village Politicians." [n] That was the wonder, — at once!
"At once, my dear Lady Mulgrave, at once!"
See [Life of Benjamin Robert] Haydon. [1853,] Vol. I. p. 42.

For *Pace*, see AC 140

[84] *Culture*
"Thank God," says Haydon, "I am capable of enjoying the sensations Raffaele intended to excite."

[Ibid.,] I. p. 174
I think I have read the like sentence from Sir Joshua Reynolds about Michel Angelo.[58]

(two-line space) "‖ . . . ‖ds, ‖ . . . ‖er" (one-line space) "‖ . . . ‖d."; p. [79]: "Pre‖ . . . ‖ ⟨‖ . . . ‖⟩ ‖ . . . ‖ an‖ . . . ‖ ch‖ . . . ‖ a‖ . . . ‖ pe‖ . . . ‖ ⟨gra⟩‖ . . . ‖". These pages probably bore an earlier version of the "Speech at the Dinner to Dr Holmes," pp. [87]–[100] below. Emerson indexed p. [74] under Opinion and Rhetoric.
[56] The entry on p. [81] is heavily lined through in ink, probably to indicate use; it is used in the speech at the dinner to Dr. Holmes, August 29, 1859. See pp. [87]–[100] below.
[57] *Life of Benjamin Robert Haydon, historical painter, from his autobiography and journals*, ed. Tom Taylor, 3 vols. (London, 1853), in Emerson's library.
[58] This sentence is struck through in pencil with a vertical use mark. Emerson uses the Reynolds remark in "Michael Angelo," *W*, XII, 232. See p. [209] below.

[8⟨6⟩5]   Will

The reactions of the world make freedom necessary.

The existence of those who take a bee-line, as soon as they are born, to the axe of the tyrant & the fagot of the Pope.[59]

[86]   Temperament.

Best example is the snapping turtle, whose life & biting begin[n] before he is born, & who bites still after he is or ought to be dead.[60]

⸻

↑Printed ⟨?⟩ in "Courage"↓

[87][61] *Speech at the Dinner to Dr Holmes, 29 Aug[us]t, 1859*
Mr President,

—————When I read the Atlantic, I have had much to think of the beneficence of wit, its vast utility, & the extreme rarity, out of this presence, of the pure article. Science has ⟨⟨measured⟩never⟩ ↑never↓ measured the immense profundity of the Dunce-power. The globe of the world—the diameter of the solar system, is nothing to it. [88] Everywhere, a thousand fathoms of sandstone⟨, &⟩to a teaspoonful of wit. And yet people speak ⟨of the⟩with apprehension of the dangers of wit, as if there were or could be ⟨to⟩an excess.

We all remember, in 1849, it was thought California would make gold so cheap, that [89] perhaps it would drive lead & zinc out of use for covering roofs & sinkspouts.

But here we have had a Missisippi river of gold pouring in from California, Australia, & Oregon for ten years, & all has not yet displaced one pewter basin from our kitchens, and I begin to believe that if Heaven had sent us a dozen [90] men as electrical as Voltaire or Sidney Smith[,] the old Dulness would hold its ground, & die hard.

Why, look at the fact. Whilst, once, wit was extremely rare & sparse-sown,—rare as cobalt, rare as platina,—here comes [91] the Doctor, & flings it about like sea-sand, threatens to make it common as newspapers, is actually the man to contract to furnish a

⸻

[59] See Journal SO, p. [201] above.

[60] "Best example . . . dead.", struck through in ink with three diagonal use marks, is used in "Courage," *W*, VII, 256–257.

[61] The entries on pp. [87]–[100] are Emerson's speech at Oliver Wendell Holmes's fiftieth birthday dinner, held by the Saturday Club.

chapter of Rabelais or Sidney Smith once ↑a month; — ↓bucketsful of Greek fire against tons of paunch & acres of bottom. Of course, the danger was that he [92] would throw out of employment all the dunces, the impostors, the slow men, the stock writers, in short, all the respectabilities & professional learning of the time. No wonder the world was alarmed.

And yet the old House of Unreason stands firm at this day, when he is fifty years old,ⁿ ↑& [93] he is bound to live a hundred in order to ⟨make his due impression⟩ ↑spend the half of his treasure.↓↓

Sir, I have heard that when nature concedes a true talent, she renounces for once all her avarice & parsimony, & gives without stint. Our friend here was born in happy hour, with consenting stars. I think his least merits are not small. He is the best critic who constructs. Here is [94] the War of Dictionaries in this country. In England, a philological Commission to draft a new Lexicon. All very well; but the real Dictionary is, the Correct writer, who makes the reader feel, as our friend does, the delicacy & inevitableness [95] of every word he uses, & whose book is so charming, that ⟨he⟩ ↑the reader↓ ⁿ has never a suspicion, amid his peals of laughter, that he is learning the last niceties of grammar & rhetoric.

What shall I say of his delight in manners, in society, in elegance, in short, of his delight in *Culture*, [96] which make him a Civilizer whom every man & woman secretly thanks for valuable hints.

What then of his correction of popular errors in taste, in behavior, in the uncertain sciences, & in theology, attested by the alarm of the synods.

[97] And this is only possible to the man who has the capital merit of healthy perception, who can draw all men to read him; whose thoughts leave such cheerful & perfumed memories, that when the newsboy enters the car, all over the wide wildernesses of America, the tired traveller says, "Here [98] comes the Autocrat to bring me one half hour's absolute relief from the vacant mind."

Now when a man can render this benefit to his country, or when men can, — I cannot enter into the gay controversy between the rival Helicons of Croton & Cochituate, but I advise [99] all men of sense to come into a mutual admiration society, to praise & honor

316

that power.[62] ↑The heartier the praise, the better for all parties.↓ For, really, this is not praise of any man. I admire Perception where-ever it appears. That is the one eternal miracle. I hail the blessed mystery with ever new delight. It lets me into the same joy. Who is Wendell Holmes? [100] If it shines through him, it is not his, it belongs to all men, & we hail it as our own.

[101] George Bancroft said, he does not consider a man worth anything, until he is sixty. And here is the newspaper account of Dr Burnap's death in his 57th year, saying, that "he was in the prime of life." [63]

[102] [blank]
[103] ↑Honor to the Gymnasium & the Riding School!↓
When the learned Thynnius took his first ride, ⟨he⟩ — was it the earnest look of the rider, or some disharmony between the rider & the horse, — he could not fail to notice the sympathizing looks of all the passengers, ⟨nay,⟩ ↑and↓ the ⟨o⟨v⟩bvious⟩ goodnatured endeavor to look away, which ↑all↓ his acquaintances ⟨showed⟩ ↑made↓. But the excellent Thynnius did not like it[.] [64]

[10⟨6⟩4]   ↑Mr Crump↓   Aug., Sept., 1859.
The unfortunate days of August & September, when the two cows were due from the Temple Pasture, & did not arrive, & we learn that they strayed on the way, & are lost. When the Muster approached bringing alarms to all housekeepers & orchard-owners. When the foot was lame, & the hand was palsied, & the foot mending

---

[62] Croton and Cochituate are reservoirs for New York City and Boston, respec-tively.
[63] The first sentence is struck through in ink with a vertical use mark; for the second sentence, see p. [120] below. George W. Burnap was a fellow student of Em-erson at Harvard Theological School.
[64] Edward Emerson notes the autobiographical nature of this entry: "Mr. Em-erson always wished that, in his youth, he had been made to learn to dance and ride. Poverty, of course, forbade. He took pains that his son had these advantages. Once about this time when his son, returning from a ride, was about to lead the wide-awake but gentle Morgan 'Dolly' to the barn, Mr. Emerson stopped him, mounted the mare, and rode off in the twilight, the only occasion that his son recalls his rid-ing" (J, IX, 229).

was lame again. When a strong southw⟨ind⟩est wind blew in vicious gusts, all [10⟨7⟩5] day, stripping every loaded pear-tree of its fruit, just six weeks too early. The beggars arrive every day, some on foot, the Sardinians & Sicilians, who cannot argue the question of labor & mendicity with you, since they do not speak a word of English; then the Monumentals, who come in landaus or barouches, & wish your large aid to Mt Vernon; Plymouth; Ball's Webster; or ⟨Judge⟩ President Quincy in marble; then the chipping lady from the Cape who has three blind [106] sisters, & I know not how many dumb ones, & she had been advised to put them in the Poor House. No, not she. As long as she had health, she would go about & sell these books for them, which I am to buy, and she tosses her head, & expects my praise & tears for her heroic resolution; though I had a puzzled feeling, that, if there was sacrifice anywhere it was in me, if I should buy them; & I am sure I was very little inclined to toss my head on the occasion.

[107] Mr Crump remarked that he hated lame folks: there was no telling how hypocritical they were. They are dreadful lame when you see them, but the lamest of them, if he wants something, & there's nobody will help him to it, will manage to get ⟨up⟩it himself, though it were a mile off; *if you are not by.*

But the fortnight of vexations is not over. I receive a letter, last night, to tell me that Phillips & Sampson will fail in a week.[65]

[108]   ↑Dr Johnson↓

Dr Johnson said of some ode "Bolder words & more timorous meaning, I think were never brought together." ↑Boswell[n] [*Life of Samuel Johnson,* 1827,] p. 433.↓ The language might be well applied to Dr Walker's sermons.[66]

---

[65] In a letter of September 8, 1859, Emerson writes to his brother William, "I have had so many frets lately that I am asserting all the claims of Mr Crump in the comedy" and tells of his lost cows and fallen pears. In the same letter, Emerson foresees that the death of Moses D. Phillips on August 20 will cause trouble; Phillips, Sampson & Co. had suspended payment by September 10 (*L,* V, 172).

[66] Dr. Walker is probably James Walker, 1794–1874, president of Harvard, 1853–60.

"Sir, if you had been dipped in Pactolus, I should not have noticed you."
                                                [*Ibid.*, p. 468]

———

"But were there not 6 horses to each coach, (at Garrick's funeral)?"
"Madam, there were no more 6 horses than 6ⁿ Phoenixes." B[oswell,
ibid., p.] 494

[109] "A man may write at any time, if he will set himself doggedly
to it;" said Johnson. [Boswell, *ibid.*, p. 51]

Among Dr J's negligences, (some of which I have noted in ⟨()   ⟩
I observe, "Taylor once challenged me to talk Latin with him. I
quoted some of Horace, which he took," &c. Boswell↑, [*ibid.*,] p.
411↓

↑Of↓ Beauclerk, "No man was ever so free, when he was going to say a
good thing, from a *look* that expressed that it was coming, or, when he had
said it, from a look that expressed that it had come." Dr J.   *Boswell*,
[*ibid.*, p.] 423 [67]

    [110] Phillips's letter to the Judge & the President on dining
at the Revere House is only a logical hit.[68] They are formalists, &
he shows them they have outraged their own forms. But he who is
not a formalist, had not a good right to write the letter.
I think wealth has lost much of its value, if it have not wine. I ⟨do⟩
abstain from wine only on account of the expense. When I heard
that Mr Sturgis had given up wine, I had the same regret that I had
lately in hearing that Mr B↑owditch↓ had broken his hip; a millionaire
without wine, & a millionaire ⟨with⟩that must lie on his bed.

[111] "We draw back into ourselves, & penetrate the false illusions,
in order that we may better enjoy the true illusions." *Herman Grimm*

———

↑Dr Johnson.↓
"He is poor & honest, which is recommendation enough to Johnson"

    [67] "Of Beauclerk . . . come.' " is struck through in ink with a vertical use
mark.
    [68] Wendell Phillips addressed an open letter to Chief Justice Lemuel Shaw and
President James Walker of Harvard University criticizing them for attending a ban-
quet at a hotel that was defying a Massachusetts Prohibition statute. See *J*, IX, 232.

said Goldsmith of Levet; and, of a certain bad pensioner, "He is now become miserable, & that insures the protection of Johnson" [Boswell, *The Life of Samuel Johnson*, 1827, p. 138]

Mrs Thrale quoted with pleasure Garrick's line "I'd smile with the simple, & feed with the poor." Johnson said, "what folly! who would feed with the poor that could help it? No, no, let me smile with the wise, & feed with the rich." [Boswell, *ibid.*, p. 162]

[112] The inconceivable frivolity of people, a ribband, a cigar, rum, a muster, it makes no difference what the bawble is, they are drunk with delight if they have it, they are peevish if they want it[.]

Johnson said of a Jamaica gentleman then lately dead, "He will not, whither he is now gone, find much difference ⟨in⟩either in the climate or the company." Piozzi [69]

———

N. tried to look as much like a piece of meat as she could.

[113] Mr W. W. said to me "All genial men are insincere."

Mrs Piozzi says of Johnson "and whatever work he did, seemed so much below his powers of performance, that he appeared the idlest of all human beings." [70]

"*diligence passe sense,*" Henry VIII was wont to say from the French.[71]

[114]   *Æsthetics*
Definition of Imagination & of Fancy —
    See *IL* 70, *PY* 260, 270, *TO* 171, *IT*

———

Realism of Demosthenes

———

[69] See Piozzi, *Anecdotes of the Late Samuel Johnson, LL.D.*, 1897, I, 211.
[70] See *ibid.*, I, 160.
[71] This sentence, struck through in ink with a vertical use mark, is used in "Power," *W*, VI, 77.

Classic & Romantic
> *SO* 74, 75, 76, 77, 82, Zweck Atlantis Feb 1857 p. 144
> Classic in landscape ⟨p 141⟩S 177

[115]   *Æsthetic Class*
Plotinus's Dance
Hamlet's Soliloquy
Sigurd & Eystein.

———

List of sentences agreeable to the Human Mind. See *BL* 40

———

Wordsworth's classification of Characters. "Yarrow ⟨V⟩Revisited," p.

———

See list of Fables &c. *BL* 40

———

Socrates's Apology. See BL, 40

———

Conclusion of the Mahabarat. See *Alger's* [72]

———

Gibbon's Autobiography

———

Portia uxor Bruti

———

Saint Anthony's address to the fishes ↑TU 106↓

———

Michel Angelo's First Sonnet.

———

Literature of Culture
[116]———
Aristotle's definition of Shipbuilder's art.

———

Story of Marsilius Ficinus

———

Aristotle's dying speech.

———

[72] William Rounseville Alger, *The Poetry of the East* (Boston, 1856), pp. 37–45.

Chief Justice Crewe's Opinion

———

⟨Prize shooting of Zeus & Apollo.⟩

———

Tennyson's Ode on Wellington.

———

Makaria

———

Mme. Recamier

———

Fable of Sphinx. *BL* 24⟨4⟩1, *Plotinus* p. 539

———

Lord Bacon's "Wisdom of the Anc[ien]ts" Explanations of fables.

———

Troilus & Cressida

———

Milton's prose

———

Male & female souls   AC 253, 4, 5,

———

Elegance of demonstration ⟨of Thales, &⟩ of the equality through & over the hill [73]

[117] There is a literature of Culture;
        Horace
        Plato, Plotinus, Apuleius,
        Michel Angelo's ⟨Sonnets⟩ poems.
        Dante's "Vita Nuova"
        Shakspeare's Sonnets

———

[73] On p. [115] "Plotinus's Dance" and "Socrates's . . . BL, 40" are struck through in pencil with single vertical use marks, "Michel Angelo's . . . Sonnet" is struck through in pencil with two vertical use marks and canceled in pencil, and "Wordsworth's . . . Revisited,' p." is struck through in ink with three diagonal use marks. The "'s'" is added to "*Alger*" in pencil. On p. [116] "Aristotle's defini- tion . . . art." and "Fable of . . . p. 539" are struck through in pencil with single vertical use marks; "Aristotle's dying speech." and "Tennyson's . . . Wellington." are struck through in ink with three diagonal use marks. "Elegance . . . hill" is marked by two vertical lines in ink in the left margin.

"Wilhelm Meister"
Landor's "Pericles & Aspasia"
C[harles]. K[ing]. N[ewcomb].'s Edith
"Charles Auchester," & "Counterparts."
Chronicle of the Cid.
Matthew Arnold's Tracts "on Homer"
Richter's Titan
Arnold's Lectures on Translating Homer
Winckel⟨l⟩mann [74]

[118] What is the ivory gate?
What the Barmecide feast?
What is the meaning of the Sphinx? *BL* 241

[119]   ⟨Pied piper, Verstegan, Tholuck⟩
Seven sleepers, Sleepy Hollow ↑Rip Van Winkle↓
Ring of Gyges
Fortunatus↑'s↓ cap
                  cloak   Aladdin's lamp.
Transformations of Indra
Wandering Jew
Thawed Tune
Sphinx   *BL* 241 [75]
     Diving in the lake & rising in a cave   *HO* 230
Winged horse
Phaedrus in Plato. Body & Soul.
Charlemagne's talisman & Bishop Turpin
Faeries
And if Newton, Laplace, Davy, Agassiz, Brewster, Jackson, & Da-
guerre, kept their secrets, what daemons!

[120] Old age ⟨looks⟩ ↑is↓ comely enough in the country, but
if you look at the faces of the people ⟨as they pass⟩ in Broadway,

[74] "Arnold's Lectures . . . Homer" is in pencil.
[75] "Pied . . . Tholuck" is canceled in pencil and "Rip Van Winkle" is in
pencil. "Seven sleepers," and "Ring . . . Sphinx *BL* 241" are struck through in
pencil with single vertical use marks and "Sleepy Hollow" in pencil with a diagonal
use mark.

there is depression or indignation in the old ones,—a determination not to mind it,—a sense of injury. Old age is not disgraceful, but immensely disadvantageous.[76]

The newspaper says, that Dr Burnap was in the prime of life, being in his 57th year.[77]

↑["I am very particular."]↓

Misuse of the word *"mortify"*
          moiety

[121]   ↑*Conversation.*↓
The clergyman walks about the streets from house to house, all day, all the year, to give people the comfort of good talk. The physician helps them mainly in the same way, by healthy talk, giving a healthy tone to the patient's mind. The dinner, the club, the walk, all have that for their main end.[78]

Agassiz	Woodman
Lowell	Holmes
Longfellow	Whipple
Dana	Ward
Motley	⟨Motte⟩Felton
Pierce	Forbes
Dwight	Hawthorn
Hoar	Emerson [79]

[122]   Pay every debt, as if God wrote the bill,
            So to shut up the avenues of ill.

            To barricade the avenues of ill,
            Pay every debt, as if God wrote the bill.

[76] This paragraph, struck through in ink with two vertical use marks, is used in "Old Age," W, VII, 320.
[77] This sentence is struck through in ink with two vertical zigzags, probably intended to cancel; see p. [101] above.
[78] This paragraph is used in "Clubs," W, VII, 227.
[79] "Agassiz . . . Emerson" lists members of the Saturday Club. See Journal VO, p. [87] above.

He could condense cerulean ether
Into the very best sole leather

Wilt thou shut up the avenues of ill?
Pay every debt, as if God wrote the bill.[80]

[123] We live, late in life, by memory, and in our solstices, or periods of stagnation, we live on our memories; as the starved camel lives on his humps.[81]

⟨Ask not for ⟨|| ... ||⟩wealth⟩ ↑Better than mines↓ or crops
    profuse,
⟨But ask⟩ ↑Love thou↓ the just amount for use.

Let restless nature cumulate
And centuple her vast estate
Crumble abraded crags to soil,
⟨Thence⟩ ↑To↓ honey, milk ⟨w⟩spice, wine, & oil,
But all is waste & worthless ⟨st⟩ till
Arrives the wise selecting will,
And out of slime & chaos, wit
/Choose/Take/ the threads of fair & fit
Which knows to resume his own
In wood & iron air & stone [82]

[124] For the noble vulgar speech, the best ⟨proof⟩ ↑praise↓ is, that all poetry must be written in it.

[80] The third couplet is used in "Fragments on the Poet and the Poetic Gift," XXIII, *W*, IX, 332; cf. the S'wétás'watara Upanishad, *The Taittaríya, Aitaréya . . . Upanishads*, 1853, p. 68: "Until man is able to compress the ether like leather, there will be no end of misery, except through the knowledge of God." See Journal SO, p. [222] above. The other couplets, each struck through in ink with a vertical use mark, are versions of "Suum Cuique," in "Fragments on Nature and Life," XXXII, *W*, IX, 357.
[81] This sentence, struck through in pencil with two vertical use marks, is used in "Memory," *W*, XII, 94.
[82] "But all . . . fit" is used in "Wealth," ll. 30–33, *W*, IX, 286.

The ⟨bird⟩ ↑sparrow↓ is rich in ⟨his⟩ ↑her↓ nest
The bee has ⟨all she wants⟩ her desire
The lover in his love is blest
The poet in his ⟨verse⟩ ↑brain↓ of fire

Then build the house
Then ⟨deck⟩ ↑gild↓ the shrine
Then spend on the ⟨state⟩ school
Enrich the orphan & [83]

[125] Aristotle said, that there was the same difference between one learned & unlearned as between the living & the dead. Boswell [*The Life of Samuel Johnson*, 1827,] p 433

[126]   ↑M[*ary*]. M[*oody*]. E[*merson*].↓
Dr Johnson is a good example of the force of temperament. 'Tis surprising how often I am reminded of my Aunt Mary E. in reading ⟨over⟩ Boswell lately. Johnson impresses his company as she does, not only by the point of the remark, but ↑also↓ when the point fails, because he makes it. Like hers, his obvious religion or superstition, his deep wish that they should think so or so, weighs with them, so rare is depth of feeling, or a constitutional value for a thought or opinion, among the lightminded men & women who make up society.[84] And this, though in both cases, [127] their companions know that there is a degree of shortcoming, & of insincerity, & of talking for victory. — Yet the existence of character and habitual ⟨faith⟩ reverence of principles over talent ⟨&⟩or learning is felt by the frivolous.

[128] What is a "cento"?   See *Boswell* [*The Life of Samuel Johnson*, 1827,] p. 166

Are you everywhere? then you misspend a great deal of money on buying railroad tickets: and that property is worthless.

[129] The imagination enters into all the details & ennobles

---

[83] These two stanzas are canceled in ink with looping vertical and horizontal lines which are finger-wiped.

[84] A discontinuous pencil line in the left margin marks "only by the . . . society."

life. ↑Even↓ the ⁿ ⟨Collegian⟩ ↑shopboy↓ smoking his cigar assumes the attitude & air of rich gentlemen, & is raised in his own eyes.

See also IO 270

⟨We pay a debt quicker to a rich man⟩

[130] [blank]
[131] [85] ↑Sept.↓   Chelmsford
I knew well the town in which they lived; the landscape which they saw. I spent an autumn & winter among these hills & plains. I knew where the chestnut forest spread its brown harvest on a frosty morning, for the boys; where the apples covered the ground with white fruit. I saw the last fires that burned in the old limekiln. I knew the ripples of the Baptist Pond, and the woods that grew where the corn is now ripening[.]
Plain homely land[,] ↑sandy fields which the Merrimack washes,↓ but the sun & stars do not disdain to fill it with magnificence ⟨& sublime beauty⟩ in June, and with sublime lights in Autumn. And I can easily believe that the soldiers you celebrate deserved your praise. For I had an acquaintance [132] with the young men & young women who grew up here in a poverty ⟨almost⟩ ↑I suppose↓ as severe, with manners as hardy & plain; and I know that their feeling was as tender & their intellect as vigorous as that which opens under softer skies, & in city palaces. I read & conversed with friends here, children of the soil, who showed that force of thought, & that sense of right, which are the warp & woof of which greatness is woven; that curiosity for knowledge & that delight in intellectual conversation which is the purest joy of youth, & the beginning of all national greatness.

[133] I suppose it is fair to judge the tree by its fruits, the fathers by the children[.]

These people were original authors of liberty, & not plagiarists, not

[85] The entries on pp. [131]–[136₂] are Emerson's notes for a speech at the dedication of a monument to Revolutionary soldiers in Chelmsford, Mass., on September 22, 1859. Emerson taught in Chelmsford in 1822 before beginning theological studies at Harvard. Inflammation of his sprained ankle apparently prevented Emerson from attending the dedication, and he sent a letter to be read (L, V, 174).

sentimental nations like the Italians, French, & Hungarians & Germans. These all learned it of our people. ⟨The⟩Our farmers were all orthodox Calvinists, mighty in the scriptures, had[n] learned that life was a preparation "& probation,"[n] to use their word.[86] They read ⟨in⟩ no romances, but with the pulpit, on one hand, & poverty & labor on another, they had a third training in the town meeting. They held the fee of their farms: no [134] patroon[,] no ground rents & great proprietaries, but every man owned his acres.

[135] ↑?printed?↓

We go to Plutarch & ⟨the⟩ Montaigne for our examples of character, but ⟨as ther⟩ we might as well go to Pliny & ⟨Columella⟩ Varro for ⟨our⟩ oaks & firs, which grow as well in our own door yards & cow-pastures. Life is always rich; & spontaneous graces & forces ⟨of character⟩ elevate life in every domestic circle which are overlooked, whilst we are reading something less excellent [136₁] in ⟨ancient⟩ ↑old↓ ⟨book⟩authors.[87] I think as I go through the streets[,] each one of these innumerable houses has its own calendar of saints, its unpublished anecdotes of courage, of patience, of wit, cheerfulness. ↑For↓ the best I know were in the most private ⟨p⟩ corners ⟨the⟩ Every thing draws to its kind, and frivolous people will not hear of ⟨them⟩ ↑⟨nobilities⟩ noble traits↓; but let any good example of this [137₁] secret virtue come accidentally to air, like Florence Nightingale, and you will hear parallels in every direction.

From the obscurity & casualty of those ↑examples↓ which I know, I infer the obscurity & casualty of the like balm & consolation & immortality in a thousand homes which I do not know, & all round the world.[88]

Let it lie safe in the shade there, from the compliments & praise of ↑foolish↓ society. ⟨All it⟩It is safer so. All [136₂] it seems to demand, is, that we know it when we see it. This is no mean ⟨p⟩ reward. If an

[86] This sentence, struck through in pencil with one vertical and one diagonal use mark, is used in "John Brown: Speech at Salem," W, XI, 279.

[87] The entry to this point, struck through on p. [135] in pencil with two vertical use marks, is used in "The Sovereignty of Ethics," W, X, 198. "?printed?" at the top of p. [135] is inserted in pencil.

[88] This sentence, struck through in pencil with two vertical use marks, is used in "The Sovereignty of Ethics," W, X, 198.

intelligent & generous witness passing by, sees our plight, & so much as exchanges a ↑searching↓ glance of sympathy, "Well done, brave heart!" it is better than the thunder of theatres, and the world full of ⟨foolish⟩ newspapers, which only echo each other.

[1372] *Clubs.*

There are men whose opinion of a book is ⟨sovereign⟩ ↑final↓. If Ellery C[hanning]. tells me, here is a good book, I know I have a day longer to live. But there are plenty of able men whose report in that kind is not to be trusted.

And in clubs ⟨pe⟩a person of the prowess of G[eorge]. W[ashington]. Tyler is inestimable.   See *BO* 79 [89]

[138] Ellen Hooper's passionate inquiry twenty years ago was, What is the place & use of common people? or I suppose ⟨th⟩ what Tennyson also meant by "Reflections of a sensitive second class mind." [90]
Let this Question take the first page in the new Edition of "Notes & Queries."

[139] The physicians wisely say, that fevers are self-limiting; so are all diseases, sprains, & headaches, & passions; and all errors, like Jupiter's moons, periodical. [91]

[140] The resistance to slavery, — it is the old mistake of the slaveholder to impute the resistance to Clarkson or Pitt, to Channing ↑or↓ Garrison, or to some John Brown whom he has just captured, & to make a personal affair of it; & he believes, whilst he chains & chops him, — ⟨first chains, & then chops up his body,⟩ that he is getting rid of his tormentors; and does not see that the air which this man breathed is liberty, & is breathed by thousands [141] & millions; that men of the same complexion as he, will look at slaveholders as

[89] For George Washington Tyler, a Boston merchant, see *JMN*, VIII, 91.
[90] Ellen Sturgis Hooper (1812–1848) was Caroline Sturgis' sister and a contributor to *The Dial.*
[91] This sentence is struck through in ink with a vertical use mark. See p. [201] below.

felons who have disentitled themselves to the protection of law, as the burglar has, whom I see breaking into my neighbor's house; and therefore no matter how many Browns ⟨or Smiths I⟩he can catch & kill, ⟨I⟩he do↑es↓ not make the number less, for the ⟨sun & moon⟩ ↑air↓ breed↑s↓ them, every school, every church, every domestic circle, every home of courtesy, genius, & conscience is educating haters of him & his misdeeds.[92]

[142] Courage. Here was happiest example of the best blood, which, in meeting the best born & best bred people of Europe[,] speaks with their speech, & deals with their own weapons. Ah[,] I should have been so glad, if it could have said to them, Look, I do without your rococo. You have heard much ill of America, I know its good, ⟨&⟩ its blessed simplicity, nor shall I make the mistake of baptising the daylight [143] & time & space by the name of Jones or Jenkins, in whose shop I chance to behold daylight & space & time. Least of all will I call sacraments ↑those↓ legendary quips of yours which break the sacraments which are most my own, my duty to my wife, husband, son, friend, country, nor can I suffer a nasty ⟨priest⟩monk to whisper to *me, to whom God has* given such a person as S[amuel]. G[ray]. W[ard]. & such children, for my confessors & absolvers.[93]

[144] We talk of Sparta & Rome, we dilettanti of liberty. But the last thing a brave man thinks of is Sparta or Scythia or the Gauls: he is up to the ↑top of his↓ boots in his own meadow, & can't be bothered with histories. That will do for a winter evening with schoolboys. ⟨Our⟩ As soon as a man talks Washington & Putnam & General Jackson to me, I detect the coxcomb & charlatan. He is a frivolous nobody who has no duties of his own.

---

[92] The entries on pp. [140] and [141] were made after the arrest of John Brown at Harpers Ferry, Virginia, on October 18, 1859. Emerson's square brackets, probably indicating matter to be omitted, are placed around "sun & moon" and "every domestic circle,".

[93] "nor shall . . . whose" is marked by a vertical pencil line in the left margin on p. [142] and by two vertical pencil lines in the right margin on p. [143]; "Jones or Jenkins," is circled and canceled in pencil. "S.G.W." is canceled in blue-black ink, probably by Edward Emerson, who writes at the top of p. [142] "RWE's Reflections on a valued friend lately turned Romanist." See *JMN*, VII, 404.

[145] Mount Vernon. I never heard a brave man talk of Mount Vernon, or a religious man of Mount Sinai. They leave that to hypocrites. They have Mount Vernons enough in ⟨the streets every day,⟩ ↑⟨his shoes,⟩ their shoes,↓ & Mount Sinai ⟨in the thunder of their own law.⟩ ↑in their wish to pay their debts.↓

[146] [blank]
[147] Anna Ward was at a loss in talking with me, because I had no church whose weakness she could show up, in return for my charges upon hers. I said to her, Do you not see that though I have no eloquence ⟨n⟩& no flow of thought, yet that I do not stoop to accept any thing less than truth? that I sit here contented with my poverty, mendicity, & deaf & dumb estate, from year to year, from youth to age, [148] rather than adorn myself with any red rag of false church or false association?[n] My low & lonely sitting here by the wayside, is my homage to truth, which, I see is sufficient without me; which is honored by my abstaining, not by superserviceableness. I see how grand & selfsufficing it is; how it burns up, & will none [149] of your shifty patchwork of additions & ingenuities.

[150] You can always see in the eyes of your companion whether your argument hits him.[94]

High courage, or a perfect will superior to all events, makes a bond of union between two enemies. Inasmuch as Gov. Wise is a superior man, he ⟨|| ... ||⟩ distinguishes John Brown.[95] As they confer, they understand each other swiftly, each respects the other; ⟨& they prefer⟩ if opportunity allowed, [151] they would prefer each other's[n] society, & desert the rest; enemies would become affectionate. ⟨They become aware that⟩ Rivals & enemies, Hector & Achilles, Wellington & Soult, become aware that they are nearer & liker than any other two, &, if their nation & ⟨cause⟩ circumstance did not keep them apart, would fly into each other's[n] arms.

[94] This sentence, struck through in ink with a vertical use mark and in pencil with a diagonal use mark, is used in "Behavior," W, VI, 180.
[95] Henry Alexander Wise (1806–1876) was governor of Virginia, 1856–1860; see pp. [159]–[162] below.

See too what contagion belongs to it. It finds its own with [152] magnetic affinity, all over the land. Heroic women offer themselves as nurses to the brave veteran. Florence Nightingale brings ⟨her⟩ lint, & the blessing of her shadow. The troop of infantry that cut him down ask leave to pay their respects to the prisoner; Poetry & Eloquence catch the hint. Everything feels the new breath, excepting the dead old doting politicians, whom the trumpet of resurrection cannot waken.[96]

[153]   There was no need of trumpets
              There was no need of banners
              Every ⟨breeze⟩ ↑zephyr↓ was a bugle
              ⟨Every maple was a flag⟩ ↑Every woodthrush sung
                  hosannas↓ [97]
              ⟨Steel was his commission
              And powder his lieutenant⟩
              ↑Sharp↓ steel [n] was his ⟨captain⟩ lieutenant
              And powder was his men

              The land was all electric
              The ⟨woods & meadows⟩ ↑mountain echoes↓ ⟨spoke⟩ ↑roar,↓
              Every ⟨stake⟩ ↑crutch↓ became a pike
              The woods & meadows ⟨murmured⟩ ↑shouted↓ War
              Every ⟨pasture⟩ ↑valley↓ shouted, strike!

[154] Courage charms us, because it indicates that a man loves an idea better than all things in the world, that he is thinking neither of his bed, nor his dinner, nor his money, but will venture all to put in act the invisible thought of his mind[.] [98]

[155] We value idealists who ⟨can⟩ do not rest in ideas, but convey them into things[.]

[96] These two paragraphs, struck through in pencil with two vertical use marks on p. [150] and with one vertical use mark on p. [151], are used in "Courage," *W*, VII, 271–272. "The troop . . . prisoner;" is marked by a vertical pencil line in the left margin.

[97] "Every woodthrush . . . hosannas" is inserted in pencil.

[98] This sentence is used in "Courage," *W*, VII, 274.

he converts the earth to its use,
the earth is proud to bear him,
the air to feed his lungs

He accepts an ideal standard. Freedom ⟨mean⟩ is ideal. It means, not, to have land or money or pleasure, but to have no other limitation than that which ⟨our⟩ his own constitution imposes. I am free to speak the truth. I am free to do justly. I am not free to lie. And I wish to break every yoke all over the world which hinders my brother from acting after his best thought[.] [99]

[156] Brown ⟨teaches⟩ ↑shows↓ us, said H[enry]. D[avid]. T[horeau], another school to send our boys to, — that the best lesson of oratory is to speak the truth. A ⟨very⟩ lesson rarely learned — To stand by the truth. We stand by our party, our trade, our reputation, our talent, but these each lead away from the truth. That is so volatile & vital, evanescing instantly from all but dedication to it.
And yet inspiration is that, to be so quick as truth; to drop the load of Memory & of Futurity, Memory & Care, [157] & let the ⟨pres⟩ moment suffice us: then one discovers that the first thought is related to all thought & carries power & fate in its womb[.]

Mattie Griffith says, if Brown is hung, the gallows will be sacred as the cross.[100]

That is the blessing of wit, the delight that sudden eloquence gives, — the surprise that the moment is so rich[.] [101]
                                                    [printed]
            ↑Transcri⟨p⟩bed under "Inspiration," in *PH* 206↓

[99] "He accepts . . . thought", struck through in pencil with two vertical use marks, is used in "Courage," *W*, VII, 275.
[100] This sentence is struck through in ink with a vertical use mark. Emerson met Mattie Griffith, whom he describes as "a brilliant young lady from Kentucky," in September, 1857 (*L*, V, 83–84).
[101] This sentence, struck through in pencil with a vertical use mark, is used in "Eloquence," *W*, VIII, 113. "A ⟨very⟩ lesson [p. [156]] . . . so rich" is struck through in pencil with single curved vertical lines on pp. [156] and [157]. The second line ends by curving around the pencil insertion, "Transcri⟨p⟩bed under . . . *PH* 206".

[158] "Water & Milestones" were the sole advice of a physician to his patient.

[159] [102] I write most privately to make a plea for B[rown]. It cannot have escaped your sagacity that he is a person who makes friends where courage & integrity are esteemed. You have pronounced his first eulogy. His speeches to the Court have interested the nation in him & will interest England, and, in due time, France & Germany. It is not, I am sure, your wish to stand in the most unlucky position which history must give to the Governor who ⟨hangs him.⟩ ↑signs his death warrant.↓ It is very easy to see that he will be a favorite of history, which plays mad pranks [160] with dignitaries, &, if so, that he will drag gentlemen into an immortality not desireable. There must of course be a minority of intelligent gentlemen in Virginia ⟨who⟩ sufficiently catholic to appreciate the public objection of all states where slavery does not exist, & to understand therefore the inevitable sympathy which all ⟨scholars⟩ writers & through them the civilized world generally will feel with ↑Captain John Brown.↓ ⁿ And Virginians also as soon as the temporary heats are [161] forgotten. I shall not insult you by referring to a public opinion changing every day, & which has softened every hour its first harsh judgment of him. The man is so transparent that all ⟨m⟩ can see him through, that he had no second thought, but was the rarest of heroes[,] a pure idealist, with no by-ends of his own.[103] He is therefore precisely what lawyers call crazy, being governed by ideas, & not by external [162] circumstance. He has afforded them the first trait marked in the books as betraying insanity, namely, disproportion between means & ends.

[102] The entry on pp. [159]–[162] is apparently the draft of a letter to Henry Alexander Wise. It must have been written some time after Brown was captured (October 18) and before he was executed (December 2), probably before he was convicted of treason and murder. The entry is heavily lined through in ink on p. [159]. "with dignitaries . . . desireable.", p. [160], is struck through in ink with four diagonal marks, probably intended to cancel. A pencil line in the left margin marks "He is therefore . . . external" on p. [161], and a discontinuous pencil line in the left margin marks "circumstance . . . ends." on p. [162].
[103] This sentence, struck through in ink with a vertical use mark, is used in "Remarks at a Meeting for the Relief of the Family of John Brown," W, XI, 268.

[163] [blank]

[164] Ideas make real societies ⟨M⟩and states. My countryman is surely not James Buchanan, ⟨nor Fernando Wood,⟩ ↑nor Caleb Cushing,↓ nor Barnum, ↑nor Governor Gardner,↓ nor Mrs Gardner the poisoner, nor Lot Poole, nor Fernando Wood; [104] but Thoreau & Alcott & Sumner & whoever lives in the same love & worship as I; every just person, every man or woman who knows what truth means.

[two leaves cut out]

[165] It will always be so. ↑Every principle is a war-note.↓ Who ever attempts to carry out the rule of right & love & freedom ⟨wil⟩ must take his life in his hand.

"Varius Sucronensis ait, Aemilius Scauras negat; Utri creditis Quirites" *Val[erius] Max[imus]* [*Factorum Dictorumque Memorabilium,*] iii, 7.[105]
↑printed in↓

[166] Queenie's private earthquake.[106] We had disputed about the duration of the vibrations, which I thought lasted 12 seconds, and she insisted returned at intervals of two minutes. Of course our accounts could not agree; but, yesterday, it chanced to turn out, that her earthquake was *in the afternoon,* & that of the rest of the world at 6 in the morning.

↑1860↓ Earthquake 17 Oct. at 6 a.m.

[167] Pierre d'Auvergne[,] troubadour of 12th century[,] sings

[104] Emerson's references are to James Buchanan (1791–1868), president of the United States, 1857–1861; Fernando Wood (1812–1881), Democratic congressman, mayor of New York and Tammany Hall leader; Caleb Cushing (1800–1879), U.S. attorney general, 1853–1857, see Journal VO, p. [191] above; Phineas Taylor Barnum (1810–1892), American showman; Henry Joseph Gardner (1818–1892), Know-Nothing governor of Massachusetts, see Journal VO, p. [192] above. Mrs. Gardner the poisoner and Lot Poole have not been identified.
[105] This entry is struck through in ink with two diagonal use marks. The anecdote referred to is used in "Behavior," *W*, VI, 195, where "Utri creditis, Quirites?" is rendered "Which do you believe, Romans?"
[106] "Queenie" was one of Emerson's names for his wife, Lidian.

"I will sing a new song which resounds in my breast x x x Never was a song good or beautiful which resembled any other" *Fauriel II. 13* [107]

"Since the air renews itself, ⟨a⟩& softens, So must my heart renew itself &, what buds in it, buds & grows outside of it."

"The nightingale ⟨shines⟩ glitters on the bough" [108]

I see at the edge of the snowbank the hardy blades of young grass prying holes through the ice, & lifting themselves ⟨thr⟩ above it[.] [109]

[168] Queteletism. How many people in a million are there who talk to themselves? How many sibilate, or whistle the S? How many wear straight shoes & not rights & lefts? How many prefer tea to coffee?

[169] Phillips goes to the ⟨rostrum as⟩ popular assembly, as the others go to their library. Whilst he speaks, his mind feeds.

Animal spirits, enthusiasm, insight, & decision.

The intellect delights in seeing the traces of a law, which, hiding itself, yet indicates at distant points its presence. And that it is which makes us so fond of pictures of fate. We say there is no lawless particle. Fate is the superstition; Law is the science. But it needs virtue to see straight[.]

[170] Intellect pure of action is skeptical. *Being*, & so *doing*, must blend, before the eye has health to behold through sympathy & through presence, the Spirit. Then all flows, & is known without

---

[107] Fauriel, *Histoire de la Poésie Provençale*, 1847. This entry is used in "Poetry and Imagination," *W*, VIII, 60.

[108] These two quotations from Pierre d'Auvergne are translated from Fauriel, *Histoire de la Poésie Provençale*, 1847, II, 13–14. The first, struck through in pencil with a vertical use mark, is used in "Poetry and Imagination," *W*, VIII, 60, where it is attributed to Pons de Capdeuil.

[109] This sentence is struck through in ink with a vertical use mark; cf. "May-Day," ll. 119–124, *W*, IX, 167.

⟨sentences⟩ words. Power even is not known to the pure. Power indicates weakness & opposition. Health exists & unfolds in the ⟨flower⟩ rose, in the sea, in the circular & endless astronomy.[110] The electricity is not less p⟨o⟩resent in my body & ↑my↓ joy, for twenty [171] years, that I never saw or suspected it, than in the twenty first, when I drew by art a spark from my knuckle.

It may be that we have no right here as individuals; that the existence of an embodied man marks fall & sin. ⟨Pure in⟩ To be pure, we must live in God radiant & flowing, constituting the health & conservation of the universe. We have stopped, we have stagnated, we have appropriated or become selfish, before we could arrest our immortality into this callus or wen of an individual,[111][n] [172] & ↑have↓ been punished by the wars, infirmities & fate, of human life. The wise ↑east-↓Indian seeks Nirwana or reabsorption, as felicity. It is for this reason that we are dualists, & know the law of our members as opposed to the good. And hence the inexplicable jangle of Fate & freedom, matter & spirit. Hence the ⟨scorn⟩ indignation of the poet, the scorn of the idealist, to whom geology & zoology are often an impertinence.

[173] Strong will, perfect will becomes a new existence, & must be allowed for. ↑Simple↓ perception[n] is shallow & weak, as the professors & the asses were ordered to the centre, in Bonaparte's Egyptian campaign. The good again are goodies, &, as Voltaire said, "'Tis the misfortune of worthy people that they are cowards." But strong will, perfect will is electricity, is unquenchable fire, & burns like the sun, & ⟨the⟩ all creatures [174] must conform themselves accordingly. There can be no such will except through the conversion of the man into his will; he, at least, has no doubts; he is the will, & the will is him. And one may say boldly that no man has a clear perception of any truth who has not been reacted on by it so as to be its martyr.[112]

↑printed in *"Fate"*↓

---

[110] A vertical line in the left margin marks "Power even . . . astronomy."

[111] The "t's" in "appropriated", "immortality", "into", and "this" are crossed in pencil.

[112] "Simple" in the second sentence of this entry is in pencil. "There can . . . is him." is struck through in pencil with two vertical use marks; "There can . . . martyr." and "of the man . . . martyr." are struck through in ink with single

[175] [113]   Immortality
                     Nachiketas
                     Pythagoras descending into flesh

[176] Nothing so selfrighteous as the morning bath, the sleeping with the windows open, & the early walk. Dr Kirkland & Professor Brazer.[114]

The believing we do something when we do nothing, is the first illusion of tobacco.

The Bath, the cutaneous sublime, the extremes meet, the bittersweet, the pail of pleasure & of pain. O, if an enemy had done this!

[177] *Books for Concord Library.*
Browning's Poems
Channing's Poems
Aurora Leigh
Piozzi
Chemistry
Blodget
? Kohl
? Ballentyne
Mather's Magnalia [115]

[178] [blank]
[179]–[180] [leaf torn out] [116]

---

vertical use marks. "as Voltaire . . . cowards.' ", struck through in ink with a vertical use mark, is used in "Fate," *W*, VI, 29. "There can . . . martyr." is used in "Fate," *W*, VI, 29–30.

[113] The entries on p. [175] are in pencil. For Nachiketas, see Journal SO, pp. [231]–[243] above.

[114] Emerson lived in the house of President John Thornton Kirkland during his freshman year at Harvard; John Brazer was his freshman Latin teacher. See *JMN*, XIII, 126–127.

[115] Emerson's list of books includes Kohl's *Russia* . . . , 1844 (see Journal VO, p. [72] above) and Cotton Mather's *Magnalia Christi Americana, or, The Ecclesiastical History of New-England.* Chemistry, Blodget, and Ballentyne have not been identified. "Mathers Magnalia" is in pencil.

[116] Letters and portions of words are visible on the stub of p. [180], including, from the last five lines on the page: "‖ . . . ‖h ‖ . . . ‖t ‖ . . . ‖al ‖ . . . ‖th ‖ . . . ‖th." Emerson indexed p. [179] under Slow Rate.

[181] ↑*John Brown.*↓

He ⟨had⟩ drew this notice & distinction from the people among whom he fell from the fact that ⟨he⟩ ↑this boy of 12↓ had conducted his drove of cattle a hundred miles alone.[117]

[182] George Sullivan's answer to Mrs Joy concerning Wm. Emerson's health — Is he dead? "No, Madam, but he is very sick"; and Ann O'Brien's answer to me when I asked if the parrot had yet said "Ann Kelly." "No," replied Ann O'Brien, "but she made a beautiful offer to say it;" — may go together as examples of Irish courtesy.[118]

[183] Manners must be selfcontained. You shall not be leaky, but king over your word & all your gesture & action indicate power at rest[.] Then they must betray the good heart which beats for all. No beautifier of complexion or behavior like this[.] [119]

[1⟨4⟩84] Courage the old physiologists taught, and their meaning holds, if their physics are grown a little mythological[.] [120]

[185] Culture

Books. The Indian who carried a letter from the French governor through the forest, hid it when he would eat, or do any unsightly office. Atahualpa ⟨wrote⟩ caused a Spaniard to write "Dio" on his thumbnail, & when Pizarro could not read it, despised him. What a And what an ado about the invention of printing: This month again on Franklin's birthday!

wonder we make of Cadmus, or of whatever inventor of letters: Then what a debt is ours to [186₁] books. How much we owe to imaginative books! the boy has no better friend or influence than his Scott, Shakspeare, Plutarch, & Homer. And if, in Arkansaw or Texas,

---

[117] This sentence, struck through in ink with a diagonal use mark, is used in "John Brown: Speech at Salem," *W*, XI, 278.

[118] See Journal AC, pp. [107] and [184], and Journal CL, p. [48] above.

[119] This paragraph, struck through in ink with a vertical use mark, is used in "Behavior," *W*, VI, 195–196.

[120] "Courage . . . mythological" is in pencil and slants upward from left to right across the page.

I should meet a man reading Horace, I were no stranger, & should forget the dreary land.[121]

Yet there is a limit to this influence also. After reading Adam Smith or Linnaeus, I am no better mate for ↑Mr↓ Hosmer or ↑Mr↓ Potter[.]

And one book crowds out [187₁] another, so that, after years of study, we are not wiser. Then books can't teach motherwit, sagacity, ⟨&⟩ presence of mind,ⁿ & humanity.

[186₂]   Bad seat & distance be defied
       ⟨Nor⟩ ↑And lest↓ ⟨a⟩I thwart the hugest throng
       ⟨Can⟩ ↑Could↓ Kemble face or feature hide
       I Ellen & Edith's gaze prolong [122]

[187₂]   Because the theatre is wide
       And Meionaon long
       And straining eyes are badly tried
       Unless like eagles strong
       By this good glass new force supplied
       Shall rectify the wrong

       /Bad/And/seat & distance be defied
       ⟨Nor⟩ ↑Can↓ Kemble ⟨can⟩ a feature hide
       ⟨Across⟩ ↑Nor o'er↓ the hugest throng
       ⟨To⟩ Ellen & Edith ⟨belong⟩ gaze among [123]

[188]   A dangerous gift & grace is mine
       Closely dame your ear incline
       ↑A word↓ my ⁿ merits ⟨shortly to⟩ ↑shall↓ unlock
       Behold me here a ⟨silent⟩ ↑whispering↓ clock
       I ⟨can⟩ both time & silence keep

[121] "Then what . . . Homer.", struck through on p. [186] in pencil with a vertical use mark, is used in "Illusions," W, VI, 312. With "And if . . . Horace," cf. "Culture," W, VI, 159.

[122] "Bad seat . . . prolong", in pencil, is overwritten by the ink entry, "books. How . . . out".

[123] "Because the . . . among", in pencil, is overwritten by the ink entry, "another, so . . . humanity.".

⟨I⟩ Will^n not wake you when you sleep
⟨But measure all⟩ ↑Yet count as true↓ the balmy hours
As truly as
The thunderer from ⟨cathedral⟩ ↑the steeple↓ towers

⟨Feb⟩ ↑Jan↓ 18 Saratoga
  19 Hamilton
  22 Sunday Rochester
  23 Lima
  24 Buffalo
  25 Batavia
  26 Rochester
  27 Toronto
  30 Toledo
⟨1⟩31 Zanesville

Feb   1 Yellow Springs
  2 Cincinnati
  3 Richmond   J. S. Hadley
  4 Lafayette   David Spencer
  6 Chicago
  7 Rockford   Mel[ancthon] Smith
  8 Madison
  9 Racine
  10 Milwaukee   James MacAlister
  11 Kenosha   J B Wheeler
  13 Niles   F Quinn
  14 Kalamazoo   F↑oster↓ Pratt
  15 Grand Rapids   H Gaylord
[189]   16 Marshall.   J B Greenough
  17 Ann Arbor   C A Thompson
  18 Detroit   S D Elwood [124]

E. of "Strafford's memory was great, & he
made it greater by confiding in it" S:r P. Warwick

[124] This list of dates is Emerson's tentative lecture schedule for January and
February, 1860. See Pocket Diary 11, pp. [135]–[138], and Pocket Diary 12, pp.
[18]–[29] below. "A dangerous . . . towers", in pencil, underlies the ink entry
on p. [188].

[190₁]   Gt N presents
           to Mr C his compliments
           And brings him a ponderous book
           Wherein he dared not cast a look
           ⟨I⟩f↑or↓ fear
           Lest sleep himself had overtook
           He says the book was such a load
           That ⟨if⟩had the sleighing not been good
           Upon the overground railroad
           It crost his mind
           To throw the volumes overboard
           He took advice of the Professor
           Of Harvard not of college lesser
           Who said charged him with

[191₁]   But adds
           ⟨that he⟩ Natts made a stipulation
           With the bibloopolie nation
           To honor this book as an order
           For better

           And their meaning holds if their physiology has grown a
little mythical

[190₂] Saw at Utica 20 Jan. A. L. Stimson, whose address at Utica is
Care of John Munn
              at Syracuse —   W D Stewart Esq
              at Rochester —   H K Jerome, Esq
J. B. Hunter   Batavia N. Y.
G. A. Thompson, Racine
John A. Wilstach, Esq.   Lafayette, Indiana
and Lahr Hotel [125]

---

[125] Emerson had corresponded with A. L. Stimson in September and October,
1852, about a lecture (L, IV, 316). "Gt N . . . mythical", in pencil on pp. [190]
and [191], underlies the entries in ink on these pages. For "And their . . . mythical",
see p. [184] above.

[191₂] ↑1860↓ *16 Jan[uar]y.* Gave Ticknor & Fields an order on Houghton printer, to print 500 copies "Essays II Series." [126]

15 Oct[obe]r an order to print 500 Essays, I Series

↑See Journal↓

The Engineer was goading his boilers with pitchpine knots.

He looked out ↑of↓ the ↑car-↓window, the fences passed languidly by; he could scan curiously every post. But very soon the jerk of every pulse of the engine was felt; the whistle of the engineer moaned short moans, as it swept across any highway. Edwin gazed out over the fields. The fences were tormented; every rail & rider writhed & twisted past the window, the snowbanks [192] swam past like fishes; & the speed seemed to increase every moment.* [127] The ⟨lands the⟩ rocks, walls, the fields themselves ⟨were in violent motion⟩ streaming like a mill-tail. The train tore on with jumps & jerks that tested the strength of oak & iron. The passengers seemed to suffer their speed. Meantime, the wind cried like a child, complained like a sawmill, whistled like a fife, mowed like an ideot, roared like the sea, & ⟨at last⟩ yelled like a demon.

[193] At Buffalo, found William B. Wright, my former correspondent from Goshen, N. Y.[128] and ⟨at⟩ on the way from Rochester to Toronto J. B. Hunter of Batavia N. Y.[,] once of Louisville Ky.: and, at Toronto, saw two Carlyles, nephews of Thomas C., and sons of John Carlyle, of Mohawk, Canada West, his brother. Another brother ↑of T. C.,↓ Alexander Carlyle, lives at Brentford; and a sister, Mrs Haining, at ⟨Toron⟩Hamilton. ⟨They⟩ ↑The young men↓

* The near trees & bushes wove themselves into colored ribbons.

[126] After the failure of Phillips, Sampson & Co. in September, 1859, Emerson hesitated about his choice of a new publisher and then settled on Ticknor & Fields (*L*, V, 177, 190).

[127] Emerson's footnote is set off at the foot of p. [192] by a square bracket at the left; it is marked in the text and at the foot by an S-like sign.

[128] Although no letters from Wright from the 1850s seem to have survived, William Bull Wright wrote to Emerson in June, 1866, thanking him for the suggestions about his long poem *Highland Rambles* (*L*, V, 467).

JOURNALS OF RALPH WALDO EMERSON   CL

did not know that their Uncle Dr J. A. Carlyle of London, [194]
was named John like their father, but called Dr John "Uncle Aikin."
One of these young men is teacher of ⟨a⟩the "Model School" in
Toronto, & the other, I believe, is preparing for the ministry.
At Toronto I had a telegraph from James E. Day inviting me to
lecture at the Mechanics Institute, — Hamilton;[n] but could not go.
My correspondent on aesthetics at Toronto is J. D. Edgar, (care of
Hon. J. Hillyard Cameron, Toronto) to whom I must write.[129]

[195] At Kalamazoo, I had a humpbacked driver who took me
to Grand Rapids & back. His name is Church, & his father is a noted
lawyer at Syracuse; but this dwarf prefers to be an ostler. He talks
to his horses all the way & praises them. "Ha, ha; Jimmy, what are
you looking after? ha, ha, ha, ⟨T⟩take care Jimmy!" st! st! John!
"John takes it easy," he says, "but whenever he's called on, he's on
hand, ha! ha!" He says, he slept for years in the same stall with the
seed-horse, "Sir Henry," which killed ⟨his⟩ ↑its↓ Dutch ostler, & was
ironed, but ⟨he⟩ ↑Church↓ took the irons off, & gave it a barrel of
sugar.

[196] Flora Temple trotted for a purse of 3000 dollars at Kalamazoo,
& made the shortest time ever made in the Union, "⟨Nineteen⟩Two
minutes, nineteen seconds, & a half." "She flew." But, he thinks,
the "Princess"[n] which was beaten, the handsomer & the better horse.

[197]		
	Ohio	Buckeye
	Illinois	Sucker
	Indiana	Hoosier
	Michigan	Wolverine
	Wisconsin	Badger
	Missouri	Puke
	Iowa	Hawkeye

When an eastern man is cheated by a Hoosier, he is said to be
Wabashed.

[198] ⟨In⟩ Dreams[n] ⟨we keep all⟩ ↑retain↓ the infirmities of our

---

[129] J. D. Edgar wrote Emerson on January 28, 1860, to thank him for his
lecture before the Ontario Literary Society on January 27, 1860 (L, V, 192–193).

character. The good ⟨g⟩Genius may be there or not; ⟨my⟩ ↑our↓ evil genius is sure to stay.[130]

In the polar regions, the only warm weather, — the great heats, — ⟨is⟩ ↑are↓, when it is warm enough to snow.

[199] The postmaster, in each of our towns, is usually some sneak who reads the Administration paper every day, & loudly defends the last measure ↑of Government.↓ Of course, in its varying policy, he is obliged to eat his words before the year is out. The boys at School call Cicero "a regular Postmaster."

[200] [131]   Errata
    p 52 ⟨shipwreck   =   explosion⟩
       ⟨54   Oregon & Utah⟩
       ⟨60   Marchez sans le peuple⟩

       59   English virility
       ⟨68   process⟩

            snuff-boxes

       ⟨82   available material⟩

[201] An adjutant bird is near six feet high, & from 12 to 15 from the extremity of each wing.

Dr Bigelow's formula was, that fevers are self-limiting; afterwards that all disease is so; therefore no use in treatment.
Dr Holmes said,[n] No use in drugs.
Dr Sam[ue]l Jackson said, Rest, absolute rest, is the panacea.

The butchers said, there was never a time when this disease of the cattle was not in the cattle. Yes answered the Gov Banks, But there's

---

[130] This paragraph, struck through in pencil with a vertical use mark, is used in "Demonology," W, X, 20.
    [131] The entries on p. [200] are in pencil. Emerson's notations refer to the first edition of Conduct of Life (1860).

as much importance in the *degree* as in the kind of distemper. Now 'tis in overpowering [202] degree. We all carry seeds of all distempers through life latent. But if you become weak, the disease will become strong.[132]

Fate Power Wealth
Culture   Worship
Beauty
Behaviour
Worship [133]

[203] *Conduct of Life*
    Fate.
    Power
    Wealth

Vol. II
⟨Domestic Life⟩ ↑Home↓
Solitude & Society

    Culture ↑see TU 210↓
    Worship
    ⟨Natural Aristocracy⟩
    Power in Private Life
    Manners & Morals
    Beauty
    ↑Success↓

Superlative
Success
Nat. Aristocracy
Eloquence
Clubs
Country Life

    Society
    Home
    Manners
    Beauty
    ⟨Success⟩ [134]

1. Fate
2. Power
3. Wealth
4. Behavior
5. Culture
6. Worship
———

---

[132] This paragraph, struck through in ink on p. [201] with two vertical use marks and on p. [202] with one, is used in "Old Age," *W*, VII, 323–324. For Dr. Bigelow's formula, see p. [139] above.

[133] "Fate Power . . . Behaviour Worship" is in pencil, partly overwritten by "degree. We . . . strong."

[134] "Society", "Home", "Manners", "Beauty", and "⟨Success⟩" are in pencil; "Success" is canceled in ink. "see TU 210" is in pencil overwritten by "Success" (in Vol. II column) in ink. On pp. [202] and [203], Emerson lists many of the lectures used in *Conduct of Life* (1860) and *Society and Solitude* (1870).

7. Wayside Consideration

8 Beauty

9 Illusions

[204] "The two mandarins, (namely, ⟨()⟩Pik Kwei & the Tartar general)
were in full official costume, & retained throughout that charmed & delighted manner, which a Chinaman always puts on when he is powerless &
alarmed."
———————— when Lord Elgin put these two captured officials into
temporary office again, after the taking of Canton

Oliphant. p. 155 [135]

[205] 'Tis trite enough, but now & then it is seen with explaining
light, that nature is a mere mirror, & shows to each man only his own
quality.

Illusions. Color is illusion, you say; but how know I that the rock
& mountain are more real than its hue & gleam? [136]

[206] "Pardon me, but the moral impression (of Everett's Φ B K Oration)
is nothing to Cicero's. Could he with sincerity but once, if only once, have
raised his gifted voice to the Aegis of our salvation! He would then
⟨have⟩better resemble[n] Burke, who descended from a higher sphere, when
he would influence human affairs." M[ary]. M[oody]. E[merson].
1825.[137]

[207]   ↑see [Notebook] M M E I p 139↓
     Then for Culture, can Solitude be spared? Solitude, the safe-
guard of mediocrity, is to genius the stern friend, the cold obscure
shelter where moult the eagle wings which will bear one farther than
suns & stars. Byron & Wordsworth there burnished their pens. Ah![n]
that you could be disunited from travelling with the souls of other

---

[135] Laurence Oliphant, *Narrative of the Earl of Elgin's Mission to China and
Japan* . . . , 2 vols. (London, 1859), I, 155. Emerson withdrew this volume from
the Boston Athenaeum June 9–August 24, 1860.
    [136] "Illusions. Color . . . gleam?" is in pencil.
    [137] A vertical pencil line in the left margin marks "Burke, who . . . affairs.'"

men, — of living, breathing, reading, & writing, with one livelong timefated yoke, — their opinions.[138]

———

over

[208] [blank]

[209] "Thank God, I am capable of enjoying the sensations that Raffaelle intended to excite." Haydon & Reynolds [139]

All knowledge gives superiority, & it makes so little difference in what direction." p 67 sup[ra].

———

Use of a University for cherishing gifted persons, Cowley said? [n 140]

———

Egotism. Genius leaves it out   *AC* 288

Dr Chauncy must pray for "the boy that was drowned in Frog Pond," but genius can sculpture the event & never name it.[141]

Egotism   M M E. I. 73, 50,

[210] Have manners that can last: As these forms are to be repeated every day, perhaps every hour, nothing exaggerated will pass — any excess, as grimace, or affected look or word, becomes intolerable. If a man ⟨answers⟩ declines the bread or meat you offer him, with "No, I'm ⟨m⟩obliged to you;" or, when he assents to your remark, says, "Decidedly," or "Exactly," one soon hesitates to give him an opportunity. But the civility reduced to the simplest form, as "Please" "No, thank you" can be spoken ⟨a⟩ten thousand [211] times with new propriety." ⟨& giving new pleasure.⟩

[212] The least mistake in sentiment takes all the beauty out of your clothes.[142]

———

[138] This paragraph, struck through in ink with a vertical use mark, is used in "Culture," *W*, VI, 155–156.

[139] This entry, struck through in ink with a diagonal use mark, is used in "Michael Angelo," *W*, XII, 232. See p. [84] above.

[140] See p. [35] above.

[141] See Journal AC, p. [288] above.

[142] This sentence, struck through in ink with a vertical use mark, is used in "Beauty," *W*, VI, 300.

[213] ↑Travel↓   ↑Culture↓
We shall not always travel over seas & lands, with light purposes, & for pleasure, as we say. Progress of culture will give
gravity & domestic rest [t]o the ↑educated classes in this coun-
try↓[.] [143]

The costliest benefit of books is ⟨to⟩ ↑that they set us↓ free ⟨us⟩
from themselves also.

                                              LI 117

[214] Classification a necessity of the human mind, and one of
its main joys. It masters the mind, & makes rogues & thieves of
learned men. A professor of theology at Berlin ? has just been convicted of stealing books from the Library of the University. All
Collectors tend to this foible. W. S. Shaw[,] the founder of the
Boston Athenaeum[,] used to steal from the private ⟨C⟩libraries of
his friends any book he coveted to make his darling Athenaeum
complete.
Collectors of shells steal orangias from Mr Grinnell's mante↑l↓piece
& Mrs Coffin's(?) house at Siasconset.[144]
[215] All autograph names ⟨are cu⟩of distinguished persons are cut
out of the books of the Cambridge College Library.

— May 1860
Mellish Motte told me, that the ⟨most⟩ books stolen from the
Boston Athenaeum are ↑mostly↓ from the *Theological department,*
so that they are forced to lock that up, as they do the Fine-Arts
alcoves.[145] As an offset to this, Mr Jewett, ↑the Librarian,↓ assured
me at the *"City Library,"* [n] that it was necessary to guard in securest
manner the 100 vols of "Patent Reports" sent by the British Gov-
[ernmen]t[,] for lawyers who had a case requiring [216] [146] the use

---

[143] "We shall . . . country" is struck through in ink with a vertical use mark;
"educated . . . country" is in pencil.
[144] Mr. Grinnell and Mrs. Coffin are unidentified. William Smith Shaw (1778–
1826), librarian and general superintendent of the Boston Athenaeum 1810–1826,
was known as "Athenaeum Shaw."
[145] Mellish Irving Motte, Emerson's college classmate, was a Unitarian minister.
[146] "the use . . . ⟨with⟩" is on the lower half of p. [216], beneath a page-wide
rule with the notation "from p 215".

of one of these books, were utterly reckless, & would borrow & never return, or would cut out the plate or diagram they wanted. ⟨with⟩

↑*Thoreau.*↓

Agassiz says, "There are no varieties in nature. All are spe-⟨ies⟩cies." *Thoreau* says, "If ⟨he⟩ ↑A.↓ sees two thrushes so alike that they bother the ornithologist to discriminate them, he insists they are ⟨varie⟩ ↑two↓ species; but if he see Humboldt & Fred. Cogswell, he insists that they come from one ancestor."[147]

[217]   April 1860
Somebody said in my hearing lately, that a house in Concord was worth half as much again as a house in any other town, since the people had shown a good will to defend each other.[148]

↑*Nationality.*↓

"Quand Italie sera sans poison,
France sans trahison,
Angleterre sans guerre,
Lors sera le monde sans terre."
                    "Leigh's Observations" ap[ud] Southey
                    Common P. Book Vol III. p. 4 [149]

[218] The teaching of politics is that the Government which was set for protection & comfort of all good citizens, becomes the principal obstruction & nuisance, with which we have to contend. Wherever we look, whether to Kansas, to Utah, to the frontier — as Mexico & Cuba, or to laws & contracts for internal improvement, the capital enemy in the way is always this ugly government.
     [219] We could manage very well by private enterprise, for

[147] Fred Cogswell was "a kindly, underwitted inmate of Concord Almshouse" (*J*, IX, 270).
[148] On April 3 the sergeant-at-arms of the United States Senate sent Silas Carleton to arrest Franklin B. Sanborn, who had disregarded the summons of a congressional committee to appear on suspicion of having been implicated in John Brown's raid. Carleton and his aides were driven off by irate residents, leaving the prisoner nominally in the custody of local authorities (*J*, IX, 266, and *L*, V, 210).
[149] *Southey's Common-Place Book. Third Series. Analytical Readings*, ed. John Wood Warter (London, 1850). Emerson withdrew the Third Series from the Boston Athenaeum April 3–May 1, 1860.

carrying the mails, associations for emigration, & emigrant aid, for local police & defence, & for prevention of crime; but the cheat & bully & malefactor we meet everywhere is the Gov[ernmen]t.

This can only be counteracted by magnifying the local powers at its cost. Take from the U.S. the appointment of postmasters & let the towns elect them, and you deprive the Federal Gov[ernmen]t of half a million defenders.

[220] Cassius M. Clay gave Wendell Phillips his audience at New Haven, by closing his own agricultural address at 7½ & went himself to attend P's lecture at 7¾, and the whole audience with him. So ^{n} Phillips opened his lecture with some compliment to him, & referred to the fact that ⟨he⟩ Clay had said, that, in a fight between the negroes & the whites, his own part would be taken with the whites. The audience gave 3 cheers for Mr Clay. "Well," said Phillips, "This, then, we must reckon the rollcall on that side, — this distinguished leader and the white population in the slave [221] states." The Audience instantly repeated their cheers. Phillips thought himself in a bad plight, but rescued himself by saying, "Well, gentlemen, now let us see ⟨have⟩ the muster on the other side. Thomas Jefferson says, that, '*in* ^{n} ⟨a⟩ ↑*this*↓ *contest*, ⟨with the slave, there is no attribute of⟩ *the Almighty has no attribute but must take part with the slave.*' [150] ↑Mr Clay & the Southern gentlemen on one side, & all the attributes of the Almighty on the other."↓ The audience were utterly silenced, — & Phillips proceeded with his speech.

[222]   See Southey's Common Place Book

Montluc, in the collection of French memoires. Tome 22

Henry IV. called his memoires "the Soldier's Bible."

His acknowledgment, that he has often trembled with fear, & that he recovered courage when he had said a prayer for the occasion. [151]

---

[150] Cf. *The Writings of Thomas Jefferson*, 1854, VIII, 404.

[151] The entries on Montluc are from *Southey's Common-Place Book. Third Series*, 1850, III, 222 and 226. "His acknowledgment . . . occasion." is used in "Courage," *W*, VII, 261. "Henry IV . . . Bible.'" is used in "Address at the Dedication of the Soldiers' Monument in Concord, April 19, 1867," *W*, XI, 361.

[223] "We do what we must" &c

2d *Essays*, p. 60.

[224] Externality of our sects at this moment
Very slight hold or no hold ↑of↓ ⟨that⟩ christian traditions ⟨have.⟩
↑on real life.↓ [152]
We are realists through our politics, trade, & geography and all the
intellectual are emancipated. Barbarism lingers with the feeble, the
passionate, the unthinking, & they are domineered by the sect of their
fathers or their companions.

[225] Christianity is much in the way. The dogma being dropped
of the mystic offices of Christ, & his Value only as a moral teacher
owned, the majesty of morals & the impertinence of persons sets him
also aside, & makes any elaborate deference to him superserviceable[.] [153]

[226] 'Tis a skeptical time[.]
Relig[ious]. sects have been displaced by progress of opinion.[n] ⟨by⟩-
Christian [n] traditions have lost their hold on the mind. The dogma of
↑mystic↓ offices being dropped, ⟨the⟩ 'tis impossible to maintain the
emphasis of his personality, & it recedes, as all persons ⟨do⟩ must,
before the sublimity of the moral laws.[154]

Duc de Brancas said, "Why need I read the Encyclopédie? Rivarol
visits me." [155] I may well say it of Theodore Parker.

[227] Theodore Parker has filled up all his years & days &
hours. A son of the energy of New Eng[lan]d[:] restless, eager,
manly, brave, early old, contumacious, clever. I can well praise him

---

[152] "Externality . . . life." is struck through in ink with a vertical use mark;
cf. "Worship," *W*, VI, 208–209.

[153] "The dogma . . . superserviceable", struck through in ink with a vertical
use mark, is used in "Worship," *W*, VI, 209.

[154] "Relig. sects . . . laws.", struck through in ink with a vertical use mark,
is used in "Worship," *W*, VI, 209.

[155] Arsène Houssaye, *Men and Women of the Eighteenth Century*, 2 vols. (New
York, 1852), I, 216. See *JMN*, XIII, 123.

at a spectator's distance[,] for our minds & methods were unlike, — few people more unlike.[156]

All the virtues are solidaires. Each man is related to persons who are not related to each other, and I saw with pleasure ⟨who⟩ that men whom I could not approach were drawn through him to the admiration of that which I admire.

[228] 'Tis vain to charge him with perverting the opinions of the new generation. The opinions of men are organic. Simply, those came to him who found themselves expressed by him; and had they not found this enlightened mind in whom they found their own opinions combined with zeal in every cause of love & humanity, they would have suspected their opinions, & suppressed them; & so sunk into melancholy or malignity: a feeling of loneliness & hostility to what was reckoned respectable.[157]

[229] ⟨He spent himself⟩ ↑He was willing to perish↓ in the using.[158] He ⟨was not a man⟩ sacrificed the future to the present, was willing to spend & be spent, felt himself to belong to the day he lived in, & had too much to do than that he should be careful for fame. —

He used every day, hour, & minute⟨s⟩; he lived to the latest moment, & his character appeared in the last moments with the same firm control as in the day of strength.

[230] Philip J. Hoedemaker
Kalamazoo
Michigan [159]

---

[156] Theodore Parker (1810–1860), Unitarian clergyman, took a leading part in antislavery agitation, and was one of the secret committee that aided John Brown's scheme for a raid at Harpers Ferry. He died on May 10, 1860. This sentence is struck through in ink with a vertical mark, probably intended to cancel.

[157] This paragraph, struck through in ink with three vertical use marks, is used in "Theodore Parker," W, XI, 287–288.

[158] The original "He" is inadvertently canceled and a penciled "He" is inserted above it; a pencil line from the second "He" encircles the original. A penciled arrow points from "perish" to "in the".

[159] P. J. Hoedemaker wrote to Emerson on April 28, 1860, presumably about a lecture engagement (L, VI, 472).

Fault of T. Parker, that there was no beauty. What he said as mere fact, almost offended you, so bald & detached.

[231] ⟨Oxford College⟩ [160]

[232]–[235] [blank]
[236]   *Music Hall*
    The realization of Christianity is the only way to get rid of it. Divination. TO ↑110, 111,↓

———

Upanishads. *SO* 222 — 230

———

Moral values   ↑Concord↓ [161]
    as value of Concord residence   *CL* 217
        living with honest people
        benefactors
        reasonable beings

Measures of these in money. $\overline{VO}$ 123, 169

[237]

———

Classes of Men

———

        ↑Classes of mind⟨s⟩ eternal. *AZ* 282   *TU* 13↓
        Men good by sympathy   CL 243
        ⟨g⟩Greatness
            See M[ary]. M[oody]. E[merson]. & C[harles] K[ing]
                                N[ewcomb]
        Real men   CL 144 [162]

[238]–[239] [blank]

[160] "Oxford College" is canceled in pencil by a zigzag line.
[161] "110, 111," is in pencil; "Concord" is enclosed in a circle.
[162] "Classes of mind . . . CL 144" is struck through in ink with a diagonal use mark.

[240]   *Death.*

When our friends die, we not only lose them, but we lose a great deal of life which in the survivors was related to them.

[241] Is a thief all thief? Is his only proof of identity the wish to steal? ⁿ

[242] I wrote that one affectation was venial, — in prosperous men, marked attention to their blood relations.[163] I have discovered another ⟨affectation⟩ ↑of↓ which I think still better; when people have not common sense, ⟨to affect it⟩ at least ⟨to affect it.⟩ ↑to simulate it.↓

[243] If you have only sympathy, you cannot be spared. If you have a ↑finer↓ perception of beauty, — he who has a portfolio of designs in his palace becomes soon aware that his portfolio waits for your praise, & ↑he↓ must climb to your garret to obtain it.[164]

[244] *Pairs*   SO 221
Things go by pairs. *CO* 98
———

Thoughts go by pairs
———

Historical pairs of men   *AC* 284
———

I am a matchmaker, & delight in nothing more than in finding the husband or mate of the trivial fact I have long carried in my memory, (unable to ⟨give⟩ ↑offer↓ any reason for the emphasis I gave it,) until now, suddenly, it shows itself as the true symbol or expressor of some abstraction.

[245] Advantages of old age.
I reached the other day the end of my fifty seventh year, and am easier in my mind than hitherto. I could never give ⟨gr⟩ much reality to evil & pain. But now when my wife says, perhaps this tumor on

---

[163] See Journal SO, p. [188] above.
[164] This entry is struck through in pencil with a diagonal use mark.

your shoulder is a cancer, I say, what if it is? It would not make the gentleman on his way in a cart to the gallows very unhappy, to tell him that the pain in his knee [n] threatened a white swelling.[165]

[246] Of Age, see *BL* 233   *CL* 240

[247] Negatives   Will not food fat him? [166]

[248] Of friendship. There is not only the unspeakable benefit of a reasonable creature to talk to, but also a certain increase of sanity, ⟨by⟩ ↑through↓ testing one's health by the other's, & noting the accords & discords. And we appeal pathetically as ↑M.↓ M. E. did, when our sanity is questioned, to the certificate of their conversation.[167]
Friendship, — it is an order of nobility; from its elevations we come [249]–[250] [leaf torn out] [168]

[251] Plutarch, the elixir of Greece & Rome, that is the book which nations went to compose. — If the world's library were burning, I should as soon fly to rescue that, as Shakspeare & Plato, or next afterwards.

Clough says, "Plutarch's best life is Antony, I think."

[252]   God getting tired of Kings.
Antonio Perez quotes a wise counsellor of Philip II. who said to him, "Should God once get tired of monarchies, he will give another form to the political world."

See *Humboldt's letters.*[169]

---

[165] "But now . . . swelling.", struck through in ink with three vertical use marks, is used in "Old Age," *W*, VII, 323.

[166] This entry is in pencil; "Negatives" is encircled on three sides by a curved line.

[167] Emerson's square brackets, indicating matter to be omitted, are inserted around "as M.M.E. did,".

[168] Emerson indexed p. [250] under Alcott and Clubs. An ink blot on p. [248] indicates that an entry on p. [249] was struck through with a vertical use mark.

[169] *Letters of Alexander von Humboldt to Varnhagen von Ense,* trans. Friedrich Kapp (New York, 1860), p. 193. Emerson withdrew this book from the Boston Athenaeum September 5–7, 1860. Cf. "Boston Hymn," ll. 5–6, *W*, IX, 201.

"It is not at all necessary," said King Bomba in a letter to Louis Philippe, "that my people think; I think for them: the people, who have betrayed me so often, submit to my power." See *Humboldt's Letters*   Trans. [Friedrich Kapp, 1860,] p. 336

[253]   11 Sept. 1860
     Fine walk yesterday with Ellery to Estabrook Farm. Finest day in the year, & best road, almost all the way "through the lots." Birds singing; — got over their summer silence — sunlight full of gnats; crickets in full cry; goldfinches (carduelis) on the thistle ⟨‖ ... ‖⟩eating the seed, scattering the awns. Boulder field: cooper's hawk: rock of Sinai, all books & tables of law, wonderful hedges, barberry, apple, elder, viburnum, ivy, cornel, woodbine, grape, white thorn, the brook through the wood—. Benzoin. The big birch. Largeness of the estate.
Nobody can buy. Came out at Capt Barrett's & through the fields again out at Flint's.[170] [254] A cornucopia of golden joys. E[llery]. says, that he & H[enry]. T[horeau] have agreed that the only reason of turning out of the mowing, is, not to hurt the feelings of the farmers; but it never ⟨has⟩does, if they are out of sight. For the farmers have no imagination. And it doesn't do a bit of hurt. Thoreau says, that, when he goes surveying, the farmer leads him straight through the grass.

[255] 'Tis strange. The bluebirds' ⟨bring⟩ song brings back vividly the cold spring days when we first hear them; those days were so sour & unlovely, & now seem so sweet!

     [256] ↑There is one trap into which the most cautious avoider of North Street and Broadway may fall.↓ ⟨What⟩ How ⟨heedless⟩ unsuspectingly a quiet conservative assembly allows a man to speak to them! They would have called in the police, if he had come ↑in↓ with a club, but, the moment he opens his mouth, he begins to unseat

[170] The Estabrook Farm or Easterbrook Country is about two miles north of Concord center along the old Carlisle Road. Barrett's farm is about one and one-half miles north of Concord center, and Flint's farm is just north of North or Flint's Bridge.

them, bereave ⟨of⟩them of their property, their position, their reasons, their self-respect, to take them out of their possession, & into his, & if he is the man I take him for, they will ⟨never⟩ ↑not soon↓ be their own men again.

[257] The↑y↓ ⟨South⟩ ↑manage things better in the South which↓ is quite right in ⟨it⟩ sticking to its gag-laws. — [171] The poor gentle-men go out of the meeting, when this outlaw ends his speech, &, rallying to recover their disturbed associations, they fancy that all is as it was when they came; that, if they suspected a kind of threat & thunder ⟨&⟩in this strange harangue, ⟨they have heard,⟩ probably the odd things dropped by the speaker were not ⟨hear⟩ noticed or understood by most people, & will [258] be forgotten tomorrow. At all events, themselves will forget them as fast as they can, & Faneuil--Hall-⟨m⟩Market, and the Brokers' Exchange, and the Banks, stand where they ⟨were⟩ ↑did,↓ & will ↑help to↓ blot out these impertinences very soon. Never believe it. Younger people & stronger than they, heard them also; and, above all, the speaker was ⟨w⟩very well con-vinced himself, and is already today taking more outrageous [259] positions; and the speech of men & women, & the fingers of the Press, are doing their utmost to give his words currency & experiment.

Eloquence is forever a power that ⟨thrusts⟩shoves usurpers from their thrones, & sits down on them by allowance & acclaim of all.

[260] ↑See *IL* 73↓ The ⟨charm⟩ ↑⟨surprise⟩ feat↓ of the Imag-ination is in ⟨the discovery of⟩ ↑showing↓ the convertibility of every thing into every other thing.[n] ⟨or into all things.⟩ Facts which had never before left their stark common sense, suddenly ⟨become symbols & badges of larger & largest intelligence.⟩ ↑⟨show⟩ figure as Eleusinian mysteries.↓ It is as if my boots & chair & candlestick are found out to be fairies in disguise, are meteors & constellations.[172] All the facts in nature are [261] nouns of ⟨heaven⟩ the intellect, & signify what befalls in the eternal world. Every word has a double, ⟨a⟩ treble, ⟨a⟩or centuple use & meaning. ⟨'Tis as if my⟩ ↑I cry you mercy, good↓

---

[171] This sentence is enclosed by a line.

[172] "It is as if" is enclosed in square brackets, probably to indicate that it should be omitted.

shoebox↑!↓ ⟨had a false bottom, & on touching the spring were⟩ ↑I did not know you were↓ a jewel-case.

⟨I am bewitched with⟩

⟨Every th⟩ Rubbish ⁿ ⟨lump⟩ ↑& dust↓ sparkle⟨s⟩ with elemental /energies/glory/.ⁿ & ⟨I can compel⟩ ↑the laborer at my sawhorse is↓ the Lord of Nature ⟨to come & work in my acre⟩.¹⁷³ Now when I go to the Pyramid or to Fountain Abbey ⟨I find⟩ or to Stonehenge, I find the sentiment ⁿ [262] of ancient peoples, their delight in their gods, & in the future, their humanity, expressed in this ⟨immense⟩ patience of labor that ⟨hewed &⟩ staggered under the toil of ⟨lifting⟩ hewing & lifting these ⟨stones⟩ grey rocks into scientific symmetry. That sentiment of their hope & love touch me, & our associations (which are most pliant & placable) ⟨make⟩ persuade the eye to forget its mathematics & reconcile it to angles & distortions. [263] The rainbow, the sky, Niagara, the rose, a tone of music, have in them something which is not individual, but public & universal, ⟨& therein is their charm.⟩ & ⟨suggest⟩ speak to me of that central benefit which is the soul of Nature, & thereby are beautiful. And, in men & women, I find somewhat ⟨which is not⟩ in manners, in form, in speech, which is not of their person or family, but is of a public & human character, [264] but is of a solar & supersolar greatness, and I love them as the sky.¹⁷⁴ Alcott yonder never learned in Connecticut or in Boston what he sees & declares to me, & his face & manners are sublime at times. The wonder of men is that the reason of things comes to my side moulded into a person like myself & full of universal relations[.]

[265] This power of imagination[,] the making some familiar object as fire, or rain, or a bucket, or shovel, do new duty as an exponent of some truth or general law, bewitches & delights men; it is a ↑taking of dead sticks &↓ clothing about with immortality, it is music out of creaking & scouring.¹⁷⁵

---

¹⁷³ "The ⟨charm⟩ . . . acre)." is struck through in ink on p. [260] with a curved diagonal use mark and on p. [261] with a diagonal use mark.

¹⁷⁴ "The rainbow . . . sky.", struck through in ink on p. [263] with one vertical use mark and on p. [264] with two, is used in "Beauty," W, VI, 303.

¹⁷⁵ "This power . . . familiar" is struck through in ink with a vertical use mark; "bewitches . . . immortality," is struck through in ink with three vertical use marks.

⟨It seems to make⟩ All ⁿ opake things ↑are↓ transparent, and ⟨showing⟩ the light of heaven ↑struggles↓ through.ⁿ ⟨them.⟩

[266] ↑Oct. 9.↓ Henry James thinks the upper powers don't care so much for talent now as once. It was once the great point to civilize & lead by these gods of the mind. Now they are putting the material activities right, to sustain & order the masses of life. — Perhaps the Fourierists have had aⁿ ⟨upper⟩ reaction upward. *Chacun a son tour.*

He talked well about Louis Napoleon, who is absolute master of all the crowned heads, because he has the revolution in his hand, & can at any time cry *Histaboy*! to the dogs, & pull them all down. And he [267] ⟨likes th⟩ knows that England is necessary to him, & has no thought of breaking with it, but likes the prestige which these great crybabies in England by their terror give him with the French & with Europe.[176]

Then of Science[:] Mansel's Limits of Knowledge.[177] The blunder of the savans is to fancy science to be a finality; that it contains & is not contained; but a scientific fact is no more than the scratching of a nail if it stops. All the life of it is in its relatedness, its implication of the All.
Only the poetic savant is right, for it is not as a finality, but as a convertibility into every other fact & system, & so indicative of First Cause, that the mind cares for it.[178]

[268] The games of Greece were in the interest & honor of manhood. They called out every personal virtue & talent. Ho! ⁿ everyone who can wrestle, run, lift, ride, fight, sing, narrate, or so much as look well!
[269] Imagination transfigures,ⁿ ⟨an object⟩so that only the cosmical relations of the object are seen.

---

[176] "likes th" is canceled in pencil.
[177] Emerson's reference may be to either of two works by metaphysician Henry Longueville Mansel (1820–1871): "The Limits of Demonstrative Science Considered" (Oxford, 1853) or *The Limits of Religious Thought Examined* (Oxford, 1859).
[178] "but a scientific . . . for it." is in pencil.

The persons who rise to beauty must have this transcendency.
The calm sky hides all wisdom & power in Beauty.
That haughty force of form, *vis superba formae*, which poets praise, —
this is that: Under calm precise outline, the immeasureable & divine.[179]

[270] It is as if new eyes were opened so that we saw under
the lilac bush or the oak or the rock or the tiger, ⟨what⟩ the spiritual
cause of the lilac, oak, stone, or tiger, the genius of that kind, ⟨& still
again under this genius of kind⟩ & so could rightly & securely use
the name for the truth it stood for in the human mind, & still again
under this genius, its origin in ↑a↓ generic law, & thence its affinities
to cosmical laws, & to myriads of particulars, & then again deeper
causes below & so on ad infinitum.[180]

[271] ⟨But I wish to know that⟩ But I do not wish ↑to find↓
that my poet ⟨is⟩be not partaker, or that he amuses me with that which
does not amuse him.[181] He must believe in his poetry. Homer, Milton,
Hafiz, Herbert, Swedenborg, are heartily enamored of their sweet
thoughts. ↑Wordsworth too.↓

Mrs Agassiz   ↑20 Oct.   1860↓
Miss Cary
Ida Agassiz
Pauline Agassiz
Ellen Hooper
Mrs Parkman
Miss Cabot
Miss Lowell
Miss Heath [182]

[179] The entries on p. [269] are struck through in ink with two vertical use
marks; the upper part of the mark, through "Imagination . . . Beauty.", has been
finger-wiped as if to cancel. "The calm . . . divine." is used in "Beauty," *W*, VI,
305. "*vis superba formae*," "tyranny of beauty" (Ed.), is quoted from Johannes
Secundus by Goethe in *Maximen und Reflexionen*. See Goethe's *Werke*, 1828–1833,
XLIX, 83, in Emerson's library.
[180] "new eyes . . . so that" is enclosed in square brackets, probably to indicate
that it should be omitted.
[181] "to find" is in pencil.
[182] "20 Oct   1860" is in pencil. The purpose of this list has not been established.

[272] We heard across the bay thirty miles where the surf of the open ocean was pounding the land.[183]

[273] Classes ↑Classes of mind eternal. *AZ* 282   *TU* 13↓
See *XO* 166, The terrible aristocracy that is in Nature.
Aristocracy. *XO* 51

___

Those who speak about things, & those who speak things themselves

___

The sympathetic class. *CL* 243

___

Subjective class, can't keep step, have no common measures, but make their own gas, their own time, ↑religion, politics,↓ their own events, persons, & estimates of all kinds. See p 56 *supra*

___

Saadi's Five Classes

___

M[ary] M[oody] E[merson] & C[harles] K[ing] N[ewcomb]

___

    Greatness
        Real men   *CL* 144
[274] *Classes*
See *S* 206

In looking at the Swiss landscapes one thinks of the heroes.[184] Rich Europe! rich in men. Themistocles has strictly applied himself to the sea & land of Salamis, and each European hero to the rivered & mountained land. Buonaparte must equal the material problem, must carry all these Swiss angles, these Rhine & Danube waterlines, Mediterranean bays, & impregnable Magdeburg, Olmutz, & Coblentz [275] or whatever fortresses, ↑the Italian quadrilateral,↓ the warlike populations, the blood lines too, or races that easily unite, & those that instinctively disjoin & quarrel, he must have Europe in his head, before he can hold Europe in his hand. Yet these are but rude

[183] Presumably when Emerson was lecturing at one of the Cape Cod towns.
[184] See pp. [277]–[279] below.

pioneers & camp guides to break ground & make way for the truer & finer European who must follow, with a grander map of Europe in his brain: as carpenter & mason build a palace, which, when they have given up the keys, they enter no more.

[276] The dialogue under the chestnut trees—the boys should not be allowed to remove anything but the greenbriar. The trees rejoice in the concavo-concave variety. O yes, there are as many as ever there were. But the lake was in perfect magic with its mists, & I wished to go to Mull & Uilsa & Skye.

[277] An old woman standing by the sea, said, "she was glad to see something that there was enough of."

_____

1860

Nov. 15. The news of last Wednesday morning (⟨6⟩7th) was sublime, the pronunciation of the masses of America against Slavery. And now on Tuesday 14th I attended the dedication of the Zoological Museum at Cambridge, an auspicious & happy event, most honorable to Agassiz & to the State. On Wednesday 7th, we had Charles [278] Sumner here at Concord & my house. Yesterday eve I attended at the Lyceum in the Town Hall the Exhibition of Stereoscopic views magnified on the wall, which seems to me the last & most important application of this wonderful art: for here was London, Paris, Switzerland, Spain, &, at last, Egypt⟨s⟩, brought visibly & accurately to Concord, for authentic examination by ⟨m⟩women & children, who had never [279] left their state. Cornelius Agrippa was fairly outdone. And the lovely manner in which one picture was changed for another beat the faculty of dreaming. Edward thought that "the thanks of the town ↑should↓ be presented to Mr Munroe, for carrying us to Europe, & bringing us home, ⟨for nothing⟩ without expense." An odd incident of yesterday was that I received a letter or envelope mailed from Frazer, Pennsylvania [280] enclosing no letter but a blank envelope containing a Ten dollar ↑bank↓ note.[185]

[185] The "news of last Wednesday", p. [277], was of Lincoln's election. The records of the Concord Lyceum show that Charles Sumner lectured on November 7 on "La Fayette" and that on November 14, "an Exhibition of the *Stereorama*

I saw at Cambridge P., who said, he could not come to the club, because he saw S there; and, in saying this, he looked so mean, that I thin⟨g⟩k I shall never esteem his high praised faculty more. ↑He was disfigured.↓

[281]   *Criticism*
The ⟨difference between writers⟩ most important difference in criticism ⟨n⟩is whether ⟨the writer⟩ ↑one↓ writes from life, or from a literary point of view. 'Tis difficult for a writer not to be bookish & conventional. If he writes from manly experience & feeling his page is a power.

———

    Whitewashing, Mahomet & ↑Lord↓ Jeffreys [186]

———

[282] [187] 1861
Jan. 4   I hear this morning, whilst it is snowing fast, the chicadee singing.
Hyperion, Thalia,

Jan. 19: Alcott's Conversation on Health. No inspiration this time.
I affirmed, that health was as the perfectness of influx & efflux. A man must pump up the Atlantic Ocean, the whole atmosphere, all the electricity, all the Universe, & pump it out again. Any obstruction[,] [285] any appropriation ⟨was⟩ ↑is↓ tumour & mortification.

How a boy tilts a mountain over.

———

    My measure of a picture is its power to speak to the imagination,

———

was given before the Lyceum this evening, embracing views of scenery and celebrated buildings in this country and Europe. This exhibition was repeated on Thursday evening (15th), and again on Friday evening, the last exhibition being given to the children."
    [186] "Whitewashing . . . Jeffreys" and the rules above and below it are in pencil.
    [187] Emerson numbered the verso of p. [281] [282] and then changed this to [284].

and I can buy a few stereoscope views at shop prices, more potent in this way than costly works of art.

———

[28⟨4⟩6] *Subjects*; Caprice; Sympathy; For the second; — We can easily come up to the average culture & performance; not easily go beyond it. I often think of the poor caterpillar, who, when he gets to the end of a straw or a twig in his climbing, throws his head uneasily about in all directions; he^n is sure he has legs & muscle & head enough to go further indefinitely, — [287] but what to do? he is at the end of his twig.

[288] *"Conduct of Life"* to be ^{n} sent to [188]
   x Mary [Russell] Watson
   x C[yrus]. A[ugustus]. Bartol
   x O[liver]. W[endell]. Holmes

[188] This list is in four columns, here indicated by breaks. The list is in ink except for "Mrs L M Child", "W Whitman", "Mrs Fields", "Abel Adams", "Susan Jackson"; in pencil and canceled in pencil "Paul Hayne", "H D Thoreau", "W Emerson"; and in pencil and canceled in ink "W E Channing" and "N Hawthorne". "H W Longfellow" is overwritten by "Rev Mr Reynolds" in ink. The "x" beside a name probably indicates that a copy was sent. Recipients who have not been previously identified or who are not easily recognizable include Mary Russell Watson, once Waldo's teacher and the wife of Benjamin Marston Watson of Plymouth; Charles Eliot Norton (1827–1908), Emerson's friend and a member of the Saturday Club; Harrison Gray Otis Blake of Worcester, Mass., a Unitarian minister and friend of Thoreau; Mrs. Elbridge Dudley, the wife of the organizer of Emerson's lectures to the Parker Fraternity; Marshall M. Strong of Racine, Wis., who visited Emerson in Concord in 1856 and accompanied him from Madison, Wis., to Chicago, Ill., in February, 1860; William G. Bryan of Batavia, N.Y., who corresponded with Emerson about his January 25, 1860, lecture there; Moncure Daniel Conway (1832–1907), a clergyman in Cincinnati, who arranged a series of lectures there for Emerson in January and February, 1857, and edited *The Dial*, Cincinnati, 1860–1861; Ainsworth Rand Spofford (1825–1908), bookseller, editor, publisher, associate editor of the *Cincinnati Commercial*, and author of *The Higher Law Tried by Reason and Authority*; Thomas Hill (1818–1891), a Unitarian minister and mathematician; Amory Dwight Mayo, pastor of the Independent Christian Church at Gloucester, Mass., and then of a church in Cleveland; Grindall Reynolds, who succeeded Barzillai Frost as pastor of the First Church in Concord on July 8, 1858; Ephraim Wales Bull (1806–1895), American horticulturist and developer of the Concord grape, Emerson's neighbor; Benjamin Peter Hunt of Philadelphia, once Emerson's pupil; LeBaron Russell, a physician; John Haven Emerson, son of Emerson's brother William; Dr. Henry MacCormac of Belfast, who published a translation of *The Meditations of Marcus Aurelius Antoninus, with*

x H[oratio]. Woodman
x J[ames]. E[lliot]. Cabot
E[benezer]. R[ockwood]. Hoar x
x J[ames]. R[ussell]. Lowell
F[ranklin]. B[enjamin]. Sanborn x
A[mos] B[ronson] Alcott x
x G[eorge]. P[artridge]. Bradford
C[aroline]. Tappan
E[lizabeth] Hoar x
M[ary] M[oody] Emerson
x W[illiam]. E[merson].
x C[harles]. K[ing]. Newcomb
Alex[ander]. Ireland
Arthur Helps
Arthur H[ugh]. Clough
x C[harles]. E[liot]. Norton
x H[arrison]. G[ray]. O[tis]. Blake

x P. Hayne
S. A. Clarke
x ↑Mrs↓ E[lbridge]. G. Dudley
x M[arshall]. M. ⟨‖ . . . ‖⟩Strong
x W[illiam]. G. Bryan
x M[oncure]. D[aniel]. Conway
x A[insworth]. R[and]. Spofford

---

the Manual of Epictetus in 1844; George Barrell Emerson, Emerson's second cousin, a noted teacher; William Allen Wall, of New Bedford, the painter who copied "The Three Fates" for Emerson's study; Charles Chauncy Shackford, Unitarian minister; Sarah Alden Bradford Ripley, scholar in several languages and wife of the Reverend Samuel Ripley of Waltham; Paulina (or Pauline) Shaw, a close friend of Emerson's daughter Edith; Philip Randolph, grandson of the surgeon, Philip Syng Physick Randolph, whom Emerson probably met in Philadelphia in January, 1854; Frederic Henry Hedge, a Unitarian minister; Emily Mervine Drury, of Canandaigua, N.Y., who met Emerson on a Mississippi steamboat in 1850; Sara Hammond Palfrey, novelist and poet; Robert Montgomery Smith Jackson (1815–1865), a botanist and geologist; Alice Bridge Jackson, daughter of Charles T. Jackson; and Mrs. Lucy Cotton Brown, sister of Lidian Emerson.

⟨T[homas]. Carlyle⟩
⟨W[illiam]. E. Forster⟩
                Wiman
x Rev. Thos. Hill.
x Rev. A[mory] D[wight] Mayo
x E[dwin] P[ercy] Whipple
x Mrs L[ydia] M[aria] Child
 ⟨Paul Hayne⟩
  W[alt] Whitman x
x Mrs [James T.?] Fields
 ⟨H[enry] D[avid] Thoreau⟩
x⟨W[illiam] Emerson⟩
 ⟨H W Longfellow⟩Rev Mr [Grindall] Reynolds x
 ⟨N Hawthorne⟩
  Paulina [Tucker] Nash x

  E[lizabeth] P[almer] Peabody   x
 ⟨W[illiam] E[llery] Channing⟩
  Mme D'Agout
  Mr Bull   ?
x William [Morris ?] Hunt
x William Goodwin
  E[phraim]. Bull
  John Chapman
  J[ames] J[ohn] G[arth] Wilkinson
  W[illiam] Allingham
  Coventry Patmore
 ⟨Rev.   Alger⟩Mayo
  Concord Library
x N[athaniel]. Hawthorne x
x H[enry]. W[adsworth]. Longfellow
x W[illiam] H[enry] Furness
x B[enjamin] P[eter] Hunt
x G[eorge]. S. Phillips
  W[illiam] E[llery] Channing x
  H[enry] D[avid] Thoreau x
x Mrs Silsbee

x Miss M[ary] H[owland] Russell
x Dr LeBaron Russell
x A[insworth] R[and] Spofford
  Hermann Grimm
x George Bancroft
x J[ohn] H[aven] Emerson

[289] Dr. [Henry] McCormac
    x Geo[rge]. B[arrell]. Emerson
    x W[illia]m. A[llen]. Wall
    x Rev D V Frothingham
    x Rev C[harles] C[hauncy] Shackford
      J[ohn]. M[ilton]. Cheney x
      L[idian] E[merson] x
      Edith E[merson] x
      Mrs. [Sarah Alden Bradford] Ripley x
      Paulina Shaw x
    x J. S. Stillman
    x P[hilip]. P[hysick]. Randolph
    x Dr. F[rederic]. H[enry]. Hedge
      Mrs Forbes x
    x Abel Adams
    x Susan [Bridge] Jackson
    x Mrs [Emily Mervine] Drury
    x Miss [Sara Hammond] Palfrey
      Miss Bartlett x
    x Rev Mr Sears
      Henry James x
      Mrs S[amuel] G[ridley] Howe x
      Jo[hn]. H[aven]. Emerson x
    x R[obert] M[ontgomery] S[mith] Jackson
      [John Greenleaf] Whittier
      Miss Duncan
      Alice [Bridge] Jackson
      Ellen Emerson
      Mrs L[ucy] C[otton] Brown
      Horace Mann

[290] [Index material omitted]
[291] [blank]
[292] [Index material omitted]
[inside back cover] [Index material omitted]

frequent every year. The 141
difficulty of executing the
Fugitive Slave law always great.
The literature of Slave states, the science,
the morals, not encouraging.
there's a kind of deviltry here as
in the Brockhams. the wine tastes
fiery. the women have a worm
between their lips. Not a gentleman,
not a hero, not a poet, not a
woman, born in all that
immense country! There must be
such, for nature avenges herself,
but they lie perdus, & make no
sign in the reign of terror.
In fifty years, since our Jefferson,
not a breath of air has come
to the intellect or heart.

Plate I   Notebook WO Liberty, page 141   Text, page 406
An outburst on the South

229   <u>Song of the Soul</u>

                            he

         red
If the Slayer think, I Slay,
                        he is
Or if the Slain think, I am Slain,
They   He knows not well the Subtle way
      I keep & pass & turn again.

       Far or
       What is forgot to me is near,
Shadow & sunlight
       And night & splendor are the same,
The vanished gods   not less
       Things disappeared to me appear,
And one to
       Alike to me are shame & fame.

      They reckon ill who leave me out,
        me
   And when they fly me, I am the wings
   I am   I am
   Of the doubter & I am the doubt
   And I the hymn the bramin sings.

    The strong gods pine for my abode
   And pine in vain the sacred Seven
            meek lover of the
   But thou, joy fearing, loving good,
   Find me, & turn thy back on heaven.

Plate II   Journal SO, page 229   Text, pages 102–103
                       "Brahma"

" Know that which does not see
by the eye; and by which they see
the eyes, as Brahma, & not what
is worshipped as this.

" Know that which does not think
by the mind, & by which they say
the mind is thought, as Brahma,
& not what is worshipped as
as this.

The gods pine for my abode
pine
But The gods desire to know thy side
in vain the sacred seven,
But thou, prime holder of the good,
Hast turned thy back on heaven

Plate III   Journal SO, page 230   Text, page 103
Passages from the Talavakára Upanishad
with another version of stanza four

136

I have now for more
than a year, I believe, ceased
~~almost wholly~~ to write in
my Journal, in which I
formerly wrote almost daily.
I see few intellectual persons,
& even those to no purpose, &
sometimes believe that I
have no new thoughts, and
that my life is quite at an
end. But the magnet that
lies in my drawer for
years, may believe it has
no magnetism, and, ~~at the~~ on
touching it with steel, it-

Plate IV   Journal AC, page 136   Text, page 248
The magnet in the drawer

knows the old virtue; and, this
morning, came by a man
with knowledge & interests
like mine, in his head,
and suddenly I had thought,
again.

Plate V   Journal AC, page 137   Text, page 248
                    A mysterious visitor

142 The whig poetry lasts as long as
their hurras. Could never be
heard of the next day. Nobody
could be hired to read it.
Their respectability is of the
same fatal kind. Every one of
them puts on stateprison trousers
in the dark, & struts in statestreet
with one leg red & one blue.

—

What real aid has come to
the cause of freedom is
always unlooked for. Nothing
calculated has ever succeeded.

Plate VI   Notebook WO Liberty, page 142   Text, pages 406–407
One leg red & one blue

PART TWO

Miscellaneous Notebooks

WO Liberty

1854? – 1857?

Notebook WO Liberty is devoted to material about abolition, slavery, and human liberty and contains the text of several speeches. Although there are no dated entries in Notebook WO Liberty, Emerson probably used it from 1854 to 1857. The entries on pp. [3] and [4] refer to books Emerson withdrew from the Boston Athenaeum in July, 1854; more than a quarter of the notebook pages bear draft material for his speech "American Slavery," first delivered on January 25, 1855; on p. [45] Emerson refers to events in Kansas in 1856; and pp. [227$_2$]–[239$_2$] bear drafts of his July 4, 1857, "Ode" on liberty. A few later entries date from the 1860s and 1870s.

The covers of the copybook, brown paper marbled with green over boards, measure 17.8 x 21.5 cm. The spine strip and the protective corners on the front and back covers are of tan leather. "WR" is written and crossed out and "WO" is written below it in the upper right and left corners of the front cover. In the upper left side of the front cover "1847" and "Antislavery & War" are written, probably not in Emerson's hand. A piece measuring 2.0 x 1.5 cm is missing from the top of the spine. "WO" is written near the top of the spine and beneath this, lengthwise, "LIBERTY". "WO" is written in the upper right corner of the back cover.

Including flyleaves (1, 2, 249, 250) there were originally 266 unlined pages measuring 17.2 x 20.8 cm, but twenty-one leaves are torn or cut out: the leaves bearing pages 51–52, 163–166, 209–210, and seventeen leaves following page 226. The page following 226 is numbered page 227 despite the absence of seventeen leaves. Three of the leaves cut out are replaced in the notebook and are here designated pages [225$_2$]–[226$_2$], [227$_1$]–[228$_1$], [229$_1$]–[230$_1$]. Page 137 is misnumbered 135. One page was numbered correctly and then misnumbered: 5⟨3⟩1. It has been regularized to 53. Forty-seven pages were misnumbered and corrected: 4⟨6⟩8, ⟨79 2/3⟩ 81, 8⟨6⟩8, 8⟨7⟩9, ⟨88⟩ 90, ⟨89⟩ 91, ⟨90⟩ 92, 9⟨2⟩4, 9⟨3⟩4, 10⟨0⟩2, 11⟨2⟩3, ⟨118⟩ 120, ⟨119⟩ 121, 12⟨0⟩2, 12⟨1⟩3, 12⟨2⟩4, 12⟨3⟩5, ⟨124⟩ 126, ⟨126⟩ 128, ⟨127⟩ 129, ⟨128⟩ 130, ⟨130⟩ 132, ⟨131⟩ 133, 13⟨2⟩4, ⟨133⟩ 135, ⟨134⟩ 136, ⟨136⟩ 138, ⟨137⟩ 139, ⟨138⟩ 140, 14⟨2⟩1, 14⟨0⟩2, 15⟨0⟩2, ⟨160⟩ 162, 16⟨5⟩7, 17⟨0⟩2, 17⟨2⟩4, 17⟨4⟩6, 18⟨0⟩2, ⟨188⟩ 190, 19⟨0⟩2, 20⟨0⟩2, 20⟨1⟩3, ⟨216⟩218, 22⟨4⟩6$_1$, 22⟨6⟩8$_2$, and ⟨2⟨2⟩39⟩ 229. Two pages were numbered correctly, then misnumbered, and then corrected: ⟨80⟩ ⟨79 1/2⟩ 80 and ⟨8⟨2⟩0⟩ 82. Fifty-nine pages are numbered in ink: 1, 3–5, 7, 9, 10–17, 22, 23, 26–39, 46–49, 53–55, 60–62, 64, 66, 68–75, 78, 79,

169, 225_2, 227_1, 229_1, 244, 245, 248. Seventy-eight pages are numbered in pencil: 42–44, 76, 77, 80, 81, 83–91, 93, 96–100, 103–110, 112–114, 116, 118, 120–122, 130, 131, 141, 143, 144, 146, 148, 150, 154, 156, 158, 160, 170, 183, 184, 186, 188, 193, 194, 196, 198, 200, 203, 204, 206, 212, 214, 216, 220, 222, 224, 227_2, 229_2, 230_2, 232_2, 234_2, 236_2, 238_2, 240_2, 242_2. Seventy-four pages are unnumbered: 2, 6, 8, 18–21, 24, 25, 45, 50, 56–59, 63, 65, 67, 101, 111, 115, 117, 119, 127, 145, 147, 149, 151, 153, 155, 157, 159, 161, 171, 173, 175, 177–181, 185, 187, 189, 191, 195, 197, 199, 201, 205, 207, 211, 213, 215, 217, 219, 221, 223, 225_1, 226_2, 226_3, 228_1, 230_1, 231, 233, 235, 237, 239, 241, 243_1, 246_1, 247_1, 249_1, and 250. Four pages are numbered in pencil and then in ink: 40, 41, 168, and 208. Thirty-three pages are numbered in ink and then in pencil: 82, 92, 94, 95, 102, 123–126, 128, 129, 132–136, 138–140, 142, 152, 162, 167, 172, 174, 176, 182, 190, 192, 202, 218, 226_1, and 228_2. Fifty-four pages are blank: 16, 18–20, 22, 30, 40, 46, 48, 54, 56–59, 73, 98, 128, 148–157, 161, 169–173, 191, 194, 195, 203, 211, 221, 225_1, 232_1, 234_1, 236_1, 238_1, 240_1, 242_1, 244_1, 246_1, 238_2, 243_2, 244_2, 246_2, 247_2, and 249_2. Page 149 is blank except for a tipped-in clipping about Salem, Massachusetts, shipping. Single clippings are tipped in on pages 37, 47, 82, 125, and 128.

Laid in between page 250 and the inside back cover are seven newspaper clippings and a flyer: a clipping of "I Still Live," an eight-quatrain poem by Morgan; a clipping from the Boston *Evening Telegraph*, Monday, September 1, 1856, of a letter from F. B. Sanborn to the Kansas State Committee of Massachusetts and the Committee for Middlesex County describing emigrant roads to Kansas through Nebraska and Iowa; a clipping from the *Christian Inquirer*, Saturday, September 4, 1858, a letter to the editor on homesickness from J. C. Gangooly of India; a clipping from the Boston *Evening Telegraph*, September 4, 1856, reporting on the National Kansas Committee's interview with President Pierce; a clipping from a Boston newspaper in April (?), 1851, reporting on the refusal of the Supreme Court to grant a habeas corpus in the case of Sims; a clipping from the New York *Weekly Tribune*, Saturday, June 17, 1854, reprinting the speech of Judge Wade of Ohio in the U.S. Senate on the night of the final passage of the Kansas-Nebraska Act ("the humiliation of the North is complete and overwhelming"); a clipping from *The Independent*, "Kossuth on War" in his letter in "Answer to the Christian Appeal of the Society of Friends of Great Britain" dated London, January 15, 1855; and a printed flyer, a "Memorial of the Citizens of Virginia to the General Assembly, asking for certain reforms in the Laws concerning Slaves and Free Persons of Color."

[front cover]   ⟨WR⟩   ⟨WR⟩
                WO   WO

[front cover verso]
[Index material omitted]

"Domus sua cuique est tutissimum refugium."
"Nemo de domo sua extrahi debet."   *Common Law.*[1]

"All party spirit produces the incapacity to receive natural impressions from facts."   Niebuhr [2]

[1]   ↑*Liberty.*↓

                              WO

Higher Law.

"That which is willing & able always follows the Gods."   Socrates

              Ask not, Is it constitutional? Ask, is it right? [3]

[2] Thoughts are free.
Culture is the school of freedom.
The higher the organization, the more freedom.
          Slavery & unbelief
Connexions of Slavery
Unbelief of Slavery
Slavery an Index of the [4]

[3] "But in truth, & to speak without perverse affectation, all laws in general are originally equally ancient. All were grounded upon nature, & no nation was, that out of it took not their grounds; &, nature being the same in all, the beginning of all laws must be the same." *Selden. Note to Fortescue De laud. Ang. Legg. Chap XVIII* [5]

[1] "One's home is the safest refuge to everyone" (Sir Edward Coke, *Pandects,* Lib. II, Tit. IV, *De in Jus vocando*) and "No one can be dragged out of his own house" (Ed.).

[2] Niebuhr, *Life and Letters,* 1852, III, 204. Emerson withdrew this volume from the Harvard College Library on May 18, 1855. This quotation is used in "Speech on Affairs in Kansas," *W,* XI, 256.

[3] "Ask not . . . right?" is used in "American Slavery."

[4] "Slavery & . . . of the" is in pencil.

[5] This quotation and the citation to John Selden's note on John Fortescue, *De Laudibus Legum Angliae* (Of the Praiseworthy Qualities of the Laws of England), are found in Francis Lieber, *Manual of Political Ethics,* 1838–1839, I, 179. Emerson withdrew this work from the Boston Athenaeum July 8–25, 1854.

"Over the Soul can & will God allow no one to rule but himself alone."
Luther.[6]

[4] ↑*Higher Law*↓

"Lord Coke (8 Coke 118) Chief Justice Hobart (in Day v. Savage, Hob. 87) and Chief Justice Holt (City of London, v. Wood 12 Mod. 687) held & decided that even in England, where Parliament is technically termed omnipotent, acts of Parliament may be controlled either by common law or ↑natural↓ equity."[7] *Lieber* [*Manual of*] Pol[*itical*]. Ethics [1838–1839,] Vol. II. p. 283

[5]   Higher Law

Webster received at Charleston 7 May 1847.[8]

↑"Even↓ the[n] canon law says, 'In malis promissis non expedit servare fidem.' So that neither allegiance nor oath can bind to obey that which is unlawful."[9] *Lieber.* [*Manual of*] Pol[*itical*]. Eth[*ics*]. [1838–1839,] II 377

See Mackintosh Hist of England. I. 264[10]
See *VS* p. 245

See Bracton & Fleta as quoted by Milton.
                    Bohn's Milton Vol. 1, p. 175.[11]

[6] The wisdom of our laws is most apparent in this, that any de-

[6] Quoted *ibid.*, I, 171.
[7] Emerson refers to this decision in "The Fugitive Slave Law" (1851), *W*, XI, 191. In the Senate on March 11, 1850, William Henry Seward (1801–1872) had declared that there was a "higher law" than the Constitution. His remark became a catch phrase of the antislavery forces. See p. [193] below.
[8] On May 7, 1847, Daniel Webster, on a campaign tour of the South for the Whigs, was enthusiastically received at Charleston, S.C. See *JMN*, XI, 347–348: "Mr. Webster has deliberately taken out his name . . . from all association with liberal, virtuous, & philanthropic men, and read his recantation on his knees at Richmond & Charleston." This entry is encircled by a line.
[9] This quotation is used in "The Fugitive Slave Law" (1851), *W*, XI, 191, and in "American Slavery."
[10] Sir James Mackintosh, *The History of England*, 3 vols. (Philadelphia, 1830–1833); this volume is in Emerson's library.
[11] *The Prose Works of John Milton*, 5 vols. (London, 1848–1853), in Emerson's library. This entry and the rule above it are in pencil.

parture from their established principles, altho at the time wearing the specious appearance of advantage, never fails to bring along with it such a train of unforeseen inconveniences, as to demonstrate their excellence, & the necessity of again having recurrence to them.

Lord Coke, ap[ud]. Sir F. Burdett's speech, in Cobbett. June, 1809. Vol XV 973 [12]

[7] Lord Mansfield said, in case of ↑slave↓ Somerset, wherein the dicta of Lords Talbot & Hardwicke had been cited to the effect of carrying back the slave to the W. Indies, "I care not for the supposed dicta of judges, however eminent, if they be contrary to all principle. The dicta cited were probably misunderstood, &, at all events, they are to be disregarded." *Campbell, Lives* II, p. 419.[13]

[8] "The Creator has laid down only such laws as were founded in those relations of justice that existed in the nature of things antecedent to any positive precept: these are the eternal immutable laws of good & evil. x x x such, among others, are these principles, — that we should live honestly, should hurt nobody, & should render unto every one his due; to which three general principles, Justinian has reduced [9] the whole doctrine of law." Blackstone [14]

He says of "Ethics or Natural law"[:]

"This law of nature being coeval with mankind & dictated by God himself, is, of course, superior in obligation to any other. It is binding all over the globe in all countries & at all times. *No human laws are of any ⟨vitality⟩ validity if contrary to this* & such of them as are valid, derive all their force & all their authority mediately or immediately from this original" ——

"Nay, if any human law should allow or enjoin us to [10] commit it, (i.e. "murder"), we are bound to transgress that human law, or else, we must offend both the natural & divine."   Blackstone. Vol I Sect 2.[15]

[12] William Cobbett, *Cobbett's Political Register*, 88 vols. (London, 1802–1835); Emerson withdrew volume XV (January–June 1809) from the Boston Athenaeum October 25–November 9, 1852. See *JMN*, XI, 280. This quotation is used in "American Slavery."

[13] John Campbell, *The Lives of the Chief Justices of England*, 2 vols. (London, 1849). Emerson withdrew volume 2 from the Boston Athenaeum June 4–August 25, 1851. This quotation is used in "The Fugitive Slave Law" (1851), *W*, XI, 191. See *JMN*, XI, 281.

[14] Sir William Blackstone, *Commentaries on the Laws of England*, 2 vols. (New York, 1843), I, 27. See *JMN*, XI, 281.

[15] *Commentaries on the Laws of England*, 1843, I, 27–29. "*No human . . . this*" and " 'Nay, if . . . divine.' " are used in "The Fugitive Slave Law" (1851), *W*, XI, 191. See *JMN*, XI, 281–282.

Lord Coke says "That the common law shall control acts of Parl[iamen]t & sometimes shall adjudge them to be merely void for where an act of Parl[iamen]t is against common right & reason the common law shall control it & adjudge it to be void." 8 Rep. f. 118 a   ap[ud] Campbell Lives Vol. 1. p. 290 [16]

[11] It was a proverb in the country, "If I knew as much as Daniel Webster." [17]

The letter to Webster, dated *Boston 25 March, 1850,* ⟨was⟩ signed by 987 persons, says, "We desire to express our deep obligations for what this speech has done & is doing. You have pointed out to the whole people the path of duty, have convinced the understanding & touched the conscience."

[12] What is the use of logic & legal acumen if it be not to demonstate to the people what is metaphysically true? [n] The fact that a criminal statute is illegal is admitted by lawyers, & that fact, once admitted, the whole structure of the new tyranny falls to the ground. Why do not the lawyers, who are professionally its interpreters, put this home to the people? There is for every man a statement possible of that truth which he is most unwilling [13] to receive, — a statement possible so pungent & so ample, that he cannot get away from it, but he must either bend to it, or die of it. Else, there would be no such word as eloquence, which means this. Mr Webster did that thing in his better days for Hayne. Mr Hayne could not hide from himself that something had been shown him & the whole world, which he did not wish to see. He left public life & retired, &, it is said, died of it. Webster, in his turn, chose evil for good, less innocently than Hayne, & Hayne is avenged. [14] For it is certain that he will be cast & ruined. He fights with an adversary not subject to casualties.[18]

[16] *The Lives of the Chief Justices,* I, 290. Emerson withdrew volume 1 from the Boston Athenaeum May 6–15, 1851. This quotation is used in "The Fugitive Slave Law" (1851), *W,* XI, 191. See *JMN,* XI, 282.

[17] See *JMN,* X, 144.

[18] "There is . . . to see.", struck through in ink with a vertical use mark on p. [13], is used in "Eloquence," *W,* VII, 91–92. For the whole entry, see *JMN,* XI, 357–358. In 1830 Robert Young Hayne (1791–1839) of South Carolina

Tout est soldat pour vous combattre[.]

Everything that can walk turns soldier to fight this down.[19]

"Leges legum," says Lord Bacon, "ex quibus informatio peti possit, quid in singulis legibus aut bene aut perperam positum aut constitutum sit."   De fontibus juris. aph[orism]. 6 [20]

[15] Cannibalism, tattooing, Vikings, torture, the duello, ⟨burking⟩ inquisition, burking.[21]

Law.

"There is no encourager nor discourager of him, in a great battle or a small." *Vedas*.[22] See *NO* 166

———

↑*Higher Law*↓

This old bible, if you pitch it out of the window with a fork, comes bounce back again.

[16] [blank]

[17] Demosthenes said to the Athenians, "If it please you to note it, my counsels unto you are not such whereby I should grow great among you, & you become little among the Grecians: but they be of that nature, as they are sometimes not good for me to give, but are always good for you to follow." ap[ud]. Bacon Adv[*ancement*]. [*of*] Learning [*Works*, 1824, I,] p 22 [23]

———

debated Daniel Webster in the U.S. Senate on principles of the Constitution, authority of the federal government, and states' rights.

[19] "Tout est . . . combattre" is from the fourth verse of "La Marseillaise"; "Tout est . . . down." is used in "The Fugitive Slave Law" (1854), *W*, XI, 237; see *JMN*, XI, 357–358.

[20] Francis Bacon, *The Works* . . . , 10 vols. (London, 1824), VII, 440, in Emerson's library. Translated by Joseph Devey (1853) as: "[We shall, therefore, here offer, according to the best of our judgment,] certain laws, as it were, of laws; from whence an information may be derived as to what is well or ill laid down, or established by particular laws." See *JMN*, XI, 283.

[21] "Cannibalism . . . burking." is used in "American Slavery."

[22] *Rig-veda-sanhitá: A Collection of Hindu Hymns*, trans. Horace Hayman Wilson, 2 vols. (London, 1850–1856), I, 113. Emerson withdrew this work from the Boston Athenaeum May 5–9, 1855.

[23] This quotation is used in "The Celebration of Intellect," *W*, XII, 120. See *JMN*, VI, 326.

[18]–[20] [blank]

[21]   *To the Whigs.*

"Fear not the rogues & wicked. Soon or late they unmask themselves. Fear the honest man deceived. He means well, & all the world trusts him. But, unhappily, he is mistaken in the means of procuring it for men." *Galiani.* [Sainte-Beuve, *Causeries du Lundi*, 1851–1862, II, 339][24]

These men meant well, but they
allowed the Missouri Compromise;
meant well, but allowed Texas;
meant well, but allowed Mexican War;
meant well, but allowed Fugitive Slave Law.
They resisted Nebraska, ↑but it is too late.↓ — Let^n them resist forever. They must now be convinced that we have no guards, — that there is no proposition — too audacious to be offered us by the Southerner.

[22] [blank]

[23] I do not wish now to raise a company of ablebodied men & employ them to catch flies.

[24] It is not pleasant to have a gentleman murdered in his house by masked robbers; but neither is it pleasant to me to see a nation (the African,)^n systematically ⟨murdered or⟩ pillaged, & ⟨mutilated⟩ whipped, mutilated, & at will murdered, by unmasked robbers.

[25] A sphere of power belongs to every atom of substance, & refuses to be detached from it.

———

From a great heart secret magnetisms flow incessantly to draw great events.[25]

———

[26]   "The wish which ages have not yet subdued
          In man, to have no master save his mood."
                        Byron. [*The Island*, I, ii]

[24] See *JMN*, XIII, 282.
[25] This sentence, struck through in ink with single vertical and diagonal use marks, is used in "Beauty," *W*, VI, 283.

[27] "If that cannot be which thou wilt, will that which can be."
"Quando non potest id fieri quod vis, id velis quod possit."
Andriae (of Terence) ii. l. 5.[26]

"At the Diet of Tours, in 1433, the clergy & nobility insisted that the Third Estate should pay the expenses of all three estates incurred by travelling to & living at the diet, because made to support the two other estates." Apud Lieber [*Manual of*] *Pol*[*itical*]. *Eth*[*ics*]. [1838,] Vol. 1.
p. 363
As late as 1614, the Third estate in France were forced to address the King on their knees, the others standing. [*Ibid.*, I, 442]

[28] "No historical argument is ever capable of deciding a present question of equity."   See [Dove] "*Theory of Human Progression.*" p. 412 [27]

[29] This making laws against humanity, this making laws to steal & kidnap, only unmakes laws, & does not legitimate the stealing & kidnapping. You strike a good sword against an anvil, & only break your rivets & your sword.

———

"God himself cannot procure good for the wicked" [28]   *Welsh Bards.*

———

[30] [blank]
[31] Caius Gracchus, says Plutarch, first among the Romans turned himself, in addressing the people, from facing the Senate-house, as was usual, & faced the Forum.[29]
One day, the kneeling Third Estate in the Diet of Tours refuses to kneel.[30]

———

[26] Both the English and Latin versions of this statement are in Lieber, *Manual of Political Ethics*, 1839, II, 43.
[27] Patrick Edward Dove, *The Theory of Human Progression, and Natural Probability of a Reign of Justice*, 1851, pp. 411–412. See *JMN*, XIII, 174.
[28] This quotation occurs in Edward Davies, *The Mythology and Rites of the British Druids* (London, 1809), p. 79; Emerson withdrew this book from the Boston Athenaeum July 8–17, 1852. This sentence, struck through in ink with a vertical use mark, is used in "Fate," *W*, VI, 21, and "Poetry and Imagination," *W*, VIII, 58. See *JMN*, XIII, 150 and 171.
[29] *Plutarch's Lives*, trans. John and William Langhorne, 8 vols. (New York, 1822), VI, 216; in Emerson's library.
[30] See p. [27] above. "Caius . . . kneel." is struck through in ink with a vertical use mark.

[32] A great step in history of liberty taken by Nectarius, at the advice of Eudaemon, a priest at Constantinople, to disuse penitentiaries, i.e. public confession of communicants. See *Hooker* B. VI. p 343[–344] [31]

↑N.B. See of Galileo, an article in the (London) "Academy" of 3 February 1877.↓

Pius VII. procured, in 1818, a repeal of the edicts against Galileo & the Copernican system. He assembled the Congregation, & the late Cardinal Toriozzi, assessor of the Sacred Office, proposed, that they should wipe off this scandal from the Church. The repeal was carried with the dissentient voice of one Dominican only.   See *Lyell.* I. 69 [32]

———

[33] In the 12 (?) century, the principal cities in the north of Italy, having grown strong & populous, reduced the castles of the rural nobility & compelled them to reside in towns. [33]

———

See some extracts from John Pym's Speeches, in △ 63[.]

———

During the mild administration of Cardinal Fleury, 54000 /*lettres du cachet*/↑warrants↓/ were issued in France, on the single ground of the Pope's bull, Unigenitus.   *Blackstone.* [34]

[34] "I am sorry for such as wish absolutely that their epoch should be, in all respects, like the preceding; but can any thing proclaim so loudly the uncertainty of their minds? What mean these retrospective discussions, so passionate, if not, that we are not satisfied with ourselves, that we regret much, that we hope little, &, above all, that we have no actual principle, which makes [35] us live, & holds to us the place of the Past. I do not say the axiom is true, "Happy they who have no history," but, we may safely say, "Happy the generations who do not occupy themselves with history; happy the men who do not turn their eyes to the Past; who have nothing to

[31] *The Works of . . . Mr. Richard Hooker, in Eight Books of Ecclesiastical Polity* . . . (London, 1676). Emerson withdrew this volume from the Boston Athenaeum September 11, 1854–April 17, 1855. See *JMN*, XIII, 358.
[32] Charles Lyell, *Principles of Geology*, 2 vols. (London, 1830–1832), I, 69. "Pius . . . 69" is struck through in ink with a vertical use mark. See *JMN*, V, 228.
[33] This sentence is used in "War," *W*, XI, 157. See *JMN*, XII, 222.
[34] See *JMN*, VI, 15.

regret; whom the present suffices; because they find in it, at once, a principle of action, & a moral end." Revue des D[*eux*]. M[*ondes*]. T. VII p 584 [35]

[36] "Quant à la multitude, il n'existe plus chez elle que deux choses, — des passions, et des intérêts; — et chacun sait, qu'on n'éclaire jamais les passions, et qu'on ne persuade jamais les intérêts."   *Revue* [*des Deux Mondes*] T. VII. p. 593

[37] [36] La revolution de fevrier —
"Ceux qui croyaient à la puissance de l'opinion,[n] n'ont pas voulu croire qu'au hasard; et ceux qui avaient des intérêts a proteger, n'ont pas voulu ↑croire↓ qu' à la force. La force et le hasard! Voila les dernières divinités auxquelles nous ayons érigé les autels." [*Revue des Deux Mondes*,] T. VII. 594

[38] Let Christianity speak ever for the poor & the low. My opinion is of no worth, but I have not a syllable of all the language I have learned to utter for the planter. If by opposing slavery I undermine institutions, I own I do not wish to live in a nation where slavery exists. The life of this world has but a limited worth in my eyes, & really is not worth such a price as the toleration of slavery. &c *B* 14

[39] *Axioms of general agreement*

———

That the greater good is to be chosen before the less.

———

Others to be used by us as we ⟨ourselves⟩ would be by them.

———

⟨Parents to be honoured.⟩

———

Truth to be spoken.

———

[35] This entry and those on pp. [36] and [37] are from Emile Montégut, "Perspectives sur le temps présent de l'homme éclairé," *Revue des Deux Mondes,* July 1, 1854, pp. 582–597. Emerson withdrew this volume from the Boston Athenaeum December 11–20, 1854.

[36] A newspaper clipping, "Napoleon's Perjury," is tipped in on p. [37] beneath Emerson's entry. Louis Napoleon Bonaparte (Napoleon III) had said, according to the story, "Never will I try to clothe myself in imperial robes."

That children should not whip their parents; but should honor them.

———

That men should not eat men[.]

[40] [blank]
[41] They are more than present[.]

Eo ipso praefulgebant, quia non visebantur[.] [37]

This country has its proper glory
Though now shrouded & unknown
We will let it shine
We go to Europe to be Americanized.[38]

———

Extirpation is the only cure[.] [39]

———

If this be law, &c *p. 61*
They have eaten too much cake[.] 79 2/3

———

Providence meant liberty should be no hasty fruit[.] [40] *VS* 38

———

Summary of the argument of slavery   *GO* 140
Cowardly interpretation [41]

[42] This abjectness to forms argues an incurable frivolity of character[.]

———

The thunderbolt goes to its mark[.] [42]

---

[37] Cf. Bacon, *Of the Advancement of Learning*, Bk. II, in *The Works*, 1824, I, 20: ". . . learned men, forgotten in states, and not living in the eyes of men, are like the images of Cassius and Brutus in the funeral of Junia; of which not being represented, as many others were, Tacitus saith, [they 'shone brighter than all by the very fact that their portraits were unseen' (*Annals*, III, lxxxvi)]." See *JMN*, V, 42. "They . . . visebantur" is in pencil.

[38] This sentence is used in "Culture," *W*, VI, 147.

[39] This sentence is used in "Speech on Affairs in Kansas," *W*, XI, 261.

[40] This sentence is used in "The Fugitive Slave Law" (1854), *W*, XI, 240.

[41] "If this . . . interpretation" is in pencil.

[42] "this abjectness . . . character" is in pencil. For "The thunderbolt . . . mark", see *JMN*, XIII, 434.

It is not possible to extricate oneself from the questions in which your age is involved[.]

———

He only who is able to stand alone is qualified for Society.

[43] Liberty is aggressive. Liberty is the crusade of all brave & honest men. It is the epic poetry, the new religion, the chivalry of all gentlemen. This is the oppressed Lady whom all true Knights on their oath & honor must rescue & save.[43]

[44] [44] I own it would be extreme affectation to speak respectfully of this transparent canting[.]

———

Carolina is earnest because she is interested[.]

———

[45] The case is so bad, that all the right is on one side. The gov[ernmen]t orators in the ⟨ho⟩ Senate denounce the Kansas Code. The President himself falters when the committee question the right of the Legislature, & declines to discuss it. ⟨All that is⟩ The only word the ruffian press can say about it, is, "the reports ⟨of⟩ from Kansas are exaggerated." Exaggerated! Is it not true that Mr Hopps was killed? Mr Jennison
Mr Nute [45]

[46] [blank]
[47]   Webster's Poem [46]

---

[43] This paragraph, written in pencil and overwritten in ink, is used in "The Fugitive Slave Law" (1854), W, XI, 244. The pencil version ends "rescue and save." and the ink reads "reserve and save."

[44] The entries on p. [44] are in pencil. Laid in between pp. [44] and [45] is a single leaf of white paper 24.9 x 19.3 cm, folded once to make four pages; on it in ink in a hand not Emerson's are passages on "God," "Nature," "Method of Knowledge," and "Love."

[45] "The case . . . Mr Nute" is used in "Speech on Affairs in Kansas," W, XI, 255–256.

[46] Tipped in on p. [47] is a newspaper clipping of an album poem, evidently what "Webster's Poem" refers to; "may not perhaps be literally true to the original." is written at the top of the clipping, and printed "absurd" (l. 13) is canceled and "obscure" is inserted in pencil in the right margin. Emerson's anthology

[48] [blank]

[49] "It has never been the case, that, when a man in a place where no mulberry trees yet grew, could cause the aged to wear silks, &, where there were no breeders of fowls or hogs, could cause the aged to eat flesh, — he did not become Emperor." *Chinese Classic* [47]

[50]

↑After the death of *Theodore Parker.*↓

[51]–[52] [leaf torn out] [48]

[53] The 4th letter in *Des Droits et des Devoirs du Citoyen,* (Par M. l'Abbe de Mably,) is a commentary of a passage of Cicero's chapter on Laws, "qu'on ne doit point obeir aux lois injustes." [49]

[54] [blank]

[55] [50] We are not so simple as to suppose a king comes only with a crown on his head, &c. See *CO* 184   O no, — he very carefully hides it in his pocket when he enters.

[56]–[59] [blank]

[60]   *Colonization*

S.J. May said, ⟨here⟩ in Concord, in 1835, of the question between the Colonizationist & the Abolitionist, — it was "Whether you should

---

Parnassus (1874), p. 281, prints Webster's poem "Lines Written in a Lady's Album Below the Autograph of John Adams."

[47] Apparently part quotation, part paraphrase, from "Shang Mung," p. 15, in *The Chinese Classical Work, Commonly Called The Four Books,* trans. Reverend David Collie (Malacca, 1828). A similar passage occurs on pp. 5–6 of this work. See *JMN,* VIII, 383.

[48] Emerson indexed p. [51] under Theodore Parker. Parker died in Florence in May, 1860. Emerson spoke at a "Memorial Meeting at the Music Hall, Boston, June 15, 1860"; see "Theodore Parker," *W,* XI, 285–293, and Journal CL, pp. [226]–[230] above. The circled word "his" is halfway down the inner margin of p. [50]; glue along the stub of p. [51] indicates that a clipping, presumably with reference to Theodore Parker, was tipped in on p. [51].

[49] Gabriel Bonnet de Mably, *Des Droits et des Devoirs du Citoyen* (Kell, 1789), pp. 137–182.

[50] The entry on p. [55] is in pencil.

remove them (negroes) from the prejudice, or the prejudice from them." [51]

[61] "If that be Law," said Webster, "it were better to run a plough-share under the foundations of this Court House." [52]

[62] 'Tis pleaded that the slave is brought from barbarous Africa to an improved condition. ⟨Yes, was brought before 1803.⟩ But how long is that plea to last? Six months? a year? two years? Well, the last was brought fifty years ago. It will not do to play Providence much nor long. He is there to have all his earnings taken ⟨to be⟩ and the earnings of all that shall come from him, his children's children forever.[53] To take the earnings of women & children is a little the meanest ⟨fraud⟩ stealing that one knows of. [63] But if heedless of his improved condition he tries to run away from his master

Jan. 17 1855
Lewis B. Monroe
Charlestown, Mass [54]

In the first ages, they bite & tear. I fear they were cannibals[;] they made prisoners slaves. Manners softened; Christianity came. Still pirates roamed the seas & made prisoners, not only from Sallee, but from Iceland, & the mouth of the Elbe. Well, people mitigated, & this usage was dropped[.]
But not in Carolina[.]

[64] 'Tis a gentle joyous race very capable of social virtues & graces. Where manners are such an aristocratic element, why not theirs? They are not in a hurry, they have dignity, grace, repose. They have

---

[51] For the visit of the abolitionist Reverend Samuel J. May to Concord, see *JMN*, V, 71 and 73–74.
[52] Daniel Webster, "The Murder of Captain John White," *The Works*, 6 vols. (Boston, 1851), VI, 76. This sentence is used in "Speech on Affairs in Kansas," *W*, XI, 261. See *JMN*, XIII, 415.
[53] This sentence is used in "Speech on Affairs in Kansas," *W*, XI, 260.
[54] "Jan 17 . . . Mass" is set off by an encircling line.

produced ⟨m⟩ some persons of ability. But now, to be sure, we are told, they are not men, but chimpanzees. Montesquieu said, "It will not do to grant them to be men, lest it appear that the whites are not." [55]

[65] Well now, these kindly useful people fall among the white races with these serviceable talents of theirs. It is not to the praise of the whites, that they have continued ⟨a⟩down to this day this mild form of cannibalism as the obsolete piece of barbarism has survived in the South the wreck & ruin of the old barbarities: they do not eat men, but only steal them, & steal their earnings. Occasionally these poor creatures not relishing their part in [66] [56] trade run away & come to Massachusetts. Then we are to hunt them & hold them & give them back to the ⟨dog & the whipper that have⟩ ↑thief↓ come for them. ↑Pleasant, is not it? Manly, is it not? Right, is it not?↓ If you try to save them from the scoundrel that hunts them, or to take them away from him[,] that is treason against the United States!
And this precious bit of old world legislation that you would think Layard had exhumed from the brick mountains of Nineveh [67] grown men that have learned to spell here in our schools, — not showmen, but judges — will read & affirm.
You would think we should go to the savages for a powow[,] for a medicineman; but no, a man born in Boston & bred at Harvard[.]
And when a reasonable man or two gets up & says, this abominable nonsense affronts the sun, down [n] with it altogether these

[68] [57] When a man is born into the world he expects good treatment,

[55] Translated and altered from Charles de Secondat de Montesquieu, *L'esprit des lois, Oeuvres*, 8 vols. (Paris, 1819), II, 54: "Il est impossible que nous supposions que ces gens-là soient des hommes, parceque, si nous les supposions des hommes, on commenceroit à croire que nous ne sommes pas nous-mêmes chrétiens." The quotation is used in "Emancipation in the British West Indies," *W*, XI, 141. "But now . . . whites are not.'" is used in "The Fugitive Slave Law" (1854), *W*, XI, 238. See p. [69] below.
[56] Laid in between pp. [66] and [67] is a sheet of blue paper 17.2 x 18.2 cm bearing two sentences in different inks: "Carlyle's points and commas speak" and "Damnation follows death with common men"; see *JMN*, VI, 92 and 77.
[57] Laid in between pp. [68] and [69] is a newspaper clipping about a European who resented the American press for saying that Europeans were "not fit for liberty." "Kossuth?" is written on the clipping in pencil.

& has some right to it. Nature has done her best. She surrounds him with smiling mother & father, ⟨broth⟩ smiling brothers & sisters. But not so in Carolina. There he is born into a den of thieves; and all that he has or has[n] the power of creating, is stolen & to be stolen, alike the fruit of his body, & the genius of his soul.

[69] Montesquieu said, "It would not do to suppose that negroes were men, lest it should turn out that whites were not."[58]

[70] Don't let us take a tone too high, but converse as a man with his friend.

The committee have invited eagerly gentlemen from the Slave states to take a part in this course to defend slavery. ⟨the⟩ Eagerly the ablest defender of the system[,] Mr Calhoun, Mr McDuffie, Mr Webster, Mr Wise, would be patiently heard to know what could be said [71] on the subject. We would even affect to be ignorant, affect to be open to conviction, try not to prejudge. But 'tis plain why ⟨all th⟩ these were asked: because the committee did not believe anything could be said, & heartily wished the community here to know the utter imbecility & destitution of the Cause.
But certain I am that the South has never offered anything, not the first ⟨thread⟩ ↑line↓ of a plan for the gradual or present abatement of the evil.

[72] Alcott said, Civility is a scale of temperaments, or, perhaps, the History of liberty everywhere is a scale of temperaments[.]

[73] [blank]
[74] England makes the golden mean of temperament neither too sandy nor too limy. To understand Shakspeare's performance you must see how English workmen hold out. The Peels & Eldons & Gibbons & Hallams & Dugdales are prosy Shakspeares. The people have that saving stupidity which masks & protects their power as the curtain of the eagle's eye. Americans when they first go there pronounce them stupid.

[58] See p. [64] above.

2 esthetic dark sharp dark dark dark dark dark dark dark dark dark dark dark dark dark dark dark dark dark dark dark dark dark dark dark dark dark

[75] The Eng[lish]. nation always resist the immoral action of their gov[ernmen]t. They think humanely on the subject of France, of Turkey, of Poland, of Hungary, of Schleswig Holstein, though overborne by the statecraft of the rulers at last.

↑Seashell should be the arms of England↓[.] [59]

[76] [60] It seems a mistake that Kossuth & Mazzini should believe that Europe will revolt according to the programme of a committee, and that they can manage that wild chaos in their London chambers like the Marshal of a City Procession.

[77] The subject seems exhausted. Who can long continue to feel an interest in condemning homicide or counterfeiting ↑or wifebeating↓? [n] [61] All the variation the subject admits will be soon exhausted, and we only find reli↑e↓f in large considerations of the fate of empires, when slavery & war come in as the necessary shadows, as the Painter & Poet must draw on night, earthquake, & chaos to temper their ideal lights.

[78] [62] One talks for victory, the other is curious to know how it stands, — had as lief be worsted as not
like ⟨an artist⟩ ↑a chemist↓ in search of sulphur he thinks it is not there. You show it him, he is all the more delighted to find it & had rather be in the wrong than not. Si non errasset, fecerit ille minus. [63]

[79]   diggers eat pounded snails
        Abolition a substitute for a ⟨home⟩house on fire
        "The abolitionists met & all went off delightfully."

[59] "Seashell . . . England" is in pencil.

[60] Laid in between pp. [76] and [77] is a four-column newspaper clipping from the Boston *Journal*, July 7, 1858. On the recto is the text of "Oration by John S. Holmes, Esq., before the Citizens of Boston, July 6, 1858," and on the verso that of "Hon. Rufus Choate's Oration, Delivered before the Democratic Club of Boston, July 5, 1858."

[61] "The subject . . . wifebeating." is used in "American Slavery."

[62] The entry on p. [78] is in pencil.

[63] "Had it not erred, it had achieved less." Martial, *Epigrams*, I, xxi. See *JMN*, IX, 360.

390

Impoverishing skepticism scatters poverty disease & cunning through the world[.] [64]

They are beggars, & yet a man, a mind, is a fagot of thunderbolts. All the elements pour in torrents through Wilkinson's mind.[65]

[80] [66] It rests on skepticism
which is not local, but universal,
tone of press not /more criminal/lower/ in slavery than on everything else
Young men ⟨don't⟩ want object
foundation ideal object they would gladly have somewhat that calls them with trumpet to be heroes, and finding no first best, they take a second best & slip into some niche or crevice of the state, some counting room or railroad or other creditable employment not the least of whose uses is the covert it affords[.] [67]

Solitaries

[81] I call slavery & the tolerance that it finds, — worst in this, the stupendous frivolity it betrays. We are dying of inanition.[68]

⟨W⟩[n] In my circle, what is so bad as the eternal inquisition, the looking round for deep minds; the "How long o Lord?" the doubt & despair whether imaginative souls will appear.

The scholars & learned believe that the age of poetry is past.[69] When the last boy is born & turns away from the last girl, I may believe the unbelief.

[82] Whig Party   nails the star to the sky
retrospective,   & so convicts itself[.] [70]

---

[64] This sentence is used in "American Slavery"; "diggers . . . world" is in pencil.

[65] "They are . . . mind." is written in ink over substantially the same matter in pencil. Cf. "Beauty," *W*, VI, 283.

[66] The entries on pp. [80]–[88] are in pencil.

[67] "It rests . . . affords" is used in "American Slavery."

[68] "I call . . . inanition." is used in "American Slavery."

[69] This sentence is used in "American Slavery."

[70] "Whig . . . itself" is used in "American Slavery."

Gentlemen will not go into politics. They are disgusted. Those who have gone did not well. Those who have gone — I heard it from those who knew them intimately, — were honest men — meant well — we could perfectly rely on them, — yet they voted with the basest of the populace, they ate dung, & saw not the sneer of the bully that duped them[.] [71]

[83] Well what refuge[?] they become apathized indifferentists [72] they become ashamed of idleness[,] do not quite like to encounter the honest face of manly labor in the streets & sneak into a counting--room & play business.

The fine young people, the flower of Society[,] go into the soft & tempered brilliancy of the saloons of N.Y. & B[oston]. O here is one who aspired for a time, & resisted to contumacy the soft appliances of fashion. But they tired of withstanding — they fell into the silken file & great is [84] congratulation of the refined[.] [73]

Sinai growls at a distance[.]
War is the state of man[.]

Boundless skepticism — they find bargain & hypocrisy. Egypt is a humbug; England a flash in the pan; Lycurgus was a slyboots; Sumner, — Cobden — o yes he got a comfortable stipend out of free trade, 80,000 pounds. Kossuth, — o he got enough money in this country to make him comfortable for the rest of his life, & Sumner — O yes, he is in the Senate; you see what his virtue meant! [74]

[85] Hide thy head oh /all seeing/starry/ [n] muse of History! See

---

[71] "Gentlemen . . . duped them" is used in "American Slavery," with "dirt" for "dung". Tipped in at the bottom of p. [82] is a newspaper clipping with an item on "Brains" and another on "Fanaticism in Old Times" quoting Washington and Jefferson in opposition to slavery.

[72] "Well what . . . indifferentists" is used in "American Slavery."

[73] "The fine . . . refined" is used in "American Slavery."

[74] "Egypt . . . pan;" is used in "Art and Criticism," W, XII, 302; "Cobden . . . life," is used in "Worship," W, VI, 211. For "Egypt . . . pan;", see JMN, XIII, 177; for "Lycurgus . . . slyboots;", see JMN, IX, 338.

not the stooping judges of Massachusetts. Omit to ⟨record⟩ register
that evil day[.]

[86] Stones have roots[.]
A mind like Wilkinson's, — what a revelation is that[:] Showing that
man is all related, that he is the exhalation & elixir of every thing
that is, — flood & fire, ice & snow, salt, sulphur, lime, & slate, blue
sky, & crystal orbs, & illimitable ether[.]

[87] Every[n] ⟨instinct⟩ soliciting instinct is only a hint of a coming fact
as the air & water that are now invisible, will presently become solid
in the form of oak timber.

[88] A man is not a man unless he have this meliorating advanc-
ing habit.
I see not what can be gained by any system which holds the mind
fast in four walls.
Man is in transition, that is the attitude of Power; — take away his
motive & ⟨power⟩ growth, & he dwarfs & dies.
Men interest only as long as they advance; all the rest is mummy &
old clothes.
And a judge who has not the meliorating leaven in [89] him, — it
is to choose an ox or ass.[75]

For this, some dreadful realist is sent, some sharp Bonaparte, some
anvilheaded Luther, some serious fooling Cromwell, who will fool
your head off.
Yet there is but one Realist, namely, Reality; as your own comic poet
has said, with a touch of tragedy, —
"You must rise up early, if you wish to swindle God." [76]

[90] [77] Moments of occultation the ebb of mind leaving all our
cisterns dry

[75] "him, — it . . . ass." is in pencil.
[76] Cf. James Russell Lowell, *The Biglow Papers* . . . (Boston, 1856), p. 5:
       "An' you've gut to git up airly
           Ef you want to take in God."
This book is in Emerson's library.
   [77] The entries on p. [90] are in pencil.

In the Fr. Revolution they took a strumpet from the street, carried her in a chariot, & worshipped her as the Goddess of Reason; and in America we ⟨p⟩ took a statute which uprooted the foundations of rectitude, & declared over our signatures that there was no Higher Law.[78]

[91]   Univ. Skepticism
                                    in youths
                                       maids
                                       ↑men↓
                                    politicians
                                    Knownothing Party
      ⟨This is⟩
This devastation reached its crisis in the acquiescence in slavery here, & the cruel political servitude in Europe. It celebrated its moment of total eclipse here in the passage of the statute, & in the maintaining it by courts of law, the frantic yell — No higher law.[79]

———

987 men enrolled their names to thank God, that Webster had touched their conscience — touched their conscience! — Yes, seared it with a red hot iron. See above p. 11.[80]

[92][81] But Cause & Effect exist; things are good as they are true, — calicoes, temples, codes, poems —
There is a truth translateable into the languages of all arts & works. And as men are perceivers of the truth, they command so much of the secret of creation.
Whatever is false cannot be enacted. This law of nature is universal: gravity is only one of its languages; justice is another. [93] Any attempt to violate it is punished, & recoils on the man. If you take advantage of a man, & steal from him, he watches his opportunity to make accounts square with you. If he is not strong enough to resist,

---

[78] "Moments of . . . Law." is used in "American Slavery."
[79] "Univ. Skepticism . . . law." is in pencil. "This devastation . . . law." is used in "American Slavery."
[80] "987 men . . . p. 11." is in ink over substantially the same matter in pencil, and the rule above it is in pencil.
[81] The entries on pp. [92]–[96] are in pencil.

why then he is cunning enough to cheat you; or if he cannot do that, he comes when you are asleep & steals.[82]

If the south country thinks ⟨he⟩it is enriched by Slavery — read the census, read their valuation table, or ⟨visit⟩ ↑weigh↓ the men. I think it impoverished.

[94] If they ⟨think⟩ ↑reckon↓ the slavery they have cherished, & you have connived at a ⟨blessing⟩ benefit — ⟨they are⟩ ↑I find them↓ saddled with a crime which demoralizes their people & is grown to be the poison which infects all politics in this country[.] [83]

[95] ↑Truth exists;↓

There's a sound healthy universe; the sky has not lost its azure because our eyes are sick; the seas & waters are not wasted if the cholera has swept the men.

And there is a healthy interior Universe as well.

And men are great & powerful in proportion as they conform themselves to, or become recipient of the great equal general laws, & not local.[84]

[96] Yet Deucalion's & Noe's Flood are partial deluges & not Universal submersions:

And so the periods of unbelief always leave a little faith alive.

[97] Judges are rare & must be born such. K[ing] James said, "O ay, I can mak him a lord, but I canna mak him a gentleman." [85] And Governors & Presidents can give a seat on the Bench, but only wisdom from above can make a right judge[.]

Infer from their judgments in one case, what light they have for all.

[82] "Any attempt . . . cheat you;" is used in "American Slavery."
[83] "If the south . . . country" is used in "American Slavery."
[84] "Truth exists . . . local." is used in "American Slavery."
[85] See *JMN*, XIII, 170.

[98] [blank]

[99] [86] The ebb of thought drains the law, the religion, the education of the land. We send our boys to the Universities; they go thither, they look the teachers[,] so called teachers[,] in the eye; — what can they teach? the boy has doubts, — he looks at the professor with his grammar & his drill, but with frightful penetration; he says, I do not see that the professor himself is [100] better or stronger for all he knows; — he looks into the stable at the horses, & on the whole concludes, — & I am not sure that he is not right, — that the horses can teach him most: they give him vigor & aplomb with no false pretention.

Why the presidents & professors of the ⟨colleges⟩ University [101] were in this very insane rabble that voted down the moral sense of mankind.[87]

———

Worst to find this in the seats of Ideas — in Courts.

Now the Idea of abstract right exists in human mind, & lays itself out in the equilibrium of nature, — the level of seas, the action & reaction of forces is the symbol of it in nature; Justice satisfies every body. Benefit being the law, & violation of individual being the crime[.]

This is so in nature & so lies in all minds. And the perceivers of this right, the ordainers of the application of right to man, were Judges.

[102] One touch makes the whole world kin[.] [88]
Skepticism dwelling in the senses
/power/cause/ being out of sight is out of mind
            poverty in young men & maids
                        in scholars,
                        in education
                        in politics
            and the whole carrying in the world
You shall find it everywhere[.]

[86] The entries on pp. [99]–[108] are in pencil.
[87] "The ebb [p. [99]] . . . mankind." is used in "American Slavery."
[88] Cf. Shakespeare, *Troilus and Cressida*, III, iii, 175.

If this is frightful it is in the seats of ideas namely in Courts & Church

> Judges rest on Laws of Menu
> Laws of Moses
> Laws of Confucius
>
> Real Judges   Laws of Jesus
> Seers of right [89]   Laws Code of Justinian

[103] I should find it in the Science
>   in the philosophy of France
>   phil[osophy] of Eng[lan]d[.]

But it is not in societies that this law is revealed but to private persons[,] to each man when he goes alone & yields himself up to his mind. All the great affections are muses; they teach & inspire & guide & enrich. Hope is a muse; Love is a muse; but Despair is none; & never gave sage counsels.

[104] Here is the secret[:]
A man is a very small thing whilst he works by & for himself but an immense & omnipotent worker as soon as he puts himself right with the law of nature. A judge who ⟨attempts⟩ gives voice as a judge should to ⟨the ⁿ law of the world⟩ the ⟨law⟩ ↑rules↓ of love & justice, ⟨speaks in thunder⟩ ↑is godlike↓ & his word is ⟨sterling⟩ ↑current↓ in all countries & times   but a man sitting on the Bench[,] a windy politician or a dangler striving to give authority to the notions of his superiors or of his set, [105] pipes & squeaks & cheeps very small & ridiculously[.]
It is as when you come to a conflagration with your fire engine, — no matter how good the machine, you will make but a feeble spray, whilst you draw from your ↑town↓ tub: But once get your /hose/pipe/ screwed on to a hose which is dipped in the river, or in the harbor, and you can pump as long as the sea holds out.[90]

[106] How
This is the open secret of the world, the art of animating a private

---

[89] "Real Judges" and "Seers of right" are joined at the right by a large brace.
[90] "A man [p. [104]] . . . holds out." is used in "American Slavery."

soul with inspirations from the great & public soul which we call
Nature or God.
When a man speaks from this, he is interesting; when he acts from
it, he is strong, effective.
His very silence, if conformed to it[,] we call character,
one of the potencies of the world.

[107] How else is man or woman fascinating to us but because the
abode of mystery & meanings never told & that cannot be exhausted[.]
How did Channing preach, except that that puny form was expanded
by a sentiment vaster than America[?]
The words national, public, sentiment, opinion, &c, all have real
meaning in real nature though they have become disgusting cant.
The King, or political head, was awful in the eyes of men: would
still be so, if the man who really represented [108] the laws & genius
& future of this nation sat in the seat. But now we put ignoble obscure
persons without character or representative power of any kind, there,
& get a figure awful — to office seekers[.]

[109] It has always seemed to me that the ⟨profligate⟩ politics of
New Hampshire in relation to Slavery would not have been so
profligate, if her people had not considered that Massachusetts &
Vermont & New York would balance their action, & hinder it of ⟨a⟩
any fatal consequence to liberty. The sannup does not hesitate to
get drunk; he knows the squaw is sober: but if the squaw is already
drunk, he will wait.

[110]^{91} All goes well whilst we put a^n private action in accord with
the powers, beauties, beneficences of the Universe as the farmer, the
sailor, the artist, the saint, the seer do, so long we ride well the sun
& wind, the elements, the men & angels work for us. We are strong
with the strength of the whole[.]
But the moment we detach our prosperity, or thinking, or endeavor,
or selfesteem, from the general good, and attempt, as fools do, to set
up an egotism & clothe [111] it with regard as if it were the will of
nature things work against us[;] we are jostled by ⟨th⟩ all these forces

[91] The entries on pp. [110]–[120] are in pencil.

& crushed. We are like one in, who does not know the order of, a dance & is jostled & trod upon by the dancers[.] [92]

[112] Slavery a symptom of skepticism which infects the age
    Society
    Education
    Religion
    Politics
Instead of a deep insight every one lives at the surface, — believes in chance, & ignorant of Law naturally blows his own trumpet & becomes Egotist. This idolatry of Self Opinion, of the interest of our set, & cool belief in the counterpoise of our set to the whole world appears general[.]

    We must have foundations[.]
We must   Is there then no truth
Is there no north & may every man set the compass to suit his hour & [113] call that north the direction toward which the wind of the moment blows him?[n]
There must be foundations[.] [93]
Nor can we quite lose the elements of belief or unmoor ourselves from ⟨the⟩ Nature. I met a man who thought colors

But colors /go by/please/ ⟨la⟩ optic law
Greek architecture   and all works of art
Rainbow
Gems not accidental

    The skepticism grew out of prosperity & sensualism[.]
    Worst when it invades Courts
Old people complain the streets are dark[.]

[114] But the Law is never violated without harm. The Fathers in 178⟨7⟩9 made a bargain, & thought they had cheated the devil. It

[92] Cf. *JMN*, XIII, 388–389.
[93] "We must have foundations" (p. [112]) and "There must be foundations" are used in "American Slavery."

returns on us. It would have been better to have gone without Union. Many ways could have been taken. If they had made a separate peace with Eng[lan]d. then slaves would have been emancipated with W. Indies & then the colonies could have been annexed to us.[94]

[115] Public opinion has a real meaning though there is so much counterfeit afloat with this name[.]
A ⟨people can⟩ wise man delights in the powers of many people. Fourier. And we shall have to call them all out.[95] ⟨Why do we not⟩ We inspire each other. The affections are muses[:] Hope is[,] Love is[,] Despair is not. & Selfishness drives away the angels. ↑It is so delicious to act with great masses to great aims.↓ [96] We shall one day bring the states shoulder to shoulder & the citizens man to man to exterminate slavery[.]
It will cost 2 000 000 000. We will have a chimney tax. We will call on these rich benefactors who found asylums, Hospitals, City Libraries, Lowell Institutes, Pea[bo]dy institutes. We will call on wealthy bachelors & wealthy maidens. We will [116] call on the mechanics, on the needlewomen, on the cent societies[.] [97]

[117]   ↑Superficial↓
There is no faith in the intellectual
        none   in the moral universe
There is faith in meat & wine, in wealth, in machinery, in Opinion, but not in Causes[.] [98]
We are like our own engineers. Every new step in improving the engine restricts one more act of the engineer, unteaches him, at last he knows his coppers, knows his handles, but knows nothing more, & if anything gets out of order, he is helpless to [118] repair it. So we

[94] "The Fathers . . . to us." is used in "American Slavery." Cf. *JMN*, XIII, 333–334.
[95] "Public opinion . . . all out." is expanded in "American Slavery": "Patriotism, public opinion, have a real meaning, though there is so much counterfeit rag money abroad under it, that the name is apt to disgust. A wise man delights in the powers of many people. Charles Fourier, noting that each man had a different talent, computed that you must collect 1800 or 2000 souls to make one complete man. We shall need to call them all out."
[96] "We inspire . . . great aims" is used in "American Slavery."

are removed from Nature & Deity by our Division of labor[,] cannot do anything ourselves but live in a hall full of bellhandles[.] [99]

[119] Social action real also[.]

Public   The king is representative

———

The state or age has a public soul or sentiment[.]

———

The state has a public action[.]

[120] These are all straws to show which way the wind goes — In the society education, law, direction of surplus capital, trade, indifferently you may see the credence of men. It is a small helm which turns them all about[.]
I fear now you will find non credence which produces nothing but leaves sterility & littleness[.]
Artists look at surface effect
Churchmen at forms
Physicians at symptoms
Science at facts which lead nowhere
Statesmen at elections & office
Judges at ↑keeping↓ the status quo
and nobody at melioration

[121] A man may come who has no egotism, who is nothing, but filled with all things, some profoundhearted child[.]

[122]   *History of Liberty*
"In Niebuhr's view the foundation of ⟨liberty⟩political liberty was municipal

---

[97] "We shall [p. [115]] . . . cent societies", struck through in pencil with a vertical use mark on p. [115], is used in "American Slavery" and "The Fugitive Slave Law" (1851), *W*, XI, 208–209. Cent societies were organizations of women whose members contributed one penny each week to buy Bibles, hymnbooks, and other religious materials.

[98] "There is no . . . Causes" is used in "Worship," *W*, VI, 208.

[99] "We are like [p. [117]] . . . repair it." is used in "Works and Days," *W*, VII, 165. With this paragraph, cf. *JMN*, XIII, 46.

self-government, or, as he used to call it, a free administration *freie Verwaltung.*" *Bunsen* [100]

Emperor Charles V.'s motto was, "Plus Ultra," More, More! [101]

---

[123]   ↑*History of Liberty*↓
     Do not be so afraid of Anarchy. See *JK* 75

'Tis a picture of misrule to see King John marching from Dover to Berwick with an army of mercenaries, devastating all but crown--lands, & burning towns & castles in revenge for the constrained concessions of Magna Charta. A.D. 1215 [102]

In 1215, there were 1115 castles in England. [103]

---

[124]   June 1855
Young [Charles] Lowell said to me that he thought if we had such a tract written for Liberty now, as Milton wrote for unlicensed printing in 16[44], it would have more than equal effect.

---

[125] [104] I↑n↓ ⟨24th⟩ year of Edw[ar]d I. he decreed that no tax should be levied without consent of Lords & Commons.
Which DeLolme reckons the basis of English liberty[.] [105]

Philippe de Comines thinks as Montesquieu afterwards;

[100] Christian Bunsen, "Niebuhr's Political Opinions and Character," *Life and Letters*, 1852, III, xxvii.

[101] See *JMN*, VI, 28, 208.

[102] Paraphrased from David Hume, *The History of England*, 6 vols. (New York, 1850), I, 435–436. See *JMN*, VI, 20.

[103] See *JMN*, VI, 35, 211.

[104] A newspaper clipping from the Boston *Daily Advertiser*, May 8, 1862, bearing an obituary of Thoreau written by Emerson is attached to p. [125] with sealing wax. A vertical ink line on p. [125] may be a use mark or may have been a border for the clipping. "1862" is written on the clipping and on p. [125]. A second piece of sealing wax covers the "r" in "peculiar".

[105] John Lewis DeLolme, *The Constitution of England* . . . (Dublin, 1793), pp. 24–25; Emerson withdrew this book from the Boston Athenaeum June 18– October 8, 1855. "⟨24th⟩ year . . . liberty" is used in "Considerations by the Way," *W*, VI, 253.

"Now in my opinion, among all the sovereignties I know in the world, that in which the public good is best attended to, & the least violence exercised on the people, is that of England." Memoires de Comines. Tom I. lib. v. chap. xix [106]

"'Tis the peculiar & inimitable excellence of the British legislation, that no law can anticipate the ↑progress of↓ public opinion." *Niebuhr.*[107]

[126] The defenders of the institutions ⟨excuse themselves from⟩ ↑disavow↓ all the designs with which they are charged, & point to the resolutions ⟨of⟩ & platforms of their parties, & the unmeaning protestations of patriotism, &c. with which those papers abound.
Cardinal de Retz insists much on the folly of speaking as badly as you act. In politics [127] 'tis a capital fault to omit the forms & professions of keeping the law, & keeping personal respects of all kinds, at the very moment that you are levying war against the king, & breaking all the laws.[108]

[128][109] [blank]
[129] Abbe Gregoire tells, "that on the arrival of bloodhounds from Cuba in the island of S. Domingo, *on leur livra par manière d'essai, le premier nègre qui se trouve sous la main. La promptitude avec laquelle ils dévorèrent cette curée réjouit des tigres blancs à figure humaine"*
Gregoire "Sur la litterature des Negres."
ap[ud]. Prichard.[110]

[130]   *Carnot organisa la victoire*
"il est de bornes que l'honneur autant que la raison ↑imposent↓ a la reconnaisance nationale. Si ce citoyen a restauré la liberté publique, sera-ce une récompense à lui offrir, que le sacrifice de cette même liberté?"

[106] This quotation is given in DeLolme, *The Constitution of England* . . . , 1793, p. 25; it is used in "Ability," *W*, V, 82.
[107] *Life and Letters*, 1852, III, 111. See Journal SO, p. [130] above. This quotation is used in "Result," *W*, V, 305.
[108] See *JMN*, XIII, 351.
[109] Tipped in on p. [128] is a newspaper clipping of a letter to the editor by C. Cushing, dated Washington, Oct. 29, 1853, opposing a coalition of Democrats and Free-Soilers and denouncing Abolitionism. Democrats who ally themselves with Free-Soilers, writes Cushing, "have done worse than to commit a fatal error."
[110] James Cowles Prichard, *The Natural History of Man* . . . (London, 1843), p. 7. Emerson withdrew this book from the Boston Athenaeum September 4–October 8, 1855.

Said Carnot, as Tribun⟨e⟩, in 1802, in opposition to the establish-ment of the Consulship for life.

[131] "If you pass this law,"ⁿ said Mirabeau to the Assembly, "I swear to disobey it."

Smith & Quesnay exploded the policy of checks.[111]

[132]   *The Two Ways.*
          There are two ways of attacking slavery.
1. The *man*-way of voluntary cooperation by parties, by legislation, by compromise, by treaty, &c. This way is inefficient. Party besets party. The more you attack, the more you exasperate defence. Then there are certain impediments that do not fail to appear. Hopeful young gentlemen are found to be dead against you. Expense makes young voters Whigs. Christian Observer, Christian Register, [133] Tract Society, Methodist Church, a universal Tartuffe. If the devil himself (See *DO* 104)
Area of freedom. And the general confusion inevitable. Few people are moralists, few have discernment, most are quadrupeds, and the deliberate shutting of their eyes on one commandment blurs all their perception[.]

'Tis against the plain interest of young men to allow freedom. Young man! the poor Kansas settlers give no elegant suppers, no Saturday dinners, no private box have they at the opera.

[134] If you vote to garotte them, & stand by Missouri & the Union, you can just as well praise the Kansas of a thousand years ago, namely, Marathon; talk just as glibly of Milton & the Puritans. You can edit Landor; you can, like Guizot & Sparks, write eulogies of Washington. Judges, Bank Presidents, Railroad men, men of fashion, lawyers universally all take the ⟨& the⟩ side of slavery. What a poor blind devil are you to break your shins for a bit of moonshine against the goodwill of the whole [135] community. "Meanness!" do you say? Yes, but when meanness is in such good company[,] when ⟨Presidents

---

[111] See *JMN*, VI, 61.

of Colleges⟩ ↑the↓ University, & the faculty of law, & of medicine, & of Divinity itself, are infinitely mean, ⟨why⟩ who knows which is meanness? What a fool, when the whole world has lost its wits, to be the only sane man!

⟨This is all⟩ 'Tis matter of certainty that the base side will win. My rule of political prophecy, is, to ascertain which is the worst party, & the meanest action, ⟨& to know⟩ that is the thing which will be done and [136] I am seldom disappointed.

Down it will go, the banner of freedom & justice; the Whig party will certainly prevail, the smooth chuckle, the well-dressed expensive man, the democrat knowing his men, managing the caucus, — these will triumph. Everett & Hallet, Mr Morey & Winthrop & Greene & the Journal of Commerce, & the pious Editors of the ↑N.Y.↓ *Observer*, will prevail, & will piously burk the poor farmers of Kansas. [137] Mr Winthrop & at a humble distance Mr Hillard will have the satisfaction of ⟨soon⟩ hearing the last scream of these fellows. Well, what's the harm of it? They had no business to go there. Besides, what's dying? What signifies a little hardship more or less, a ⟨w⟩ knife wound or a gunshot? We all must die. Mortal men.

Another thing; the friends of freedom fall out: the Abolitionists are waspish egotistical Ishmaelites, not cunning. In short the [138] man-
-way does not prosper.

As for these gentlemen, they have no insight, they have passions & interests: and we know therefore they are beyond argument: for, 1. the belly has no ears: &, 2. Interests were never persuaded. Can you persuade the shoe-interest, or the iron-masters,[n] by reading Milton or Montesquieu?

Now the skepticism of the gentlemen is very sincere: they are in the quadruped state: & 'tis better they should not cant, nor be forced into a theatrical attitude, as Boston was in Burns' case,[112] but let them

---

[112] Anthony Burns (1834–1862), a fugitive slave arrested in Boston, May 24, 1854, was returned to Virginia over Abolitionist protests. See pp. [225₂]–[230] below.

neigh, & bray, & follow a handful of oats, as they genuinely will. If 'tis *in*, better let it come *out*, as Swedenborg thinks of fornication. Let them "mind the hand that feeds them," as G[eorge] S[tillman] H[illard].

[139] ↑The Godway↓ [113]
2. But the friction ↑or judgement of God↓. There is strangely enough another element which does not prove so friendly to Slavery, as the Whig or ↑fine-↓gentleman party;[n] and that is,[n] an unexpected hitch in the working of the thing. There's something always wrong in the machinery. It is out of gear. In spite of the open friendship of the democratic party, & the warmer aid of the fine gentlemen, ⟨the⟩ with everything for it, it does not seem to get on.
[140] California did not behave well,[n] but voted to be free. Texas is not quite to be trusted lest it vote itself free. The census is incendiary, & the tables must be cooked. The Whites of the South threaten to be troublesome. Gen. Shields finds a difficulty in sending Irishmen into ⟨Missou⟩Kansas who will take up the land in their own name, & then give him back the land warrants. The valuation of the Slave states is not satisfactory. The escape of fugitives is easier & more [141] frequent every year. The difficulty of executing the Fugitive Slave ⟨bill⟩ ↑law↓ always greater. The literature of slave states, the science, the morals, not encouraging. There's a kind of deviltry here as in the Brockhaus. The wine tastes fiery. The women have a worm between their lips. Not a gentleman, not a hero, not a poet, not a Woman, born in all that immense country! There must be such, for nature avenges herself, but they lie perdus, & make no sign in the reign of terror. ↑In fifty years, since Mr Jefferson,↓ not[n] a breath of air has come to the intellect or heart.

[142] The Whig poetry lasts as long as their hurras. Could never be heard of the next day. Nobody could be hired to read it. Their respectability is of the same fatal kind. Every one of them puts on stateprison trowsers in the dark, & struts in Statestreet with one leg red & one blue.

------

[113] "The Godway" is in pencil.

What real aid has come to the cause of freedom is always unlooked for. Nothing calculated has ever succeeded.

[143]–[147] [...] [114]
[148]–[157] [115] [blank]
[158] [116] I wish to tell you something, gentlemen. Eternity is very long[;] opportunity is a very little portion of it, but worth the whole of it. If God gave me my choice of the whole planet, or my little farm, I should certainly take my farm.[117]

[158$_a$] ⟨I do not share⟩
    ⟨I am ashamed of this⟩
    I am glad to see the ⟨effeminate⟩ terror at disunion & anarchy which I hear expressed disappearing. Massachusetts, in its great day, had no government: was an anarchy[;] every man stood on his own feet, & was his own governor; & there was no breach of the peace from the capes to the mountains. California, a few years ago, by the testimony of [158$_b$] all people in that country, had the best government that ever existed. Pans of gold ↑to the amount of hundreds of dollars↓ lay drying at outside of every man's tent ↑in perfect security.↓ A bit of land that your hand ⟨w⟩could cover was worth one or two hundred dollars ↑& there was no dispute.↓ Every man throughout the country was armed with knife & revolver & perfect peace reigned. Instant justice was administered to each offence[.] [118]

[114] Pp. [143]–[147] bear the text of Emerson's speech on the assault upon Charles Sumner in the U.S. Senate on May 22, 1856, as printed in the Boston *Evening Transcript*, May 31, 1856 ("Remarks of Mr. R. W. Emerson at a meeting in Concord on the 26th, to Consider the outrage upon Mr. Sumner."), and in "The Assault upon Mr. Sumner," *W*, XI, 247–252. The text is not in Emerson's hand.

[115] A newspaper clipping on "An American Trader for Japan" is tipped in on p. [149]. The story, reprinted from the Newburyport *Herald*, tells of the first clearance from any port in the United States direct for Japan for commercial purposes and notes that "Salem ships were among the first, if not the very first, for ordinary commercial pursuits, on the west shores of Africa."

[116] Laid in between pp. [158] and [159] are two leaves bearing inscriptions by Emerson: a sheet of blue paper 12.6 x 20.2 cm with an ink inscription printed here as pp. [158$_a$] and [158$_b$], and a sheet of off-white paper 12.2 x 18.1 cm with a pencil inscription printed here as p. [158$_c$].

[117] See *JMN*, XIII, 10.

[118] This paragraph is used in "Speech on Affairs in Kansas," *W*, XI, 261–262. See *JMN*, XIII, 49, and pp. [213] and [215] below.

[158ₑ] C[hief] J[ustice] Sewall in 1700 wrote to Judge Addington[:] The poorest boys & girls within this prov[ince]. such as are of the lowest condit[ion] whether they be Eng[lish] or Ind[ian] or Ethiop may have the same right to religion & life that the richest heirs have. And they who go about to deprive them of their right, attempt the bombarding of Heaven & the shells they throw will fall down on their own heads[.]

C[*hristian*] R[*egister*]   June 11 1853

[159] Tisso, a bramin, suffered from an ulcer in his foot, occasioned from the puncture of a thorn. His brother inquired what would cure it; and Tisso replied; "a palm-full of clarified butter;" but he forbade that he should seek for it (at an unorthodox time) in the afternoon. If, in thy morning pilgrimage to beg thy daily alms, thou shouldst receive some clarified butter, that thou mayest bring. [160] But no palm full of clarified butter ⟨was⟩ having been ⟨giv⟩ offered him, ⟨a disease⟩ in his morning round, — a disease was engendered which could not be subdued by a hundred cauldrons of clarified butter. By this disease the hero[n] was brought to the close of his existence[.] [119]

[161] [blank]
[162] "Le grand défaut de ce siècle philosophique est de ne l'etre pas encore assez. Il ne l'est pas envers les femmes: mais, quand la lumière sera plus libre de se repandre, plus etendue, et plus egale, nous cesserons de tenir les femmes sous le joug, et dans l'ignorance; et les femmes cesseront de seduire de tromper et gouverner leurs maitres."   *D'Alembert.*[120]

[163]–[166] [121] [two leaves cut out]

[119] Emerson found this story in George Turnour, *The Maháwanso in Roman characters, with the translation subjoined; and an introductory lecture on Páli Buddhistical literature* (Ceylon, 1837). He withdrew this volume from the Boston Athenaeum December 1, 1854–January 16, 1855.

[120] Quoted on p. 457 of Saint-Marc Girardin's "Jean-Jacques Rousseau," *Revue des Deux Mondes*, Aug. 1, 1854, pp. 453–487.

[121] Emerson indexed p. [166] under History of Liberty and Montesquieu. On the stub of p. [163] the following words or portions of words are visible: "He

[167] "For stories teach us, that liberty sought out of season, in a corrupt & degenerate age, brought Rome itself to a farther slavery; for liberty hath a sharp & double edge fit only to be handled by just & virtuous men: to bad & dissolute it becomes a mischief unweildy in their own hands." ↑&c   See Milton Vol V p 239↓ [122]

[168]   *History of Liberty*
"Dr Reinhold Pauli in London is printing his history of Simon de Montfort, Earl of Leicester, the founder of the House of Commons."   *Publishers Circular* Dec., 1866 [123]

[169]–[173] [blank]
[174] The wonderful change. The idea of liberty was the essence of this country. It was like the climate or the mountain chains or the ⟨wild American⟩ ↑red man↓ ⟨peculiar⟩ ⟨|| ... ||⟩ ↑native↓ & inseparable to this region. ⟨The starry sky of⟩ ⟨one third of the starry sky was the measure of⟩ Our Star-Spangled banner was the pride of young imaginations. A true emblem, as we then thought, that one third of the ⟨starry⟩ sky that covers the globe, one third of the sky [175] with its galaxies of stars ⟨was the measure of our banner of Liberty⟩ covering the land & waters of America, — was the measure of the banner of liberty.

[176] [124]
_____
↑(s)Sketch of an undelivered speech, May 1853↓
I do not often touch the subject of slavery, being preoccupied, like others, by nearer & imperative duties. If I may dare to say so, I have my own slaves to free, spirits in other prisons, whom no man visits, & whom I am sent to help, if I can. [125] And in all my life, until the

---

|| ... || Per|| ... || Foxe|| ... || Bec|| ... || In|| ... || in the || ... || intim|| ... || that || ... || a libe|| ... || wish || ... || him, || ... ||." See *JMN*, XIII, 332.

[122] *The Prose Works of John Milton*, 1853. "&c" and "See Milton Vol V p 239" are in pencil. Another "Milton" is added in ink.

[123] Reinhold Pauli, *Simon von Montfort, Graf von Leicester, der Schöpfer der Hauses der Gemeinen* (Tübingen, 1867).

[124] The speech on pp. [176]–[190] was probably intended for a May 5, 1853, dinner in honor of John Parker Hale (1806–1873), Free-Soil senator from New Hampshire (*L*, IV, 354–355).

[125] "I do not . . . I can." is used in "The Fugitive Slave Law" (1854), *W*, XI, 217. For "I have . . . I can.", see *JMN*, XIII, 80.

disastrous legislation ⟨on the⟩ ⟨two⟩ ↑three↓ years ago on the Fugitive bill, operated by the misguided & [177] misguiding genius of a great man now no more, the evil of slavery has been remote, & has never practically come to our doors (except in the case of the imprisonment ↑at the South↓ of ↑some of our↓ colored citizens). Now, we have all been polluted by it. I know, that, when seen near & in detail, it is disheartening. Yet I am accustomed to regard it as a subject of that slow [178] & secular melioration which expels in time every wrong. Nature is not so helpless but it can rid itself at last of every crime. An eastern poet in describing the golden age, said, that God had made justice so dear to the heart of nature that if any injustice lurked anywhere under the sky the blue vault would shrivel to a snakeskin & cast it out [179] by spasms. I believe it will still. For what is the golden age, but the healthy condition at which all things are aiming? If anything is pure, the riddance of this piece of barbarism cannot long be postponed. In the infancy of society, all the institutions are on a war-foundation, & slavery came in. Now the institutions are all on a commercial [180] foundation, & it must go out. The very despotism of commerce which unmans our trading community, & this once heroic town, & has thrown all timid persons into a conservative or shop-till party, may be relied on, in the sequel, to break up Slavery, once for all. Once it was believed to be cheap to buy & hold, & the planter bought. But when he ciphers better, & [181] has learned, that it is dear to hold, & cheap to emancipate, he will emancipate. That slavery is bad economy, all shrewd men know by Cocker's Arithmetic, by census, & valuation tables. No sensible man believes that beggary or thieving are, on the whole, lucrative professions, though there have been paupers with fortunes sewed into their rags; & though there have been successful Captain Kidds & even Louis Napoleons.

[182] Neither can slavery, — which is the worst, as it is chronic & perpetual ⟨thieving⟩ stealing, — be economical, or anything else but bankruptcy. Down in Alabama & Missisippi, it may take half a century to show this, but they will find it out, & act on it. For the human mind has no predilection for absurdity.

Meantime, what they learn slow, the senator has learned fast,[126]

[126] Senator John Parker Hale; see p. [176] above.

& has read the law of [183] nature so truly, that he can afford to be good humoured, & wait till duller men have blundered & blundered out. It requires wide mental vision, or what is perhaps better, the wisdom of the heart to forgive difference of opinion, & only they who are secure by being in the right, can be so generous[.]

The senator has not failed in his part. Justice has been done to his merits. And yet I cannot help adding a word of homage [184] because they are so signal, & because I wish to extend my thanks to the like merits of others besides himself[.]

Sir, whilst this inconsistency of slavery with the principles on which the world is built, guarantees its downfall,ⁿ I own that the patience it requires is almost too sublime for mortals, & it seems to demand of us a little more than ⟨hoping⟩mere [185] hoping; & when one sees how vast the mischief is & how it ⟨poisons⟩ ↑embitters↓ everything it touches, I think we demand of superior men, that they be superior in this; that the mind & the virtue in the country give their verdict in their day, & accelerate so far the progress of civilization.[127] I do not wonder that feeble men are advocates for slavery. No feeling of worthiness [186] assures them of their own safety in a new state of things.[128]

Fear is cruel. But strong men are always humane; for they know, that, whatever comes, they will always be wanted. As Luther said, "God himself cannot do without wise men."[129]

Yet ⟨in⟩ ↑who can ever forget↓ that widespread treason to justice, which wasted like a cholera ⟨striking d⟩the land, striking down the [187] highest & learnedest, the rich & the refined, & the profound feeling of desolation & skepticism which it produced?
That period will hereafter be looked upon as rivalling (in the unexpectedness of the succumbing, — down they all went, like reeds before the wind, ——) the baseness of Charles II's age, or of the

---

[127] "whilst this . . . civilization." is used in "The Fugitive Slave Law" (1854), W, XI, 240–241.

[128] For "I do not . . . things.", see JMN, IX, 133.

[129] This sentence is used in "Nature," W, III, 187.

French regency. And, as Macaulay has impeached the Penns & Sidneys of England, — [188] so I am ashamed to think what havoc the truth of history will make with our laurels & respectabilities.

↑I don't
I hold men to their order↓ [130]

Meantime, the senator has done his part. Whoever has been faithless, he has been faithful. By singular wisdom & temperance, has approved his fidelity against roaring majorities, & won the praises of his opponents. We who [189] see him here today, can now understand the prevailing charm of his sweetness joined with ↑this↓ courage. He is the living hero of the old minnesinger's song —

"Oft have I heard, & now believe it true,
Whom man delights in, God delights in too." [131]

The genius of life is friendly to the noble, & in the dark brings them friends from far. Courage loves courage, & he has friends in all the west & south country. He may suffer from present opprobrium among the [190] timid & mean. But freedom has a long memory, & remembers her own. And it is easy already to read the names that in America will be luminous in the next generation.

[191] [blank]

[192] Shall man be treated as leather? Negroes are money. Slavery is a factory for converting men into monkeys[.] [132]

[193]   *Higher Law.*
"My dominion ends," said Napoleon, "where that of conscience begins." [133]

[130] "I don't . . . order" is in pencil.

[131] Emerson found these lines from the twelfth-century Provençal poet Pons de Capdueil in *Lays of the Minnesingers or German Troubadours of the Twelfth and Thirteenth Centuries* . . . , [ed. Edgar Taylor] (London, 1825), p. 220, which he withdrew from the Harvard College Library January 14, 1847. See *JMN*, IX, 357. The first line is "Oft have I heard and deemed the witness true." The lines are used in "Success," *W*, VII, 306, and "Poetry and Imagination," *W*, VIII, 37.

[132] "Shall man . . . monkeys", in pencil, is used in "The Fugitive Slave Law" (1854), *W*, XI, 227. See *JMN*, V, 295.

[133] Quoted in [Ainsworth Rand Spofford], *The Higher Law Tried by Reason and Authority* (New York, 1851), p. 34. See p. [212] below.

[194]–[195] [blank]

[196] I believe papers are of no use, ↑resolutions of↓ public meetings, platforms of conventions, nor laws nor constitutions any more:
they are all declaratory of the will of the moment, & are passed with
⟨as much⟩ ↑more↓ levity, & on grounds ⟨as petty as⟩ ↑much less honor-
able↓ than ordinary business transactions in the street. You relied on
the constitution. What has that availed?ⁿ It has been shown [197]
over & over again to be insufficient guaranty of slavery. You relied
on the Missouri Compromise. That is ridden over. You relied on the
rights of the States to protect their citizens. They cannot. And now
you relied on these dismal guaranties so much admired by Mr
Everett & Mr Webster of 1850. And before the body of Webster is
yet crumbled, it is found that they are no guaranty to the ⟨shuffling⟩
free states[,] are only a guaranty to the slave states that as they have
[198] hitherto met with no repulse they shall meet with none.

⟨I believe that⟩ These ⁿ events teach us that no help is but in ourselves:
that they are putting it home to every man that ⟨he⟩ in him is the
only bulwark against slavery[.]

> None any work can frame
> Unless himself become the same [134]

[199] There is no reliance on churches nor scriptures. For one would
have said "that a Christian would ⟨be a lover & benefactor⟩ not keep
slaves;" but Christians keep slaves. "Of course they will not dare
open the bible:" Of course they quote the bible, & ⟨the⟩ Christ &
Paul, to defend slavery. These are dead forms that will cover anything. To use laws, it needs ⟨an upright judge.⟩ ↑a loyal man↓[;] to
⟨use⟩ interpret Christ, it needs a Christ; to understand the Spirit, it
needs the Spirit.
[200] Therefore to make good the cause of Freedom against Slavery
you must be citadels & warriors & for God himself & Declarations of
Independence walking. Cromwell said only we can resist the superior
training of the King's soldiers, by having godly men[.]

---

[134] This couplet is attributed to Dante in a translation from Pico della Mirandola
in Thomas Stanley, *The History of Philosophy* . . . , 1701, p. 197. The couplet
is also used in "Poetry and Imagination," *W*, VIII, 43. See *JMN*, XIII, 285.

And no man has a right to hope that the laws of New York will defend him from the contamination of slaves another day, [201] until he has made up his mind that he will not owe his protection to the laws of New York but to his own spirit & arm. Then he protects New York. He only who is ⟨sufficient to himself⟩ ↑able to stand alone↓ is ⟨fit⟩ ↑valuable↓ for society ⟨& union⟩.[135]

It has all sorts of guards[,] poverty & temperance and spiritual aims[.]
He who takes his own life in his hand can command any other life and no^n man is yet fit for any great action or any [202] who holds his life dear.

Elizur Wright said, "All we ask for the negro, is, that he be removed from under Mr Lash, & put under Mr Cash." [136]

[203] [blank]
[204] [137]   Mrs Stowe
        The heroes & orators truly American
When shall we send home the dexterous officials good at dinner speeches but who cannot stand before Barabbas[?]
        The mountains of Nebraska sit heavy on his soul. Ah[,] those accusing snow crests loom up in the morning light[.]

[205] Day when no slave breathes in America
When the ⟨children⟩ ↑sons↓ of the mad men
When the star spangled banner of half the heaven is
        Science of liberty
        World exists for benefit   Talent of welldoing
        Culture is not stealing
        All action reacts
        Who steals another's steals his own

[135] "I believe . . . for society." on pp. [196]–[201] is used in "The Fugitive Slave Law" (1854), *W*, XI, 232–235.
[136] Elizur Wright (1804–1885), editor of the *Massachusetts Abolitionist*, organ of the conservative opponents of Garrison and the *Liberator*, was tried and acquitted for aiding the escape of the fugitive slave Shadrack.
[137] The entries on pp. [204] and [205] are in pencil.

And liberty is the highest good
As a man thinks he is free
thinks wholly & ship minds the helm
Liberty not cheap
Severely guarded
free of debt & passion
        neither chain nor chain of chain

[206] The Whigs say politely that all sensible people supported
the Fugitive Slave law. They mean that all persons who are sensible
in regard to property, did so. When they say that all sensible & good
citizens support it, the remark only exposes their own idea of sense &
goodness. It sounds to me as if they said, a law has been passed to
enable debtors to ⟨swin⟩ defraud their creditors, & all sensible & good
men support the law. [207] I never ↑knew↓ one virtuous man on the
side of the law[.] [138]

I observe that our Whigs are only brave ⟨to⟩ in a cowardly cause.
They are brave to call Theodore Parker hard names, brave to mob
Garrison & Phillips, brave to mob quakers & Miss Lucy Stone, but
when the State of Massachusetts is threatened & insulted & disfranchised, they are as gentle & peaceable as whipt dogs.

[208] [139] [blank]
[209]–[210] [leaf cut and torn out]
[211] [blank]
[212] [140] "Countries not cultivated in proportion to their fertility but
in proportion to their liberty."   Montesq[uieu] [141]

[138] A small portion of p. [207] bearing the "new" of "knew" was torn away
when a newspaper clipping tipped in on p. [208] was removed. "knew" is written
in pencil beneath the hole.
[139] Two clippings were tipped in on p. [208]; when they were removed a
small piece was torn out of the top and another piece was cut out at the lower edge
of the leaf. The remaining piece of the clipping on the left is headed "for publication
in the Evening Telegraph."; a penciled note referring to the clipping on the right
reads "They call it stealing".
[140] The entries on pp. [212]–[217] are in pencil.
[141] L'esprit des lois, Oeuvres, 1819, II, 111: "Le pays ne sont pas cultivés en
raison de leur fertilité, mais en raison de leur liberté." The English version of this
quotation is used in "American Slavery" and in "Civilization," W, VII, 34.

"My dominion ends where that of Conscience begins," said Napoleon[.] [142]

The mountains of Nebraska sit heavy on his Soul.[143]

day coming when the star spangled banner which now is broad as half the heaven, shall cover no slave [144]

[213] We are brave only in a cowardly cause, brave to mob Quakers & Miss Lucy Stone[,] but when the state of Mass is threatened, insulted, disfranchised, we are as gentle & amiable as whipt dogs[.] [145]

———

our weather cock government

———

California has the best government that ever existed[.] [146]
no fear of anarchy

When the Extinguisher takes fire it's an awkward business[.] [147]
When ⟨go⟩ judges do not judge, when governors do not govern, when Presidents do not preside but sell themselves to somebody who bargains to make them presidents again [148]
[214] When the people do not elect but allow a caucus to ⟨elect⟩ take the trouble of thinking out of their hands & make a ticket for them. When all is done at second hand you have taken the commodore & the captain & the sailing master & the helmsman & the sailors from their posts & put the Bowditch's navigator ⟨into the⟩ under the boiler, & the steam ship is rushing on the rocks with a whirlwind[.]
The Excellence of our government is the cause of our ruin[.]
We are spoiled by selfpraise & our institutions[.]

[142] See p. [193] above.
[143] See p. [204] above.
[144] See p. [205] above.
[145] See p. [207] above.
[146] For "California . . . existed", see p. [158ᵦ] above.
[147] See *JMN*, XIII, 226.
[148] "When ⟨go⟩ judges . . . preside" is used in "American Slavery." For "When ⟨go⟩ judges . . . again", see p. [235₁] below.

[215] California
    Massachusetts[,] when every man stood on his feet and was his own governor[,] was united & perfect in word & work[.]
California had the best government that ever existed[.]
For the Saxon man when he is fairly awake is not a pirate but a perfect citizen, all made of hooks & eyes, he links himself naturally to his brothers as ⟨a swarm⟩ bees hook themselves to each other & to their queen in a loyal swarm.[149]

[216] Nature has made up its mind on one point, that races or men who can't sustain themselves shall go to the ground[.]
    It is of no use to put arms into hands that dare not use them. It's of no use to give ⟨good laws⟩ ↑Bills of rights↓ ⟨good⟩ constitutions to Sicilians, or Mexicans, or South Americans, (if the minds of the people are servile) and it is of no use to give writs of replevin or jury trial or state sovereignty as means offset & balance to the [217] federal arm, if we have lost the spirit which first enacted these defences of liberty. They who made them, made them for brave men only. ⟨If the⟩ If they are not rooted in the determination of the people they are nothing but a costume for the day ↑of no more importance than the color or cut of the garment you wear.↓ As the King of Naples said, when his officers were discussing a new uniform for his troops, It was no matter how you dressed them, they were sure to run away.

[218]   ↑*Exordium of Kansas Relief Lecture.*↓
In the stormy election through which we have just passed, the day has gone against the interests of political liberty, on great & vital issues, & with some sequel so dangerous before us, that it requires regard to the largest views & resources to console the friends of freedom & of man. It seemed as if nothing were left us but suicide or emigration. Well, no; I don't think 'tis come to that yet. Neither will New England take to drink. 'Tis more likely her enemies will, & she will meet "Those sons of Belial flown with insolence & wine,"[150]

---

[149] "Massachusetts . . . swarm." is used in "Speech on Affairs in Kansas," *W*, XI, 261–262. For "California . . . existed", see p. [213] above. For "Massachusetts . . . existed", see p. [158ᵇ] above.
    [150] John Milton, *Paradise Lost*, I, 501–502.

⟨another day⟩ with ⟨more⟩better advantage, another day, from her own habit of good sense & sobriety.

[219] [151] What's the use of telegraphy? What of newspapers? To know how men feel in Indiana, in Wisconsin, in Illinois, in ⟨O⟩ Minesota I wait for no mails. I read no telegraphs. I ask my own heart. If they are made as I am, if they breathe the like air, eat the same wheat or corn bread, have wi⟨f⟩ves & children, I know their resentment is boiling & will boil until this wrong is righted. The [n] interest of human labor[,] the selfrespect & love of mankind that engages man not to be to man a wolf[,] secures their everlasting hostility to this shame [220] of human nature.[152]
In haying time farmers can't come[.]

Better is justice in the Sovereign than plenty in the season[.] [153]

Nature has made up her mind on one point[:] that what can't defend itself shall not be defended[.] [154]
I do not think we are safe when I see this fatal reliance on laws & machinery of gov't.
Why we are spoiled by the very goodness of the laws.   See [Notebook] MO[rals] p 49

[221] [blank]
[222] [155] I shall not feel safe until I see that the people are alarmed
We credulous
Evils of this machinery
Attention is fixed on details of measures[,] on parliamentary order[,]

[151] The entries on pp. [219] and [220] are in pencil.
[152] "What's the . . . boil" is used in "Progress of Culture," W, VIII, 227–228. In JMN, VI, 139, Emerson quotes "Man has been to man a wolf" from Thomas Hobbes. For this paragraph, see JMN, XIII, 306.
[153] Quoted in Practical Philosophy of the Muhammadan People, exhibited in its professed connexion with the European, so as to render either an introduction to the other; being a translation of The Akhlāk-I-Jalāly, the most esteemed ethical work of middle Asia, from the Persian of Fakir Jāny Muhammad Asäad, trans. W. F. Thompson (London, 1839), p. 457. This sentence is used in "The Emancipation Proclamation," W, XI, 318. See JMN, IX, 286–287, and p. [225₂] below.
[154] See p. [216] above.
[155] The entries on pp. [222]–[224] are in pencil.

& the ⟨gist⟩ ↑core↓ of the question[,] the ⁿ issue for which parliaments exist is not secured. Somebody has swindled it away whilst the eyes of all were fastened on the forms. It wants a church of freedom[,] it wants serious thoughtful men & women who hold the forms very cheap[,] [223] do not care for Whig or democrat or free soil or Union, but for Rights & Wrongs only; who must have equity, who will extirpate crime & will have ↑to every man↓ the largest liberty ⟨to every man, that is⟩ compatible with liberty to every other man.[156] I am ashamed of this effeminate terror at ⟨agitation & change⟩ dis-union. ⟨Let us⟩ We are losing for the sake of Union, the good which the Union was adopted to guard[.]
Saxon men must not lose sight of the main chance.

[224] Lord Nelson. To obey orders is thought all perfection but in case of confusion of signals ⟨or⟩ no officer can go wrong who brings his ship close alongside of ⟨the enem⟩ a ship of the enemy.[157] So every wise legislator will say in the collision of statutes or the doubtful interpretation. No citizen will go wrong who does to others as he would have others do to him & who on every question leans to the side of general liberty[.] [158]

[225₁] [blank]
[226₁] Private liberty, according to the definition of the English lawyers, consists, 1. of the right of property, that is, of the right of enjoying exclusively the gifts of fortune, & all the various fruits of one's industry.

     2. of the right of personal security.

     3. of the locomotive faculty, taking the word liberty in its more confined sense.

———

[225₂] [159]   Sketch of an undelivered speech.

[156] "who will . . . other man." is used in "American Slavery."

[157] "To obey . . . enemy." is quoted from Robert Southey, *The Life of Nelson* (New York, 1830), pp. 193 and 289. See *JMN*, XIII, 319.

[158] "Lord Nelson . . . liberty" is used in "American Slavery."

[159] Sixteen leaves here were cut out, but the first three of them, bearing pp. [225₂]–[226₂], [227₁]–[228₁], and [229₁]–[230₁], are laid in at this point. Nine additional leaves, seven inscribed on recto only, bearing pages [231₁]–[248₁],

The farmers have begun their haying, & could come only at much inconvenience; but I found no unwillingness. They were of the opinion of the Chinese who say "Better is justice in the sovereign, than plenty in the season." [161]

'Tis high time the people came together. I know the objections commonly urged by the best against popular meetings. They bring out individualisms, impracticable local views, side-issues & each speaker forms a republic which has room in it for only one, namely, himself.

[226₂] You get abstractionists, you breed discontent & ill blood, &, in place of the quiet business & lawabiding habit of our people, you exasperate party-spirit.

But higher reasons exist, transcending these timid considerations. No doubt, many people, in 1776, thought the meetings of the people in town houses & the hanging ⟨of⟩ in knots about the meetinghouse door, & in the taverns, quite needless; [227₁] a waste of the farmers' time. But hereby the whole country is turned into a busy school where every student learns his lesson and all are put in training for what may come.

The natural check on side issues & partial & private views, is, a great & common danger which is sinking, at this moment, every man's whim in the necessity of bringing all men to meet the common enemy [228₁] of everything that does not walk on all fours.

As to visionary & abstract, you will forgive me if I do not see any harm in that. I think we need that: It is curious that now liberty is grown passive & defensive: Slavery alone is inventive & aggressive. Slavery reads the Constitution with a very shrewd & daring & innovating eye. Liberty is satisfied with literal [229₁] construction.

are now in Houghton MS. Am 1280. 202 (9), ff. 12–20, "American Slavery, 6 Feb 1855, Preliminary notes."

[160] The speech on pp. [225₂]–[248₁] undoubtedly concerned the capture of Anthony Burns; see p. [138] above.

[161] For "The farmers . . . the season.' ", see p. [220] above.

The Declaration of Independence is an abstraction. Every man is an abstractionist on Sunday morning. The gospel of Christ is an abstraction; and by debate & study, new views & broader principles are given to fit the natural expansion of the times. That is the sole consolation to the wounds inflicted, in evil times, on the commonwealth; that ⟨the⟩ in the glare of passion the foundations of ⟨p⟩law are searched, & men become masters of the science of liberty.

[230_1] Abstract! the more abstract the better. It is a law which is found to hold in history, that, it is not their climate, not their race, not their government, or their employment, which determines the destinies of men, but their credence. As is their way of thinking & belief, will their power & fortune be, & their influence on mankind.

[231_1] And the greatest dominion will be to the deepest thought. The establishment of Christianity in the world does not ⟨depend⟩rest on any miracles, but the miracle of being the broadest & most humane doctrine. "Revolutions" said Metternich, "begin in the highest classes, & are communicated to the lower."

[232_1] [blank]

[233_1] These are things which are lost sight of, in legislatures, but are always looming up in primary assemblies.

But besides the manifold benefits of primary assemblies, — in the extraordinary crisis at which we have arrived, there is no other way.

This has ceased to be a Representative Government.

I do not wish to hear, until I forget the experience of the last years, anything farther [234_1] [blank] [235_1] on the excellence of American laws & institutions.

What avails the correctness of the theory, ⟨if⟩when the practice is despotism? When judges do not judge; when governors do not govern; when Presidents do not preside, but sell themselves to somebody who bargains to make them Presidents again; [162] when the People do not elect, but suffer a Caucus to take from them the trouble of electing, &, last & worst of all, when Representatives do

[162] For "When judges . . . again;", see p. [213] above.

not represent, (for there is some⟨th⟩ poison in the water of the Potomac River which [236₁] [blank] [237₁] none but the strongest stomachs can resist,—) what matters how good or wise the theory may be? And how wide is the departure of the practice of gov[ernmen]t from the theory, the late history shows. All government is, by the recent events, brought into disrepute. ↑In Massachusetts, we found,↓[163] laws[n] maintaining the personal liberty, & the sovereignty of this Commonwealth, are sure not to be enforced. Laws enacting a crime, are enforced.

The statute fastens penalties of treason on acts of common humanity & of imperative moral obligation.

[238₁] [blank]

[239₁] The Governor is not worth his own cockade. He sits in his chair to see the laws of his Commonwealth broken, & to sanction the proceeding to see every peaceable citizen endangered[,] every ⟨‖ ... ‖⟩patriotic citizen insulted & hurled to the wall by the riff raff of the dance cellars & the jails of the metropolis. I thought the successor of ⟨G⟩Hancock & of Caleb Strong & of Elbridge Gerry[164] who knew their office would have exhausted the stores of legal ingenuity for the security & honor of that state whose sovereignty he represents. If he [240₁] ⟨found no⟩[n] [241₁] found no guard, no reserve of liberty, no security for it, in the capital city of Massachusetts[,] I thought[n] he would have convened the legislature, or made his proclamation to the people that he found himself powerless, they must strengthen his hands or else resign the sword, when he found it was of wood.

When the governor contents himself with sitting by, to see the state dishonored; & compliments the troops, at public dinners, for their alacrity on this ominous occasion; [242₁] [blank] [243₁] when the judges of Massachusetts who, I am told, might with a bare word order the Suffolk Court House to be cleared, suffer the building to be occupied as a military fortress by the vilest of mankind,[n] to the pointed exclusion of the citizens of Mass[achuse]tts;

[163] "In Massachusetts, we found," is in pencil.
[164] John Hancock (1737–1793), Caleb Strong (1745–1819), and Elbridge Gerry (1744–1814) were governors of Massachusetts.

whilst the laws say, that the officers of the state shall not aid in the capture, & the public buildings shall not imprison the fugitive.

When the guards of personal liberty, writ of habeas corpus & the like, are not used or not enforced [244₁] [blank] [245₁] for fear of bringing the state & federal courts into collision.

When the old safeguards by which every prisoner is assumed to be innocent, until proved guilty, &, in case of any doubt, he has the benefit of it, — are all sacrificed — interpreted in favor of the kidnapper

When the statute itself fastens penalties of treason on acts of common humanity, & of imperative moral obligation; and when the United States Congress passes a law to stop the [246₁] [blank] [247₁] march of human civility & virtue, by preestablishing the barbarous institution of Slavery over a vast territory that had been pledged by law to freedom, and this is done by the help of Northern men.

— I submit that all government is bankrupt, all law turned upside down; that the government itself is treason: you ↑the constituency,↓ are swindled in the face of the world.

and that nothing remains but to begin at the beginning to call every man in America [248₁] to counsel, Representatives do not represent, we must ⟨now⟩ take new order & see how to make representatives represent us.

[227₂] [165]   The heavy blue chain of the sea didst thou just man
                    endure [166]

    The heavy blue chain
    Of the circling main
    Did the brave old exile wear

    And the mountains dungeon doors
    And the gaoler was the law

[165] The entries on pp. [227₂]–[237₂] are in pencil. The entries on pp. [227₂]–[237₂] are early versions of "Ode: Sung in the Town Hall, Concord, July 4, 1857," ll. 1–12, 16–24, 26–36, 39–40, W, IX, 199–200, and "Boston," ll. 11–12, 17–18, 29–36, 53–54, and 99, W, IX, 212–217. For "For what . . . fail", see Journal VO, p. [118] above.

[166] This sentence, from Edward Davies, *The Mythology and Rites of the British Druids*, 1809, p. 515, is used in "Poetry and Imagination," W, VIII, 59. See JMN, XIII, 32.

An union then
Of honest men
Or union none for me

For what avail the plough & sail
Or ⟨life⟩ ↑land↓ or ⟨love⟩ ↑life↓ if freedom fail

[228₂]   O Tenderly the haughty day
Fills its urn with fire
One morn is in the mighty heaven
And one in our desire

The cannon booms from town to town
Our pulses are not less
The ⁿ ⟨bells⟩ joybells fill from sea to sea
⟨But more⟩ The ⁿ children's voices bless

For he that flung ⟨abroad the dawn⟩ the broad blue folds
⟨of the⟩ O'erarching ⁿ ⟨sky⟩ ↑land & sea↓
One third of heaven assigned
The banner of the free

[229₂]   The land that has no song
Shall have a song today

The world was made
For honest trade   To plant & eat
The honest waves   be none afraid
Refuse to slaves
The empire of the sea
Let Freedom's area ⟨extend⟩ ↑reach beyond↓
To nations o'er the sea

And make the broad Atlantic pond
A ferry of the free

[230₂]   O tenderly the haughty day
Fills its blue urn with fire.

424

One morn is in the mighty heaven
And one in our desire

The cannon booms from town to town
Our pulses are not less
The joybells /peal/chime/ ⟨o'er dale &⟩ ↑their tidings↓
    down
The children's voices bless

For he that flung the broad blue folds
O'erarching land & sea
One third of heaven unrolled
The banner of the free

[231₂]   ⟨Let Freedom's area extend⟩ ↑O'er mighty States & aye
        beyond↓
As wide as rolls the sea
We'll make the broad Atlantic pond
A ferry of the free

And aye they say in chorus loud
Or in an undersong
Go put your creed into your deed
The rights to all belong
Nor speak with double tongue
For sea & land don't understand
The lies of tyrant⟨s⟩ men

⟨The⟩ ↑⟨How⟩↓ ↑Nor || ... ||↓ rights by one hand ⟨achieve⟩
    ↑for which the one ↑hand↓ fights↓
By the other cloven down

[232₂]   And henceforth there shall be no chain
Save underneath the sea
The wire /wove cable/shall whisper/ thro the main
The secrets of the free

425

For sea & land can't understand
Nor ⟨skies⟩ ↑Jove↓ without a frown
See right for which the one hand fights
By the other cloven down

[233₂] The conscious stars above
The waters free below
And underneath the cable wove
The ⟨sparkling⟩ ↑fiery↓ errands go

And underground a railway found
To pass ⟨t⟩from wrong away

[234₂] O tenderly the haughty day
Fills his blue urn with fire
One morn is in the mighty heaven
And one in our desire

The cannon booms from town to town,
Our pulses are not less;
The joybells chime the tidings down,
Which children's voices bless.

For he that flung the broad blue fold
O'erarching land & sea
One /third /part/ of the galaxy unrolled
/For the banner of the free/Starspangled flag of the free/

[235₂] And aye ⟨they say⟩ in chorus loud
↑Heaven ⁿ & earth in thunder ⟨they⟩ plead↓
Or in an undersong
Go put your creed into your deed
Nor speak with double tongue

For sea & land don't understand
Nor /Jove/skies/ without a frown

426

See rights for which the one hand fights
By the other cloven down.

⟨O'er mighty states⟩ ↑Mountain & coast↓ & aye beyond
As wide as rolls the sea
We'll make the broad Atlantic pond
⟨The⟩A ferry of the free

And henceforth there shall be no chain
Save underneath the sea
The wires shall whisper thro the main
The secrets of the free

[236₂] ↑Freedom↓
            The conscious stars above
            The ⟨ocean⟩ ↑waters↓ wild below
            And underneath, thro cable wove,
            ⟨The⟩ ↑Her↓ fiery errands go

Saying to you men of this land I give a new law[:] Be strong
through freedom. Make your duty your fate & see that you cling to it
while you live[.]

[237₂]   O Sun! take off thy cloudy hood
            O land! take off thy chain
            And fill the earth with happy mood
            And love from main to main.

            For men & planet both are wise
            Upon the selfsame plan
            I'll take the sun out of the skies
            ⟨And⟩ ↑Ere↓ freedom out of man

[238₂] [blank]
[239₂]   We will not ⟨soil⟩ ↑stain↓ the whitest day
            In all the shining year

427

Blaspheme the goddess Freedom
We came to celebrate

Disloyally ⁿ withold
↑Free air from captive men↓
Her privilege
↑By pirates↓ where ⁿ man is bought & sold

⟨We will not⟩ ↑Ye shall not↓ stain this shining day
Nor ⁿ disloyally withold
Free air & soil from captive men
By pirates bought & sold

[240₂] In an age that produced Wellington[,] an English family-
-man, who never rising above the morale of his countrymen was yet
the embodiment of that, & won all his battles, & governed all his
countries, *as a family-man,* — won & kept every thing by having more
conscience of every kind than other people, & so had the boundless
confidence of all Europe, — Webster distrusted moral power, & sold
himself. [241₂] He was coarsely bribed as being of a coarse character.
Wellington saw the empire of Buonaparte to be inconsistent with
even the existence of civilized society. How much more should
Webster have seen the impossibility of ⟨|| ... ||⟩ slavery.

[242₂]   Miscellany.
_____

The two liberties, liberty to do what I please, & liberty to compel
every body else to do as I like to have them.[167]
Abolition   E 204
negroes   E 204

[243₂]–[244₂] [blank]
[245₂]   *Free Trade.*
"It is certainly no accident that the degree of less or more free trade
coincides with the degree of lessened or enlarged political freedom;
the feeling of material, economic, & industrial self-subsistency begets

[167] See *JMN,* VIII, 158.

also the feeling of political independence, which must express itself in corresponding state-forms."   Atlantis Feb. 1857 p 123 [168]

[246₂]–[247₂] [blank]
[248₂] Servile races! forsooth, Mr Justice Taney! "et velut in copuia canum constringuntur," says the chronicler, of the English. ap[ud]. Thierry p 156 (London) [169]   See VS 131

"No historical argument is ever capable of deciding a present question of equity."
     [Dove,] Theory of Hum[an]. Prog[ression]. p 412 [170]

"Sir, I say that it is employment that makes ⟨men happy⟩the people happy."
              Webster.
"It is the Senate that determines when the fourth of March arrives."
              Webster.

[249] [blank]
[250] [171] [Index material omitted]
[250ₐ]   Antislavery Almanac
1850 March 7
     Daniel Webster's speech (for Fugitive Slave Law)
March 25   Boston letter to Webster signed by 987 names (*WO* 11)
Sept. 18. Fugitive Slave law ⟨p⟩ received President Fillmore's signature.
Oct. 25   Attempt to seize Wm. & Ellen Craft in Boston.
      They escaped to England.
Dec   Castle Garden Committee in N.Y. volunteered their aid, & retained Geo. Wood as counsel of the claimant of alleged fugitive Henry Long. He was sent to Richmond.
1851 Feb 15   Arrest & rescue of Shadrack in Boston.

[168] "Der Handel als Kosmopolit," *Atlantis*, VI, ii, 119–126. "Atlantis . . . p 123" is in pencil.
[169] Augustin Thierry, *History of the Conquest of England by the Normans* (London, 1841). Emerson withdrew this book from the Boston Athenaeum June 13–July 12, 1853.
[170] See p. [28] above.
[171] Laid in inside the back cover is a single sheet of white paper 19.8 x 24.7 cm folded lengthwise to form four pages, the first two of which, printed here as pp. [250ₐ] and [250ᵦ], bear inscriptions in ink.

Apr 4.   Arrest of Thomas Sims in Boston.
chains around the Court House
he was surrendered ↑by Curtis↓ & carried to Savannah
Oct.   24   Died   D. Webster.

[250ᵦ]   1854
May.   Kansas-Nebraska bill was enacted repealing the Missouri Compromise.
May 24.   Anthony Burns arrested in Boston: Loring Commissioner; Pierce President; J.V.C. Smith mayor. J.A. Wright commander Mass[achuse]tts troops. Col. B.F. Edmands commanding a Reg't. of infantry posted on the Common.

1856
May 22   Assault of Brooks & Keith on Charles Sumner in the Senate Chamber
1859. Oct. 15.   Seizure of Harper's Ferry, by John Brown.

[inside back cover] [Index material omitted]

Pocket Diary 7

1 8 5 6

Pocket Diary 7 is devoted primarily to recording Emerson's lecture engagements for 1856. It also contains miscellaneous expenses, addresses, quotations, and memoranda. A few entries may have been made late in 1855 or early in 1857.

The notebook, bound in purple stamped leather, is a commercially published diary entitled "POCKET DIARY, / OR / DAILY REMEMBRANCER / FOR / 1856: / CONTAINING / A BLANK FOR EVERY DAY IN THE YEAR, / FOR THE RECORD OF / Interesting Events, Appointments, &c.", published by John Marsh and Co., Boston. The covers measure 7.7 x 12.6 cm. The back cover extends into a tongue which, when the book is closed, fits into a loop on the front cover; the back cover also contains an expandable pocket. A paper label fastened to the spine is inscribed "1856 x".

The light blue, unnumbered pages, whose edges are gilt, measure 7.5 x 12.6 cm; pages 15–162 are faintly lined. The book consists of front flyleaves (i, ii, 1, 2); a title page (page 3); information on eclipses in 1856 (page 4), rates of U.S. and foreign postage (pages 5 and 6), the salaries of President Franklin Pierce and his cabinet members (page 6); interest tables (pages 7–8); tables of the moon's phases (pages 9–14); daily appointments for 1856, three to a page (pages 15–136); pages for cash accounts (pages 137–146); and pages for notes (pages 147–166). The leaf bearing pages 161–162 is torn out and laid in.

Entries by Emerson occur on sixty-five pages. Printed matter in Pocket Diary 7 is reproduced here only in the section on daily appointments, in which dates are supplied where relevant. Otherwise, pages are designated as blank if they bear no inscription by Emerson; the presence or absence of printed matter is not specified.

[front cover verso] [blank]
[i] [1] [blank]
[ii] [2] Sumner

⟨Rhoades⟩

---

[1] "FL/56", apparently a stationer's mark, is written in pencil in the upper right-hand corner of this page.
[2] The entries on pp. [ii]–[2] are in pencil.

⟨Cord⟩
⟨M[erchan]ts. B[an]k.⟩
E Taylor
⟨Billings⟩
⟨E⟩L. Ripley   Waterford

Sydney Smith
Wit & Wisdom [3]

Rust

[1]   Boston to Albany   200
          Albany to Buffalo   298
          Buffalo to Erie   88
          Erie to Cleveland   95
          Cleveland to Toledo   112
          Toledo to Chicago   242
          ────────

                                        1035

          Chicago to R[ock]. Island   182

          Concord Bank
          179.50

[2]   S[amuel] G[ray] W[ard]
          Bhagvat
          Tremont Temple
          Lowell St.   Rust & Co

          P[hillips]. & S[ampson].   T[homas]. C[arlyle].
                    Errata
                    1855
                    Copies of Poems

---

[3] E. A. Duyckinck, *Wit and Wisdom of the Rev. Sydney Smith*, . . . *With a biographical memoir and notes* (New York, 1858).

Eng[lish] T[raits]
Miscellany

1 Essay[s] 223   not st[ereotyped]
Poems   373. st[ereotyped].
2 Essay[s] 358
   do St[ereotyped].   141
Rep[resentative] Men St[ereotyped]   208 [4]

Agassiz   Concord L[yceum] [5]
Lowell
Dana
____

Furness
Whitmore
Lowell St
Woodman
Cobb
Ward

[3]–[14] [blank]
[15] [6] [Tues., Jan. 1] Davenport.   W. Hall Esq
                          J.A. Jameson
Rock Island   H H Taylor
   Mixter, Esq   Geo. Purinton
                          ____

Judge Wilkinson   Freeport, Ill.
                          ____

[4] "1 Essay . . . 208" is written vertically in the left margin next to "Lowell St. . . . Miscellany". Editions of *Essays, First* and *Second Series*, and of *Poems* and *Representative Men* were issued in 1857 by Phillips & Sampson.

[5] Emerson was a curator of the Concord Lyceum for the 1856–1857 season. The records of the Concord Lyceum show that Agassiz lectured on "the different forms of Animal Life" on March 20, 1857. See p. [159] and Pocket Diary 8, p. [39] below.

[6] The entries on this page are in pencil, except for "J.A. Jameson   H H Taylor   Geo. Purinton   Freeport, Ill." (enclosed at top left and bottom by an ink line), "D", and "G.H. Wyman . . . 15 Jan". Henry H. Taylor of Freeport, Ill., was Emerson's "general committee for ten or eleven towns" in January, 1856 (*L*,

433

[Wed., Jan. 2] La Salle   W.W. Welch   D[ixon]   Dr Hitt   G.H. Wyman   Cleveland   10 or 15 Jan
[Thurs., Jan. 3] Dixon   Aldridge   J.W. Camp   James W C.

[16] [Fri., Jan. 4] Freeport   H H Taylor
[Sat., Jan. 5] Galena   McMasters   Jas. W. Camp
[Sun., Jan. 6] Sunday P.M. sent L[idian]. E[merson]. a draft of $150. by mail.

[17] [Mon., Jan. 7] Belvidere   Fuller, Esq.
[Tues., Jan. 8] Elgin
[Wed., Jan. 9] Beloit   Bushnell House   J.M. Bundy, Esq.

[18] [Thurs., Jan. 10] ⟨Freeport⟩   Janesville   N H Wood, Esq [7]
[Fri., Jan. 11] ⟨Galena⟩ ⟨Whitewater⟩ ?   Waukesha   Prof Sidney A. Bean   Irving M. Bean   Prof. Daniels
[Sat., Jan. 12] ⟨Waukesha⟩

[19] [Sun., Jan. 13] At Chicago   E.L. Pierce Esq

[20] [8] [Wed., Jan. 16] Galesburg ⟨?⟩   J H MacMonagle   D H ⟨Brithe⟩Blake   W E Phelps   Artos.
[Thurs., Jan. 17] Peoria ⟨?⟩   Mr Elwood   Borland   Harding   Rev. J.R. McFarland.

[21] [Sat., Jan. 19] Ann Arbor   ?   A K Spence
[Mon., Jan. 21] Adrian ?   J R Smith   Mr Lyon [9]

[22] [Tues., Jan. 22] Sandusky ?   ⟨Mansfield Ohio⟩ ?   W.J. Kennedy

---

V, 5). Emerson stayed with George H. Wyman of Cleveland on January 23 (L, V, 7).

[7] "N H Wood, Esq" is set off by square brackets with rules drawn above and below to form a discontinuous rectangle.

[8] On p. [20] "W E Phelps   Artos." and the cancellations of the two question marks are in pencil.

[9] "Mr Lyon" is in pencil. For "my banker here at Adrian, Mr. Lyon", see Journal RO, p. [103] above.

[Wed., Jan. 23] Cleveland ?
[Thurs., Jan. 24] Columbus ⟨?⟩ [10]

[23] [Fri., Jan. 25] Mansfield, O.   J.E. Wharton   Massillon O
Akron
[Sat., Jan. 26] Hudson [11]

[24] [12] [Mon., Jan. 28] Ravenna
[Tues., Jan. 29] Harvard   Salem
[Wed., Jan. 30] Exeter   Canton

[25] [Thurs., Jan. 31] Worcester   Massillon [13]

[26] [Mon., Feb. 4] Taunton   W Dickinson M D
[Tues., Feb. 5] Danvers

[27] [Wed., Feb. 6] Gloucester
[Thurs., Feb. 7] Wrentham 2.45   B[oston]. & P[rovidence].   leave
cars at N. Wrentham   Tickets Mr Thayer at Gate

[28] [Sat., Feb. 9] At Dr Keep's   lost money [14]
[Mon., Feb. 11] ⟨Yarmouth   Mr A B Wiggin⟩   Hallowell ?   W B
Glazier

[29] [Tues., Feb. 12] Gardiner   F. A. Butman
[Wed., Feb. 13] Bath   J O Fiske
[Thurs., Feb. 14] Bangor   S H Dale [15]

---

[10] The question mark after "Columbus" is canceled in pencil.

[11] "Akron" and "Hudson" are in pencil.

[12] The entries on p. [24] except for "Harvard" and "Exeter" are in pencil.

[13] "Massillon" is in pencil.

[14] "At Dr . . . money" is in pencil. Dr. Nathan C. Keep was the Emerson family dentist.

[15] In a letter to John O. Fiske on November 5, 1855, Emerson accepts an appointment for February 13, 1856, at Bath and notes that "Mr Butman invites me to Gardiner, on Tuesday"; Samuel H. Dale, Bangor, Me., asked on November 2, 1855, that Emerson lecture there on February 14. Emerson failed to arrive on February 14 "from detention of the cars beyond Portland" and was reannounced for the next evening (L, IV, 535).

[30] [Fri., Feb. 15]
Belfast ⟨?⟩   A T Wheelock

```
        50
        50
        90
      3.00
      2.⟨13⟩25
      1.50
       .50
    ⟨3⟩2.00
      4.00
      1.50
       .50
      2.25
        60
      ————
        00 16
```

[31] [Mon., Feb. 18] Berkshire
[Tues., Feb. 19] B
[Wed., Feb. 20] B

[32] [Thurs., Feb. 21] B

[33] [Mon., Feb. 25] W Newton ?   H Lambert 17
[Tues., Feb. 26] So Danvers

[34] [Wed., Feb. 27] Harvard ?
[Thurs., Feb. 28] N Bedford

[35] [blank]
[36] [Tues., March 4] Lincoln
[Wed., March 5] Cambridge
[Thurs., March 6] Exeter 18

16 The column of figures is in pencil.
17 The entries for February 25 are in pencil.
18 "Exeter" is in pencil.

[37] [blank]
[38] [Tues., March 11] Great Barrington   11½ o'clock[19]
[Wed., March 12] Lee

[39] [Thurs., March 13] Pittsfield
[Fri., March 14] N. Adams.

[40] [blank]
[41][20] [Thurs., March 20] D[artmouth] College

[42] [blank]
[43] "Si Dieu a fait l'homme a son image l'homme le lui a bien rendu"[21]

[44] [blank]
[45] [Wed., April 2] Wood burned in P M by freight train. Fr.
Wheeler & W Benjamin

   Smith

[46]–[74] [blank]
[75][22] [Mon., June 30]
     1.00   to Mrs Lewis
      .50   to Mrs Clark for Cream
     1.00   for Strawberries &
      .15   or 16 or 17 cts. for Mr ⟨Emerson[?]⟩Adams
                 Mrs Brooks for cake

[76]–[90] [blank]
[91] La quantite d'action necessaire pour produire un changement dans
le mouvement des corps est toujours un minimum.
Il entendait par quantité d'action le produit d'une masse par sa vitesse et

   [19] "11 ½ o'clock" is in pencil.
   [20] The entries on pp. [41], [43], and [45] are in pencil.
   [21] For this quotation, see Journal SO, p. [265], and Journal VO, p. [274]
above.
   [22] The entries on p. [75] are in pencil.

par l'espace qu'elle parcourt. See Principes de l'equilibre et du mouvement de Carnot. 2^d Edit p 163

Biog. Universelle.
ad verbum Maupertuis.[23]

[104] [Fri., Sept. 26] Mr. Lee says that 1000 copies of each series of Essays, were printed in February.

[105]–[112] [blank]
[113] [Thurs., Oct. 23] Marlboro

[114]–[119] [blank]
[120] [Wed., Nov. 12] Watertown   Jos. Crafts.
[Thurs., Nov. 13] So. Reading   J. Winship [24]

[121] [blank]
[122] [Mon., Nov. 17] Roxbury   John B[ackup]   West Newton
[Tues., Nov. 18] ⟨Roxbury   John Backup⟩ [25]   Social Circle
[Wed., Nov. 19] Danbury ?

[123] [Thurs., Nov. 20] New Haven   M T Brown [26]
[Fri., Nov. 21] Danbury ?

[124]–[126] [blank]
[127] [Tues., Dec. 2] ↑Roxbury↓   ⟨Taunton⟩   ⟨Taunton⟩ [27]

[128] [Sun., Dec. 7] ⟨Roxbury ?⟩Roxbury ? [28]

[129] [Tues., Dec. 9] ⟨Taunton ?⟩   Groton ?

[23] For this quotation, see Journal SO, p. [165] above.
[24] In a letter to Emerson on about October 1, 1856, John Winship, of South Reading, Mass.(?), says November 13, the evening Emerson has proposed, will be satisfactory (L, V, 38).
[25] "Roxbury John B" is struck through with three diagonal lines; "⟨Roxbury John Backup⟩" is struck through with two horizontal lines and one diagonal line. On November 3, 1856, H. Lambert of West Newton, Mass., asked for a lecture on November 17; Emerson answered that he would come then (L, V, 42). On September 4, 1856, John Backup of Roxbury, Mass., asked permission to list Emerson as a lecturer in the course at Roxbury beginning in November (L, V, 35).
[26] "New Haven   M T Brown" is in pencil.
[27] The first "Taunton" is in pencil canceled in ink.
[28] "Roxbury ?" in pencil is overwritten by the same in ink and the ink is wiped.

[Wed., Dec. 10] Lynn   Wm Howland [29]

[130] [Thurs., Dec. 11] ⟨Waltham ?⟩
[Fri., Dec. 12] Newb[ur]yp[or]t. ⟨?⟩

[131] [Mon., Dec. 15] Malden
[Tues., Dec. 16] ⟨9 or⟩ 16 [30]   Cambridgeport   Mr Livermore

[132] [Wed., Dec. 17] ⟨Waltham⟩ [31]   Whitinsville   H A Goodell
[Thurs., Dec. 18] Blackstone
[Fri., Dec. 19] Taunton ?

[133] [Mon., Dec. 22] New Bedford [32]

[134] [Tues., Dec. 23] ⟨Taunton ?⟩   Lincoln
[Wed., Dec. 24] Waltham [33]
[Thurs., Dec. 25] S. Danvers   B.C. Perkins

[135] [Fri., Dec. 26] ⟨Lynn   Wm Howland⟩   Wrentham [34]

[136] [Mon., Dec. 29] N. Bridgewater
[Tues., Dec. 30] Fitchburg   W.P. Tilden
[Wed., Dec. 31] Cambridge [35]

[137] Brooklyn	70	280
Clinton	15	100
Salem	50	87
Davenport	40	25
Rock Island	40	
Dixon	40	492
Freeport	40	LaSalle 20

[29] In a letter to William Howland on September 4, 1856, Emerson says that he will speak in Lynn on Friday, December 26 (*L*, V, 35).
[30] "9 or", in pencil, is canceled in ink.
[31] "Waltham" is canceled in pencil with four diagonal lines.
[32] "New Bedford" is in pencil.
[33] "Waltham" and the cancellation of "Taunton ?" are in pencil.
[34] "Wrentham" is in pencil.
[35] "Cambridge" is in pencil.

439

Galena	40
Belvidere	40
Elgin	
Beloit	40
Janesville	37
Waukesha	30
Galesburg	50
Peoria	50
Ann Arbor	25 [36]

1857   6 Jan. Concord N.H.
       13 Buffalo
       15 Rochester
       16 Syracuse

[138] Lit[erary]. Gaz[ette]. Sept. 1849

6 Concord
7
8 Paterson
9 Phila[delphia]

[139] Grote's History of Greece
       Mayne Reid's
          Island Home
          Desert Home
          Young Voyagers
          Boy Hunters
          Bush

[36] The entries to this point on p. [137] are in pencil, except the "40" after "Belvidere", "Elgin", "Beloit 40", "Janesville 37", and "Waukesha". "Elgin" is written after "Beloit", then square brackets are added in ink with an ink line indicating that 'Elgin" should precede "Beloit". This list of lecture payments, although not inclusive, spans the period from December 11, 1855 (Brooklyn, N.Y.) to January 19, 1856 (Ann Arbor, Mich.). Emerson lectured in La Salle, Ill., on January 2, 1856, between his engagements in Rock Island and Dixon, Ill. Emerson does not seem to have lectured in Elgin, Ill.

         Miss Bremer's
            Home
            Brothers & Sisters
      Lewes' Life of Goethe
            Talssa
            Tennyson
            Browning[37]

[140] March 18 Gloucester

[141] ——
         Muldar chemist 'no philosophy'
         ——
         2 ways. California not discov. by geologist ↑it was chance
         but not chaos.↓
         ——
         Superlative. abime sur abime Boy with thorn in the
         foot[38]
         ——

[142] [blank]
[143][39]   Henry Avery   Commercial St

[144]–[145] [blank]
[146]   1856   March 21, Weight lb 154½

[37] The entries on p. [139] are in pencil, except for "Grotes History of Greece" and "Talssa" in ink. Emerson withdrew volume 8 of George Grote's *History of Greece*, 12 vols. (London, 1846–1856) from the Boston Athenaeum March 15–June 18, 1859. The works of Thomas Mayne Reid (1818–83), author of popular adventure novels, included *The Desert Home, or the adventures of a lost family in the wilderness* (London, 1852), *The Young Voyageurs, or the Boy Hunters in the North* (London, 1854), *The Boy Hunters; or, Adventures in Search of a White Buffalo* (London, 1853), and *The Bush-boys; or, the Adventures of a Cape Farmer and his family in the wild Karoos of Southern Africa* (London, 1856). "Island Home" has not been identified. The works of Swedish novelist Fredrika Bremer (1801–1865) included *The Home; or, Family cares and family joys,* trans. Mary Howitt (New York, 1843), and *Brothers and Sisters; a tale of domestic life,* trans. Mary Howitt (New York, 1846). Emerson withdrew volume 2 of George Henry Lewes' *The Life and Works of Goethe,* 2 vols. (Boston, 1856) from the Boston Athenaeum April 25–May 14, 1870.
[38] For "Muldar . . . foot", see Journal SO, pp. [2]–[3] above.
[39] The entries on pp. [143], [146], [148], [149], and [153] are in pencil.

[147] [blank]

[148] The Eng[lish]. mind conditioned. I am aware of the vices of the poetic mind[:] it runs into luxury & an ideal pedantry as common-sense into stagnation. But a healthy greatness, must have both elements and there can be no real & puissant mind that does not [149] combine them. Aristotle, Plato, Bacon, Pascal, Goethe had both genius & good sense. And ⟨the height of⟩ⁿ both tendencies have run to their height in England[.]

[150]–[152] [blank]

[153]   Margaret Topp   116 Mt Pleasant   Liverpool

[154]–[157] [blank]

[158]   Concord Lyceum

    Dec. ⟨2⟩3

          10   E P Whipple

          17   G S Boutwell

          24   T. Parker

          31

    Jan.   7

          14   W. Phillips

          21

          28

    Feb.   7

      Aphorismen Aus Schellings Werke   1850 [40]

[159]   Agassiz
           Pierce

[40] "T. Parker" and "W. Phillips" are in pencil. "Aphorismen . . . 1850", in pencil, is upside down on the page and is separated from the other entries by a page-wide rule in pencil. The records of the Concord Lyceum show that E. P. Whipple lectured on "Courage" on December 11, 1856; G. S. Boutwell lectured on "Education" on December 17. F. D. Huntington lectured on "The Hand, the Head, the Heart" on December 26; Emerson lectured on "The Times, politics, preaching, bad boys, clean shirts &c &c" on January 2, 1857; Arthur Gilman lectured on "New England Wit & Humor" on January 8; Wendell Phillips lectured on "European Street Life" on January 14; Prof. Gajani lectured on "Dante" on January 29; and Dr. Joseph Reynolds lectured on the "Science of Agriculture" on February 4. For Parker's and Agassiz' lectures, see Pocket Diary 8, pp. [33], [39], and [178] below.

Longfellow
Ward
Whipple
Billings
Woodman
Hoare
Sanborn
Lowell
Alger
E[merson] [41]

[160] [42]	Joseph Barker		pd.
	x H D Thoreau	1.00	
	Wm F. Channing		
	S.K. Lothrop		
	Alfred Norton		
	Miss A Thaxter		
	J.A. Andrew		
	H.A. Page		
	R.W. Emerson	⟨100.⟩	pd.
	C.F. Hovey	10.00	
	Charles Morgan		
	Manning		
	H.W. Bellows		
	Sam[ue]l Johnson		

[161]–[162] [blank]

[163]	Fund	500.	
	T. Davis	100.	pd
	RWE	100.	
	HW Longfellow	50.	pd
	TS King	50.	pd
	Seth Cheney	50.	pd.
	H. Woodman	50.	

[41] This list is in pencil; the names of Agassiz, Billings, Hoare, and Lowell are ticked off in ink with a small diagonal mark.

[42] The entries on p. [160] are in pencil, except for "Wm F. Channing . . . R.W. Emerson" in ink.

J G Fisher
T. Parker
E.P. Whipple
R. E. Apthorp
A. Norton
F. Beck   20.   pd.
W R Alger.   20.   pd
S. G. Ward.
Wendell Phillips   50.   pd.
          Congden
⟨JF⟩C.C. Hovey.   10.   pd.[43]

[164][44]   ˣDavenport   ⟨La Salle⟩ I
            ˣRock Island   Peoria
            ˣDixon   Muscatine
            ˣFreeport   Iowa City
            ⟨Galena⟩   Galena   Lyons Ia
            ⟨Elgin⟩[45]   ⟨Elgin⟩Belvidere   Galesburg
            ⟨Bel⟨videre⟩oit⟩   Elgin   Mt Morris
            Beloit.   Wright   ⟨Waukesha⟩
               ↑Whitewater↓   Whitewater
            Janesville
            ⟨Whitewater⟩   M
            Waukesha

                                          Ann Arbor Mich
                                          Adrian Mich
                                          Sandusky O
                                          Yellow Springs O
                                          Columbus
                                          Cleveland
                                          Erie Pa

[43] "pd" after Longfellow and King, the "20.   pd" after F. Beck, the "⟨JF⟩"
before Hovey, and the "10.   pd." after Hovey are in pencil. A curved pencil line
under the lower "20.   pd" after Beck seems to indicate that the contribution is his
and not W.R. Alger's. The entries on pp. [160] and [163] relate to the Alcott Life-
Annuity Fund. See *L*, IV, 511–514, and V, 159–160.
[44] The entries on pp. [164]–[166] are in pencil.
[45] An s-shaped mark and "tr[anspose]." beside it indicate that "⟨Galena⟩",
listed first, should follow "⟨Elgin⟩".

[165]   W W Welch
             J R Mc Farland
             D F Wells
             J Van Valkensburg
             J J Mathews
             D H Blake   J H M Monagle
             E W Little
             G W Burchard
             H.J. Curtin

                                              Binghamton
                                              W Stuart

             ——
             J R Smith
             A K Spencer
             W S Kennedy

             ——
             Wilson Laird & others

[166] ⟨A Ally [?]⟩Geo. Sumner   ⟨⟨T⟩Care T. Murphy⟩22 Jan   74A
St. S. Boston
             Thomas Murphy
      Kate Francis   At Mrs Dill's   4 Belcher Lane
                                       Forthill, Boston

             1845
      Nov 29
             41 acres 52 rods
                  1239.56 [46]

[inside back cover] Miss D[elia]. S[alter]. Bacon, Care of Mrs Farrar,
17 Pembridge Place   Bayswater   London

[46] "1845 . . . 1239.56" is upside down.

445

Pocket Diary 8

1857

Pocket Diary 8 is devoted primarily to Emerson's lecture engagements for 1857. It also contains miscellaneous expenses, addresses, quotations, and memoranda. A few entries may have been made late in 1856 or early in 1858.

The notebook, bound in black stamped leather, is a commercially published diary entitled "POCKET DIARY / FOR / 1857; / FOR REGISTERING EVENTS OF / PAST OR PRESENT OCCURRENCE . . . ," published by Whittemore, Niles, and Hall, 114 Washington Street, Boston. The covers measure 7.4 x 12.4 cm. The back cover extends into a tongue that, when the book is closed, fits into a loop on the front cover; the back cover also contains an expandable pocket. A paper label fastened to the spine is inscribed "1857. x".

The light blue, unnumbered pages, whose edges are marbled, measure 7.2 x 12.1 cm; pages 13–172 are faintly lined. The book consists of a front flyleaf (i, ii); a title page (page 1); a list of Sundays (page 2); a calendar for 1857 (page 3); a table showing the number of days from any day in one month to the same day in another month (page 4); rates of postage (page 5); eclipses in 1857 (page 6); the moon's phases for 1857 (pages 7–12); daily appointments for 1857, three to a page (pages 13–134); pages for memoranda (pages 135–147); pages for cash accounts (pages 148–160); and blank pages for notes (pages 161–172).

Entries by Emerson occur on fifty-four pages. Printed matter in Pocket Diary 8 is reproduced here only in the section on daily appointments, in which dates are supplied where relevant. Otherwise, pages are designated as blank if they bear no inscription by Emerson; the presence or absence of printed matter is not specified.

[front cover verso] D.B. O'Bannon Esq   of   Jones & O'Bannon Attys. at Law   Keokuk. Ia.

Stallo
W H Channing
M Wilson

⟨C. Beecher⟩
D S Bacon

[i] [1] R.W. Emerson.
    Concord, Masstts

Feb	9	Chicopee
	10	Springf[iel]d
Feb	12	Littleton
	19	Bedford
	20	Salem
	26	Taunton [2]

Mr Wood   27 Dover St

[ii] [blank]
[1]–[13] [blank]
[14] [Mon., Jan. 5] Woburn.   J. M. Masters
[Tues., Jan. 6] Concord N H

[15] [Thurs., Jan. 8] Paterson N J
[Fri., Jan. 9] Philadelphia   W H Richardson, Jr.   376 Chestnut St [3]

[16] [4] Mary Eliza Summers
        24 years
    ↑child born↓

---

[1] "LT/21–", apparently a stationer's mark, is written in pencil in the upper right-hand corner of this page. The entries on p. [i] are in pencil, except for "R.W. Emerson. Concord, Masstts".

[2] This is a partial list of lecture engagements for January and February, 1858. The lectures in Littleton, Bedford, Salem, and Taunton, Mass., were in January, not February. See Pocket Diary 9, pp. [16]–[21] below.

[3] William H. Richardson wrote September 4, 1856, to say that Emerson's reply encouraged him to hope for a lecture before the People's Literary Institute (*L*, V, 33).

[4] The entries on p. [16] are in pencil, except for "MacLean . . . Welles" in ink; "Waterloo . . . Welles" is struck through with two diagonal lines in pencil.

447

Sick 8 June 1856
    died 1⟨5⟩6 June
affectionate   sincere   playful   good house keeper
churchwoman   born on the sea
[Mon., Jan. 12] ⟨MacLean   N.Y.⟩   ⟨Waterloo, Seneca Co   E.R.
Welles⟩

[17] [Tues., Jan. 13] Buffalo
[Thurs., Jan. 15] Rochester

[18] [Fri., Jan. 16] Syracuse

[19] [Mon., Jan. 19] Columbus ?   "Conduct of Life"
[Tues., Jan. 20] Columbus ?   "Poetry."

[20] [Thurs., Jan. 22] Chicago Y.M.A.   J H Thompson [5]
[Fri., Jan. 23] Waukegan   J L Clarke

[21] [Mon., Jan. 26] Lafayette   Indiana
[Tues., Jan. 27] Cincinnati   Telegraphed home at 10. P.M. [6]

[22] [Wed., Jan. 28] Sandusky.

                    at home, they rec'd my telegraph.
                    "Beauty"
[Thurs., Jan. 29] Cleveland [7]   J M Jones   "Conduct of Life"

[23] [Sat., Jan. 31] ⟨Cin⟩Cincinnati   Beauty
[Mon., Feb. 2] ↑Cincinnati↓   ⟨Cin⟩Poetry [8]

[5] John Howland Thompson, attorney and corresponding secretary for the
Young Men's Association, wrote to Emerson on September 16 and October 6, 1856,
to arrange this lecture (L, V, 22, 38).
    [6] "Lafayette   Indiana" is in pencil. "Cincinnati" is written in pencil and over-
written in ink. From Cincinnati Emerson telegraphed home for "the Amherst-
Williamstown Discourse, 'the Scholar' ", which he received on February 3 and read
on February 6 (see pp. [24]–[25] below and L, V, 60).
    [7] "Cleveland" is written in pencil and overwritten in ink.
    [8] "Cin" is in pencil both times on p. [23] and is canceled each time by being
overwritten in ink.

[24] [Tues., Feb. 3] ⟨Charlestown⟩   at 2 P.M. I received the Concio ad Clerum for which I sent to Concord last Tues.⁹
[Wed., Feb. 4] Cin[cinnati]   Works & Days
[Thurs., Feb. 5] ⟨Worcester⟩ ?   Yellow Springs

[25] [Fri., Feb. 6] Cin[cinnati]   Scholar ¹⁰

[26] Davis   100
     E[merson]   100
     L[ongfellow]   50
     P[hillips]   50
     K[ing]   50
     W[oodman]   50
     C[heney]   50
     ⟨B. & H.   50.⟩
[Tues., Feb. 10] ⟨Charlestown⟩
[Wed., Feb. 11] ⟨S⟩Salem ¹¹

[27] [Thurs., Feb. 12] Worcester ?   N.Y.   D.H. Olmstead ¹²
[Fri., Feb. 13] O.B. Frothingham

[28] [blank]
[29] [Wed., Feb. 18] Manchester, N H G.A. French   Works & Days
[Thurs., Feb. 19] ⟨Newport   F.A. Tenney, ↑37 Pelham   leave Boston at 11 A.M.↓⟩ ¹³

⁹ Emerson telegraphed to Concord for "A Plea for the Scholar," given Aug. 8, 1855, in Amherst, Mass. (*L*, V, 60, 62).
¹⁰ "Cin . . . Yellow Springs" on p. [24] and "Cin   Scholar" on p. [25] are in pencil.
¹¹ "B. & H. . . . Charlestown" is struck through with a diagonal line in pencil; "S", in pencil, is overwritten by "Salem" in ink. "Davis   100 . . . C   50" is another memorandum of the Alcott Life-Annuity Fund; see Pocket Diary 7, pp. [163] and [165] above.
¹² "Worcester ?" is in pencil. In a letter of December 11, 1856, to William Emerson, Emerson wrote that he was corresponding with a Mr. Olmstead in New York about an appointment "not yet fixed." Dwight H. Olmstead was listed as a lawyer in *Trow's New York City Directory* for the year ending May 1, 1857 (*L*, V, 46).
¹³ "Works & Days" is in pencil; "Newport . . . 11 A.M." is struck through with a diagonal line in pencil.

[30] [blank]
[31] [Tues., Feb. 24] Wrentham   ⟨N.Y.   D H Olmstead⟩
[Wed., Feb. 25] Phila ?   J. Edmonds.

[32] [Sat., Feb. 28] Club—   due to Woodman

[33] [Tues., March 3] Roxbury   J. Backup
[Wed., March 4]
————
——
     Parker at Concord [14]

[34] [Fri., March 6] Charlestown

[35] [Tues., March 10] ⟨Charlestown⟩

[36] [Thurs., March 12] Mrs Parkman

[37] [Mon., March 16] Brighton [15]

[38] [Tues., March 17] ⟨Gloucester ?⟩
[Wed., March 18] Gloucester
[Thurs., March 19] ⟨Worcester⟩

[39] [Fri., March 20] Mr Agassiz at Concord [16]

[40] [Mon., March 23] Mrs Copeland [17]
[Wed., March 25] Milton

[41] [Thurs., March 26] Worcester
[Fri., March 27] Newport ?
[Sat., March 28] Club—   due

[14] Theodore Parker lectured at the Concord Lyceum on March 4 on "America, its history, people, resources, capacities, & probable destiny."
[15] "Mrs Parkman" on p. [36] and "Brighton" on p. [37] are in pencil.
[16] On March 20, Agassiz lectured on "the different forms of Animal Life."
[17] "Mrs Copeland" is in pencil.

[42] [Tues., March 31] Nantucket

[43] [Wed., April 1] Nantucket
[Fri., April 3] Concord

[44] [Sat., April 4]
        Pierce
        Woodman
        Agassiz
        Lowell
        Prescott
        Motley
        Whipple
        Ward
        Dwight
        Dana
        Emerson [18]

[45] [Thurs., April 9] Teaparty

[46] [blank]
[47] [Wed., April 15] Concord [19]

[48]–[56] [blank]
[57] [20] [Wed., May 13] Charge Kate   2 yds flannel at 37½ pr yd
4 yds velvet rib. at 14 cts pr yd   2 yds brilliant at 12½ cts yd

---

Qu.   1.00

[58]–[59] [blank]
[60] [Fri., May 22]
        Poems Apr
        now just exhausted

[18] This list of the members of the Saturday Club is in pencil. "Hoar" and "Longfellow" are added in pencil in a hand not Emerson's. See Journal VO, p. [89] above.

[19] The records of the Concord Lyceum show that "R. W. Emerson gave a lecture, the proceeds of which is to make up the deficiency in the Treasury."

[20] The entries on pp. [57] and [60] are in pencil.

[61]	1855	Dec	500	Rep[resentative]. Men.
	1856	Dec 22	500	Miscellanies
	1856	Sept 30	1000	Essays Vol 1
			1000	Essays Vol 2
		Sept	500	Poems
		Dec 5	Seventh 1000	[English] Traits
	1857	Apr. 2	⟨3⟩500	"Poems"
		Eighth	1000	"Traits"
	1856,	Dec,	500	Rep[resentative]. Men
			250	Poems fine
			250	Mis[cellanies]. fine
			250	Essays I
			250	Essays II
			250	[English] Traits[21]

[62]–[66] [blank]
[67] [Fri., June 12] Paid Woodman
    old clubs   21.00
  and pd Parker   6.46
[Sat., June 13] Dined with G. Ripley & a company at Parker's[22]

[68]–[72] [blank]
[73] [Tues., June 30] Dined with club

[74] [Fri., July 3] B[oston] & P[rovidence].   Atl[antic Monthly].
P[hillips]. & S[ampson].   Field. Hovey. Bond. Keep[23]

[75]–[112] [blank]
[113] [Wed., Oct. 28] Watertown   J. Crafts
[Thurs., Oct. 29] Nantucket

[114]–[116] [blank]

[21] "1856, Dec . . . 250 Traits" is in pencil.
[22] The entries on p. [67] are in pencil; Emerson adds rules on either side of the printed "Saturday 13".
[23] "B & P. . . . Keep" is in pencil.

[117] [Tues., Nov. 10] Social Circle

[118] [Fri., Nov. 13] Winchendon ?

[119]–[123] [blank]
[124] [Tues., Dec. 1] Taunton ? [24]

[125] [blank]
[126] [Tues., Dec. 8] ⟨New Bedford.⟩ ⟨Cadwell⟩ [25]   Woburn

[127] [blank]
[128] [Mon., Dec. 14] Westminster

[129] [Tues., Dec. 15] Athol   D C O'Daniels
[Wed., Dec. 16] Amherst. ⟨?⟩   W.S. Dickinson
[Thurs., Dec. 17] New Haven

[130] [blank]
[131] [Tues., Dec. 22] New Bedford
[Wed., Dec. 23] Melrose [26]

[132] [Thurs., Dec. 24] Bartol
[Fri., Dec. 25] Newburyport

[133]–[157] [blank]
[158] Bad use of money at C. It does little good to the owners. I
saw the house of a poor bachelor who died alone of cholera being
worth a million. Mr O's coachman owns $30,000.[27]

[159]–[160] [blank]
[161]   Virginia Vaughan   No 8 Union Place   Hoboken   N.J.

[162]–[170] [blank]

[24] "Taunton ?" is in pencil.
[25] Emerson corresponded with William(?) Cadwell of New Bedford, Secretary
of the Lyceum, concerning his December 22 lecture and payment for it (L, V, 93–95).
[26] "Melrose" is in pencil.
[27] "Bad use . . . $30,000." is in pencil.

453

[171]   cigars [?]   glasses

———

P. Kaufmann, care of   Wright, Gillett, & Rawson   Commission Merchants,   No 1 Front St. N.Y.[28]

———

————

and

————

M.M. Caleb.   Agent of American Transportation Company. Pier No 7 Coenties Slip. New York.

[172]   Concord Lyceum

Jan 7	Mr Gilman
14	Mr W. Phillips
⟨21⟩23	T.S. King
28	⟨Agassiz⟩
Feb 4	
⟨11⟩13	Geo Sumner
18	
25	⟨Agassiz⟩ R.W.E.
March 4	T. Parker
13	D Foster
20	Agassiz [29]

[173] [blank]

[174] A Adams.   Dubuque

P.R. Paulding.   Tarrytown

P G Webster   Fort Plains

H A Rockafield   Lancaster Pa

C Wheaton   Po'keepsie

S G Paddock   Princeton, Ill

---

[28] "cigars" and "glasses", in pencil, are overwritten by "P. Kaufmann, care of" in ink. For Peter Kaufmann, see Journal VO, pp. [83]–[84] above, and L, V, 66–69, 73–74, and 77.

[29] See Pocket Diary 7, p. [160] above.

Andrew Howell.   Adrian, M.
Horace Rublee   Madison, W.
J L Clarke   Waukegan Ill
G T VanArsdale,   Kenosha, Wis.
H A Barnum   Syracuse
J M Jones   Cleveland

[inside back cover]
Gray Mem[oria] Tech[nica]

1858
Feb. 9 Tues. Taunton

Vacherot Hist Critique de l Ecole d Alexandrie Paris Libraire
Philosophique de Ladrange 1846 3 vols 8VO [30]

[30] The entries on the inside back cover are in pencil except for "1858 . . .
Taunton" in ink. For Grey's *Memoria Technica*, see Journal VO, p. [39] above.
For Vacherot, see Journal VO, front cover verso above.

Pocket Diary 9

1 8 5 8

Pocket Diary 9 is devoted primarily to recording Emerson's lecture engagements for 1858. It also contains miscellaneous expenses, addresses, quotations, and memoranda. A few entries may have been made late in 1857 or early in 1859.

The notebook, bound in black stamped leather, is a commercially published diary entitled "POCKET DIARY / FOR / 1858; / FOR REGISTERING EVENTS OF / PAST OR PRESENT OCCURRENCE . . . ," published by Denton and Wood, Cambridgeport, Mass. The covers measure 7.4 x 12.3 cm. The back cover extends into a tongue that, when the book is closed, fits into a loop on the front cover; the back cover also contains an expandable pocket. A paper label fastened to the spine is inscribed "1858   x".

The light blue, unnumbered pages, whose edges are marbled, measure 7.5 x 12.1 cm; pages 13–172 are faintly lined. The book consists of a front flyleaf (i, ii); a title page (page 1); a list of Sundays (page 2); a calendar for 1858 (page 3); a table showing the number of days from any day in one month to the same day in another month (page 4); rates of postage (page 5); eclipses in 1858 (page 6); the phases of the moon (pages 7–12); daily appointments for 1858, three to a page (pages 13–134); pages for memoranda (pages 135–147); pages for cash accounts (pages 148–160); and pages for bills payable (pages 161–172). The lower half of the leaf bearing pages 167–168 and the leaf bearing pages 173–174 are torn out.

Entries by Emerson occur on forty-three pages. Printed matter in Pocket Diary 9 is reproduced here only in the section on daily appointments, in which dates are supplied where relevant. Otherwise, pages are designated as blank if they bear no inscription by Emerson; the presence or absence of printed matter is not specified.

In the expandable pocket in the back cover are two tickets, each 4.3 x 1.5 cm, one pink and one green, on the East Boston Omnibus Line.

[front cover verso]   Urbino
                        Linnaeus
                        Compass
                        ⟨Mrs L[ucy]. C[otton]. B[rown].   Hauy⟩

4 5 6

Reynolds
Atlantic B[an]k
Warren
American H[ouse]
Channing

[i]   Baltimore
Brooklyn
Albany
Phila[delphia]
Ann Arbor
Providence
Bangor
Boston 28th Cong[regational] Ch[urch].
Cortland
Cleveland
Salem
⟨Cambridgeport⟩
Auburn
⟨Blackstone⟩
Hartford [1]

[ii]   Atl[antic]. B[an]k. 24–91
Chandler 1½ yd
Lowell letters.

———

Books

—

Cambridge Essays 1857
Geology by Wm Hopkins

Edw. Emerson married Rebecca Waldo
lies in Malden graveyard [2]

[1] "Cambridgeport" and "Blackstone" are canceled in pencil.
[2] Mary Moody Emerson wrote to Emerson in January or February, 1856, that her great-grandfather was "Edward Emerson, Esq. of Newburyport, who lies buried in Malden. His wife lies beside him, or did" (L, V, 99). "Atl. . . . graveyard" is in pencil.

[1]–[12] [blank]
[13] Oct 7 to Dec 14
        9 w.   3 d
        MME pays   37.⟨4⟩71
        RWE pays   9.42
                       ―――――
                       47.13 [3]

[14] [4] Mr R whipped P. Robinson for she was his blood relation &
Mrs R whipped Daniel Farnham for he was hers. The Dr R,
(M M E remembers) used to wake up the boy by slapping [15] for
the back of the body, he said, was made to whip. [5]

[16] [Tues., Jan. 12] Littleton

[17]–[18] [blank]
[19] [Tues., Jan. 19] Bedford
[Wed., Jan. 20] Salem

[20] [blank]
[21] [Tues., Jan. 26] Taunton [6]

[22] [blank]
[23] [Tues., Feb. 2] ⟨Phil ?⟩Philadelphia

[24] [Fri., Feb. 5] Phil ? [7]

[25] [blank]
[26] [Tues., Feb. 9] ⟨Taunton⟩   Chicopee [8]
[Wed., Feb. 10] Springfield

---

[3] "MME . . . 47.13" is in pencil. Mary Moody Emerson had refused to pay
more than $3 a week to her Concord landlady. "Emerson and Elizabeth Hoar, seeing
that $5 was not too much for such a boarder, paid the difference themselves" (L,
399). See p. [169] below.
  [4] The entries on pp. [14]–[16] are in pencil.
  [5] Daniel Farnham was Emerson's cousin (L, I, 91–92).
  [6] "Taunton" is in pencil.
  [7] On p. [23] "Phil ?" in pencil is overwritten by "Philadelphia" in ink.
"Phil ?" on p. [24] is in pencil.
  [8] "Taunton" is struck through in pencil with two diagonal lines.

[27] [Fri., Feb. 12] Phil ? [9]

[28]–[32] [blank]
[33] [Wed., March 3] Freeman Chapel.   Country Life.

[34] [blank]
[35] [Wed., March 10] Freeman Chapel   Works & Days

[36]–[37] [blank]
[38] [Wed., March 17] Freeman Chapel   Powers of the Mind

[39] [blank]
[40] [Wed., March 24] Freeman Chapel   Lecture on Nat Method of Mental Phil.

[41] [blank]
[42] [Wed., March 31] Freeman Chapel   "Memory."

[43]–[44] [blank]
[45] [Wed., April 7] Freeman Chapel   Self-possession

[46]–[47] [blank]
[48] [Fri., April 16] Worcester

[49] [Tues., April 20] Lynn

[50]–[51] [blank]
[52] [Wed., April 28] Lynn   4½ P.M.   Mr Wright,   3 P.M.

[53] [blank]
[54] [Tues., May 4] Jamaica Plains

[55]–[107] [blank]

[9] "Phil ?" is in pencil.

459

[108] [Thurs., Oct. 14]
⟨Bangor

—

Mrs Appleton

—

Sec[retar]y Mrs. G. W Ingersoll⟩ [10]

[109]–[112] [blank]
[113] [Thurs., Oct. 28] Bangor

[114] [blank]
[115] [11] [Thurs., Nov. 4] Salem

[116] [blank]
[117] [Tues., Nov. 9] Salem
[Thurs., Nov. 11] Salem

[118] [blank]
[119] [Tues., Nov. 16] Salem
[Wed., Nov. 17] Peterboro

[120] [Thurs., Nov. 18] ⟨Cambridgeport ?   J W Cotton⟩   Salem [12]
[Fri., Nov. 19] Billerica

[121]–[123] [blank]
[124] [Thurs., Dec. 2] ⟨Peterboro   ?⟩ [13]

[125] [blank]
[126] [Mon., Dec. 6] Lynn
[Tues., Dec. 7] Boston Fraternity

[127] [blank]

[10] "Bangor . . . Ingersoll" is struck through in ink with a diagonal mark.
[11] The entries on pp. [115], [117], and [119] are in pencil.
[12] "Cambridgeport . . . Salem" is in pencil; "Cambridgeport . . . J W Cotton" is struck through in pencil with a diagonal line.
[13] "Peterboro   ?" is in pencil.

[128] [14] [Mon., Dec. 13] Mr King   3½
[Tues., Dec. 14] Hartford

[129] [Wed., Dec. 15] Brooklyn
[Thurs., Dec. 16] Phila ⟨?⟩

[130] [blank]
[131] [Thurs., Dec. 23] Hamilton

[132] [blank]
[133] [Tues., Dec. 28] ⟨Lynn⟩   Auburndale ?
[Wed., Dec. 29] Salem

[134] [Thurs., Dec. 30] East Boston

[135]   Ask Dr Jackson — of sulphur, and limestone, whence it
comes to coral?   and Hauy.[15]

[136] [16] Jan.   1   Saturday
                   2   S
                   3   M
                   4   Tu   Baltimore
                   5   W
                   6   Th
                   7   Fri
                   8   Sat
                   9   Sun
                  10   Mon

[14] The entries on pp. [128], [129], and [131] are in pencil.
[15] For Emerson's query to Dr. Jackson, see Journal VO, p. [252] above. For
Haüy, see Journal VO, p. [209] above.
[16] Pp. [136] and [137] list Emerson's tentative lecture schedule for January
and February, 1859. On p. [136], "Brooklyn", "Port Byron", and "Brighton" are
in pencil. "Auburn" and the two "Cortland" entries are written in pencil and overwritten in ink. A curved line in pencil with a penciled quotation mark to the right
of it links "Auburn" and "Batavia ?". A slanting ink line connects "27 Th" to
"So Danvers" on the line below. On p. [137], "Hartford" is canceled in pencil
and the "Lynn" after it is in pencil; "Brooklyn Bovee" is canceled in pencil;
"Salem", in pencil, is canceled in pencil.

11	Tu. —	Brooklyn			
12	Wed				
13	Th —	Albany			
14	Fri	Auburn			
15	Sat	Cortland			
16	Sun	Cortland			
17	M	Port Byron			
18	Tu	Batavia ?			
19	W				
20	Th	Cleveland ⟨?⟩			
21	Fr	Ann Arbor			
22	Sat				
23	Sun				
24	M				
25	Tu	Taunton	Burns		
26	W	Providence			
27	Th	⟨Blackstone⟩	⟨Natick⟩		
28	Fr		So Danvers		
29	Sat				
30	Sun				
31	Mon	Brighton			

[137] Feb.

1	Tues.	⟨Hartford⟩ Lynn	
2	W	⟨Brooklyn Bovee⟩ ↑Grafton↓	
3	Th	Lancaster	
4	Fr		
5	Sat		
6	S		
7	Mon		
8	Tu	Lynn	
9	W		
10	Th		
11	Fr		
12	Sat		
13	S.		
14	Mon		
15	Tu	Cambridgeport	

462

16	Wed	
17	Th	
18	Fr	
19	Sat	
20	S	⟨Salem⟩
21	M.	
22	Tu	
23	W	
24	Th	Bangor ?
25	Fr	
26	Sat	
27	S	
28	M	

[138]–[168] [17] [blank]
[169] [18] In the country sleep is better cheaper & more of it

    ⟨2⟩7 Oct.

        pd Mrs Wright for boa[r]d of M M E

                5 weeks   25.

        pd M M E   2.

[170] [blank]
[171]   J. Howland
        Eliz Howland married J Chipman
   Lydia [?] C mar John Sargent
       Sargent m Jos. Warn
   Hannah↑?↓ Wm Phineas Upham
   Hannah Upham
     J H

[172] 2 Mad River & Lake Erie Bonds dated 1 Feb. 1851, & fall due
1 Feb 1866 and are of a series of one thousand of like tenor & date[.]

[17] The lower half of the leaf bearing pp. [167] and [168] is torn away.
[18] The entries on pp. [169] and [171] are in pencil. For "⟨2⟩7 Oct . . . pd
MME   2.", see p. [13] above.

7 Union Building
46 State St [19]

[173]–[174] [leaf torn out]
[inside back cover] J S Babcock   93 Revere St [20]

Horticulturist Vol 1 p 226 [21]   restoring cracked pears

[19] The final figure in "1851," is heavily blotted; "7 Union . . . St" is in pencil. Emerson wrote to his financial adviser, Abel Adams, on January 18, 1858, saying "I am sorry that the Mad River Road will not pay", and on February 24, 1858, he asks Adams for an exact description of the bonds. Adams' reply, February 25, 1858, stated that Emerson's Mad River & Lake Erie bonds were dated February 1, 1851, were due February 1, 1866, and belonged to a series of one thousand (*L*, V, 96, 100).

[20] "J S Babcock . . . St" is in pencil.

[21] Emerson owned volumes 1 and 2 (1846–1847 and 1847–1848) of *The Horticulturist, and journal of rural art and rural taste*, ed. A. J. Downing.

Pocket Diary *II*

1 8 5 9

Pocket Diary 11 is devoted primarily to recording Emerson's lecture engagements for 1859. It also contains miscellaneous expenses, addresses, quotations, and memoranda. A few entries may have been made late in 1858 or early in 1860.

The notebook, bound in black stamped leather, is a commercially published diary entitled "POCKET DIARY / FOR / 1859. / FOR REGISTERING EVENTS OF / PAST OR PRESENT OCCURRENCE . . . / NEW YORK: / PUBLISHED ANNUALLY / FOR THE TRADE." The covers measure 7.5 x 12.4 cm. The back cover extends into a tongue that, when the book is closed, fits into a loop on the front cover; the back cover also contains an expandable pocket. A paper label fastened to the spine is inscribed "1859. 1860. x".

The off-white, unnumbered pages measure 7.5 x 12.1 cm; pages 13–172 are faintly lined. The book consists of a front flyleaf (i, ii); a title page (page 1); a table showing the number of days from any day in one month to the same day in another month (page 2); a list of Sundays (page 3); a calendar for 1859 (page 4); rates of postage (page 5); eclipses in 1859 (page 6); the phases of the moon (pages 7–12); daily appointments for 1859, three to a page (pages 13–134); pages for memoranda (pages 135–147); pages for cash accounts (pages 148–160); and pages for bills payable (pages 161–172).

Entries by Emerson occur on forty-seven pages. Printed matter in Pocket Diary 11 is reproduced here only in the section on daily appointments, in which dates are supplied where relevant. Otherwise, pages are designated as blank if they bear no inscription by Emerson; the presence or absence of printed matter is not specified.

Laid in between pages 26 and 27 is a sheet of white paper 12.8 x 6.2 cm bearing an inscription in ink; the editors have numbered it pp. [26a] and [26b].

[front cover verso] [blank]

[i]   Mirabeau Letters
           p 218 [1]

---

[1] "Mirabeau . . . p 218" is in pencil. Cf. *JMN*, XIII, 221, where Emerson, in an 1853 entry, refers to "Clubs Mirabeau's Letters Vol 1 p 218". His reference is to *Mirabeau's Letters during his Residence in England (with notes on his life, writings and character)*, 2 vols. (London, 1832).

[ii]–[13]² [blank]
[14] [Tues., Jan. 4] Baltimore   G A Pope³

[15] [blank]
[16] [Mon., Jan. 10] Mr King⁴
[Tues., Jan 11] Brooklyn   M[ercantile] L[ibrary]

[17] [Thurs., Jan. 13] Albany
[Fri., Jan. 14] Auburn
[Sat., Jan. 15] Cortland

[18] [Mon., Jan. 17] ⟨P & B⟩
[Tues., Jan. 18] Batavia

[19] [Thurs., Jan. 20] Cleveland
[Fri., Jan. 21] Ann Arbor

[20] [Mon., Jan. 24] Taunton

[21] [Tues., Jan. 25] Burns Club
[Wed., Jan. 26] Providence
[Thurs., Jan. 27] So. Danvers   King⁵

[22] [blank]
[23] [Mon., Jan. 31] Brighton   King
[Tues., Feb. 1] ⟨Lynn⟩⁶
[Wed., Feb. 2] Grafton

[24] [Thurs., Feb. 3] Lancaster ?   ⟨Auburndale ?⟩Auburndale⁷
King   3 p m

[25] [Tues., Feb. 8] ⟨Lynn⟩

² "38", in pencil on pp. [ii] and [3], may be a stationer's mark.
³ "G A Pope" is in pencil.
⁴ "Mr King" is in pencil.
⁵ "King" is in pencil.
⁶ "King" is in pencil; "Lynn" is struck through in ink with a diagonal mark.
⁷ "Auburndale ?" in pencil is overwritten by "Auburndale" in ink.

[26] [Wed., Feb. 9] Concord [8]
[Thurs., Feb. 10] Phil[adelphia]   ?   F C Herbrager

[26$_a$]   April [8a]
          Art. 1 Hazewell
                2. Underwood
                3. Burleigh
                4. Ruffini
                5. Mrs Hopkinson
                6. Dr G. Ellis
                7   T.B. Read
                8   W W Story
                9   T W Higginson
               10   A Browne
               11   J.W. Deforest

[26$_b$]   Some   adjective
                     not adverb

[27] [blank]
[28] [Tues., Feb. 15] Cambridgeport   Mr King [9]

[29] Some   adjective
               not adverb

[30] [Tues., Feb. 22]
               King
               Lowell Club   5.

[31] [Thurs., Feb. 24] Bangor ?
[Sat., Feb. 26] Club
               J.I. Wyer — S. Groton.   Dr C[harles]. T. J[ackson]. [10]
               J[ames]. E[lliot]. C[abot].

[8] "Concord" is in pencil. The records of the Concord Lyceum show that Emerson
lectured on "the Law of Success."
    [8a] The following list names the contributors to *The Atlantic Monthly* for April,
1859.
    [9] "Mr King" is in pencil.

[32] [Sun., Feb. 27] 28th Cong[regational].[11]
[Mon., Feb. 28] King
[Tues., March 1] ⟨Lynn⟩

[33]–[34] [blank]
[35] [Tues., March 8] Lynn

[36]–[41] [blank]
[42] [Tues., March 29] Lynn

[43]–[52] [blank]
[53] [Sun., May 1] Music Hall

[54]–[56] [blank]
[57] [Sun., May 15] Natick

[58] [12] [Wed., May 18] 10 A.M.   Oriental Society   Amer. Academy

[59] [blank]
[60] [Sun., May 22] Music Hall

[61]–[63] [blank]
[64] [Fri., June 3] pd Reuben Hoar   67.11
                    pd N B Robbins   2⟨1⟩3. ⟨50⟩66
                    pd. O.F. Seavy   21.50
                                            ───────
                                            112.27
[Sat., June 4]
              pd carriage at Littleton   .65
              Fare to & from Littleton   .70
              pd. for Turkey   2.08 [13]

[10] In a letter to James I. Wyer on March 18, 1859, Emerson wrote "When I saw you on the Fitchburg train, I promised to send you any information I might procure respecting the 'Scientific School.'" He adds information on the fees for a chemistry course at Harvard and says that he "inquired of Dr C T Jackson, what he tho't would be the value of a Chemical Course to your son" (L, V, 136).

[11] Emerson spoke to the Fraternity of the Twenty-eighth Congregational Church, or Parker Fraternity, on February 27, 1856.

[12] The entries on pp. [58], [60], and [64] are in pencil.

[13] Emerson's feeble-minded brother, Robert Bulkeley Emerson, died May 27,

[65]–[117] [blank]
[118] [Sun., Nov. 13] Music Hall

[119] [Tues., Nov. 15] Newton
[Thurs., Nov. 17] E. Abingdon

[120] [blank]
[121] [Tues., Nov. 22] Social Circle

[122] [Thurs., Nov. 24] Thanksgiving

[123] [Tues., Nov. 29] Bedford

[124]–[125] [blank]
[126] [Tues., Dec. 6] Lynn
[Wed., Dec. 7] Danbury
[Thurs., Dec. 8] Greenfield

[127] [blank]
[128] [Mon., Dec. 12] Malden

[129]–[130] [blank]
[131] [Wed., Dec. 21] Concord [14]

[132] [blank]
[133] [Wed., Dec. 28] Norwich

[134] [blank]
[135] [15]   1860
⟨S.⟩ Jan   1
2

1859. Emerson wrote his brother William on June 8, 1859, that he "went on Friday to Littleton, & settled his affairs there." Bulkeley had boarded with Mr. and Mrs. Reuben Hoar (L, V, 148–152).

[14] The records of the Concord Lyceum show that Emerson spoke on "Manners."

[15] The entries on pp. [135]–[138] are Emerson's tentative lecture schedule for January and February, 1860. He does not seem to have spoken in Sherburne, N.Y., Norwich, N.Y., Richmond, Ind., or Cambridgeport, Mass.

3
4
5
6
7
8
9
10
11
12
13
14
15
16
17 Poughkeepsie
18 Hamilton

[136]   1860
     Jan 19 Sherburne
          20 Norwich
          21
          22
          23 Lima
          24 Buffalo
          25 Batavia
          26 Rochester
          27 Toronto
          28
          29
          30 Toledo
          31 Zanesville
           1 Yellow Springs
           2 Cincinnati
           3 Richmond
           4 Lafayette
           5

[137]   1860
               Feb   6
                      7
                      8
                      9
                     10
                     11
                     12
                     13
                     14
                     15
                     16
                     17
                     18
                     19
                     20
                     21 Cambridgep[or]t.
                     22

[138]   1860
               Feb 23
                     24
                     25
                     26
                     27
                     28 New Bedford

[139] [blank]
[140]   Dec   5
               pd S[amuel]. G[ray]. Ward
               for Edmund Hosmer
               for invest[men]t   206.50
               pd S[amuel]. G[ray]. W[ard] for 3 [?] £   15.
               Charge E. Hosmer   6.50
               Charge Alice MacGuire   5.00
               pd. Dr Peabody   ·37
          Pd Knott for Edith   3.50

[141] For Dec 25
      Conversation
      Character
      Criticism
      Immortality
            See *CL* 175 p.[16]

[142]–[166] [blank]
[167]   Feb   paid let. Sh in   State Prison

      Harrison Ritchie, 30 Court St.
      Sam[ue]l El⟨l⟩iot. Hartford
      J. Quincy, Jr.

[168]–[169] [blank]
[170] Corn — eastern valley of Rocky Mts.[17]

[171]–[172] [blank]
[173][18]   Rockford   6   Feb
             Madison   7
             Milwaukie   8
             Chicago   9
             Racine   10
             Kenosha   11
             Niles   13
             Kala[mazoo]   14
             G[rand] Rapids   15

---

[16] "For Dec 25" is set off by a curved line at bottom and right. Journal CL, p. [175] above, bears words and phrases used in "Immortality," *W*, VIII, 323–352. Emerson spoke at the Dowse Institute, Cambridgeport, Mass., on December 25.

[17] "Corn . . . Mts." is in pencil.

[18] The entries on pp. [173] and [174] are upside down; the entries on p. [174] and the inside back cover are in pencil. The entries on p. [173] are Emerson's tentative lecture schedule for February, 1860. He spoke in Rockford, Ill. on February 7, in Madison, Wis., on February 8, in Milwaukee, Wis., on February 9, in Racine, Wis., on February 10, in Kenosha, Wis., on February 11, in Niles, Mich., on February 13, in Kalamazoo, Mich., on February 14, in Grand Rapids, Mich., on February 15, in Marshall, Mich., on February 16, and in Ann Arbor, Mich., on February 17. See Pocket Diary 12, pp. [25]–[27] below.

Marshall   16
Ann Arbor   17

[174]   1 Dr ⟨William⟩ Cheever [19]
          2 L Hale
          3 Fullerton (sitting by the dead)
          4
          5
          6 Mayers   [Birthmark]
             Mrs Howe
             Brown
↑Inscrip↓   Dr Parsons

             Dawson Shanley

[inside back cover]
        Rahel
        Westminster [*Review*]   Vol 32   1839   p 60
        ————

        For[*eign*]. Quar[*terly*]. Rev[*iew*]   1841   Vol 27 p 57
        Apr 1841 [20]

[19] In a letter of May 23, 1859, Emerson wrote to his brother William that he "saw in town Dr Cheever by chance"; this was probably David W. Cheever, apparently a nephew of Susan Haven Emerson (*L*, **V**, 146).

[20] Karl August Varnhagen von Ense's *Rahel*, 3 vols. (Berlin, 1834), and *Galerie von Bildnissen aus Rahel's Umgang und Briefwechsel* . . . , 2 vols. (Leipzig, 1836) were reviewed in the *Westminster Review*, XXXII, 32–44, and the *Foreign Quarterly Review*, XXVII, 57–74.

Pocket Diary 12

1860

Pocket Diary 12 is devoted primarily to recording Emerson's lecture engagements for 1860. It also contains miscellaneous expenses, addresses, quotations, and memoranda. A few entries may have been made late in 1859 or early in 1861.

The notebook, bound in black stamped leather, is a commercially published diary entitled "POCKET DIARY / FOR / 1860. / FOR REGISTERING EVENTS OF / PAST OR PRESENT OCCURRENCE . . . ," published by Brown, Taggard & Chase, Boston. The covers measure 7.5 x 12.5 cm. The back cover extends into a tongue that, when the book is closed, fits into a loop on the front cover; the back cover also contains an expandable pocket. A paper label fastened to the spine is inscribed "1860. x".

The white, unnumbered pages, whose edges are marbled, measure 7.3 x 12.1 cm; pages 13–171 are faintly lined. The book consists of a front flyleaf (i, ii); a title page (page 1); a calendar for 1860 (page 2); advertisements for music books (page 3) and other assorted books (page 4) published by Brown, Taggard & Chase; rates of postage (page 5); eclipses in 1860 (page 6); the phases of the moon (pages 7–12); daily appointments for 1860, three to a page (pages 13–132); pages for memoranda (pages 133–145); pages for cash accounts (pages 146–158); and pages for bills payable (pages 159–170). The leaf bearing pages 151–152 is torn out.

Entries by Emerson occur on forty-three pages. Printed matter in Pocket Diary 12 is reproduced here only in the section on daily appointments, in which dates are supplied where relevant. Otherwise, pages are designated as blank if they bear no inscription by Emerson; the presence or absence of printed matter is not specified.

Laid in between pages 32 and 33 is a sheet of white paper 12.5 x 20.2 cm bearing a pencil inscription; the editors have numbered it pp. [32a]–[32b].

[front cover verso] [blank]
[i] [1]   Send books to
                    President Hill

[1] "17h/30", apparently a stationer's mark, is written in pencil in the upper right-hand corner of this page. The entries on p. [i] are in pencil.

Mr Bryan
Mr Wiman
Mme D'Agout
C.G. Leland

[ii] [blank]
[1]–[13] [blank]
[14] [Wed., Jan. 4] Waltham
[Fri., Jan. 6] Salem   Brown R[elief] Meeting [2]

[15] [Sat., Jan. 7] Dr Keep   J R Manley [3]

[16] [Wed., Jan. 11] Salem

[17] [blank]
[18] [Tues., Jan. 17] Poughkeepsie
[Wed., Jan. 18] ⟨Hamilton⟩   Saratoga

[19] [Thurs., Jan. 19] Hamilton   Madison Co
[Fri., Jan. 20] Pt Byron ? [4]   ⟨Hamilton C.W.⟩

[20] [Sun., Jan. 22] Rochester   ⟨S B Anthony⟩Eagle Hotel [5]   Wor-
ship
[Mon., Jan. 23] Lima   W H Webster   Manners
[Tues., Jan. 24] Buffalo   Manners

[21] [Wed., Jan. 25] Batavia   Manners
[Thurs., Jan. 26] Rochester   G. H Humphry   Manners   C
[Fri., Jan. 27] Toronto   Manners

———

[2] "Salem . . . Meeting" is in pencil. For Emerson's "John Brown: Speech at
Salem, January 6, 1860," see W, XI, 277–281.
[3] "Dr . . . Manley" is in pencil. J. R. Manley wrote Emerson June 7, 1860,
about Emerson's remarks at Music Hall ceremonies honoring Theodore Parker
(L, V, 220). See W, XI, 285–293.
[4] "Pt Byron ?" is in pencil.
[5] "Rochester", in pencil, is overwritten by the same in ink; "S B Anthony",
in pencil, is overwritten by "Eagle Hotel" in ink to cancel.

[22] [Sun., Jan. 29] ⟨Rochester   Susan B Anthony⟩ 6
[Mon., Jan. 30] Toledo   J.W. Fuller   Manners

[23] [Tues., Jan. 31] ⟨Zanesville   B F Hersh⟩ 7
[Wed., Feb. 1] Yellow Springs   Manners
[Thurs., Feb. 2] Cincinnati   Theo. Cook.   Mr. T. Williamson
⟨Success⟩   Manners

[24] [Fri., Feb. 3] ⟨Richmond   ⟨Lafayette⟩, Ind.   J.S. Hadley.⟩
Cincinnati. "Success"
[Sat., Feb. 4] Lafayette, Ind   David Spencer   "Conduct of Life"
[Sun., Feb. 5] Lahr House 8

[25] [Mon., Feb. 6] Chicago   Manners   P L Sherman   E S
Wells   Wiley   Thompson
[Tues., Feb. 7] Rockford   "Manners"   Melanchthon Smith
[Wed., Feb. 8] Madison   S G Benedict   "Manners"   Rublee 9

[26]   Milwaukee
              Racine
              Kenosha
              Niles
              Kalamazoo
              G[rand] Rapids
              Marshall

6 "Rochester   Susan B Anthony", in pencil, is struck through in pencil with
nine diagonal zigzag lines.
7 "Zanesville . . . Hersh" is struck through in pencil with thirteen diagonal
zigzag lines.
8 "Richmond . . . Hadley." is struck through in ink with two diagonal marks
and in pencil with one diagonal mark. "Lahr House" is in pencil.
9 "Wiley", "Thompson", and "Rublee" are in pencil. Emerson corresponded
with Penoyer L. Sherman, a lawyer, and Edwin S. Wells, proprietor of Metropolitan
Hall, concerning his February 6 lecture. In a letter of February 10, 1860, Emerson
writes Ellen "Saw Mr Wiley at Chicago Mr Thoreau's friend who attended me like
a friendly shadow." Emerson apparently wrote Benjamin B. Wiley about speaking
in Racine, Wis., on February 10. Emerson corresponded with Stephen G. Benedict
of Madison, Wis., about his lecture at Madison on February 10 (L, V, 180–183,
196–197).

Ann Arbor
Detroit

J MacAlister
[Thurs., Feb. 9] ⟨Racine⟩ Milwaukie   ⟨W H Baker⟩   "Success"
Caverno   Chapman   Staples
[Fri., Feb. 10] ⟨Milwaukie⟩   Racine   ⟨Jas. Mac Alister⟩   W.H.
Baker.   M M Strong
[Sat., Feb. 11] Kenosha   J.B. Wheeler   Manners [10]

[27] [Mon., Feb. 13] Niles.   F Quinn   Manners   Mr Glenn
[Tues., Feb. 14] Kalamazoo.   ↑Dr↓ Foster Pratt   Holden   Manners   Anderson   Dr & Mrs Stone   Olney [11]

[28] [Wed., Feb. 15] Grand Rapids   H. Gaylord   Manners / Babcock
[Thurs., Feb. 16] Marshall,   Mr Brown   J.B. Greenough   Conduct of Life [12]
[Fri., Feb. 17] Ann Arbor   C A Thompson   Manners

[29] [Sat., Feb. 18] Detroit   S D Elwood   ⟨M⟩"Manners" [13]

[30] [Tues., Feb. 21] ⟨Cambridgeport   W W Wellington⟩   Zanesville, ⟨R⟩B. F. Hersh   Manners—

[10] "Milwaukee . . . Detroit", the original entry on p. [26], extends through
the spaces for February 9 and 10. "J MacAlister . . . Strong" is written over it.
"W H Baker" is canceled in pencil. "Caverno . . . Staples" and "M M Strong"
are in pencil. "Milwaukee . . . Detroit" is a list of Emerson's lecture engagements
for February 9–18, 1860. Emerson corresponded with the Reverend Carlton Albert
Staples, pastor of the Unitarian church in Milwaukee, about lectures there in 1865
(L, V, 397–399). Marshall M. Strong corresponded with Emerson in August, 1856,
on Oriental readings and sought to interest Emerson in his studies in the philosophy
of crime; Strong met Emerson in Madison, Wis., on February 10 and accompanied
him to Racine, Kenosha, and Chicago (L, V, 27, 197–198).
    [11] "Manners   Mr Glenn" under February 13 is in pencil; the inserted "Dr"
and "Holden . . . Olney" are in pencil. Two diagonal marks in pencil after
"Stone" may be intended to set it off from "Olney". Rusk, L, V, 199, says the five
people were doubtless L. E. Holden, Edward Anderson, Edward Olney, and J.A.B.
Stone and his wife, all members of the faculty of Kalamazoo College.
    [12] "Manners / Babcock", ",   Mr Brown", and "Conduct of Life" are in pencil.
    [13] The penciled "M" is overwritten by " 'Manners' " in ink.

[Wed., Feb. 22] Zanesville   Conduct of Life [14]

[31] [Sun., Feb. 26] Music H[all].   ?

[32] [Tues., Feb. 28] New Bedford.   Z S Durfee   W.A. Wall [15]

[32a]   Urbino
               Paulina
               Bond
               Peabody
               Ward
               Mitchell
               Keep
               Knife [16]

[32b] [blank]
[33]–[37] [blank]
[38] [Sun., March 18] Music Hall, Boston   "Moral Sentiment"
on   basis of Sermon on Wonder

[39] [blank]
[40] [Thurs., March 22] ⟨Concord Lyceum   "Clubs"⟩ [17]   ↑Christian
Union   New York   "Manners."↓

[41]–[44] [blank]
[45] [Fri., April 6] Mrs J.I Wyer   S. Groton

[46]–[118] [blank]
[119] [Tues., Nov. 20] Fraternity Lecture   Boston

[120] [Sat., Nov. 24] Club

[14] "Cambridgeport . . . Wellington" is struck through in ink with three
diagonal marks; "Zanesville . . . Life" (February 22) is in pencil.
[15] William A. Wall of New Bedford, whom Emerson had known for many
years, painted the copy of "The Three Fates" still hanging in the reconstructed
Emerson library at the Antiquarian House in Concord (L, VI, 322).
[16] "Urbino . . . Knife" is in pencil.
[17] The records of the Concord Lyceum show that Emerson lectured on "Conversation and Clubs" on March 14, 1860.

[121] [Tues., Nov. 27] ⟨*L̄ynn*⟩   ↑Teachers' Convention Concord↓
Lynn
[Wed., Nov. 28] Concord Lyceum

[122] [Thurs., Nov. 29] Thanksgiving

[123] [Sun., Dec. 2] Music Hall

[124] [Wed., Dec. 5] Roxbury —   J. Backup   "Clubs"
[Thurs., Dec. 6] Chelsea   Mr J.F. Pickering   "Clubs"

[125] [blank]
[126] [Tues., Dec. 11] ⟨Fraternity Lecture   Music Hall⟩ [18]   ⟨Lynn⟩
   Concord N.H.   "Clubs"
[Wed., Dec. 12] Bedford   "Clubs"
[Thurs., Dec. 13] Andover

[127] [Fri., Dec. 14] Beeson [19]

[128] [Tues., Dec. 18] Dowse Institute   Cambridgeport
[Wed., Dec. 19] Salem   H.J. Cross [20]

[129] [Sat., Dec. 22] Class

[130] [Tues., Dec. 25] Dowse Institute

[131] [Wed., Dec. 26] Nashua
[Fri., Dec. 28] Andover   ?

[132]–[139] [blank]
[140] Geo L Brown. [21]

[141]–[142] [blank]

[18] "Fraternity . . . Hall" is struck through in ink with two diagonal marks.
[19] "Beeson" is in pencil.
[20] H.J. Cross, corresponding secretary of the Salem Lyceum, wrote October 9, 1860, to say that he had put Emerson down for December 19 (*L*, V, 226).
[21] "Geo L Brown.", in pencil, is not in Emerson's hand.

[143] [22] 100
    100
    200   Cin[cinnati]
    100   Chi[cago]
    1⟨0⟩10 Mil[waukee]
    50.   Cin[cinnati]

[144] [23] 1860
25 Jan. Bought at Bank of City of Buffalo a draft on N. York for $90.
payable to J.M. Cheney Cash[ie]r

3 Feb. Sent from Cincinnati by mail to B. Dodd Cash[ie]r Atlantic
B[an]k Boston a draft on Commercial B[an]k Boston for $200.00
From Chicago   100
From Milwaukee   100
               10

[145]	Po'keepsie	40.
	Saratoga	40
	Hamilton	40
	Rochester	25
	Lima	40
	Buffalo	50
	Batavia	50
	Rochester	50
	Toronto	75
	Toledo	50
	Yellow Springs	50
	Cincinnati	100
		50
	Lafayette	50
	Chicago	75
	Rockford	50
	Madison	50
	Milwaukie	50

[22] The entries on p. [143] are in pencil.
[23] The entries on p. [144] are in pencil, except for "3 Feb. . . . $200.00".

Racine	50
Kenosha	50 [24]

[146] Jan. 16

Expenses to N[ew] Y[ork]	6
Coach in Boston	1.75
Astor House	2.75
Coach & porter	75
Ticket to Po[ugh]keepsie	1.80
Rutzer House 4.60	2.60
Ticket to Troy	1.50
to Saratoga	1.00
dinner	50
Saratoga	1.50
Ticket to Schenectady	75
to Utica	1.56
Utica expenses	3.
Exchange on N[ew] Y[ork]	.50
Ticket to Rochester	2.68
To Lima	1.50
Expense at Rochester	4.00
To ⟨|| ... ||⟩Buffalo	1.
Porters &c	1.

[147] [blank]

[148]

Niles	31
Kalamazoo	50
Grand Rapids	50
Marshall	40
Ann Arbor	25
Detroit	
Zanesville	100 [25]

[24] "Chicago . . . Kenosha   50" is in pencil. This list of lecture payments spans the period from January 17 (Poughkeepsie, N.Y.) to February 11, 1860 (Kenosha, Wis.).

[25] "Niles . . . Marshall   40" is in pencil. This list of lecture payments spans the period from February 13 (Niles, Mich.) to February 22, 1860 (Zanesville, O.).

[149]–[150] [blank]
[151]–[152] [torn out]
[153]²⁶   Feb 27   90
                Feb 1   50
                Copyright   100

[154]–[167] [blank]
[168]   H D Thoreau's note May 1860 gives 5 acres 56 rods as the burned area in my woodlot[.]²⁷

[169]–[170] [blank]
[171]   Ticknor & F[ields]
                  H[enry] D[avid] T[horeau']s books
                  H[enry]. James
                      Mrs Drury
                      Century
                      Pres[byterian] Mag[azine]
              "Tom Brown"
              Lockhart
              Longfellow &c Longf
              Bond
              Foils
                  City Lib[rar]y
              Knife²⁸

[172] [blank]
[inside back cover] [blank]

²⁶ The entries on p. [153], [168], and [171] are in pencil.
²⁷ For the fire, see Pocket Diary 7, p. [45] above.
²⁸ Emily Mervine Drury, of Canandaigua, N.Y., wrote to Emerson on December 23, 1860, inviting him to be a guest on January 25, 1861 (*L*, V, 234). Thomas Hughes, *Tom Brown at Oxford* . . . , 2 vols. (New York, 1860–1861), is in Emerson's library, with Ellen Emerson's inscription.

Appendix

Textual Notes

Index

Appendix

The following table shows which of Emerson's journals and miscellaneous notebooks are already printed in the Harvard University Press edition (*JMN*, I–XIII), and where they may be found, by volume and volume page numbers. Because this edition prints Emerson's manuscript page numbers of the journals and notebooks in the text, the reader should have no difficulty in locating cross-references to previously printed journals or notebooks. These are listed alphabetically, as designated by Emerson or others; the dates are supplied by Emerson, or the editors, or both. Since some passages are undated and some dates are doubtful, scholars should look at individual passages before relying on their dating.

Designation	Harvard edition
A (1833–1834)	IV, 249–387
AB (1847)	X, 3–57
AZ (1849–1850)	XI, 183–278
B (1835–1836)	V, 3–268
Blotting Book I (1826–1827)	VI, 11–57
Blotting Book II (1826–1829)	VI, 58–101
Blotting Book III (1831–1832)	III, 264–329
Blotting Book IV (1830, 1831? 1833)	III, 359–375
Blotting Book IV[A] (1830, 1832–1834)	VI, 102–114
Blotting Book Psi (1830–1831, 1832)	III, 203–263
Blotting Book Y (1829–1830)	III, 163–202
Blue Book (1826)	III, 333–337
BO (1850–1851)	XI, 279–365
BO Conduct (1851)	XII, 581–599
Books Small [I] (1840?–1856?)	VIII, 442–479
Books Small [II]	VIII, 550–576
C (1837–1838)	V, 277–509
Catalogue of Books Read (1819–1824)	I, 395–399
CD (1847)	X, 58–123
Charles C. Emerson (1837)	VI, 255–286
CO (1851)	XI, 366–452
Collectanea (1825–1828?)	VI, 3–10
College Theme Book (1819–1821, 1822? 1829?)	I, 161–205
Composition (1832?)	IV, 427–438

APPENDIX

Designation	Harvard edition
D (1838–1839)	VII, 3–262
Delta (1837–1841, 1850, 1857, 1862)	XII, 178–268
Dialling (1825? 1841? 1842)	VIII, 483–517
DO (1852–1854, 1856, 1858)	XIII, 3–57
E (1839–1842)	VII, 263–484
ED (1852–1853)	X, 494–568
Encyclopedia (1824–1836)	VI, 115–234
England and Paris (1847–1848)	X, 407–445
F No. 1 (1836–1840)	XII, 75–177
F No. 2 (1840–1841)	VII, 485–547
France and England (1833)	IV, 395–419
G (1841)	VIII, 3–77
Genealogy (1822, 1825, 1828)	III, 349–358
GH (1847–1848)	X, 124–199
GO (1852–1853)	XIII, 58–128
H (1841)	VIII, 78–145
HO (1853–1854)	XIII, 207–289
Index Minor (1843–1847?)	XII, 518–580
IO (1854)	XIII, 290–378
Italy (1833)	IV, 134–162
Italy and France (1833)	IV, 163–208
J (1841–1842)	VIII, 146–197
JK (1843?–1847)	X, 365–404
Journal 1826 (1825, 1826, 1827? 1828)	III, 3–41
Journal 1826–1828 (1824, 1825, 1826–1828)	III, 42–112
Journal at the West (1850–1853)	XI, 510–540
K (1842)	VIII, 198–247
L Concord (1835, 1838)	XII, 3–32
L Literature (1835)	XII, 33–55
LM (1848)	X, 288–362
London (1847–1848)	X, 208–287
Maine (1834)	IV, 388–391
Man (1836)	XII, 56–74
Margaret Fuller Ossoli (1851)	XI, 455–509
Memo St. Augustine (1827)	III, 113–118
Meredith Village (1829)	III, 159–162
N (1842)	VIII, 248–308
NO (1855)	XIII, 379–469
No. II (1825)	II, 413–420
No. XV (1824–1826)	II, 272–351
No. XVI (1824–1828?)	II, 396–412
No. XVII (1820)	I, 206–248

486

Designation	Harvard edition
No. XVIII (1820–1822)	I, 249–357
No. XVIII[A] (1821?–1829)	II, 355–395
Notebook 1833 (1833–1836)	VI, 235–254
O (1846–1847)	IX, 355–470
Phi (1838–1844? 1847–1851?)	XII, 269–419
Platoniana (1845–1848)	X, 468–488
Pocket Diary 1 (1820–1831)	III, 338–348
Pocket Diary 1 (1847)	X, 405–406
Pocket Diary 2 (1833)	IV, 420–426
Pocket Diary 3 (1848–1849)	X, 446–457
Pocket Diary 4 (1853)	XIII, 473–482
Pocket Diary 5 (1854)	XIII, 483–501
Pocket Diary 6 (1855)	XIII, 502–515
Psi (1839–1842, 1851)	XII, 420–517
Q (1832–1833)	IV, 3–101
R (1843)	VIII, 349–441
RO Mind (1835)	V, 269–276
RS (1848–1849)	XI, 3–86
Scotland and England (1833)	IV, 209–235
Sea 1833 (1833)	IV, 236–248
Sea-Notes (1847)	X, 200–207
Sermons and Journal (1828–1829)	III, 119–158
Sicily (1833)	IV, 102–133
T (1834–?)	VI, 317–399
Trees[A:I] (1843–1847)	VIII, 518–533
Trees[A:II]	VIII, 534–549
TU (1849)	XI, 87–182
U (1843–1844)	IX, 3–92
Universe 1–7, 7[A], 8 (1820–1822)	I, 358–394
V (1844–1845)	IX, 93–181
VS (1853–1854)	XIII, 129–206
W (1845)	IX, 182–255
Walk to the Connecticut (1823)	II, 177–186
Warren Lot (1849)	X, 489–493
Wide World 1 (1820)	I, 3–32
Wide World 2 (1820–1821)	I, 33–58
Wide World 3 (1822)	I, 59–90
Wide World 4 (1822)	I, 91–113
Wide World 6 (1822)	I, 114–158
Wide World 7 (1822)	II, 3–39
Wide World 8 (1822)	II, 40–73
Wide World 9 (1822–1823)	II, 74–103

Designation	Harvard edition
Wide World 10 (1823)	II, 104–143
Wide World 11 (1823)	II, 144–176
Wide World 12 (1823–1824)	II, 187–213
Wide World XIII (1824)	II, 214–271
Xenien (1848, 1852)	X, 458–467
Y (1845–1846)	IX, 256–354
Z (1831? 1837–1838, 1841?)	VI, 287–316
Z[A] (1842–1843)	VIII, 309–348

Textual Notes

RO

4 the ⟨L⟩Rome ["the" not canceled] | less | Throw **5** of | de*l*e | Heedless | how **6** of | Britain. | who [not canceled] **8** know↑.↓ | strange↑,↓ **10** point. **11** , An **15** interest, [comma in pencil] **18** No | T'was **20** aright. ⟨But⟩ **22** articlle **23** commons ["c" underscored twice] **24** youth, | Concord, [comma in pencil] | ⟨at⟩ at [cancellation in pencil] **26** ⟨here,⟩↑,↓ **27** discount. **29** ⟨Judge⟩ | Ohio. **34** despotisms.↓.

SO

46 nourishment↑,↓ **48** landing." | de. **49** enormous↑,↓ | Day;↑—↓Zeus **51** he | purchased↑,↓ **53** ↑"↓I | land?↑"↓ ↑"↓Yes | value.↑"↓ ↑"↓Is | more?↑"↓ ↑"↓Perhaps, | wait.↑"↓ ↑"↓So | it;⟨"⟩ **54** tavern, **58** cent.; **59** every | ⟨are⟩ **62** Sevres, | A.B.H.W. **65** Nusketaquid **67** thou↑,↓ | She | She [92] She **70** Do **72** A **74** to those who hear it [finger-wiped and then canceled] **76** Wa[122]chusett | b*a*ck **77** "emb*o*dy" | history **78** ↑(↓to | be,↑)↓ **commission.** | European [blotted] **80** he **83** others, **85** day. **87** occurred," **89** A.B.H.W. **91** brook↑,↓ | dentatum↑,↓ | vero*n*ica **93** science. **97** experience **100** my an **103** to [not canceled] | when | thou↑,↓ | me↑,↓ **106** unborn **107** in | also↑:↓ **111** world. **112** phan[263]toms | intelligence. **113** He **114** usages₂ & foundations₁ | man. | dephth **115** engine: | Adrastia he | period. **117** not;

VO

120 *Cat. Per. Virg. Ven.* **121** said↑,↓ **123** ↑savants↓ **128** affirmations. | nonintervention↑?"↓ — ↑"↓Sire | intervention.↑"↓ **134** ⟨S⟩A **135** beli⟨↑l↓⟩eve **137** barrel, | in **138** preva-[73]lence **139** in **140** thought⟨s⟩ ["s" canceled in pencil] | flows. [period in pencil] | The **144** ↑cones↓ [91] cones **150** deli-[111]cately | ⟨⟨i⟩↑im↓mensity⟩ **151** ⟨or⟩ **153** Upon **154** their **155** ⟨"⟩I | ⟨t⟩They | ⟨wi⟨f⟩ves⟩ **156** tempera-[131]ment **157** Light **158** lightning.⟨"⟩— **159** *tu* **161** ⟨must⟩ **162** Amphi⟨↑o↓t⟩carp⟨i⟩aea, **163** can't [blotted] | must be [blotted] **166** said, a **167** benefit,? | the **169** ↑h↓in⟨s⟩ts **170** politics. **171** pains to ⟨put⟩ ["to" not canceled] | we **172** neither **174** An | ↑£↓10,000 | Here **175** The **176** wh↑i↓ch **177** Such **178** *ghestly* **179** ⟨the[?]⟩ **180** [ampersand in pencil] | ↑animals | ↑sheen↓ **183** she **184** coal, [comma in pencil] | remark↑(?)↓. **186** In | The **193** "his sought **194** fig-[260]ure | People **198** Montesquieu*[.] **199** [274a] [superscript "a" in pencil] | [275a] [subscript "a" in pencil] **203** *the*, **204** artist⟩↑.↓

AC

210 melioration. **223** beauty's [apostrophe in pencil] | miss **224** ↑"↓C.↑ounterparts,"↓ **228** "the . . . air, . . . night—" [quotation marks and comma in pencil] **230** stutute" **233** left. **234** ⟨&⟩And **236** doubt. **237** mud-hole, [hyphen in

pencil] **240** S⟨*hd*⟩*ould* | this | m⟨n⟩onotines **241** ⟨to **242** precedent↑?↓ | obey it↓
it, it **243** 'O'Neal's **245** Mallows⟨—⟩: [colon inserted over dash] **247** off, [comma in pencil] **250** Why↑?↓ | ⟨&⟩, [comma not canceled] **253** street; [semicolon in pencil] | Whipple's [apostrophe in pencil] **254** through, **256** self-conceit. [hyphen in pencil] **258** Bonaparte's [apostrophe in pencil] **263** Drive | self↑–↓executing **264** ⟨fury of⟩ **265** & puff & [not canceled] **269** poets, [comma in pencil] **270** revolvers,— [period changed to comma and dash added in pencil] | beans,↑?↓ **271** Sailed **273** hill, river, wood, hummock, . . . perspective, [commas in pencil] | with↑al↓ ⟨a⟩ a **274** noise: [colon in pencil] | journal, [comma in pencil] **275** ⟨asteroid⟩ [the dot of the "i" and the "d" are on p. [265]] **284** H.D.T.↑—↓ **288** unchange[294]able

CL

293 Irenaeus↑'↓, ⟨Martyr⟩ **300** Varnhagen,↑'s↓ **301** tis **302** read. **303** ↑A.↑dam↓↓ **304** "*33.* **305** ⟨MST[?]⟩ | Necessary, ⟨Fate.⟩ **306** quadru[42]ped **307** All | ⟨me⟩. ↑us.↓ **308** Bigelow." | hog↑s↓h⟨s⟩ead. | me↑—↓is | line. **309** ⟨forever⟩, [comma not canceled] | argument, **310** of of **312** duns↑.↓ ⟨are hated⟩. [original period not canceled] | Madeleine /?/ are | ↑(↓if | survivor⟨,⟩↑!)↓ **314** Village Politicians." [capitals underscored twice] **315** begins begin **316** old⟨.⟩, [period changed to comma] | that ⟨he⟩ ↑that the reader↓ **318** Bo↑s↓well **319** than⟨6⟩ 6 **327** The **328** ⟨th⟩ad | probation⟨.⟩↑,↓ **331** association. | others' | others' **332** Steel **334** ↑Captain John Brown↓ B. **337** individ-[172]ual | Perception **340** mind. | My **341** will **344** ↑—↓Hamilton; | ⟨the⟩ the "Princess" | dreams, [comma not canceled] **345** said. **347** resembled | Ah↑!↓ **348** direction.⟨"⟩ | said.? | propriety↑.↓ **349** ↑"↓*City Library,*↑!↓ **351** ⟨P.⟩S. *"in* | *slave."* **352** opinion⟨,⟩. ⟨by⟩Xn **355** steel? **356** knee [wiped] **358** thing↑.↓ **359** rubbish | /energies./glory./ | senti[262]ment **360** all | through↑.↓ | an | Ho↑!↓ | transfigures↑,↓ **365** He | *to be*

WO Liberty

376 The **378** true. **380** let | (, the African,) **383** ⟨l⟩ ↑l↓opinion **388** sun. Down **389** has, **390** wifebeating↓. **391** W [not canceled] **392** /all seeing/starry,/ **393** every **397** the [not canceled] **398** an **399** him. **404** law↑,↓ **405** ironmasters(?)↑,↓ **406** party; [period changed to semicolon in pencil] | is, [comma in pencil] | well, [comma in pencil] | Not **408** thero **411** downfal, **413** availed. | these **414** and he no **418** the **419** The **422** Laws | found no [not canceled] | thought **424** The | the | o'erarching **426** heaven **428** disloyally | Where | nor

Pocket Diary 7

442 the ⟨height of⟩ ["the" not canceled]

490

Index

This Index includes Emerson's own index material omitted from the text. His index topics, including long phrases, are listed under "Emerson, Ralph Waldo, INDEX HEADINGS AND TOPICS"; the reader should consult both the general Index and Emerson's. If Emerson did not specify a manuscript page or a date to which his index topic referred, the editors have chosen the most probable passage(s) and added "(?)" to the printed page number(s). If Emerson's own manuscript page number is an obvious error, it has been silently corrected.

References to materials included or to be included in *Lectures* are grouped under "Emerson, Ralph Waldo, LECTURES." References to drafts of unpublished poems are under "Emerson, Ralph Waldo, POEMS." Under "Emerson, Ralph Waldo, WORKS" are references to published versions of poems, to lectures and addresses included in *W* but not in *Lectures*, and to Emerson's essays and miscellaneous publications. Kinds of topics included under "Emerson, Ralph Waldo, DISCUSSIONS" in earlier volumes are now listed only in the general Index.

497

Herschel, Sir William, 10, 15, 44
Hersh, B. F., 476, 477
Higginson, Thomas Wentworth, 467
Higher Law, 376, 394, 412
Hill, Thomas, 367, 474
Hillard, George Stillman, 97, 143, 171, 405, 406
Hindu(s), 77
Hippias, 168
Hitt, Dr., 434
Hoar, Mrs., 67
Hoar, Ebenezer Rockwood, 37, 270n, 324, 366, 443
Hoar, Edward, 161
Hoar, Elizabeth, 37, 67, 73, 366
Hoar, Reuben, 468
Hoar, Samuel, 113
Hobbes, Thomas, 253, 418n
Hoboken, N.J., 453
Hoe, Robert, 250
Hoedemaker, Philip J., 353
Holden, L. E., 477
Holmes, John, 270n
Holmes, John S., 390n
Holmes, Oliver Wendell, 143–144, 146n, 173, 269n, 270n, 313–314, 315–317, 324, 345, 365; *The Autocrat of the Breakfast Table*, 145n, 316
Homer, 80, 109, 179, 180, 193, 199, 262, 281, 288, 339, 361; *Iliad*, 287; *Odyssey*, 121n
Hood, Thomas, "The Last Man," 67n
Hooke, Robert, 19
Hooker, Richard, *Works* . . . , 382
Hooper, Mr., 196
Hooper, Ellen, 361
Hooper, Ellen Sturgis, 329
Hopkins, Samuel, 277
Hopkins, William, *Geology*, 457
Hopkinson, Mrs., 467
Hopps, Mr., 385
Horace, 322, 340; *Odes*, 41
Hornellsville, N.Y., 294
Hosmer, Edmund, 243, 244n, 251, 340, 471
Hottentots, 197
House of Representatives, U.S., 117
Houssaye, Arsène, *Men and Women of the Eighteenth Century*, 352n

Hovey, 452
Hovey, C. C., 444
Hovey, C. F., 443
Howard, John, 30, 42
Howe, Mr., of Nova Scotia, 269
Howe, Mrs., 473
Howe, Estes, 270n
Howe, Julia Ward, 38
Howe, Mrs. Samuel Gridley, 368
Howell, Andrew, 455
Howland, Elizabeth, 463
Howland, J., 463
Howland, William, 439
Hubbard, Cyrus, 157
Hubbard, Ebba, 162
Huber, François, 81, 82
Hudson, O., 435
Hughes, Thomas, *Tom Brown at Oxford* . . . , 482
Hugo, Victor Marie, *Cromwell*, 142n
Humboldt, Baron Alexander von, 73, 350; *Letters of Alexander von Humboldt to Varnhagen von Ense*, 356–357
Hume, David, 89; *The History of England*, 402n
Humphry, G. H., 475
Hunt, Benjamin Peter, 367
Hunt, William Morris, 246, 367
Hunter, J. B., 342, 343
Hunter, John, 173
Huntington, F. D., 442n
Hungarian(s), 328
Hungary, 390
Hutchinson, Lucy, 13
Hutchinson, Peter, 149
Hyde, Lawrence, 1st Earl of Rochester, 276
Hyperion, 364

Iamblichus, *Life of Pythagoras*, 245n, 274n; *On the Mysteries of the Egyptians* . . . (tr. Thomas Taylor), 130n, 131
Iceland, 387
Illinois, 27–29, 31, 58, 59, 107, 196, 344, 418
Illinois Central Railroad, 30, 42
Illusion(s), 160, 302
Imagination, 326, 358, 359, 360

Olympus, 108, 178
O'Neal, 243
Oregon, 315, 345
Orpheus, 282
Osborn, Mr., 231
Osman, 226, 279
Ossian, 281, 288
Owego, N.Y., 292, 294
Owen, Sir Richard, 68, 184, 285
Owen, Robert, 65
Oxford University, 50, 114, 354
Ozman, 64

P., 364
P., F., 93
Paddock, S. G., 454
Page, H. A., 443
Paley, William, 192
Palfrey, Sara Hammond, 368
Palmerston, Henry John Temple, 3rd
    Viscount, 247, 287
Paris, France, 48, 61, 97, 120, 132, 280,
    307, 363
Paris, University of, 114
Parker, Theodore, 37, 83, 168, 352, 353,
    354, 386, 415, 442, 444, 450, 452,
    454, 475n
Parker Fraternity, Boston, 293, 457, 460,
    468, 478
Parker House, Boston, 143n, 269n, 452
Parkman, Mrs., 361, 450
Parkman, Rev. Francis, 18
Parsons, Dr., 473
Parthia, 45
Pascal, Blaise, 198, 277, 442
Paterson, N.J., 440, 447
Patmore, Coventry Kersey Dighton, 367;
    The Angel in the House, 33, 35n
Paul, Saint, 237, 285, 413
Paulding, P. R., 454
Paulet, Mr., 10
Pauli, Reinhold, Life of Alfred the Great,
    258; Simon von Montfort . . . ,
    409n
Peabody, Dr., 471, 478
Peabody, Elizabeth Palmer, 37, 367;
    "Primeval History," 188
Peabody Institute, 400
Peel, Sir Robert, 389

Peirce, Benjamin, 143, 156, 166, 324,
    442, 451
Pélissier, Aimable Jean Jacques, Duc de
    Malakoff, 12
Penn, Sir William, 412
Peoria, Ill., 26, 31, 434, 440, 444
Pericles, 49, 151, 311
Perkins, B. C., 439
Pervigilium Veneris, 120
Peterboro, N.H., 460
Petty, Sir William, 19
Phelps, W. E., 434
Phenix, The . . . , 54n
Pherecydes, 47
Philadelphia, Pa., 32, 440, 447, 450,
    457, 458, 459, 461, 467
Phillips, George S., 367
Phillips, Jonathan M., 54
Phillips, Moses Dresser, 31n, 146n, 318n
Phillips, Wendell, 310, 319, 336, 351,
    415, 442, 444, 449, 454
Phillips, Sampson & Co., 31, 318, 343n,
    432, 433n, 452
Philolaus, 131n
Phipps, Constantine Henry, 1st Marquis
    of Normanby, 128, 129, 274
Phocion, 309
Photographer, 126
Pickering, J. F., 479
Pierce, E. L., 434
Pierce, Franklin, 170, 430
Pigeon Cove, Mass., 100, 108
Pindar, 132, 282, 297; Odes, 121-122
Piozzi, Hester Lynch, Anecdotes of the
    Late Samuel Johnson, LL.D., 11n, 320,
    338
Pisistratus, 288
Pitt, William (1759-1806), 329
Pittsburgh, Pa., 292
Pittsfield, Mass., 44, 437
Pizarro, Francisco, 339
Plato, 12, 80, 84, 115, 116, 168, 250,
    256, 268, 272, 285, 322, 356, 442;
    Phaedrus, 323; Theaetetus, 218n;
    Timaeus, 216; Timaeus Locrus, 165;
    Works . . . (tr. F. Sydenham and T.
    Taylor), 216n, 218n; Works, A new
    and literal version . . . , 165
Pliny, 328; Natural History, 57n